The Almanac of

BRITISH
POLITICS

The Almanac of
BRITISH
POLITICS

ROBERT WALLER

CROOM HELM London
ST. MARTIN'S PRESS New York

©1983 Robert Waller
Croom Helm Ltd, Provident House, Burrell Row,
Beckenham, Kent BR3 1AT

British Library Cataloguing in Publication Data

Waller, Robert
  The almanac of British politics.
  1. Election districts -- Great Britain -- History
  I. Title
  324.41   JN558
  ISBN 0-7099-2767-3

©1983 Robert Waller
All rights reserved. For information, write:
St. Martin's Press, Inc., 175 Fifth Avenue,
New York, NY 10010

First published in the United States of America in 1983

Library of Congress Cataloging in Publication Data
Waller, Robert.
  The almanac of British politics.
  1. Great Britain. Parliament. House of Commons --
Election districts. 2. Election districts -- Great
Britain. 3. Great Britain -- Economic conditions --
1945-   . 4. Great Britain -- Social conditions --
1945-   . I. Title.
JN561.W28 1983   328.41,07345   83-3100
ISBN 0-312-02136-4

Printed and bound in Great Britain by
Biddles Ltd, Guildford and King's Lynn

CONTENTS

ACKNOWLEDGEMENTS

I would like to thank David Croom and the staff at Croom Helm for their faith in backing a particularly risky project. Most of the finance for the research needed for this book was provided by a Prize Fellowship awarded by Magdalen College, Oxford. Sydney Elliott of Queen's University, Belfast, provided essential help for the Northern Irish section of the Almanac. John Whitehead of CACI Market Analysis Group, 58-62 High Holborn, London, provided the 1981 census ward statistics, which make the social and economic information for the new constituencies authoritative. Michael Hart, Fellow in Politics at Exeter College, Oxford, read the whole typescript in draft form. The BBC and ITN kindly allowed me to use their expertly calculated 1979 notional General Election results, where these were available. Where the BBC-ITN figures are not yet available, I have included my own estimates, which are distinguished by the symbol (RW). Academic assistance and encouragement was offered by, amongst others, David Butler, John Curtice, David Denver, Paul McKaskle, Henry Pelling, Andrew Robertson and Michael Steed. Local advice and accomodation was provided by Peter Andrews, Jonathan Beveridge, Graham Fife, Richard Fisher, John O'Reilly, Tony Sharp, Chris Warmoth, David Wilson, Graham Wood and many others. Stephen Cope operated the word-processor and Jayne Lewin drew the maps, both with admirable efficiency. The book is dedicated to PME and BJCR.

Magdalen College, Oxford, 1980-83.   Robert J. Waller

INTRODUCTION

This book attempts to describe the political geography or electoral anatomy of the United Kingdom. By means of individual constituency profiles, an assessment is made of what influences the various parts of the country to vote as they do. How do social and economic characteristics affect political behaviour and preference? What are the local and national determinants of voting patterns? What makes each parliamentary seat 'tick'? How strong are regional factors, or the personal votes of MPs and candidates? The title of the book, and its approach and format, owe much to Michael Barone's illuminating, enjoyable and unique Almanac of American Politics, to which a great debt must be acknowledged. No similar work relating to the United Kingdom has been published, apart from Henry Pelling's Social Geography of British Elections, which dealt with the period 1885-1910. It is hoped that this Almanac of British Politics will fill such a gap.

Certain national themes are illustrated. A high proportion of owner-occupiers in a seat usually implies an abundance of Conservative voters, and conversely council estates are generally bedrocks of Labour support. Those parts of the country which have a concentration of middle-class residents - those who work in non-manual occupations - tend to the right, working-class manual employees to the left. Districts favoured by non-white voters, whether Asian or West Indian in origin, often provide a reliable source of support for the Labour Party. The heaviest concentrations of blacks and Asians are to be found in various parts of London (such as Southall, Brent, Hounslow, Newham, Haringey, Lambeth and Hackney), in Birmingham and the West Midlands, and in the smaller towns of Manchester, Bradford, Leeds, Leicester, Blackburn, and Slough. Agricultural areas are very poor ground for Labour. They are much more fertile territory for the Conservatives, and in some parts of Britain (particularly the 'Celtic fringe') for the Liberals. Certain types of industry, such as coal mining, nurture Labour strongholds. A high proportion of military voters, such as are found at Portsmouth and Gosport in Hampshire, skew the political characteristics of a constituency to the Tories.

These variable indicators, and others too, are incorporated in the text describing each seat, or in the statistics associated with it. In the text, any features of specific interest relating to a constituency and its history are recorded. These short essays are inevitably impressionistic; they try to point out the individuality of each locality. The electoral histories of British constituencies reveal changing trends and developments since the Second World War. The Conservatives have done increasingly well in the south of England in recent years, while Labour have prospered more in the North, thus raising the spectre of 'Two Nations' once again in British politics. Unemployment also varies greatly between North and South, between depressed and affluent districts; but somewhat surprisingly there seems little direct, independent correlation between rates of unemployment and voting preferences in a constituency, and unemployment figures are not included in this book for every seat. Several cities have swung to Labour as the population has dropped, as the middle-classes have fled to the suburbs, as non-white immigrants became more numerous, or where old religious cleavages have declined in importance, as in the case of the end of the working-class Orange Protestant Tory vote in Liverpool and Glasgow. In some places such as the Forest of Dean (West Gloucestershire) and Leicestershire the exhaustion of coalfields has sapped Labour strength. Norfolk's unusual agricultural Labour support has all but vanished in the last twenty years. Such long-term patterns superimpose themselves upon the uniform and regular swings between the political parties, which are to be found at each General Election.

It is likely that a thorough local knowledge will aid in predicting and understanding the results of the next General Election as well. It may well be that the North of England, far removed from the centre of government in London, and suffering more heavily than the South from unemployment, will show more favour to the Labour Party than the national average. The Conservatives have been doing exceptionally well in London in local elections recently, even enjoying a further positive swing since the 1979 General Election. In Scotland there may be a revival of Nationalist support. In some parts of England, such as Berkshire, the issues of defence and nuclear disarmament may become important. The newly-founded Alliance will be attempting to break through the traditional pattern of British politics, although it seems at present that the SDP's vote is spread very evenly across classes and across the country, which means that they could poll 25-30% in many seats without winning any of them. The SDP will probably rely heavily on the survival of their existing MPs: 25 defectors from the Labour Party, one from the Conservatives and two byelection victors (Roy Jenkins and Shirley Williams). Individual and local factors alone may therefore decide which of the SDP members are returned. Liberal hopes are also heavily reliant upon local organisation and activity.

But it is hoped that this Almanac will be more than a guide to the political and electoral map of Britain. It is hoped that electoral evidence, together with the social and economic information, will help to produce a series of thumbnail sketches which build up to a characterisation of the United Kingdom and what makes it behave as it does. Elections offer a mass of evidence relating to the history and traditions of each part of the country. The Almanac should be able to tell the reader where the leafy residential areas of a town are to be found, where the council estates are, where one can discern that divide between the 'right and wrong side of the tracks', the 'east and west ends of town'. All kinds of political cleavage are illustrated: between North and South, England and Scotland, urban and rural areas. There are electorally significant distinctions of class and tenure, race and language. The Almanac aims to be more than a handbook for elections. The political topography of the nation should have a wider relevance. Elections inform social and economic history and sociology. British society should not be analysed as if it were of secondary importance, offering clues to election results, to the reasons behind the short-term success and failure of mere political parties.

It should be noted that this Almanac deals with a <u>new</u> political map of Britain. The constituencies which form the basic units of description have never been tested in a General Election. They are the product of the work over the last seven years of a Boundary Commission which has been responsible for drawing revised parliamentary divisions. This is a task which has to be undertaken regularly – every 15 years – due to the shifts of population which are continually taking place within Britain.

This is a very major revision compared with previous redistributions, partly because it has been necessary to bring the constituency boundaries into line with the new local government units created in the early 1970s. Only 59 seats are unaltered this time, or altered in name only – 90% of the seats are in some ways new. In the previous redistribution, which came into effect at the February 1974 election, 220 seats were left unaltered. In 1955, the boundaries of only 243 seats were changed at all, under half of the total. In 1950 there was a major redrawing as the boundaries were revised on a national basis for the first time since 1918 – but even then 80 seats survived intact.

In the present boundary changes there has been a general shift in seats away from the depopulated inner cities to the expanding shire counties of the southern half of England. London loses eight seats, Glasgow three, Liverpool and Manchester two each, other cities one. On the other hand Essex is granted two extra seats, and most other English shire counties one more. This phenomenon means that the boundary changes' overall effect is to help the Conservatives electorally, as undersized urban Labour seats are abolished or merged and new rural and suburban divisions created. The only type of place where Labour does well out of the boundary changes are those where the growth of New Towns now entitles them to a seat of their own, usually a good Labour bet, undiluted by Conservative rural hinterland territory. New Towns are the only predominantly working-class areas which are still growing in population. Examples of this are the new constituencies of Stevenage, Basildon, Peterborough, The Wrekin and Cumbernauld. If the 1979 General Election had been fought on the new boundaries, the Conservative majority over Labour would have increased by between 30 and 40 seats. The outcome as calculated by 'notional' results would have seen the Tories win 360 seats (instead of their actual 339), Labour 257 (268), the Liberals 10 (11), the Welsh and Scottish Nationalists 5 (4) and there would have been 17 seats in Northern Ireland rather than 12. The new House will have 650 members, compared with 635 at present. Besides the five extra seats granted to N Ireland, Scotland has one more, Wales two and England seven. Maps of the new constituencies are to be found at the back of the book.

The Almanac of British Politics is a personal and impressionistic description of the country. The author fully realises that he cannot know as much about each district as the inhabitants themselves. He welcomes corrections and improvements which might be incorporated in possible revised editions, which would strive for a more accurate and penetrating understanding of the electoral reflection of the character of the United Kingdom.

THE STRUCTURE OF THE BOOK

The new constituencies are described in the following order:

(i) Seats in Greater London, within London Boroughs in alphabetical order.

(ii) Seats in Metropolitan Counties, in alphabetical order of county: Greater Manchester, Merseyside, West Midlands, Tyne and Wear, South Yorkshire, West Yorkshire. Within the Metropolitan counties, the seats are placed in order of Metropolitan Borough - for example, within Greater Manchester, Bolton Borough comes before Bury. In a few cases, Metropolitan Boroughs have been amalgamated by the Boundary Commission for their own purposes - for example, Stockport/Tameside, Manchester/Trafford, Leeds/Wakefield. These are treated as single units in this book.

(iii) Non-Metropolitan Counties within England, in alphabetical order.

(iv) Scotland, within Regions.

(v) Wales, within Counties.

(vi) Northern Ireland, as a whole.

The County or Region name will be found on the top line of each entry, on the left. The constituency number is on the top line on the right. The name of the constituency is on the second line. Where the seat is in a London or Metropolitan Borough, the Borough's name is on the right hand of the second line.

EXPLANATION OF STATISTICAL TERMS

Housing Tenure

The first two of the statistics at the foot of each entry refer to housing tenure. The figures are taken from the raw material in the 1981 Census. If the figures are not defined beyond the decimal point, they are to be taken as estimates. The variable 'Own Occ' refers to the percentage of all households in the seat owned or being bought by the occupiers - this includes ownership with the aid of a mortgage. The 'Loc Auth' indicator shows the percentage of housing in a constituency owned by the local authority and rented to the tenants: in other words, council houses.

In recent years it has become clear that housing is an important determinant of voting preferences, regardless of other variables. Owner-occupiers of all classes tend to support the Conservatives, while council tenants are in the main pro-Labour. The percentage of owner-occupiers has risen greatly during the century, even in the apparently depressed and stagnant 1970s, and owner-occupied houses now form over 55% of the total stock in Britain. 31% of the housing in the nation is now local-authority owned. The two figures, for owner-occupied housing and council housing, will not add up to 100% in each seat. Housing Association property is included with the coucil tenancy figures. The third type of housing tenure is privately rented, which at one time formed a majority of all accommodation, but which has all but disappeared in the twentieth century. Only about 12% of the total housing stock is now in the privately rented sector. Private tenants are usually more inclined to Labour than owner-occupiers, but less so than council tenants.

Black/Asian

The statistic '% Black/Asian' refers to the estimated percentage in each seat living in a household headed by a person born in the New Commonwealth or Pakistan. This is not quite the same as the percentage of non-white residents, but no direct racial question was asked in the 1981 Census, and this is the best alternative. Non-whites, both of Asian and West Indian origin, tend to be strong supporters of the Labour party regardless of their occupation. Largely white seats on the neighbourhood of concentrations of immigrants have shown some signs of reacting to racial change by swinging to the Right. There is no point in including such information for Wales and Scotland, where the number of non-white residents is insignificant in all but a very few urban divisions. In Wales, the percentage of non-whites is replaced by the percentage who can speak Welsh. This is an accurate indicator of the strength of Plaid Cymru, the Welsh Nationalist Party. In Northern Ireland, the only social statistic which is significant enough as a political indicator to warrant inclusion is of a religious nature: an estimation of the percentage of Roman Catholics in each constituency.

Middle-Class and Professional-Managerial

The two socio-economic class variables included for each seat are '% Mid Cl" and '% Prof Man'. The percentage 'Middle Class' refers to those in the Registrar-General's socio-economic categories 1, 2, 3, 4, 5, 6 and 13 - those in non-manual occupations. The percentage 'Professional and Managerial' refers to those in groups 1, 2, 3, 4 and 13 - professions such as the law and teaching, higher management, and independent farmers. This 'Prof Man' variable is often described by election experts as the best predictor of the Labour and Conservative shares of the vote - the higher the percentage, the more Conservative a seat is likely to be. The full figures for the 1981 Census are not yet fully available so some figures have been estimated in order to provide a comparison between constituencies. These figures do not include decimal points. It should be noted that the middle-class percentage in Britain increased by approximately 10% between 1971 and 1981. Due to the nature of their economy, the 'middle-class' figure tends to be unusually low in agricultural districts, and high in urban areas, especially in the capital cities of London, Edinburgh and Cardiff.

Electorate

The 'electorate' figure is the number of voters on the electoral roll in each seat as announced by the Boundary Commission. The Commission began work in England in 1976, in Scotland in 1978, in N Ireland in 1979, and in Wales in 1981. 1982 figures were not all available at the time of going to press. The electoral quota, the average size of all the seats, is 65,753 for England, 53,649 for Scotland, 58,753 for Wales and 61,206 for N Ireland.

Notional Result

The 'notional result' is the estimated majority which would have been achieved by the winning party if the newly drawn seat had existed at the time of the last General Election in 1979. It is not in any way a prediction, and it does not of course take account of the SDP or the Alliance which did not exist in 1979. The notional result is calculated by assessing how the wards which make up the new constituencies did vote in 1979. This task is assisted by the fact that local elections were fought in most parts of Britain on the same day as the General Election. It can be established that most people vote the same way in local contests as in parliamentary elections, at least in urban areas, although the Liberals and other small parties tend to do somewhat better locally. The political colour and preference of most wards can be estimated quite accurately,

8

but it must be remembered that these are only guesses and some degree of uncertainty must be expected. The BBC and ITN set up an expert working-party to assess notional results for the 1979 Election, and they have been kind enough to allow their figures to be used in this book, where they are available. Where the BBC-ITN estimates are not yet available, I have included my own figures, with the symbol (RW) attached.

Alliance

The 'Alliance' indicator at the foot of each entry reveals to which partner, Liberals or Social Democrats, the seat has been allocated. These assignments should not be regarded as final. They may in some cases be subject to renegotiation before the General Election. If local difficulties prove insuperable, the two Alliance parties may end up fighting each other in a limited number of seats. Some allocations had not been made at the time of going to press, and the Alliance indicator has in this case been left blank. Although the strength of the Social Democrats cannot be taken into account in the 1979 General Election notional results, it is possible in some cases to assess their chances by considering their performance in the 1982 local government elections, their first nationwide campaign. This information is frequently included in the textual description of each constituency.

Core Seat and New Seat

The figures on the right hand side of the statistics at the foot of the page usually refer to a 'core seat'. This is the old parliamentary constituency which the new seat most resembles. Its 1979 General Election result and a list of present and former MPs is appended. Byelection results between 1979 and the present are not reported in full at the foot of the relevant entry, because it is usually found that the General Election result is a more useful indicator of the political characteristics of a seat. Where the byelection result is of interest, it is described in the text. The historical list of MPs may begin at various dates since 1945. This is due to the fact that the core seat may have effectively been created in 1950, 1955 or 1974, and previously the seat would have been so different that to include information about it would have been misleading. Where an MP was elected as a member of one party, but subsequently changed his allegiance, as in the case of the defectors to the SDP in 1981-2, the new party is included in brackets. In some cases there will be no appropriate former division which can be defined as a core seat, either because several small seats have been collapsed into one new constituency, or because a new seat is an extra and additional division in a county. In these cases it is categorised as a 'New Seat', and no previous results or list of MPs is given.

RESULTS OF GENERAL ELECTIONS SINCE 1945

	Conservative	Labour	Liberal	Others
1945	213	393	12	22
1950	298	315	9	3
1951	321	295	6	3
1955	345	277	6	2
1959	365	258	6	–
1964	303	317	9	2*
1966	253	363	12	2*
1970	330	287	6	7*
1974 (Feb)	296	301	14	24*
1974 (Oct)	276	319	13	27*
1979	339	268	11	17*

* Includes Speaker

UNALTERED SEATS IN THE PRESENT REDISTRIBUTION

Where only the name has been changed, the former name is in brackets

3	Barnet, Chipping Barnet
4	Barnet, Finchley
9	Old Bexley and Sidcup (Sidcup)
13	Bromley, Beckenham
14	Bromley, Chislehurst
25	Ealing, Southall
34	Fulham
35	Hammersmith (Hammersmith North)
40	Havering, Hornchurch
41	Havering, Romford
42	Havering, Upminster
43	Hillingdon, Hayes and Harlington
44	Hillingdon, Ruislip-Northwood
45	Hillingdon, Uxbridge
46	Hounslow, Brentford and Isleworth
47	Hounslow, Feltham and Heston
60	Merton, Mitcham and Morden
61	Merton, Wimbledon
62	Newham North East
63	Newham North West
64	Newham South
67	Redbridge, Wanstead and Woodford
73	Carshalton and Wallington (Carshalton)
74	Sutton and Cheam
81	Wandsworth, Putney
127	Southport
214	Bath
261	Redcar
270	Carlisle
271	Copeland (Whitehaven)
274	Workington
305	Darlington
323	Southend East
324	Southend West
330	West Gloucestershire
368	Great Grimsby (Grimsby)
372	Isle of Wight
378	Folkestone and Hythe
387	Tonbridge and Malling
388	Tunbridge Wells (Royal Tunbridge Wells)
390	Blackpool North
391	Blackpool South
405	Blaby
407	Harborough
457	Shrewsbury and Atcham (Shrewsbury)
464	Burton

11

469   South Staffordshire (South West Staffordshire)
482   East Surrey
487   North West Surrey
489   Spelthorne
497   Hove
501   Chichester
523   York
545   Orkney and Shetland
547   Western Isles
582   Kilmarnock and Loudoun
611   Rhondda
631   Ynys Mon (Anglesey)
633   Montgomery

(Total 59)

ABBREVIATIONS

All	Alliance Party (Northern Ireland)
C	Conservative Party
Comm	Communist
CW	Common Wealth
Dem	Democrat
Dem Lab	Democratic Labour
DUP	Democratic Unionist Party (Northern Ireland)
E	Ecology Party
Eng Nat	English Nationalist
IIP	Irish Independence Party
Ind	Independent
L	Liberal Party
L-C	Liberal-Conservative
Lab	Labour Party
Loc Auth	Local Authority Housing
Meb Ker	Mebyon Kernow (Cornish Nationalists)
Mid Cl	Middle Class
Mod Lab	Moderate Labour
NEC	National Executive Committee (Labour Party)
NF	National Front
Oth(s)	Other(s)
OUP	Official Unionist Party (Northern Ireland)
Own Occ	Owner Occupier
PC	Plaid Cymru (Welsh Nationalists)
Prof Man	Professional and Managerial Classes
R	Ratepayer
RC	Roman Catholic
Rep C	Republican Clubs (Northern Ireland)
SDLP	Social Democratic and Labour Party (Northern Ireland)
SDP	Social Democratic Party
SLP	Scottish Labour Party
SNP	Scottish National Party
Spkr	The Speaker
UPNI	Unionist Party of Northern Ireland
UU	Ulster Unionist
UUUP	United Ulster Unionist Party
Wessex R	Wessex Regionalist
WRP	Workers Revolutionary Party

LIST OF MAPS

1   South West England
2   Wessex
3   Home Counties (South)
4   South London
5   North London
6   Home Counties (North)
7   East Anglia
8   Welsh Marches and Warwickshire
9   West Midlands
10 East Midlands
11 North Midlands
12 Greater Manchester
13 Lancashire and Merseyside
14 South and West Yorkshire
15 North Yorkshire and Humberside
16 Northern England
17 South Wales
18 Mid and North Wales
19 Southern Scotland
20 Strathclyde
21 Northern Scotland
22 Northern Ireland

Barking   Barking/Dagenham

Barking is very much the older half of the East End Borough
of Barking and Dagenham. Once a fishing village by the
Thames, Barking grew up around its creek, not far from the
heart of London's dockland. It still presents a uniformly
industrial aspect, while the housing stock is divided between
council estates and older terraces. Barking is to all
appearances a Labour stronghold, then. But the swing to the
Tories here at the 1979 Election was 14%, the highest
anywhere in Britain.

Barking and Dagenham lie at the heart of the wedge NE of
London which demonstrated the largest swings away from
Labour in 1979. There is little social change visible in the
census figures, and the proportion of owner-occupiers is not
increasing rapidly; the skilled workers of this district near
the Ford motor works simply shifted their preferences to the
Tories in large numbers. Barking is still a Labour seat, of
course; Tom Driberg held it for many years until 1974, when
he was replaced by the Tribunite Josephine (Jo) Richardson.
But it now harbours a considerable minority of working-class
Conservative voters. Only one ward, Longbridge on the Ilford
border, is regularly Conservative in Borough Council
elections, but in the 1982 municipal contests Gascoigne was
won by the Liberals, who have the Alliance nomination for
Barking constituency.

There are only minor boundary changes – Goresbrook ward is
transferred from Dagenham to help to equalise the electorates
of the two seats in the Borough, although Barking remains
well below the average size for England (65,000) with its
electorate of 55,000. Both seats will surely still be safe for
Labour; the main interest lies in the size of the swing, and
the size of the majority.

1981	% Own Occ	23.6	1979 core seat Barking		
1981	% Loc Auth	73.3	Lab	18,111	52.8
1981	% Black/Asian	6	C	11,103	32.4
1981	% Mid Cl	41.8	L	3,679	10.7
1981	% Prof Man	8.8	NF	1,021	3.0
1982	electorate 53,318		Ind Lab	400	1.2
1979	notional result		MPs since 1945		
	Lab 8,300		1945-59 S. Hastings Lab		
Alliance		L	1959-74 Tom Driberg Lab		
			1974- Jo Richardson Lab		

Dagenham   Barking / Dagenham

The present MP for Dagenham is John Parker, the Father of
the House, which means that he has sat in the Commons for a
longer continuous period than anyone else. He is the only
pre-Second World War MP left, having first been elected at
Romford in 1935 and for Dagenham in 1945.

His move was enforced by the rapid growth of Dagenham's
population, due to the construction of the massive Becontree
council estate, one of the largest local authority developments
there has ever been in Britain. The population of the new
community of Dagenham rose from 2,000 in 1922 to 103,000 in
1932, as the vast and monotonous layout of semi-detached
council houses was completed. Dagenham has been a Labour
stronghold since its creation, although it suffered a 13.5%
swing to the Tories at the 1979 General Election. This was
probably due to a combination of factors - the regional
variation in swing north and east of London, together with
the movement of opinion among the car workers of Fords,
Dagenham's largest employer. Other constituencies with a
large number of skilled manual workers also showed a large
swing to the Tories, particularly those like Birmingham
Northfield with a connection with the automobile industry.
There are also very few non-whites here among the council
houses in Outer London - this paucity also does not help
Labour.

Dagenham's borders are little altered by the Boundary
Commission. It remains a long, thin seat, stretching from the
Thames river frontage north to Chadwell Heath and Mark's
Cross. It is still a largely council-owned and working-class
seat, and Labour should win easily, despite the intervention
for the first time of an SDP candidate. John Parker is
retiring after nearly 50 years in the House; his replacement
is another man from the centre of the party, Bryan Gould,
formerly the MP for the ultra-marginal Southampton Test.

1981	% Own Occ	38.1	1979 core seat Dagenham		
1981	% Loc Auth	58.6	Lab	24,707	52.6
1981	% Black/Asian	3	C	14,600	31.1
1981	% Mid Cl	41.1	L	5,583	11.9
1981	% Prof Man	8.7	NF	1,553	3.3
1982	electorate 63,826		Comm	553	1.2
1979	notional result		MP since 1945		
	Lab 8,800		1945-	John Parker Lab	
Alliance		SDP			

Chipping Barnet   Barnet

Chipping Barnet is a constituency on the very outermost fringe of North London. It is semi-rural, reaching into the green belt itself. Indeed it is the successor to the Hertfordshire county seat of Barnet, which was represented by Reginald Maudling from 1950 to 1974, when it became part of Greater London and the Borough of Barnet. Maudling died just before the 1979 General Election, and was replaced by another man on the liberal wing of the Conservative Party, Sydney Chapman, the former MP for Handsworth, Birmingham.

Chipping Barnet is a safe Tory seat. Some of the most expensive housing in suburban North London is to be found along the A5109 road at Totteridge, which still has the air of a wealthy village. Most of the other districts are solidly middle class and owner-occupied: East Barnet, Arkley, Cockfosters, Hadley, Brunswick Park. There is scarcely any industry in the constituency, and the only feature which prevents it from appearing a monolithic identikit Tory stronghold is the rather high proportion of non-white residents - over 8%.

The seat, like many in London, is unaltered in the present boundary revision. The Liberals have the Alliance nomination in Chipping Barnet, but this is not their strongest seat in the Borough, and they can hope for no better than second place. Sydney Chapman will find Chipping Barnet a less volatile constituency than the socially changing Birmingham Handsworth.

1981	% Own Occ	72.5	1979 same seat	Chipping Barnet	
1981	% Loc Auth	17.9	C	25,154	57.1
1981	% Black/Asian	8.2	Lab	11,147	25.3
1981	% Mid Cl	67.9	L	6,867	15.6
1981	% Prof Man	26.1	NF	865	2.0
1982	electorate	58,915	MPs since 1950		
Alliance		L	1950-79 Reginald Maudling C		
			1979- Sydney Chapman C		

Finchley   Barnet

Margaret Thatcher achieved a great triumph in leading the
Conservatives to a decisive victory at the General Election of
May 1979, thus becoming Britain's first female Prime
Minister. She had displaced Edward Heath from the leadership
in February 1975, so 1979 was her first contest as party
leader in her own constituency of Finchley in NW London. Yet
she did not do outstandingly well in Finchley. Surprisingly,
the swing to the Conservatives there was only 4.7%, lower
than the London average. Mrs Thatcher's majority was still
under 8,000. It is still by no means a Tory citadel.

Why is Finchley not a true-blue suburban walkover for a
successful party leader? One of the reasons is that the
housing stock is older and poorer than in, say, Chipping
Barnet to the north. There is quite a high percentage of
privately rented accommodation – over 20% of the total.
Connected with this is another feature of Finchley: over 16%
of the population is non-white, a figure which has doubled in
the 1970s. In this respect it is more like neighbouring
Hornsey in Haringey than like Outer London. Many of the
non-whites are Asians, living in wards like East Finchley,
where Labour is the strongest party. Finchley itself and the
separate community of Friern Barnet are much more
Conservative.

However, it is likely that the political and social trend in
Finchley is still favourable to Labour. It seems inconceivable
that Mrs Thatcher could lose her own seat, even if her
government should be defeated. But Finchley has a large and
active Labour presence, and the Prime Minister can never
rely on a massive majority.

1981	% Own Occ	61.7	1979 same seat Finchley		
1981	% Loc Auth	17.0	C	20,918	52.5
1981	% Black/Asian	16.4	Lab	13,040	32.7
1981	% Mid Cl	65.5	L	5,254	13.2
1981	% Prof Man	24.9	NF	534	1.3
1982	electorate 56,098		Oth	86	0.2
Alliance		L	MPs since 1945		
			1945-59 J.F.E. Crowder C		
			1959- Margaret Thatcher C		

Hendon North   Barnet

Hendon North is the most marginal of the four Conservative constituencies in the Borough of Barnet. It is divided into two quite distinct halves. In the north, on the edge of the city, are the middle-class suburbs of Edgware and Mill Hill. In the latter there is a touch of genuine affluence: expensive houses enjoying something of a rural village ambience around a famous public school. To the south, though, is the vast inter-war council estate of Burnt Oak, also known as Watling. There is a very modern local authority development nearby at Grahame Park, and the Colindale ward is also predominantly working class.

The political pattern of the constituency matches its social divisions. Mill Hill and Edgware are very Conservative, Burnt Oak and Colindale Labour. The Conservatives have always won the seat since 1950, but in 1966 Sir Ian Orr-Ewing's majority was only 600, and in October 1974 Orr-Ewing's successor John Gorst won by just 1,750. Labour's vote is holding up better than elsewhere in London, probably because of the solidity of their support in the council estates - the swing against them was 5% between 1974 and 1979, and a further 3% between 1979 and the May 1982 local elections. But Labour still polled more votes in May 1982 than the Alliance in the wards which constitute Hendon North.

This is the only one of the four Barnet seats to be allocated to the SDP. But they have as yet made no impact here, despite the relative success of the Liberal-led Alliance in next-door Hendon South. There are only minor boundary changes affecting the seat. The Conservative northern half should continue to dictate the destiny of Hendon North, despite Labour's votes in Burnt Oak.

1981	% Own Occ	54.4	1979 core seat Hendon North		
1981	% Loc Auth	33.4	C	20,766	52.1
1981	% Black/Asian	11	Lab	14,374	36.0
1981	% Mid Cl	59.3	L	4,113	10.3
1981	% Prof Man	22.0	NF	638	1.6
1982	electorate 55,219		MPs since 1945		
1979	notional result		1945-50 Mrs B. Gould Lab		
	C 6,500		1950-70 Ian Orr-Ewing C		
Alliance		SDP	1970- John Gorst C		

Hendon South

Hendon South is more Conservative than Hendon North, with fewer council houses and some great affluence in the heavily Jewish districts of Golders Green, Childs Hill and Hampstead Garden Suburb. The centre of Hendon is to be found in the seat, and Labour's best ward of West Hendon. But it is the Liberals who have recently been active in Hendon South, at least in local politics, winning 32% of the vote in the municipal elections in 1982. The Liberals may take second place, but the former Welsh Secretary Peter Thomas should hold Hendon South comfortably for the Conservatives.

1981	% Own Occ	59.1	1979 core seat Hendon South			
1981	% Loc Auth	17.4	C	19,981	52.8	
1981	% Black/Asian	15	Lab	11,231	29.7	
1981	% Mid Cl	68.9	L	5,799	15.3	
1981	% Prof Man	31.6	E	563	1.5	
1982	electorate 54,490		NF	290	0.8	
1979	notional result		MPs since 1945			
	C 8,700		1945-70 Hugh Lucas-Tooth C			
Alliance		L	1970- Peter Thomas C			

Bexleyheath   Bexley

When Bexleyheath was created in 1974, it was felt that the constituency might just be vulnerable to Labour. This theory turned out to be inaccurate. Cyril Townsend won it easily for the Conservatives, which is scarcely surprising considering that Bexleyheath is a suburban Outer SE London seat with over 80% owner occupiers and very few non-whites. It will be even better ground for the Conservatives now, with the transfer of Barnehurst from Erith and Crayford.

1981	% Own Occ	81.5	1979 core seat Bexleyheath			
1981	% Loc Auth	12.5	C	21,888	53.7	
1981	% Black/Asian	4	Lab	13,342	32.7	
1981	% Mid Cl	60.8	L	4,782	11.7	
1981	% Prof Man	16.9	NF	749	1.8	
1982	electorate 59,965		MP since 1974			
1979	notional result		1974- Cyril Townsend C			
	C 10,400					
Alliance		L				

Erith and Crayford   Bexley

The political situation in Erith and Crayford is very
complex. This seat on the Thames marshes, on the very
border with Kent, is a three-way marginal. At the last
General Election, Jim Wellbeloved won Erith and Crayford for
Labour by a narrow margin - 2,733 votes. In the 1982 local
elections, the Conservatives actually received more votes than
Labour in the wards which made up the old constituency. But
the removal of middle-class Barnehurst in the boundary
changes now gives the advantage back to Labour.

But by this time Wellbeloved had defected to the SDP. Due to
the even split of votes between the major parties, the
Alliance's 25% in the new seat in 1982 was little over 10%
behind both Labour and Conservative. Wellbeloved must
believe he has a reasonable chance of closing that gap in the
General Election. 35% may suffice to win the contest in Erith
and Crayford.

Erith and Crayford now includes a very substantial amount of
council housing. The ultra-modern Thamesmead estate near
the river is partly within the seat, as are estates at
Belvedere and North End. Erith and Crayford are themselves
both strongly Labour. The only Conservative ward left after
Barnehurst's departure is Bostall. The Alliance were strongest
in May 1982 in Northumberland Heath, but even there they
only obtained a 29% level of support. Indeed, their vote
ranged from 20% to 30% in nearly every ward, confirming the
national impression that their vote is evenly spread
geographically and among social classes. But it also means
that Wellbeloved will have to find a boost above the level from
somewhere, if he is to hold Erith and Crayford.

1981	% Own Occ	57.1
1981	% Loc Auth	36.6
1981	% Black/Asian	6
1981	% Mid Cl	52.7
1981	% Prof Man	13.3
1982	electorate 50,927	
1979	notional result	
	Lab 4,500	
Alliance		SDP

1979 core seat Erith and
Crayford

Lab	22,450	47.2
C	19,717	41.5
L	4,512	9.5
NF	838	1.8

MPs since 1950
1950-65 N.N. Dodds Lab
1965-   James Wellbeloved Lab
                        (SDP)

Old Bexley and Sidcup   Bexley

Edward Heath represented the Bexley constituency from 1950 to 1974, for the last four years as Prime Minister. Bexley was split up in the boundary changes which took effect in February 1974, and Heath preferred to contest Sidcup to the more marginal Bexleyheath. Sidcup has remained loyal to Edward Heath, even though his government lost the February 1974 Election, and again finished second in October, and he was ousted by Margaret Thatcher as Conservative leader in 1975. He is still in Parliament, a dignified if isolated figure on the back benches, critical of the policy of the new Conservative regime and making a statesmanlike contribution to world affairs.

It seems unlikely that the mainstream of the Conservative Party will move back towards Heath and his way of thinking in the immediate future. But he has not announced his retirement from Parliament, and he seems intent on continuing to represent Sidcup. He should have few worries in this regard. There is a higher proportion of owner occupiers in Sidcup and Bexleyheath than anywhere else in London - about 81% in each constituency. By contrast only 12% of the housing in Sidcup is council owned. Here on the very edge of SE London there are virtually no non-white residents, again unusual in the cosmopolitan capital city. The Alliance may push their way into second place here, and they have local strength in Blackfen ward, but no one can challenge Edward Heath's hold on a part of Kentish London he has represented for over 30 years.

The seat is unaltered in boundary changes, but renamed Old Bexley and Sidcup. It is one of the smallest seats in London, with around 50,000 electors. Indeed Bexley Borough is fortunate to retain three seats, especially since the neighbouring Borough of Bromley has four small seats. But the Commission decided not to cross London Borough boundaries to equalise electorates.

1981	% Own Occ	80.6	1979 same seat Sidcup		
1981	% Loc Auth	12.7	C	23,692	59.8
1981	% Black/Asian	2.5	Lab	10,236	25.8
1981	% Mid Cl	66.5	L	4,908	12.4
1981	% Prof Man	21.7	NF	774	2.0
1982	electorate 50,927		MP since 1974		
Alliance		L	1974-	Edward Heath C	

Brent East   Brent

The controversial Greater London Council leader Ken
Livingstone has never made a secret of his parliamentary
ambitions. But his hopes of transforming his energy and
vision to the national scene came up against the problem of
finding a suitable seat. Livingstone was born in South
London, but his home and political base have been north of
the river for many years - he was a Camden councillor before
he took over the GLC, and he contested Hampstead at the
1979 General Election. The best Borough for Labour in NW
London is now Brent, which has not shared the general swing
to the Tories of recent years, mainly because of its large
non-white population. The seat which Livingstone decided to
aim for was Brent East - but his route was blocked by the
sitting Labour MP, Reg Freeson.

Brent East gains one Conservative ward, Chamberlayne, from
Brent South. But it should remain a safe Labour seat. 30% of
the population is non-white. Over 30% of the housing is still
privately rented. This part of London has long been known
for receiving immigrants - once Irish, now West Indian and
Asian. Many of the neighbourhoods reflect this tradition:
Kilburn, Queens Park, Willesden Green, Cricklewood,
Brondesbury Park, Neasden, Church End. There is relatively
little council housing here, except in the south towards the
near-slums of North Paddington and North Kensington.
It would be surprising if any Labour candidate were to lose
Brent East. The constituency is set in the heart of the
nation's largest West Indian community. Most of London seems
to be moving towards the Tories, but the swing in Brent East
was only 3% in 1979, and the Labour vote held up well in the
1982 local elections. The Alliance has shown little strength in
Brent East. It would form a sound platform for Livingstone,
the sprightly left-wing Londoner who has become so nationally
known and notorious while still a local leader.

1981	% Own Occ	41.1	1979 core seat Brent East		
1981	% Loc Auth	27.7	Lab	20,351	53.3
1981	% Black/Asian	30	C	14,008	36.7
1981	% Mid Cl	52.8	L	2,799	7.3
1981	% Prof Man	16.0	NF	706	1.9
1982	electorate 61,631		WRP	290	0.8
1979	notional result		MPs since 1974		
	Lab 5,900		1974-	Reg Freeson Lab	
Alliance		SDP			

Brent North   Brent

The MP for Brent North is an old-fashioned Tory, a devotee
of the personality, principles and policies of Margaret
Thatcher. Rhodes Boyson is the Minister in charge of higher
education: a suitable post for a well-known disciplinarian
headmaster who is also the holder of a PhD in History and
has several books to his credit. After a trial contest in a safe
Labour seat in his native Lancashire in the 1970 General
Election, Boyson entered Parliament at Brent North in
February 1974.

Brent North is, according to most indicators, a very safe
Conservative seat. Three quarters of the housing is owner
occupied, and nearly 60% of the employed workers have non-
manual jobs - the most commonly accepted definition of the
middle class. There are many respectable suburbs, some
bordering the Borough of Harrow: Kenton, Kingsbury,
Queensbury, Sudbury and Preston. But there is also just one
unusual feature which might have political consequences. 26%
of the population in the present Brent North is non-white,
the highest proportion of any Tory seat in Britain. The
further south one goes, the blacker Brent North becomes.
One ward from this cosmopolitan district, Tokyngton, has
been transferred to Brent South, but Brent North will still
have a significant non-white minority.

This does not mean that Boyson may lose his seat, even
though he only benefited from a 3% swing in 1979 - he still
has a comfortable 10,000 majority. None of the wards in Brent
North elected a Labour councillor in the 1982 Brent Borough
elections, when the Alliance only achieved 20% in their first
contest. With his stern morality and his mutton-chop
whiskers, Rhodes Boyson may seem to be a Victorian, even a
Dickensian figure; but as a militant Thatcherite he also seems
to represent a highly successful philosophy for the 1980s.

1981	% Own Occ	72.5	1979 core seat Brent North		
1981	% Loc Auth	16.4	C	29,795	53.8
1981	% Black/Asian	24	Lab	18,812	34.0
1981	% Mid Cl	66.1	L	5,872	10.6
1981	% Prof Man	25.9	NF	873	1.6
1982	electorate 63,401		MP since 1974		
1979	notional result		1974-	Rhodes Boyson C	
	C 12,000				
Alliance		SDP			

Brent South   Brent

Brent South is the most heavily West Indian parliamentary constituency in Britain. The proportion of the population which is non-white (43% in 1981) is likely to be exceeded in the new Parliament only by Southall in Ealing. As in Southall, the impact of this characteristic can be seen in the recent political history of the seat. The swing to the Conservatives in 1979 was a minimal 0.5%. Brent South, little altered in the boundary changes, will now rank as one of the safest Labour seats in the nation's capital.

This constituency is a long strip on the southern border of the Borough of Brent, from Alperton in the west to Kensal Rise in the east. The heaviest non-white concentration is near the Park Royal industrial estate, at Harlesden and Stonebridge (a ward which already has a well-known black councillor, Merle Amory). In the north, the seat extends as far as the centre of Wembley and its great stadium, mecca of the footballing world. The constituency is divided by many railway lines, and by the A406 North Circular Road. Seedy owner-occupied and privately rented houses outnumber the council estates.

Like Brent East, Brent South has seen a challenge to the sitting Labour MP. It was felt in some quarters that Laurence Pavitt was no longer left-wing enough for this constituency; and indeed it may well be true that social change is pushing Brent South not only towards Labour but also towards radical left-wing politics. The traditional and rather conservative London working classes once formed the backbone of the electorate and also of the Labour support in Brent South. But the seat has changed out of recognition since Pavitt was first elected in 1959.

1981	% Own Occ	49.4	1979 core seat Brent South		
1981	% Loc Auth	33.6	Lab	24,178	59.4
1981	% Black/Asian	43	C	12,562	30.9
1981	% Mid Cl	44.2	L	2,859	7.0
1981	% Prof Man	11.5	NF	811	2.0
1982	electorate 63,625		WRP	277	0.7
1979	notional result		MP since 1974		
	Lab 12,700		1974–	Laurence Pavitt Lab	
Alliance		L			

Beckenham   Bromley

Bromley is a large suburban middle-class residential Borough
in outer SE London. It has four safe Tory constituencies,
none of which is substantially altered in the boundary
changes. Beckenham is the most compact of the four, tucked
into the north-west corner of the Borough towards the centre
of London. It is predominantly affluent, but the further in
one progresses towards Crystal Palace the less Tory it
becomes. Anerley and Penge were Labour wards, with a
substantial non-white population, and are now inclined to the
Alliance, which may take second place in Beckenham next
time. The MP is a very senior and experienced Conservative,
Philip Goodhart.

1981	% Own Occ	62.8	1979 same seat Beckenham	
1981	% Loc Auth	21.3	C	22,607	56.9
1981	% Black/Asian	6.5	Lab	10,056	25.1
1981	% Mid Cl	69.1	L	6,450	14.9
1981	% Prof Man	24.1	E	762	1.8
1982	electorate 59,471		NF	606	1.4
Alliance		L	MPs since 1950	

1950-57 P. Buchan-Hughes C
1957-   Philip Goodhart C

Chislehurst   Bromley

The NE part of the Borough of Bromley enjoys some social
and political contrasts, even though it is not really marginal.
Chislehurst itself has some of the best residential areas in
Outer London, especially around the Common. But there are
also two large, albeit respectable, council estates –
Mottingham and St Paul's Cray – which were mainly
responsible for electing a Labour MP in 1966. This was but an
aberration in Pat Hornsby-Smith's 25-year tenure. The
boundaries were changed in 1974, but are unaltered now.

1981	% Own Occ	63.0	1979 same seat Chislehurst	
1981	% Loc Auth	29.2	C	23,259	54.4
1981	% Black/Asian	3.0	Lab	13,494	31.6
1981	% Mid Cl	66.5	L	5,335	12.5
1981	% Prof Man	26.8	NF	564	1.3
1982	electorate 55,296		MPs since 1950	
Alliance		L		

1950-66 P. Hornsby-Smith C
1966-70 Alistair Macdonald Lab
1970-74 P. Hornsby-Smith C
1974-   Roger Sims C

Orpington   Bromley

In March 1962 a new political phenomenon was born -
'Orpington Man', the symbol of the rebellion of traditional
Tory voters against the goverment of Harold Macmillan (whose
own seat of Bromley was right next to Orpington). Liberal
Eric Lubbock was elected after a massive swing. Lubbock held
on to this seat on the very fringes of rural Kent until 1970,
but he was then ousted by Ivor Stanbrook, who has since
consolidated the Tory position. The Orpington byelection was
the high-water mark of the 1960s Liberal revival, but it
foretold neither a great national upsurge for the party nor a
long-lasting impact here in comfortable commuterdom.

1981	% Own Occ	77.1	1979 core seat Orpington		
1981	% Loc Auth	17.5	C	32,150	58.0
1981	% Black/Asian	2.5	L	16,074	29.0
1981	% Mid Cl	70.4	Lab	6,581	11.9
1981	% Prof Man	25.8	NF	516	0.9
1982	electorate 59,110		Oth	146	0.3
1979	notional result		MPs since 1945		
	C 13,000		1945-55 Sir W. Smithers C		
Alliance		L	1955-62 W.D.M. Sumner C		
			1962-70 Eric Lubbock L		
			1970- Ivor Stanbrook C		

Ravensbourne   Bromley

Ravensbourne takes in that south-eastern part of the Borough
which is most associated with the community of Bromley itself,
which was held by Harold Macmillan from 1945 to 1964. It also
includes the communities of West Wickham, Keston, Hayes,
and now Biggin Hill and Darwin wards are transferred from
Orpington. Ravensbourne is the most Conservative of the four
Bromley Borough seats, the most completely given over to
purely residential middle-class occupation. It will remain safe
for Macmillan's successor at Bromley, liberal Tory John Hunt.

1981	% Own Occ	76.3	1979 core seat Ravensbourne		
1981	% Loc Auth	12.8	C	22,501	60.9
1981	% Black/Asian	2.5	L	7,111	19.3
1981	% Mid Cl	70.6	Lab	6,848	18.5
1981	% Prof Man	25.8	NF	478	1.3
1982	electorate 59,313		MP since 1974		
1979	notional result		1974- John Hunt C		
	C 18,300				
Alliance		SDP			

Hampstead and Highgate   Camden

Few parts of London have so clear or well-publicised an image as Hampstead. But the legend of affluent middle-class radicalism is in danger of fostering several myths. It is true that Hampstead is more inclined to Labour than most constituencies of its economic composition, and it did once elect a Labour MP (in 1966). But this is a seat of 75,000 electors, and it spreads far beyond the fashionable Hampstead Town district near the Heath. In fact the Labour votes come mainly from far less attractive areas - Kilburn, ex-Irish and now largely West Indian, and West Hampstead. The politically and socially mixed Swiss Cottage, Fortune Green and Belsize Park are also in the seat. The name is changed as Highgate ward comes in from St Pancras N. The Hampstead Town ward itself is easily Conservative.

Nor is it true that Hampstead is especially good ground for the Alliance, despite the presence of radical lawyers, academics and writers. The Alliance candidates only polled 25.6% in the new constituency in the 1982 Camden Borough elections, which put them into a mediocre third place. The Conservatives remain in the lead here, although Labour's vote has held up far better here than elsewhere in London. To challenge another myth, the Labour candidate at the last General Election restrained the pro-Tory swing to 2%, one of the lowest figures in London. That candidate was the supposedly unpopular 'Red Ken' Livingstone, now leader of the GLC.

Livingstone has moved to better ground. But Labour, not the SDP, remains the strongest threat to Tory MP Geoffrey Finsberg. Hampstead is certainly a vibrant and intellectually distinguished part of London, if a little incestuous - over 80 MPs live in the division! But its politics are not so abnormal as is rumoured. Perhaps the Labour vote is a little more solid than elsewhere, because it is drawn from the very top and the bottom of the social scale, rather than from the more volatile middling orders.

1981	% Own Occ	33.6	1979 core seat Hampstead		
1981	% Loc Auth	28.7	C	20,410	47.3
1981	% Black/Asian	10	Lab	16,729	38.8
1981	% Mid Cl	72.6	L	5,753	13.3
1981	% Prof Man	30.3	NF	255	0.6
1982	electorate 68,211		MPs since 1945		
1979	notional result		1945-50 C. Challen C		
	C 3,800		1950-66 Henry Brooke C		
Alliance		SDP	1966-70 Ben Whitaker Lab		
			1970- Geoffrey Finsberg C		

Holborn and St Pancras   Camden

Camden is now entitled only to two parliamentary constituencies rather than three. The northern half of the Borough is little affected by the redistribution, for Hampstead just picks up one ward, Highgate, from St Pancras N. But the two seats in the southern half are effectively merged, bringing together two Labour MPs, Frank Dobson of Holborn and St Pancras S and Albert (Jock) Stallard of St Pancras N. Thus one Labour seat is lost, and one Labour MP must look elsewhere.

The new Holborn and St Pancras seat will contain many famous neighbourhoods in the capital city. Moving north from the centre of London, it includes Holborn, Bloomsbury, King's Cross, St Pancras, Somers Town, Kentish Town, Primrose Hill, Haverstock Hill and Gospel Oak. Despite the distinguished nature of the public buildings here, commercial in Holborn and academic and scientific in Bloomsbury, this will be a safe Labour seat. Only 15% of the housing is owner occupied, and over half the residents are tenants of the local authority, often living in blocks of council flats. Young professionals are in evidence too, as in Islington districts like Barnsbury to the east, but Holborn and St Pancras is still predominantly working class.

The southern half of the Camden Borough typifies the way that the depopulated inner city seats of Britain are being eliminated in the redistribution. As here, such seats are usually Labour strongholds, and as here Labour members are left without seats, having to fight it out for fewer, enlarged divisions.

1981	% Own Occ	14.5	New seat
1981	% Loc Auth	62.2	
1981	% Black/Asian	10.5	
1981	% Mid Cl	52.4	
1981	% Prof Man	15.3	
1982	electorate 71,044		
1979	notional result		
	Lab 7,900		
Alliance		L	

Croydon Central   Croydon

Croydon is not just a major commuting base for the centre of London. It is also in its own right the commercial and shopping metropolis of South London, attracting daily its own influx of workers. It has an impressive cluster of skyscrapers at its heart, the district Americans would call the 'downtown'. It also has its own electoral anatomy, its own Labour council estates and Tory leafy suburbs.

The 'downtown' is, logically enough, in Croydon Central constituency. Central was created in the early 1970s, and it immediately became clear that it was the most marginal of Croydon's four Conservative seats. In October 1974 John Moore's majority over Labour was reduced to just 164 votes. Indeed, in 1966 Labour's David Winnick actually won a seat similar to this one, although it was then named Croydon South. There are seedy 'inner city' areas in Central Croydon, which harbour most of the constituency's non-white population. But most of the heavy Labour minority vote in the seat comes from a district which is in no way central - the large council estate of New Addington on the edge of Croydon and of London itself. Central also includes the strongly Conservative wards of Spring Grove, Heathfield and Fairfield.

Croydon Central has swung a long way to the Conservatives since October 1974. In the 1979 General Election, John Moore secured a 7.7% swing which increased his majority to 8,000. The 1982 local elections recorded a further 8% movement towards the Tories. In the boundary changes the marginal inner Broad Green ward is moved to Croydon NW. This will make it even harder for Labour to recover to win Croydon Central, which now looks like a safe Conservative seat, despite the presence of New Addington and the Croydon 'downtown'.

1981	% Own Occ	50.9	1979 core seat Croydon Central	
1981	% Loc Auth	37.7	C	26,457	52.5
1981	% Black/Asian	8	Lab	18,499	36.7
1981	% Mid Cl	60.6	L	5,112	10.1
1981	% Prof Man	19.8	Oth	354	0.7
1982	electorate 56,959		MP since 1974	
1979	notional result		1974-	John Moore C
	C 8,800			
Alliance		SDP		

Croydon North-East   Croydon

The MP for Croydon NE is Bernard Weatherill, a senior and
respected Conservative who is probably the favourite to
succeed George Thomas as Speaker of the House of
Commons. If he does so, his seat may not be fought on party
lines. But this sector of Croydon is a near-certainty for the
Conservatives now in any case.

It is not particularly affluent, but consists of the swathes of
mainly owner-occupied housing running down the southern
slopes from the Crystal Palace ridge. The neighbourhoods are
respectable enough, but rarely rich - Selhurst Park,
Addiscombe, Thornton Heath, South Norwood and now Upper
Norwood, taken from Croydon NW. The most up-market ward
is Monks Orchard, on the border with the Borough of
Bromley.

Like much of outer south London, Croydon NE has swung
heavily to the right of late. In October 1974, Weatherill's
majority was only a little over 2,000. By 1979 it was nearly
7,000. Upper Norwood will make it safer still. But the revival
is not connected just with Weatherill's popularity. In the local
elections of May 1982, the Tory candidates polled 24% more
than Labour in the new Croydon NE wards. The Alliance
could not do better than a poor third place. This does not
bode well for the Liberal MP Bill Pitt who sits for the next-
door constituency of Croydon NW, although it is the SDP who
have the nomination in NE. Bernard Weatherill can count on
support from his constituency, even if he cannot yet be sure
that his fellow members will honour him with the Speakership.

1981	% Own Occ	63.3	1979 core seat Croydon North-
1981	% Loc Auth	19.3	East
1981	% Black/Asian	14	C 21,560 51.0
1981	% Mid Cl	62.9	Lab 14,784 35.0
1981	% Prof Man	18.3	L 5,459 12.9
1982	electorate 63,378		NF 464 1.1
1979	notional result		MPs since 1955
	C 7,800		1955-64 J. Hughes-Hallett C
Alliance		SDP	1964- Bernard Weatherill C

Croydon North-West   Croydon

In retrospect, it may well come to seem that the Liberal byelection victory at Croydon NW in October 1981 marked the high-water mark of the Alliance's thrust of the early 1980s. It was a remarkable performance. The Liberal candidate, Bill Pitt, had lost his deposit in the 1979 General Election; in the 1981 GLC election just six months before the byelection Pitt had scarcely done any better. Croydon NW had been regarded as a Tory marginal vulnerable to Labour. But the seat fell in the first flush of enthusiasm of the young Alliance in the first British byelection after Roy Jenkins's inaugural campaign at Warrington in July 1981.

Croydon NW is not archetypal Liberal country. To the south it approaches the seedy inner part of Croydon, where Labour is traditionally ahead. To the north the leafy slopes of Beulah Hill offer the strongest Conservative support. Altogether over 20% of the population is non-white. The acquisition of Broad Green ward and the loss of Upper Norwood in the boundary changes would help Labour in a normal year, in normal circumstances. Indeed it may well be that Bill Pitt will not be able to repeat his byelection triumph. The omens of the May 1982 local elections are not promising. In the old constituency the Alliance candidates polled only 26%, compared with 50% for the Conservatives and 23% for Labour. With the inclusion of Broad Green, Labour would actually have pushed the Alliance into third place.

Many Liberal MPs first returned in byelections have consolidated their hold on their constituency subsequently. David Steel, first elected at Roxburgh, Selkirk and Peebles in 1965, is one good example. Cyril Smith (Rochdale, 1972) is another. But some enjoy only a brief political career in the House before returning to obscurity. Unfortunately for Bill Pitt it seems very likely that it is the latter fate that will befall him.

1981	% Own Occ	63.6	1979 core seat Croydon North-
1981	% Loc Auth	19.8	West
1981	% Black/Asian	23	C 19,928 49.4
1981	% Mid Cl	54.4	Lab 16,159 40.1
1981	% Prof Man	14.6	L 4,239 10.5
1982	electorate 58,946		MPs since 1955
1979	notional result		1955-70 F.W. Harris C
	C 1,400		1970-81 Robert Taylor C
Alliance		L	1981- Bill Pitt L

Croydon South   Croydon

In 1966 Labour's David Winnick won the Croydon South constituency, albeit by only 81 votes. But that seat was in no way similar to the present division of the same name. The Croydon South Winnick held from 1966-70 was the forerunner of the present Croydon Central, and included the massive New Addington council estate. The current Croydon South, which came into existence in time for the February 1974 Election, consists of ultra-middle-class suburbs formerly in East Surrey county constituency - in fact the E Surrey MP William Clark moved to Croydon South due to the boundary changes.

Indeed, the records that Croydon South breaks now have nothing to do with marginality. It is the most middle-class seat in Britain, in the sense that 76% of its working population were employed in non-manual jobs in 1981. 80% of the housing is owner occupied, only 10% rented from the local council. Small wonder that it was the second safest Tory seat in London at the 1979 General Election. The Liberals were second, and Labour obtained a derisory vote, near deposit-losing level. The seat is uniformly affluent - Purley, Coulsdon, Woodcote, Sanderstead and Selsdon, where the Conservatives once held a conference which marked a right-wing turn in economic policy.

That Selsdon Park Hotel meeting typifies the politics of Croydon South. Sir William Clark is a Thatcherite loyalist, a reincarnation of 'Selsdon Man', and his position here is impregnable. Labour obtained less than 10% of the votes in the 1982 local elections, and the Alliance only 25%. The constituency is little altered in the boundary review.

1981	% Own Occ	80.0	1979 core seat Croydon South		
1981	% Loc Auth	10.6	C	30,874	64.9
1981	% Black/Asian	5	L	10,006	21.0
1981	% Mid Cl	76.0	Lab	6,249	13.1
1981	% Prof Man	29.7	NF	469	1.0
1982	electorate 64,930		MP since 1974		
1979	notional result		1974- Sir William Clark C		
	C 21,400				
Alliance		L			

33

Acton   Ealing

Before the 1974 redistribution Acton was a marginal seat which usually fell to the Labour Party. The wards at the eastern end of Ealing Borough, on the border with Hammersmith, are still politically closely contested. But in 1974 the Hanger Lane district was added to Acton, which effectively gave it to the Conservative Party and to Sir George Young. Hanger Lane and Ealing Common are comfortable and Conservative residential areas, with large Victorian mansions and leafy green parks.

In the present boundary changes, more of the Hanger Hill middle-class bloc is added, in the form of the Pitshanger ward. Pitshanger is also strongly Conservative, and it reinforces Sir George Young's position while helping Labour in the more marginal Ealing North, from whence it came. These western wards do contrast strongly with Acton town centre, which has a high proportion of privately rented accommodation and a large number of non-white residents. There are few council houses anywhere in the Acton seat.

Sir George Young is not a crabbed and crusty aged knight of the shires. Although he was educated at Eton and Christ Church, Oxford, he is a hereditary baronet and was elected at the age of 32 in February 1974. He is a moderate junior minister who cycles to work at Westminster and leads anti-smoking campaigns. His position is again strengthened in Acton by boundary changes, for the second time in a decade.

1981	% Own Occ	48.3	1979 core seat Acton			
1981	% Loc Auth	22.2	C	21,056	51.9	
1981	% Black/Asian	14	Lab	15,258	37.6	
1981	% Mid Cl	64.1	L	3,549	8.7	
1981	% Prof Man	23.6	NF	501	1.2	
1982	electorate 62,132		Oth	243	0.6	
1979	notional result		MPs since 1945			
	C 8,700		1945-59 J.A. Sparks Lab			
Alliance		SDP	1959-64 Philip Holland C			
			1964-68 B. Floud Lab			
			1968-74 Nigel Spearing Lab			
			1974- Sir George Young C			

Ealing North   Ealing

In general, Labour has not done well out of the present boundary review. Overall, between 30 and 40 seats have been added to the Conservative majority in Parliament by the redrawing of lines. But here and there Labour have been given a boost. One example occurs in the closely contested London Borough of Ealing. The strongest Tory ward in the highly marginal Ealing North seat, Pitshanger, is moved into Acton. This relatively minor change would have been sufficient to wipe out Harry Greenway's slender 1,480 majority in 1979 and give Labour this west London seat by a very narrow margin. Ealing N will remain extremely tight, but Labour should now be favourites in an even year.

Ealing North is a classic marginal, consisting of a variety of mixed neighbourhoods. It is situated in the NW section of the Borough, on each side of the A40 as it leaves London on its way towards Oxford. West End, Mandeville and Hobbayne wards consist of large council estates, where Labour is strong. Greenford, Wood End and Costons are very close. Perivale and Argyle (near Hanger Hill) are more Conservative. Around 15% of the population is non-white: high, but nowhere near as high as in neighbouring Southall. There is a considerable quantity of light industry and warehousing in the constituency.

Despite periodic boundary changes, Ealing North has been one of the closest constituencies in London for many years. Its percentage of owner occupiers and council tenants, of working-class and middle-class residents, of non-white residents, are all close to London's average. It should fall to the winning party in a General Election. The Alliance received only 23% of the vote in the wards constituting the new seat in May 1982 - their highest figure in Ealing, but not enough to worry the two major parties in Ealing North.

1981	% Own Occ	58.9	1979 core seat Ealing North		
1981	% Loc Auth	32.0	C	27,524	46.0
1981	% Black/Asian	15	Lab	26,044	43.6
1981	% Mid Cl	55.5	L	5,162	8.6
1981	% Prof Man	16.0	NF	1,047	1.8
1982	electorate 68,649		MPs since 1950		
1979	notional result		1950-55 J.H. Hudson Lab		
	Lab 1,400		1955-64 J.W. Barter C		
Alliance		L	1964-79 William Molloy Lab		
			1979- Harry Greenway C		

Southall   Ealing

The politics of Southall are dominated by one issue - that of
race. In the 1981 census, 43.7% of the population lived in
households where the head of the family was born in the New
Commonwealth or Pakistan. This is likely to prove to be the
highest non-white proportion in any constituency in the new
Parliament. In 1971 25% were black or Asian, so the trend
suggests that some time during the 1980s Southall may become
the first seat in Britain with a non-white majority.

Southall is the southern part of the Borough of Ealing. Why
has it become the most heavily Asian part of London? Partly
the cause was the easy availability of inexpensive private
housing - only 16% of the housing in the seat is council
owned. Once the district had initially become popular with
Asian immigrants in the 1950s and 1960s, many others
followed, to be concentrated in the Northcote and Glebe wards
south of the A4020 Uxbridge Road. This district, and the
centre of Southall around the High Street, is almost entirely
occupied by Asian families and businesses. The eastern end
of the constituency, Hanwell and West Ealing, is much more
white.

The party political preferences of Southall reflect its changing
racial composition. Although there are often independent
Asian candidates in both local and General Elections, Labour's
vote has held up here very well. The swing to the
Conservatives in 1979 was only 0.3%, Labour's best result in
London. In local elections too, Labour remains well ahead in
Southall. The MP is still a white man, the active Tribunite
Syd Bidwell, and he has nothing to fear from Tories and
Alliance in this outpost of Asia in West London.

1981	% Own Occ	64.7
1981	% Loc Auth	19.2
1981	% Black/Asian	43.7
1981	% Mid Cl	45.5
1981	% Prof Man	12.9
1982	electorate 71,085	
Alliance		L

1979 same seat Southall

Lab	28,498	54.4
C	17,220	32.9
L	3,920	7.5
NF	1,545	2.9
Oths	1,229	2.3

MPs since 1945
1945-50 W.H. Ayles Lab
1950-66 G.A. Pargiter Lab
1966-   Sydney Bidwell Lab

Edmonton   Enfield

The Boundary Commission's proposals for redrawn
constituencies in the London Borough of Enfield were delayed
for nearly two years by a protracted legal wrangle concerning
the new local government ward boundaries. The Commission's
provisional recommendations were eventually published in
August 1980, well after those for the other 31 London
Boroughs, all of which appeared in June 1979. In the end,
only minor adjustments have been made to the three Enfield
constituencies, but for a while it looked as if the whole
process of redistribution may be held up by Enfield alone.
Edmonton is situated in the SE corner of Enfield. It is the
most strongly Labour of the three seats in the Borough –
held continuously since 1935, although sometimes by narrow
margins. For the first time in nigh on 50 years, Edmonton
now looks very vulnerable to the Conservatives. Edward
Graham's majority in 1979 was a shaky 1,980, but the
boundary adjustments will eat into his lead as more territory
is transferred from Enfield North and Southgate. The best
part of Edmonton for Labour is the east end, on the bank of
the River Lee, around the A1010 (the old road to Hertford
and Cambridge). To the west it becomes more middle class,
more residential, more white, more Conservative.
In the 1982 local elections in Enfield, the Conservatives
achieved a small majority in the wards which make up the new
Edmonton. Even under the new boundaries, it would take a
further swing to the Tories since 1979 for Edmonton to fall.
But such an event would be a powerful symbol of the long-
term decline of London Labour – for the last time it happened
was in Labour's disastrous year of 1931.

1981	% Own Occ	62	1979 core seat Edmonton		
1981	% Loc Auth	28	Lab	20,713	47.1
1981	% Black/Asian	19	C	18,733	42.6
1981	% Mid Cl	48	L	3,276	7.5
1981	% Prof Man	14	NF	1,213	2.8
1982	electorate 64,953		MPs since 1945		
1979	notional result		1945-48 E.F.M. Durbin Lab		
	Lab 900		1948-74 Austen Albu Lab		
Alliance		L	1974- Edward Graham Lab		

Enfield North   Enfield

Enfield North is an archetypal marginal seat. Like Edmonton,
it verges from the Conservative green belt in the west, to
tower blocks and industry east of the Cambridge Road.
Enfield Town and Chase are Conservative, Ponders End and
Enfield Lock and Wash are Labour. Tim Eggar gained the seat
for the Tories in the 1979 Election, and he seems comfortable,
for the 1982 local election results indicated that the Tory lead
had stretched to 17%. Like Edmonton, its housing tenure
pattern fits closely the London average, but there are few
non-whites here in outermost North London.

1981	% Own Occ	61	1979 core seat Enfield North
1981	% Loc Auth	29	C 24,927 48.1
1981	% Black/Asian	7	Lab 21,444 41.3
1981	% Mid Cl	50	L 4,681 9.0
1981	% Prof Man	14	NF 816 1.6
1982	electorate 68,184		MPs since 1974
1979	notional result		1974-79 Bryan Davies Lab
	C 4,100		1979- Tim Eggar C
Alliance		SDP	

Enfield, Southgate   Enfield

Southgate is the only truly safe Tory seat in Enfield. It is
typical middle-class suburbia, with almost entirely inter-war
private housing stock. All the constituent neighbourhoods are
Conservative - Winchmore Hill, Cockfosters, Palmers Green,
Oakwood, Arnos Park. This haven on the edge of the
Hertfordshire green belt will remain super-safe for
Government Whip Anthony Berry. The Alliance is not strong
anywhere in Enfield, and only reached 23% in Southgate in
1982; they can hope for no better than second place next
time.

1981	% Own Occ	75	1979 core seat Southgate
1981	% Loc Auth	11	C 31,663 61.6
1981	% Black/Asian	16	Lab 11,584 22.6
1981	% Mid Cl	68	L 7,223 14.1
1981	% Prof Man	26	NF 895 1.7
1982	electorate 65,376		MPs since 1950
1979	notional result		1950-64 A.B. Baxter C
	C 18,400		1964- Anthony Berry C
Alliance		L	

Eltham   Greenwich

The new Eltham division is very similar to the old Woolwich
West; only minor changes resulting from ward boundary
alterations are made. Like Woolwich West, Eltham will be
marginal. The independently-minded Peter Bottomley gained
Woolwich W for the Tories in a byelection in 1975, during the
final period of unpopular Wilsonian Labour government.
Bottomley did well to hold the seat in 1979, and now seems to
have consolidated his position. In the 1982 local elections the
Conservatives were 10% ahead of Labour in the new Eltham,
and Bottomley will start favourite to win next time.
The constituency takes in the southern portion of the
Borough of Greenwich, away from the Thames river-
frontage. In general, it becomes more Conservative the
further south one progresses towards the border with
Bromley Borough. Nearly half the housing is council owned,
and Labour does best in the estates at Shooters Hill and Well
Hall. Much of Eltham itself has owner-occupied houses used as
commuting bases, and this is strongly Conservative,
particularly around the Palace and in New Eltham.
Eltham will be the only Liberal-led seat in Greenwich
Borough, but prospects for the Alliance are not good in this
Tory-Labour marginal. The Liberals only polled 9.7% in
Woolwich West in 1979 and lost their deposit. In the 1982 local
elections, Alliance candidates received only 23.7%, and won
just one ward, Avery Hill.

1981	% Own Occ	46.2	1979 core seat Woolwich West
1981	% Loc Auth	47.4	C 21,222 47.3
1981	% Black/Asian	5	Lab 18,613 41.5
1981	% Mid Cl	59.0	L 4,363 9.7
1981	% Prof Man	15.7	NF 630 1.4
1982	electorate 55,661		MPs since 1945
1979	notional result		1945-50 H. Berry Lab
	C 2,900		1950-59 W.A. Steward C
Alliance		L	1959-64 C.W.C. Turner C
			1964-75 William Hamling Lab
			1975- Peter Bottomley C

Greenwich   Greenwich

On the south bank of the Thames, opposite the Isle of Dogs, in the heart of London's East End and dockland, lies Greenwich. Despite its ability to attract tourism, with its Royal Naval College and observatory at the meridian, Greenwich is part of London's working-class inner city. Heavy industry lines the river-bank. More housing is council owned than owner occupied, some in the form of towers and tenements. Greenwich has been safely Labour since the war. From 1959 to 1971 it was held by Richard Marsh, once the Transport Secretary in Harold Wilson's government, and later Chairman of British Rail. Marsh later joined the Conservative Party, but Greenwich has not altered its allegiances.

This is not to say that there are no Conservative districts in the Greenwich constituency. Blackheath is a fashionable residential area, on the border with Lewisham East division. Vanbrugh ward also fell to the Tories in the 1982 local elections, when overall they were only 12% behind Labour in the constituency as a whole. The Conservative candidate at the General Election was Narindar Saroop, an Asian businessman. (The Conservatives have shown themselves as willing as the other parties to adopt non-white candidates.)

Labour still pull ahead due to their heavy vote in Greenwich itself and in Charlton, and Richard Marsh's successor Guy Barnett should have little difficulty retaining this little altered seat next time.

1981	% Own Occ	30.6	1979 core seat Greenwich		
1981	% Loc Auth	54.1	Lab	18,975	52.1
1981	% Black/Asian	8	C	12,133	33.3
1981	% Mid Cl	54.0	L	3,870	10.6
1981	% Prof Man	15.9	NF	951	2.6
1982	electorate 52,197		Oth	460	1.3
1979	notional result		MPs since 1945		
	Lab 7,000		1945-59 J. Reeves Lab		
Alliance		SDP	1959-71 Richard Marsh Lab		
			1971- Guy Barnett Lab		

Woolwich   Greenwich

The south-east London district of Woolwich has long played a
prominent role in Labour politics. It was first won by the
infant party in 1903, when Will Crooks was elected. Woolwich
East, the predecessor of the new Woolwich, was held by
Labour continuously from 1922 to the 1970s, even surviving
Labour's disaster of 1931. The formidable former trade union
leader Ernie Bevin, who was Foreign Secretary in Attlee's
government, moved to Woolwich East in 1950 when his
Wandsworth Central seat suffered boundary changes. Bevin
only represented his constituency for a year, and on his
death Christopher Mayhew was elected. Then in the 1970s
Woolwich East began to suffer from defections. Mayhew became
a Liberal in July 1974, but he didn't defend Woolwich East in
the October Election. Then his successor John Cartwright left
Labour to become a founder member of the SDP in 1981.
Will Cartwright hold Woolwich, or will Labour's long tradition
of winning at General Elections here continue? The best
evidence we have is that of the local elections of May 1982,
when the Alliance candidates polled only 30% in Woolwich to
Labour's 48%. Clearly Cartwright will have to hope for a
sizeable personal vote as well as an improvement in the
general level of Alliance support.
There are some middle-class residential districts in the seat,
around Plumstead, but Woolwich is a working-class and
industrial division. Down on the marshes the tower blocks of
the new Thamesmead development have risen in the last
decade. Woolwich still looks the part of a Labour heartland.

1981	% Own Occ	38.5	1979 core seat Woolwich East		
1981	% Loc Auth	52.5	Lab	21,700	58.9
1981	% Black/Asian	11	C	11,240	30.5
1981	% Mid Cl	45.5	L	2,998	8.1
1981	% Prof Man	8.4	NF	884	2.4
1982	electorate 56,037		MPs since 1945		
1979	notional result		1945-50 E.G. Hicks Lab		
	Lab 10,600		1950-51 Ernest Bevin Lab		
Alliance		SDP	1951-74 Christopher Mayhew Lab		
			(L)		
			1974- John Cartwright Lab		
			(SDP)		

Hackney North and Stoke Newington   Hackney

Rather like its neighbouring Borough, Islington, Hackney is
to be reduced from three seats to two by the Boundary
Commissioners. Again, the Central division disappears, and
its consituent wards are shared between North and South. In
Hackney, however, it is the Labour Party and not the SDP
which faces the most major problems as a result of this
pruning. The Labour MP for Hackney Central, Stanley Clinton
Davis, was only reselected narrowly in 1981 after a battle
with the left in the constituency. Now he has to enter
another intra-party election contest, probably against two
left-wing candidates: Ernie Roberts, the MP for Hackney N,
and Brian Sedgemore, a former MP who has been chosen to
stand against the SDP's Ron Brown in Hackney South. Davis's
chances of survival this time seem slim.

The most likely Labour standard-bearer in the new enlarged
Hackney N/Stoke Newington is Ernie Roberts, a long-serving
left-wing AUEW official who entered Parliament for the first
time at the age of 67 in 1979. The constituency will include
some middle-class terrain, and one Conservative ward,
Springfield. Some tip Hackney as good ground for future
gentrification. But the percentage of blacks and Asians is
very high, over 30%, and only 22% of the housing in the seat
is owner occupied. Although more socially mixed than its
neighbour Hackney South, it is a predominantly working-class
NE London constituency.

The Alliance will be Liberal-led here - it will be the only seat
in Hackney and Islington where there will be no sitting SDP
member. But the Alliance obtained only 17% of the vote in the
new Hackney N. Labour - and Ernie Roberts - remain strong
favourites to win next time.

1981	% Own Occ	22.3	1979 core seat Hackney North/	
1981	% Loc Auth	54.3	Stoke Newington	
1981	% Black/Asian	31	Lab 14,688	51.6
1981	% Mid Cl	47.9	C 9,467	33.2
1981	% Prof Man	11.9	L 3,033	10.6
1982	electorate 66,491		NF 860	3.0
1979	notional result		Comm 440	1.5
	Lab 9,300		MPs since 1950	
Alliance		L	1950-79 David Weitzman Lab	
			1979- Ernest Roberts Lab	

Hackney South and Shoreditch   Hackney

Ron Brown is the brother of Lord George-Brown, the former Labour Deputy Leader. Both brothers have now left the party, which means that Ron will be seeking to defend his Hackney South and Shoreditch seat as an SDP candidate at the next General Election. He faces several difficulties. The Alliance candidates polled only 20% in Hackney at the 1982 local elections, trailing over 30% behind Labour. Hackney South is also expanded greatly to take in half of the abolished Hackney Central seat - the wards of Homerton, Kings Park, Westdown and Wick. Central was the safest of the three Labour seats in Hackney, and of course Brown will not be able to claim a personal vote as a long-serving MP here.

Hackney South and Shoreditch is an inner urban seat. In the south it borders on the City of London itself. A quarter of the population is non-white. In Haggerston, Kings Park and Wenlock wards over 90% of the housing is council owned. There is actually also a strong National Front presence: their leader John Tyndall obtained nearly 8% of the vote as candidate here in the 1979 Election, their best performance anywhere in Britain. The NF have been particularly active around Hoxton market, but the period when they threatened to become a serious political force in Hackney seems to have passed.

The Alliance won Haggerston, Moorfields and Wenlock wards in the 1982 local elections, but Ron Brown is not one of the SDP defectors who has a good chance of retaining his seat flying his new colours. The local Liberals are reluctant to support him. The most likely winner is Brian Sedgemore, formerly a leading Tribunite as MP for Luton West in the late 1970s. Hackney, like Islington, will in all likelihood return to the Labour fold at the General Election.

1981	% Own Occ	10.9	1979 core seat Hackney South/		
1981	% Loc Auth	74.9	Shoreditch		
1981	% Black/Asian	25	Lab	14,016	54.1
1981	% Mid Cl	41.3	C	7,312	28.2
1981	% Prof Man	9.5	L	2,387	9.2
1982	electorate 70,730		NF	1,958	7.6
1979	notional result		WRP	215	0.8
	Lab 11,400		MP since 1974		
Alliance		SDP	1974-	Ron Brown Lab (SDP)	

Fulham   Hammersmith and Fulham

The former Labour Foreign Secretary Michael Stewart represented a Fulham constituency from 1945 to 1979. But as time passed the Labour majority was eroded by the colonisation of the Fulham bend of the river by the middle classes, who sought an opportunity to move back in closer to the centre of London. Stewart retired in 1979, and an 8.2% swing gave the Conservative Martin Stevens the seat. By the 1982 local elections the Conservatives had clearly increased their lead, as they won 45% of the vote to Labour's 35%.

The social transformation of Fulham, which is unaffected by boundary changes, is reflected in the 1981 census figures. The percentage of owner occupiers went up from 20.2% in 1971 to 33.6% in 1981, one of the highest rises in Britain. The percentage of middle-class residents has now swept past the 50% mark. There was a far smaller number of non-white residents than in neighbouring Hammersmith. Fulham is still a marginal - even in 1982 Labour won the wards of Eel Brook, Gibbs Green, Sands End, Margravine and Normand. But most of the wards gave a lead to the Tories. The Alliance made no impact in Fulham, taking only 18% of the vote in 1982.

Fulham is becoming an increasingly fashionable part of West London, more like Chelsea just to the east than Hammersmith to the north and west. It is set in a loop of the Thames opposite Putney, which is also becoming a desirable residential area. Martin Stevens has consolidated his position as the favourite to retain the seat for the Conservatives at the next General Election.

1981	% Own Occ	33.6	1979 same seat Fulham		
1981	% Loc Auth	31.7	C	20,249	46.7
1981	% Black/Asian	11.6	Lab	18,750	43.2
1981	% Mid Cl	59.8	L	3,882	8.9
1981	% Prof Man	20.5	NF	499	1.2
1982	electorate 54,687		MPs since 1955		
Alliance		L	1955-79 Michael Stewart Lab		
			1979- Martin Stevens C		

Hammersmith   Hammersmith and Fulham

There are no boundary changes in the London Borough of
Hammersmith and Fulham, but the former Hammersmith North
seat is renamed. Labour held on here by just 3,506 votes in
1979, as Clive Soley replaced the veteran Frank Tomney as
candidate. Tomney had been a crusty eccentric on the far
right of the party, and at one time the only Labour MP in
favour of the noose. Labour have continued to decline in
strength in London since 1979, but Soley has less to fear
than some sitting Labour MPs with equally thin majorities. In
the 1982 local elections the Labour candidates remained well
ahead in the wards which make up the new Hammersmith
seat. The Labour vote is holding up better in this
constituency than elsewhere in London and elsewhere in the
Borough.

The reasons for this are connected with social change in this
part of West London. Unlike Fulham, which is moving up the
social scale through gentrification, Hammersmith is rather
seedy, cosmopolitan and far from affluent. The proportion of
non-white residents is high and rising, and indeed the
population is amongst the most international in Britain, for it
also has the second highest proportion of Irish-born.
Districts like Wormwood Scrubs, Old Oak Common and
Shepherds Bush remain unattractive to middle-class
Londoners. Over 40% of the housing is still privately rented,
but council houses make up the majority of the remainder -
there is a large estate at White City, near the stadium and
the BBC TV Centre.

Clive Soley can expect to be returned in Hammersmith next
time. This part of London is still descending the ladder of
status, and the Conservatives are no growing force. Neither
do the Alliance pose much of a threat - in 1982 they polled
only 23%. The SDP has the Alliance nomination in
Hammersmith.

1981	% Own Occ	26.2	1979 same seat Hammersmith		
1981	% Loc Auth	44.4	North		
1981	% Black/Asian	18.2	Lab	17,241	48.2
1981	% Mid Cl	52.9	C	13,735	38.4
1981	% Prof Man	15.4	L	4,147	11.6
1982	electorate 48,976		NF	462	1.3
Alliance		SDP	WRP	193	0.5

MPs since 1950
1950-79 Frank Tomney Lab
1979-   Clive Soley Lab

45

Hornsey and Wood Green   Haringey

In the present review, no part of Britain has given the
Boundary Commission so much trouble as the London Borough
of Haringey. The first problem was that the Borough's 1976
electorate of 159,500 entitled it only to two very large seats –
another thousand electors or so and it would have been able
to retain its present allocation of three. The larger of the two
seats proposed, Hornsey and Wood Green, had a 1976
electorate of 84,401 – the highest in the country except for
the Isle of Wight, and far in excess of the smallest seat in
London, Surbiton (46,493).

The second problem was that the way the boundaries were
drawn would undoubtedly cause political controversy.
Haringey is a socially divided Borough, with a middle-class
Tory west end (Hornsey) and a working-class Labour east
end (Tottenham). The third seat in the old Parliament was
more marginally Labour Wood Green. If the Borough was
divided into northern and southern constituencies, Labour
may be able to win both and eliminate the sole Tory Hugh
Rossi. Eventually, after two inquiries and the suggestion of
many possible permutations (Hornsey and Tottenham, Wood
Green and Tottenham...), western and eastern seats were
proposed. Hornsey and Wood Green should be Conservative,
Tottenham Labour – so it is Labour who have ended up losing
a seat in Haringey.

The old Hornsey did have Labour elements – there was a
strong non-white presence in Hornsey itself, for example. But
it was still influenced most strongly by the wooded and
affluent middle-class residential district east of Hampstead
Heath, from Highgate through Fortis Green to Muswell Hill.
The half of Wood Green which is added is also the more
Conservative part, around Alexandra Palace and Bowes Park,
and certainly it shouldn't reduce Hugh Rossi's majority in this
huge new seat.

1981	% Own Occ	45.7	1979 core seat Hornsey		
1981	% Loc Auth	25.9	C	20,225	49.4
1981	% Black/Asian	23	Lab	16,188	39.5
1981	% Mid Cl	64.6	L	4,058	9.9
1981	% Prof Man	22.2	NF	337	0.8
1982	electorate 76,970		Ind C	156	0.4
1979	notional result		MPs since 1945		
	C 4,300		1945-57 L.D. Gammans C		
Alliance		SDP	1957-66 Lady Gammans C		
			1966- Hugh Rossi C		

Tottenham   Haringey

Haringey is a long, thin Borough, stretching all the way from
the edge of upper-crust Hampstead Heath in the west to the
industrial and working-class valley of the River Lee in the
east. It is a far cry, socially and politically, from Highgate to
Tottenham. Tottenham has been a safe Labour seat for many
years, although in the 1959 Parliament the Labour MP A.G.
Brown defected to the Conservatives. But he was beaten
easily in 1964 by Norman Atkinson, a leading Tribunite who
was for some years elected Treasurer of the national Labour
Party. But now Atkinson's seat takes in half of the abolished
division of Wood Green, which is at present held by another
left-winger, Reg Race. It is presumably Race who will have to
move to fight another seat.

The enlarged Tottenham will remain strongly Labour. Here
can be found one of the largest communities of West Indians
in the country, and nearly 40% of the population is non-
white. There is much heavy industry here in east Haringey,
along the A10 trunk road north from the City towards
Cambridge, and near the River Lee. The wards which are
transferred to Tottenham for the first time are also strongly
Labour - Harringay, White Hart Lane (home of Spurs FC),
Coleraine and Park. It is not that Tottenham is now
vulnerable that worries Labour in Haringey - it is that all the
Labour strength in the Borough seems to be concentrated in
this one seat, making it difficult to win the other, Hornsey
and Wood Green.

Labour undoubtedly made Haringey one of the leading issues
in their court case against the Boundary Commission. Its
three seats are reduced to two of the largest divisions in the
country. Labour's two seats are reduced to one. Three left-
wing candidates collide, and only the one chosen for
Tottenham has a good chance of victory.

1981	% Own Occ	41.2	1979 core seat Tottenham
1981	% Loc Auth	42.7	Lab 16,299 56.9
1981	% Black/Asian	36	C 9,166 32.0
1981	% Mid Cl	41.4	L 2,177 7.6
1981	% Prof Man	9.7	NF 833 2.9
1982	electorate 70,670		Oths 165 0.5
1979	notional result		MPs since 1950
	Lab 9,900		1950-59 F. Messer Lab
Alliance		L	1959-64 A.G. Brown Lab (C)
			1964- N. Atkinson Lab

Harrow East   Harrow

If Labour suffers from the reduction of Haringey's
representation from three seats to two, it seems at first sight
that it must be the Conservative Party which is hit by a
similar diminution in Harrow. In 1979 all three Harrow seats
were safely Conservative. Harrow Central, the constituency of
Anthony Grant, has been abolished, and its wards shared
between Harrow East and West. So, a net loss of one for the
Conservatives, apparently. Yet in fact the situation is not
quite so simple - for Harrow Central had been one of the best
Alliance hopes in London, and their candidates (mainly
Liberals) had won 12 council seats and 37% of the vote there
in the Borough elections of 1982. This was only 3% behind the
Tories. The destruction of Harrow Central means the
dissolution of Liberal hopes as well as of a Conservative
constituency.

The east end of Harrow is the less affluent part of the
Borough. Labour's Roy Roebuck actually won the old Harrow
East in the 1966 General Election. Labour can still count on a
lead in normal years in Kenton East, Stanmore South and
Wealdstone, but the Alliance has replaced them as the main
opposition in parts of the seat such as Marlborough ward.
The Liberal activity in Harrow is of recent origin and at
present confined only to local contests - there was no hint of
it in the 1979 General Election results. It may well be that
their support could not be translated into parliamentary
elections anyway, even if it had not been fragmented by the
boundary changes.

In any case, the strong favourite in Harrow East, in
Stanmore, Kenton, Harrow Weald and Wealdstone, is the
moderate Conservative sitting MP Hugh Dykes, who defeated
Roy Roebuck in 1970. Dykes should be able to hold this large
seat of 80,000 electors against a Liberal challenge which is as
yet only potential.

1981	% Own Occ	73.4	1979 core seat Harrow East		
1981	% Loc Auth	14.7	C	20,871	54.3
1981	% Black/Asian	18	Lab	12,993	33.8
1981	% Mid Cl	62.9	L	3,984	10.4
1981	% Prof Man	21.8	NF	572	1.5
1982	electorate 80,539		MPs since 1945		
1979	notional result		1945-50 F.W. Skinnard C		
	C 9,100		1950-59 Ian Harvey C		
Alliance		L	1959-66 A.T. Courtney C		
			1966-70 Roy Roebuck Lab		
			1970- Hugh Dykes C		

Harrow West   Harrow

The Harrow West constituency consists of the neighbourhoods of Pinner, Hatch End, Headstone, North Harrow, Roxbourne, Roxeth and Harrow on the Hill. Much of this is high-class residential territory - Pinner and Hatch End are very similar in character to the next-door seat of Ruislip-Northwood. Harrow on the Hill still has the atmosphere of a prosperous village, rather like Mill Hill, Dulwich and Highgate elsewhere in London. It is well known for its elite public school, attended by Winston Churchill among other prominent figures.

It is scarcely surprising that Harrow West has long been a very safe conservative seat, represented since 1960 by right-winger John Page. Now it takes in part of the much more marginal Harrow Central, but the Liberal and Labour votes there should be absorbed easily by the large Tory majority. 76% of the housing is owner occupied, and only 14% council owned. 70% of the population was middle class in 1981, one of the highest figures in London.

Both new Harrow seats are larger than average, West with an electorate of 72,000, East with over 79,000. The seats in London do vary in size considerably, due to the Boundary Commission's decision to assess London Boroughs individually, and not to cross Borough boundaries. But nobody can claim that the situation is as unsatisfactory as it was before the 1945 redistribution, which was the first since 1918. This part of London grew extraordinarily rapidly in the inter-war period. The Middlesex county seat of Harrow (once held by Oswald Mosley) rose from 38,000 electors in 1924 to 168,594 at the time of the 1941 byelection. Harrow West is one of the more affluent parts of inter-war suburban London; its electorate is large, but it might be argued that its comfortable residents need the services of an MP no more than most.

1981	% Own Occ	76.0	1979 core seat Harrow West
1981	% Loc Auth	14.0	C 26,007 58.1
1981	% Black/Asian	13	Lab 10,794 24.1
1981	% Mid Cl	70.3	L 7,350 16.4
1981	% Prof Man	25.9	NF 646 1.4
1982	electorate 73,881		MPs since 1945
1979	notional result		1945-51 N.A.H. Bower C
	C 18,500		1951-60 Sir A.N. Braithwaite C
Alliance		SDP	1960- John Page C

Hornchurch   Havering

When the NE London Borough of Havering was divided into
three seats in 1974, it was generally thought that there would
be one safe Tory (Romford), one marginal (Upminster) and
one safe Labour (Hornchurch). But in 1979 the Conservative
Robin Squire ousted Labour MP Alan Lee Williams by an 8.5%
swing, destroying a majority of nearly 7,000. By the 1982
local elections, the Conservatives had pulled further ahead,
although the picture was clouded by the success of Residents
candidates. But the outlook for the Labour Party in Havering
is hardly promising; by tradition they should be expecting to
win majorities in seats like Hornchurch in the middle of a
Parliament.

Some of Labour's problems are caused by Hornchurch's social
and economic characteristics. On the one hand it is true that
Hornchurch is scarcely a glamorous part of the world, set in
the SW corner of Havering just beyond Dagenham, which is a
massive working-class council estate. South Hornchurch and
Rainham are overshadowed by scenes of heavy industry,
including the Ford Motor Works. Nor are any of the other
residential areas very affluent - Elm Park, Hacton and
Hylands. But on the other hand over three-quarters of the
housing is owner occupied. Very few non-whites have come to
live in Havering, which is very much part of Outer London,
indeed set on the very edge of rural Essex. Labour did
unusually badly in the wedge N and E of London last time.

Robin Squire is one of the most moderate of the 1979 intake
of young Conservative MPs. He must have been surprised as
well as gratified to win in 1979, and he must still be
somewhat surprised to be regarded as the favourite to win
the seat again next time. The Alliance is quite strong,
especially in Rainham, and may well split the anti-Tory vote.
Hornchurch is not affected by the Boundary Commission's
revisions.

1981	% Own Occ	76.1	1979 same seat Hornchurch		
1981	% Loc Auth	18.0	C	21,340	44.9
1981	% Black/Asian	3.0	Lab	20,571	43.3
1981	% Mid Cl	54.7	L	4,657	9.8
1981	% Prof Man	13.7	NF	994	2.1
1982	electorate 62,417		MPs since 1974		
Alliance		SDP	1974-79 Alan Lee Williams Lab		
			1979- Robin Squire C		

Romford   Havering

The constituency of Romford became safely Conservative in
1974, when the Harold Hill GLC housing estate was
transferred to the new Upminster division. Romford is the NW
part of Havering. Unchanged by the Boundary Commission, it
is mainly residential, and indeed mainly owner occupied.
There are wealthy suburbs like Gidea Park, and in the 1982
local elections the Tories won every ward, gaining 56% of the
vote compared with Labour's 22% and the Alliance's 21%.
Michael Neubert seems to face few problems winning re-
election at Romford.

1981	% Own Occ	73.4	1979 same seat Romford		
1981	% Loc Auth	19.7	C	22,714	53.8
1981	% Black/Asian	2.4	Lab	13,902	32.9
1981	% Mid Cl	57.4	L	4,818	11.4
1981	% Prof Man	17.2	NF	820	1.9
1982	electorate 56,496		MP since 1974		
Alliance		L	1974-	Michael Neubert C	

Upminster   Havering

Upminster is a long thin strip on the eastern edge of
Havering, which means the eastern edge of London too. It is
socially and politically divided. In the north is the Harold Hill
council estate, with its three safe Labour wards of Gooshays,
Heaton and Hilldene. In the south are the middle-class
residential areas of Cranham and Upminster, and the affluent
and leafy Emerson Park and Ardleigh Green. When Upminster
was first contested in the February 1974 Election, the
Conservatives won by only a thousand votes. But by 1979
John Loveridge had benefited from an 8% swing, and
Upminster now seems a safe Tory seat.

1981	% Own Occ	67.4	1979 same seat Upminster		
1981	% Loc Auth	28.1	C	27,960	52.7
1981	% Black/Asian	1.7	Lab	18,895	35.6
1971	% Mid Cl	58.8	L	5,216	9.8
1971	% Prof Man	19.2	NF	965	1.8
1979	electorate 67,124		MP since 1974		
Alliance		SDP	1974-	John Loveridge C	

Hayes and Harlington   Hillingdon

After a long battle with left-wingers in his own party, the Labour MP for Hayes and Harlington, Neville Sandelson, became a founder-defector to the SDP in 1981. This was fully expected, for he had been an outspoken member of the far right of the Labour Party for a number of years. Sandelson had unsuccessfully stood for election to Parliament eight times before his success at the Hayes-Harlington byelection of 1971. What are his chances of winning the seat as an SDP candidate at the next Election?

Judging by the evidence of the 1982 London Borough elections, Sandelson is in a more hopeful position than most SDP MPs. The Alliance won 27.9% of the vote in the wards which make up the Hayes division, to Labour's 33.3%. The largest percentage, however, went to the Conservatives - 37.6%. Sandelson can expect something of a personal vote to add to the general level of Alliance support, so it seems as if Hayes and Harlington could well turn into a genuine three-party marginal.

Marginal status would be a new phenomenon in the constituency, which had been safely Labour since its creation in 1950. Hayes and Harlington is the most plebeian part of Hillingdon Borough, situated just north of Heathrow Airport. Although it borders heavily Asian Southall, it is often regarded as a white working-class council estate seat. Yet in fact, over half the housing is now owner occupied, which may account partly for the improving Tory performance. It may well be possible to win Hayes-Harlington with little over 35% of the vote next time: the Labour and Conservative candidates, and Sandelson himself, will all think this within their capabilities. It will be a cracking contest, and perhaps a bitter one too.

1981	% Own Occ	57.0	1979 same seat Hayes and	
1981	% Loc Auth	34.2	Harlington	
1981	% Black/Asian	11.0	Lab 20,350	48.3
1981	% Mid Cl	47.6	C 17,048	40.5
1981	% Prof Man	12.2	L 3,900	9.3
1982	electorate 57,982		NF 582	1.4
Alliance		SDP	Comm 249	0.6

MPs since 1950
1950-53 W.H. Ayles Lab
1953-71 Arthur Skeffington Lab
1971-   Neville Sandelson Lab
                    (SDP)

Ruislip-Northwood   Hillingdon

There are some highly attractive middle-class private
residential areas on the NW edge of London, on the
Hertfordshire border. The Ruislip-Northwood constituency,
which also contains Eastcote, is of this nature. Socially and
economically similar to neighbouring Harrow West and SW
Herts, it is a rock-solid Tory seat, containing some of the
most affluent housing in Outer London. The three seats in
the Borough of Hillingdon are unaltered in the present
boundary review.

1981	% Own Occ	71.9	1979 same seat Ruislip-		
1981	% Loc Auth	18.6	Northwood		
1981	% Black/Asian	4.0	C	26,748	61.3
1981	% Mid Cl	65.7	Lab	9,541	21.9
1981	% Prof Man	23.5	L	6,867	15.7
1982	electorate 56,773		NF	477	1.1
Alliance		L	MPs since 1950		
			1950-79 Petre Crowder C		
			1979- John Wilkinson C		

Uxbridge   Hillingdon

There was a time when the three seats in Hillingdon seemed
to consist of one safe Tory (Ruislip-Northwood), one Labour
(Hayes-Harlington) and one marginal (Uxbridge). But now
Hayes is an SDP seat vulnerable to a possible Tory victory;
and Uxbridge has a Conservative majority of 8,000. On the
Borough Council, the Tories outnumber Labour by 57 to 10.
Although the Conservatives do much better in Ickenham,
Hillingdon and W Drayton than in Harefield and Yiewsley,
they did lead in every ward in the constituency in the 1982
local elections. The Alliance only polled 22%, and pose no
threat to the continued tenure of MP Michael Shersby.

1981	% Own Occ	55.4	1979 same seat Uxbridge		
1981	% Loc Auth	34.6	C	24,967	52.5
1981	% Black/Asian	4.5	Lab	16,972	35.7
1981	% Mid Cl	53.4	L	5,031	10.6
1981	% Prof Man	17.9	NF	595	1.3
1982	electorate 62,129		MPs since 1945		
Alliance		SDP	1945-59 F. Beswick Lab		
			1959-66 Charles Curran C		
			1966-70 J. Ryan Lab		
			1970-72 Charles Curran C		
			1972- Michael Shersby C		

Brentford and Isleworth   Hounslow

When the Brentford and Isleworth seat was first contested in February 1974 it appeared to be one of the most marginal in London. Two sitting MPs battled it out - Barney Hayhoe, the Conservative member for Heston and Isleworth, and Michael Barnes, the Labour MP for Brentford and Chiswick. In the February Election, Hayhoe emerged victorious by 726 votes. In October of the same year, his majority was cut to just 232. The pro-Tory swing of 1979 improved Hayhoe's position to one of relative comfort, but it is still just conceivable that one day Labour might win Brentford and Isleworth - the Labour vote seems not to have crumbled here as it has elsewhere in London.

Brentford and Isleworth is the eastern half of the long thin Borough of Hounslow. For much of its length the seat hugs the north bank of the Thames as the river curves around past Kew Gardens, the Old Deer Park and Syon Park. The housing is very mixed. There are some affluent Tory wards like Spring Grove and Hounslow South. Almost a quarter of the housing is council owned, though, which tips wards like Gunnersbury to Labour. Over 13% of the electorate is non-white. Some older private housing, rented and owner occupied, is of a poorer quality. This means that Labour does well in Hounslow Central and Isleworth N and S wards.

All in all, this large west London constituency has many of the characteristics of a marginal. Competition here is intense in local and General Elections. Labour won control of the Hounslow Borough Council in 1982, and remain a force to be reckoned with in Hounslow. Barney Hayhoe is a popular local MP who stands on the moderate wing of the Conservative Party. He has already shown an ability to survive narrowly in Brentford and Isleworth, and may yet be severely tested again.

1981	% Own Occ	52.8	1979 same seat Brentford and		
1981	% Loc Auth	28.8	Isleworth		
1981	% Black/Asian	13.7	C	27,572	49.4
1981	% Mid Cl	59.0	Lab	22,533	40.4
1981	% Prof Man	20.0	L	4,208	7.6
1982	electorate 72,521		NF	738	1.3
Alliance		SDP	Oths	712	1.3
			MP since 1974		
			1974-	Barney Hayhoe	C

Feltham and Heston   Hounslow

Feltham and Heston is the western end of the Borough of
Hounslow, situated north and east of Heathrow Airport. Its
boundary with Brentford and Isleworth cuts through the
community of Hounslow itself, which is divided between the
two seats. Feltham and Heston is decidedly the more working-
class end of the Borough. It has a higher proportion of
council tenants, a higher proportion of non-whites and a
higher proportion of Labour voters than Brentford-Isleworth.
The Australian Tribunite Russell Kerr was MP for Feltham in
1966, and he has had little trouble winning Feltham and
Heston since its creation before the 1974 Elections.

In 1974 the area of west London covered by Hounslow
Borough was reduced from three seats to two. In the present
redistribution its boundaries are not disturbed further,
although this leaves Feltham and Heston as a very large
constituency of nearly 80,000 electors. Although his majority
in 1979 was reduced to a shaky 4,000, Russell Kerr has less
cause for worry than some London Labour MPs. In the local
elections of 1982, fought when the Conservatives were still
benefiting from the 'Falklands Factor', Labour candidates still
won most of the wards within the Feltham/Heston division:
Cranford, East Bedfont, the council estate of Hanworth,
Feltham Central and North, the heavily Asian Hounslow West
and Hounslow Heath. The Conservatives come out on top only
in Heston and in Feltham South. The Alliance did not do well
in the 1982 local elections in Hounslow, their first major
campaign in the Borough. In both constituencies they
registered only 18% of the vote.

With its growing non-white population (which more than
doubled in the 1970s), and a large number of workers in
threatened British Airways, Feltham and Heston looks likely
to stay Labour - even when other London Labour
constituencies of similar safeness seem highly vulnerable.

1981	% Own Occ	53.5	1979 same seat Feltham and			
1981	% Loc Auth	38.5	Heston			
1981	% Black/Asian	19.6	Lab	28,675	48.3	
1981	% Mid Cl	48.9	C	24,570	41.4	
1981	% Prof Man	13.2	L	5,051	8.5	
1982	electorate 82,028		NF	898	1.5	
Alliance		L	WRP	168	0.3	
			MP since 1974			
			1974-	Russell Kerr Lab		

Islington North   Islington

Islington was the scene of some of the first triumphs of the SDP, and also of its first disaster. In 1981 and 1982 all three Labour MPs in this inner North London working-class Borough defected to the SDP. Enough Labour councillors also defected to create the first SDP-controlled local authority in Britain. But in May 1982, the municipal election results produced a devastating disappointment for the youthful party. Only one of their councillors retained his seat, facing a solid phalanx of 51 Labour members. The voters of Islington had decisively rejected their SDP council. The Alliance only polled 22% in the Borough to Labour's 51.5%. Clearly the defecting MPs have as much to worry about as the councillors had.

The three SDP members in Islington have another problem. There will be only two Islington seats at the next Election, and one of the MPs must move elsewhere. Islington North takes in part of the abolished Islington Central, represented by John Grant, whereas North has been held since 1969 by Michael O'Halloran. O'Halloran was one of the earliest members of the SDP, a man long unhappy in the ideological Labour Party of recent years, who owed his selection and influence more to his local connections than to any espousal of socialist theory. O'Halloran is of Irish descent, as are many of his constituents here in Finsbury Park and Highbury, Tufnell Park and Upper Holloway - in 1971 Islington N had the third highest proportion of Irish-born in the country. Much of the housing is nineteenth-century terraced.

The SDP's chances of re-election are slim. The Alliance polled only 18.5% of the vote in the new Islington N in the 1982 Borough elections, the lowest figure in any seat where they have an MP at present. Labour achieved 57%, which makes their new candidate Jeremy Corbyn firm favourite to win Islington N.

1981	% Own Occ	21.6	1979 core seat Islington North		
1981	% Loc Auth	56.0	Lab	12,317	52.6
1981	% Black/Asian	20	C	7,861	33.6
1981	% Mid Cl	49.8	L	2,079	8.9
1981	% Prof Man	13.4	NF	501	2.1
1982	electorate 60,540		Oths	655	2.8
1979	notional result		MPs since 1945		
	Lab 6,700		1945-50	L. Haden-Guest	Lab
Alliance		SDP	1950-51	R.M. Hughes	Lab
			1951-58	W. Fienburgh	Lab
			1958-69	G.W. Reynolds	Lab
			1969-	M. O'Halloran	Lab
					(SDP)

Islington South and Finsbury   Islington

The present Islington South and Finsbury seat is held by Social Democrat George Cunningham. It takes in the Canonbury and Holloway wards of Islington Central, which is represented by Social Democrat John Grant. Whichever SDP defector contests the enlarged seat, he will have a difficult task - in the local elections of 1982 the Alliance candidates here were 27% adrift of the Labour candidates.

South and Finsbury is generally more typical of London's inner city than Islington North. Most of the housing is council owned, and this means that there are fewer non-white residents. Its politics are, however, similar - all three seats in Islington were safely Labour until the redistribution despite large swings to the Conservatives in 1979. Parts of the South/Finsbury seat are well known as undergoing gentrification, as middle-class Londoners re-colonise districts such as Barnsbury, Canonbury and Finsbury in order to cut transport costs from the suburbs. It is unclear if this phenomenon is likely to have any significant political impact. It is after all unlikely to change the character of the whole of the seat. Over half of the housing is immune from such changes in status, since it is local authority owned - council estates dominate the wards of Clerkenwell, Bunhill and Thornhill for example.

Islington once offered a false dawn of hope for the SDP, but Labour produced by far their best results in London here in 1982. As well as boasting almost a full slate of Labour councillors, Islington can be expected to return two Labour MPs at the next General Election instead of the present three Social Democrats.

1981	% Own Occ	12.1	1979 core seat Islington South/			
1981	% Loc Auth	72.0	Finsbury			
1981	% Black/Asian	12	Lab	12,581	52.0	
1981	% Mid Cl	47.4	C	8,237	34.1	
1981	% Prof Man	13.6	L	1,991	8.2	
1982	electorate 60,289		NF	824	3.4	
1979	notional result		Oths	544	2.3	
	Lab 6,300		MPs since 1950			
Alliance		SDP	1950-70 A. Evans Lab			
			1970-	George Cunningham Lab		
				(SDP)		

Chelsea   Kensington

Chelsea is the safest Conservative seat in London, and the
fourth safest in Britain. This southern half of the Borough of
Kensington contains some of the most valuable property and
wealthiest residents in affluent west London. This is terrain
of elegant tree-lined squares and select mews cottages tucked
away behind the larger dwellings. Here are to be found such
London landmarks as the Royal Hospital, the Chelsea
Embankment, the Kings Road, the Earls Court Exhibition Hall,
the Natural History Musuem, the Victoria and Albert Museum
and Sloane Square. Indeed the recently publicised myth of
the 'Sloane Ranger' captures the essence of the more brusque
variety of Chelsea Conservatism.
More than half of the housing here is privately rented.
Labour's only strength here lies in South Stanley ward, where
there is a small council estate next to the electric power
station, Chelsea Dock and the gasworks. In other wards
Labour obtain a derisory vote - in the 1982 local elections
they polled 5% in Cheyne, Brompton and Hans Town, 4% in
Royal Hospital ward. They would barely have saved their
deposit overall. Nor did the Alliance do much better, polling
22% in the new Chelsea constituency. The Liberals hold the
Alliance nomination.
Chelsea is little altered in the boundary changes. It still
extends from the Thames to the Cromwell Road, and as far as
Kensington High Street beyond Earls Court. It will remain
super-safe for Tory MP Nick Scott. Despite the extreme
strength of Chelsea's Conservatism, Scott is a well-known
moderate in the party, noted for his club for wet Tories -
Nick's Diner. He appears to have settled his differences with
the party, which would pose the only threat to his continued
tenure in Chelsea.

1981	% Own Occ	34.5	1979 core seat Chelsea		
1981	% Loc Auth	18.7	C	21,782	66.1
1981	% Black/Asian	7	Lab	6,092	18.5
1981	% Mid Cl	69.8	L	4,544	13.8
1981	% Prof Man	29.7	NF	342	1.0
1982	electorate 53,895		Oths	195	0.5
1979	notional result		MPs since 1974		
	C 15,900		1974-	Nicholas Scott C	
Alliance		L			

Kensington   Kensington

When the Borough of Kensington was reduced from three seats to two in the last redistribution a decade ago, ultra-Tory South Kensington was brought together with Labour North Kensington in a single seat. This clash resulted in the creation of a marginal seat - won narrowly by the Tories in 1974, then more comfortably in 1979. It also gave rise to one of the most starkly socially divided constituencies in Britain, an epitome of the 'two nations' within three square miles of west London.

South Kensington is one of the nation's wealthiest districts. It is scarcely surprising that many embassies are situated near Kensington Palace Gardens in the seat's Campden ward (72% Conservative, 6% Labour in 1982). Holland Park is politically similar, and wealthy enough as a catchment area to create a nationally known model comprehensive school. North of Notting Hill Gate, at first the mansions are still grandiose and well maintained. Then suddenly as one travels north along Ladbroke Grove, everything changes. The property becomes more decrepit. Affluence gives way to squalor. Tory wards are succeeded by Labour strongholds. This abrupt political reversal occurs just north of Stanley and Lansdowne Crescents, where Pembridge and Norland wards are replaced by Colville and Avondale.

Notting Hill is commonly thought to be one of London's black ghettoes. This is actually a false impression, based on the fame and notoriety of the annual carnival in the streets of North Kensington. In fact Kensington is only 11% non-white overall, no more than average in London. Nevertheless, it is ironic that North Kensington, the site of riots in the 1950s and of Oswald Mosley's racist candidature in 1959, should be represented by a Tory MP. It would be just as ironic if South Kensington were ever to fall into Labour hands!

1981	% Own Occ	28.8	1979 core seat Kensington		
1981	% Loc Auth	34.3	C	17,361	51.3
1981	% Black/Asian	11	Lab	11,898	35.1
1981	% Mid Cl	61.4	L	3,537	10.4
1981	% Prof Man	24.3	E	698	2.1
1982	electorate 50,371		NF	356	1.1
1979	notional result		MP since 1974		
	C 5,200		1974-	Sir Brandon Rhys	
Alliance		SDP		Williams C	

Kingston upon Thames   Kingston upon Thames

Kingston upon Thames will be an almost unchanged seat at
the next Election, and the result is likely to be unchanged
too - with the exception that the Liberals will probably over-
take Labour to finish second. Something of the Liberal enthusiasm current in the neighbouring Borough of Richmond seems
to have infected Kingston in recent years: the Alliance polled
33% in the 1982 local elections here. As before, Labour show
only in Norbiton. The Conservatives are strongest in wealthy
Coombe at the top of Kingston Hill, and in New Malden; but
they should collect enough votes across the constituency to
hold on to a seat they haven't lost this century.

1981	% Own Occ	67.3	1979 core seat Kingston upon
1981	% Loc Auth	18.2	Thames
1981	% Black/Asian	6	C 24,944 57.9
1981	% Mid Cl	67.4	Lab 11,400 26.4
1981	% Prof Man	24.7	L 6,771 15.7
1982	electorate 57,449		MPs since 1945
1979	notional result		1945-72 John Boyd-Carpenter C
	C 13,500		1972- Norman Lamont C
Alliance		L	

Surbiton   Kingston upon Thames

Kingston is a small London Borough, and it is only just
entitled to two seats. As a result, Surbiton becomes the
smallest seat proposed in the capital, at just 47,000 electors.
This is only just over half the electorate of the largest -
Hornsey, with 84,000. Yet it is difficult to see why this seat
needs such over-representation. It is solidly Tory, as the
homogeneous lower middle-class semis of Hook, Chessington,
Tolworth and Berrylands have turned out regularly to vote
for liberal Conservative Sir Nigel Fisher since the seat's
creation in 1955. Sir Nigel retires at the next Election, but
there will be no problems for his successor Dick Tracey.

1981	% Own Occ	67.3	1979 core seat Surbiton
1981	% Loc Auth	18.2	C 20,063 56.6
1981	% Black/Asian	5	Lab 9,261 26.1
1981	% Mid Cl	66.4	L 6,093 17.2
1981	% Prof Man	22.8	MP since 1955
1982	electorate 47,313		1955- Sir Nigel Fisher C
1979	notional result		
	C 10,800		
Alliance		SDP	

Norwood   Lambeth

The south-eastern part of the London Borough of Lambeth is to continue to be known as the constituency of Norwood. This is something of a misnomer, since Upper Norwood is in the Borough of Croydon, and the Norwood seat spills down from the ridge of London's southern heights from Knight's Hill and Gipsy Hill, Tulse Hill and Herne Hill to the environs of Brixton. In the present redistribution, the only change is that the boundaries of Norwood constituency will be extended further northwards towards the inner city of London, to include the ward of Angell, formerly in the abolished Lambeth Central division.

As might be expected, the effect of this addition is to give Labour a boost in a critical marginal seat. The Tory strength in the Norwood seat is concentrated around the crest of the hills, as in Thurlow Park ward, which in 1981 had 8% unemployment, a 12% black population and 48% owner occupiers. Here green parks offer dramatic views of the nation's capital to the north. Tulse Hill ward, though, the home area of GLC leader Ken Livingstone, contains Railton Road, the 'front line' of the Brixton riots of 1981. Tulse Hill is 39.8% black, and unemployment reaches a figure of nearly 20% amongst males.

Angell ward, newly attached to the constituency, is socially and economically similar to Tulse Hill, and its inclusion would have doubled Labour MP John Fraser's 2,000 majority in the 1979 General Election. He should be able to look forward to representing this socially divided seat with renewed hope, despite Labour's poor showing in Lambeth in recent years.

1981	% Own Occ	29.0	1979 core seat Norwood		
1981	% Loc Auth	50.2	Lab	16,282	47.4
1981	% Black/Asian	24	C	14,342	41.7
1981	% Mid Cl	53.6	L	3,051	8.9
1981	% Prof Man	13.6	NF	707	2.1
1982	electorate 56,549		MPs since 1945		
1979	notional result		1945-49 R. Chamberlain Lab		
	Lab 3,300		1950-66 Sir J.G. Smyth C		
Alliance		SDP	1966- John Fraser Lab		

Streatham   Lambeth

At first sight Streatham might seem to be a marginal seat.
The Conservative majority in October 1974 was under 3,000.
In 1979 it was still only about 5,500. In the boundary
changes the Labour ward of Town Hall, which encompasses
the centre of Brixton, is transferred from the Labour
constituency of Lambeth Central – Town Hall ward is over 25%
black, and solidly working-class. Yet in fact Streatham has
never been won by Labour, and it can still be counted as a
safe Tory seat. In fact, no part of Britain has swung more to
the Conservatives in the early 1980s.

In the 1982 local elections, the Conservatives polled 53% of
the vote in the old Streatham seat, Labour 20%: a swing of
10% to the Tories since 1979. Even in the new Streatham, with
Town Hall ward included, Labour was still in third place with
23% to the Alliance's 27% and the Conservatives' 50%. Why has
there been such a landslide shift of votes in the Tories'
favour? The Borough of Lambeth has seen an unpopular left-
wing Labour local authority under 'Red Ted' Knight, briefly
ousted by the voters in 1982. It also bore the brunt of the
riots in London in 1981. Neither of these features appealed to
respectable citizens of Streatham, SW Lambeth, which is the
most middle-class part of the Borough. There are more rate-
paying owner occupiers here than elsewhere, and down in
Streatham South and Streatham Wells Lambeth takes in some
outer London suburbia – a far cry from the Thames frontage
of Vauxhall. The residents in Lambeth's Deep South did not
enjoy their experience of Knight or their proximity to
Brixton.

William Shelton was originally elected MP for Clapham in 1970,
benefiting from a large swing against the West Indian Labour
candidate David Pitt. He moved to Duncan Sandys' old seat of
Streatham in 1974, and now seems to have a safe
constituency. Labour can hardly expect to recover from their
disastrous position by General Election time.

1981	% Own Occ	38.3	1979 core seat Streatham		
1981	% Loc Auth	33.7	C	19,630	51.4
1981	% Black/Asian	21	Lab	14,130	37.0
1981	% Mid Cl	62.5	L	3,779	9.9
1981	% Prof Man	18.2	NF	523	1.4
1982	electorate 60,958		Oth	120	0.3
1979	notional result		MPs since 1945		
	C 4,800		1945–50 D. Robertson C		
Alliance		L	1950–74 Duncan Sandys C		
			1974– William Shelton C		

Vauxhall   Lambeth

The north end of the Borough of Lambeth is part of London's true inner city. At present two small seats are to be found here, Vauxhall and Lambeth Central. Both are represented by Labour MPs - Stuart Holland and John Tilley respectively. Effectively, the two are merged to form the new Vauxhall seat, which had a rather large electorate of 75,000 in 1976, but which is losing population rapidly through redevelopment and rehousing.

Vauxhall should be an iron-clad safe Labour seat, but Labour has been doing very badly in Lambeth in recent years, at least in the local elections. It is true that the Conservatives have little solid support, and that confined mainly to the more gentrified parts of Clapham near the Common. But the Alliance did very well in the northern wards of Bishop's and Prince's near Lambeth Palace in the 1982 London Borough elections, and the SDP do pose a threat to Labour in this new division. Vauxhall is situated next door to Bermondsey and Peckham in Southwark Borough, both of which have recently seen Labour perform unconvincingly in parliamentary byelections.

It is a measure of Labour's decline in inner south London that one can even talk of their failing to win Vauxhall. The seat possesses only 14% owner occupiers and a majority of council tenants. It is nearly 30% non-white - in one ward, Ferndale, the figure reaches 43.3%. Only 12% of the population are in the professional and managerial classes, one of the lowest figures in London. Yet Labour's grasp is shaky. Nowhere is the unpopularity of the London Labour Party so evident as in the Borough of Lambeth.

1981	% Own Occ	13.7	New seat
1981	% Loc Auth	64.6	
1981	% Black/Asian	27	
1981	% Mid Cl	46.6	
1981	% Prof Man	11.9	
1982	electorate 64,437		
1979	notional result		
	Lab 8,700		

Alliance   SDP

Lewisham, Deptford   Lewisham

Labour's poor performance in south London's inner city has
not yet affected their hold on Deptford, Lewisham's northern
riverside seat. Deptford's MP is John Silkin, one of the
unsuccessful candidates for the Deputy Leadership of the
party in 1981. Silkin is an intellectual and a solicitor, a
member of the Garrick club and the son of a peer, but the
signs are that he will hold Deptford easily. Tory strength is
confined to the southern end of the seat at Crofton Park and
Blythe Hill, while the Alliance only polled 24% here in 1982.

1981	% Own Occ	28.7	1979 core seat Deptford		
1981	% Loc Auth	55.1	Lab	19,391	54.2
1981	% Black/Asian	24	C	11,638	32.5
1981	% Mid Cl	47.5	L	2,774	7.8
1981	% Prof Man	10.7	NF	1,490	4.2
1982	electorate 59,309		Oths	472	1.4
1979	notional result		MPs since 1945		
	Lab 7,500		1945-50 J.C. Wilmot Lab		
Alliance		SDP	1950-51 J. Cooper Lab		
			1951-63 Sir L.A. Plummer Lab		
			1963- John Silkin Lab		

Lewisham East   Lewisham

Labour's vote has held up better in the Borough of Lewisham
than in most of London. Lewisham East was held marginally
for Labour by Roland Moyle in 1979, and Labour was still just
ahead in the 1982 London Borough elections. The Tory
strength is around Blackheath at the north end of the
constituency, while Labour fights back in the council estates
of the south, at Grove Park and Downham. Owner-occupied
and local authority housing are both numerous in Lewisham
East. The SDP are likely to be squeezed into third place in
this SE London marginal.

1981	% Own Occ	38.5	1979 core seat Lewisham East		
1981	% Loc Auth	49.3	Lab	22,916	46.0
1981	% Black/Asian	10	C	21,323	42.8
1981	% Mid Cl	54.9	L	4,265	8.6
1981	% Prof Man	14.1	NF	1,168	2.3
1982	electorate 61,978		WRP	190	0.4
1979	notional result		MP since 1974		
	Lab 2,100		1974- Roland Moyle Lab		
Alliance		SDP			

Lewisham West   Lewisham

Lewisham is a Borough which could be described as 'Middle
London'. It stretches from Deptford, decidedly in Inner
London, to the borders of Bromley and Beckenham, in Outer
SE London. It also enjoys a cross-section of social
characteristics. Lewisham West, for example, has
approximately 40% council housing and 40% owner occupied. It
has a non-white population of 10% - larger than most seats in
England but average for London. Finally, Lewisham West is a
super-marginal constituency, held for Labour by Christopher
Price by 1,050 votes in 1979. In the 1982 local elections the
Conservatives built up a similarly tiny lead in the Lewisham
West wards.
This microcosm of London and England is not of an internally
uniform nature. Labour has some very strong wards, such as
the inter-war council estate of Bellingham, at Sydenham East
and in Forest Hill. The Conservatives do best in Catford, and
on the boundary with Dulwich in Upper Sydenham. None of
the Lewisham seats is significantly altered in the
redistribution. The apparently featureless landscape east of
Crystal Palace which makes up the Lewisham West division has
in fact seen some titanic political battles, as the major parties
fight street by street for a vital marginal seat.
There have been six different MPs since the war, three
Labour and three Conservatives. Only once has the majority
been over 5,000. Lewisham West has usually fallen to the
winning party in the General Election, which indicates that
Price did well to hold on last time, after an unusually small
swing to the Tories compared with the rest of the capital.
The Alliance polled 28% here in 1982, their best showing in
Lewisham Borough - but the Liberals still seem likely to be
relegated to third place in another tight contest in this key
seat.

1981	% Own Occ	43.4	1979 core seat Lewisham West
1981	% Loc Auth	41.7	Lab	20,932	46.4
1981	% Black/Asian	12	C	19,882	44.1
1981	% Mid Cl	57.1	L	3,350	7.4
1981	% Prof Man	14.6	NF	901	2.0

1982   electorate 63,782   MPs since 1945
1979   notional result   1945-50 Arthur Skeffington Lab
        Lab 900   1950-64 H.A. Price C
Alliance   L   1964-66 P. McNair-Wilson C
                                 1966-70 James Dickens Lab
                                 1970-74 John Selwyn Gummer C
                                 1974-   Christopher Price Lab

Mitcham and Morden   Merton

In June 1982 the Conservatives won the Mitcham and Morden
byelection in south London. This was the first byelection gain
by a governing party for over 20 years, and it was achieved
in rather extraordinary circumstances. Bruce Douglas-Mann
was one of 29 MPs who defected from their parties to the new
Social Democratic Party after its foundation in 1980. Unlike
the other 28, Douglas-Mann nobly decided to resign from
Parliament in order to seek a fresh mandate from the electors
of Mitcham and Morden, who had elected him as a Labour
candidate since 1974. These electors preferred to choose Tory
Angela Rumbold, by a 4,000 majority over Douglas-Mann, with
Labour third.
Mitcham and Morden is the southern half of the two-seat
Borough of Merton, which is unaffected by the boundary
changes. The seat was created in 1974, and appeared to be a
marginal Labour constituency until Douglas-Mann's
conversion. Together with the Falklands Factor and the great
unpopularity of London Labour, this gave it to the Tories. It
does have underlying Labour strength at both ends of the
seat - in the north in the rather dingy terraces of Colliers
Wood, and in the south in the vast council estate of St
Helier, part of which lies in the seat, and part in
Carshalton. The Conservatives do best in Morden and around
Mitcham Common. The Alliance vote appears to have been
spread fairly evenly, as is its wont nationally.
Mitcham and Morden is in the Wandle Valley, the southern arm
of London's working-class and industrial 'cross' of rivers
(Lee, Thames and Wandle). In normal times, Labour should
win. But the impact of the SDP, and Douglas-Mann's uniquely
principled stand, has made it a three-way fight. The Tories
seem the most likely victors at present.

1981	% Own Occ	55.5	1979 same seat Mitcham and
1981	% Loc Auth	35.5	Morden
1981	% Black/Asian	11.6	Lab 21,668 45.2
1981	% Mid Cl	52.3	C 21,050 43.9
1981	% Prof Man	13.3	L 4,258 8.9
1982	electorate 63,999		NF 966 2.0
Alliance		SDP	MPs since 1974

1974-82 Bruce Douglas-Mann
              Lab (SDP)
1982-   Angela Rumbold C

Wimbledon   Merton

Wimbledon is best known as the home of the (ultra-conservative) lawn tennis Establishment. It is indeed a safe Tory constituency, the seat of Attorney General Sir Michael Havers. Around the Common and Wimbledon Park are comfortable detached houses reminiscent of outer Surrey. But there are unfashionable parts of Wimbledon, across the railway tracks to the east towards the River Wandle. Here are terraced houses, not dissimilar to those of Tooting over the Wandsworth border. There is hardly any council housing in Wimbledon, which should remain safe for the government's senior Law Officer.

1981	% Own Occ	67.6	1979 same seat Wimbledon		
1981	% Loc Auth	13.2	C	27,567	55.1
1981	% Black/Asian	9.6	Lab	14,252	28.5
1981	% Mid Cl	69.9	L	7,604	15.2
1981	% Prof Man	25.8	NF	612	1.2
1982	electorate 64,962		MPs since 1945		
Alliance		L	1945-59 Arthur Palmer Lab		
			1950-70 Sir Cyril Black C		
			1970- Sir Michael Havers C		

Newham North-East   Newham

Newham NE reached the headlines when its long-standing MP Reg Prentice defected to the Conservatives in October 1977 after a protracted and bitter battle with left-wingers within his own constituency. Prentice departed to greener pastures (in every sense) at Daventry in 1979. The quiet Labour loyalist Ron Leighton succeeded to the NE seat with remarkably little fuss - even facing a lower swing to the Tories than most. Newham NE is East Ham, from Manor Park south almost to the docks. The Tories left several wards here uncontested in the 1982 elections, and seem to be ceding the main opposition role to the Alliance.

1981	% Own Occ	57.5	1979 same seat Newham NE		
1981	% Loc Auth	26.0	Lab	22,818	54.5
1981	% Black/Asian	32.6	C	12,778	30.5
1971	% Mid Cl	44.8	L	4,027	9.6
1971	% Prof Man	8.8	NF	1,769	4.2
1979	electorate 64,012		Oths	480	1.2
Alliance		L	MPs since 1974		
			1974-79 Reg Prentice Lab (C)		
			1979- Ron Leighton Lab		

Newham North-West   Newham

As in the neighbouring NE seat, Newham NW has seen a well-publicised takeover by the left within the local Labour party in recent years. In autumn 1982, Arthur Lewis, an MP since 1945, failed to be reselected as candidate, being replaced by a leading GLC activist, Tony Banks. This had been on the cards for some time. Lewis is a bombastic tough East End eccentric. He has been known to ask over 2,000 questions in a single parliamentary session, many of them trivial. He is one of a handful of Labour MPs to support hanging. His demise was predicted by many, including himself - he claimed that his party was now 100% Communist. He may yet stand as an Independent candidate.

This would be the only development which could threaten Labour's hold on Newham NW, which is the north end of West Ham. Here are to be found many of the classic neighbourhoods of the East End - Upton, Plashet, Stratford (East), Forest Gate. As in neighbouring Newham NE, over 30% of the population is non-white, a proportion which has more than doubled in the 1970s. The immigrants have been attracted by the availability of cheap private housing. This is not all flattened, council-block, new East End; many of the straight treeless streets are Victorian. There is however an ultra-modern source of employment at the Chobham Farm container freightliner terminal.

It is difficult to assess Arthur Lewis's chances should he stand as an Independent in Newham NW. No one has been an MP for a longer time. But it is generally reckoned that a member, however experienced, rarely has a significant personal vote in Britain, at least outside byelections. Lewis will probably need to try to enlist an ideological dislike of the Left among traditional Labour voters to add to his personal appeal; yet the Alliance did not do well here in 1982. He may yet think better of trying to win election for a 12th time here in the heart of the East End.

1981	% Own Occ	38.9	1979 same seat Newham North-
1981	% Loc Auth	41.2	West
1981	% Black/Asian	32.7	Lab 18,392 61.5
1981	% Mid Cl	42.9	C 7,937 26.5
1981	% Prof Man	9.2	L 2,377 7.9
1982	electorate 50,122		NF 1,217 4.1
Alliance		SDP	MP since 1950
			1950- Arthur Lewis Lab

Newham South   Newham

Newham South is truly the heart of east London's dockland. Here are the 1,000 acres of the Royal Victoria Dock, the Royal Albert Dock and the King George V Dock - the largest area of impounded dock water in the world and the employer of over 10,000 people. The Thames loops around Woolwich Reach and Bugsby's Reach through a stark industrial scene and past little riverside communities like North Woolwich, Silvertown and Cyprus. Further inland can be found the heavily redeveloped tower block landscape of Canning Town and Plaistow.

This is all traditional Labour territory, and Labour have received no unpleasant shocks in recent years. There has however been a rather large National Front vote for some time, over 6% in 1979 and higher still in the three elections in 1974, including the May byelection at which Nigel Spearing was first elected MP. The NF support derives from the social and racial characteristics of Newham South: a mainly white working-class enclave. The other two Newham seats are over 30% black/Asian, a proportion rising very rapidly. Here in dockland only 13% are non-white, and many communities have resisted social and racial change. Another factor is the high percentage (59%) of council accommodation, which throughout Britain tends to house whites rather than immigrant families.

There is, however, no suggestion that the NF might win Newham South, or indeed anyone other than Labour. The Conservatives left many seats uncontested in the 1982 Newham Borough elections, and the Alliance didn't win a single seat either. The East End docks were among the first part of the country to vote Labour, in the early years of the century. They seem likely to be among the last that would abandon the party of the traditional working class.

1981	% Own Occ	25.4	1979 same seat	Newham	South
1981	% Loc Auth	62.6	Lab	19,636	64.4
1981	% Black/Asian	13.0	C	6,863	22.5
1981	% Mid Cl	37.1	L	2,085	6.8
1981	% Prof Man	7.4	NF	1,899	6.2
1982	electorate 51,509		MPs since 1950		
Alliance		SDP	1950-74 Sir Elwyn Jones Lab		
			1974- Nigel Spearing Lab		

Ilford North   Redbridge

Ilford North was always the more Conservative of the two
marginal Ilford seats. Labour failed to win it even in 1966,
and Millie Miller's triumph of October 1974 was to be short-
lived, for she died in 1978 and the seat returned to the Tory
fold at the subsequent byelection. In 1979 the Conservative
majority was increased to over 7,000, and by the 1982 local
elections they were well ahead, winning every ward in the
constituency except one. Overall they polled 57% in Ilford
North wards, to Labour's 26% and the Alliance's 17%. In the
boundary changes a few thousand voters in Newbury Park are
lost to the Ilford South seat, but this will not make the seat
any closer.

The one ward that Labour did win in Ilford North in 1982 is
the large peripheral GLC estate of Hainault, the end of a
tube line and almost in the heart of rural Essex. But Hainault
is very untypical of Ilford. Most of North is owner-occupied,
residential, lower middle-class Conservative territory like
Barkingside, Aldborough and Fullwell. There are relatively
few non-white immigrants, although part of the sizeable
Jewish community centred on Gants Hill is included in the
seat. Most of the housing is more modern than in the
neighbouring Ilford South, although Seven Kings is
nineteenth century (and the second most Labour part of the
seat).

Ilford North seems set now to remain loyally Conservative. Its
recent history also demonstrates the strength of party
labels. The Conservative MP for twenty years, Tom
Iremonger, was dropped as candidate before the 1978
byelection. He stood as an Independent both then and in the
1979 General Election. But clearly his years of service
counted for little. On both occasions he won a negligible vote
of under 1,000, and his intervention did not worry the
official Conservative Vivian Bendall, even in a seat which was
still regarded as a marginal. Bendall looks safe enough now.

1981	% Own Occ	71.5	1979 core seat Ilford North		
1981	% Loc Auth	21.1	C	26,381	51.3
1981	% Black/Asian	8	Lab	19,186	37.3
1981	% Mid Cl	60.9	L	4,568	8.9
1981	% Prof Man	16.7	NF	804	1.6
1982	electorate 61,082		Ind C	452	0.9
1979	notional result		MPs since 1945		
	C 6,500		1945-50 Mrs M. Ridealgh Lab		
Alliance		SDP	1950-54 G.C. Hutchinson C		
			1954-74 Tom Iremonger C		
			1974-78 Millie Miller Lab		
			1978- Vivian Bendall C		

Ilford South   Redbridge

Ilford South is a marginal seat. For nearly 30 years Labour's Arnold Shaw and Conservative Albert Cooper divided the representation between them. The seat is very heavily owner occupied, although much is low-quality terraced housing, and 20% of the population is non-white. Labour does best in the far south, near the Barking-Dagenham border; the Conservatives' best ward is Cranbrook near Wanstead Park and the River Roding. The Alliance is very weak throughout Redbridge, so it seems that Ilford South will remain a major-party battle.

1981	% Own Occ	72.8	1979 core seat Ilford South		
1981	% Loc Auth	11.9	C	19,290	46.8
1981	% Black/Asian	20	Lab	17,602	42.7
1981	% Mid Cl	59.8	L	3,664	8.9
1981	% Prof Man	16.8	NF	636	1.5
1982	electorate 59,058		MPs since 1945		
1979	notional result		1945-50 J. Ranger Lab		
	C 2,400		1950-66 Albert Cooper C		
Alliance		L	1966-70 Arnold Shaw Lab		
			1970-74 Albert Cooper C		
			1974-79 Arnold Shaw Lab		
			1979- Neil Thorne C		

Wanstead and Woodford   Redbridge

Some seats will eternally be associated with a single MP. In the case of Wanstead and Woodford, it will always be remembered as Winston Churchill's division, and one he held till he was 90 years of age in 1964. Churchill's successor is a Tory Cabinet Minister, Patrick Jenkin, but his name is not coupled with that of Woodford in the same way. The seat has unchanged boundaries, and will remain a solidly middle-class super-safe Tory seat between the Roding and Epping Forest.

1981	% Own Occ	74.6	1979 same seat Wanstead and		
1981	% Loc Auth	16.2	Woodford		
1981	% Black/Asian	5.5	C	26,214	62.2
1981	% Mid Cl	70.2	Lab	8,464	20.1
1981	% Prof Man	25.8	L	6,535	15.5
1982	electorate 57,790		NF	957	2.3
Alliance		L	MPs since 1945		
			1945-64 Winston Churchill C		
			1964- Patrick Jenkin C		

Richmond and Barnes

Richmond on Thames

The No.1 target seat in Britain for the Liberal Party is probably Richmond and Barnes. For a number of years they have been building up their local support in the Borough of Richmond upon Thames, the only London authority which straddles the river. Their particular strength lies on the southern shore, although they have of late made strides in Twickenham too. In the 1982 local elections in Richmond Borough, the Tories and the Alliance ended up tied at 26 seats each. In the 1981 GLC elections, the Liberal candidate Adrian Slade won the Richmond ward, which is the same as the old constituency, by just 115 votes. The Tories are resisting vigorously, and all the signs point to another neck and neck battle in Richmond at the next Election.

Richmond and Barnes will also be the only seat in London which crosses the river, for the East Twickenham ward is added to the seat. This should not hurt the Liberals here, for E Twickenham elected three Liberal councillors in May 1982. The Liberals are also ahead in Kew, Mortlake, Richmond town, Ham and Petersham. Barnes, East Sheen and Palewell still have nor cracked before their advance - but the Alliance was 12% ahead in the seat as a whole in 1982. The Labour Party has already been squeezed to a deposit-losing level.

Richmond is an intellectual and affluent part of London, 60% middle class, predominantly private housing, and with scarcely any non-white population. The Liberal strength is a product of the attitudes of the progressive middle classes, combined with Liberal activism in a neglected Tory area. But the Conservatives have put their house in order, and will enter the General Election with a new candidate, Jeremy Hanley. This will be no Liberal pushover, but it remains their best chance of a gain in London, and indeed in Britain as a whole.

			1979 core seat Richmond
1981	% Own Occ	55.3	(Surrey)
1981	% Loc Auth	19.1	
1981	% Black/Asian	4	C 19,294 46.7
1981	% Mid Cl	71.1	L 16,764 40.5
1981	% Prof Man	29.9	Lab 4,692 11.3
1982	electorate 57,276		NF 244 0.6
1979	notional result		Oths 349 0.9
	C 2,500		MPs since 1945
Alliance		L	1945-59 Sir G.S. Harvie-Watt C
			1959- Sir Anthony Royle C

Twickenham   Richmond on Thames

Twickenham was one of the few constituencies where the
Liberals increased their vote between the October 1974 and
1979 General Elections. The candidate John Waller pushed
their share up from 24% to 30%, and moved past Labour into
second place. This progress has continued since 1979. In the
1981 GLC elections, the Liberals came within 2,000 votes of
Tory councillor George Tremlett, whose ward was identical to
the old Twickenham seat. In the 1982 Richmond Borough
elections, the Alliance vote in the constituency passed 40% for
the first time. This phenomenon is clearly a result of local
Liberal activity, which started over the river in Richmond. If
it can be fully translated into parliamentary votes, it may well
turn Twickenham into a Liberal-Conservative marginal.

Twickenham has up to now always been a safe Tory seat. It
is associated by many with the home of English Rugby Union,
a game dominated by Establishment conservatism. But more
importantly its electorate tends to the right too. Over half
work in non-manual (i.e. middle-class) occupations. Nearly
70% live in owner-occupied houses, and only 15% in council
houses. The percentage of non-whites is one of the lowest in
London. The character of the constituent neighbourhoods
varies little, from Hampton to Whitton, Teddington to
Twickenham itself.

In the boundary changes, East Twickenham is lost to the
Richmond-Barnes seat. This should help Twickenham Tory MP
Toby Jessel to defend the seat, for the ward was one of
those which had succumbed to the Liberal infection from
across the Thames - those which remain which were won by
Liberals in 1982 are South Twickenham, Teddington and West
Twickenham. The Labour Party is now being thoroughly
eliminated from the scene in Twickenham, and may well lose
its deposit at the next Election. Jessel faces a tough fight,
but Twickenham is less likely to fall to the Liberal assault
than its neighbour Richmond on the other bank of the river.

1981	% Own Occ	68.9	1979 core seat Twickenham		
1981	% Loc Auth	15.7	C	30,017	52.2
1981	% Black/Asian	4.5	L	17,169	29.9
1981	% Mid Cl	67.3	Lab	9,591	16.7
1981	% Prof Man	26.0	NF	686	1.2
1982	electorate 65,148		MPs since 1945		
1979	notional result		1945-55 E.H. Keeling C		
	C 12,900		1955-70 R.G. Cooke C		
Alliance		L	1970- Toby Jessel C		

Dulwich   Southwark

Dulwich is a super-marginal and socially divided seat.
Labour's former Attorney-General, Sam Silkin QC, held it by
122 votes in 1979, defeating Tory beauty contest organiser
Eric Morley. Dulwich Village, and the district around the
College (one of London's top independent schools), is one of
the most attractive and expensive residential areas in the
city, as well as a cultural and educational centre. But this
core of Dulwich is untypical of the constituency which bears
its name. The Labour strength comes from further north,
from East Dulwich, Peckham Rye and Nunhead, which are
similar to the neighbouring inner-city territory of the
Peckham and Deptford seats.

Together the two constituency halves of Dulwich create a
balance, a tension, which accounts for the tight contests. But
that balance will be slightly yet significantly tipped by the
boundary changes. Only one ward is removed from Dulwich –
but it is the safest Labour ward, Barset, near Peckham and
New Cross. This relatively minor modification would have been
sufficient to put Dulwich into the Conservative column in the
1979 General Election.

Sam Silkin was one of the first Labour MPs to announce that
he would not stand at the next Election, and his successor as
Labour candidate is Kate Hoey. She will have to engineer a
positive swing from the Conservatives from 1979 to 'hold'
Dulwich. But with the continued unpopularity of Labour in
London and the gentrification of parts of the Dulwich seat, it
seems increasingly likely that it will in future take its
political colour from the affluent Village rather than the seedy
hinterland.

1981	% Own Occ	38.0	1979 core seat Dulwich		
1981	% Loc Auth	41.9	Lab	18,557	43.0
1981	% Black/Asian	16	C	18,435	42.7
1981	% Mid Cl	58.7	L	4,759	11.0
1981	% Prof Man	18.1	NF	920	2.1
1982	electorate 57,273		E	468	1.1
1979	notional result		MPs since 1945		
	C 500		1945-51 W.F. Vernon Lab		
Alliance		SDP	1951-64 R.C.D. Jenkins C		
			1964- Sam Silkin Lab		

Peckham   Southwark

Labour won an unconvincing victory at the Peckham byelection of 1982. Harriet Harman was returned with a 4,000 vote majority over the SDP's Dick Taverne, with the Conservative losing his deposit in a poor third place. But despite winning the seat, Labour's performance was unimpressive, for Peckham should be one of the party's true strongholds, according to all social and economic variables.

It is an inner-city south London seat, with three-quarters of the population living in council accommodation, often in tenement blocks and high-rise towers. Under 10% of the housing is owner occupied. Only 5% of the population work in professional or managerial occupations. 20% are black or Asian. Unemployment exceeds 20% in some wards. Poverty and degradation seems just around the corner in Peckham, yet no more than 50% of those who voted chose Labour in 1982; and under 40% of the total electorate did turn out to vote. In minor boundary changes Peckham loses Consort ward to Southwark and Bermondsey and gains Barset from Dulwich. The political effect of this exchange will be negligible. The constituency is part of the old Camberwell Borough, consisting of Walworth, the Old Kent Road, and Peckham - but not Peckham Rye, which is in the Dulwich division.

Harriet Harman must hope and expect to improve her majority in the General Election, and it is unclear whether Dick Taverne will again contest Peckham. Taverne was one of the pioneers of independent social democracy, for he retained his Lincoln seat after his resignation from the Labour Party - in the 1973 byelection, and again in February 1974. He must be one of the SDP's strongest and most experienced candidates, and having made his mark in Peckham in 1982 he may well move on to a more winnable seat at the General Election.

1981	% Own Occ	8.0	1979 core seat Peckham		
1981	% Loc Auth	82.9	Lab	20,364	59.8
1981	% Black/Asian	20	C	9,553	28.1
1981	% Mid Cl	40.2	L	2,607	7.7
1981	% Prof Man	7.5	NF	1,503	4.4
1982	electorate 59,709		MPs since 1945		
1979	notional result		1945-50 Lewis Silkin Lab		
	Lab 10,500		1950-74 Freda Corbet Lab		
Alliance		SDP	1974-82 Harry Lamborn Lab		
			1982- Harriet Harman Lab		

Southwark and Bermondsey   Southwark

The new seat of Southwark and Bermondsey is the former
Bermondsey with the addition of one ward, Burgess, from
Peckham. Bermondsey engaged national attention in the early
1980s. After a long power struggle within the local Labour
Party, the long-serving right-wing MP Bob Mellish, a papal
knight, and Chief Whip under Harold Wilson, was so alienated
that he supported Independent Labour candidates against the
official choices in the 1982 local elections. This action led to
Mellish's expulsion from the party. He resigned his seat in
autumn 1982, precipitating its long-awaited byelection.

The ructions caused by the local quarrel reached the very
top of the Labour Party. For when the left-dominated General
Management Committee of the constituency party selected
Peter Tatchell, a radical of Australian origin, as prospective
parliamentary candidate, Michael Foot declared that Tatchell
would never be endorsed by the NEC. This unexpected and
intemperate intervention rebounded on Foot, for Tatchell was
subsequently re-selected by the local party, and he was
accepted by the national body. However right-wingers such
as John O'Grady, leader of Southwark Borough for 14 years
before he was ousted by the left-wingers, continued to
oppose Tatchell bitterly.

Many thought that the main electoral contest at Bermondsey
would be fought between opposing factions of the Labour
Party; for Bermondsey is in the heart of south London's
working-class dockland, across the river from the massive
wealth of the City itself. But the Liberals had long been
locally active, and the Battle for Bermondsey was decisively
won by their candidate Simon Hughes, who monopolised the
anti-Tatchell vote and secured the largest byelection swing in
living memory.

1981	% Own Occ	2.5	1979 core seat Bermondsey		
1981	% Loc Auth	87.7	Lab	19,338	63.6
1981	% Black/Asian	10	C	7,582	24.9
1981	% Mid Cl	39.4	L	2,072	6.8
1981	% Prof Man	7.6	NF	1,175	3.9
1982	electorate 56,495		WRP	239	0.8
1979	notional result		MPs since 1950		
	Lab 12,700		1950-82 Robert Mellish Lab		
Alliance		L	1983- Simon Hughes L		

Carshalton and Wallington   Sutton

Despite the reputation of Carshalton Beeches as a fashionable ex-Surrey top residential area, the Carshalton constituency is not iron-clad Conservative country. In October 1974 Robert Carr, the former Conservative Home Secretary, won by little over 3,000 votes. This is because the seat takes in the bulk of the huge GLC council estate of St Helier, which is as Labour as Carshalton, Beddington and Wallington are Conservative. The name of the seat is altered, but its boundaries remain the same.

1981	% Own Occ	58.6	1979 same seat Carshalton		
1981	% Loc Auth	33.2	C	26,492	51.3
1981	% Black/Asian	3.5	Lab	16,121	31.2
1981	% Mid Cl	61.6	L	8,112	15.7
1981	% Prof Man	19.2	NF	919	1.8
1982	electorate 69,199		MPs since 1945		
Alliance		SDP	1945-60 A.H. Head C		
			1960-74 Walter Elliot C		
			1974-76 Robert Carr C		
			19760 Nigel Forman C		

Sutton and Cheam   Sutton

Graham Tope won Sutton and Cheam for the Liberals in a byelection in July in the great year of 1972; but his tenure was to last little over a year, and the Liberal challenge has gradually faded in subsequent years. Former oil executive Neil Macfarlane (now Minister of Sport) has a 15,000 majority in 1979. This is not surprising, for much of the seat is affluent commuterdom: Cheam South is the most middle-class ward in the whole of London, and Labour obtained a derisory 2.7% of the vote there in 1982. Sutton and Cheam remains a Liberal target, but a repeat of Tope's success is unlikely.

1981	% Own Occ	78.1	1979 same seat Sutton & Cheam		
1981	% Loc Auth	12.7	C	28,842	58.0
1981	% Black/Asian	4.0	L	13,136	26.4
1981	% Mid Cl	68.9	Lab	7,126	14.3
1981	% Prof Man	24.2	NF	465	0.9
1982	electorate 63,653		Ind	128	0.3
Alliance		L	MPs since 1945		
			1945-54 S.H. Marshall C		
			1954-72 Richard Sharples C		
			1972-74 Graham Tope L		
			1974- Neil Macfarlane C		

Bethnal Green and Stepney   Tower Hamlets

The Borough of Tower Hamlets encompasses the inner East End, the traditional working-class communities beyond the Tower of London. Under the old parliamentary boundaries, Stepney was associated with Poplar in a riverside constituency, while Bethnal Green was placed together with Bow in the northern half of the Borough. Now the boundaries have been redrawn, so that the dividing line runs from north to south. Bethnal Green comes together with Stepney in the western Tower Hamlets seat, leaving Bow with Poplar in the east.

At one time such a revision would have made little difference, politically, for the whole of Tower Hamlets used to be as solid a Labour stronghold as any in the country. But in recent years the Liberals have made a great impact, at least in local elections. They have done much better inland, in Ian Mikardo's old Bethnal Green/Bow seat than in Peter Shore's Stepney/Poplar. In the 1982 local elections, for example, the Liberals won every seat in Bethnal Green, and were well ahead in the wards which make up Mikardo's constituency. The new Bethnal Green and Stepney would have been close, but Labour would have retained a lead.

It is difficult to imagine Labour losing a seat in Tower Hamlets. Bethnal Green enjoyed a Liberal tradition in the inter-war years when Percy Harris was MP, but social and economic characteristics seem more suitable for Labour. There is scarcely any private housing, and here in the old East End the working-class neighbourhoods have a history of Labour activism dating back to the beginning of the century. In Spitalfields and in Whitechapel Asians form only the latest in the series of immigrant communities who have congregated here beyond the Tower - at one time this was the centre of the Jewish East End. But perhaps Labour has taken the support of Tower Hamlets too much for granted, and allowed Liberal local activism too much room for manoeuvre. Both Peter Shore and Ian Mikardo have cause for worry, even in London's working-class heartland.

1981	% Own Occ	3.6	1979 core seat Bethnal Green
1981	% Loc Auth	85.1	and Bow
1981	% Black/Asian	24	Lab 14,227 49.8
1981	% Mid Cl	35.3	L 6,673 23.4
1981	% Prof Man	8.7	C 5,567 19.5
1982	electorate 54,640		NF 1,740 6.1
1979	notional result		Oths 336 1.1
	Lab 9,500		MP since 1974
Alliance		L	1974- Ian Mikardo Lab

Bow and Poplar   Tower Hamlets

Peter Shore is probably the favourite to succeed Michael Foot
as Leader of the Labour Party. Like Foot, at present he
represents one of the safest Labour seats in Parliament,
Stepney and Poplar. But Shore is posed problems by the
Boundary Commission, and not for the first time. Between
1964 and 1974 he represented Stepney alone, but Tower
Hamlets's entitlement was then reduced from three seats to
two, and Peter Shore had to win selection for the new seat of
Stepney and Poplar. Now Stepney and Poplar is divided, and
each half is combined with parts of Bethnal Green and Bow.
Not only is there the question of which seat Shore and
Mikardo should fight; more seriously, both seem vulnerable to
the Liberal challenge which has grown in Tower Hamlets in
the last ten years.

The Liberals do better in Bow than in Poplar. In the 1982
local elections the Alliance, usually Liberal-led, won in Bow,
Park and Grove wards - Grove being the only ward with a
significant number of owner occupiers in the whole of the
Borough. Labour still presents a monolithic front down in the
old dockland by the Thames at Poplar, Millwall and the Isle of
Dogs in the loop of the river. The docks are now closed, and
much speculation concerns the direction the redevelopment will
take.

The early stages of the birth of the SDP were negotiated in
David Owen's home at Limehouse in the Bow and Poplar
constituency. But it is unlikely that the SDP will make a
breakthrough here. The Alliance strength in Tower Hamlets is
strongly associated with Liberalism. Yet still London's East
End is traditionally its most working-class and Labour
terrain. The true Cockney, it is said, is born within the
sound of Bow Bells. Should Bow fall into Liberal hands, an
element of that old-fashioned Cockney spirit may well seem to
have been eroded.

1981	% Own Occ	5.6	1979 core seat Stepney/Poplar		
1981	% Loc Auth	87.8	Lab	19,576	62.6
1981	% Black/Asian	16	C	6,561	21.0
1981	% Mid Cl	37.7	L	2,234	7.1
1981	% Prof Man	7.2	NF	1,571	5.0
1982	electorate 57,432		Oths	1,320	4.2
1979	notional result		MP since 1974		
	Lab 12,200		1974-	Peter Shore Lab	
Alliance		L			

Chingford   Waltham Forest

One of Mrs Thatcher's most ardent Cabinet devotees is the
brusque Employment Minister Norman Tebbit, a former airline
pilot once described as the 'Skinhead of Chingford'. His
constituency, the northern middle-class part of the Waltham
Forest Borough, remains virtually unaltered. Squeezed
between the River Lee and Epping Forest, Chingford is the
epitome of an owner-occupied white dormitory, somehow more
reminiscent of Essex county than of the capital city.

1981	% Own Occ	69.4	1979 core seat Chingford		
1981	% Loc Auth	22.2	C	24,640	56.1
1981	% Black/Asian	5.0	Lab	12,257	27.9
1981	% Mid Cl	59.2	L	5,225	11.9
1981	% Prof Man	18.0	NF	1,157	2.6
1982	electorate 57,080		E	649	1.5
1979	notional result		MP since 1974		
	C 12,400		1974- Norman Tebbit C		
Alliance		L			

Leyton   Waltham Forest

Philosopher, academic and TV host Bryan Magee defected from
Labour to the SDP a few months after the new party's
foundation. The Alliance did quite well in his Leyton seat in
the 1982 local elections, polling 32% to Labour's 39%. Leyton is
the southernmost seat in Waltham Forest, and that most
similar to the traditional East End - much terraced housing,
some redevelopment and a large non-white population. Magee's
chances seem to be improved by the fact that Leyton's
boundaries are scarcely altered, and if he can add the
personal vote of a long-serving MP to the basic Alliance
strength here, he could well hold on.

1981	% Own Occ	49.6	1979 core seat Leyton		
1981	% Loc Auth	28.3	Lab	21,095	51.4
1981	% Black/Asian	26.6	C	15,361	37.4
1981	% Mid Cl	48.3	L	3,425	8.3
1981	% Prof Man	10.0	NF	1,179	2.9
1982	electorate 58,604		MPs since 1950		
1979	notional result		1950-65 R.W. Sorenson Lab		
	Lab 5,700		1965-66 R.C. Buxton C		
Alliance		SDP	1966-74 Patrick Gordon Walker		
				Lab	
			1974- Bryan Magee Lab (SDP)		

Walthamstow   Waltham Forest

Walthamstow was the scene of two of the disastrous byelection results which befell Harold Wilson's 1966-70 government. Both seats were lost to the Tories following the deaths of their Labour members, West in 1967 and East in 1969. The loss of Walthamstow West was an especial blow. Not only did it require an 18% swing, but West had been the seat of Labour Party leader Clement Attlee from 1950 until his retirement in 1955. Labour went into the 1970 Election holding neither of the Walthamstow seats. But they found a saviour in the form of Eric Deakins.

Deakins first of all won back Walthamstow West, defeating the Tory byelection victor Fred Silvester in 1970. Then in 1974 the two seats were merged into a unified Walthamstow constituency. The East MP since 1967, Michael McNair-Wilson, wisely moved to stand at Newbury, for Deakins won the new seat easily. Walthamstow is little altered in the present redistribution. It remains the centre of the three Waltham Forest seats, a working-class and industrial enclave between the River Lee and Tory Woodford. Much of the housing is elderly, private and terraced; nearly 20% of the population is non-white.

Deakins should have little difficulty retaining Walthamstow. The Conservatives are still unable to approach victory, despite a typically large NE London swing of 9% in 1979. The Alliance, SDP-led in Walthamstow, only polled 23% in the 1982 local elections. With Bryan Magee's defection in the neighbouring, socially similar Leyton, Deakins is now the only Labour MP in Waltham Forest. But Attlee's old stamping ground seems safe for Labour under his stewardship.

1981	% Own Occ	45.1	1979 core seat Walthamstow	
1981	% Loc Auth	33.8	Lab	17,651	50.2
1981	% Black/Asian	19.5	C	13,248	37.7
1981	% Mid Cl	46.4	L	3,117	8.9
1981	% Prof Man	11.1	NF	1,119	3.2
1982	electorate 49,331		MP since 1974	
1979	notional result		1974- Eric Deakins Lab	
	Lab 4,500			
Alliance		SDP		

81

Battersea   Wandsworth

Wandsworth is one of the eight London Boroughs which have
lost a seat in the boundary changes. The two old Battersea
seats had both been reduced to around 40,000 electors by the
early 1980s, and now effectively they are merged to provide a
single large Battersea division, although the Nightingale,
Springfield and Earlsfield wards are transferred from
Battersea South to Tooting.

The two former Batterseas were of different character. North
was an inner-city, riverside seat next door to Lambeth's
Vauxhall. North contained several well-known London
landmarks – Battersea Park, the Power Station, the Dogs'
Home, Clapham Junction, the new Covent Garden Market. It
was a Labour stronghold, represented from 1946 to its
abolition by Douglas Jay, a senior anti-EEC intellectual in the
party, and a Fellow of All Souls, Oxford. Jay's career will
end with that of Battersea North. Both have been greatly
loyal to Labour for many years. Battersea South, on the
other hand, was one of the most marginal seats in London. It
stretched from gentrified, fashionable Wandsworth Common on
the southern region BR line to seedy Balham. Over 20% of the
population were non-white. Yet there were also pockets of
affluence, especially between the two Commons – Wandsworth
and Clapham. Alf Dubs held Battersea South for Labour by
only 332 votes in 1979.

The combination of a Labour stronghold and a marginal will
make the new Battersea a moderately safe Labour seat. The
Conservatives were only 4% behind Labour in the 1982 local
elections, so they too may entertain expectations in a very
good year. The Alliance however did very badly in Battersea,
achieving only 17% of the total vote – one of their worst
results in London.

1981	% Own Occ	28.9	New seat
1981	% Loc Auth	47.8	
1981	% Black/Asian	22	
1981	% Mid Cl	54.3	
1981	% Prof Man	17.3	
1982	electorate 65,829		
1979	notional result		
	Lab 7,000		
Alliance		SDP	

Putney   Wandsworth

In some ways Putney is socially similar to its neighbour to the
west, Richmond on Thames. It is over 50% middle class, with
a strong academic and intellectual presence, and a reputation
for progressive politics. Comfortably set between Barnes
Common, Putney Heath and Richmond Park, there is
considerable affluence here in Putney, and a lower than
average non-white population. Unlike Richmond, it is not the
Liberals but Labour who have received the benefit of the
non-Tory vote, although this is partly due to the large
council estate majority in Roehampton ward. The model cottage
estate of Roehampton was one of the earliest local authority
housing developments in Britain, and in more recent years
there have been further developments to the west of
Roehampton Lane.

Roehampton is undoubtedly Labour's stronghold in Putney,
but the former Arts Minister Hugh Jenkins needed middle-
class support as well to hold the seat from 1964 to 1979. But
the Conservative David Mellor gained Putney in Mrs
Thatcher's year of triumph, and it is generally felt that
Labour will find it hard to regain the constituency. Putney is
becoming more affluent, more exclusive, as property values
rise. It is an attractive residential area, relatively close to
the centre of London - just the kind of place which becomes
gentrified in a period of increasing transport costs. This
development may be partly responsible for a long-term swing
to the Tories.

The Labour candidate in Putney is the former Young Liberal
and student activist, Peter Hain. Hain will be a well-known
candidate, both locally and nationally, but his task seems
difficult. The Tories were 16% ahead in the 1982 local
elections, a gap it will be hard to close. The Alliance are not
strong in Wandsworth, and only attained 20% of the vote in
Putney in 1982. The constituency boundaries are unchanged.
David Mellor was the first Tory MP of the 1979 intake to join
the front bench team, and he seems to have a bright future
ahead of him.

1981	% Own Occ	34.6	1979 same seat Putney		
1981	% Loc Auth	46.0	C	23,040	46.8
1981	% Black/Asian	8.8	Lab	20,410	41.5
1981	% Mid Cl	61.8	L	5,061	10.3
1981	% Prof Man	20.6	NF	685	1.4
1982	electorate 63,991		MPs since 1945		
Alliance		L	1945-64 Sir H.N. Linstead C		
			1964-79 Hugh Jenkins Lab		
			1979- David Mellor C		

Tooting   Wandsworth

In the 1982 London Borough elections, the Conservatives polled a majority of votes in the wards which make up the old Tooting constituency in Wandsworth. There can be no more compelling example of the decline of Labour in London. In 1979 - a year in which they lost the General Election by a clear 7% or two million votes - Tom Cox held Tooting for Labour with a 5,200 majority. But a further swing of 8% to the Tories was recorded between 1979 and 1982. If Labour is in danger of losing Tooting, very serious doubts must be cast upon their chances of approaching the 100 gains needed to win an overall majority at the next General Election.

The boundary changes make Tooting even more vulnerable. Three wards are wholly or partly taken from the old Battersea South seat. The Conservative Nightingale and Springfield wards are now completely within Tooting - previously they were shared with Battersea S. The more Labour-inclined Earlsfield is gathered in from the same source. The constituency already included Tooting Bec and Tooting Graveney and Tooting Broadway; the area around Graveney and Tooting High Street is the best for Labour. Tooting is a cosmopolitan seat. A quarter of the population is non-white, and there are still many Victorian terraced houses. Tooting has a high proportion of privately rented housing, a favourite form of tenure for Asian and West Indian residents.

That Tooting could ever be considered a marginal would have been surprising when it was created in 1974. Why has Labour come to be in such a parlous state in London? A number of guesses may be mentioned: the relatively low unemployment in the capital, the distaste for left-wing Labour local government in London, a reaction to the increasing non-white population. Whatever the reason, the omens foretold by Tooting's voters in 1982 bode ill for Labour's future.

1981	% Own Occ	43.0	1979 core seat	Tooting	
1981	% Loc Auth	27.1	Lab	18,642	51.9
1981	% Black/Asian	24	C	13,442	37.4
1981	% Mid Cl	57.2	L	2,917	8.1
1981	% Prof Man	16.6	NF	682	1.9
1982	electorate 68,894		Comm	233	0.6
1979	notional result		MP since 1974		
	Lab 5,000		1974-	Tom Cox Lab	
Alliance		SDP			

City of London and Westminster South   Westminster

It could fairly be said that the very heart of the nation lies
in this constituency, the City of London and Westminster S.
Only a few thousand electors live in the square mile of the
City proper (although it had two MPs until 1950), but it is
the hub of the British economic empire. The seat also
includes the West End, with its retail shopping centre of the
capital, and the meccas of entertainment. Here are most of
the tourist 'sights' of London - St Paul's Cathedral and
Westminster Abbey, the Tower and Buckingham Palace.
Finally, in Westminster itself can be found the legislative and
executive pinnacle of the British constitution - the Houses of
Parliament and Whitehall.

It might be thought that few people live in this pulsating
vortex of British affairs. Yet in fact the seat will be a
populous one, of 75,000 electors, for it has absorbed the
southern wards of the abolished St Marylebone seat in
addition to retaining its previous 50,000 voters. Where are all·
these full-time residents of the 'downtown' area of London?
Some live in the super-rich neighbourhoods, in the plush
apartments of Mayfair, Knightsbridge and Belgravia. The
district of Pimlico is in the constituency, with its renovated
cottages and rather raffish reputation. There is council
housing at Millbank and in the Churchill estate, and the up-
market Barbican development in the City itself.

There are Labour voters scattered amongst the wealthy, but
this will be an even safer Tory seat now that the St
Marylebone wards of Bryanston, Baker St and Cavendish have
been added, and Hyde Park from Paddington. The Alliance
did very badly here in 1982, reaching only 18% in the local
elections. Conservative Peter Brooke, son of a former Home
Secretary, educated at Marlborough, Balliol and Harvard
Business School, will continue to represent the elite
constituency in the nation's capital city.

1981	% Own Occ	21.1	1979 core seat City of London
1981	% Loc Auth	35.2	and Westminster South
1981	% Black/Asian	6	C 16,851 60.7
1981	% Mid Cl	63.3	Lab 7,067 25.4
1981	% Prof Man	27.2	L 3,375 12.2
1982	electorate 69,251		NF 478 1.7
1979	notional result		MPs since 1950
	C 15,800		1950-59 Sir H. Webbe C
Alliance		L	1959-65 Sir Harry Hylton-Foster
			C (Speaker)
			1965-70 John Smith C
			1970-77 C. Tugendhat C
			1977- Peter Brooke C

Westminster North   Westminster

The Cities of Westminster and London lose one of their three seats in the redistribution. Westminster North is made up of wards in the old Paddington and St Marylebone constituencies. It will be a socially divided seat. St Marylebone was an affluent Tory stronghold, but Paddington was very marginal. North Paddington included some very low-status working-class and Labour-voting neighbourhoods: Harrow Road, Queens Park, Maida Vale and Westbourne wards. But Paddington also contained the mixed Little Venice and Bayswater, and Lancaster Gate and Hyde Park, which were strongly Conservative. John Wheeler defeated Tribune Group chairman Arthur Latham by only 106 votes to record a Tory gain in Paddington in 1979. But it was very much a winnable seat for both major parties - indeed, it is Ken Livingstone's seat on the GLC.

Westminster North will not be much worse for Labour than the super-marginal Paddington. Hyde Park is lost to Westminster S, and the parts of St Marylebone added include its one Labour ward, Church Street, as well as affluent St John's Wood and Regents Park. Westminster North should still be a possible Labour win in a very good year. This is surprising considering the reputation of St John's Wood and other wealthy areas in the seat, but that merely illustrates the political and economic contrasts which can be found within a few hundred yards of each other in the capital.

The Conservatives were only 3% ahead in the wards which make up Westminster North in the 1982 London Borough elections, polling 41% to Labour's 38%. The Alliance made little impact, achieving only 18% in the new constituency, their best performance being 20.9% in Lord's ward. There may well be another tight two-party contest next time.

1981	% Own Occ	19.7	1979 core seat Paddington		
1981	% Loc Auth	43.1	C	16,189	45.5
1981	% Black/Asian	15	Lab	16,083	45.2
1981	% Mid Cl	57.7	L	2,815	7.9
1981	% Prof Man	22.2	NF	402	1.1
1982	electorate 70,895		WRP	117	0.3
1979	notional result		MPs since 1974		
	C 2,400		1974-79 Arthur Latham Lab		
Alliance		SDP	1979- John Wheeler C		

Bolton North-East   Bolton

In recent years Bolton has been noted for its tight contests
between Labour and Conservative candidates. In 1979 both
Labour MPs, David Young (East) and Ann Taylor (West) did
well to resist the Thatcherite landslide. The old Bolton East
was until then a bellwether of British politics, falling to the
winning party in each General Election since its creation in
1950.
But now all has changed. The new, enlarged Bolton
Metropolitan Borough takes in much territory from outside the
former Bolton town boundaries, and earns three seats in
Parliament. None of these is very similar to any previous
division. But Bolton NE consists of much of the former East
division plus the highly Tory, ultra-middle-class wards of
Bradshaw and Bromley Cross from the old Turton Urban
District, which used to be in Darwen constituency. South
Turton is a rapidly developing private residential area, and
the inclusion of the outer wards would undoubtedly have
tipped Bolton NE to the Conservatives in 1979. Labour has
considerable strength in Breightmet and Tonge, where there
are a considerable number of council houses, and in the
depressed Central ward. But the Conservatives also have the
old middle-class ward of Astley Bridge, north Bolton, on the
road to Blackburn.
Bolton NE will be a socially divided seat. In Central ward,
26% of the population are non-white, and only 26% of all
families have a car. In Bradshaw 1% is non-white, and 72%
own a car. The seat will provide a tough fight to the finish,
but Labour has an uphill task to win it. The Alliance have
made no impact here as yet, so it seems like a two-horse
race.

1981	% Own Occ	62.8	1979 core seat Bolton East		
1981	% Loc Auth	33.2	Lab	21,920	47.6
1981	% Black/Asian	5.1	C	20,068	43.6
1981	% Mid Cl	47.9	L	3,603	7.8
1981	% Prof Man	16.1	NF	457	1.0
1982	electorate 59,870		MPs since 1950		
1979	notional result		1950-51 A. Booth Lab		
	C 1,400		1951-60 P.I. Bell C		
Alliance		SDP	1960-64 E. Taylor C		
			1964-70 R.L. Howarth Lab		
			1970-74 Laurance Reed C		
			1974- David Young Lab		

Bolton South-East   Bolton

Labour held both the former Bolton seats, but seem favourites in only one of the three new divisions created by the Boundary Commissioners. One reason for this is that most of the Labour support has been packed into a single safe seat, the new Bolton SE. Actually only half of the SE division was formerly inside the Bolton boundaries, and the outlying communities of Farnworth, Little Lever and Kearsley have been added since Bolton became a Metropolitan Borough. These were previously in the Farnworth constituency of Social Democrat John Roper, which has been irretrievably split asunder.

Roper is in a parlous state, worse off than most SDP MPs. Worsley has been detached from his constituency because it is in Salford Metropolitan Borough. The Alliance did not do very well in Kearsley, Little Lever and Farnworth in the 1982 local elections. In any case these towns, which have been used to voting for Roper for more than a decade, seem liable to be smothered by heavily Labour wards from Bolton. Harper Green is a peripheral council estate. Derby and Burnden are inner Bolton wards, which harbour a concentration of privately rented housing and the town's black and Asian community. 38% of the population of Derby ward originated in the New Commonwealth and Pakistan, by far the highest proportion in Bolton.

Bolton SE looks like a Labour stronghold, and although it is as near a successor to Farnworth as there is, it is doubtful whether Roper will contest it.

1981	% Own Occ	61.8	1979 core seat Farnworth
1981	% Loc Auth	32.6	Lab 27,965 50.1
1981	% Black/Asian	10.8	C 19,858 35.5
1981	% Mid Cl	35.6	L 8,043 14.4
1981	% Prof Man	9.7	MPs since 1945
1982	electorate 68,788		1945-52 G. Tomlinson Lab
1979	notional result		1952-70 E. Thornton Lab
	Lab 12,500		1970- John Roper Lab (SDP)
Alliance		L	

Bolton West   Bolton

West Bolton includes some exceedingly fine affluent residential areas. In Heaton ward, around Bolton School and along the A673 Chorley New Road, the nineteenth-century mansions of Bolton's textile magnates can still be seen. Yet the existing seat of Bolton West has rarely had a Conservative MP. From 1951 to 1964 there was a curious electoral pact between the Liberals and Conservatives in Bolton, rather like that in another textile town over the Pennines in Huddersfield. The Tories gave Liberal MP Arthur Holt a free run in Bolton West, while the Liberals stood down in turn in East. In 1964 the pact ended. Labour won both seats, and Arthur Holt finished bottom of the poll in Bolton West.

Ann Taylor was only 27 years of age when she won Bolton W in October 1974. She did exceedingly well to hold the highly marginal seat in 1979, restricting the swing to the Tories to 0.4%. But boundary changes will make her task considerably harder. Besides Bolton's best residential areas of Heaton and Smithills wards, which are already in the West division, there arrives the 84% owner-occupied Hulton Park ward. Also from Westhoughton constituency come Blackrod, Horwich and Westhoughton itself, which are much more inclined to Labour. However, overall Labour will need a 5% swing next time to take the new Bolton West.

Like many Lancashire textile towns, Bolton has a tradition of owner occupation. Over 74% of families in Bolton West own their own houses, which makes it a microcosm of the property-owning democracy. This doesn't ensure that it will be a Tory seat, but there is a strong correlation between house ownership and Conservative support - at the last election it is probable that even working-class homeowners gave Mrs Thatcher a majority. This makes a Labour victory in Bolton West all the more unlikely.

1981	% Own Occ	74.6	1979 core seat Bolton West
1981	% Loc Auth	19.4	Lab 17,857 44.8
1981	% Black/Asian	3.0	C 17,257 43.3
1981	% Mid Cl	50.0	L 4,392 11.0
1981	% Prof Man	17.4	NF 348 0.9
1982	electorate 67,705		MPs since 1950
1979	notional result		1950-51 J. Lewis Lab
	C 5,600		1951-64 Arthur Holt L
Alliance		SDP	1964-70 Gordon Oakes Lab
			1970-74 Robert Redmond C
			1974- Ann Taylor Lab

Bury North   Bury

In the 1979 General Election, Labour did very well to hold
two Greater Manchester marginal seats, Bury-Radcliffe and
Middleton-Prestwich. In both cases, the sitting MP managed to
restrict the pro-Tory swing to a much lower percentage than
average. But now the Boundary Commission's work is to pose
greater problems still for Labour, as they try to cling on to
two of their most vulnerable seats. Bury and Radcliffe was
held by locally popular moderate Frank White by just 38
votes. But Radcliffe, the more strongly Labour part of the
seat, is moved into the new Bury South division; and the
extremely Conservative town of Ramsbottom is brought in from
the Rossendale constituency. As a result, Labour would have
been at least 3,000 votes behind in Bury North in 1979, even
allowing for something of a personal vote for Frank White.
Bury always was one of the more prosperous of the
Lancashire textile towns. There is an area of low-price
terraced nineteenth-century housing in East ward, but very
few council estates of any size, and much solid owner-
occupied property. Even more Tory than Bury, though, are
the small communities of Tottington and Ramsbottom.
Ramsbottom was once a valley mill town, but its neat cottages
have become increasingly valued by Manchester commuters,
especially since the M66 has been open, cutting journey time
to the south.
The long-term swing to Labour in this district has continued,
however, and in the early 1980s Labour was still doing better
in the NW of England than in the Midlands or the SE. This
was one of the seats Labour held in 1979 but not in 1970.
The Alliance has made little impact here, securing under 25%
of the vote in the 1982 local elections in Bury North wards.
Labour still have a chance here, even though the boundary
changes have threatened to stymie their valiant and
exceptional efforts in the Bury neighbourhood.

1981	% Own Occ	74.5	1979 core seat Bury/Radcliffe
1981	% Loc Auth	20.5	Lab 29,194 45.3
1981	% Black/Asian	2	C 29,156 45.2
1981	% Mid Cl	51.3	L 5,711 8.9
1981	% Prof Man	17.8	NF 414 0.6
1982	electorate 66,716		MPs since 1945
1979	notional result		1945-55 W. Fletcher C
	C 3,000		1955-64 J.C. Bidgood C
Alliance		L	1964-70 David Ensor Lab
			1970-74 Michael Fidler C
			1974- Frank White Lab

Bury South   Bury

If Bury North consists basically of the more Conservative
parts of the marginal Bury/Radcliffe seat, Bury South
includes the more Tory sections of Middleton and Prestwich.
Middleton is now in the Borough of Rochdale, and part of the
fairly safe Heywood-Middleton division. But Prestwich has the
reputation of being one of the most exclusive and desirable
residential areas north of Manchester. It is also reputed to be
very Jewish in population and character. Neither of these
stereotyped views is quite correct, although it is true that
many members of the Manchester Jewish community did do
well, and moved north up and out of the original Cheetham
Hill ghetto. Prestwich is pleasantly situated on the edge of
Heaton Park, but there has always been a large Labour
minority there. Middleton and Prestwich were never quite as
different as chalk and cheese.

Bury South also includes Radcliffe, which is generally
favourable to Labour; and the Besses o' the Barn ward,
which is one of the Tories' weakest areas in the whole Bury
Borough. All this means that Bury South is a better bet for
Labour than Bury North. Although the Conservatives would
probably have won it by about 400 in 1979, Labour was ahead
in the 1982 local elections. The Alliance did very badly in
their first full-scale venture into municipal elections, polling
little over 20% in Bury South as a whole in 1982.

Bury is the smallest of the Boroughs of Greater Manchester,
and one of the most marginal. Both new Bury seats seem to
have been 'nominal' Conservative victories last time, and likely
Labour 'gains' next time. The present MP for Middleton/
Prestwich is James Callaghan - not the former Prime Minister,
but a rather more left-wing, younger member. If he retains
his connection with Prestwich rather than following Middleton,
he should still be a narrow favourite to win the Bury South
battle.

1981	% Own Occ	67.8	1979 core seat Middleton/	
1981	% Loc Auth	26.6	Prestwich	
1981	% Black/Asian	2	Lab	27,918	45.8
1981	% Mid Cl	52.6	C	26,820	44.0
1981	% Prof Man	17.2	L	5,888	9.7
1982	electorate 65,802		NF	350	0.6
1979	notional result		MPs since 1945	
	C 400		1945-51 E.E. Gates C	
Alliance		SDP	1951-66 Sir J.D. Barlow C	
			1966-70 D.W. Coe Lab	
			1970-74 Alan Haselhurst C	
			1974- James Callaghan Lab	

Altrincham and Sale   Manchester/Trafford

This constituency might well have been renamed Altrincham
and Hale, for most of Sale has been transferred to the newly
created Davyhulme division. Still, Sale Moor and Brooklands
remain, and Altrincham and Sale is a long-standing name.
Altrincham incorporates the community of Timperley and the
ward of Broadheath. Hale and Bowdon arrive from the old
Knutsford constituency.

This is part of Cheshire's middle-class belt, south-west of
Manchester. Altrincham and Sale, however, were large enough
to be more than dormitories; they have a life and character of
their own, and can act as minor economic counter-attractions
to Manchester. This was not, in general, true Rolls-Royce or
stockbroker country as found in some of the smaller
communities further out. But Hale and Bowdon are two of the
five highest-status small towns in the country. Each reached
a level of 69% non-manual workers in 1971. This figure was
exceeded in England only by Harpenden and Chorleywood in
Hertfordshire and by Formby in Shirley Williams's Crosby
seat. There really are millionaires in Hale, secluded in leafy
private roads and luxury houses, especially out towards
Halebarns. Not surprisingly, Labour polls under 10% in Hale
and Bowdon, whose addition should make this seat even safer
for the Conservatives.

The MP here is Fergus Montgomery, who has wandered more
almost than any other member in search of a constituency. He
has represented both Newcastle upon Tyne East (where he
was defeated by Labour), and Brierley Hill in the West
Midlands (where he was ousted by the last Boundary
Commission), but surely his travels have come to a happy
end, for the new Altrincham and Sale cannot be detached
from the Tory grasp in any normal circumstances.

1981	% Own Occ	72.6	1979 core seat Altrincham and		
1981	% Loc Auth	17.0	Sale		
1981	% Black/Asian	1	C	29,873	51.6
1981	% Mid Cl	65.2	Lab	14,543	25.3
1981	% Prof Man	25.8	L	12,603	21.8
1982	electorate 66,800		E	796	1.4
1979	notional result		MPs since 1945		
	C 18,900		1945-65 F.J. Erroll C		
Alliance		L	1965-74 Anthony Barber C		
			1974- Fergus Montgomery C		

Davyhulme   Manchester/Trafford

Winston Churchill, the present MP for Stretford, would be
well advised to seek nomination for the new Davyhulme
constituency at the next election. Davyhulme contains the
Conservative western half of his present seat - Urmston,
Flixton and Davyhulme itself. It also includes the north-
western part of Sale around Ashton on Mersey. The only
Labour stronghold is Bucklow ward, which basically consists
of Partington, the working-class community which serves the
massive ICI chemical works at Carrington.
Urmston, Flixton and Davyhulme are mainly middle-class
owner-occupied suburbs west of Manchester. They never
blended very well with Stretford itself and Old Trafford,
nearer inner-city Manchester, which were much more inclined
to the Labour Party and which form the core of the new
Stretford seat. There is a Labour presence in Sale,
particularly in St Martin's ward. But despite this, and the
anomalous Partington, which used to be the only Labour ward
in Knutsford constituency, the Tories can count on
Davyhulme as an extra safe seat.
Davyhulme is essentially the north-western end of the
Cheshire belt which girdles southern Manchester and houses
so many of that city's commuters. About three-quarters of the
housing in Davyhulme division is owner occupied. There is no
significant black or Asian population. It is not the direct
successor to any old seat, but seems an ideal haven for
Winston Churchill, should he wish to secure his parliamentary
future.

1981	% Own Occ	65.2	New seat
1981	% Loc Auth	25.7	
1981	% Black/Asian	2	
1981	% Mid Cl	57.1	
1981	% Prof Man	17.0	
1982	electorate 65,835		
1979	notional result		
	C 10,700		
Alliance	L		

Manchester Blackley   Manchester/Trafford

In the redistribution, Manchester loses three of its eight
seats; admittedly, both Openshaw and Gorton were only half
composed of city wards, also including Failsworth and Denton.
But Manchester's parliamentary representation has been
dramatically adjusted to take into account its loss of
population. Blackley is less affected than most. Blackley is
North Manchester - Blackley ward itself, Charlestown,
Moston, Lightbowne and Crumpsall. Now a section of the true
inner city is added - Harpurhey, 75% local authority housing,
with 25% male unemployment, 70% Labour in 1979. Blackley is
a mixed constituency. Crumpsall is a Conservative ward in a
normal year, and all the other wards have large Tory
minorities. Council estates like those at Charlestown and
Higher Blackley stand shoulder to shoulder with private
residential areas like Shackcliffe Green and old terraces in
Lightbowne and the centre of Moston.

Harpurhey should reinforce a trend to Labour in Blackley
which has been operating since the war. In the 1950s, the
Tories held this seat, but new council housing developments
have combined with some middle-class out-migration to lower
the status of the area. Manchester has also been one of the
kinder cities to Labour in the last twenty-five years,
swinging below the average in good Tory years and above the
average in good Labour years.

Blackley Labour MP Paul Rose retired in 1979, professing
himself disillusioned with Parliament. But Blackley should
remain loyal to the new member, Ken Eastham, and to the
Labour Party, despite its hefty Conservative minority.

1981	% Own Occ	44.0	1979 core seat Manchester

1981 % Own Occ   44.0   1979 core seat Manchester
1981 % Loc Auth   46.3   Blackley
1981 % Black/Asian 0.5   Lab   20,346   50.4
1981 % Mid Cl   41.4   C   15,842   39.2
1981 % Prof Man   9.9   L   3,868   9.6
1982 electorate 60,627   NF   328   0.8
1979 notional result   MPs since 1945
      Lab 5,800   1945-51 J. Diamond Lab
Alliance   L   1951-64 E.S.T. Johnson C
                           1964-79 Paul Rose Lab
                           1979-   Kenneth Eastham Lab

Manchester Central   Manchester/Trafford

The old Manchester Central seat was one of the anomalously small inner-city constituencies which most clearly revealed the need for boundary changes. In 1979 there were only 31,000 electors on the roll, and even this number was still dropping rapidly. Now the old seat has disappeared into a relatively vast division comprising the whole of central and inner-city Manchester.

Central now includes part of several former seats: Newton Heath and Bradford from Openshaw, Hulme from Moss Side, Ardwick from the constituency of the same name, as well as most of the old Central seat. Every ward is strongly Labour. Most are extremely poor, and many of the most deprived redevelopments in Manchester are to be found here: the notorious Bison-constructed 'Fort' Beswick, half-abandoned and due for demolition; the planning disasters of Hulme; the remnants of the working-class Jewish quarter of Cheetham Hill, now skeletal and gutted. Here too are the fine buildings of the commercial centre, which still hint that Manchester was once the second city of the Empire. But most of the residential areas are not so fine. The highest proportion of non-white residents are to be found in other wards, but Cheetham is 30% black and Asian, Hulme and Rusholme 20%. Overall, the figure reaches about 9%, less than Gorton and Stretford.

The central division of Manchester has always provided one of the safest Labour seats in England. Now, with its newly enlarged electorate of 71,000, it should produce one of the largest majorities too - over 20,000. This is wretched ground for the Tories, and the only real contest will be for the Labour nomination.

1981	% Own Occ	19.2	1979 core seat Manchester
1981	% Loc Auth	72.4	Central
1981	% Black/Asian	9	Lab 14,117 70.8
1981	% Mid Cl	28.1	C 4,413 22.1
1981	% Prof Man	6.4	L 2,082 5.3
1982	electorate 70,893		NF 365 1.8
1979	notional result		MPs since 1974
	Lab 21,000		1974-79 Harold Lever Lab
Alliance		SDP	1979- Bob Litherland Lab

95

Manchester Gorton   Manchester/Trafford

The new Gorton seat bears little resemblance to the previous
constituency of that name. Like the old Openshaw seat,
Gorton used to cross the city boundary to take in Lancashire
towns beyond – in this case Audenshaw and Denton, both of
which had substantial middle-class and Tory minorities. After
the redrawing Gorton stands as one of the five new
Manchester city seats, but besides Gorton itself it also
contains most of the old Ardwick division – the wards of
Levenshulme, Longsight and Rusholme. The specification is
completed by the new Fallowfield ward, which was only
created in 1981.
The parts of this urban constituency vary somewhat in
character. Longsight is the south-eastern part of Manchester's
belt of inner-city desolation. It is strongly Labour and over
30% non-white. Levenshulme, a little further out from the
centre, is a Liberal target ward, and includes only 7% council
housing. Rusholme and Fallowfield also contain many owner
occupiers, and were once part of Manchester's southern
middle-class area, but have declined as the more affluent
Mancunians have fled further south and out to Cheshire.
The Tories cannot usually win any of the wards in the new
Gorton seat nowadays, and it should be regarded as a Labour
banker despite the fact that half its housing is owner
occupied – an increasing proportion of this will probably be
occupied by Asians, in any case. It is not clear as yet
whether Ardwick's Gerald Kaufman or Gorton's Kenneth Marks
has the best claim to the Labour nomination in this new seat
in SE Manchester.

1981	% Own Occ	50.3	1979 core seat Manchester	
1981	% Loc Auth	27.5	Ardwick	
1981	% Black/Asian	13	Lab 17,235	56.7
1981	% Mid Cl	38.0	C 9,963	32.8
1981	% Prof Man	9.8	L 2,934	9.6
1982	electorate 65,903		Oth 287	0.9
1979	notional result		MPs since 1950	
	Lab 9,900		1950–70 Leslie Lever Lab	
Alliance		L	1970– Gerald Kaufman Lab	

Manchester Withington   Manchester/Trafford

For some years, Withington has been the only Conservative seat in Manchester. It used to include the classic middle-class suburbs of south Manchester - Didsbury, always the strongest Tory ward in the city, Barlow Moor, Burnage, and Withington itself. But by the 1970s the Conservative majority here was reduced to shaky proportions. The big houses were being multi-occupied, broken up or slipping down the scale of social status. Council estates had been established at Old Moat and Burnage in the inter-war years - Burnage Garden Village is one of the oldest and most desirable council developments in Britain. By 1979 Withington's housing was over 30% local authority owned. Tory MP Fred Silvester could win only a 3,000 majority as his party was swept to power in 1979.

With the reduction of seats in Manchester from eight to five, it might be thought that the redistribution would sweep away this last Conservative enclave. But in fact the reverse has happened. Help had been provided for Silvester, in the form of Chorlton cum Hardy. Chorlton, Manchester's second strongest ward, has been added to Withington. Previously Chorlton had formed the outermost segment of the curiously divided Moss Side seat, but it never sat logically or happily with the troubled inner-city wards of that division. Chorlton will bring a much needed boost of 1,500 to the Conservative majority.

Withington might seem embattled and besieged, totally surrounded by Labour seats. But this very fact might keep it Conservative, as its voters contrast their lot with the encroaching tide of poverty nearby. The last Tory redoubt in Manchester will probably prove a hard nut to crack.

1981	% Own Occ	47.1	1979 core seat Manchester
1981	% Loc Auth	33.1	Withington
1981	% Black/Asian	4	C	18,862	47.3
1981	% Mid Cl	56.6	Lab	15,510	38.9
1981	% Prof Man	17.3	L	5,387	13.5
1982	electorate 65,947		Feudal	157	0.4
1979	notional result		MPs since 1945
	C 4,700		1945-50 E.L. Fleming C
Alliance		SDP	1950-51 F.W. Cundiff C
			1951-74 Sir Robert Cary C
			1974- Fred Silvester C

Manchester Wythenshawe   Manchester/Trafford

The least altered seat in Manchester is the council estate
constituency of Wythenshawe at the southern end of the city,
in the lee of Manchester International Airport (Ringway). It
consists basically of the same wards as before, although there
may be minor changes in the ward boundaries following local
government redistribution in Manchester.
It is fair to describe Wythenshawe as a council estate seat,
for nearly 80% of the housing is rented from the local
authority, and since the inter-war years Wythenshawe has
been noted as one of the largest municipal overspill
developments in Europe, growing to a population of roughly
60,000. It is on the edge of the city, 6-8 miles from
Piccadilly, but it has not suffered from the inadequate
services and other economic and social deprivations in the
way that its counterparts in Liverpool and Glasgow have. The
Wythenshawe estate has had a relatively happy history. But it
is resolutely and remorselessly working class, and a solid
area of Labour support. This seat is not entirely composed of
the Wythenshawe estate. North of the A560 road are to be
found good residential areas: in Brooklands, near the city's
boundary with the Cheshire commuter belt of Sale; and in
mixed Northenden. Before 1964 this kind of area was enough
to give the Conservatives victory. But as the council estate
has continued to grow, the seat has slipped away from the
Tory Party.
Labour MP Alf Morris had the largest numerical majority in
Manchester in 1979. Morris is a member of a well-known local
political family - his brother Charles has held the Openshaw
seat since 1963. Alf Morris is also known for his specialist
work on behalf of the disabled. As a popular and active
member, he seems invulnerable in Wythenshawe. This is not
good territory for the Alliance.

1981	% Own Occ	20.5	1979 core seat Manchester		
1981	% Loc Auth	77.5	Wythenshawe		
1981	% Black/Asian	1	Lab	26,860	59.1
1981	% Mid Cl	39.7	C	14,747	32.4
1981	% Prof Man	10.7	L	3,853	8.5
1982	electorate 62,140		MPs since 1950		
1979	notional result		1950-64 Mrs E. Hill C		
	Lab 12,100		1964-	Alf Morris Lab	
Alliance		L			

Stretford   Manchester/Trafford

The seat called Stretford is at present held by Conservative
Winston Churchill, the grandson of the former Prime Minister.
But the new constituency of Stretford should be a Labour
seat in most years, and probably it would even have voted
Labour by a narrow margin in 1979. What is more, this is not
just because the seat now crosses the Trafford Borough
border to annex parts of the city of Manchester, including
the ward of Moss Side.
The mystery is explained by the character of the old
Stretford seat. Stretford itself, which includes Old Trafford,
made up but half of that constituency named after it. These
wards - Clifford, Longford, Park, Stretford and Talbot - are
clearly Labour except in a good Tory year, when they are
close. The Conservative lead in Stretford constituency came
from Davyhulme, Flixton and Urmston, further west and now
in the new Davyhulme seat. Now two wards from Manchester
are added, both formerly in the Moss Side constituency, but
of a very different nature. Whalley Range, like its neighbour
Chorlton, is a Conservatively inclined private residential area
of SW Manchester. Moss Side is an inner-city ward, mainly
new council houses and blocks, and the heart of Manchester's
West Indian community. Moss Side was one of the unfortunate
districts to hit the headlines through rioting in summer 1981,
and it shares the housing blight, multiple deprivations and
unemployment of Manchester's inner-city belt.
Moss Side's Labour sympathies should outweigh Whalley
Range's Toryism, and the boost offered thereby should tip
the balance of the new Stretford seat. But it would be too
bold to describe it as more than a Labour marginal, despite
the poverty and the black population of about 18%. It will be
one of the most politically interesting divisions in the new
Parliament.

1981	% Own Occ	50.7	1979 core seat Stretford
1981	% Loc Auth	33.5	C 25,972 48.3
1981	% Black/Asian	18	Lab 21,466 39.9
1981	% Mid Cl	47.2	L 6,369 11.8
1981	% Prof Man	12.7	MPs since 1945
1982	electorate 58,969		1945-50 H.L. Austin Lab
1979	notional result		1950-66 S. Storey C
	Lab 3,600		1966-70 E.A. Davies Lab
Alliance		SDP	1970- Winston Churchill C

Heywood and Middleton   Oldham/Rochdale

This seat, entirely within the Metropolitan Borough of
Rochdale, combines Heywood, the most Labour part of
Heywood and Royton, with Middleton, the most Labour part of
Middleton and Prestwich. Both of these old seats had paper-
thin Labour majorities, but Heywood and Middleton should be
a much safer bet for Labour. Probably they would have
obtained a lead of about 9,000 here in 1979, princely
compared to the photo-finish victories they achieved in some
adjacent seats.
Both Heywood and Middleton are towns of varied political
composition. Middleton ranges from the comfortable and even
plush semis and detached houses of Alkrington Garden Village
in the south of the town to the huge overspill council estate
of Langley in the NW. The growth of Langley significantly
swung this seat to Labour through the 1950s and 1960s. West
Heywood has a clutch of tower blocks which forms a notable
landmark off the M66 motorway. Heywood South, on the other
hand, is usually a Tory ward.
This outlying part of Rochdale Borough traditionally did not
share the Liberalism of Cyril Smith's Rochdale itself. But the
Alliance did quite well here in 1982, polling 26.3% of the vote,
to Labour's 40% and 33% for the Conservatives. The SDP took
Heywood N. If the Alliance should take off, they could well
pose a greater threat to Labour here than the Tories do. It
is unclear whether the Labour candidate will be the right-
wing Joel Barnett (a former Cabinet Minister) of Heywood and
Royton or left-wing James Callaghan (not the former Prime
Minister) of Middleton and Prestwich. Both have done well to
hold their seats in the Commons so far, and seem popular
locally.

1981	% Own Occ	50.5	1979 core seat Middleton and
1981	% Loc Auth	44.6	Prestwich
1981	% Black/Asian	1	Lab 27,918 45.8
1981	% Mid Cl	40.6	C 26,820 44.0
1981	% Prof Man	11.6	L 5,888 9.7
1982	electorate 60,894		NF 350 0.6
1979	notional result		MPs since 1945
	Lab 9,100		1945-51 E.E. Gates C
Alliance		SDP	1951-66 Sir J.D. Barlow C
			1966-70 D.W. Coe Lab
			1970-74 A. Haselhurst C
			1974- J. Callaghan Lab

Littleborough and Saddleworth   Oldham/Rochdale

Littleborough and Saddleworth is one of those seats which
crosses Metropolitan Borough boundaries, in this case
Rochdale and Oldham. It should provide a fascinating battle,
for it also crosses the historic county boundaries to include
Saddleworth from the Yorkshire constituency of Colne Valley.
Colne Valley had a dramatic and famous electoral history and
its last MP in its old form was a Liberal, Richard
Wainwright. Now it is broken in two, although the name of
Colne Valley lives on in association with the half on the
Yorkshire side of the border.
  Colne Valley was a Labour-Liberal marginal. However, the
little ex-mill towns which join Saddleworth are full of spry,
neat owner-occupied cottages. They are also full of
Conservatives. Littleborough, Milnrow, Wardle, Crompton and
Shaw are all consistently Tory wards, mainly transferred from
the marginal Heywood and Royton. They do not possess a
strong Liberal tradition. Who will win this western Pennines
seat? Labour has less chance than the other contestants, for
their only stronghold is the little town of Lees, and the
Saddleworth end of the Colne Valley was not their best - they
run a poor third here in local elections. The Liberals won
Saddleworth in the 1982 elections, but only polled 29%, the
same as Labour, in the new seat as a whole. The
Conservatives achieved 42% in 1982, and polled most votes, as
they would have in 1979.
  The Tories must be favourites to pick up a seat here.
However it should be remembered that 1979 and 1982 were
both good Tory years. In the event of serious government
unpopularity, either of the other two groupings could pull off
a victory.

1981	% Own Occ	68.4	New seat
1981	% Loc Auth	24.5	
1981	% Black/Asian	1	
1981	% Mid Cl	51.5	
1981	% Prof Man	18.0	
1982	electorate 64,114		
1979	notional result		
	C 5,600 (over Lab)		
Alliance		L	

Oldham Central and Royton   Oldham/Rochdale

Most of the old County Borough of Oldham is included in this
new seat, together with Royton. Royton is the more heavily
owner occupied (75%) and Conservative element of Heywood
and Royton. But Oldham Central and Royton should still be a
safe Labour seat. This is where Oldham's Asian population is
to be found, although it is less noticeable than in
neighbouring Rochdale. Only a quarter of the population is
employed in non-manual ('middle-class') jobs.

Oldham is a hilly ex-textile town, and some of the most
dramatic industrial scenery of the Lancashire cotton age can
be glimpsed here, as one sweeps down from the Pennines on
the M62. William Cobbett was MP at one time here, in 1832
when cotton was king. Many of the mills have been converted
to other uses now, but the economy is relatively healthy.
Unemployment is around average for the industrial North
West.

There have been indications that the local political temper is
out of tune with the left-wing member, James Lamond. But
there is no sign of any Alliance strength here, and Labour
should hold on easily.

1981	% Own Occ	55.9	1979 core seat Oldham East		
1981	% Loc Auth	39.1	Lab	18,248	50.7
1981	% Black/Asian	6	C	13,616	37.8
1981	% Mid Cl	36.2	L	4,549	11.5
1981	% Prof Man	10.5	MPs since 1950		
1982	electorate 68,195		1950-51 F. Fairhurst Lab		
1979	notional result		1951-59 I.A. Horobin C		
	Lab 6,100		1959-70 Charles Mapp Lab		
Alliance		SDP	1970- James Lamond Lab		

Oldham West   Oldham/Rochdale

Oldham West is now comprised mainly of the towns of
Failsworth and Chadderton, not of Oldham itself. The seat
straddles the road north-east from Manchester nearly to the
centre of Oldham.

Failsworth is at present part of a Manchester seat, Openshaw,
which is abolished in the redistribution. Chadderton is
already included in the current Oldham West division. Both
Chadderton and Failsworth are marginally inclined to Labour.
The two wards from Oldham itself which are to be included in
the new Oldham West, Werneth and Hollinwood, are strong
Labour areas, especially the latter, which is a peripheral
council estate.

Despite the owner-occupier majority in this seat, it should
belong to Labour, and it should be won by Michael Meacher,
a leading intellectual left-winger in the party and a lieutenant
of Tony Benn. The Liberals have the Alliance nomination for
Oldham West, but they lost their deposit in both the Oldham
constituencies in the 1979 General Election.

1981	% Own Occ	63.3	1979 core seat Oldham West		
1981	% Loc Auth	30.8	Lab	17,802	52.4
1981	% Black/Asian	1	C	12,025	35.4
1981	% Mid Cl	39.4	L	3,604	10.6
1981	% Prof Man	10.6	NF	515	1.5
1982	electorate 57,590		MPs since 1950		
1979	notional result		1950-68 Leslie Hale Lab		
	Lab 3,600		1968-70 K.B. Campbell C		
Alliance		L	1970- Michael Meacher Lab		

Rochdale   Oldham/Rochdale

In the autumn of 1972, the massive Cyril Smith caused a
political earthquake when he seized Rochdale from the Labour
Party in a byelection. A series of landslides to the Liberals
followed, the abortive third party revival of the early 1970s.
The Liberal tide ebbed, but Cyril Smith remained
representing Rochdale in the Commons, like a rock in the
ocean of major party MPs. With the revival of centre politics
in the early 1980s, he seems invulnerable to mortal opponents
in Rochdale. In 1982 the Alliance obtained a clear majority in
the local elections in Rochdale, and Cyril Smith has always
run ahead of his municipal colleagues.

Rochdale is little altered in the redistribution. Where does
the weight of the Liberal strength come from? The bulk has
traditionally been concentrated in the centre of the town, in
wards like Spotland where the Conservatives have given up
the contest, and Labour comes second and last. There is a
sizeable Asian population here, but it does not seem to
benefit Labour. Labour does best in peripheral council
estates, such as those in the south-eastern Newbold ward.
The Conservatives have been badly squeezed by the two-
horse character of the Rochdale race, and even their hilly
western stronghold ward, Norden and Bamford, now seems
vulnerable to the Liberals.

Cyril Smith receives a considerable personal vote over and
above the municipal Liberal strength. He has done much to
put Rochdale on the map, and he is one of the most active
and visible members in the Commons. Barring sudden
disaster, Cyril Smith's name should continue to be coupled
with the politics of Rochdale for the foreseeable future.

1981	% Own Occ	56.4	1979 core seat Rochdale		
1981	% Loc Auth	37.2	L	22,172	45.0
1981	% Black/Asian	10	Lab	16,878	34.3
1981	% Mid Cl	44.9	C	9,494	19.3
1981	% Prof Man	15.7	NF	690	1.4
1982	electorate 67,922		MPs since 1945		
1979	notional result		1945-50 H.B.W. Morgan Lab		
	L 4,600		1950-51 J. Hale Lab		
Alliance		L	1951-58 W. Schofield C		
			1958-72 Jack McCann Lab		
			1972- Cyril Smith L		

Eccles   Salford/Wigan

In 1979 Labour MP Lewis Carter-Jones suffered from a swing
to the Conservatives of only 2% in Eccles, a suburban district
of Manchester and Salford. Now its status as a safe Labour
seat is reinforced by the addition of 10,000 voters from the
Weaste/Seedley ward of the abolished Salford West. Seedley is
a perfectly healthy suburb of semi-detached houses. But
down the hill towards the Manchester Ship Canal is Weaste,
which is rapidly falling into decay, as any journey west along
the A57 road will testify. The old Eccles seat combined Eccles
and Swinton/Pendlebury. There is a middle-class Conservative
area around the centre of Eccles and South Swinton, but the
seat will remain easy for Carter-Jones. The Alliance has had
very little success at any level anywhere in Salford Borough.

1981	% Own Occ	52	1979 core seat Eccles		
1981	% Loc Auth	40	Lab	24,280	53.6
1981	% Black/Asian	1	C	16,221	35.8
1981	% Mid Cl	44	L	4,448	9.8
1981	% Prof Man	13	Comm	368	0.8
1982	electorate 68,996		MPs since 1945		
1979	notional Lab 10,000		1945-64 W.T. Proctor Lab		
Alliance		L	1964- Lewis Carter-Jones Lab		

Leigh   Salford/Wigan

As one moves west from Manchester towards Liverpool, from
the Borough of Salford to the Borough of Wigan, the scenery
flattens into a plain, and the traditional economic base
changes from the textiles of the Pennines to coal. But the
Lancashire coalfield has declined through the century, and as
the pits have closed smaller light industries have been
established in Leigh and the smaller towns - Atherton,
Hindley and Tyldesley. In the boundary changes Hindley
replaces Tyldesley in the seat, but this will hardly effect the
majority of NUM-sponsored Labour MP Laurence Cunliffe.

1981	% Own Occ	60.9	1979 core seat Leigh		
1981	% Loc Auth	32.7	Lab	27,736	54.1
1981	% Black/Asian	0.5	C	18,713	36.5
1981	% Mid Cl	37.0	L	4,796	9.4
1981	% Prof Man	10.0	MPs since 1945		
1982	electorate 68,896		1945-79 Harold Boardman Lab		
1979	notional Lab 10,900		1979- Laurence Cunliffe Lab		
Alliance		SDP			

Makerfield   Salford/Wigan

Makerfield is based on the former constituency of Ince, which had to be redrawn not only because of its excessive size (83,000 electors) but because it spread across three counties. The troubled New Town of Skelmersdale is in Lancashire, and now moves to the West Lancashire constituency. Billinge is in Merseyside, and now in St Helens North. The name of this seat had to be changed too, for the town of Ince itself is transferred to Wigan, and the largest town is Ashton in Makerfield. Orrell, Abram and Winstanley remain from the old Ince, and Golborne comes in from Newton.

There are substantial areas of Conservative support in Orrell and in the small Winstanley, and Golborne is a fashionable area for new private housing development. But much of this is fairly low-price, intended for first-time buyers. These are the sort of people, usually young marrieds, who might have gone into council housing twenty years ago, and they are not such good targets for the Conservatives as other owner occupiers. This seat still looks like a Labour stronghold, and the council towers of Worsley Mesnes have been added from Wigan itself, boosting the Labour majority.

In the 1982 local elections over 50% of the voters still chose Labour, in a generally poor year for the party, compared with 26% for the Alliance and 23% for the Conservatives. Makerfield may well be as safe a seat for Labour as Ince was.

1981	% Own Occ	66.1	1979 core seat Ince		
1981	% Loc Auth	29.3	Lab	34,599	56.2
1981	% Black/Asian	0.5	C	20,263	32.9
1981	% Mid Cl	42.6	L	6,294	10.2
1981	% Prof Man	12.2	WRP	442	0.7
1982	electorate 69,186		MPs since 1945		
1979	notional result		1945-64 T.J. Brown Lab		
	Lab 10,500		1964- Michael McGuire Lab		
Alliance		L			

Salford East   Salford/Wigan

Salford East will really be the whole of the town of Salford minus one western ward, Weaste/Seedley, now in Eccles. Between the wars over 200,000 people lived in Salford, widely regarded as Manchester's twin city. But at the 1981 census its population had shrunk to 98,000. The two former Salford seats, held for Labour by Frank Allaun and Stan Orme, had become indefensibly small, and basically they are now merged into the new Salford East.

In parts of the constituency, for example in Ordsall near the docks, the slum clearance has given rise to clusters of tower blocks as bleak as any in Manchester's devastated inner city belt. Salford still penetrates almost into the centre of Manchester: the boundary is the River Irwell just behind the great shopping street of Deansgate. There are still terraces of Victorian housing similar to the fictional one which became known on TV as 'Coronation Street'. But some trees do grow in Salford, in Broughton Park and Kersal in the NE near Manchester's affluent northern suburb of Prestwich, and in Claremont (formerly in the West division). But Salford, like so many north-western urban seats, has resisted the swing to the Conservatives of recent years. This must be one of the Alliance's weakest areas in England. The Liberals failed to contest only 10 seats in England in the 1979 General Election, but two of them were the two Salford seats. The SDP showed no greater keenness to fight the 1982 Salford council elections in these wards.

The main question seems to be this: which of the two distinguished Salford Labour MPs will win nomination for the single new division? Veteran peace campaigner and senior backbencher Frank Allaun is the older man, just into his seventies. He may retire to leave the field clear for a frontbencher, Stan Orme of Salford West, the former Social Security Minister. But both are popular in the party and in their old constituencies. Either would win the new Salford East easily.

1981	% Own Occ	35	New seat
1981	% Loc Auth	45	
1981	% Black/Asian	2	
1981	% Mid Cl	34	
1981	% Prof Man	8	
1982	electorate 65,366		
1979	notional result		
	Lab 11,800		

Alliance   SDP

Wigan   Salford/Wigan

Wigan is one of the stereotypes of a northern industrial town
of music-hall jokes, and George Orwell chose Wigan as the
site of one of his famous investigations into working-class and
industrial poverty in the 1930s. But Wigan now has a modern
town centre, and a variety of industries which has relieved
its historic dependence on coal-mining. It has an excellent
wooded residential district in the north of the town and
relatively few urban problems. It is a lively cultural centre,
especially noted for its popular disco music. In short, many
people find Wigan an attractive place in which to live. But it
is for other reasons, perhaps, that Nuneaton Labour MP Les
Huckfield has decided to migrate to Wigan.
The bulk of the town is to be found in the constituency,
together with Aspull, Standish and Shevington, from the
abolished constituency of Westhoughton, and Ince. Wigan's
present MP, the quiet but influential right-winger Alan Fitch,
is retiring. Huckfield, for many years the Co-op and Socialist
Societies representative on Labour's National Executive
Committee, is more left-wing. He applied for the nomination as
Fitch's successor because he felt that Nuneaton had been
made much more marginal by boundary changes. This is not a
popular move in all quarters, and Huckfield has been the
target of some criticism. But nobody can deny that Wigan will
still be an excellent prospect for Labour.
Wigan has a pleasant middle-class residential ward, Swinley,
which votes Conservative. The Liberals have achieved local
success in the small towns north of Wigan. But Labour piles
up votes in the Wigan council estates of Beech Hill, Whelley
and Norley. Huckfield's decision to take the road to Wigan
should undoubtedly pay dividends.

1981	% Own Occ	55.2	1979 core seat Wigan		
1981	% Loc Auth	37.7	Lab	26,144	59.8
1981	% Black/Asian	0.5	C	13,149	30.1
1981	% Mid Cl	38.5	L	4,102	9.4
1981	% Prof Man	11.9	WRP	348	0.8
1982	electorate 73,206		MPs since 1945		
1979	notional result		1945-48 W. Foster Lab		
	Lab 15,000		1948-58 R.W. Williams Lab		
Alliance		L	1958- Alan Fitch Lab		

Worsley   Salford/Wigan

The SDP MP John Roper finds his Farnworth constituency
split asunder in the boundary changes. The northern half
passes into Bolton SE. The southern wards, now in Salford
Borough, make up the Worsley constituency together with two
wards around Tyldesley from Wigan Borough. Worsley itself is
quite a well-known Conservative middle-class area, but
Walkden and Little Hulton, Irlam and Cadishead are solidly
Labour. The Alliance only polled 31% here in 1982, and
Worsley looks no better a bet for John Roper than Bolton SE.

1981	% Own Occ	55	New seat
1981	% Loc Auth	42	
1981	% Black/Asian	1	
1981	% Mid Cl	40	
1981	% Prof Man	14	
1982	electorate 72,137		
1979	notional result		
	Lab 8,100		
Alliance		SDP	

Ashton under Lyne   Stockport/Tameside

The constituency of Ashton under Lyne is basically that part
of Tameside north of the river Tame – the old textile-working
communities of Ashton, Droylsden and Mossley, which used to
be in Lancashire. It has held up as well for Labour in their
difficult days of the early 1980s as well as any in the
country. In the 1982 local elections Labour polled over twice
as many votes here as the Tories, with the Alliance in third
place. Labour MP Robert Sheldon can look forward to
increasing his 1979 majority of 8,000 in a virtually unchanged
seat.

1981	% Own Occ	60.1	1979 core seat Ashton under		
1981	% Loc Auth	31.0	Lyne		
1981	% Black/Asian	5	Lab	24,535	54.7
1981	% Mid Cl	38.5	C	16,156	36.0
1981	% Prof Man	11.8	L	3,699	8.2
1982	electorate 59,359		NF	486	1.1
1979	notional result		MPs since 1945		
	Lab 8,400		1945-64 H. Rhodes Lab		
Alliance		SDP	1964- Robert Sheldon Lab		

Cheadle   Stockport/Tameside

Cheadle grasped electoral fame in 1966 when Dr Michael Winstanley, soon to become an ITV personality, won the seat for the Liberals. But the brief deviation of this extremely middle-class Manchester commuter constituency from its expected Tory allegiance did not last long. Winstanley was defeated by Tom Normanton in 1970, and the vast Cheadle seat was then split. The best Liberal area went into Hazel Grove, and Normanton had increased his majority to 17,000 plus by 1979.

Another enforced change has had to be made now to Cheadle's boundaries. Wilmslow is not in Greater Manchester, and has therefore had to be transferred to a Cheshire constituency, Tatton. Cheadle's numbers are made up by Bramhall, previously associated with Hazel Grove. This hardly improves the Liberals' chances, though, for Bramhall is one of the very top affluent residential districts in the Cheshire commuter belt, 70% middle class in the 1971 census and still loyal to the Conservatives. The rest of the constituency is socially similar: Cheadle, Gatley, Cheadle Hulme and the more modern development at Heald Green. Altogether it forms a solid suburban citadel in the south-western corner of Stockport Borough.

The high-status character of Cheadle is shown by the fact that Labour scraped together less than 6% of the vote in the 1982 local elections. The Conservatives polled an overall majority there, even in the Stockport Metropolitan Council elections, in which the Liberals do unusually well. It will prove a very hard nut for the Alliance to crack in an election to decide the government of the country.

1981	% Own Occ	83.1		1979 core seat Cheadle	
1981	% Loc Auth	11.6	C	32,407	58.8
1981	% Black/Asian	1	L	15,268	27.7
1981	% Mid Cl	72.3	Lab	7,415	13.5
1981	% Prof Man	30.5	MPs since 1950		
1982	electorate 66,549		1950-66 W.S. Shepherd C		
1979	notional result		1966-70 Michael Winstanley L		
	C 17,100		1970- Tom Normanton C		
Alliance		L			

Denton and Reddish   Stockport/Tameside

The most Labour part of Stockport South used to be the
massive post-war council estate of Brinnington. The most
Labour part of Stockport North was Reddish. Now both
Brinnington and Reddish are removed from Stockport, which
should leave behind a Conservative seat. They are added to
the Tameside towns of Denton and Audenshaw in a new
constituency which crosses the Metropolitan Borough
boundary. Its origins are even more complex than this,
though, for Audenshaw and Denton were previously situated
in a Manchester city division, Gorton.

One thing is certain about this mixed bag of a seat - it
should be safe for the Labour Party. There are Conservative
wards in Audenshaw and Denton West, which have the
majority of owner occupiers. But Denton South includes the
large overspill council estate of Haughton Green, and overall
the ex-Gorton wards would have given Labour a couple of
thousand votes lead in 1979. Brinnington and Reddish would
have increased this figure to 9,000.

Brinnington achieved fame of a different kind before the 1979
election: the many hundreds of party members associated with
the social centre of Brinnington Labour Club were held
responsible for the selection of right-winger Tom McNally as
candidate for Stockport South. After being elected as MP,
McNally defected to the SDP. He would be unwise to attempt
to follow Brinnington into Denton and Reddish, though, for it
produced one of the lowest Alliance votes anywhere in the
country in 1982. This new seat would be a better bet for a
Labour man looking for greener pastures, perhaps Andrew
Bennett of Stockport North or Ken Marks of Manchester
Gorton.

1981	% Own Occ	57.8	New seat
1981	% Loc Auth	35.5	
1981	% Black/Asian	1	
1981	% Mid Cl	39.4	
1981	% Prof Man	10.6	
1982	electorate 69,366		
1979	notional result		
	Lab 10,200		
Alliance		SDP	

Hazel Grove   Stockport/Tameside

When Hazel Grove was carved out of the huge Cheadle seat in
1974, it was rightly thought to be the better bet for the
Liberals, and Michael Winstanley won its inaugural contest in
the February election. This south-eastern segment of
Stockport Borough is not quite as affluent as Cheadle in the
SW, harbouring some Labour votes in Bredbury and Romiley.
Now Hazel Grove loses its richest neighbourhood, Bramhall,
and gains the marginal Great Moor ward from Stockport
South. Hazel Grove and Marple enjoy close Liberal-Tory
battles. The Liberals have a larger Labour vote to squeeze
here than in Cheadle, and may well be able to challenge the
young sitting MP, Tom Arnold, in a very good year.

1981	% Own Occ	72.3	1979 core seat Hazel Grove		
1981	% Loc Auth	22.0	C	32,420	55.5
1981	% Black/Asian	1	L	17,148	29.4
1981	% Mid Cl	59.2	Lab	8,846	15.1
1981	% Prof Man	23.1	MPs since 1974		
1982	electorate 64,179		1974	Michael Winstanley L	
1979	notional result		1974-	Tom Arnold C	
	C 11,800				
Alliance		L			

Stalybridge and Hyde   Stockport/Tameside

The southern half of the Tameside Borough is composed of
the towns of Stalybridge, Hyde and Dukinfield. Its boundary
is not significantly altered. Labour MP Tom Pendry is
relatively safe here. Although there are Conservative wards -
Hyde Werneth and hilly Stalybridge South - the Labour vote
is very solid and resisted the Conservative and Alliance
challenges in the 1982 local elections. The seat has shown a
long-term movement to Labour due to the 1960s development
of the large Manchester overspill estate in Hattersley (east
Hyde) and Longdendale.

1981	% Own Occ	53.9	1979 core seat Stalybridge and		
1981	% Loc Auth	40.6	Hyde		
1981	% Black/Asian	1	Lab	27,082	51.9
1981	% Mid Cl	40.4	C	20,502	39.3
1981	% Prof Man	13.9	L	4,642	8.9
1982	electorate 69,101		MPs since 1945		
1979	notional result		1945-51 G. Lang Lab		
	Lab 6,600		1951-70 Fred Blackburn Lab		
Alliance		L	1970-	Tom Pendry Lab	

Stockport   Stockport/Tameside

In the 1979 General Election, Stockport's two seats both elected Labour MPs by paper-thin majorities, and they did very well to hold on to these. Since then the political situation in the town has been transformed. The member for Stockport South, Tom McNally, defected to the SDP in 1981. In the boundary changes the two small constituencies disappear and one new seat is created. What is more, the wards which depart are in the main heavily Labour: Reddish and Brinnington go to Denton and Reddish, Great Moor to Hazel Grove.
That which remains is the more Conservative western half of the old County Borough of Stockport. From North come the middle-class Heatons: Heaton Moor, Heaton Mersey, Heaton Norris and Heaton Chapel. These are socially and economically very similar to the neighbouring Conservative constituency of Manchester Withington. From South is taken the leafy Davenport, next door to Bramhall and Cheadle Hulme. There are Labour wards too - Edgeley by the railway tracks, the central ward of Manor, and the Cale Green/Adswood council estate. Labour were ahead in the new seat in the 1980 council elections. But Stockport will be even harder for Labour to win than the two old seats were. The Alliance got closer to the Tories in 1982, and the Liberals won Edgeley.
Stockport could well turn out to be a three-way marginal, especially if Tom McNally decides to contest it as the sitting SDP member. In such circumstances the Conservatives may well creep home, for their vote is very solid and the anti-Tory forces may well be split. But the North-West has been more critical of Mrs Thatcher's government than the Midlands and the South, and if there is a regional factor at work in the next Election, Labour could achieve the 5% swing needed to take the new Stockport.

1981   % Own Occ   70.1   New seat
1981   % Loc Auth   18.4
1981   % Black/Asian 1
1981   % Mid Cl   53.7
1981   % Prof Man   17.1
1982   electorate 59,701
1979   notional result
       C 4,400
Alliance   SDP

Knowsley North   Knowsley

In the post-war years much of Liverpool's poorer population has been resettled in council housing developments on the edge of the Merseyside conurbation. The best known - and most notorious - of these is Kirkby. Kirkby is not a New Town, but a series of vast council estates created in the 1950s. In 1951 its population was 3,000, in 1961 52,000.

Kirkby has had a dramatic effect on the politics of the area NE of Liverpool. Originally it was in Huyton constituency, where it played a major role in lifting Harold Wilson's majority from 834 in 1950 to 19,000 in 1964. Then in February 1974 it was moved out into hitherto rural Ormskirk, formerly a safe Tory seat, which was then immediately won by Labour's Robert Kilroy-Silk. Now it forms the basis of the Knowsley North division, and divorced from Conservative West Lancashire, it will form one of Labour's safest seats. Kirkby has many problems and deprivations, which breed vandalism and violence. It suffers from appalling unemployment and housing blight. Tower blocks only a decade old, like those at Tower Hill, have already had to be demolished. Small wonder that the BBC TV crime series Z Cars was set in Kirkby. It has a great scarcity of leisure services to offer to its large population. The Liberals form the only effective opposition to Labour, and that only in local elections. The rest of Knowsley North consists of Cantril Farm, a 1960s peripheral development just outside the Liverpool city boundary; and Prescot, an industrial 'company town' dominated by an enormous British Cables plant.

Every ward in Knowsley North is usually won by Labour. It is the poorer end of one of the most working-class Metropolitan Boroughs in England. After so many years of being absorbed in large constituencies, it is only right that Kirkby should form the core of a seat which is rather smaller than average - no other town can need effective representation more desperately.

1981	% Own Occ	25	New seat
1981	% Loc Auth	70	
1981	% Black/Asian	0.5	
1981	% Mid Cl	23	
1981	% Prof Man	6	
1982	electorate 57,064		
1979	notional result		
	Lab 16,000 (RW)		
Alliance		SDP	

Knowsley South   Knowsley

For many years Sir Harold Wilson enjoyed an excellent
relationship with his constituency of Huyton. In 1964, the
first Election after he became leader of the Labour Party, he
enjoyed a 10% swing and an increase in his majority from
6,000 to 19,000. When his first Premiership came to an end in
1970, his lead at Huyton still increased. But in 1979 he did
not do so well. There was an 8.5% swing to the Tories, who
gathered nigh on 20,000 votes in Huyton. Some people had
thought that this might be a sign that his constituents had
finally become disillusioned with Wilson, and thought it was
time he should retire.

But Huyton does have strong reservoirs of middle-class
housing, which would fairly naturally vote for Mrs Thatcher
in 1979. Although its predominant characteristics are those
associated with peripheral council estates like Page Moss/
Woolfall Heath and Longview, there are comfortable
Conservative residential areas such as Swanside and Roby.
Overall, Huyton was 37% middle class - not far from the
national average. Knowsley South is similar to the old
Huyton, but it gains Halewood, site of the Ford motor works,
and Whiston (both from Widnes). But it loses Prescot and
Cantril Farm to Knowsley North, and the Conservative ward
of Eccleston, which is really an affluent suburb of St Helens,
to St Helens South.

Harold Wilson is finally retiring at the next Election, having
represented roughly this area throughout his chequered
parliamentary career of nearly 40 years. His successor is a
locally-active moderate, Sean Hughes. Despite the continued
presence of a large minority of middle-class voters in the
seat, Hughes should inherit a safe bet from the old magician-
illusionist.

1981	% Own Occ	42	1979 core seat Huyton		
1981	% Loc Auth	50	Lab	27,449	51.9
1981	% Black/Asian	0.5	C	19,939	37.7
1981	% Mid Cl	40	L	12,812	17.6
1981	% Prof Man	12	MP since 1950		
1982	electorate 69,343		1950-	Sir Harold Wilson Lab	
1979	notional result				
	Lab 11,000				
Alliance		L			

Liverpool Broadgreen   Liverpool

Liverpool's parliamentary representation has been reduced from eight seats to six by the boundary review. This is an inescapable result of the rapid exodus which has reduced Liverpool's population from 745,000 in 1961 to 510,000 in 1981, but it poses problems for the city's sitting MPs, particularly the three Social Democrats and the Liberal David Alton. None of their constituencies survives the boundary changes intact. Alton's Edge Hill, for example, was undersized at 35,000 electors, and is irretrievably split and swamped by wards from other seats. Broadgreen is a highly complex and marginal division which bears little resemblance to any previous Liverpool seat.

Indeed, Broadgreen should be an ultra-tight three-way contest. Situated east of the city centre, it includes the Tory ward of Childwall which is predominantly owner occupied. Broadgreen, Liberal in local elections, is another outer suburban ward and probably votes Conservative nationally. Old Swan is a three-way marginal. All these three wards were previously in Wavertree constituency, which was the Conservatives' safest seat in Liverpool. The other two wards, Tuebrook and Kensington, are Liberal strongholds, where over a third of the oldish housing is still privately rented. They are situated in that belt of territory half-way from the centre to the edge of the city, which has provided the Liberals' most consistent support at local level. Kensington was in the heart of Alton's Edge Hill seat.

It is very difficult to tell what would have happened at Broadgreen in the last Election, especially since the Liberals do much better in local elections in Liverpool than in General Elections. In the 1982 Liverpool City Council contest, for example, the Alliance polled 44% in these wards and finished well clear of Labour and the Tories, who were neck and neck. It should be a photo-finish – Childwall and the other ex-Wavertree wards may have tipped the balance for the Tories at the 1979 election, but no confident analysis or prediction can be made, especially since the seat was provisionally allocated to the SDP despite the Liberals' great strength here.

1981	% Own Occ	52.4	1979 core seat L'pool Wavertree
1981	% Loc Auth	26.3	C 21,770 50.3
1981	% Black/Asian	1	Lab 14,828 34.2
1981	% Mid Cl	48.0	L 6.705 15.5
1981	% Prof Man	11.5	MPs since 1945
1982	electorate 64,376		1945-50 H.V.A.M. Raikes C
1979	notional C 600		1950-74 John Tilney C
Alliance		SDP	1974- Anthony Steen C

Liverpool Garston   Liverpool

Garston is the classical Labour-Conservative marginal in Liverpool, swinging with the national tide in 1974 and 1979, and resisting the Liberal municipal success more completely than any other area of the city. Garston constituency is composed of the south-eastern sector of Liverpool, and its marginality is assured by the fact that it contains two very different types of residential area.

Allerton and Woolton are two of the best, and most Conservative, middle-class owner-occupier suburbs in Liverpool. On the other hand Garston also includes the massive peripheral council estate of Speke, the terraced centre of Garston itself (St Mary's ward), and the half-abandoned ultra-modern horror of Netherley, a tower-block estate on the very edge of the city. Netherley, only a decade old and already in the process of demolition, is one of the most alarming of the many slums in Liverpool, reminiscent of the worst blight of United States cities or of a nightmarish vision of future urban squalor. Much of Netherley is already left to decay and the vandals.

Garston is less altered than most Liverpool constituencies in the redistribution. With 79,000 electors, it was the only over-sized seat which had to lose a ward. But the one which has gone should be crucial - Aigburth, another middle-class residential area, by the Mersey between Toxteth and Garston. Conservative Malcolm Thornton defeated Labour's sitting MP Eddie Loyden by only 2,787 in 1979, but the Aigburth-Grassendale area probably gave Thornton a majority of over 4,000 on its own. Garston is now going to be far better for Labour than before, and in most years Speke and Netherley should outvote Allerton and Woolton - as long as they come out to vote at all.

1981	% Own Occ	38.6	1979 core seat Liverpool Garston
1981	% Loc Auth	56.5	C 28,105 48.1
1981	% Black/Asian	1	Lab 25,318 43.3
1981	% Mid Cl	46.3	L 4,890 8.4
1981	% Prof Man	13.5	WRP 142 0.3
1982	electorate 66,122		MPs since 1950
1979	notional result		1950-57 H.V.A.M. Raikes C
	Lab 5,200		1957-66 R.M. Bingham C
Alliance		L	1966-74 Trevor Fortescue C
			1974-79 Edward Loyden Lab
			1979- Malcolm Thornton C

Liverpool Mossley Hill   Liverpool

Mossley Hill, SE of Liverpool's city centre, is another of the
new, highly mixed seats created in Liverpool by the Boundary
Commission. Like Broadgreen it runs the social and political
gamut. Grassendale and Aigburth have some of the best
quality housing in Liverpool, although the Liberals have made
some inroads into the Tory vote there. Church ward,
formerly the centre of Wavertree constituency, saw the start
of the Liberal revival in Liverpool when the late Cyril Carr
first took the ward in the 1960s from the Conservatives.
Progressing towards the city centre, Picton and Smithdown
are the heart of David Alton's Liberal Edge Hill stronghold,
the only part of Liverpool which votes as heavily for the
Liberals in parliamentary elections as in local contests.

David Alton has decided to contest Mossley Hill at the next
General Election. In the 1982 local elections, the Liberal
Alliance polled 45% here, over 15% ahead of the Tories. But
Mossley Hill also contains some of the most affluent districts
in the city. Grassendale has 78% owner-occupied housing, and
67% of the households possessed a car in 1981 - compare
Everton's 1% owner occupied and 9% with a car. Grassendale's
unemployment rate in 1981 was 7.6%, Everton's 39.2%. Such
are the contrasts even in England's poorest city.

The Tories are unlucky that the middle-class South Liverpool
block is split three ways - Allerton and Woolton in Garston,
Grassendale and Aigburth in Mossley Hill and Childwall in
Broadgreen. In a good year they might win all three seats, in
a bad year none. But in Mossley Hill they have as good a
chance as anywhere, for the Liberal vote in the middle-class
areas by tradition fails to hold up in General Elections.
Labour look likely to be squeezed into third place. There is
substantial council housing only in Smithdown ward where it
verges into the inner city. But Mossley Hill will provide
another dramatic and close battle in Liverpool.

1981	% Own Occ	58.2	New seat
1981	% Loc Auth	21.9	
1981	% Black/Asian	2.5	
1981	% Mid Cl	54.0	
1981	% Prof Man	16.3	
1982	electorate 63,396		
1979	notional result		
	C 9,100		
Alliance	L		

Liverpool Riverside   Liverpool

Depopulation has transformed the inner city of Liverpool. By 1979 Scotland Exchange (itself an amalgamation of two former seats) had an electorate of 32,000, Toxteth 42,000 and Kirkdale 43,000. The new Riverside seat is essentially an amalgamation of Scotland Exchange and Toxteth, and adds up to a river-front constituency stretching from the Bootle boundary almost to Aigburth. It contains some of the poorest and most deprived urban areas in Britain.

The northern wards, Vauxhall and Everton, are almost entirely white, but suffer from the worst unemployment in Liverpool - nearly 40% of males between 16 and 59 years of age. They consist of 90% council housing, often wretched and semi-abandoned blocks like the infamous Everton 'Piggeries'. West of the Scotland Road, towards the docks, lay the original Irish Catholic ghetto which sent T.P. O'Connor to Westminster as an Irish Nationalist for fifty years. Up the hill in Everton by contrast lay the heart of Orange Protestant reaction. Both are Labour strongholds now. South of Liverpool's fine city centre, in Liverpool 8 postal district, lie the multi racial wards of Granby, Arundel and Dingle, the 'Toxteth' which produced the most serious riots of the summer of 1981. The non-white population of Liverpool 8 does not show up in the census figures because it came to Britain far earlier than the post-war immigrants from the New Commonwealth found elsewhere in Britain. The Toxteth riots were, in any case, less connected with race than elsewhere, for Liverpool demonstrates a disrespect for authority, and for the police, highly untypical of England.

Toxteth constituency is held by an SDP defector, Richard Crawshaw, who is most noted for his long-distance walking. But his chances if he fights this new seat must be negligible. Riverside should be one of the safest Labour seats in the country, for the Liberals have never penetrated to the heart of inner-city Liverpool, with its varying deprivations and degradations.

1981	% Own Occ	19.5	1979 core seat Liverpool
1981	% Loc Auth	64.4	Scotland Exchange
1981	% Black/Asian	5	Lab 13,920 75.1
1981	% Mid Cl	30.6	C 2,264 12.2
1981	% Prof Man	7.8	L 1,939 10.5
1982	electorate 63,615		Comm 421 2.3
1979	notional result		MP since 1974
	Lab 19,100		1974- Robert Parry Lab
Alliance		SDP	

Liverpool Walton   Liverpool

Eric Heffer is one of the only two Labour MPs in the
depressed city of Liverpool, which also has three Social
Democrats, two Tories and a Liberal. Walton is the
northernmost constituency, and in the boundary changes it
expands to take in much of the abolished Kirkdale division,
now held by SDP MP James Dunn. Walton loses its council
estate ward, Pirrie, to West Derby, leaving a fairly average
mix of housing types in Warbreck, County, Fazakerly,
Breckfield and the footballing ward of Anfield. This is not
the Alliance's strongest area in Liverpool, and Heffer should
have little difficulty in holding a seat he first won in 1964.
The outlook for James Dunn is much more bleak.

1981	% Own Occ	45.6	1979 core seat Liverpool Walton
1981	% Loc Auth	35.1	Lab	20,231	55.2
1981	% Black/Asian	0.6	C	12,673	34.6
1981	% Mid Cl	37.0	L	3,479	9.5
1981	% Prof Man	6.5	NF	254	0.7
1982	electorate 74,140		MPs since 1950		
1979	notional Lab 11,100		1950-64 Kenneth Thompson C		
Alliance			1964- Eric Heffer Lab		

Liverpool West Derby   Liverpool

West Derby is Liverpool's council estate seat, situated on the
north-eastern edge of the city. Here are inter-war estates
like Norris Green in Pirrie ward, which joins West Derby from
Walton; and post-war Gillmoss and Dovecot. There is one
Tory owner-occupied ward, Croxteth, which is centred on
Sandfield Park and around the grounds of Croxteth Hall. West
Derby swung to Labour, like many Liverpool seats, in the
1950s and 1960s due to housing redevelopment and the
destruction of the old Orange Protestant Tory vote. But Eric
Ogden defected to the SDP in 1981, and must defend his seat
in solid Labour territory, where the Liberals have failed to
make many breakthroughs.

1981	% Own Occ	28.3	1979 core seat L'pool W Derby
1981	% Loc Auth	68.3	Lab	22,576	55.5
1981	% Black/Asian	0.5	C	14,356	35.3
1981	% Mid Cl	38.9	L	3,765	9.3
1981	% Prof Man	8.0	MPs since 1945		
1982	electorate 64,008		1945-54 Sir D.P.M. Fyfe C		
1979	notional Lab 11,100		1954-64 J.P.V. Woollem C		
Alliance			1964- Eric Ogden Lab (SDP)		

St Helens North   St Helens

This division does contain the northernmost wards of the town
of St Helens, around the A580 East Lancs trunk road. But at
least as much of its population comes from the Merseyside
part of the Newton seat, and Newton's MP John Evans, now a
moderate member of Labour's NEC, will probably stand for St
Helens N. There is a solid Conservative vote among the new
private estates of the commuter town of Rainford; and the
Liberals are locally active at Newton-le-Willows. But Labour
piles up votes in Haydock and north St Helens, and should
win easily.

1981	% Own Occ	55.8	1979 core seat Newton		
1981	% Loc Auth	38.6	Lab	41,466	51.4
1981	% Black/Asian	0.5	C	30,125	37.3
1981	% Mid Cl	44.1	L	8,471	10.5
1981	% Prof Man	13.8	NF	641	0.8
1982	electorate 71,848		MPs since 1945		
1979	notional result		1945-50 Sir R. Young Lab		
	Lab 9,800		1950-74 Fred Lee Lab		
Alliance		L	1974- John Evans Lab		

St Helens South   St Helens

Labour's new prospective candidate for St Helens, Gerald
Bermingham, is one of the party's foremost experts on
boundary changes. But he need have nothing to fear from the
destruction of the existing safe seat of St Helens, for in St
Helens S is a successor which is just as strongly Labour. The
bulk of St Helens is to be included. The town is famous for
Pilkington's glassworks, but coal mining and other heavy
industries leave their mark on the landscape. There is a large
Tory ward to the west, at Eccleston, but Gerald Bermingham
could scarcely have drawn a better seat for himself than this
one!

1981	% Own Occ	60.0	1979 core seat St Helens		
1981	% Loc Auth	30.7	Lab	32,489	59.6
1981	% Black/Asian	0.5	C	16,934	31.1
1981	% Mid Cl	41.4	L	4,587	8.4
1981	% Prof Man	11.0	WRP	471	0.9
1982	electorate 70,237		MPs since 1945		
1979	notional result		1945-58 Sir Hartley Shawcross		
	Lab 11,300			Lab	
Alliance		SDP	1958- Leslie Spriggs Lab		

Bootle   Sefton

Bootle is part of the Merseyside Metropolitan Borough of Sefton, which was brought into existence in the early years of the 1970s. But Bootle has very little in common with the middle-class commuting and seaside communities of Crosby, Maghull, Formby and Southport. This tough dockland town is far more similar to the neighbouring districts of working-class, depressed north Liverpool.

Politically too Bootle is far removed from the Tory-Liberal marginal of Southport or Shirley Williams's new SDP seat, Crosby. Bootle is a very safe Labour division. There are no Tory wards here, either in inner-city districts like St Oswald or in peripheral council estates like Netherton, which is not dissimilar from Cantril Farm or even Kirkby nearby. In the boundary changes, Bootle expands to take in the most southerly ward of Shirley Williams's seat, Seaforth - but this is the most Labour-inclined ward in Crosby, and Bootle will surely remain ultra-safe for Labour, the only Labour seat in Sefton.

The MP is Allan Roberts. Roberts is a left-winger with a very different reputation from his predecessor, Simon Mahon. Mahon was a hard right-wing Roman Catholic of Irish descent, a 'social reactionary', and a member of a long-standing and influential local political family - his brother Peter was once Labour MP for Preston South, before becoming an Independent Liberal candidate. Allan Roberts, on the other hand, was pilloried by Private Eye for his visit to a Berlin homosexual club. But despite the slurs of the muckrakers, Roberts has survived as a popular and effective local MP, and should have no trouble winning re-election.

1981	% Own Occ	40.4	1979 core seat	Bootle		
1981	% Loc Auth	46.3	Lab	26,900	61.0
1981	% Black/Asian	0.5	C	11,741	26.6
1981	% Mid Cl	41.4	L	4,531	10.3
1981	% Prof Man	8.1	Ind	911	2.1
1982	electorate 76,094		MPs since 1945		
1979	national result		1945-55	J. Kinley Lab	
	Lab 15,600		1955-79	Simon Mahon Lab	
Alliance		SDP	1979-	Allan Roberts Lab	

Crosby   Sefton

A large proportion of Merseyside's middle classes live outside
Liverpool and commute to work, either through the tunnels
from the Wirral or from the constituency of Crosby, which is
north of the city on the way to Southport. When Shirley
Williams won the Crosby byelection for the SDP in 1981, it
contained three large centres of population: Crosby itself,
Maghull and Formby, together with some farming villages on
the rich Lancashire plain. In the redistribution, Crosby is to
lose some 10,000 electors - the southernmost ward of Church
to Bootle, but the whole of Maghull is now in the seat.
  Except for the southern fringe, which more resembles
neighbouring working-class Bootle, Crosby is a constituency
of middle-class owner occupiers. There are differences, it is
true, between the mansions of Formby and the standard new
private estates which have boosted Maghull's post-war
population from under 10,000 to 25,000. But all voted solidly
Tory until the SDP's miraculous year of 1981, and all
provided SDP majorities then. Perhaps the older population of
Formby and Crosby's seaside retirment ward of Blundellsands
proved less fertile ground for Shirley Williams than the newly
marrieds of Maghull - but the seat is one of economic and
social homogeneity.
  Can Shirley Williams hold the new Crosby? The detachment of
a ward like Church may mean the loss of Labour supporters
who would vote SDP tactically to keep the Tory out. But
basically the redrawing alone would not lead to Shirley
Williams's second successive defeat in a General Election. It
looks as if Crosby, with its inbuilt Toryism, will be a hard
seat to hold anyway, unless the enthusiasm and the level of
support achieved in the historic byelection can be recaptured.

1981	% Own Occ	81.5	1979 core seat Crosby		
1981	% Loc Auth	10.4	C	34,768	56.9
1981	% Black/Asian	0.4	Lab	15,496	25.4
1981	% Mid Cl	67.2	L	9,302	15.2
1981	.% Prof Man	21.5	E	1,489	2.4
1982	electorate 84,359		MPs since 1945		
1979	notional result		1945-53 M. Bullock C		
	C 19,600		1953-81 Graham Page C		
Alliance		SDP	1981- Shirley Williams SDP		

Southport   Sefton

The genteel resort of Southport, 20 miles north of Liverpool, should by all indicators be a Tory citadel. Besides its characteristics as an up-market seaside town, less working-class in nature and appeal than the bustling Blackpool further up the coast, and noted more for its flower show than its fun-fair, Southport is a desirable commuting base for more affluent Merseyside commuters. It couldn't be more different from the other end of the Borough of Sefton, or further from the poverty and unemployment of Bootle. Yet Southport, like so much of Merseyside county, of all classes, shares a predilection for the Liberal Party.

In local elections the Liberals come at least second throughout the Southport wards, and Norwood is a real Liberal stronghold. Labour has been eliminated from any kind of contention. Southport does possess terraces of modest housing inland from the promenade and the broad main street, Lord St, but these are good ground for the Liberals. There are scarcely any substantial pockets of council housing for Labour to exploit. The Conservatives do best in the top residential areas of Birkdale and Ainsdale, where there are most commuters to Liverpool; everywhere new private estates burgeon in this popular area for development.

Southport is left unaltered in the present boundary review. The Conservative MP here is Sir Ian Percival, the Solicitor-General. Although Southport has figured on the list of best Liberal chances since at least 1970, one somehow feels that the last breakthrough is always beyond them. Perhaps the Liberal Party will eternally be second in Southport.

1981	% Own Occ	74.2	1979 same seat Southport		
1981	% Loc Auth	9.3	C	25,953	50.8
1981	% Black/Asian	0.5	L	19,426	38.0
1981	% Mid Cl	59.4	Lab	5,725	11.2
1981	% Prof Man	22.1	MPs since 1945		
1982	electorate 70,793		1945-52 R.S. Hudson C		
Alliance		L	1952-59 R.F. Fleetwood-Hesketh C		
			1959- Sir Ian Percival C		

Birkenhead   Wirral

The centre of Birkenhead is only a little over a mile through the Mersey tunnels from the city centre of Liverpool. Birkenhead is therefore a closer constituency physically to inner Liverpool than some of the peripheral Liverpool seats like Garston and West Derby, and very much part of the heart of Merseyside.

This has been accentuated by the fact that the constituency has never included the whole of the former County Borough of Birkenhead, but omitted the western peripheral Prenton and Upton wards. This reduced the Birkenhead electorate to only 56,000 in 1979. Now, more of the western edge is to be included, such as the modern council estate of Bidston, but Birkenhead is still centred on the shipbuilding and industrial area of the town. Here are to be found solidly Labour wards like Birkenhead itself and Tranmere (Rock Ferry). The only Conservative strength lies in Claughton, near Birkenhead Park, and in Oxton. As across the Mersey, there have been many Liberal successes at local level, but they have never been able to transfer this achievement to parliamentary elections. This suggests that although the Alliance polled over 31% and reached 'second place' in the 1982 local elections, this should not be regarded as a sign that the Liberals could easily win this seat at a General Election.

The MP here is Frank Field, who was well known before his election in 1979 as a director of Shelter, the housing pressure group. Field stands in the centre of the party, but to the left of the former Birkenhead Labour MP Edmund Dell, a financial expert who is now a Social Democrat. Field should have little trouble with the expanded Birkenhead division at the next election.

1981	% Own Occ	50.3	1979 core seat Birkenhead		
1981	% Loc Auth	33.6	Lab	20,803	49.9
1981	% Black/Asian	1	C	14,894	35.7
1981	% Mid Cl	43.4	L	5,708	13.7
1981	% Prof Man	13.4	WRP	306	0.7
1982	electorate 68,802		MPs since 1950		
1979	notional result		1950-64 P.H. Collick Lab		
	Lab 8,100		1964-79 Edmund Dell Lab		
Alliance		L	1979- Frank Field Lab		

Wallasey   Wirral

Labour have come very close to winning Wallasey on several occasions, cutting Ernest Marples's majority to 589 votes in 1966, and getting within 2,000 votes of victory in October 1974. It must therefore rank as a marginal, even though Labour have never won it, not even in 1945.

This compact constituency, situated across the Mersey from Liverpool in the NE Wirral, is one of contrasts. The two Labour wards are at opposite ends of the seat: Seacombe is just across the docks to the north of Birkenhead town centre, and shares many of the qualities of the true Merseyside inner-city district. Leasowe, on the other hand, is an isolated council estate on the north coast of the Wirral peninsula. In between these, there are the Tory strongholds of Wallasey itself, Liscard and New Brighton. New Brighton, as its name implies, is a seaside resort which once boasted a tower higher than Blackpool's, but now the tower is gone and New Brighton has lost its popularity as the Mersey has silted up.

Wallasey is a mixed seat, including as it does residential areas for Liverpool commuters, inner-city dockland, council estates and seaside resort territory. It is an interesting constituency, politically, but the Conservatives have always seemed to have a little extra in hand. The Alliance only polled 25% here in the 1982 elections. The MP now is Lynda Chalker, one of the women members thought to have a promising career in government in prospect. Wallasey is scarcely altered in the boundary changes, and it should continue to provide close contests, but it would be a surprise if Labour were to break through here, and interrupt Lynda Chalker's progress.

1981	% Own Occ	62.7	1979 core seat Wallasey		
1981	% Loc Auth	22.2	C	26,548	49.6
1981	% Black/Asian	1	Lab	21,167	39.6
1981	% Mid Cl	48.2	L	5,269	9.9
1981	% Prof Man	13.7	NF	491	0.9
1982	electorate 69,977		MPs since 1945		
1979	notional result		1945-74 Ernest Marples C		
	C 5,400		1974- Lynda Chalker C		
Alliance		SDP			

Wirral South   Wirral

The new Wirral South is an amalgamation of Bebington, from
the old Bebington/Ellesmere Port seat, and the Heswall area
of the former oversized Wirral division. Bebington was the
more Conservative half of its marginal seat, and Heswall was
an 85% Tory ward in 1979. The only Labour votes of any
number come from the centre of chemical-land, Bromborough
and Port Sunlight, but South Wirral should be a safe extra
Conservative seat in the Wirral commuter belt. The Alliance
has a local election base here in Eastham, but can hope for
no more than second place in the new South Wirral
constituency.

1981	% Own Occ	72.2	New seat
1981	% Loc Auth	17.0	
1981	% Black/Asian	0.5	
1981	% Mid Cl	48.2	
1981	% Prof Man	13.7	
1982	electorate 61,585		
1979	notional result		
	C 14,200		
Alliance		SDP	

Wirral West   Wirral

The north-west corner of the Wirral peninsula is mainly
residential. Most typical are the seaside towns of Hoylake and
West Kirby, whose popular appeal as resorts is limited by the
mudbanks off the Wirral, and the absence of the sea, but
which serve as extremely Tory middle-class commuter bases
for Liverpool and Birkenhead. The constituency also includes
the wards of Upton and Prenton on the edge of Birkenhead,
both of which contain a mixture of private and council
housing of post-war vintage. Wirral was a very large seat, of
over 97,000 electors in 1979, and it is now reduced to a solid
Conservative core, losing Heswall and Neston.

1981	% Own Occ	70.6	1979 core seat Wirral		
1981	% Loc Auth	22.1	C	44,519	59.0
1981	% Black/Asian	0.5	Lab	21,188	28.1
1981	% Mid Cl	60.7	L	9,769	12.9
1981	% Prof Man	22.6	MPs since 1945		
1982	electorate 61,799		1945-76 Selwyn Lloyd C (The		
1979	notional result			Speaker)	
	C 15,200		1976- David Hunt C		
Alliance		L			

Birmingham Edgbaston   Birmingham

Edgbaston is probably the best known middle-class residential area in Birmingham. Situated just SW of the city centre, it still contains large mansions, many of which are converted to institutional use, but some of which are still occupied by single families. Edgbaston ward has leafy parks, the Test cricket ground, the BBC TV studios at Pebble Mill and ranks as the educational centre of the city, harbouring Birmingham University and King Edward's Grammar School. But despite all these marks of distinction, the Conservative majority in October 1974 was reduced to little over 2,000.

The Tories' problem was that under the old boundaries Edgbaston constituency stretched into the inner-city region to take in Deritend ward, which was heavily Labour, 63% council housing and 44% non-white. Now however the picture is very different. Edgbaston is to consist simply of the middle-class Harborne, Edgbaston and Quinton wards. The first two are mainly composed of older housing, wooded and low-density, while Quinton is typified by much more modern private estates, even less inclined, if anything, to grant Labour more than a derisory vote.

The MP for Edgbaston since 1966 has been Jill Knight, a vivacious right-winger with forthright views on law and order, immigration, and the other issues of Tory populism. She must have had her worries in the mid-1970s, as the non-white population of Deritend increased, but the new Edgbaston will be the most middle-class and Conservative seat within Birmingham itself. In the 1982 local elections the Conservative candidates gained 55% of the vote in Edgbaston's three remaining wards, compared with 25% for the Alliance and 20% for Labour.

1981	% Own Occ	56		1979 core seat Birmingham		
1981	% Loc Auth	25		Edgbaston		
1981	% Black/Asian	9		C	25,192	54.1
1981	% Mid Cl	57		Lab	15,605	33.5
1981	% Prof Man	18		L	4,377	9.4
1982	electorate 55,433			E	852	1.8
1979	notional result			Oth	538	1.1
	C 12,800			MPs since 1945		
Alliance		SDP		1945-53 Sir P.F.B. Bennett C		
				1953-66 Dame Edith Pitt C		
				1966- Jill Knight C		

Birmingham Erdington   Birmingham

Labour lost three seats in Birmingham to the Tories in the 1979 General Election, and they only just held two others in the north of the city - Perry Barr and Erdington. Erdington, NE Birmingham, showed a 9.4% swing away from the veteran sitting MP, Julius Silverman, who held on by only 680 votes.

Erdington is a mixed constituency, but it had always been regarded as safe for Labour. It includes a good residential area in Erdington ward itself, up against the border with affluent Sutton Coldfield. Stockland Green also voted Conservative, narrowly, in 1979, but as one progresses further into the city, at Gravelly Hill, the Labour vote strengthens. But the best area for Labour should be the new Kingsbury ward, which is basically the large ultra-modern tower block estate of Castle Vale, on the very edge of the city. However the Alliance came out on top in Kingsbury when it was first contested in the 1982 Birmingham City Council elections. Despite this blow, Labour polled the highest number of votes in Erdington, with the Alliance in third place, although it was all fairly close and Erdington certainly looks like the Alliance's best chance in Birmingham. Among the prominent landmarks in Erdington constituency are the huge tyre works at Fort Dunlop and the 'Spaghetti Junction' motorway junction at Gravelly Hill.

Erdington loses a few thousand voters in the redistribution, mainly in the district of Witton near Stockland Heath. There shouldn't be a notable impact on the political characteristics of Erdington, which will remain a mixed marginal seat with a large proportion both of council housing and owner occupied. Julius Silverman has been a Birmingham MP since 1945, and he is now nearly 80 years old. He will retire at the next election, and his successor must prepare for another close contest in Erdington.

1981	% Own Occ	47	1979 core seat Birmingham
1981	% Loc Auth	39	Erdington
1981	% Black/Asian	7	Lab 20,105 46.0
1981	% Mid Cl	39	C 19,425 44.4
1981	% Prof Man	9	L 3,487 8.0
1982	electorate 57,020		NF 687 1.6
1979	notional result		MP since 1945
	C 1,400		1945- Julius Silverman Lab
Alliance		SDP	

Birmingham Hall Green   Birmingham

Hall Green is one of the two Birmingham seats which have
never fallen to the Labour Party. It is not so much a classic
old upper-class district like Edgbaston, the other perpetually
Tory division. Rather it is a peripheral constituency on the
south and south-eastern edge of Birmingham. Billesley and
Brandwood wards contain a complex mixture of council
housing and owner-occupied dwellings, but Hall Green ward
itself is 78% owner occupied and only possesses 12% council
tenants.
The political characteristics reflect these other indicators.
Billesley and Brandwood are very marginal, Billesley tending
to be slightly better ground for Labour, because of the tower
block cluster at Highter's Heath on the very southern edge of
Birmingham. Hall Green is one of the most Conservative wards
in the city. Unemployment runs at only 10% in the Hall Green
seat, less than half of the central city average. Only 5% of
the population is non-white. In many ways, this suburban
constituency is far removed from the turmoil and tensions of
Birmingham city centre five miles to the north.
The MP is Reginald Eyre, who has had a long career as
junior minister and a vice-chairman of the national
Conservative Party. His majority sank to 2,000 in the Tories'
bleak election of October 1974. But there should be few
problems now, although the Boundary Commission's changes
are minor and do not particularly favour the Conservatives. A
small district around Stirchley has been removed to Selly
Oak. Hall Green's owner-occupier majority will almost certainly
continue to make this seat safe for Reginald Eyre.

1981	% Own Occ	52	1979 core seat Birmingham Hall		
1981	% Loc Auth	33	Green		
1981	% Black/Asian	5	C	27,072	54.5
1981	% Mid Cl	50	Lab	17,508	35.3
1981	% Prof Man	15	L	4,440	8.9
1982	electorate 62,038		NF	615	1.2
1979	notional result		MPs since 1950		
	C 9,000		1950-65 Aubrey Jones C		
Alliance		L	1965- Reginald Eyre C		

Birmingham Hodge Hill   Birmingham

Hodge Hill, East Birmingham, is basically the successor to the
Stechford seat which achieved note when it elected a
Conservative in the 1977 byelection cause by Roy Jenkins's
move to EEC headquarters in Brussels. At the 1979 General
Election, the Labour loser at the byelection, Terry Davis,
regained the seat, but only by 1,649 votes. Ironically Terry
Davis was also the Labour candidate in their only byelection
gain anywhere in the 1970s, at Bromsgrove in 1971. There
were signs that the Stechford byelection had left a lasting
impact on its politics. There was a swing of 13% to the Tories
between the October 1974 and 1979 General Elections. In 1979
the majority council estate ward of Shard End voted
Conservative. It would obviously be a while before the level
of Labour support in Stechford returned to 'normal'.
The name of Stechford died before this could ever happen.
But the new Hodge Hill seat is very similar to Stechford,
losing 7,000 voters to Yardley and gaining 3,000 from Small
Heath and 4,000 back from Yardley. Hodge Hill is almost
evenly divided between owner occupiers and council tenants.
Less than in most parts of the country, however, can the
political tastes of Hodge Hill be predicted from tenure. The
council estates on the eastern edge of Birmingham, in Shard
End and Hodge Hill wards, are full of white skilled workers,
who have shown an inclination to prefer the Tories in recent
years. The most owner-occupied ward is nearer the city
centre, Washwood Heath. This is actually the strongest
Labour area, which might not be unconnected with the fact
that 24% of the population in Washwood Heath is non-white.
This eastern wedge of Birmingham demonstrates a range of
attributes, from the Labour-voting Asian owner occupiers of
the inner segment to the Tory working classes of the
peripheral council estates. One feels that its volatile and
unpredictable political behaviour may not yet be over.

1981	% Own Occ	45	1979 core seat Birmingham		
1981	% Loc Auth	45	Stechford		
1981	% Black/Asian	11	Lab	21,166	48.4
1981	% Mid Cl	38	C	19,517	44.6
1981	% Prof Man	9	L	2,349	5.4
1982	electorate 62,214		NF	698	1.6
1979	notional result		MPs since 1950		
	Lab 3,700		1950-77 Roy Jenkins Lab		
Alliance		L	1977-79 Andrew MacKay C		
			1979- Terry Davis Lab		

Birmingham Ladywood   Birmingham

Ladywood, the western part of Birmingham's inner city, has had a complex and fascinating electoral history. There was a time in the 1920s when it was the constituency of Neville Chamberlain. In 1924 the future Conservative Prime Minister beat the Labour candidate, one Oswald Mosley, by 77 votes. In 1929 Labour captured Ladywood by 11 votes (Chamberlain had departed to safer pastures in Edgbaston). After World War Two Ladywood seemed like a safe Labour seat due to residential and population decline and the end of the business vote. But in the 1969 byelection the Liberal Wallace Lawler swept home. His stewardship of the seat only lasted a year before the seat returned to Labour. John Sever did well to hold Ladywood for Labour in another byelection in 1977, but now Sever has not been reselected, and is replaced by left-wing city councillor Albert Bore.

Ladywood includes the city centre - which Americans would call the 'downtown': the Bull Ring, New Street, Paradise Circus and so on. It also has the aptly named Rotton Park area, and the most heavily non-white area in the city, Soho ward (71% black and Asian). But Ladywood was far too small, at 33,000 electors, in 1979. Now it expands to the north to take in a very different kind of ward, Sandwell. Sandwell, on the eastern edge of the park of the same name, is predominantly owner occupied, and it votes Conservative. But even Sandwell has a 37% non-white population, and Ladywood will be one of the most heavily non-white seats in Britain - certainly the most in the cosmopolitan city of Birmingham. It's all a far cry from the days of Neville Chamberlain.

Sandwell, which was previously the minority Tory ward in another multiracial seat, Handsworth, will certainly reduce Labour's majority. But with Ladywood being 42% black/Asian in 1981, and this percentage rising fast, the seat must be swinging to the left. The Alliance won two of the three Labour seats in Ladywood ward itself in 1982, only Albert Bore surviving, but the chances of a repeat of Wallace Lawler's victory for the Liberals is unlikely.

1981	% Own Occ	48	1979 core seat B'ham Ladywood
1981	% Loc Auth	32	Lab 13,450 63.5
1981	% Black/Asian	42	C 5,691 26.9
1981	% Mid Cl	30	L 2,030 9.6
1981	% Prof Man	7	MPs since 1945
1982	electorate 60,687		194%-69 Victor Yates Lab
1979	notional result		1969-70 Wallace Lawler L
	Lab 6,400		1970-74 Doris Fisher Lab
Alliance		L	1974-77 Brian Walden Lab
			1977- John Sever Lab

Birmingham Northfield   Birmingham

Birmingham Northfield caused one of the greatest upsets in the West Midlands – and indeed in the country – in the 1979 General Election when the young Conservative candidate Jocelyn Cadbury overturned a 10,597 Labour majority with a 10% swing. Northfield is a working-class seat, and half its population live in council houses. It is situated on the SW edge of Birmingham, and BL's Longbridge car manufacturing plant lies in the constituency. It seemed as if the skilled motor workers had abandoned Labour en masse.

Then in the summer of 1982 Jocelyn Cadbury, aged 33, shot himself in the garden of his parents' home in Birmingham. He had been one of the most left-wing of the Tory intake of 1979, and one of the things which depressed him was the failure of the government to achieve more for the areas where unemployment was high. Labour might have been expected to win the subsequent byelection (held in October 1982) easily. Even with a powerful right-wing candidate in the shape of John Spellar, right-hand man to Electricians' leader Frank Chapple, Labour only managed to achieve a majority of 289 – scarcely larger than Cadbury's had been. The Liberal candidate polled very well – 26% – despite Northfield's status as a two-party marginal. Ironically Labour's previous gain in a byelection, 11 years before, had been in the neighbouring seat of Bromsgrove.

Northfield is little altered in the redistribution. It still consists of a mix of council and private housing in the white, skilled, working-class territory of SW Birmingham – Longbridge, Northfield, King's Norton and Weoley wards. It is still a rather large and very marginal seat. It has shown itself to be volatile in the past, and John Spellar cannot be sure of consolidating his tenuous hold on Northfield in the next General Election.

1981	% Own Occ	42
1981	% Loc Auth	48
1981	% Black/Asian	3
1981	% Mid Cl	45
1981	% Prof Man	10
1982	electorate 75,121	
1979	notional result	
	C 100	
Alliance		L

1979 core seat Birmingham Northfield

C	25,304	45.4
Lab	25,100	45.1
L	4,538	8.1
NF	614	1.1
WRP	144	0.3

MPs since 1950
1950-51 A.R. Blackburn Lab
1951-70 Donald Chapman Lab
1970-79 Ray Carter Lab
1979-82 Jocelyn Cadbury C
1982-   John Spellar Lab

Birmingham Perry Barr   Birmingham

Labour left-winger Jeff Rooker did extremely well to hold on
to Perry Barr in NW Birmingham in the 1979 General Election,
when so many Labour seats were falling in England's volatile
second city. The pro-Tory swing was restrained to 3.5%, and
Rooker scraped in by 491 votes. Perry Barr was a nearly all-
white peripheral suburban seat, just the type of constituency
which abandoned Labour elsewhere in the West Midlands -
Northfield   and   Yardley   in   Birmingham,   Dudley   West,
Aldridge-Brownhills and Meriden.

There is evidence that the active Rooker won by a personal
vote in Perry Barr last time. His running mates in the local
elections of the same day (3 May 1979) polled fewer votes
than their Tory opponents. Perry Barr ward itself and Oscott
are predominantly owner occupied, though skilled working
class rather than professional and managerial voters dominate.
Kingstanding is a large semi-detached council estate. But now
Rooker receives a great boost from the Boundary Commission.
The strongly West Indian ward of Handsworth (54% non-white)
is transferred from the abolished seat of that name.
Handsworth swung progressively to Labour as post-war
immigrants settled in the inner north-western section of the
city. Unemployment in Handsworth in 1981 was over 25%; in
Perry Barr ward 9%.

Perry Barr will now be a curiously divided marginal seat. In
the 1982 local elections, Conservatives did very well in the
white owner-occupied Perry Barr and Oscott wards, and
polled a majority even in the new seat with Handsworth
included. Rooker may need another personal vote to persuade
Perry Barr to re-elect him next time, although it must be a
better bet for him than before.

			1979 core seat Birmingham
1981	% Own Occ	59	Perry Barr
1981	% Loc Auth	28	Lab 18,674 47.6
1981	% Black/Asian	16	C 18,183 46.3
1981	% Mid Cl	40	L 1,811 4.6
1981	% Prof Man	8	NF 582 1.5
1982	electorate 75,053		MPs since 1950
1979	notional result		1950-55 C.C. Poole Lab
	Lab 4,600		1955-64 C.B. Howell Lab
Alliance		L	1964-66 W.R. Davies C
			1966-70 Christopher Price Lab
			1970-74 Joseph Kinsey C
			1974- Jeffrey Rooker Lab

Birmingham Selly Oak   Birmingham

Selly Oak was one of the urban seats which slipped away from
the Conservatives due to social change in the 1950s and
1960s. This SW Birmingham seat was once typified by some of
the best housing areas in the city, similar in standard to the
neighbouring Edgbaston. But the proportion of non-white
immigrants increased in Moseley, Selly Oak and Selly Park,
the districts nearest to the city centre; and council estates
were built near the edge of the city at Kings Norton. It
seemed only a matter of time before the veteran right-winger
Harold Gurden, MP since 1955, lost Selly Oak. The blow fell
in October 1974. The new Labour member was a prominent
left-winger, Tom Litterick, who made his mark in the 1974-79
Parliament. But Litterick's hold actually proved no more
secure than Gurden's, and he was comfortably ousted by
Anthony Beuamont-Dark in the year of Mrs Thatcher's
success. Tom Litterick died shortly afterwards.
Selly Oak is only slightly altered in the boundary changes,
gaining the Stirchley district from Hall Green. All four wards
are fairly marginal - the outermost, Kings Norton, is
probably best for Labour and the innermost, Moseley, is best
for the Conservatives. The centre of the constituency is Selly
Oak itself and the Cadbury's model community of Bournville.
It is a predominantly owner-occupied seat, with a middling
proportion of non-white - around 10%.
Labour could only win Kings Norton when the newly drawn
city council wards were fought for the first time in 1982, and
the Alliance came a clear third in the Selly Oak seat. Its long
swing to Labour seems to have stopped, and it should remain
Conservative in an even year. Certainly it is still the third
most Tory seat in the city, after Edgbaston and Hall Green.

1981	% Own Occ	57
1981	% Loc Auth	16
1981	% Black/Asian	9
1981	% Mid Cl	47
1981	% Prof Man	14
1982	electorate 72,476	
1979	notional result	
	C 6,800	
Alliance		SDP

1979 core seat Birmingham Selly
Oak

C	23,175	49.7
Lab	18,400	39.5
L	4,470	9.6
NF	401	0.9
Oth	190	0.4

MPs since 1955
1955-74 Harold Gurden C
1974-79 Tom Litterick Lab
1979-   Anthony Beaumont-Dark
                    C

Birmingham Small Heath   Birmingham

If Ladywood is the constituency which makes up the western half of Birmingham's depressed inner city, its twin to the east is Small Heath. Like many inner-city seats, Small Heath was undersized before the boundary changes, and it takes Aston ward from the old, abolished Handsworth division.

Small Heath comprises both heavily non-white owner-occupied districts like Saltley and Small Heath itself, and inner-city tower blocks and council estates like Duddeston and Newtown. In general it is true in Birmingham, as elsewhere, that Asians and West Indians live in housing of private ownership and not in local authority developments, but in Small Heath the proportion of non-whites is so high - over 35% - that they are to be found throughout the constituency. In the old Parliament, there were four Birmingham seats with over 35% living in households headed by someone born in the New Commonwealth or Pakistan - Small Heath, Sparkbrook, Handsworth and Ladywood. The last two had the highest proportion of any seats in Britain, between 45% and 50%.

Not surprisingly, Small Heath is safely Labour, and it should pose no problems for Denis Howell, a Labour frontbencher who has taken on a series of off-beat portfolios from sport to assorted disasters connected with the weather.

1981	% Own Occ	36
1981	% Loc Auth	53
1981	% Black/Asian	36
1981	% Mid Cl	30
1981	% prof Man	6
1982	electorate 60,315	
1979	notional result	
	Lab 15,900	
Alliance		SDP

1979 core seat Birmingham Small Heath

Lab	17,735	60.5
C	6,268	21.4
L	4,470	15.2
NF	490	1.7
Oth	349	1.2

MPs since 1950
1950-52 F. Longden Lab
1952-61 W.E. Wheeldon Lab
1961-   Denis Howell Lab

Birmingham Sparkbrook   Birmingham

Sparkbrook is a long thin wedge of a constituency stretching from the City Centre of Birmingham to the south-eastern edge. Socially too it runs the gamut from the heavily Asian inner areas of Sparkbrook and Sparkhill to the almost all-white peripheral council estate of Fox Hollies.

All the wards are now safely Labour, Sparkbrook having swung very sharply away from the Conservatives along with non-white colonisation - the Tories won the seat as recently as the 1959 General Election. It was gained from them in 1964 by the present MP, Roy Hattersley.

Hattersley is a fast-rising, plausible, witty politician who is widely regarded as one of the two or three most likely to become a future Labour Party leader. Hattersley should have no trouble with Sparkbrook, a constituency which offers him the experience of a variety of urban problems. In the boundary changes it takes the Labour-voting inner-city Deritend ward from Edgbaston. The Liberals did not even bother to contest Sparkbrook in 1979, and have willingly ceded the Alliance nomination to the SDP.

1981	% Own Occ	44	1979 core seat Birmingham
1981	% Loc Auth	38	Sparkbrook
1981	% Black/Asian	36	Lab 18,717 62.7
1981	% Mid Cl	35	C 10,398 24.9
1981	% Prof Man	7	Comm 715 2.4
1982	electorate 54,516		MPs since 1945
1979	notional result		1945-59 P.L.E. Shurmer Lab
	Lab 10,600		1959-64 L.G. Seymour C
Alliance		SDP	1964- Roy Hattersley Lab

Birmingham Yardley   Birmingham

Yardley is a typical West Midlands marginal. Situated on the SE edge of the city, it contains a mixture of council and private housing, and its social makeup is composed mainly of white skilled workers. In 1979 not only was the Yardley constituency decided by only 1,164 votes, but the wards within it were all tight contests in the municipal elections of the same day. Acocks Green was Conservative by 193, Sheldon Labour by 187, and Yardley ward Conservative by 682 (out of 15,000 cast in all in the ward).

Yardley is little altered in the redistribution, simply swapping a few thousand voters with Stechford (the new Hodge Hill seat). It has changed hands six times since the war, being gained by whichever party won the General Election in 1945, 1959, 1964, 1970, February 1974 and 1979. Yardley's seventh MP since 1945 is local product David Gilroy Bevan, a former Birmingham City Councillor. History suggests that his chances of holding Yardley depend very much on the result of the next General Election.

But there are one or two favourable factors running in Bevan's direction. The council estates of the eastern edge of Birmingham are among the most desirable in the city, and council house sales are reducing the percentage of local authority tenants here. New private developments continue when council house building has stopped. And the white suburbs are always likely to react to the increase of non-whites in the conurbation by moving to the right. Yardley is 96% white. In many ways the Conservatives already do well to make Yardley a marginal, for there are no Tory seats in Britain with a lower proportion of professional and managerial workers. According to this indicator, Birmingham Yardley shares with Gosport the title of the most working class Conservative seat.

1981	% Own Occ	59	1979 core seat Birmingham		
1981	% Loc Auth	33	Yardley		
1981	% Black/Asian	4	C	20,193	47.6
1981	% Mid Cl	45	Lab	19,029	44.8
1981	% Prof Man	10	L	2,491	5.9
1982	electorate 58,446		NF	749	1.8
1979	notional result		MPs since 1945		
	C 3,300		1945-50	W. Perrin	Lab
Alliance		SDP	1950-59	H.C. Osborne	Lab
			1959-64	L.H. Cleaver	C
			1964-70	Ioan Evans	Lab
			1970-74	Derek Coombs	C
			1974-79	Sydney Tierney	Lab
			1979-	David Bevan	C

Sutton Coldfield   Birmingham

Sutton Coldfield is the safest Conservative seat in Britain. It is also the least working-class constituency outside London. Like another dormitory seat east of Birmingham, Solihull, this prosperous and affluent town breaks records as an overwhelming stronghold for the Conservative Party. It is set in leafy surroundings around Sutton Park, which is so large that it gives a pleasant rural ambience. Sutton Coldfield is the goal for many aspiring West Midlanders, and offers the material ultimate in what has been accused of being an over-materialist part of Britain. The fortunate MP is Social Services Secretary Norman Fowler.

1981	% Own Occ	78.8	1979 core seat Sutton Coldfield			
1981	% Loc Auth	15.2	C	34,096	68.9	
1981	% Black/Asian	2	L	7,989	16.1	
1981	% Mid Cl	68.4	Lab	6,511	13.1	
1981	% Prof Man	27.6	NF	466	0.9	
1982	electorate 67,624		Ind C	459	0.9	
1979	notional C 26,100		MPs since 1945			
Alliance		L	1945-55 Sir J.S.P. Mellor C			
			1955-74 Geoffrey Lloyd C			
			1974- Norman Fowler C			

Coventry North-East   Coventry

Coventry NE is the Labour stronghold in the second city of the West Midlands. It is similar to Richard Crossman's old Coventry East seat, which he held from 1945 to 1974, when Coventry gained a fourth seat in boundary changes. There are no significant changes in the present redistribution. Foleshill will remain Labour's strongest ward, Wyken the most marginal. Near the centre of the city there are rows of terraced houses and a substantial proportion of Coventry's non-white population. Further out is a mixture of council estates and low to medium cost private housing. It will remain safe for Crossman's successor, George Park.

1981	% Own Occ	61.7	1979 core seat Coventry NE		
1981	% Loc Auth	29.0	Lab	27,010	57.3
1981	% Black/Asian	16.6	C	16,487	35.0
1981	% Mid Cl	36.5	L	2,291	4.9
1981	% Prof Man	8.9	NF	546	1.2
1982	electorate 67,665		Oths	768	1.6
1979	notional Lab 11,700		MP since 1974		
Alliance		L	1974- George Park Lab		

Coventry North-West   Coventry

Coventry has been for much of the twentieth century the hub
of Britain's motor industry. Many car manufacturers have
been based in the motor city, ever since Daimler and Humber
were the first to be founded in 1896. In the inter-war years
Coventry was a 'new industry' town, attracting migrants from
more depressed districts such as South Wales. The city
showed considerable resilience in recovering from the wartime
devastation it suffered. But now Coventry's automobile
industry is in decline. Many of the famous marques have
closed down, or merged. Car manufacture seems to be
running out of steam in Britain, just as coal mining, textiles
and shipbuilding were in the 1930s.

Coventry NW is the home of the Jaguar-Daimler division of
BL, which has two large plants in the constituency. Rather
appropriately - but also, perhaps, rather surprisingly - the
Labour MP is an ex-Jaguar chief executive, Geoffrey
Robinson. Robinson seems to be able to count on a personal
vote in Coventry NW. He did very well to retain this seat,
which is by no means a Labour stronghold, in the 1976
byelection at a time of unpopular Labour government. In 1979
Robinson did better than his local election running mates. In
1982 the Conservatives polled more votes than Labour at the
local level, but it would be premature to write off Geoffrey
Robinson's chances. The boundary changes in Coventry NW
are not major, and he did hold it by nearly 4,000 at the last
General Election.

This was a considerable achievement, if the social and
economic character of Coventry NW is considered. Over 70% of
the housing is owner occupied, and Bablake ward is one of
the best residential areas in the city. Only 20% of the houses
in NW are council owned. The percentage of non-white
residents is below the city-wide average. Coventry NW seems
to be the home of the affluent, white, skilled worker, rather
like Birmingham seats such as Northfield. But as yet it has
not demonstrated Northfield's volatility, but rather a loyalty
to Labour, and to Geoffrey Robinson.

1981	% Own Occ	70.4	1979 core seat Coventry North-		
1981	% Loc Auth	20.9	West		
1981	% Black/Asian	7.4	Lab	19,460	50.1
1981	% Mid Cl	42.1	C	15,489	39.9
1981	% Prof Man	10.8	L	3,413	8.8
1982	electorate 52,552		NF	359	0.9
1979	notional result		Oth	98	0.3
	Lab 4,200		MPs since 1974		
Alliance		L	1974-76 Maurice Edelman Lab		
			1976- Geoffrey Robinson Lab		

Coventry South-East   Coventry

William Wilson has been the MP for Coventry SE since its creation in 1974, and before that he represented Coventry South from 1964. But now Wilson is retiring, and the constituency Labour party caused some ructions when they selected Militant supporter David Nellist as his successor. Like the other Militant candidates, Nellist's position was placed under pressure after the attempt at the 1982 Labour Party Conference to declare Militant a banned organisation. It is also widely thought that extreme left candidates prove to be electoral liabilities. However Nellist did win the Coventry SE ward (which is identical to the old constituency itself) to join the West Midlands County Council in December 1982. If he is confirmed as candidate, Nellist probably will win Coventry SE at the next General Election.

Coventry SE includes the city centre, which is largely situated in St Michael's ward. The centre was almost completely destroyed in the war - the best known of the many works of reconstruction is the new cathedral, replacing the one burnt down in 1940, and consecrated in 1962. St Michael's also includes the second highest number of non-white residents of any ward in Coventry (Foleshill in NE is over 50% black/Asian). Binley and Willenhall ward contains sizeable council estates. Lower Stoke has a Talbot car works. The best ward for the Conservatives is Cheylesmore, which is almost entirely owner occupied and forms part of the middle-class south Coventry belt.

The SDP have the Alliance nomination for Coventry SE, but Coventry has not shown any sign of being a good area for the new party. In the 1982 local elections, only 22% voted for the Alliance candidates in each of the three seats NE, NW and SE. Labour remain the favourites to win SE, whoever their candidate turns out to be.

1981	% Own Occ	59.2	1979 core seat Coventry South-		
1981	% Loc Auth	32.3	East		
1981	% Black/Asian	10.9	Lab	19,583	55.0
1981	% Mid Cl	41.0	C	12,097	34.0
1981	% Prof Man	11.0	L	2,984	8.4
1982	electorate 53,069		NF	513	1.4
1979	notional result		WRP	426	1.2
	Lab 5,700		MP since 1974		
Alliance		SDP	1974-	William Wilson Lab	

Coventry South-West   Coventry

Coventry SW is the most marginal and the most middle-class
seat in the city. In 1974, when Coventry was first granted
four constituencies, Labour won all four, but Audrey Wise's
majority scarcely exceeded 2,000 even in October; and in 1979
the far left activist Mrs Wise was swept away by over 5,000
votes. But this is not necessarily a personal condemnation.
Nearly three-quarters of the housing is owner occupied, and
only 2.5% of the population is non-white: by far the lowest
proportion in the city. Audrey Wise did well to win Coventry
SW in the first place.
   Much of the constituency consists of the most fashionable
residential areas in Coventry, such as Gibbet Hill, the classic
avenue of large detached mansions along the road to
Kenilworth in Wainbody ward. Earlsdon ward is also very
Conservative. Labour fights back in pockets of council
housing in Woodlands and Westwood wards in west Coventry;
there is an old Standard-Triumph motor works in Whoberley
ward; and the campus of the radically-inclined 1960s
University of Warwick is also in the constituency.
   It is unlikely that Labour will regain Coventry SW. In the
1982 local elections in Coventry they actually sunk to third
place, as the Alliance (SDP-led here) produced their best
result in Coventry - nearly 28%. The Tories polled 46% and
seem capable of making SW a safe seat. There are few
boundary changes of significance in any of the Coventry
constituencies.

1981	% Own Occ	73.6	1979 core seat Coventry South-	
1981	% Loc Auth	19.4	West	
1981	% Black/Asian	2.5	C	27,928	49.3
1981	% Mid Cl	55.1	Lab	22,274	39.3
1981	% Prof Man	18.5	L	5,921	10.4
1982	electorate 66,090		NF	482	0.9
1979	notional result		Oth	78	0.1
	C 5,400		MPs since 1974	
Alliance		SDP	1974-79 Audrey Wise Lab	
			1979- John Butcher C	

Dudley East   Dudley

Dudley is the south-westernmost Metropolitan Borough in the
West Midlands county. It would be fair to say that it consists
of one safe Labour seat, one safe Conservative and one
marginal. Unlike many West Midlands Boroughs, Dudley does
not have a particularly large population of Asians and West
Indians, but most of them are concentrated in Dudley East,
which is the one strongly Labour seat. Dudley East also used
to be the smallest seat in rather a large Borough, but now it
is to be the largest, with over 75,000 electors. This is the
result of a couple of minor changes: East picks up Cradley
from Halesowen and Stourbridge, and Quarry Bank from West.
These modifications should reinforce John Gilbert's 8,000
majority.

Dudley East is centred on the old iron-working town of
Dudley, set on its industrial Black Country hill, and on
Coseley at the NE end of the borough. The only regularly
Conservative ward is Coseley West; and this is not strong
Alliance country, for the Liberals were always very weak in
Dudley, and the SDP have made few inroads against a
moderate Labour party. East is the successor to the old
Dudley seat, which was held by George Wigg for many years,
but which temporarily fell to the Tories in the 1968 byelection
in a 21% swing, one of the worst results of Harold Wilson's
first government. But this was clearly an exceptional result.

East is one of those constituencies with a council estate
majority, and it is sure to remain the best Labour bet in
Dudley borough. In many ways it resembles the next-door
seats in the Metropolitan Borough of Sandwell - West
Bromwich West and Warley West. Together they form a solidly
Labour triangle in the heart of the vast West Midlands
industrial belt.

1981	% Own Occ	45	1979 core seat Dudley East
1981	% Loc Auth	50	Lab 22,521 53.8
1981	% Black/Asian	9	C 14,834 35.5
1981	% Mid Cl	38	L 3,639 8.7
1981	% Prof Man	11	NF 844 2.0
1982	electorate 75,728		MPs since 1945
1979	notional result		1945-68 George Wigg Lab
	Lab 9,500		1968-70 W.D. Williams C
Alliance		SDP	1970- John Gilbert Lab

143

Dudley West   Dudley

Dudley West was one of the Conservatives' most impressive gains in the 1979 General Election. They took the seat with an 8.5% swing, overturning a Labour majority of 8,500. Since then their position has improved even further. In the 1982 local elections their lead over Labour was 15%, and the minor boundary changes are in the Tories' favour.

Dudley West loses about 6,000 electors net, but this is mainly due to the loss of a Labour ward, Quarry Bank, to East, and the picking up of some more marginal territory from Halesowen and Stourbridge. This should add a small but vital boost to John Blackburn's 1,139 vote Tory majority. Dudley West is rather similar to the old Brierley Hill seat, which was abolished in 1974. Brierley Hill itself is a strongly Labour ward, as are the other eastern wards of Gornal and Brockmoor-Pensnett. But on the western edge of the constituency, and the Borough itself, are to be found some of the desirable middle-class residential districts which fringe the South Staffordshire countryside. Sedgley is an old market town, but more modern private housing predominates in Wall Heath, Kingswinford and Wordsley. Their Conservatism has tipped the balance in Dudley West in recent years.

Dudley West is one of the 'snow-white' seats on the periphery of the West Midlands conurbation. These districts have had a tendency to swing to the right, and West may well become a Conservative seat in an even year. The Alliance only polled 28% in 1982, and the Liberals did not even contest Dudley West at the last election, leaving it as one of the only three straight fights in Great Britain.

1981	% Own Occ	62	1979 core seat Dudley West
1981	% Loc Auth	33	C	30,158	51.0
1981	% Black/Asian	1	Lab	29,019	49.0
1981	% Mid Cl	48	MPs since 1950
1981	% Prof Man	16	1950-59 C.J. Simmons Lab
1982	electorate 77,422		1959-67 J.E. Talbot C
1979	notional result		1967-74 Fergus Montgomery C
	C 2,100		1974-79 Colin Phipps Lab
Alliance		L	1979- John Blackburn C

Halesowen and Stourbridge   Dudley

When Halesowen and Stourbridge were first coupled in
parliamentary terms in 1974, the seat could be considered
marginal. In October 1974 John Stokes's majority for the
Conservatives was reduced to 850. But Mrs Thatcher's appeal
proved to the taste of this constituency - John Stokes himself
is one of the far right Monday Club stalwarts in the House of
Commons - and the Tory majority shot up to 9,000 in 1979.
  Halesowen and Stourbridge makes up the southern section of
Dudley borough, situated on the very border between the
West Midlands urban sprawl and the Worcestershire
countryside. Both Stourbridge and Halesowen are prosperous
and independent towns, and much inclined to the
Conservative Party. But there are Labour wards in this
constituency, most notably Lye and Wollescote, which lies
between the two main centres, and Belle Vale. The Alliance
have not made much impact, and only reached 26%, below the
national average, in their first full scale try-out here in
1982.
  John Stokes's hard-line right-wing politics suit an almost all-
white district not out of contact with the multiracial tension of
the centre of the West Midlands metropolis. It seems doubtful
that Halesowen-Stourbridge will again be reduced to marginal
status. It has lost about 10,000 of its 1979 electorate of
84,000 in minor boundary changes, which should not
significantly affect the outcome.

1981	% Own Occ	65	1979 core seat Halesowen-
1981	% Loc Auth	27	Stourbridge
1981	% Black/Asian	2	C 33,247 49.6
1981	% Mid Cl	49	Lab 24,282 36.2
1981	% Prof Man	19	L 8,597 12.8
1982	electorate 77,172		NF 921 1.4
1979	notional result		MP since 1974
	C 9,800		1974- John Stokes C
Alliance		SDP	

Warley East   Sandwell

The bearded actor Andrew Faulds, who is MP for Warley
East, manages at the same time to be a vocal Labour partisan
in the Commons and to be widely regarded as on the right of
his party. Warley East is based on the old Smethwick
constituency, which came to national prominence in 1964 when
Labour's Patrick Gordon Walker was defeated against the
national swing by Conservative Peter Griffiths, who was
accused of adopting a racist campaign. Andrew Faulds won
back Smethwick in 1966, and has remained in Parliament ever
since, although his majority in 1979 was only 5,000.
As its history might suggest, Warley East possesses both a
large immigrant community and a substantial Tory vote. It is
a starkly divided seat. In its northern and eastern sectors
can be found the strongly Labour Soho/Victoria and
Smethwick wards, which abut on to the heavily non-white
Soho and Handsworth wards of west Birmingham. This is
where the immigrants, mainly of Asian origin, congregate. On
the other hand, to the south is a Tory area around Old
Warley and Warley Abbey, with its parks and comfortable
private housing. This is the kind of 'snow-white' region near
to a concentration of immigrants which is keenly aware of the
racial question. Old Warley is just over the border from
Birmingham's middle-class Harborne/Quinton district. There
are only minor boundary changes in the Sandwell Metropolitan
Borough, but a favourable one for Labour is the transfer of
St Paul's ward from Warley West to East. This is north of
Smethwick itself and strongly Labour.
There was a suggestion that Andrew Faulds might be the kind
of member who might be tempted by the SDP. But in fact he
has stayed with Labour, and was one of the first sitting MPs
to be reselected, unopposed. His presence must blunt the
Alliance's appeal in an area of great Liberal weakness – the
Liberals did not even contest Warley East in 1979. The
Alliance only polled 15% here in the 1982 local elections, and
Labour's vote held up strongly. This augurs very well for
Andrew Faulds's chances, in this most divided division.

1981	% Own Occ	48.3	1979 core seat Warley East	
1981	% Loc Auth	43.0	Lab 21,333	55.0
1981	% Black/Asian	21.3	C 16,236	41.9
1981	% Mid Cl	35.4	NF 1,204	3.1
1981	% Prof Man	8.9	MP since 1974	
1982	electorate 58,454		1974– Andrew Faulds Lab	
1979	notional result			
	Lab 6,200			
Alliance		SDP		

Warley West   Sandwell

Warley used to be in Worcestershire before it was merged with
Staffordshire's West Bromwich in the new West Midlands
Metropolitan Borough of Sandwell. If Warley East was based
on Smethwick, Warley West takes in Oldbury and Rowley
Regis, together with Blackheath, Tividale, Cradley Heath and
Langley. It is the south-west corner of Sandwell. Unlike
Warley East, there has never been any doubt about its safety
for Labour, and for the former Solicitor-General, Peter
Archer - all the wards were won by Labour, even in 1979.

1981	% Own Occ	44.0	1979 core seat Warley West		
1981	% Loc Auth	49.9	Lab	25,175	58.4
1981	% Black/Asian	7.2	C	15,074	35.0
1981	% Mid Cl	32.8	L	2,864	6.6
1981	% Prof Man	8.9	MP since 1974		
1982	electorate 58,335		1974- Peter Archer Lab		
1979	notional result				
	Lab 9,100				
Alliance		L			

West Bromwich East   Sandwell

West Bromwich East is the most marginal of the four Sandwell
Labour seats. Witty and able MP Peter Snape won by under
2,000 votes in 1979, and at local level the Conservatives
achieved a majority then. The Tory vote here comes from the
rather detached district east of the Tame Valley, in Great
Barr and Newton wards, together with Charlemont. Labour
fights back in the Friar Park council estate and in central
West Bromwich, but the constituency remains balanced. A
further complication arose in 1982, when the Liberals seized
two of the middle-class wards and the Alliance won a majority
in the seat as a whole, although they've never performed well
in General Elections here.

1981	% Own Occ	48.4	1979 core seat West Bromwich		
1981	% Loc Auth	48.0	East		
1981	% Black/Asian	8.5	Lab	19,279	47.0
1981	% Mid Cl	40.5	C	17,308	42.2
1981	% Prof Man	11.8	L	3,228	7.9
1982	electorate 60,317		NF	1,175	2.9
1979	notional result		MP since 1974		
	Lab 2,400		1974- Peter Snape Lab		
Alliance		L			

West Bromwich West   Sandwell

Neither of the West Bromwich seats has been significantly altered in the most recent boundary changes. As in the case of all the Sandwell constituencies, they were already of the right size and their population is at a stable level. They were however very much changed in the boundary redistribution which came into effect in 1974, and West Bromwich West is really the successor to the old Wednesbury division, which was held by John Stonehouse to the end of its days.

West is the safer of the two West Bromwich seats for Labour, and NEC women's section member Betty Boothroyd won a comfortable 9,468 majority in 1979. Unlike Warley West, though, there is a Conservative district in this seat – Wednesbury North is a Tory ward, and Wednesbury South went the same way in the 1982 local elections when an Asian Labour candidate was selected. Although there is of course a scattering of non-white voters throughout the West Midlands, the only concentration in Sandwell Borough is in Warley East, on the Soho border with Birmingham. Most of West Bromwich West is the old Black Country – Wednesbury and Tipton, Greets Green and Great Bridge. With its variety of engineering and metalworking industries, and few favoured residential areas, it is similar socially and economically to neighbouring constituencies like Dudley East and Wolverhampton SE.

The Tories pressed Labour hard here in the 1982 municipal elections, but that was their best ever result. The Liberals have been very weak through much of the Midlands for many years, and did not contest West Bromwich West in 1979; the Alliance achieved only 18% in 1982. Betty Boothroyd is a Labour right-winger, and should have little to fear from the SDP; and the Tories are unlikely to produce a further 12% swing from 1979 to defeat her either.

1981	% Own Occ	32.2
1981	% Loc Auth	63.8
1981	% Black/Asian	10.0
1981	% Mid Cl	31.7
1981	% Prof Man	8.6
1982	electorate 58,803	
1979	notional result Lab 9,000	

Alliance   SDP

1979 core seat West Bromwich West

Lab	23,791	60.3
C	14,323	36.3
NF	1,351	3.4

MP since 1974
1974-   Betty Boothroyd Lab

Meriden   Solihull

Meriden is a constituency with a complex electoral history.
Labour won the seat when it was first contested in 1955, the
Conservatives came out first in 1959, Labour in 1964 and
1966, the Tories again in the 1968 byelection and 1970. The
boundary changes of the early 1970s were felt to favour
Labour, as was the construction of the tower-block
Birmingham overspill estate of Chelmsley Wood, and John
Tomlinson won Meriden for Labour in both 1974 Elections. But
a 9% swing gave Tory Iain Mills a 4,000 majority in 1979 - the
fifth time the seat had changed hands in under 25 years.
 Once again Meriden had grown too large, passing 100,000
electors as the 1980s began. Now it has been drastically split
- the northern half, around Coleshill and Atherstone, is now
in North Warwickshire Borough, and the new constituency of
that name. The parts of Meriden within the Solihull Borough
and West Midlands county are now joined by two wards from
the slightly oversized Solihull seat, Knowle and Packwood. It
might be thought unlikely that the space-age towers of
Chelmsley Wood should ever again be in a Conservative
constituency, but this is what is likely to happen. Of course
the overspill estate does create four Labour wards, but the
ex-Solihull districts included are the most desirable and most
Conservative residential areas in that ultra-middle class town
- Knowle and Packwood on their own produced a Tory
majority of 8,000 in 1979. Lady Byron Lane in Knowle is
widely regarded as the wealthiest road in Solihull, or even in
the whole West Midlands. Its includion in the same seat as
Chelmsley Wood is one of the most bizarre effects of the
Commission's work.
 Meriden seems to continue to produce large swings. There
was a photo-finish in the local elections of 1980 and 1981, but
the Tories were well ahead in 1979 and 1982. Meriden does
not seem to be good ground for the Alliance.

1981	% Own Occ	55.1	1979 core seat Meriden		
1981	% Loc Auth	40.6	C	37,151	48.8
1981	% Black/Asian	2.5	Lab	33,024	43.3
1981	% Mid Cl	52.9	L	4,976	6.5
1981	% Prof Man	18.9	NF	1,032	1.4
1982	electorate 74,235		MPs since 1955		
1979	notional result		1955-59 R. Moss Lab		
	C 10,000		1959-64 G.R. Matthews C		
Alliance		SDP	1964-68 C.J.S. Rowland Lab		
			1968-74 Keith Speed C		
			1974-79 John Tomlinson Lab		
			1979- Iain Mills C		

Solihull   Solihull

In 1979 Solihull was the second safest of all the 339
Conservative seats, and returned the second largest majority
of the 623 seats in Great Britain (not including Northern
Ireland) - 32,207. Ironically the one safer Tory constituency
is also an affluent suburb of Birmingham, Sutton Coldfield.
Solihull was a larger seat than average, with over 84,000
electors, and its chances of breaking records will now be
reduced, for two of the most Conservative wards, Knowle and
Packwood, have been moved out into Meriden. But it should
remain an ultra-safe division for whoever is fortunate enough
to succeed Percy Grieve, who is retiring.
Solihull does contain the Rover motor works, and the
territory north of the railway line is slightly less fashionable
- Elmdon and Lyndon wards. But all are safely Conservative
- Shirley and Silhill, St Alphege and Olton. There is no
substantial block of council housing, and almost uniquely for
a large town the percentage of non-manual workers climbs
past 60%.
Why is Solihull so Conservative? Perhaps it is because so
many of the middle-class commuters to Birmingham are
concentrated in restricted areas, here and in Sutton
Coldfield, whereas in London such people are spread much
more widely in the West End, Outer London and the Home
Counties, and as far afield as Brighton and Oxford. Yet
Birmingham is the nation's second city, and the home of much
prosperity and affluence. Another point is that Solihull is
almost all-white, but the cosmopolitan racial mixture of the
West Midlands is a pervasive factor in the politics of the West
Midlands conurbation. The white middle classes and skilled
workers are particularly prone to the appeal of the
Conservative Party as one which can maintain law and order,
protect property, and control immigration. Whatever the
reasons, Solihull will certainly remain one of the ten safest
Tory seats in Britain.

1981	% Own Occ	78.9	1979 core seat Solihull		
1981	% Loc Auth	14.7	C	43,027	66.2
1981	% Black/Asian	1.3	Lab	10,820	16.6
1981	% Mid Cl	63.8	L	10,214	15.7
1981	% Prof Man	24.6	NF	978	1.5
1982	electorate 74,407		MPs since 1945		
1979	notional result		1945-64 M.A. Lindsay C		
	C 26,500		1964- Percy Grieve C		
Alliance		L			

Aldridge-Brownhills   Walsall

When Aldridge-Brownhills was created in 1974, it was
regarded as an ultra-marginal seat; and indeed its first
contest in February of that year produced a victory by only
366 votes for Labour's Geoffrey Edge over Conservative Dame
Patricia Hornsby-Smith. Edge increased his majority in
October 1974, but lost in 1979 by over 5,000 to Richard
Shepherd. It is a seat of two distinct halves. Brownhills is an
ex-mining town, 83% working class according to the last
available figures, formerly in Labour Walsall North. Aldridge
is much more middle class, largely private post-war housing,
and it was largely responsible for the Conservative character
of the Walsall South seat which existed before 1974. Now
Aldridge-Brownhills has been incorporated as the eastern end
of the enlarged Metropolitan Borough of Walsall.
Aldridge is growing much more rapidly than Brownhills, and
Labour's chances of regaining the seat do not seem to be
good. The Labour Party did very badly in the Walsall local
elections of 1982, partly because of the left-wing reputation
of the local Labour council, and polled only 18% in Aldridge-
Brownhills. Besides Brownhills, Labour can count on support
only from the small community of Pelsall. The Conservatives
have Aldridge, Walsall Wood, and the best residential area in
the seat, Streetly, which like many other districts on the
edge of Sutton Park, houses some of the wealthiest West
Midlanders.
The Alliance won 35% in 1982, not as excellent a result as in
neighbouring Walsall North, but probably enough to split the
anti-Tory vote at the next Election and let Richard Shepherd
in again. Aldridge-Brownhills seems likely to swing to the
right to become another all-white Tory residential district on
the edge of the West Midlands conurbation. It is little altered
in the boundary changes.

1981	% Own Occ	61.8	1979 core seat Aldridge-	
1981	% Loc Auth	33.4	Brownhills	
1981	% Black/Asian	1.0	C	26,289	50.3
1981	% Mid Cl	50.1	Lab	20,621	39.4
1981	% Prof Man	17.2	L	5,398	10.3
1982	electorate 61,678		MPs since 1974	
1979	notional result		1974-79 Geoffrey Edge Lab	
	C 7,000		1979- Richard Shepherd C	
Alliance		SDP		

Walsall North   Walsall

Labour lost Walsall North in the 1976 byelection caused when vanishing ex-Cabinet Minister John Stonehouse's political career came to an enforced end when he was convicted for fraud. But the Tory victory seemed to be but an aberration, for Walsall North is a solidly working-class seat, 63.6% council housing in 1971, and Labour Tribunite David Winnick easily recaptured it in 1979.

Walsall North consists of Willenhall, traditionally the centre of the Black Country lock and key industry, Bloxwich, Birchills-Leamore and Short Heath, and the most Conservative ward, Blakenall. Compared with South, North has far fewer non-whites, and more post-war council estates, although both are part of the South Staffordshire engineering and metalworking belt forged in the Industrial Revolution. In the boundary changes Walsall North loses about 8,000 electors in the Bentley area to Walsall South.

Now a new threat to David Winnick has arisen - not the Conservatives this time, but the Alliance. The Liberals took Bloxwich West, both Willenhall seats and Short Heath in the 1982 borough council elections. They polled 42% across the seat, to Labour's 29%. A Liberal victory in the industrial West Midlands would be quite a shock, but they are threatening to break through at West Bromwich East and here at Walsall North. It is unclear whether the Liberals can sustain this impact in a General Election, but Walsall North must remain a seat to be watched closely next time.

1981	% Own Occ	35.3	1979 core seat Walsall North		
1981	% Loc Auth	60.5	Lab	26,913	50.9
1981	% Black/Asian	4.7	C	21,047	39.8
1981	% Mid Cl	31.7	L	3,778	7.2
1981	% Prof Man	9.0	NF	1,098	2.1
1982	electorate 69,873		MPs since 1950		
1979	notional result		1950-74 William Wells Lab		
	Lab 4,200		1974-76 John Stonehouse Lab		
Alliance		L	1976-79 Robin Hodgson C		
			1979- David Winnick Lab		

Walsall South   Walsall

Walsall South is supposedly the more marginal of the two
Walsall Labour seats, but MP Bruce George restricted the
swing to the Tories to 3.6% in 1979, and held on by 1,588
votes. Since the Liberals have no solid base here, and did
not even contest the seat at the last General Election, they
pose much less of a menace than in Walsall North. The
Conservatives have a massive lead in one ward, Paddock, SE
of the town centre, but Labour fight back in Darlaston,
Pleck, Pheasey and the central ward, St Matthew's. The
Conservatives took the lead in the local elections in Labour's
black year of 1982, but Bruce George is popular locally and
again has a good chance of survival next time.

1981	% Own Occ	51.0	1979 core seat Walsall South		
1981	% Loc Auth	41.7	Lab	22,539	50.9
1981	% Black/Asian	15.4	C	20,951	47.3
1981	% Mid Cl	40.6	NF	795	1.8
1981	% Prof Man	13.0	MP since 1974		
1982	electorate 68,193		1974-	Bruce George Lab	
1979	notional Lab 4,600				
Alliance		L			

Wolverhampton North-East   Wolverhampton

By tradition, the industrial Black Country town of
Wolverhampton, NW of Birmingham, has three safe
parliamentary seats, two Labour and one Conservative. It is
left almost untouched by the Boundary Commissioners, but
some doubt arises about the safe Labour status of
Wolverhampton NE. This seat, despite its council housing
majority, voted Conservative in the 1982 local elections,
Labour redoubts like Bushbury falling for the first time since
the war. Oxley is the best Conservative ward, Low Hill the
best Labour, and Wednesfield is marginal. But if Renee Short
should lose NE, it would still be a major surprise.

1981	% Own Occ	35	1979 core seat Wolverhampton		
1981	% Loc Auth	60	North-East		
1981	% Black/Asian	10	Lab	24,046	50.0
1981	% Mid Cl	35	C	17,986	37.4
1981	% Prof Man	10	L	4,760	9.9
1982	electorate 64,104		NF	1,283	2.7
1979	notional Lab 4,700		MPs since 1950		
Alliance		L	1950-64 J. Baird Lab		
			1964-	Renee Short Lab	

Wolverhampton South-East   Wolverhampton

South-East is clearly the safer of the two Labour seats in
Wolverhampton. The Labour vote held up much better than in
North East in the 1982 local elections, for example; this may
well be due to the high percentage of non-whites in South
East, whereas NE is a largely white council estate and modern
residential area. Neither division is altered much in the
boundary redistribution.
South-East is the most recent of the constituencies to be
designated as a Wolverhampton seat. In the mid-1960s the
County Borough of Wolverhampton was expanded to include
the town of Bilston, which had formed the base of its own
seat in association with Coseley and Sedgley, now in Dudley
Borough. Besides Bilston itself, SE includes the working-class
East Park ward of Wolverhampton and the more marginal
Blakenhall, south of the town centre. The Conservatives can
only approach Labour's vote in this latter ward, and in
Bilston North and Bilston Spring Vale. The Alliance only
polled 22½% in 1982. The Borough of Wolverhampton is
dominated by a mixture of industries, many of them heavy,
and this seat is set amongst some of the most scarred and
polluted townscape in Britain. The train journey from
Wolverhampton to Birmingham takes the traveller through a
stark panorama created by the Industrial Revolution. It looks
every inch the Labour stronghold.
The MP for Wolverhampton South-East, and formerly for
Bilston, is Robert (Bob) Edwards. Edwards, a veteran of the
Republican forces in the Spanish Civil War, is now in his late
seventies, but he has not announced his retirement, and he
may well be one of the oldest and most senior members of the
new Parliament. Certainly his constituency doesn't seem to
offer too many threats to the continuation of his long political
career.

1981	% Own Occ	36	1979 core seat Wolverhampton		
1981	% Loc Auth	57	South-East		
1981	% Black/Asian	18	Lab	20,708	55.7
1981	% Mid Cl	32	C	12,807	34.5
1981	% Prof Man	9	L	2,499	6.7
1982	electorate 57,047		NF	1,139	3.1
1979	notional result		MP since 1974		
	Lab 8,600		1974-	Robert Edwards Lab	
Alliance		L			

Wolverhampton South-West   Wolverhampton

Wolverhampton South-West will forever be associated with Enoch Powell. Powell represented this seat from 1950 to February 1974, but then refused to contest the General Election as the Tory candidate, voted Labour himself, and called on his anti-Common Market supporters to do the same. In October of the same year he returned to Parliament after having migrated to South Down in Northern Ireland, and to the Ulster Unionist party.

SW is of course the safe Conservative seat in Wolverhampton, although Powell clearly had a personal vote and personal influence as well. Ironically, SW also includes the highest proportion of non-white voters in the town, and one of the thirty highest in Britain - around 20% in 1981. The immigrants are concentrated in the town centre, in St Peter's ward, and in Graiseley. Both of these are strong Labour wards, but the rest of SW is a solidly middle-class peripheral residential area on the edge of the West Midlands conurbation. Tettenhall, Penn and Merry Hill are strongly Conservative and mainly modern. Park is the old west end of the town, and traditionally the educational centre, containing the girls' and boys' grammar schools.

Powell's successor was Nicholas Budgen, who lacks his notoriety, his fame and his charisma, but who increased his majority to 10,760 at the 1979 General Election. This constituency is less likely to swing than many, for it contains two very solid blocs of opposing supporters - the growing non-white Labour vote in the central district of Wolverhampton, and the Conservative strongholds of the western edge of the town, and indeed the western edge of the whole Black Country.

1981	% Own Occ	64	1979 core seat Wolverhampton
1981	% Loc Auth	20	South-West
1981	% Black/Asian	20	C	26,587	52.5
1981	% Mid Cl	52	Lab	15,827	31.2
1981	% Prof Man	19	L	6,939	13.7
1982	electorate 69,157		NF	912	1.8
1979	notional result		Ind	401	0.8
	C 10,100		MPs since 1950
Alliance		SDP	1950-74 Enoch Powell C
			1974- Nicholas Budgen C

Blaydon   Gateshead / Newcastle

The Metropolitan Borough of Gateshead lies on the south bank
of the Tyne, facing Newcastle. At the western end of the
Borough can be found the constituency of Blaydon, whose
name has become renowned in Geordie folklore through the
popular song about working people trekking to see the
'Blaydon Races'. The constituency formerly consisted of the
small urban districts of Ryton, Whickham and Blaydon. The
boundary changes are only minor: the innermost ward on the
Tyne, Dunston, is removed to the controversial new Tyne
Bridge seat; the Birtley-Lamesley wards come in from
Chester-le-Street. Basically Blaydon still comprises the SW
edge of the Tyneside conurbation.
Even though it is far from the inner city, Blaydon is still a
safe Labour seat. Here can be found the old mining village of
Chopwell, which achieved a reputation for red radicalism in
the 1920s. Over 40% of the electorate live in council housing,
like that at the Winlaton estate at Blaydon. Labour normally
comes out on top in the upland villages of the Crawcrook/
Greenside and Lamesley wards - for in Tyne and Wear,
industry is always just over the horizon. Mining has declined
here - there is no pit at Chopwell now - but the working-
class industrial traditions encaptured in the 'Blaydon Races'
still survive in the district's solid Labour politics. The worst
side of this one-party loyalty was seen in the Poulson
scandals, when corruption dogged local Labour parties
permanently in office; but now the party is purged, and still
as popular electorally as ever.
Conservatives can win the Whickham South ward, and the
Liberals do well in local elections in the Ryton area. But this
will probably only be enough to leave the Alliance and the
Tories fighting it out for second place behind sitting Labour
MP John McWilliam.

1981	% Own Occ	52	1979 core seat Blaydon
1981	% Loc Auth	41	Lab	24,687	53.4
1981	% Black/Asian	0.5	C	16,178	35.0
1981	% Mid Cl	48	L	5,364	11.6
1981	% Prof Man	14	MPs since 1945
1982	electorate 65,984		1945-56 W. Whiteley Lab
1979	notional result		1956-79 Robert Woof Lab
	Lab 11,000		1979- John McWilliam Lab
Alliance		SDP	

Gateshead East   Gateshead/Newcastle

Gateshead East was by far the larger of the two Gateshead
seats in the old Parliament, and it survives the sweeping
redrawing of central Tyneside without being changed too
dramatically. It does gain around 7,000 electors at Saltwell
from Gateshead West, but it remains recognisably the same
seat that has sent Labour MP Bernard Conlan to Westminster
with comfortable majorities ever since 1964.

East is not true inner city territory, like West was, although
it does reach the Tyne at Felling, opposite the St Anthony's
district of dockland Newcastle. But more typical are the vast
windy council estates of Wrekenton, set high on the hills of
the south-eastern edge of the Gateshead-Newcastle
conurbation. There is also one very Conservative middle-class
enclave, Low Fell, two or three miles south of the Tyne
bridges on the old A1. But Gateshead East should remain a
very safe Labour seat, with over half its housing council
owned and under a third of its population non-manual
workers.

The next-door seat, Gateshead West, is at present held by
SDP MP John Horam. But East is not to be the target of an
SDP challenge. The Alliance only contested three of the nine
wards within the constituency in the 1982 local elections, and
the seat has been allocated to the Liberal Party, which lost
its deposit last time. With unemployment running at around
20% in 1981, a further swing to Labour at the next General
Election seems the only plausible forecast.

1981	% Own Occ	29	1979 core seat Gateshead East		
1981	% Loc Auth	55	Lab	28,776	61.2
1981	% Black/Asian	0.5	C	14,078	29.9
1981	% Mid Cl	39	L	4,201	8.9
1981	% Prof Man	10	MPs since 1950		
1982	electorate 69,137		1950-64 A.S. Moody Lab		
1979	notional result		1964- Bernard Conlan Lab		
	Lab 14,900				
Alliance		L			

Newcastle upon Tyne Central   Gateshead/Newcastle

To the uninitiated, Newcastle Central might provide the greatest shock of the next Election. For it should be won by the Conservatives, and the present Newcastle Central is one of the safest Labour seats in the country. But the new Central will have nothing at all in common with the tiny division of 23,000 electors which bears the name now.

Central will in future surround the Town Moor, the large stretch of open land just north of the city centre. As in most cities, the housing on the edge of the main park tends to be desirable and up-market, so it is scarcely surprising that Central will now be the Conservatives' best seat in Newcastle. But it is a little unusual that the seat entitled Central should no longer include the commercial and shopping centre of the city, which is in the Tyne Bridge seat (which crosses the river to include part of Gateshead). The new Newcastle Central will be geographically in the centre of the city, but not socially or politically so.

The former North seat was narrowly Conservative in 1979 – from it come the Moorside, Jesmond and Wingrove wards. From the old Newcastle West come Kenton, Blakelaw and Fenham. From Wallsend comes South Gosforth. Much of all this consists of owner-occupied middle-class housing, although in the Moorside-Jesmond area some mansions are run down, privately rented and multi-occupied. Many students live here, and a sizeable non-white minority is to be found in Wingrove and Jesmond. Kenton and Blakelaw have much more council housing, and Blakelaw is very inclined to Labour; South Gosforth is the most Conservative ward, with many up-market detached houses. Central would have been won by the Tories in 1979. But like the old North, it contains enough socially disparate elements to prevent it from seeming impregnable.

1981	% Own Occ	44	1979 core seat Newcastle North
1981	% Loc Auth	34	C	12,721	47.6
1981	% Black/Asian	4.5	Lab	11,010	41.2
1981	% Mid Cl	45	L	2,983	11.2
1981	% Prof Man	13	MPs since 1945
1982	electorate 62,188		1945-51 Sir C.M. Headlam C
1979	notional result		1951-57 G. Lloyd George C
	C 5,800		1957- Sir R.W. Elliott C
Alliance		SDP	

Newcastle upon Tyne East   Gateshead/Newcastle

Newcastle upon Tyne East is a very diverse and mixed constituency. In leafy Jesmond Dene there is perhaps the most wealthy and attractive Tory residential area in Newcastle itself. On the other hand, East possesses in Byker a famous working-class inner-city development, a ward in which the Conservatives polled just 158 votes, or 6% of the total, in 1982. Walker is another Labour citadel, down among the Tyne shipyards, but Heaton is a large owner-occupied middle-class district. Add to this mixture the spice of an SDP defector as MP, Mike Thomas, and the appetite is whetted for a fascinating political battle on Tyneside.

Mike Thomas is one of the most aggressive and determined of the founder members of the SDP. But his chances of re-election in East under his new colours do not seem good. The Alliance did not win a single ward within the seat on its first major attempt in 1982. In the areas which come into East (which is 20,000 voters larger than it was before the boundary changes), the Alliance do not do very well. Sandyford is a marginal ward from the former Tory North seat. Byker is a dramatic Labour stronghold on top of its hill just east of the city centre, famed for its imaginative redevelopment as a 'wall' of housing along the skyline.

East has been held by the Conservatives, from 1959-64, by Labour, and now by the SDP. All parties will contest the seat strongly next time, and Mike Thomas will hope that his personal vote carries him home. But probably the favourite should be the moderate Labour candidate selected to replace Thomas.

1981	% Own Occ	36	1979 core seat Newcastle East		
1981	% Loc Auth	46	Lab	18,257	55.1
1981	% Black/Asian	1.5	C	12,087	36.4
1981	% Mid Cl	41	L	2,818	8.5
1981	% Prof Man	10	MPs since 1945		
1982	electorate 59,998		1945-59 Arthur Blenkinsop Lab		
1979	notional result		1959-64 Fergus Montgomery C		
	Lab 9,800		1964-74 Geoffrey Rhodes Lab		
Alliance		SDP	1974- Mike Thomas Lab (SDP)		

Newcastle upon Tyne North   Gateshead/Newcastle

It is confusing. If the new Newcastle Central is based on the
old Newcastle North, the new Newcastle North is centred on
the abolished Newcastle West constituency. As such, it should
be a safe Labour seat. Yet a further element of disruption is
introduced by the fact that in the 1982 local elections the
Alliance polled most votes of any grouping in the new North,
a seat ascribed to the Liberals in the carve-up. It is ironic to
discover that the Liberals may well have the best chance of a
gain in the North East, one of the heartlands of the SDP
defector MPs.

The Liberals are particularly strong in Castle and Grange
wards, north of the old city boundaries in Gosforth and
beyond. Another victory came in 1982 in the predominantly
council estate Fawdon ward, formerly a Labour stronghold.
The constituency sweeps down to the Tyne west of Newcastle
through the mixed Newburn area - Tory Westerhope, Labour
Denton and Leamington. West has lost some wards to the new
Central, but it forms the majority of the new North, which
also picks up some outlying territory now in the City of
Newcastle but formerly out in Hexham and Wallsend divisions
- North Gosforth and the villages around Newcastle Airport.

North is almost equally balanced between peripheral council
estates and peripheral owner-occupied suburbs. The Liberals
have made inroads in both, but they have done well in local
elections before, only to suffer drastic disappointment at
parliamentary level. It would be a great breakthrough for the
Liberals to build on their tiny 9.6% vote in Newcastle West in
1979, and Labour must remain favourites to win the new
North division.

1981	% Own Occ	46	1979 core seat Newcastle West
1981	% Loc Auth	48	Lab 32,827 54.5
1981	% Black/Asian	1	C 21,591 35.9
1981	% Mid Cl	46	L 5,801 9.6
1981	% Prof Man	13	MPs since 1945
1982	electorate 70,314		1945-66 E. Popplewell Lab
1979	notional result		1966- Robert Brown Lab
	Lab 5,400		
Alliance		L	

Tyne Bridge   Gateshead/Newcastle

One of the more controversial decisions of the Boundary
Commission has been to deal with the problem of two grossly
undersized seats, Gateshead West and Newcastle Central, by
crossing the Borough boundaries and the natural barrier of
the River Tyne to create the new constituency of Tyne
Bridge. It was certainly true that something had to be done
about the two tiny inner-city divisions - Newcastle Central's
electorate in 1979 was but 23,000, Gateshead West's 29,000.
But a particularly harsh blow has thus been struck against
the SDP founder-member who defected from Labour,
Gateshead West MP John Horam, whose seat will form less
than half of Tyne Bridge, diminishing any personal vote he
may have.
In many ways, though, Tyne Bridge is a logical creation. The
south bank of the Tyne, the Teams, Bensham, Dunston and
Bede wards of Gateshead, are socially and economically similar
to the inner city of Newcastle, and Elswick, Benwell and
Scotswood west of the city centre. This is one of the most
blighted areas of the North East, with nearly 25%
unemployment in 1981, and 60% council housing, much of it
blocks of flats erected in post-war slum clearance schemes.
The western inner city is more depressed than Byker to the
east, with less of a community spirit. Although as in
Newcastle as a whole there are hardly any non-white
residents, most of the other problems of central conurbations
are present in Tyne Bridge. Central Gateshead's
unemployment approaches 40%, as bad as any region in
Britain.
Given the multiple deprivations suffered by Tyne Bridge, it
would be surprising if Labour were not elected with a large
majority such as they enjoyed in the two 'parent' seats in
1979. Indeed the local elections in 1982 offer John Horam
scant comfort, for Labour won every ward in Tyne Bridge
and the Alliance polled under 20%. Horam will probably do
better to seek greener pastures far from the industrial north-
east.

1981	% Own Occ	21	New seat
1981	% Loc Auth	60	
1981	% Black/Asian	2	
1981	% Mid Cl	30	
1981	% Prof Man	6	
1982	electorate 61,881		
1979	notional result		
	Lab 18,000		
Alliance		SDP	

Tynemouth   North Tyneside

The only truly safe Conservative constituency in the Tyne and Wear county is the North Tyneside seat of Tynemouth. For many years until 1974 Tynemouth was represented by Dame Irene Ward, who became known as the 'Mother of the House of Commons' (she first entered Parliament in 1931). Now it is held by Tory MP Neville Trotter, who stands on the right of his party, by over 7,500 voters. Why is Tynemouth so favourable to a party which has always lagged far behind in the industrial North East?

Tynemouth does have its share of heavy industry and Labour supporters. Squeezed into the SE corner of the old Northumberland county, in the angle of the River Tyne and the North Sea, it is a split constituency. Along the river bank can be found the furthest downstream of the shipyards and docks of the Tyne, and council estates behind them – Chirton, Collingwood, North Shields. This is the Labour section of the seat. But as one turns the corner at the mouth of the Tyne, one enters a different kind of country – the seaside resorts and middle-class residential areas on the rocky North Sea coast – Tynemouth, Cullercoats, Whitley Bay, Seaton Sluice. The owner-occupied estates behind Whitley Bay, around Monkseaton, bare and treeless as they are, house many Conservative commuters to Newcastle.

Tynemouth is little altered in the redistribution, and with the Alliance apparently making some inroads into the Labour wards on the Tyne, it should remain safe for Neville Trotter at the next Election. Indeed, if there is a general swing to Labour, it may well prove to be the only Conservative seat in Tyne and Wear at the next Election, and indeed in the whole of the urban North East.

1981	% Own Occ	58	1979 core seat Tynemouth		
1981	% Loc Auth	27	C	29,941	51.6
1981	% Black/Asian	0.5	Lab	22,377	38.5
1981	% Mid Cl	56	L	5,736	9.9
1981	% Prof Man	19	MPs since 1945		
1982	electorate 75,973		1945-50 G.M. Colman Lab		
1979	notional result		1950-74 Irene Ward C		
	C 7,700		1974- Neville Trotter C		
Alliance		L			

Wallsend   North Tyneside

Wallsend used to be a very large and a very disparate division. At the 1979 Election it possessed over 90,000 electors. Nearly 40,000 of them voted for the sitting Labour MP, Ted Garrett, but a substantial minority of over 20,000 preferred the Conservative candidate. Many of these came from the middle-class North Newcastle suburb of Gosforth, whose respectable roads harbour many of Tyneside's more affluent commuters, and the British headquarters of the multinational Procter and Gamble corporation. Gosforth always seemed an unlikely place to be associated with Labour Wallsend, and now it has been removed to be incorporated in Newcastle City constituencies.

Wallsend does reach the Tyne east of Newcastle, around the spot fixed as the eastern extremity of Hadrian's Wall (hence the name). But most of the population of the seat is far from the river, concentrated in mining villages, new private estates, and large council developments. The best known of the latter is the grim fort-like redoubt known as Killingworth Township, perhaps the most stark and dramatic of all the North-Eastern housing redevelopments created by post-war reconstruction. There are still active mines in villages like Backworth and Dudley, and like much of the constituency these retain a great loyalty to the Labour Party. But there are also ex-colliery villages where private housing is burgeoning - at Wideopen and Seaton Burn on the A1, and elsewhere.

Gosforth's departure will make Wallsend a smaller, more compact but more solidly Labour seat. There will still be a significant Conservative vote, but with a council housing majority there is no doubt that Ted Garrett will be the victor next time. The Alliance has not yet made any kind of breakthrough here.

1981	% Own Occ	30	1979 core seat Wallsend		
1981	% Loc Auth	55	Lab	38,214	55.1
1981	% Black/Asian	0.5	C	21,695	31.3
1981	% Mid Cl	41	L	8,514	12.3
1981	% Prof Man	9	MPs since 1945		
1982	electorate 77,363		1945-64 J. McKay Lab		
1979	notional result		1964- Ted Garrett Lab		
	Lab 22,200				
Alliance		SDP			

Jarrow   South Tyneside

The stereotype of the 1930s as a period of economic depression in Britain is now known to be an over-simplification. The decade also saw the greatest period of house-building in the history of Britain, and also the booming growth of new industries such as cars, chemicals and electricity, in towns like Oxford, Slough and Luton. But the pattern was very geographically varied, depending on the staple industry on which the local economy depended.

The south bank of the Tyne east of Newcastle achieved a kind of notoriety as the most depressed part of Britain in the inter-war slump. As a result of the collapse of the Tyne shipbuilding industry, the male unemployment rate in the town of Jarrow rose to 70%, which accounts for the famous 'hunger march' to London in 1934. The unemployment rate was even higher in the next town on the Tyne, Hebburn, and both Jarrow and Hebburn are still Labour strongholds. The unemployment rate on South Tyneside is now again up to 20%. Behind the battered river-front districts, large council developments like Jarrow's Primrose estate still turn in heavy Labour margins. The third town in the constituency is the more marginal Boldon. West Boldon is an old colliery village, but East Boldon/Cleadon is a residential area and the only Conservative ward.

A few thousand voters are picked up from South Shields to equalise the numbers in South Tyneside - this is mainly the modern Biddick Hall council estate, which should increase Don Dixon's Labour majority by a couple of thousand. As Britain enters a more generalised economic slump, with fewer bright spots on the horizon, Jarrow's name remains a poignant and relevant reminder of the inequality and suffering associated with the blight of unemployment.

1981	% Own Occ	32	1979 core seat Jarrow			
1981	% Loc Auth	65	Lab	24,057	55.8	
1981	% Black/Asian	0.5	C	12,259	29.1	
1981	% Mid Cl	40	L	3,907	9.1	
1981	% Prof Man	11	Ind Lab	2,247	5.2	
1982	electorate 64,660		WRP	374	0.9	
1979	notional result		MPs since 1945			
	Lab 15,200		1945-47 Ellen Wilinson Lab			
Alliance		L	1947-79 Ernest Fernyhough Lab			
			1979- Don Dixon Lab			

South Shields   South Tyneside

South Shields is many towns in one - a shipbuilding
metropolis at the mouth of the Tyne, an active coal mining
community, a holiday resort on the North Sea. Its politics are
similarly varied. The Conservatives do not contest local
elections, but their allies, known as Progressives, are very
competitive in municipal contests, particularly in middle-class
areas like Harton and Cleadon Park. But the industrial
section is politically dominant; the Tories run behind the
Progressives in national elections, and South Shields has been
safely Labour since 1935.

1981	% Own Occ	30	1979 core seat South Shields
1981	% Loc Auth	50	Lab 28,675 57.1
1981	% Black/Asian	0.5	C 15,551 31.0
1981	% Mid Cl	40	L 6,003 12.0
1981	% Prof Man	10	MPs since 1945
1982	electorate 62,843		1945-64 J.C. Ede Lab
1979	notional result		1964-79 Arthur Blenkinsop Lab
	Lab 9,400		1979- David Clark Lab
Alliance		SDP	

Houghton and Washington   Sunderland

The parts of the Metropolitan Borough of Sunderland,
formerly in Durham County, which lie outside the big
Wearside town itself are collected together in the new
Houghton and Washington division. The halves of the seat are
very different in character. Houghton-le-Spring is an old
mining district, incorporating colliery villages like Shiney
Row, Fence House and Hetton-le-Hole. Washington is a New
Town, designated in 1964, and now sprawling across its
windy hills west of Sunderland. But both halves have been
and remain solidly Labour, producing a majority between them
of around 20,000 in 1979.

1981	% Own Occ	35	1979 core seat Houghton-le-
1981	% Loc Auth	60	Spring
1981	% Black/Asian	0.5	Lab 30,181 68.5
1981	% Mid Cl	41	C 9,105 20.7
1981	% Prof Man	10	L 4,479 10.2
1982	electorate 74,526		WRP 326 0.7
1979	notional result		MPs since 1945
	Lab 20,600		1945-64 W.R. Blyton Lab
Alliance			1964- Tom Urwin Lab

Sunderland North   Sunderland

Wearside is one of the most depressed industrial areas in
Britain, with unemployment running at over 20%, and
particularly severe amongst the young. It is scarcely
surprising that both the Sunderland seats are safely Labour.
The North division does include Tory wards by the sea at
Fulwell and Roker, but these are outvoted by massive council
estates like Hylton Castle three or four miles inland, and by
the banks of the Wear, which offers one of the most stark
industrial scenes in Britain. Now North is to take in more
terrain south of the Wear, including part of the middle-class
Thornhill district, and it will be one of the largest seats
drawn by the Commission. The long-serving Labour MP, Fred
Willey, is retiring, and there may yet be trouble over the
nomination of the left-wing Rob Clay as his successor.

1981	% Own Occ	39	1979 core seat Sunderland North		
1981	% Loc Auth	51	Lab	29,213	57.5
1981	% Black/Asian	0.5	C	16,311	32.1
1981	% Mid Cl	41	L	5,238	10.3
1981	% Prof Man	10	MP since 1950		
1982	electorate 79,573		1950-	Fred Willey Lab	
1979	notional Lab 12,200				
Alliance					

Sunderland South   Sunderland

Sunderland is a great north-eastern Labour stronghold,
suffering from the decline of its staple industries of coal and
shipbuilding. But there was a time (1953-64) when the South
division was held by the Conservatives. It is true that there
is a substantial middle-class residential area here, south-west
of the town centre. But the NE has been swinging surely to
Labour for many years, and now the Tory bloc is to be
broken up by the Boundary Commissioners. South will be
every bit as safe as North for Labour now. Moderate MP
Gordon Bagier has been reselected as candidate.

1981	% Own Occ	40	1979 core seat Sunderland South		
1981	% Loc Auth	52	Lab	29,403	53.1
1981	% Black/Asian	0.5	C	21,002	37.9
1981	% Mid Cl	42	L	4,984	9.0
1981	% Prof Man	11	MPs since 1950		
1982	electorate 76,157		1950-53 R. Ewart Lab		
1979	notional Lab 9,100		1953-64 P.G. Williams C		
Alliance			1964-	Gordon Bagier Lab	

Barnsley Central   Barnsley

Surrounded by pits and slag heaps, Barnsley is one of those towns which are usually regarded as a stereotype of heavy industry and grimy Northern popular culture. This is the headquarters of the powerful Yorkshire NUM, for so long the seat of the 'court' of 'King' Arthur Scargill. In fact Barnsley is the centre of the older western coalfield in South Yorkshire - the most prosperous and largest modern pits are to be found further east, around Doncaster. Pit closure has even affected this part of South Yorkshire, even though this field has more coal reserves than most. But all around Barnsley, the debris of mining and other industry dominates a landscape which enjoys fewer redeeming features than most even of the working-class stereotypes. There really are no leafy suburbs, no Conservative wards here.

Barnsley's Labour MP is a very different figure from Arthur Scargill. Roy Mason is a staunch and tough right-wing front-bencher, himself a miner at the age of 14. He has held this seat since 1953. The only serious opposition has come from within his own party, and he has faced a long series of threats to his candidacy. But his electoral popularity is undeniable. His majority in 1979 was over 22,000, even in a year of Labour defeat. No Labour candidate has many worries in Barnsley - at local level there are very few Conservative candidates, the burden of opposition being taken by Ratepayers. The Alliance has no tradition here and little appeal.

In the redistribution, Barnsley Metropolitan Borough is lucky to be granted three MPs. Barnsley Central is really the core of the old Barnsley division, less three wards - Darton, Park and Worsborough. It takes Royston from Wakefield. Though numerical majorities will be smaller, a Labour victory will be just as certain as before, here amongst the miners' cottages, council estates and colliery communities of this scarred townscape.

1981	% Own Occ	47.2	1979 core seat Barnsley		
1981	% Loc Auth	45.3	Lab	36,276	64.0
1981	% Black/Asian	0.5	C	13,654	24.1
1981	% Mid Cl	33.6	L	5,751	10.1
1981	% Prof Man	9.3	Oth	986	1.7
1982	electorate 55,515		MPs since 1945		
1979	notional result		1945-51 F. Collindridge Lab		
	Lab 12,200		1951-53 S. Schofield Lab		
Alliance		L	1953- Roy Mason Lab		

Barnsley East   Barnsley

When the new Metropolitan Counties of West and South
Yorkshire were created, the mighty Labour mining stronghold
of Hemsworth was split in two. Hemsworth itself is in W
Yorkshire, and it takes its electorally famous name with it.
But half of the population of the old Hemsworth forms the
basis of the new Barnsley East - Cudworth, Thurnscoe,
Goldthorpe, Bolton upon Dearne. With Wombwell and Darfield
from the abolished Dearne Valley division, this creates a
compact ultra-solid Labour constituency of small mining towns
in the heart of the S Yorkshire coalfield - in all probability
one of the ten safest Labour seats in Britain.

1981	% Own Occ	42.6	New seat
1981	% Loc Auth	44.2	
1981	% Black/Asian	0.5	
1981	% Mid Cl	29.2	
1981	% Prof Man	8.6	
1982	electorate 54,241		
1979	notional result		
	Lab 18,600		
Alliance		L	

Barnsley West and Penistone   Barnsley

Half of the old Penistone seat has been transferred to the
City of Sheffield, and its Hillsborough division. The
remainder rolls down from sheep-farming Pennine moorland at
the north end of the Peak District, through the small towns
of Penistone, Dodworth and Hoyland to the outskirts of
Barnsley. As it does so, it becomes progressively more
dominated by mining and by Labour. Now it takes the towns
of Darton and Worsborough and the ward of Park from the old
Barnsley seat. There is a Tory presence in Penistone itself,
but with the departure of the Liberal-inclined parts of the old
Penistone this seat will be safer for Labour than before.

1981	% Own Occ	50.2	1979 core seat Penistone
1981	% Loc Auth	41.0	Lab 28,010 49.1
1981	% Black/Asian	0.5	C 18,309 32.1
1981	% Mid Cl	38.0	L 10,772 18.9
1981	% Prof Man	12.8	MPs since 1945
1982	electorate 60,939		1945-59 H.G. McGhee Lab
1979	notional result		1959-78 John Mendelson Lab
	Lab 14,300		1978- Allen McKay Lab
Alliance		SDP	

Doncaster Central   Doncaster

The 'Socialist Republic of South Yorkshire' has not always been as monolithically Labour as it is now. From 1951 to 1964 the Doncaster constituency was held by Conservative Anthony Barber, a future Chancellor of the Exchequer. Even in 1970 and 1979 his successor Harold Walker had a Labour majority of only 3,000. Doncaster is surrounded by one of the most modern and productive coalfields in Britain, but it is itself a mixed town of many industries. What is more, it possesses several middle-class residential areas of firm Tory persuasion, most notably in SE Doncaster, beyond the racecourse. For much of the post-war period it has been a marginal seat.

But the latest redistribution should finally put paid to any remaining Conservative hopes. The best Tory ward, South East, is moved out into the Don Valley seat, where it will be swamped by colliery communities. There are still Conservative wards such as Town Field and Bessacarr, but SE has effectively been replaced by Armthorpe, a mining village east of the town. Armthorpe is heavily Labour, and the consequence of this relatively minor exchange should be to raise Harold Walker's majority by at least 4,000.

The Conservatives must count themselves a little unfortunate. SE was a ward remote from the town centre, but very much part of Doncaster - its most favoured wooded residential area. Armthorpe has always had a separate identity, as the colliery village for a massive 1920s coal mine, one of the last to be developed in South Yorkshire. Unusually, this is an example of Labour doing very well out of the present boundary changes.

1981	% Own Occ	52.6	1979 core seat Doncaster	
1981	% Loc Auth	36.8	Lab	22,184	48.9
1981	% Black/Asian	2	C	19,208	42.4
1981	% Mid Cl	40.6	L	3,646	8.0
1981	% Prof Man	12.5	NF	300	0.7
1982	electorate 71,261		MPs since 1945	
1979	national result		1945-50 E. Walkden Lab	
	Lab 7,000 (RW)		1950-51 Ray Gunter Lab	
Alliance		SDP	1951-64 Anthony Barber C	
			1964- Harold Walker Lab	

Doncaster North   Doncaster

The new Doncaster North will be a coal-mining constituency,
set on the flat plain of the Don north and NE of Doncaster.
From the old massive Don Valley seat come the large colliery
villages of Bentley, Adwick-le-Street and Askern. From Goole
(now split between four different counties), comes the most
modern mining area - Thorne, Stainforth and Hatfield, low-
lying amongst the dykes, where the elevation reads
remorselessly in single figures. Only man-made excrescences
break the monotony of the featureless landscape. There are
some Conservative owner-occupiers in Stainforth and Hatfield,
but this will be a relentless Labour stronghold.

1981	% Own Occ	49.6	New seat
1981	% Loc Auth	39.0	
1981	% Black/Asian	0.5	
1981	% Mid Cl	32.2	
1981	% Prof Man	9.8	
1982	electorate 72,403		
1979	notional Lab 16,500		
Alliance		SDP	

Don Valley   Doncaster

The present Don Valley seat completely surrounds Doncaster,
a necklace of colliery villages which produce a massive
majority for Labour. The new seat of the same name still
curls around the south side of Doncaster in a kidney shape,
but its character is somewhat changed. It includes SE, the
best Tory ward in Doncaster itself. There are Conservative
votes too in isolated non-mining country towns in this large
division, at Bawtry, Tickhill and in the villages around
Hooton Pagnell and Hickleton. These should still be outvoted
by the mining villages of Rossington and New Edlington, and
the ex-Dearne Valley towns of Conisbrough and Mexborough -
but this will be a much closer contest than before.

1981	% Own Occ	56.3	1979 core seat Don Valley		
1981	% Loc Auth	34.7	Lab	39,603	55.6
1981	% Black/Asian	0.5	C	22,243	31.2
1981	% Mid Cl	41.3	L	8,228	11.6
1981	% Prof Man	13.7	Oth	1,118	1.6
1982	electorate 73,739		MPs since 1945		
1979	notional Lab 13,400		1945-59 T. Williams Lab		
Alliance		L	1959-79 Richard Kelley Lab		
			1979- Michael Welsh Lab		

Rotherham   Rotherham

Like Sheffield, Doncaster and Barnsley, the Metropolitan
Borough of Rotherham is a Labour stronghold in South
Yorkshire. As in Barnsley, the Conservatives find it very
difficult to win a single seat on the Rotherham council, and
there is no doubt that the three constituencies ascribed to
the Borough by the Boundary Commission will all be safe for
the Labour Party. This is the land of heavy industry, where
coal and steel are both major sources of employment, and the
gritty landscape and sprawling communities bear the impress
of function rather than beauty or elegance.

Rotherham itself is ringed by coal mines, but its most famous
and dramatic industrial scene is certainly provided by the
great British Steel works along the road SW to Sheffield
beside the River Don. Rotherham has been a Labour seat
since a byelection in 1933 ended an anomalous two-year period
of Conservative representation. There is a pleasant middle-
class residential area in SE Rotherham, which provides some
Tory votes, but more typical are the council estates and
terraces of districts like Kimberworth, Greasbrough and
Thorpe Hesley.

Rotherham is little changed in the redistribution, and it
should continue to provide a safe platform and an appreciative
audience for the town's singing MP, Stan Crowther. This is
not good Alliance country, and the Liberals, who have won
the nomination for Rotherham in the carve-up of seats, will
be lucky to save their deposit, lost last time.

1981	% Own Occ	40.7	1979 core seat Rotherham		
1981	% Loc Auth	53.7	Lab	26,580	60.5
1981	% Black/Asian	2	C	13,145	29.9
1981	% Mid Cl	41.2	L	3,686	8.4
1981	% Prof Man	11.9	NF	490	1.1
1982	electorate 61,709		MPs since 1945		
1979	notional result		1945-50 W. Dobbie Lab		
	Lab 13,300		1950-63 J.H. Jones Lab		
Alliance		L	1963-76 Brian O'Malley Lab		
			1976- Stan Crowther Lab		

171

Rother Valley   Rotherham

Rather as Don Valley surrounds Doncaster, the former Rother Valley seat wrapped itself around Rotherham like a red blanket. For this constituency returned the third largest Labour majority in 1979 (26,002), and the largest Labour vote (45,986). This was partly due to its extreme size (99,000 electors). But this will be modified at the next Election, as the 40,000 who live north of Rotherham are transferred into the new Wentworth seat. Peter Hardy's majority will be reduced, but not the safeness of the seat. Rother Valley will still be composed of little colliery communities like Maltby, Kiveton Park and Thurcroft. They offer rich seams of Labour support, with no sign as yet of exhaustion or decay.

1981	% Own Occ	55.1	1979 core seat Rother Valley
1981	% Loc Auth	34.1	Lab 45,986 62.2
1981	% Black/Asian	1	C 19,984 27.0
1981	% Mid Cl	41.7	L 7,937 10.7
1981	% Prof Man	13.0	MPs since 1945
1982	electorate 65,183		1945-70 D. Griffiths Lab
1979	notional Lab 14,900		1970- Peter Hardy Lab
Alliance	SDP		

Wentworth   Rotherham

The industrial region north of Rotherham is again to be known as Wentworth, after the country house which is now an adult education centre. There was a Wentworth seat before 1950, which gave Labour a majority of over 17,000 even in their black year of 1931. The new seat includes electors from towns and villages like Rawmarsh and Wickersley, formerly in Rother Valley; and Swinton and Wath from the old Dearne Valley seat. Coal production dominates the economy, and this seat will be amongst the ten in Britain employing most miners. It will also be a Labour stronghold of formidable proportions; they would probably have piled up a majority of around 18,000 in this rather small seat even in 1979.

1981	% Own Occ	41.7	New seat
1981	% Loc Auth	49.8	
1981	% Black/Asian	1	
1981	% Mid Cl	36.0	
1981	% Prof Man	10.3	
1982	electorate 62,444		
1979	notional Lab 18,700		
Alliance	SDP		

Sheffield Attercliffe   Sheffield

The east side of Sheffield offers one of the most stark and
dramatic industrial vistas in Britain. Heavy industry and
steelworks pack the valley of the Don as it flows not so
quietly towards Rotherham, dominating the scene by day and
night, as the great blast furnaces burn. The British Steel
works at Tinsley cross the border into Rotherham. High-
density housing sprawls and climbs over Sheffield's many
hills. It is easy to see why Sheffield has been the most loyal
of England's major cities to the Labour Party since 1918.
Attercliffe is south-east Sheffield, resolutely working class
and one of the city's three super-safe Labour seats. A higher
proportion of the housing here is owner-occupied, often old
terraced streets, than in Sheffield's other Labour citadels.
However, as in the whole of Sheffield, the proportion of non-
whites is relatively low for an industrial metropolis.
All the wards are solidly Labour - Birley, Darnall,
Mosborough and Handsworth. Attercliffe is little altered in the
boundary changes, and will surely remain safe for Dr Patrick
Duffy, who has been the Labour MP since 1970.

1981	% Own Occ	43.4	1979 core seat Sheffield		
1981	% Loc Auth	50.4	Attercliffe		
1981	% Black/Asian	4	Lab	29,702	64.9
1981	% Mid Cl	39.4	C	11,599	25.3
1981	% Prof Man	9.6	L	4,017	8.8
1982	electorate 63,644		NF	457	1.0
1979	notional result		MPs since 1945		
	Lab 16,200		1945-70 John Hynd Lab		
Alliance		SDP	1970- Patrick Duffy Lab		

Sheffield Brightside   Sheffield

Brightside, north-east Sheffield, is the steel city's peripheral council estate constituency. Over two-thirds of the housing is owned by the local authority, and only 4% of the population falls into the professional and managerial class category. Unemployment is very high; it had already reached a level of 17% at the time of the 1981 census. Brightside is a seat of multiple social deprivation.

Most of the constituency - Firth Park and Southey Green, Parsons Cross and Shiregreen - was constructed in the inter-war years, and consists of semi-detached council houses very unlike the massive tower blocks found in the centre of the city. In the redistribution Brightside gains Owlerton, an older working-class neighbourhood north of the city centre, from Hillsborough.

Brightside will remain one of the safest Labour seats in Britain. It will be retained by Joan Maynard, hard-line left-winger who (ironically for this most industrial of cities) has been a doughty fighter for agricultural workers all her life.

1981	% Own Occ	25.2	1979 core seat Sheffield		
1981	% Loc Auth	69.9	Brightside		
1981	% Black/Asian	2	Lab	25,672	68.5
1981	% Mid Cl	30.5	C	7,979	21.3
1981	% Prof Man	7.1	L	3,482	9.3
1982	electorate 68,122		NF	354	0.9
1979	notional result		MPs since 1945		
	Lab 20,600		1945-50 F. Marshall Lab		
Alliance		L	1950-68 R.E. Winterbottom Lab		
			1968-74 Eddie Griffiths Lab		
			1974- Joan Maynard Lab		

Sheffield Central   Sheffield

Sheffield was heavily bombed in the war, and due to this and slum clearance programmes the face of the central city has been transformed by the massive new developments of commerce and working-class accommodation. Often these rise above the city in soaring towers, on occasion enjoying greater architectural originality and interest than most, and made more impressive by the hilly setting of this switchback city. Hyde Park, a great wall of flats within a few hundred yards of Park Square itself, is a good example. The central Sheffield seat, formerly called Park, is of course an ultra-safe Labour seat, awarding Fred Mulley a majority of over 20,000, and of over 50% of the votes cast, in 1979.

Fred Mulley is a former Cabinet Minister, Defence Secretary in James Callaghan's government. But he failed to be reselected for Park constituency in 1982, being replaced as prospective Labour candidate by the more left-wing Sheffield Euro-MP Dick Caborn. Park has to be renamed as a result of the boundary changes, for the Park ward itself has been moved into Heeley. Netherthorpe has been added from Hillsborough, and Burngreave ward has expanded to take in part of Attercliffe. Much of the new Central will consist of high-rise buildings or council house estates like Castle/Manor SE of the centre, but there are also older terraces in places like Sharrow which afford homes for Sheffield's small immigrant population. Despite its poverty, Sheffield has fewer inner-city problems and fewer racial tensions than most large British conurbations.

Sheffield is a gritty northern city with as strong an industrial and working-class character as any in England. It has not reacted favourably to Mrs Thatcher's government. It was one of the few places where Labour did better in 1982 than 1979, and despite the Liberals' local activism in Burngreave ward here, their candidate Francis Butler seems unable to make any kind of breakthrough in parliamentary elections - he lost his deposit in Park in 1979. The SDP have gained the Alliance candidature here now, but seems just as unlikely to break the Labour stronghold.

1981	% Own Occ	24.1	1979 core seat Sheffield Park			
1981	% Loc Auth	63.7	Lab	27,483	68.6	
1981	% Black/Asian	7	C	7,159	17.9	
1981	% Mid Cl	30.3	L	4,737	11.8	
1981	% Prof Man	7.1	NF	302	0.8	
1982	electorate 67,756		Comm	279	0.7	
1979	notional result		WRP	111	0.3	
	Lab 20,700		MP since 1950			
Alliance		SDP	1950-	Frank Mulley Lab		

Sheffield Hallam   Sheffield

Many people regard Sheffield as the archetype of an industrial and working-class city. Such an impression is encouraged by the most common travellers' view of Sheffield, from the M1 as it passes the mighty steelworks of Rotherham and the east end of Sheffield. However, as in the case of many British towns, there is a sharp divide between the west end of Sheffield, upwind of industry, dirt and smoke, and the classic east end areas. In Sheffield, the middle-class residential area which serves England's third largest city is situated almost entirely within the city boundaries. This creates the possibility of a safe Conservative seat within the 'Socialist Republic of South Yorkshire'; indeed, Sheffield Hallam is the only Tory seat in Sheffield and in the whole county.

SW Sheffield, from the bohemian University area of Broomhill through Ecclesall and Fulwood out to the fringe of the Peak District at Dore and Totley, is a leafy neighbourhood of outstanding residential quality. There are many dark-stone mansions standing solidly among the wooded hills, and only some of them are now broken up into flats and bed-sits. Further out can be found modern semis and detached houses in great numbers, as Sheffield's professional and managerial groupings gather together in as concentrated a pattern of residential segregation as may be found in Britain. Hallam loses about 7,000 voters from the inner section of the constituency in the boundary changes.

Hallam has provided a safe haven for Tory John Osborn since 1959. Little altered in the present review, it remains as safe a Conservative seat as any in the urban North of England.

1981	% Own Occ	72.7
1981	% Loc Auth	12.8
1981	% Black/Asian	3
1981	% Mid Cl	71.2
1981	% Prof Man	29.4
1982	electorate 73,572	
1979	notional result	
	C 18,500	
Alliance		L

1979 core seat Sheffield Hallam

C	31,436	54.9
Lab	16,502	28.8
L	8,982	15.7
NF	300	0.5

MPs since 1945
1945-59 Sir R. Jennings C
1959-   John Osborn C

Sheffield Heeley   Sheffield

Sheffield has one of the most progressive and successful local
authorities in the country. It provides a cheap and efficient
public transport, and has an enviable record of social
services. But despite this municipal radicalism it has not
seriously fallen out with the Conservative government, as
have Labour councils in London and Lothian, for example.
What is more, it remains popular with the Sheffield electorate,
securing a positive swing in the 1982 local elections, when
high-spending authorities like Walsall and Lothian were lost to
Labour's grasp. Now one of the Sheffield City Council
leaders, Bill Michie, has achieved national press coverage
through his selection as candidate for the Heeley division in
place of sitting MP Frank Hooley. It will be interesting to see
if Michie can achieve as much in national politics as in local
affairs.

Heeley is south Sheffield. In the past it has been the one
Sheffield seat which changed hands with the political tide,
and could be regarded as a Con-Lab marginal. But its
boundaries were altered in Labour's favour in the early 1970s,
and will be again in the early 1980s. The ultra-Labour inner
city ward of Park is picked up as the Heeley electorate is
increased from 64,000 to over 75,000. Much of the southern
edge of Sheffield is composed of newish council estates, like
those in the spectacular Gleadless Valley where tower blocks
climb up the steep sides of the hills. But there is one strong
Conservative area over in the SW, towards Hallam
constituency, in Beauchief ward.

The Boundary Commission's original proposals for Sheffield
split the middle-class bloc of SW Sheffield into two parts, one
in Hallam and one in Heeley. This would have given the
Conservatives a good chance of winning both. But after an
inquiry, Heeley was redrawn as a safe Labour seat, and it
seems as if there will be no Conservative versus Labour
marginal contest in Sheffield in the foreseeable future.

1981	% Own Occ	40.4	1979 core seat Sheffield Heeley		
1981	% Loc Auth	53.5	Lab	24,618	49.8
1981	% Black/Asian	1	C	19,845	40.1
1981	% Mid Cl	41.6	L	4,708	9.5
1981	% Prof Man	11.0	NF	274	0.5
1982	electorate 75,362		MPs since 1950		
1979	notional result		1950-66 Sir P.G. Roberts C		
	Lab 12,700		1966-70 Frank Hooley Lab		
Alliance		SDP	1970-74 John Spence C		
			1974- Frank Hooley Lab		

Sheffield Hillsborough   Sheffield

The old constituency of Hillsborough, in NW Sheffield, was a safe Labour seat. But the expansion of Sheffield City boundaries in the early 1970s seems likely to turn Hillsborough into one of the very few Liberal-Labour marginals, at least according to local election results. The new additions - a mixture of modern private and council housing - usually elect Liberals at all levels from Parish Councils to County Council. But they were previously in Penistone constituency, where the Liberals failed to make any great impact in parliamentary elections.

This would seem to make Labour the favourites to win the new Hillsborough, even though their best wards, Netherthorpe and Owlerton, have been removed in the redistribution - these were the districts nearest to the city centre. The wards which remain from the old division are Walkley and Hillsborough, which are typified by terraced owner-occupied housing of middling status - skilled working class or lower middle class. The Liberals lost their deposit in the old Hillsborough seat at the 1979 General Election. The Conservatives have some support in Hillsborough ward itself, but are not in a position to challenge for victory in this seat. They may beat the Liberals into second place, for another disappointment for the Alliance at parliamentary level may well be in the offing here.

Hillsborough is the most detached of the Sheffield seats from the city itself. Half of it was not included within the city boundaries until ten years ago, or a city seat till now. The other half is based on a busy community in Hillsborough itself, with its famous Sheffield Wednesday Football Club as but one example of independence. Nevertheless the present MP, former headmaster Martin Flannery, should be returned to join the growing and tightly-knit battery of Sheffield left-wing Labour activist MPs.

1981	% Own Occ	60.4	1979 core seat Sheffield
1981	% Loc Auth	30.6	Hillsborough
1981	% Black/Asian	1	Lab 20,556 56.8
1981	% Mid Cl	48.0	C 12,206 33.7
1981	% Prof Man	12.9	L 3,088 8.5
1982	electorate 75,062		NF 326 0.9
1979	notional result		MPs since 1945
	Lab 9,600		1945-50 A.V. Alexander Lab
Alliance		L	1950-74 George Darling Lab
			1974- Martin Flannery Lab

Bradford North   Bradford

Bradford North is one of the constituencies which has reached
the news headlines through the deselection of its sitting
Labour MP, Ben Ford, and his replacement by a far-left
activist, Militant supporter Pat Wall. Like all the seats in
Bradford itself, it has not been significantly altered in the
redistribution, since it was already of the right size. The
only disruption to its electoral future is likely to be caused
by the quarrels within the Labour Party.

Despite its name, Bradford North is in fact a kidney-shaped
seat nestling around the eastern side of the city: the Bowling
ward is actually south of the centre. Bowling also happens to
be a Labour stronghold, like Bradford Moor. The Liberals
have managed to win the Idle ward for several years, and the
Conservatives do best in Bolton ward. Eccleshill and
Undercliffe are marginally Labour. North used to be the best
Labour bet in Bradford. It does not have many council
estates, but a considerable quantity of old private housing,
ranging from near-slum terraces to substantial Victorian
houses at the north end of the city. There is a substantial
Asian population in the inner part of the seat; Bradford has
become known as one of the chief recipient areas of
immigrants from the Indian sub-continent and from East
Africa.

The Alliance won 27.4% of the vote in the wards composing
this seat in the 1982 local elections. There is a clear
possibility that the arguments in the Labour Party could lead
to an Alliance gain, although Pat Wall is an eloquent and
experienced campaigner of notable personal presence.
Bradford North should provide one of the most interesting
contests in the next election, with the ideological battle within
the Labour Party being fought out in a fairly typical northern
working-class seat little changed by the Boundary
Commission.

1981	% Own Occ	62.1	1979 core seat Bradford North		
1981	% Loc Auth	29.8	Lab	25,069	50.9
1981	% Black/Asian	12	C	17,548	35.7
1981	% Mid Cl	40.5	L	5,819	11.8
1981	% Prof Man	10.7	NF	614	1.2
1982	electorate 66,841		WRP	158	0.3
1979	notional result		MPs since 1945		
	Lab 7,600		1945-50 Mrs M.E. Nichol Lab		
Alliance		SDP	1950-64 W.J. Taylor C		
			1964-	Ben Ford Lab	

Bradford South   Bradford

If one consults the 1979 General Election results, Bradford
South appears to be the least safe of the three Labour seats
in the city. The majority was only 4,318 in a large seat. Yet
Labour probably has a better chance of winning it next time
than either of the other two. This is only partly because of
the slight boundary changes which have removed marginally
Conservative Clayton and Shelf. More importantly, South has
avoided the internecine strife which has affected North and
West Labour parties, and its Tribune MP Tom Torney should
survive to contest and win his constituency again.
    South is the Bradford seat with the fewest Asian voters and
the most council housing. These indicators are connected, for
few immigrants from the New Commonwealth have found their
way into council estates in Britain. Here in Bradford South
are the inter-war estate of Buttershaw, in the south-west of
the city, and the more modern developments of Tong ward in
the south-east. The best ward for the Tories is Queensbury,
outside the old Bradford city limits, but long included in a
Bradford seat. The wards of Great Horton, Odsal, Wibsey and
Wyke are all fairly marginal.
    However, the Conservatives did not achieve a majority of
votes in these wards in 1982, although this was a very good
year for them in West Yorkshire. The Alliance also polled
disappointingly - only 25%, their weakest performance in the
city. South was the only constituency where the Alliance
didn't win a council seat in 1982. Bradford looks like it could
well become a three-way marginal city. But it is a sign of the
volatility of politics that the most marginal seat in 1979 should
look the least marginal now.

1981	% Own Occ	70.3	1979 core seat Bradford South		
1981	% Loc Auth	22.1	Lab	26,323	47.1
1981	% Black/Asian	1	C	22,005	39.4
1981	% Mid Cl	44.6	L	7,127	12.8
1981	% Prof Man	12.6	NF	422	0.8
1982	electorate 70,072		MPs since 1945		
1979	notional result		1945-70 George Craddock Lab		
	Lab 5,000		1970- Tom Torney Lab		
Alliance		SDP			

Bradford West   Bradford

Bradford West is a constituency of complexity and even contradictions. It contains much of the heavy Asian population of inner-city Bradford, but also western communities like Clayton and Thornton which are almost outside the built-up area of the city. It includes some of the poorest parts of Bradford, but also the best residential areas. It provided the biggest of the rare swings to Labour at the 1979 General Election. And although its MP Edward Lyons has defected from Labour to the SDP, it was the Conservative Party which achieved the most votes here in the 1982 local elections.

West includes Manningham, one of the neighbourhoods most associated by many people with Asian immigration to Britain. Probably one of the main reasons for Labour's abnormally good result in 1979 was their successful mobilisation of the Asian vote. Manningham was once the fashionable west end of the city, but its wool merchants' mansions are now often faded, often multi-occupied. The University ward is an area of multiple social deprivation and squalor. Yet West also includes the leafy middle-class Heaton, and the comfortable expanded villages to the west of the city. It is little altered by the Boundary Commission, although Clayton is taken from the South division.

Edward Lyons may have a better chance of retaining his seat than most SDP converts. The Alliance won 28.3% of the votes here in 1982, only 7% behind Labour and 8% behind the Conservatives, and Lyons may well be able to claim a personal vote over and above that. However, Labour and the SDP may well split the Asian and left-of-centre vote to let in the Tories, who have a solid base in Heaton and on the edge of the city. Bradford West looks like a three-way marginal, and as close and bitter a battle as any in the country at the next Election.

1981	% Own Occ	61.2	1979 core seat Bradford West		
1981	% Loc Auth	27.2	Lab	24,309	53.8
1981	% Black/Asian	28	C	16,554	36.7
1981	% Mid Cl	41.9	L	3,668	8.1
1981	% Prof Man	12.4	NF	633	1.4
1982	electorate 71,847		MP since 1974		
1979	notional result		1974-	Edward Lyons Lab	
	Lab 7,900			(SDP)	
Alliance		SDP			

Keighley   Bradford

In the 1979 General Election, Labour's Bob Cryer held Keighley by only 78 votes. Cryer is a left-wing activist, involved in many causes and often associated in the Commons with Dennis Skinner because of his vocal criticism of the Thatcher government. However, his chances of retaining this most marginal of seats have become considerably more dubious now that the Boundary Commission has added Ilkley to the constituency.

Ilkley is an ultra-Conservative residential spa town from the old Ripon seat, where Labour have finished a poor third for many years. Labour did not contest Ilkley ward in the 1979 local elections, and only managed 9% of the vote there in 1982. Labour's strength lies in the woollen textile town of Keighley itself, particularly in the South and West wards. Keighley is not big enough for a seat of its own, though, and the small towns among the moors which make up the balance of the seat are all Conservative - Ilkley, Silsden and the Brontёs' Haworth. The old Keighley was too small, at 54,000 electors; but even a slight alteration has tipped the scales in this division to the Conservative side.

Cryer's struggle to win Keighley against the odds will be one of the most watchable contests of the next election. But another factor has to be taken into account: the Alliance. In the 1982 local elections, the Alliance won the Craven ward, based on Silsden, and polled 31% of the vote in the new Keighley as a whole, compared to the Conservatives' 40% and Labour's 29%. In a good year, the Alliance could make a breakthrough here; and Cryer cannot be happy with the threat of a Labour third place, faced with defeat at the hands of the twin evils of Right and Centre.

1981	% Own Occ	74.8	1979 core seat	Keighley	
1981	% Loc Auth	16.2	Lab	19,698	45.0
1981	% Black/Asian	3	C	19,620	44.8
1981	% Mid Cl	46.1	L	4,062	9.3
1981	% Prof Man	17.3	NF	234	0.5
1982	electorate 63,911		E	208	0.5
1979	notional result		MPs since 1945		
	C 2,400		1945-50 I. Thomas Lab		
Alliance		L	1950-59 C.R. Hobson Lab		
			1959-64 W.M.J. Worsley C		
			1964-70 John Binns Lab		
			1970-74 Joan Hall C		
			1974- Bob Cryer Lab		

Shipley   Bradford

In 1979, Shipley was the only Conservative parliamentary constituency in the Bradford Metropolitan Borough. It has not been won by Labour since 1945, and it has been consistently shifting to the Conservatives for over 50 years - Labour won it several times between the wars. Now a further boost has been administered to the Tory vote by the Boundary Commissioners, while Labour slipped into third place here in the May 1982 local elections.

The seat used simply to consist of the towns of Shipley, Bingley and Baildon. Now it is extended to the north and the south - north to take in Menston and Burley in Wharfedale across Ilkley Moor, and south to take Denholme, Cullingworth and Wilsden from Keighley. All these small communities are highly Conservative, and their inclusion would have boosted the Tory majority of 8,000 in 1979 to around 12,000. Bingley and the western half of Shipley were always Conservative. Baildon has often voted Liberal in municipal elections, but the Liberals never did as well as in neighbouring Pudsey in General Elections. The only Labour strength comes from Shipley East ward, which stretches from Titus Salt's planned nineteenth century industrial village of Saltaire through Shipley town centre to the old Bradford city boundary.

The Alliance polled 29% in 1982 to take second place to the Conservatives, but this was more due to Labour's disastrous showing (22%) than to any deep potential of their own. This seems a safe seat for the sitting MP Marcus Fox, who is a highly placed figure in the organisation of the party. Shipley has been becoming steadily more middle class and owner occupied throughout the twentieth century, as the woollen industry has declined in importance, and as commuters have moved into the smaller towns of West Yorkshire.

1981	% Own Occ	70.3	1979 core seat Shipley		
1981	% Loc Auth	23.2	C	22,641	52.6
1981	% Black/Asian	0.5	Lab	14,281	33.1
1981	% Mid Cl	58.0	L	5,673	13.2
1981	% Prof Man	21.5	E	486	1.1
1982	electorate 68,025		MPs since 1945		
1979	notional result		1945-50 A.C. Jones Lab		
	C 11,500		1950-70 G.A.N. Hirst C		
Alliance		L	1970- Marcus Fox C		

Calder Valley   Calderdale

As the fast-moving streams rush down the eastern slope of the Pennines into Yorkshire, they forge a landscape of valleys which were transformed in the earliest days of the Industrial Revolution. The damp climate and the easy water-power made this rugged district suitable for the manufacture of woollen textiles, and little industrial communities hug the valley bottoms and the steep-sided hills. This new constituency follows the river Calder and its tributaries as it winds south of Halifax, from the topmost town of Todmorden amongst the moors, as far as Brighouse.

Calder Valley would have been Conservative in 1979, even more so in fact than its core seats of Sowerby and Brighouse/Spenborough, which are very marginal. It consists of Sowerby minus Sowerby Bridge itself (the most Labour area), plus Brighouse and Rastrick, which are Conservative. More Tory still are the precipitous and dramatic Hebden Bridge and the smaller towns and villages along the Calder and Ryburn, its southern tributary passing through Ripponden. Todmorden, which suffers from high unemployment, is a three-way marginal, and Labour and Liberals battle it out in Elland. This is good Liberal country, at least in local elections - Richard Wainwright's nearby Colne Valley seat is of a very similar nature - but the Liberals have never managed to do as well in parliamentary elections in Sowerby. In the 1982 local elections the Tories managed to stave off an Alliance assault by just 66 votes, if the wards that make up Calder Valley are aggregated. But the Conservative Party must remain the favourites in a three-way marginal.

Why are working-class Pennine seats like Calder Valley so Conservative? Perhaps it is partly the result of the fact that the textiles industry has many female workers and little tradition of highly organised, militant trade unionism. But also it should be noted that there is a tradition of owner-occupation, and relatively few council houses among the neat stone terraces. Finally there is now a scattering of commuters who prefer living in these small valley communities amongst the hills to the grime and bustle of the northern cities.

1981	% Own Occ	69.0	1979 core seat Sowerby		
1981	% Loc Auth	21.6	C	16,797	42.2
1981	% Black/Asian	1	Lab	15,617	39.3
1981	% Mid Cl	45.5	L	7,565	13.9
1981	% Prof Man	17.0	NF	518	1.0
1982	electorate 72,064		MPs since 1950		
1979	notional result		1950-74 Douglas Houghton Lab		
	C 1,300		1974-79 Max Madden Lab		
Alliance		L	1979- Donald Thompson C		

Halifax   Calderdale

Halifax is one of the northern marginals that Labour did well to hold in the 1979 General Election: Shirley Summerskill restricted the pro-Conservative swing to 3%, and crept in again by 1,234 votes. But this has been a close seat for over thirty years, and the Conservative Maurice Macmillan, son of Harold, held it between 1955 and 1964. Shirley Summerskill's chances are slightly improved by the Boundary Commission, who have added Sowerby Bridge, the best Labour ward in the old Sowerby seat, as well as Shelf from Bradford South.

There are few marginal wards within Halifax. Labour does best in the north of the town, where council estates of varying vintage are to be found in Illingworth, Mixenden and Ovenden, and in the central St John's ward. The Conservatives win Northowram/Shelf, the western Warley ward, and the best residential area of Skircoat, south of the town centre. The Alliance is likely to be squeezed into third place in so marginal a seat. The Labour activists here, and Shirley Summerskill herself, are reckoned to owe allegiance to the moderate wing of the party – which suits the tastes of this Yorkshire electorate.

With its prominent mills and chimneys among the dark terraces, Halifax is one of those hilly Pennine towns whose industrial townscape betokens a Labour stronghold to the untutored observer. But there are many solid gritstone houses here, and Halifax has a large owner-occupier majority. It seems destined to continue to produce close results and small swings for years to come.

1981	% Own Occ	66.9	1979 core seat Halifax	
1981	% Loc Auth	26.2	Lab 21,416	43.8
1981	% Black/Asian	5	C 20,182	41.3
1981	% Mid Cl	39.9	L 6,853	14.0
1981	% Prof Man	11.8	NF 455	0.9
1982	electorate 73,872		MPs since 1945	
1979	notional result		1945-55 D. Brook Lab	
	Lab 900		1955-64 Maurice Macmillan C	
Alliance		SDP	1964- Shirley Summerskill Lab	

Batley and Spen   Kirklees

The creation of the new Metropolitan Boroughs such as
Kirklees in the early 1970s cut the long-established
boundaries of many parliamentary constituencies. The
Commissioners are not statutorily compelled to respect
metropolitan borough boundaries outside London, but have
chosen to do so unless this causes great problems concerning
the size of constituencies. The new Batley and Spen division
is a good example: the textile town of Batley was previously
conjoined with Morley in a safe Labour seat, but Morley is
now in Leeds City. Spenborough was formerly associated with
Brighouse, which is now in Calderdale.
Brighouse and Spenborough was a marginal, won narrowly by
Conservative Gary Waller in 1979. But Brighouse was the
more Conservative half, and Labour held its own in the
composite district of Spenborough (Cleckheaton, Gomersal,
Birkenshaw, Oakenshaw, Birstall, etc.) and Heckmondwike
even in the bad year of 1979. Batley is Labour territory, and
all in all this northernmost Kirklees seat should have been
won by Labour by about 2,000 votes at the last Election.
This is not the best area for the Alliance in West Yorkshire.
The SDP won two seats from Labour in Spen ward in the 1982
local elections, but this was achieved without Conservative
opposition. Throughout this new seat the Alliance polled 26%,
no more than the national average, to the Tories' 31% and
Labour's 42% - and Labour is highly likely to improve its
position at the next General Election compared with its poor
performance in 1982.

1981	% Own Occ	63	
1981	% Loc Auth	26	
1981	% Black/Asian	4	
1981	% Mid Cl	39	
1981	% Prof Man	12	
1982	electorate 74,433		
1979	notional result		
	Lab 1,700		
Alliance		SDP	

1979 core seat Brighouse and
Spenborough
  C   23,448   44.7
  Lab 21,714   41.4
  L   7,278   13.9
MPs since 1950
1950-51 F.A. Cobb Lab
1951-60 L.J. Edwards Lab
1960-64 Michael Shaw C
1964-70 Colin Jackson Lab
1970-74 Wilfred Proudfoot C
1974-79 Colin Jackson Lab
1979-   Gary Waller C

Colne Valley   Kirklees

Colne Valley is one of the best known and historic of constituencies, the seat of Victor Grayson and Philip Snowden and Richard Wainwright. Grayson was elected as socialist MP here before the First World War, and enjoyed a meteoric career before disappearing in obscure circumstances. Snowden was the first Labour Chancellor of the Exchequer in the 1920s. But Richard Wainwright is a Liberal, and for many years now Colne Valley has been the only true Liberal-Labour marginal in the country. Small wonder that a former Labour MP for Colne Valley, David Clark, has been able to write a book about the history of this one seat.

Now Colne Valley suffers the greatest disruption in its long existence. It used to straddle the Pennines, but now Saddleworth, the western tip, is in Greater Manchester and must be removed. Denby Dale is lost too, and all that remains is the Holme Valley and Colne Valley communities of Holmfirth, Meltham, Golcar, Linthwaite, Slaithwaite and Marsden. To make up the numbers, Colne Valley must take population from Huddersfield, Crosland Moor and Lindley wards. In fact the redrawn seat was originally named Huddersfield West by the Boundary Commission, and only altered after entreaties at the inquiry that the Colne Valley name should not die.

Huddersfield West was a Conservative seat in 1979, and the best residential areas in the town are in Lindley ward. But the controversial member, Geoffrey Dickens, is not to stand again, and the Yorkshire end of the Colne Valley was never good for the Tories - who were reduced to 8% here in 1966, their vote squeezed as right-wingers chose Wainwright rather than Labour. The Tories have recovered greatly since then, but Labour may just have polled more votes in the new seat in 1979. Wainwright faces a tough fight to hold the seat, since the Liberals' once proud tradition in Huddersfield West has been dead for some years. But in 1982 the Alliance polled 35% to Labour's 33% and the Tories' 32% - so Colne Valley may produce yet another dramatic result next time.

1981	% Own Occ	73	1979 core seat Colne Valley		
1981	% Loc Auth	15	L	20,151	38.4
1981	% Black/Asian	2	Lab	17,799	33.9
1981	% Mid Cl	46	C	14,450	27.5
1981	% Prof Man	18	Ind	101	0.2
1982	electorate 69,995		MPs since 1945		
1979	notional result		1945-63 W.G. Hall Lab		
	Lab 2,200 (over C)		1963-66 Patrick Duffy Lab		
Alliance		L	1966-70 Richard Wainwright L		
			1970-74 David Clark Lab		
			1974- Richard Wainwright L		

Dewsbury   Kirklees

Dewsbury was a moderately safe Labour seat in 1979, and its
basic political composition should not be altered by the loss of
Ossett to Wakefield and the gain of Kirkburton (from
Huddersfield East) and Denby Dale (from Colne Valley). But
David Ginsburg, MP since 1959, switched his allegiance to the
Social Democrats in 1981, to add some spice to the electoral
mixture in this woollens town in the heart of rugby league
land. Ginsburg's chances do not appear good, for the Alliance
achieved a mediocre 26.4% in the 1982 Kirklees elections in
this constituency, and failed to come near winning a single
ward. The Labour vote held up excellently, which bodes well
for local councillor Denis Ripley, the new candidate.

1981	% Own Occ	60	1979 core seat Dewsbury	
1981	% Loc Auth	31	Lab	22,829	46.7
1981	% Black/Asian	7	C	18,448	37.8
1981	% Mid Cl	43	L	7,850	15.5
1981	% Prof Man	15	MPs since 1945	
1982	electorate 70,261		1945-59 W.T. Paling Lab	
1979	notional result		1959- David Ginsburg Lab	
	Lab 5,200		(SDP)	
Alliance		SDP		

Huddersfield   Kirklees

Huddersfield East lacked the political marginality and
excitement of its western neighbour and Colne Valley, which
are now combined in the super-marginal Colne Valley seat.
The new Huddersfield is based on East, but gains the centre
of the town from West and loses Tory Kirkburton to
Dewsbury. It contains Huddersfield's eastern council estates,
most of its large Asian population, and all its safe Labour
wards. Labour's Ben Sheerman should retain his seat easily
next time, although there is localised Alliance activity in
Almondley and Paddock wards.

1981	% Own Occ	54	1979 core seat Huddersfield East	
1981	% Loc Auth	37	Lab	19,040	47.5
1981	% Black/Asian	19	C	15,945	39.7
1981	% Mid Cl	39	L	4,890	12.2
1981	% Prof Man	12	Ind	243	0.6
1982	electorate 68,689		MPs since 1950	
1979	notional result		1950-79 J.P.W. Mallalieu Lab	
	Lab 4,300		1979- Barry Sheerman Lab	
Alliance		L		

Elmet   Leeds/Wakefield

Elmet is an entirely new constituency, made up of the eastern
wards of the enlarged City of Leeds. Most of it is situated
beyond the edge of the main built-up area: Wetherby,
Barwick and Kippax, Garforth and Swillington. One ward from
Denis Healey's Leeds East seat is included, Whinmoor. Most of
Elmet was formerly in Tory Michael Alison's Barkston Ash
seat, but Barkston Ash stretched as far as the Selby and
Tadcaster districts, which are now in North Yorkshire.

Elmet should be a marginal seat. Whinmoor is part of the
sprawl of vast council estates in east Leeds, and votes
Labour. Both Barwick-in-Elmet and Garforth-Swillington are
marginal wards. The south end of Garforth is a council estate
where many miners live, and votes Labour heavily. Wetherby
on the other hand is the strongest Conservative ward in the
whole of the City of Leeds Council. This market town ten
miles NE of Leeds has expanded in recent years to take in
many affluent commuters. It produced a 9% vote for Labour in
1982, 70% for the Conservatives.

Wetherby should swing the balance of the Elmet division in
most years. The Conservatives were 4,000 votes ahead in
Wetherby in 1982, and 4,000 votes ahead in the whole of
Elmet. The other wards all had majorities within 500 votes.
Elmet will rank as a marginal seat, and it is unlikely that any
sitting MPs will venture the contest. The Alliance have no
history of success here.

1981	% Own Occ	61.3	New seat
1981	% Loc Auth	32.6	
1981	% Black/Asian	0.5	
1981	% Mid Cl	53.2	
1981	% Prof Man	19.7	
1982	electorate 66,850		
1979	notional result		
	C 5,000 (RW)		

Alliance   SDP

Hemsworth   Leeds/Wakefield

Hemsworth is a famous name, in electoral history at least. This is the seat which has produced the largest Labour majority in so many General Elections, remaining over 30,000 from 1950 to 1974. This is where it has been said that the Labour votes are weighed and not counted. The majority will not be quite so large as before, for Hemsworth's electorate is to be reduced; but it will be every bit as safe as before.

The constituency has had to be redrawn, for it was split between two of the new adminstrative counties which were created in the early 1970s, West Yorkshire and South Yorkshire; and according to the Boundary Commission's rules, county boundaries must never be crossed. Cudworth, Goldthorpe, Thurnscoe and Bolton on Dearne are lost to the new South Yorkshire seat of Barnsley East. Hemsworth is now entirely within Wakefield City. The mining towns of Hemsworth, South Kirkby and South Elmsall remain the core of the seat, but an important addition is Featherstone from Pontefract and Castleford. Featherstone is a large mining village of 10,000 souls, with a famed community spirit - its rugby league team has frequently reached the Cup Final at Wembley.

Hemsworth is a mining seat. Together with Bolsover in Derbyshire, a higher proportion of its population is employed in the coal industry than any other constituency in the UK - over 30%. It will remain the ideal Labour seat, now more compact than ever. The surprising victory of an Asian SDP candidate in Hemsworth ward itself in 1982 in the local elections looks likely to be a flash in the pan.

1981	% Own Occ	35	
1981	% Loc Auth	45	
1981	% Black/Asian	0.5	
1981	% Mid Cl	30	
1981	% Prof Man	8	
1982	electorate 54,876		
1979	notional result		
	Lab 20,500		
Alliance			

1979 core seat Hemsworth

Lab	36,509	69.6
C	10,466	20.0
L	5,474	10.4

MPs since 1945
1945-46 G.A. Griffiths Lab
1946-59 H.E. Holmes Lab
1959-74 Alec Beaney Lab
1974-   Alec Woodall Lab

Leeds Central   Leeds/Wakefield

Inner-city Leeds used to be divided between more than one constituency. The seat nearest to the centre was Leeds South East, which was grossly undersized at 43,000 electors in 1979, and most of Leeds SE is included in the new Central. Central also incorporates Beeston and Holbeck, the innermost wards of Merlyn Rees's Leeds South citadel.

Depopulation certainly made the creation of a large centre-city seat necessary in Leeds, as in many other conurbations. Leeds Central takes in the commercial area, the University buildings and part of the city's black and Asian population. Much of the old back-to-back housing for which Leeds was once famous has given way to modern redevelopment, sometimes high-rise. As one would expect, this is archetypal working-class Labour territory. The Conservatives undoubtedly don't have a chance here, but there is a considerable amount of Alliance local effort. In 1982 the Alliance polled a third of the votes cast in the division in the local elections, and won the Richmond Hill ward. The Liberals had high hopes of the old Leeds SE for many years, but their challenge always faded at General Election time, and they never made the same impact in the district which has come from Leeds South. The Alliance may meet a similar fate.

Catholic Labour MP Stanley Cohen failed to be reselected for Leeds SE after a well-publicised battle with the left-wing of his own party. There is likely to be further strife over the nomination for Leeds Central, and the Liberal Alliance could benefit from this. But Leeds Central, with only about 4% of professional and managerial workers, will be a hard nut to crack for any party other than Labour when it comes to a national Election.

1981	% Own Occ	32.9	1979 core seat Leeds South East		
1981	% Loc Auth	53.0	Lab	15,921	56.3
1981	% Black/Asian	10	C	6,549	23.2
1981	% Mid Cl	33.1	L	5,430	19.2
1981	% Prof Man	7.5	Comm	190	0.7
1982	electorate 64,212		NF	168	0.6
1979	notional result		MPs since 1955		
	Lab 14,500		1955-70 Alice Bacon Lab		
Alliance		L	1970- Stan Cohen Lab		

Leeds East   Leeds/Wakefield

Denis Healey's seat is essentially the Leeds council housing constituency. Massive post-war estates like Gipton and Seacroft sweep up and down the hills of eastern Leeds to the edge of the city. Over 60% of East Leeds is now composed of local authority housing, and this has been the source of Denis Healey's safe margin for thirty years. Leeds East has always included the rather isolated Conservative enclave of Halton. The seat is slightly changed in the redistribution. Whinmoor is lost from the eastern end of the constituency, and is replaced by Burmantofts and Harehills from nearer the inner city. Burmantofts was formerly in Leeds SE, Harehills in Leeds NE.

Burmantofts and Harehills will change the character of Healey's seat, but they will not weaken his grip. Burmantofts is essentially part of the inner city, once the back-to-back heart of the Leeds East End, but now almost completely rebuilt. Harehills was the inner segment of Sir Keith Joseph's seat. Its rapid swing to Labour, as its terraced housing was colonised by Leeds's Asian and black population, was responsible for a gradual reduction of Joseph's majority, even in 1979 when his party was swept to national power.

Leeds East will now be less of a purely peripheral constituency, but will include two types of inner-city housing - desiccated post-war council and heavily immigrant owner-occupier and privately rented. With the exception of the anomalous middle-class Halton, Denis Healey will have a seat which provides a cross-section of urban problems, characteristics highly suitable for a potential Labour Party leader.

1981	% Own Occ	44.2		1979 core seat Leeds East	
1981	% Loc Auth	49.2	Lab	26,346	55.4
1981	% Black/Asian	12	C	15,810	33.3
1981	% Mid Cl	40.8	L	4,622	9.7
1981	% Prof Man	9.8	NF	445	0.9
1982	electorate 64,638		Oths	309	0.6
1979	notional result		MP since 1955		
	Lab 15,300		1955-	Denis Healey Lab	
Alliance		L			

Leeds North-East   Leeds/Wakefield

Sir Keith Joseph had a cause to worry about his old Leeds NE
constituency. Long a safe Tory seat, it was changing in
social and political character, and it actually produced one of
the few swings to Labour at the 1979 General Election. Leeds
NE was a wedge of the city, stretching from Harehills nearest
the centre out to the affluent northern edge of Leeds. It was
Harehills which caused the problems for Joseph, for here
many Asians and West Indians were settling in the rows of
oldish private houses. But now Harehills has been moved into
Denis Healey's seat next door at Leeds East, and Leeds NE
becomes more of a uniformly middle-class suburban unit.

Leeds is the home of one of the three biggest Jewish
communities in Britain, along with Manchester and London.
When the Jews stopped off at Leeds, having arrived at East
Coast ports nearly a century ago, they settled in the
Chapeltown-Harehills area which is now popular with another
type of immigrant incomer. With success and affluence born of
hard work and skill, they moved out into Leeds's northern
middle-class area - Moortown, the Allertons and beyond. Now
they tend to vote Conservative, and to vote for a Jewish MP,
Sir Keith Joseph.

There will still be Labour elements in the constituency,
principally in Chapel Allerton, but it stretches out to the
most fashionable residential areas in the city, at Roundhay
and the newer developments at Alwoodley on the brink of the
countryside. This is solid Tory country, and Sir Keith Joseph
need have fewer fears about his political future after the
Boundary Commission's work.

1981	% Own Occ	64.6	1979 core seat Leeds North East		
1981	% Loc Auth	26.0	C	20,297	49.0
1981	% Black/Asian	7	Lab	14,913	36.0
1981	% Mid Cl	64.1	L	5,329	12.9
1981	% Prof Man	25.1	E	813	2.0
1982	electorate 65,701		Oth	103	0.2
1979	notional result		MPs since 1955		
	C 14,000		1955-56 O. Peake C		
Alliance		SDP	1956- Sir Keith Joseph C		

Leeds North-West   Leeds/Wakefield

North Leeds is the major middle-class residential area in the West Yorkshire conurbation. A large proportion of the non-manual workers of Leeds live within the city limits, rather than commuting from outside. This has meant that for many years Leeds has been able to sustain two safe Conservative constituencies, NE and NW.

Like its neighbour, Sir Keith Joseph's NE, North West has been affected by the declining status of the innermost section of its wedge. Kirkstall has been a Labour ward for some years, and in the 1970s for the first time Headingley went the same way. Headingley is one of the best known names associated with Leeds, with its rugby league and Test cricket grounds, and its large houses. Once it was the city's 'west end', where the woollen manufacturers lived, but now it is reduced to multi-occupation, for example for student accommodation. Kirkstall is removed by the boundary changes, but Headingley remains. NW passes out through middle-class Cookridge and Weetwood beyond the old city border to Otley and Wharfedale. This used to be in the old Ripon county constituency. Like Ripon it is basically Tory, but enjoys a strong Liberal presence which can on occasion pull off a victory.

The Alliance did manage to poll 34% to the Tories' 44% in the new NW seat in the 1982 local elections, and may well pose a greater threat than Labour, despite the latter's lead in Headingley. But the Conservatives would have been 10,000 votes clear here in 1979, and to lose Leeds NW would be a disastrous result for the Government.

1981	% Own Occ	60.5	1979 core seat Leeds North West		
1981	% Loc Auth	25.3	C	23,837	47.5
1981	% Black/Asian	2	Lab	17,623	35.1
1981	% Mid Cl	61.8	L	7,899	15.7
1981	% Prof Man	22.2	E	847	1.7
1982	electorate 68,408		MP since 1950		
1979	notional result		1950- Sir Donald Kaberry C		
	C 11,800				
Alliance		SDP			

Leeds West   Leeds/Wakefield

West Leeds is a working-class district, but it has for many years been the scene of Liberal hopes - one of the few Liberal assaults on a Labour parliamentary seat. The Liberal Party flag was flown by local government activists Michael Meadowcroft and Chris Greenfield, but they never achieved better than a good second place; in 1979 the Liberals slipped to third, as Labour's Joe Dean held Leeds West by nearly 10,000 votes.

Of the four wards in Leeds West, Armley and Bramley are Labour-Liberal contests at local level; Wortley is a three-sided battle; and Kirkstall, although it was in Leeds NW, is a Labour stronghold. Leeds West is divided almost equally between owner-occupied and local authority housing.

In the 1982 local elections, the Alliance forged its way back into second place in the local elections in the Leeds West constituency, polling 32% to Labour's 42% and 26% Conservative. This indicates that if their fortunes improve, and if they can translate local support into General Election votes, they might be able to challenge Labour here. But disappointment has been the lot of the Liberals here so often, that it would be unwise to predict that the seat which elected Charles Pannell for thirty years will desert Labour.

1981	% Own Occ	47.4	1979 core seat Leeds West		
1981	% Loc Auth	44.2	Lab	21,290	49.4
1981	% Black/Asian	2	C	11,626	27.0
1981	% Mid Cl	39.7	L	9,734	22.6
1981	% Prof Man	9.4	NF	466	1.1
1982	electorate 68,656		MPs since 1945		
1979	notional result		1945-74 Charles Pannell Lab		
	Lab 12,800		1974- Joe Dean Lab		
Alliance		L			

Morley and Leeds South   Leeds/Wakefield

This new constituency brings together two wards from former Home Secretary Merlyn Rees's seat, Leeds South, and half of the more marginally Labour Batley and Morley division. Morley always returns a Labour majority though, and the two Leeds wards are overwhelmingly strong for the party. Middleton is a vast inter-war council estate on the southern edge of Leeds, while Hunslet is a much redeveloped inner-city area. In the 1979 local elections Labour outvoted the Tories by 4 to 1 here, and Merlyn Rees achieved the highest numerical and percentage majority in Leeds at the last General Election. The Alliance has no local base here, and Hugh Gaitskell's old seat should remain safe for Labour.

1981	% Own Occ	44.1	1979 core seat Leeds South		
1981	% Loc Auth	48.1	Lab	22,388	65.0
1981	% Black/Asian	2	C	8,058	23.4
1981	% Mid Cl	39.8	L	3,568	10.4
1981	% Prof Man	12.1	NF	416	1.2
1982	electorate 61,395		MPs since 1945		
1979	notional Lab 11,900		1945-63 Hugh Gaitskell Lab		
Alliance		SDP	1963- Merlyn Rees Lab		

Normanton   Leeds/Wakefield

Before the redistribution Normanton was a predominantly coal-mining constituency situated SE of Leeds. The three main communities were Rothwell, Normanton and Stanley. They are still in the division, but now joined by a town of a different kind, with a different economic base – the wool weaving Ossett, formerly in Dewsbury. Normanton is a safe Labour seat, although unlike the coalfield Ossett has a substantial Conservative and Liberal presence. Normanton is the only seat which crosses the border of the City of Leeds and the Borough of Wakefield – Rothwell is a Leeds ward. Veteran right-wing Labour MP Albert Roberts, noted for his support of Franco and hanging, is retiring.

1981	% Own Occ	60	1979 core seat Normanton		
1981	% Loc Auth	32	Lab	26,591	56.4
1981	% Black/Asian	0.5	C	14,398	30.6
1981	% Mid Cl	40	L	6,134	13.0
1981	% Prof Man	11	MPs since 1945		
1982	electorate 61,633		1945-47 T. Smith Lab		
1979	notional Lab 8,900		1947-51 G.O. Sylvester Lab		
Alliance			1951- Albert Roberts Lab		

Pontefract and Castleford   Leeds/Wakefield

As one travels eastwards from Leeds, the Pennine countryside gradually flattens into a plain, and the traditional base of the economy changes from textiles to coal. Great rivers like the Aire and the Ouse water the low-lying land, and have been tapped by massive power stations which tower over the landscape. This is scenery dominated by heavy industry, by the production of power and energy. One travels too from the City of Leeds into the City of Wakefield, where there are no Tory or marginal seats. Wakefield is a Labour powerhouse in every sense.

Pontefract and Castleford used to be one of the strongest coal-mining constituencies in West Yorkshire. Now the big colliery village of Featherstone has been transferred to Hemsworth, and been replaced by the equally Labour town of Knottingley, which lies beside the vast Ferrybridge power station. Knottingley was formerly in Goole, a seat forcibly split four ways by its division between the counties of West, South and North Yorkshire and Humberside. Pontefract town has a Tory vote in its southern ward, and is a historic town with a notable castle. But Castleford is one of the largest towns created by mining in the country, with over 30,000 electors; it is the largest influence in the constituency, for Pontefract has 20,000 electors and Knottingley 10,000.

An SDP candidate might push the Alliance up into second place here, although some of the respectable SDP percentages obtained in the 1982 local elections were achieved without Conservatives standing. Pontefract and Castleford will remain one of the safest Labour seats.

1981	% Own Occ	45	1979 core seat Pontefract and
1981	% Loc Auth	45	Castleford
1981	% Black/Asian	0.5	Lab 30,566 68.2
1981	% Mid Cl	37	C 10,665 23.8
1981	% Prof Man	10	L 3,616 8.1
1982	electorate 65,754		MPs since 1950
1979	notional result		1950-62 G.O. Sylvester Lab
	Lab 17,400		1962-78 Joseph Harper Lab
Alliance			1978- Geoffrey Lofthouse Lab

Pudsey   Leeds/Wakefield

Pudsey is the least altered seat in the Leeds area after the redistribution. It still consists of three units: Pudsey itself, Horsforth, and Aireborough, which is a composite ward made up of the towns of Guiseley, Yeadon and Rawdon in the Aire Valley. Although technically now within the City of Leeds, Pudsey retains an independence and unity which justifies its continued existence in its present form as a constituency.

Much of the housing in the division is made up of neat Pennine stone terraces dating from the period before the First World War. But an untutored impression of its appearance can mislead: this is a comfortable, middle-class seat. Horsforth is a dormitory town for Leeds, 53% middle class in 1971. Both Pudsey and Aireborough contain over 40% non-manual workers, well above the national average, and all the towns have less than 25% council housing.

The Conservatives have held Pudsey since 1950. It is true that both Labour and the Liberals have entered strong challenges, and in 1974 Pudsey was as close as any constituency in the country to a three-way marginal. But in 1979 Giles Shaw returned an 8,739 majority for the Tories, and they seem always to be able ultimately to hold on. The opposition is divided: Labour is very weak in Horsforth, and the Liberals usually come third in Pudsey itself. In the 1982 local elections, the Alliance attained a level of 35% in the wards which make up the Pudsey constituency - within 7% of the Conservatives. In a breakthrough year, Pudsey will be one of the best third party bets.

1981	% Own Occ	70.1	1979 core seat Pudsey		
1981	% Loc Auth	24.3	C	24,591	45.1
1981	% Black/Asian	0.7	L	15,852	29.1
1981	% Mid Cl	53.7	Lab	13,727	25.2
1981	% Prof Man	18.4	E	340	0.6
1982	electorate 71,037		MPs since 1945		
1979	notional result		1945-50 M. Stoddart-Scott C		
	C 9,600 (over L)		1950-59 C. Banks C		
Alliance		L	1959-74 J. Hiley C		
			1974- Giles Shaw C		

Wakefield   Leeds/Wakefield

Wakefield was the capital of the old West Riding, and it retains its status as the administrative headquarters of the Metropolitan County of West Yorkshire. It is a cathedral city and a historic market centre, with many fine buildings. But its political preferences are shaped more by the fact that it is also the focus of a heavy industrial belt and a working coalfield.

It has been held by Labour since 1932, when it was won in a byelection by Arthur Greenwood, who had been Minister of Health in Labour's second government (1929-31), but who had lost his seat at Nelson and Colne in the debacle of 1931. The present MP for Wakefield is Walter Harrison, the party's tough 'sergeant-major' - Deputy Chief Whip.

There are Conservative residential districts in the Wakefield constituency, concentrated in the Tory South ward around Sandal and Crigglestone. But Labour are ahead everywhere else, in the colliery communities like East Moor and Lupset, and in the outlying town of Horbury - although their stronghold at Royston has had to be removed since it is now in the Barnsley Borough. This should reduce the Labour majority slightly - it would have been around 6,000 in 1979. But it is inconceivable that Labour should lose this seat in the very heart of its West Yorkshire citadel. The Alliance has made little impact as yet in local elections in Wakefield.

1981	% Own Occ	51	1979 core seat Wakefield		
1981	% Loc Auth	42	Lab	27,124	50.9
1981	% Black/Asian	2	C	19,571	36.7
1981	% Mid Cl	48	L	6,059	11.4
1981	% Prof Man	15	NF	530	1.0
1982	electorate 69,134		MPs since 1945		
1979	notional result		1945-54 A. Greenwood Lab		
	Lab 5,800		1954-64 A.C. Jones Lab		
Alliance			1964- Walter Harrison Lab		

Bath

The City of Bath remains a single complete parliamentary constituency - one of the few seats in the United Kingdom unaltered as a result of the redistribution. The most well-known features of this West Country spa town and tourist resort are the Royal Crescent, the Roman Baths and the Abbey. But despite the apparent elegance and affluence of Bath, it is by no means a Conservative stronghold. Labour came within 800 votes of winning Bath in 1966, and in 1974 the seat looked like a three-way marginal as Liberal Christopher Mayhew forced his way into a strong second place.

From where does the anti-Tory vote come? There are indeed many comfortable up-market residential roads in Bath, in Lyncombe, Combe Down, Lansdown, Lambridge and elsewhere. But here the Liberals have a strong appeal, based not only on hard local work in the wards but in the importation in the 1970s of a 'big-name' candidate, Christopher Mayhew, who had defected from Labour with much publicity during the Liberal revival of those years. Mayhew's drive was directed against a criticised and ailing Conservative MP. Moreover, there is a substantial element of Labour support in west and south west Bath, in council estates like Southdown and Twerton, which create some of the safest Labour wards in Avon, and in older working-class areas.

The Conservatives have won Bath with a minority vote since 1959. Now, with a highly promising and moderate new member, Christopher Patten, they may be in a better position to defend the seat than for some years. Patten increased the majority to 9,000 when first elected in 1979. But if one of the opposing parties, probably the Liberals, could gather in all the non-Tory votes, and squeeze Labour, this cultured city could again become one of the Tories' most vulnerable seats.

1981	% Own Occ	57.9	1979 same seat Bath		
1981	% Loc Auth	27.2	C	23,025	46.4
1981	% Black/Asian	2.5	L	13,913	28.0
1981	% Mid Cl	57.4	Lab	11,407	23.0
1981	% Prof Man	17.5	E	1,082	2.2
1982	electorate 64,896		NF	202	0.4
Alliance		L	MPs since 1945		

MPs since 1945
1945-64 I.J. Pitman C
1964-79 Sir Edward Brown C
1979-   Christopher Patten C

Bristol East

In the present revision of seats, Bristol loses one of its five representatives. This pattern is of itself unsurprising. Most of the large cities in Britain have shed seats as their population has declined of recent decades. But in Bristol the constituency to vanish is Bristol South-East, a seat famous in electoral history. Bristol SE has elected Tony Benn twelve times in all, remaining loyal throughout his struggle to renounce his peerage in the early 1960s. Now Tony Benn must find another seat, and the nearest successor to his old stamping-ground is the new Bristol East.

Bristol E is to consist of Brislington, Stockwood, Hengrove and Lawrence Hill from the old SE seat; and Easton and Eastville from the NE division at present held by retiring Labour member Arthur Palmer. It is a long strip of the eastern fringe of the city, and its political and social makeup is very mixed. Many of the wards are classic marginals, like Brislington with its skilled working-class owner occupiers. Being drawn basically from two seats with Labour MPs, it should return a Labour MP in an even year. But the most solid part of Benn's seat have been transferred elsewhere, to Bristol South, and it is thought that Benn entertains ambitions for that seat.

Benn, or any other Labour candidate who contests Bristol East, must start favourite; but they are likely to find themselves vulnerable not so much to any Alliance effort, but to a resurgent Conservative Party which could flourish in an affluent and owner-occupied working-class constituency such as this.

1981	% Own Occ	66	
1981	% Loc Auth	25	
1981	% Black/Asian	4	
1981	% Mid Cl	46	
1981	% Prof Man	12	
1982	electorate 66,876		
1979	notional result		
	Lab 4,300		
Alliance		L	

1979 core seat Bristol South-East

Lab	24,868	45.4
C	22,981	41.9
L	6,371	11.6
NF	321	1.0
Ind	62	0.1

MPs since 1945
1945-50 Sir Stafford Cripps Lab
1950-61 A. Benn Lab
1961-63 M. St Clair C
1963-   A. Benn Lab

Bristol North-West

North-West Bristol has traditionally been politically the most marginal part of the city. Since the war, the representation has changed hands between the two major parties in 1955, 1959, 1966, 1970, October 1974 and 1979. In the redistribution the boundaries of Bristol NW are extended beyond the district of Bristol to take in Filton and Stoke Gifford from the District of Northavon and the present parliamentary division of South Gloucestershire.

The changes should make this super-marginal constituency a better bet for Labour. This is not so much because of the additions from beyond the city limits, although Filton is the site of Rolls-Royce aero engine factory and has a considerable, if affluent, working class population. Rather more crucially, the stronghold Conservative ward of Stoke Bishop, which includes the mansions of Sneyd Park north of Clifton Downs, has been transferred out of the seat to Bristol West. There still remain the middle-class owner-occupied wards of Westbury on Trym and Horfield, but these are counterbalanced by the Labour vote in the port of Avonmouth and in council estates like Southmead, Kingsweston and Sea Mills; 50% of the housing in the seat is owned by the local authority.

Bristol NW will remain the most marginal of the city's constituencies, now there are only four of them. But the 5,000 majority of first-term Conservative MP Michael Colvin must be vulnerable to any kind of pro-Labour swing in a division which has one of the best of claims to be regarded as a social microcosm of urban England.

1981	% Own Occ	47
1981	% Loc Auth	50
1981	% Black/Asian	1
1981	% Mid Cl	50
1981	% Prof Man	16
1982	electorate 73,428	
1979	notional result	
	C 4,000	

Alliance   SDP

1979 core seat Bristol North-West

C	25,919	48.6
Lab	21,238	39.8
L	5,857	11.0
NF	254	0.5
Ind	73	0.1

MPs since 1950
1950-55 J.G. Braithwaite C
1955-59 T.C. Boyd Lab
1959-66 Martin McLaren C
1966-70 John Ellis Lab
1970-74 Martin McLaren C
1974-79 Ron Thomas Lab
1979-   Michael Colvin C

Bristol South

In the 1979 General Election, just as in all the elections since the Second World War, Bristol South turned in the largest Labour majority in the city, and indeed in the whole of SW England. The present benefactor of this heavy vote is Labour Chief Whip Michael Cocks - and if there is any threat to his continued tenure of the seat it comes not from the Tories but possibly from a rather unusual direction - from within his own party, from his present neighbour, Tony Benn.

The existing Bristol S seat stretches from the old working class area of Bedminster, near Temple Meads station immediately south of the city centre, to the massive post-war council estates of Bishopsworth, Hartcliffe and Whitchurch on the edge of Bristol. In 1971 52% of the housing in the old Bristol South was council owned. With only one or two pockets of middle-class semi-detached ribbon development along the main roads out of the city, the seat was clearly the Labour stronghold in Bristol. In the redistribution, however, Bristol S has been extended to include Knowle and Windmill Hill, parts of Tony Benn's Bristol SE constituency. The eastern part of Knowle is an attractive residential area, but Windmill Hill is the inner-city segment of Benn's seat and Knowle West is a large 1930s council estate - so the changes should not weaken Labour's overwhelming control over this division.

But the redrawing has given Tony Benn a claim on Bristol S, rather than the more dubious Bristol East, and it is as yet unclear what the outcome would be of a contest for the nomination between Cocks and Benn, who represent different wings of the Labour Party, and alternative solutions to the problems of the last quarter of the twentieth century. Whoever wins the Labour candidacy could not find a safer seat in southern England, outside London at least.

1981	% Own Occ	47	1979 core seat	Bristol South	
1981	% Loc Auth	48	Lab	25,038	57.9
1981	% Black/Asian	1	C	13,855	32.0
1981	% Mid Cl	39	L	3,815	8.8
1981	% Prof Man	9	NF	392	0.9
1982	electorate 73,028		WRP	135	0.3
1979	notional result		MPs since 1945		
	Lab 10,900		1945-70	W.A. Wilkins Lab	
Alliance		SDP	1970-	Michael Cocks Lab	

Bristol West

Bristol West has always been the city's Conservative heartland. Unlike many British towns, the classic west end has survived in Bristol - an attractive residential area close to the city centre, rising up the hills to the north and west of the downtown area which was rebuilt after the last War. Here we find the green parks and elegant eighteenth and nineteenth century housing of Clifton, with its chic shops and restaurants, Clifton College and Bristol Zoo, the expensive new Roman Catholic cathedral and the university. Many of the famous schools of Bristol, once direct grant and now independent, are to be found in the constituency, in Cotham and Redland as well as in Clifton. The intellectual ambience is borne out by the statistics. Bristol West has the highest proportion of students of any seat in Britain, not barring Oxford and Cambridge.

Perhaps as a concomitant of these social factors, Bristol West has had a tradition of electing Conservative MPs from the liberal wing of the party. Robert Cooke (1957-79) was considered easy-going in the extreme, and the present representative is William Waldegrave, Fellow of All Souls, Oxford. Waldegrave is a leading intellectual of the 'wet' wing of the party, elected at the age of 32 and widely tipped as a high-flyer.

Because the seat extends into the centre of Bristol, it does include part of the troubled St Paul's district, where the small West Indian population is most evident. In the redistribution the boundaries have been extended beyond Clifton Down to the north, to include the less academic but solidly middle-class ward of Stoke Bishop. Stoke Bishop lacks Clifton's radical-chic image, but in most years it returns the largest Conservative majority in the city council elections. Waldegrave should certainly be able to hold this most elegant of seats for as long as he wishes.

1981	% Own Occ	50	1979 core seat Bristol West		
1981	% Loc Auth	4	C	22,257	52.6
1981	% Black/Asian	6	Lab	9,690	22.9
1981	% Mid Cl	66	L	8,880	21.0
1981	% Prof Man	20	E	1,154	2.7
1982	electorate 73,794		Oth	339	0.8
1979	notional result		MPs since 1945		
	C 12,700		1945-50 O. Stanley C		
Alliance		L	1950-57 Sir Walter Monckton C		
			1957-79 R. Cooke C		
			1979- William Waldegrave C		

Kingswood

From its creation in 1974, Kingswood has been a super-marginal seat. Its first MP, Labour's Terence Walker (1974-79) was defeated by 303 votes by Tory Jack Aspinwall, who had previously been the seat's <u>Liberal</u> candidate. Now, although the name remains the same, the constituency will swing back to Labour due to boundary changes which significantly alter its character.

Kingswood is an urban seat. Originally it included the town of that name together with Mangotsfield and a series of suburbs on the eastern edge of the Bristol conurbation. It has always been a constituency of owner occupiers, but the northern part of the seat, Kingswood itself, and Mangotsfield, has consistently shown a preference for Labour. Many residents are skilled workers at Rolls Royce and elsewhere, living in turn of the century terraced housing. Now in the revision the wealthier southern half of Kingswood constituency has been transferred to the Wansdyke seat, and four Bristol wards have been added. Hillfields, Frome Vale, St George E and St George W are all Labour wards, and indeed Hillfields returns the Labour City Council leader. All were formerly in Bristol NE, a safe Labour seat.

In such a close division as Kingswood, these revisions should tip the balance towards Labour, and the colourful local MP, Jack Aspinwall, may well be in serious trouble. His home base is in the southern part of the old seat, which has now been removed, and he may even seek safer pastures elsewhere.

1981	% Own Occ	68	1979 core seat Kingswood		
1981	% Loc Auth	27	C	23,553	45.4
1981	% Black/Asian	1	Lab	23,250	44.8
1971	% Mid Cl	36	L	4,852	9.3
1971	% Prof Man	10	NF	258	0.5
1982	electorate 72,516		MPs since 1974		
1979	notional result		1974-79 Terry Walker Lab		
	Lab 3,900		1979- Jack Aspinwall C		
Alliance		SDP			

Northavon

In the local government reorganisation which created the new county of Avon in 1974, the District of Northavon more or less exactly reproduced the area covered by the South Gloucestershire parliamentary seat. With the exceptions of Filton and Stoke Gifford, lost to Bristol NW, the District of Northavon is now to form a new constituency of the same name.

There are no large towns in Northavon, but a surprisingly high proportion of the electorate lives in urban communities, such as the expanding Yate-Chipping Sodbury area, and like Thornbury, Patchway and Frampton Cotterell. Most of the seat does look to Bristol as an economic and social magnet, but genuine rural Gloucestershire is preserved in the Severn Valley and at the country seat of Badminton. Some of the small towns, like Yate and Patchway, have some unemployment and large council estates. But they are outnumbered by the prosperous commuter bases and soft agricultural lowlands.

There has always been a substantial Labour vote in South Gloucestershire - the seat was once held by Anthony Crosland. But the Conservative MP John Cope can have few realistic fears of losing the new seat.

1981	% Own Occ	73.1	1979 core seat South		
1981	% Loc Auth	18.8	Gloucestershire		
1981	% Black/Asian	1	C	35,627	51.2
1971	% Mid Cl	56.3	Lab	20,465	29.4
1971	% Prof Man	21.5	L	12,850	18.5
1976	electorate 73,400		E	695	1.0
1979	notional result		MPs since 1945		
	C 14,200		1945-50 J.H. Alpass Lab		
Alliance		L	1950-55 Anthony Crosland Lab		
			1955-74 Sir Frederick Corfield C		
			1974- John Cope C		

Wansdyke

Wansdyke, named after the ancient ditch that traverses this part of Avon, is effectively the successor seat to the old oversized North Somerset division. It contains the expanding middle-class commuter town of Keynsham, one of the Tory districts of North Somerset, and Midsomer Norton and Radstock, isolated Labour outposts whose preferences reveal the fact that these twin towns once formed the centre of the defunct Somerset coalfield.

However, a considerable portion of the old North Somerset seat, which extended to the coast at Portishead, has been lost to the new Woodspring constituency, not Wansdyke. Also, the Wansdyke constituency will contain parts of the District of Kingswood - Bitton, Oldland and Hanham Abbots. These are the more Conservative and affluent neighbourhoods of south Kingswood, whose loss will tip the Kingswood seat towards Labour.

Like Keynsham, the south Kingswood communities typify the social and political spirit of the new Wansdyke constituency: they are expanding private commuter bases conveniently situated between Bath and Bristol in the centre of the new county of Avon.

1981	% Own Occ	71.6	1979 core seat North Somerset			
1981	% Loc Auth	22.0	C	43,173	54.3	
1981	% Black/Asian	1	Lab	22,122	27.8	
1981	% Mid Cl	55.3	L	12,898	16.2	
1981	% Prof Man	19.7	E	1,254	1.6	
1982	electorate 70,738		MPs since 1950			
1979	notional result		1950-64 Ted Leather C			
	C 6,400		1964- Paul Dean C			
Alliance		L				

Weston super Mare

With 92,000 electors at the 1979 General Election, the constituency of Weston-super-Mare was the second seat in the ex-Somerset part of the County of Avon to rank as grossly oversized - North Somerset was the other. In Weston's case, the seat of that name has now been pared down to a smaller hinterland around the Bristol Channel resort itself. Outlying areas such as Clevedon, Nailsea and Long Ashton have overflowed into the new division of Woodspring.

Weston super Mare is a large town of over 50,000 people, and it can quite adequately form the basis of a compact constituency. It is also large enough to have a substantial Labour vote, particularly in the South ward and in the inland, eastern, part of the town, where most of the council tenants are to be found - 25% of Weston's housing is local authority owned.

But in general the seat shows all the political traits of an area dependent on tourism: the endless rows of guest houses, the fashionable residential areas in the hilly north of the town, the non-unionised and casual workers in the service and summer industries. All add to the rural votes of the remaining smaller communities like Churchill, Blagdon and Congresbury to create an ultra-safe Conservative seat.

1981	% Own Occ	66.6	1979 core seat Weston-super-
1981	% Loc Auth	21.7	Mare
1981	% Black/Asian	1	C 40,618 56.9
1981	% Mid Cl	53.3	L 16,305 22.9
1981	% Prof Man	19.1	Lab 14,420 20.2
1982	electorate 71,468		MPs since 1945
1979	notional result		1945-58 Ian Orr-Ewing C
	C 16,900		1958-69 D. Webster C
Alliance		SDP	1969- Jerry Wiggin C

Woodspring

Woodspring is the extra constituency in Avon assembled from the districts left over when the old seats of Weston-super-Mare and North Somerset were compressed into the new Weston and Wansdyke. The name is taken from the local government District of Woodspring, although that is a large unit which also includes Weston itself.

The new Woodspring division comprises Clevedon, Nailsea and the Gordano Valley (formerly in the Weston-super-Mare seat) and Portishead (ex-North Somerset). It extends as far as Long Ashton and Failand, set in wooded country just over the Clifton Bridge from the most fashionable and wealthy parts of Bristol.

It will be a safe Conservative seat. Clevedon and Portishead are elegant seaside resorts, decidedly up-market from bustling plebeian Weston a few miles down the coast. Clevedon in particular has expanded through new private housing development in recent years, and like all other parts of the Woodspring division, it houses a considerable number of commuters to Bristol.

1981	% Own Occ	73.8	New seat
1981	% Loc Auth	18.2	
1981	% Black/Asian	1	
1981	% Mid Cl	60.3	
1981	% Prof Man	24.6	
1982	electorate 70,677		
1979	notional result		
	C 20,500		
Alliance		L	

Luton South

When Luton was granted an extra seat in 1974, the result was that two marginal seats replaced one. Luton's most famous MP was the 'Radio Doctor', Charles Hill. He stood as a 'Liberal and Conservative', but voted with the Tory Party in the House. But Labour could win the old Luton, and took both the new divisions, East and West, in the 1974 Elections. Both were lost to the Conservatives by under 1,000 votes in 1979. Clearly Luton is one of the most politically marginal towns in the country. Rather like Northampton, both the Luton seats were a little small. Again like Northampton, the Boundary Commission have now brought in wards from outside the old County Borough to make up the numbers. This especially affects the new North Luton. Luton South is the successor to the old East constituency, and it contains fewer wards from outside the town - only Caddington and Slip End from South Bedfordshire.

Luton South contains most of the institutions associated in the public mind with the town: the Vauxhall motor works, the airport which is so popular with European holiday package operators, the huge Arndale shopping centre in the middle of the town. Like the constituency as a whole, many wards are closely contested. Labour will do best in the old terraces near the town centre, popular with Luton's large non-white population, and in the Farley council estate. The Conservatives' strongest ward (besides the rural Caddington) is High Town, north of the town centre. In local elections the Liberals have done well in the residential area of Stopsley.

All in all, Luton South will be a highly marginal seat. The rural additions are not populous enough to make the constituency safe for first-term Conservative MP Graham Bright, and there should therefore still be one Luton seat at least which will swing with the national tide.

1981	% Own Occ	66.0	1979 core seat Luton East		
1981	% Loc Auth	20.3	C	17,809	43.7
1981	% Black/Asian	18	Lab	16,962	41.6
1981	% Mid Cl	42.4	L	5,285	13.0
1981	% Prof Man	13.0	NF	461	1.1
1982	electorate 71,729		Oth	213	0.6
1979	notional result		MPs since 1974		
	C 900		1974-79 Ivor Clemitson Lab		
Alliance		L	1979- Graham Bright C		

Mid-Bedfordshire

Mid-Bedfordshire is in many ways typical of a Tory seat in the Home Counties. With a mixture of small market towns (Biggleswade, Ampthill and Sandy) and prosperous villages, it smoothly created a majority of over 20,000 in 1979 for Conservative Stephen Hastings, who is retiring at the next Election. He will bequeath a safe and little altered division: some villages are lost to North Luton, some to SW Beds, and the marginal town of Kempston is picked up from Bedford. But for the presence of brickfields among the more conventional type of fields, it would be almost entirely non-industrial. Mid-Bedfordshire will remain a Tory citadel, too substantial a structure for Labour or the Alliance to demolish.

1981	% Own Occ	61.4	1979 core seat Mid-Bedfordshire		
1981	% Loc Auth	25.9	C	37,724	56.9
1981	% Black/Asian	1.5	Lab	17,140	25.8
1981	% Mid Cl	49.6	L	11,467	17.3
1981	% Prof Man	18.7	MPs since 1945		
1982	electorate 75,779		1945-60 A.T. Lennox-Boyd C		
1979	notional C 16,800		1960- Stephen Hastings C		
Alliance		L			

North Bedfordshire

North Bedfordshire is dominated by the county town of Bedford, an industrial and educational centre with a large population of immigrants, both coloured and Italian. Labour won Bedford by upsetting Christopher Soames in 1966. But by 1979 the New Zealand born Tory MP Trevor Skeet had built up a lead of over 12,000. Now Bedford loses the marginal suburb of Kempston, across the Ouse. Bedford town itself is fairly marginal, ranging from Conservative wards like De Parys to Labour's Cauldwell. But the villages of the flat northern tip of the county should continue to keep Skeet in charge of this rather cosmopolitan constituency.

1981	% Own Occ	63.7	1979 core seat Bedford		
1981	% Loc Auth	23.7	C	31,140	51.2
1981	% Black/Asian	7	Lab	18,727	30.8
1981	% Mid Cl	53.9	L	10,129	16.9
1981	% Prof Man	19.0	NF	813	1.3
1982	electorate 72,696		MPs since 1950		
1979	notional C 11,400		1950-66 Christopher Soames C		
Alliance		L	1966-70 Ben Parkyn Lab		
			1970- Trevor Skeet C		

North Luton

North Luton may be based on the old marginal Luton West seat, held by leading Tribunite Brian Sedgemore from 1974 to 1979. But its political character will be much altered by the inclusion of eight rural wards from Mid- and South Bedfordshire, all in the countryside north of Luton.

The parts of Luton contained within the N Luton division are mainly residential districts. Most of the council estates in the town are situated here: as one drives through the urban part of the seat on the M1, the tower blocks of Leagrave ward are only a few yards away. Labour does well there, and in Lewsey west of the M1, and Sundon Park at the north end of the town. Many car factory employees and other skilled manual workers live in this part of Luton, which has grown rapidly since the war. Council semis and low-price private developments jostle together in bare treeless neighbourhoods. The Tories fight back in Icknield ward, along the A6 towards Bedford, probably the classiest residential area in Luton (although many managerial workers live outside the town, in dormitories like Harpenden and in wealthy villages like Studham). But the real Tory advantage will be built up in the villages in the prosperous Bedfordshire hinterland, in Flitton and Flitwick, Barton le Clay, Harlington and Toddington.

A word might be said about the name of this new seat. Why 'North Luton' when we have 'Luton South'? Why is there no standard order of town name and compass point? The answer is that the Commission is endeavouring to preserve a distinction between Borough constituencies (like Luton South), and County constituencies (North Luton). There are scarcely any significant differences nowadays between Borough and County constituencies - candidates are allowed to spend a little more in County divisions. But if the legal distinction is trifling, the political implications of the creation of North Luton are not. As in most parts of Britain, rural Bedfordshire is very Conservative. The super-marginal old Luton West seat, held by Tory right-winger John Carlisle by only 246 votes, should pass beyond Labour's grasp due to the introduction of a 'County seat' mixture of urban and rural wards.

1981	% Own Occ	67.8	1979 core seat Luton West		
1981	% Loc Auth	27.2	C	21,230	44.1
1981	% Black/Asian	5	Lab	20,984	43.6
1981	% Mid Cl	47.0	L	5,233	10.6
1981	% Prof Man	15.6	NF	701	1.5
1982	electorate 69,781		MPs since 1974		
1979	notional result		1974-79 Brian Sedgemore Lab		
	C 7,400		1979- John Carlisle C		
Alliance		SDP			

South-West Bedfordshire

The south-western strip of Bedfordshire, along the
Buckinghamshire border, might seem at first sight to be
another identikit Conservative constituency in the south-east
of England. But in fact it is based on the old South Beds
seat, which was actually held by Gwilym Roberts for Labour
between 1966 and 1970. In 1979, though, the Conservatives
won South Beds by over 16,000 votes after a 10% swing. How
did Labour ever win the seat, and why did it turn against
them so violently?

The largest town in South Bedfordshire is Dunstable, which
houses many skilled car workers – the Dunstable-Luton area
is the General Motors (Vauxhall) metropolis in England.
Dunstable is nearly all-white, and dominated by owner-
occupied semi-detached housing, and despite its frequently
drab and dreary appearance it usually returns a Conservative
majority. But it is connected to Luton by a strip of
peripheral council developments, like that at Houghton Regis,
which is the Labour stronghold in the constituency. Before
1974 South Beds also contained Lewsey, Leagrave and
Limbury, Labour wards which then passed into Luton West –
so boundary changes in the early 1970s were one reason for
South Bedfordshire's swing away from Labour. Another is the
volatility of the skilled manual class, which more than any
other rejected Mr Callaghan's government in 1979.

In theory SW Bedfordshire could move back a long way
towards Labour. It loses 15,000 rural electors. Several
villages pass to North Luton, although the Woburn district is
gained from Mid-Beds. But it should be a better bet for
Labour than the old South Beds, which only had a 4,000
Tory majority in October 1974. The Liberals did well here too
in 1974, and the Alliance could spring a surprise in this
highly unpredictable seat. But the favourite must remain the
moderate Conservative who is the sitting MP, David Madel,
unless disaster should strike the car industry – which might
affect even GM, the biggest car corporation in the world.

1981	% Own Occ	65.1	1979 core seat South		
1981	% Loc Auth	26.1	Bedfordshire		
1981	% Black/Asian	2	C	32,988	56.4
1981	% Mid Cl	51.9	Lab	16,505	28.2
1981	% Prof Man	20.4	L	8,402	14.4
1982	electorate 76,418		NF	626	1.1
1979	notional result		MPs since 1950		
	C 14,100		1950-51 E.W. Moeran Lab		
Alliance		SDP	1951-66 N.J. Cole C		
			1966-70 Gwilym Roberts Lab		
			1970- David Madel C		

East Berkshire

This is Berkshire's seventh and extra seat, created by the boundary changes. E Berks is based on the New Town of Bracknell, formerly in the large Wokingham constituency. Bracknell is politically marginal, voting almost evenly Labour and Conservative in 1979. The wards of Priestwood, Garth, Old Bracknell and Great Hollands North elected Labour councillors on the same day as the last General Election, although Bracknell is not the most working-class of New Towns. The pine-wooded wards of Harmans Water and Hanworth are among the most attractive neighbourhoods of any New Town - and usually vote Conservative. All the same Bracknell was the only source of Labour support in the Wokingham seat.

Bracknell is still not really part of a marginal seat. It is still growing. New neighbourhoods are still being carved out of the evergreen forest. But Bracknell is even yet not large enough to justify a seat of its own, and the communities which complete the specification of East Berkshire are highly affluent and ultra middle-class: Old Windsor, Sunningdale, Sunninghill and Ascot, famed for its racecourse. Ascot has a most exclusive residential area just to the west of Ascot Heath. Part of Berkshire's military establishment is also to be found in the constituency - the Sandhurst Military Academy as well as the RAF Staff College at Bracknell. Wellington College, a public school with strong military connections, and the Broadmoor secure mental hospital at Crowthorne, are other institutions within the division.

The Conservative member for Wokingham, William van Straubenzee, will probably choose to contest the newly compact Wokingham seat at the next Election. This will leave a vacancy in East Berkshire, which will probably be filled by another Conservative, despite Bracknell's increased (and increasing) influence.

1981	% Own Occ	51	New seat
1981	% Loc Auth	36	
1981	% Black/Asian	2	
1981	% Mid Cl	60	
1981	% Prof Man	21	
1982	electorate 81,226		
1979	notional result		
	C 15,300		
Alliance		SDP	

Newbury

About half of the acreage of the County of Berkshire is to be
found in the Newbury constituency. This west Berkshire seat
stretches from the edge of Reading across the Downs to the
borders with Oxfordshire, Hampshire and Wiltshire. Newbury
(population 26,000) is the only town of any size, and even its
connection with industry has declined since the sixteenth
century, when a man named Jack of Newbury is reported to
have been operating a very early woollen weaving factory.
Newbury is nowadays better known for its racecourse, and
much training takes place up on the downs above the town.
Thatcham, also in the valley of the River Kennet, is also a
centre of population, but most of the electorate is to be found
in villages and rural areas.

Newbury seems in many ways the epitome of a Tory seat in
the Home Counties of southern England. Indeed so it was
until the early 1970s, when for a while it became one of the
Liberals' top target seats in the country. In February 1974
the Conservative Michael McNair-Wilson won the seat by only
1,201 votes from Liberal Dane Clouston. Clouston cut the
majority to 1,022 in October of the same year, but there was
to be no Liberal breakthrough in Newbury. In 1979 the Tory
lead increased to 10,000, although the Liberals still have a
formidable local organisation here.

In the boundary changes, Newbury loses about 15,000 voters
in the affluent communities of the Thames Valley near Reading
- Pangbourne, Purley and that part of Tilehurst outside the
Reading boundaries. But this was not the Liberals' strongest
area, which was the Newbury-Thatcham district, where they
hold every seat on the county council. The Conservatives do
better out in the villages, but the Liberals could still
challenge strongly in Newbury at the next Election, should
time be auspicious for the Alliance.

1981	% Own Occ	63	1979 core seat Newbury		
1981	% Loc Auth	21	C	33,677	52.8
1981	% Black/Asian	1.5	L	23,388	36.7
1981	% Mid Cl	55	Lab	6,676	10.5
1981	% Prof Man	22	MPs since 1945		
1982	electorate 71,270		1945-64 A.R. Hurd C		
1979	notional result		1964-74 John Astor C		
	C 8,700		1974- Michael McNair-Wilson C		
Alliance		L			

Reading East

Reading has on several occasions seen notable examples of the Boundary Commission's willingness to mix urban and rural terrain to create new constituencies of appropriate size. In 1955 even though Reading was then a sovereign County Borough, wards were hived off into Newbury and Wokingham county constituencies. In 1974 Reading was given two seats for the first time, but South was dominated by rural and suburban additions and was designated as a county seat. Now both Reading seats are to include Tory countryside and villages as well as wards from the town itself. This is almost certain to put both beyond Labour's reach, although Labour is still quite capable of amassing an electoral majority in Reading itself. In 1981, for example, Labour took 9 of the 17 seats in Reading on Berkshire County Council.

Reading East takes wards from the town together with five suburban wards from the Wokingham district. Some of the Reading districts are heavily Labour: the inner ward of Abbey, the southern council estate of Whitley. But the constituency also includes Reading's largest middle-class (and Tory) area, Caversham, across the Thames from the town centre. Over all, Reading East can be characterised as a Conservative seat with isolated Labour enclaves.

The practice of diluting urban units with external territory is almost always likely to hurt Labour, whose strength is concentrated in towns and cities. They would have a reasonable chance in a unified Reading seat. But the lines are drawn against them here in mid-Berkshire, and they may be thankful that the Boundary Commission has not adopted this policy throughout the country.

1981	% Own Occ	65	1979 core seat Reading South
1981	% Loc Auth	19	C 30,067 53.9
1981	% Black/Asian	3	Lab 14,422 25.8
1981	% Mid Cl	55	L 10,642 19.1
1981	% Prof Man	18	E 700 1.3
1982	electorate 65,340		MP since 1974
1979	notional result		1974- Gerard Vaughan C
	C 12,800		
Alliance	SDP		

Reading West

Reading is an industrial town, noted for many years for beer, biscuits and bulbs, and now for Metal Box. It is a railway junction, but also a University town. It is in many ways a microcosm of England, and it is scarcely surprising that several sociological surveys have taken place in this British version of 'Middletown'.

There is a fair selection of council estates, such as that at Southcote on the old A4, in the Reading West division. There is a sizeable immigrant population, concentrated in the private terraces of the town centre - Katesgrove ward has a West Indian county councillor, Joe Williams. There are also swathes of middle-class owner-occupied housing, of all ages and statuses. Politically too, all three parties are well represented on the local council - Labour does well in the centre of the town, and the Liberals and Conservatives fight it out in western residential districts like Tilehurst.

But two factors make both Reading seats fairly safe for the Tories. The Liberals seem unable to translate their local support into a breakthrough in General Elections. This leaves the Conservatives well ahead among owner occupiers, who form a majority in Reading. Secondly, both Reading divisions now include thousands of electors from outside the town. The old Reading seat, which existed before 1874, could be classed as marginal. But Reading West takes the smart Thames-side villages of Pangbourne and Purley, as well as Theale and Calcot by the Kennet. This means that socially typical Reading is skewed to the right in parliamentary elections, and cannot be counted in any way as a political bellwether.

1981	% Own Occ	65	1979 core seat Reading North		
1981	% Loc Auth	20	C	25,085	50.6
1981	% Black/Asian	8	Lab	17,662	35.6
1981	% Mid Cl	52	L	6,170	12.4
1981	% Prof Man	17	NF	554	1.1
1982	electorate 66,194		Ind	126	0.3
1979	notional result		MP since 1974		
	C 8,500		1974-	Anthony Durant C	
Alliance		L			

Slough

For many years Slough was united with Eton in a constituency which had a strong claim to be regarded as the most quaintly drawn in England. Notable left-wing Labour MPs such as peace campaigner Fenner Brockway (1950-64) and Joan Lestor (1966-) have had the privilege of representing the small town of Eton, which is dominated by the most famous boys' school in the world. It has been a tradition for Labour MPs to be bombarded with flour bags on their annual visit to the school. But the anomaly has been ended: the new seat of Slough is to consist simply of Slough District - Eton has been swapped for two peripheral council estates, Wexham and Britwell, which were formerly in Beaconsfield constituency.

For most people, Slough evokes the image of one of the few 'red' enclaves in Home Counties true blue suburbia, of the vast inter-war industrial estates along the Great West Road - a very early example of such planning - and of burgeoning council housing and a large immigrant population concentrated near the centre of town. But Slough does have Conservative areas too. The strongest is the middle-class residential ward of Upton, just east of the town centre. But most Tory votes come from the western and eastern ends of the Borough, where the sizeable semi-independent communities of Burnham and Langley fall within the District boundaries, and tend to the Conservatives in a good Tory year. In 1979, the District of Slough produced only a 500 majority for redheaded Labour NEC member Joan Lestor - and she would probably have lost her seat had it not been for the intervention of an Independent Conservative candidate.

Removing Eton will not hurt Labour, but Eton never actually played a significant role in anything other than the name of the old constituency. The two 'halves' of Eton and Slough were never equal in any sense, and Slough will remain a Labour marginal.

1981	% Own Occ	56.9
1981	% Loc Auth	34.7
1981	% Black/Asian	20.9
1981	% Mid Cl	44.8
1981	% Prof Man	13.7
1982	electorate 72,104	
1979	notional result	
	Lab 500	
Alliance		SDP

1979 core seat Eton/Slough

Lab	20,710	42.6
C	19,370	39.8
L	5,254	10.8
Ind C	2,359	4.9
NF	943	1.9

MPs since 1945
1945-50 B. Levy Lab
1950-64 Fenner Brockway Lab
1964-66 Sir A. Meyer C
1966-   Joan Lestor Lab

Windsor and Maidenhead

Berkshire is known as the Royal County, and the Queen's residence at Windsor Castle is one of Britain's best-known landmarks. It is now joined by another bastion of privilege and wealth, Eton, which although just across the Thames from Windsor, used to be combined in a seat with Slough. Maidenhead, the largest town in the seat, is well known as a haunt of wealthy commuters to London. There are Labour votes at Clewer, New Windsor, but it is not surprising that Alan Glyn enjoyed a Tory majority of 25,000 last time.

1981	% Own Occ	65		1979 core seat Windsor/		
1981	% Loc Auth	19		Maidenhead		
1981	% Black/Asian	4		C	38,451	59.7
1981	% Mid Cl	58		Lab	13,321	20.7
1981	% Prof Man	25		L	11,496	17.8
1982	electorate 79,095			NF	930	1.4
1979	notional result			Oth	251	0.4
	C 22,800			MPs since 1945		
Alliance		L		1945-70 Charles Mott-Radclyffe		
					C	
				1970-	Alan Glyn C	

Wokingham

The Wokingham seat is divided in the present redistribution. Bracknell New Town becomes a major part of the new East Berkshire division. Wokingham is left as a rather compact constituency east of Reading, consisting mainly of middle-class owner-occupied Reading suburbs like Woodley and Earley. The older town of Wokingham is independent of Reading, but more Conservative still in politics. Deprived of their only core of support in Bracknell, Labour will probably slip behind the Liberals into third place in this ultra-Tory seat.

1981	% Own Occ	81.8		1979 core seat Wokingham		
1981	% Loc Auth	11.1		C	36,194	54.4
1981	% Black/Asian	2		Lab	17,448	26.2
1981	% Mid Cl	68.7		L	12,120	18.2
1981	% Prof Man	29.5		NF	722	1.1
1982	electorate 70,500			MPs since 1950		
1979	notional result			1950-59 P.F. Remnant C		
	C 19,100			1959-	William van Straubenzee	
Alliance		L			C	

Aylesbury

With the creation of the new seat of Milton Keynes at the northern end of Buckinghamshire in the present review of boundaries, a 'ripple effect' has been produced which has driven the borders of Aylesbury constituency a few miles southwards. A region of villages like Brill and Winslow has been lost to the new Buckingham seat.

This will not affect the sure grip of the MP, senior non-Cabinet Minister Timothy Raison, on Aylesbury (even though he himself lives in Brill). About half the electorate is situated in Aylesbury itself, and the rest live in villages and small towns like Great Missenden and Princes Risborough. The small communities provided the bulk of Raison's 20,000 majority at the 1979 General Election.

There are Labour votes in the constituency. Aylesbury is expanding, and on the northern side of the town this involves council housing as well as private development. But mid-Buckinghamshire will remain a solidly Conservative part of one of the most loyally Tory counties in England.

1981	% Own Occ	63	1979 core seat Aylesbury	
1981	% Loc Auth	26	C 33,953	58.2
1981	% Black/Asian	3	Lab 14,091	24.2
1981	% Mid Cl	52	L 10,248	17.6
1981	% Prof Man	20	MPs since 1945	
1982	electorate 73,049		1945-50 Sir H.S. Reed C	
1979	notional result		1950-70 Sir G.S. Summers C	
	C 17,100		1970- Timothy Raison C	
Alliance		SDP		

Beaconsfield

The Beaconsfield division of south Buckinghamshire was justifiably described by the press during the 1982 byelection as one of the classic Tory citadels of Britain. Disraeli kept his country seat here, at Hughenden, and took the title of his earldom from Beaconsfield. Sir Ronald Bell, a crusty and trenchant right-winger, had held Beaconsfield and its predecessor South Bucks since 1950, always with massive majorities. The Conservatives held the seat in 1982 with a thumping 13,000 lead.

What is more, the minor changes recommended by the Boundary Commissioners will remove Labour's only enclaves of support, the council estates of Britwell and Wexham on the edge of Slough, which are now in Berkshire. Some of London's most affluent and expensive outer commuter belt is to be found in this division, especially around Gerrards Cross.

The young byelection victor Tim Smith, briefly member for Ashfield after he upset a 23,000 Labour majority in 1976, now seems likely to be able to reproduce Sir Ronald Bell's 30 years in Parliament without any trouble at all.

1981	% Own Occ	68
1981	% Loc Auth	19
1981	% Black/Asian	2
1981	% Mid Cl	66
1981	% Prof Man	31
1982	electorate 66,619	
1979	notional result	
	C 20,300	
Alliance		L

1979 core seat Beaconsfield

C	31,938	61.7
Lab	10,443	20.2
L	8,853	17.1
NF	548	1.1

MPs since 1950
1950-82 Sir Ronald Bell C
1982-   Tim Smith C

Buckingham

Before the much-needed redrawing of boundaries, Buckingham was the most populous British constituency, with over 122,000 electors in 1982. This was largely due to the growth of the new city of Milton Keynes, which has now been almost entirely hived off into a seat of its own. In the main, Buckingham will be a rural seat containing the small town of Buckingham itself and a number of villages, some of which were formerly in the Aylesbury division.

However, Milton Keynes Borough is already so large that some wards must still be included in the Buckingham seat. Those districts which are to overflow happen to be the strongest for Labour in the new city. These are Wolverton, which is an old railway town, always an anomaly in rural Buckinghamshire; Stony Stratford; and the brand-new Milton Keynes neighbourhood of Wolverton Stacey Bushes. Wolverton was the only ward which elected a Labour County Councillor in the Tory landslide year of 1977.

The inclusion of these Milton Keynes wards should have more impact on Labour's chances of winning the prospectively marginal Milton Keynes seat, than on the Tory grip on the new, shrunken Buckingham – which will be safe for sitting MP William Benyon.

1981	% Own Occ	59.4	1979 core seat Buckingham
1981	% Loc Auth	28.5	C 41,719 51.3
1981	% Black/Asian	3	Lab 27,752 34.1
1981	% Mid Cl	53.8	L 11,045 13.1
1981	% Prof Man	23.5	NF 803 1.0
1982	electorate 63,134		MPs since 1945
1979	notional result		1945-51 Aidan Crawley Lab
	C 13,600		1961-64 Sir S.F. Markham C
Alliance		L	1964-70 Robert Maxwell Lab
			1970- William Benyon C

222

Chesham and Amersham

In the last redistribution before the present one, that of 1974, prominent Conservative Sir Ian Gilmour had to move from his abolished Central Norfolk seat to a newly created constituency in Buckinghamshire, Chesham and Amersham. This compact seat in the Chilterns has provided a firm base for the moderate Sir Ian through his political tribulations, which have included his departure from the Foreign Office rather like Lord Carrington during the Falklands Crisis.

Chesham and Amersham is nearly coterminous with the local government Chiltern District, and as that name implies, it is composed of pleasant leafy towns and villages set in the hills. This is still part of the Home Counties, and it is close enough to London to rank as a desirable commuter base.

There is a council estate at Chesham, which makes that town politically marginal. But Amersham, Chesham Bois, the Chalfonts and Hazlemere, and the numerous secluded villages, will continue to return a massive and reliable majority for Sir Ian Gilmour in the foreseeable future.

1981	% Own Occ	72	1979 core seat Chesham and			
1981	% Loc Auth	17	Amersham			
1981	% Black/Asian	2	C	32,924	61.4	
1981	% Mid Cl	64	L	12,328	23.0	
1981	% Prof Man	28	Lab	7,645	14.3	
1982	electorate 70,620		NF	697	1.3	
1979	notional result		MP since 1974			
	C 20,600		1974-	Sir Ian Gilmour C		
Alliance		L				

Milton Keynes

New Towns are often associated with working-class overspill from such big cities as London. But in the new city of Milton Keynes, designated as Britain's last great New Town project in 1967, this has not led to a notable upsurge in Labour strength. Indeed there has been a swing away from Labour in this district since the 1960s, when the controversial entrepreneurial millionaire Oxford publisher Robert Maxwell held this division's parent seat of Buckingham.

Maxwell lost Buckingham in 1970, and by 1979 his successor William Benyon had increased the Tory majority to nearly 14,000. This is partly because there is good evidence that the Labour loyalties of uprooted voters are disrupted when they move, and partly because there are substantial pockets of owner-occupier development in Milton Keynes. Existing communities like Newport Pagnell, Woburn Sands and Bletchley were never noted for strong Labour support, and the hypermodern developments of Linford, Woughton and other neighbourhoods around the hypermarkets of the new city's centre have yet to demonstrate strong political preferences one way or another.

The strongest Labour wards, Wolverton and Wolverton Stacey Bushes, are still in the Buckingham division, and this new Milton Keynes seat would probably have voted Conservative in 1979. Its political characteristics are as yet not fully clear, however, and it must be ranked as a marginal prospect. Although Milton Keynes had only 50,000 electors in 1976, by the 1980s its growth had been such that it was already over average size for an English constituency - 75,000 plus. In due course it will probably become one of the larger seats in the country, just as its parent Buckingham did.

1981	% Own Occ	48.1	New seat
1981	% Loc Auth	47.4	
1981	% Black/Asian	4	
1981	% Mid Cl	50.5	
1981	% Prof Man	16.9	
1982	electorate 76,548		
1979	notional result		
	C 6,700		
Alliance		SDP	

Wycombe

The town of High Wycombe itself has light industrial estates,
many working-class voters and a notable immigrant
community. Yet at the 1979 Election the Wycombe seat
delivered to Tory MP Ray Whitney a majority of over 20,000
votes. The explanation for this lies in the fact that more than
half of the electorate lay outside High Wycombe, in affluent
commuting Marlow on the Thames and in many solidly
Conservative villages.

High Wycombe town itself is politically marginal. The
strongest Labour wards are in the east of the town, in the
terraces near the industrial scene which can be viewed from
the M40 motorway as its swoops in switchback fashion past
the town on its way from Oxford towards London. The
Conservative suburbs sit on the slopes of the steep hills,
especially off the road north-east towards Amersham. There is
a variety of industry in High Wycombe, and a number of
modern industrial estates such as that at Cressex in the
south-west of the town.

Wycombe has lost 20,000 of the more rural voters in the
boundary changes, mainly to Aylesbury in the north; but
although Whitney's majority may be reduced, this constituency
remains safe Conservative territory. There are over 10,000
paid-up Tory Party members in this division, and a Labour
victory would still be seen as a local political earthquake in
the Chiltern foothills.

1981	% Own Occ	68	1979 core seat Wycombe		
1981	% Loc Auth	22	C	38,171	57.3
1981	% Black/Asian	7	Lab	18,000	27.0
1981	% Mid Cl	54	L	9,615	14.4
1981	% Prof Man	23	NF	833	1.3
1982	electorate 70,560		MPs since 1945		
1979	notional result		1945-51 J.E. Haire Lab		
	C 15,700		1951-52 W.W. Astor C		
Alliance		SDP	1952-78 Sir John Hall C		
			1978- Ray Whitney C		

Cambridge

In the last three decades, Labour has held Cambridge for only one year, 1966-67. Unlike the case of the rival ancient University town, Oxford, the Conservative grip on Cambridge has proved almost unbreakable. This is somewhat surprising, for at local council level the Tories have been markedly vulnerable to both Labour and Liberal challenges for several years. Why has the parliamentary performance run so unusually ahead of the Conservatives' municipal showing?

One possible explanation is that the Conservative MPs have been liberal enough to appeal to the intellectual tastes of a sophisticated electorate: on his departure to the Commission for Racial Equality in 1976 the colour-blind David Lane was replaced by historian Robert Rhodes James. It is true that in local elections the University-dominated wards show scant favour to the Conservatives. Newnham, in wooded west Cambridge, belies its appearance to vote Labour. Market ward in the centre of the city is a Liberal stronghold. Whether such seats return their allegiance to the Conservatives at General Election time is impossible to tell. Labour does well too in the rather extensive council estates such as King's Hedges and Arbury in the north of the city, and in the terraced working-class wards like Petersfield and Romsey.

The Conservatives' best wards have in the past been at Chesterton and at Queen Edith and Trumpington on the southern edge of the city; but they must be hindered now by the removal in the present boundary review of the latter two wards. Cambridge <u>was</u> 10,000 electors too large. But the Tories must count themselves unlucky to have their hold on the seat reduced to uncertainty through the exclusion of their two best wards.

1981	% Own Occ	45.0	1979 core seat Cambridge
1981	% Loc Auth	37.9	C 25,568 45.8
1981	% Black/Asian	3.5	Lab 20,672 37.0
1981	% Mid Cl	53.3	L 9,285 16.6
1981	% Prof Man	18.3	NF 311 0.6
1982	electorate 67,223		MPs since 1945
1979	notional result		1945-50 A.L. Symonds Lab
	C 1,700		1950-66 Sir H.W. Kerr C
Alliance		SDP	1966-67 R.M.D. Davies Lab
			1967-76 David Lane C
			1976- R. Rhodes James C

Huntingdon

One of the casualties of the local government reshuffle of the early 1970s was the independence of the County of Huntingdonshire. Like Rutland, Westmorland and Herefordshire, it was felt to be too small to sustain county status on its own, so it was absorbed into Cambridgeshire. Nevertheless, the population of Huntingdonshire was among the most rapidly growing in the country, and by 1979 its single parliamentary constituency had attained an electorate of 94,000.

Clearly some reduction had to be made, and the Boundary Commission has decided to move the area around the booming overspill town of St Neots to SW Cambridgeshire. St Neots had a population of 8,000 in 1961, rising to 21,000 in 1981 as there was an influx mainly composed of resettled Londoners. Huntingdon/Godmanchester itself is another expanding town of similar characteristics, and the Huntingdon constituency now includes some wards around Barnack west of Peterborough, which are to some extent affected by the growth of that New Town.

But despite its experience of ultra-modern housing development, Huntingdon will remain a predominantly rural and strongly Conservative seat, stretching across the low-lying farming land between Cambridge and Peterborough. The Conservative MP John Major won a majority of over 21,000 in his first contest here, in 1979. Though more compact, the new Huntingdon will be as safe as before for the Tory Party. The new housing is mostly owner occupied, and Labour can hope for little new sustenance here.

1981	% Own Occ	63.1	1979 core seat Huntingdon
1981	% Loc Auth	21.5	C 40,193 55.3
1981	% Black/Asian	1.5	Lab 18,630 25.7
1981	% Mid Cl	46.6	L 12,812 17.6
1981	% Prof Man	17.4	MPs since 1945
1982	electorate 75,130		1945-79 Sir David Renton C
1979	notional result		1979- John Major C
	C 20,000		
Alliance		L	

North-East Cambridgeshire

The present MP for the Isle of Ely is a most well-known personality. Clement Freud is a Liberal, a chef, a gourmet, a TV and radio star, a sometime director of the Playboy Club, and a class winner in the Daily Mail London - New York air race of 1969. He won the Isle of Ely in one of the most spectacular byelection successes of the Liberal revival of the early 1970s, and has repeated his victory in three subsequent General Elections. Last time he held off the formidable challenge of Dr Thomas Stuttaford, the former Conservative MP for Norwich South, and now he looks almost invincible for as long as he should choose to maintain active politics among his many interests.

NE Cambridgeshire should prove a suitable constituency for Freud - it is really the Isle of Ely minus Ely itself. The cathedral city of Ely is Conservative, at least in local elections, so will prove no sad loss for the Liberals. Much of Fenland is not wealthy. It is dependent on arable farming and agriculture related industries. The farms, villages and towns are functional rather than spruce. Labour used to do well in the towns here amongst the Fens - March, Wisbech, Whittlesey and Chatteris - and they nearly captured the Isle of Ely themselves in 1966. But Freud has squeezed their vote very effectively, down to a bare 12.5% in 1979.

Clearly Clement Freud can benefit from marshalling the large anti-Tory vote in the Isle of Ely, particularly in the northern half around Wisbech and March, and with his personal vote he runs far ahead of Liberal local election candidates - the Fenland people feel they benefit from having a distinctive representative, one of those recognised far beyond the confines of the House of Commons itself.

1981	% Own Occ	63	1979 core seat Isle of Ely	
1981	% Loc Auth	25	L	26,397	46.7
1981	% Black/Asian	0.6	C	23,067	40.8
1981	% Mid Cl	40	Lab	7,067	12.5
1981	% Prof Man	15	MPs since 1945	
1982	electorate 70,009		1945-73 Sir Harry Legge-Bourke	
1979	notional result		C	
	L 1,400		1973- Clement Freud L	
Alliance		L		

Peterborough

In 1966 Peterborough produced the closest contest of any constituency in post-war Elections. The sitting Conservative MP, Sir Harmar Nicholls, defeated Labour's Michael Ward by just three votes. Seven recounts were necessary. Then in 1968 this cathedral city on the edge of the Fens was designated as one of the last New Towns. The population rose from 76,000 (1961) to 115,000 (1981), largely through the acceptance of London overspill. Needless to say, this threatened the Tories' shaky grasp on the seat, and in October 1974 Michael Ward finally defeated Harmar Nicholls (having lost by 22 votes in the February Election!). But rural areas remained in the Peterborough seat, and it was their votes which were largely responsible for returning it to the Conservatives after a large swing in 1979.

Now, however, many of the outlying wards of Peterborough City Council are removed. Thorney and Eye pass into NE Cambs, Werrington and Barnack into Huntingdon. In exchange, Peterborough gains the Labour suburb of Old Fletton across the River Nene from the city centre. The number of council houses in the constituency doubled in the 1970s, and together with the boundary changes this makes Peterborough one of Labour's best hopes in the 1980s. There are still pleasant older middle-class neighbourhoods in wards like West and Park, but New Town developments march out from the heart of the city further and further towards the Fens. There is also now a substantial non-white population in the centre of Peterborough.

It would not be true to say that sociological changes generally favour the Labour Party in modern Britain. But there are places which are swinging to the left, either in inner cities or New Towns like Peterborough. Labour were ahead in the new Peterborough seat in the 1982 local elections. The present Conservative MP, Dr Brian Mawhinney, must be one of the most vulnerable to defeat at the next General Election.

1981	% Own Occ	47.8	1979 core seat Peterborough			
1981	% Loc Auth	45.3	C	27,734	48.8	
1981	% Black/Asian	7	Lab	22,632	39.8	
1981	% Mid Cl	41.4	L	5,685	10.0	
1981	% Prof Man	11.3	NF	672	1.2	
1982	electorate 78,585		WRP	106	0.2	
1979	notional result		MPs since 1945			
	C 2,900		1945-50 S. Tiffany Lab			
Alliance		SDP	1950-74 Sir Harmar Nicholls C			
			1974-79 Michael Ward Lab			
			1979- Brian Mawhinney C			

South East Cambridgeshire

The Cambridgeshire constituency held by Tory Foreign Secretary Francis Pym reached an electorate of 93,000 in 1979 - quite an achievement, considering that this seat, which surrounds the city of Cambridge, contained no towns of over 5,000 population. Clearly the Cambridgeshire seat had to be split, but the majority of it does pass into the new SE Cambs, which also annexes the city of Ely from Clement Freud's Liberal seat. But Ely was never Freud's strongest area, and there should be no problem for Francis Pym (widely tipped as a possible leader of the Tory Party), if he should decide to stay with the bulk of his electorate.

1981	% Own Occ	59	1979 core seat Cambridgeshire
1981	% Loc Auth	28	C 41,218 56.5
1981	% Black/Asian	1	Lab 17,929 24.6
1981	% Mid Cl	50	L 13,780 18.9
1981	% Prof Man	20	MPs since 1945
1982	electorate 66,566		1945-50 A.E. Stubbs Lab
1979	notional result		1950-61 S.G. Howard C
	C 15,300		1961- Francis Pym C
Alliance		SDP	

South-West Cambridgeshire

Given the rapid population growth in Cambridgeshire and Huntingdonshire in the last 15 years, it was inevitable and deserved that an extra seat should be allocated to this part of eastern England. It is, however, also inevitable that SW Cambs should be made up of a ragbag of former seats. The expanding town of St Neots comes in from Huntingdonshire, and the two safest Conservative wards in Cambridge (Trumpington and Queen Edith's) are detached to join the minority of Francis Pym's Cambridgeshire division. Like so many of the new seats in the English shire counties, it will undoubtedly provide another Conservative face in the Commons.

1981	% Own Occ	60.6	New seat
1981	% Loc Auth	27.5	
1981	% Black/Asian	1	
1981	% Mid Cl	55.0	
1981	% Prof Man	23.2	
1982	electorate 76,062		
1979	notional result		
	C 17,400		
Alliance		L	

City of Chester

In a conventionally arranged list of parliamentary constituencies, if one wishes to find Chester, one is directed to 'City of Chester' - and then it is somewhat surprising to find that this is a County, not a Borough constituency! The City of Chester seat does indeed include rural areas outside the historic city itself, although it is more compact now than previously: the district north of Chester around Elton, Mollington and Saughall has been transferred to Ellesmere Port and Neston.

As might be expected, the fertile agricultural hinterland is more Conservative than the city itself. But Chester has never really been a marginal: Labour failed to capture it either in 1945 or in 1966. Labour wins easily in the council estate ward of Blacon across the Dee from the centre of Chester and in Dee Point, but most of the city wards are marginal or Conservative. Chester is a prosperous and historic market centre, which draws tourists to see its cathedral, its walls and its 'Rows' or elevated arcades of shops. The Tories pile up the votes in Upton and in the villages which remain in the constituency, such as Christleton. It is hard to see the Labour Party pulling off their first ever victory in Chester next time.

The Conservative MP for the City of Chester is Peter Morrison, the younger brother of the member for Devizes. He is not as associated with anti-Thatcherite moderation as the elder Morrison, and seems set for a lengthy career in the House.

1981	% Own Occ	61.2	1979 core seat Chester
1981	% Loc Auth	27.3	C 28,764 51.4
1981	% Black/Asian	1	Lab 19,450 34.8
1981	% Mid Cl	54.2	L 7,711 13.8
1981	% Prof Man	18.9	MPs since 1945
1982	electorate 64,952		1945-56 B.E. Nield C
1979	notional result		1956-74 John Temple C
	C 7,700		1974- Peter Morrison C
Alliance		L	

Congleton

The Liberals caused a shock in 1981 when they polled more votes than any other party in Congleton Borough in SE Cheshire, a district in which they had previously achieved no strong showing. Congleton constituency, which is closely based on the Borough of the same name, is entirely new, drawn together from a number of old seats. Alsager, Sandbach and Haslington were formerly in the Crewe division. Congleton itself, and its surrounding villages on the Cheshire Plain, formed the southern half of Nicholas Winterton's oversized Macclesfield seat. Middlewich is transferred from Nantwich.

But no matter what their origins, in 1981 these Cheshire towns showed great favour to the Liberals, who won the county wards of Alsager, Middlewich, Moreton and Sandbach. They were second in the other two, behind Labour in Congleton and behind the Tories in Hulme (Holmes Chapel). Nor did the Liberals draw their support only from a particular social or economic category. Sandbach and Alsager, and the rural parishes, were traditionally Conservative in local and national preference. The old salt-mining town of Middlewich, and Congleton itself, have strong Labour elements.

But overall this new seat of Congleton would have been Conservative in 1979, and the Liberals would only have finished third. In such an untried division the Liberals' hopes must be regarded as somewhat speculative. A constituency of small towns and agricultural areas must usually be good Conservative ground nowadays. But there is no doubt that Congleton will all the same be one of the most interesting of the new divisions created by the latest boundary redistribution. It would still be a surprise if the Liberals were to win - but they have been known to spring one or two suprises in each General Election, and this could just be another one!

1981	% Own Occ	73.2	New seat
1981	% Loc Auth	19.9	
1981	% Black/Asian	0.5	
1971	% Mid Cl	51.6	
1971	% Prof Man	22.4	
1976	electorate 63,778		
1979	notional result		
	C 9,100		
Alliance		L	

Crewe and Nantwich

This new constituency, which consists of the whole of Crewe
and Nantwich Borough less one ward, will be one of the most
socially divided and politically marginal in the country. Even
the name reveals this. Crewe has always been seen as a
working-class island in Cheshire, famed for its railway
junction and repair works and its manufacture of Rolls Royce
cars. Nantwich is a picturesque and affluent market-town,
with a centre typified by half-timbered buildings and antique
shops; and the old Nantwich Rural District included many of
the expanded villages which house Crewe's middle class
commuters - Willaston, Wistaston, Shavington and others.

Crewe always was a Labour seat. Its terraced Victorian
streets in the centre and peripheral council estates remained
loyal successively to Scholefield Allen and Gwyneth
Dunwoody. Crewe division formerly included Alsager, now lost
to Congleton; but if anything, Alsager was the Liberals' best
area in the constituency. Nantwich, on the other hand,
formed the core of a seat which always returned
Conservatives despite the presence of Labour towns like
Middlewich and Winsford.

Crewe and Nantwich may be physically so close that their
suburbs run into each other. But they are worlds apart
economically and electorally, and the new constituency should
be as marginal as the Borough council elections have been. It
is probable that in 1979 the seat would have voted
Conservative, narrowly, and that in future it will go to the
party which wins the General Election.

1981	% Own Occ	62.7	1979 core seat Crewe		
1981	% Loc Auth	27.4	Lab	22,288	48.3
1981	% Black/Asian	1	C	18,051	39.1
1981	% Mid Cl	42.0	L	5,430	11.8
1981	% Prof Man	13.8	NF	352	0.8
1982	electorate 72,230		MPs since 1945		
1979	notional result		1945-74 S.S. Allen Lab		
	C 3,600		1974- Gwyneth Dunwoody Lab		
Alliance		SDP			

Eddisbury

The western part of the Vale Royal District comprises the new constituency of Eddisbury, which revives a name formerly used for a parliamentary division before 1950. Eddisbury Hill, near Delamere Forest, is one of a series of hills in west Cheshire, which rise above the Cheshire Plain further east. The Eddisbury seat cuts across the county from north to south, including the western halves of Runcorn, Northwich and Nantwich. This is mainly solid Tory territory, either rural villages or affluent small towns like Frodsham, Helsby and Tarporley. The only real Labour support is in the largest town, Winsford, which has been expanding through accepting Manchester overspill since the 1950s. Frodsham and Helsby were formerly in Runcorn; Winsford in Nantwich.

Eddisbury could prove a suitable refuge for any of the three Conservative MPs who sit for its constituent parts at present. All are threatened in some way. Mark Carlisle of Runcorn finds that the New Town which gives its name to his seat is placed together with Widnes across the Mersey in the new Halton division, which will be safely Labour. Nicholas Bonsor of Nantwich finds the heart of his seat merged with Labour's Crewe, producing a super-close marginal. Alastair Goodlad of Northwich has a different problem: the eastern half of his constituency is included with that of another Tory, Jock Bruce-Gardyne (Knutsford) in the new NE Cheshire seat.

Whichever Conservative wins the nomination for Eddisbury should find it a safe haven. Winsford's growth is incomplete still, for much of its road network goes nowhere, connecting as yet unbuilt neighbourhoods. But even an enlarged Winsford should be able to be absorbed by comfortable Tory west Cheshire.

1981	% Own Occ	63.2	1979 core seat Nantwich		
1981	% Loc Auth	25.8	C	25,624	50.3
1981	% Black/Asian	0.5	Lab	17,919	35.2
1981	% Mid Cl	53.7	L	6,571	12.9
1981	% Prof Man	24.3	NF	814	1.6
1982	electorate 72,004		MPs since 1945		
1979	notional result		1945-50 Sir J.D. Barlow C		
	C 11,600		1950-74 Sir R. Grant-Ferris C		
Alliance		L	1974-79 John Cockcroft C		
			1979- Sir Nicholas Bonsor C		

Ellesmere Port and Neston

The new constituency of Ellesmere Port and Neston is squeezed between the muddy, swampy estuaries of the Dee and the Mersey. This is one of Britain's most functional, industrial landscapes. By the Mersey can be found the massive complex of the oil refinery at Stanlow. There is a power station at Ince. Vauxhall Motors have a factory at the north end of Ellesmere Port. There are docks, paper-works, oil depots, sewage works, fertiliser factories and many other concerns. Chimneys and flares overshadow the council estates of Ellesmere Port, a town created by the Industrial Revolution and the Manchester Ship Canal. Just outside the boundaries of the constituency over the Welsh border lie the gaunt remains of Shotton steelworks.

But this is by no means a Labour stronghold, for the south Wirral villages and the small town of Neston on the Dee marshes have their fair proportion of commuters to Merseyside and Chester. Neston was 48% middle class in 1971, compared with Ellesmere Port's figure of 23%. Neston also possessed only 18% council housing, compared with 50% in Ellesmere Port. Neston is Conservative, particularly the Parkgate ward in the north of the town. All in all the two distinct halves of the constituency nearly cancel each other out. Neston's Conservatism is strengthened by a few thousand voters who come in from the City of Chester constituency – the village wards of Elton, Saughall and Mollington. Ellesmere Port was previously counterbalanced by a larger Tory town, Bebington, while Neston was part of the massively Conservative Wirral division.

The standard methods of calculation do not really tell us who would have been the victors in Ellesmere Port and Neston had it existed in 1979, for some of the local wards were left unfought in the council elections of the same day, which means that estimates have to be made. It is clear that the seat would have been very close; Labour would probably have been ahead, and certainly must start favourites in an even year. But this is one of the most marginal of all the new seats.

1981	% Own Occ	59.2	1979 core seat Bebington/		
1981	% Loc Auth	34.7	Ellesmere Port		
1981	% Black/Asian	0.5	C	32,488	43.9
1981	% Mid Cl	44.4	Lab	32,002	43.2
1981	% Prof Man	15.2	L	9,591	12.9
1982	electorate 70,449		MPs since 1974		
1979	notional result		1974-79 Alf Bates Lab		
	Lab 1,500 (RW)		1979- Barry Porter C		
Alliance		SDP			

Halton

Since Widnes was moved from Lancashire into Cheshire in the early 1970s, it has become possible for it to be united with the town on the opposite bank of the Mersey, Runcorn. Both are heavily dependent on the chemical industry. Now linked by the major A533 road bridge, there is no longer any need to take the ferry made famous by the music hall entertainer Stanley Holloway, which cost "2d per person per trip". But the creation of the Widnes-Runcorn Borough council, known as Halton, and now the constituency of the same name, is even more logical than ever before.

Widnes is one of the starker creations of the nineteenth century Industrial Revolution, but most of Runcorn is much newer - it was actually designated as a New Town in April 1964. Runcorn is now larger than Widnes - with a 64,000 population compared with 54,000. Runcorn is at present the centre of a safe seat held by the former Conservative Education Secretary Mark Carlisle, who was dismissed by Mrs Thatcher. But the Conservatism of the seat is somewhat misleading, for it is ensured by the rural and suburban elements of north Cheshire such as Lymm and Grappenhall, not by Runcorn itself. Widnes too is solidly Labour, except for a small middle-class residential area at the north end of the town, at Farnworth. Like Runcorn, Widnes was formerly surrounded by a large suburban hinterland for parliamentary purposes, including such places as Halewood and Whiston, which are now in Merseyside County.

Halton will be a safe Labour seat. Its proportion of council housing is nearly 50%, and was still growing rapidly in the 1970s, against the national trend. The most likely member is the sitting Labour MP for Widnes, Gordon Oakes, while Mark Carlisle must look elsewhere if he is to continue his political career.

1981	% Own Occ	48.3	1979 core seat Widnes		
1981	% Loc Auth	46.9	Lab	32,033	55.2
1981	% Black/Asian	0.6	C	21,752	37.5
1971	% Mid Cl	40.0	L	4,290	7.4
1971	% Prof Man	10.8	MPs since 1945		
1976	electorate 73,762		1945-50 C.N. Shawcross Lab		
1979	notional result		1950-71 J.E. MacColl Lab		
	Lab 5,800		1971- Gordon Oakes Lab		
Alliance		SDP			

Macclesfield

Nicholas Winterton has been one of the most vocal and well-publicised politicians of the populist right since he won Macclesfield in a byelection in 1971. His concern with law and order, immigration and trade union power was obviously to the taste of his electors in 1979, when he was returned with his largest ever majority, over 23,000. Now Macclesfield has lost 20,000 voters, to the new Congleton division, but the more compact core left should be even safer for Winterton. From where does this enthusiast derive such ardent support?

Macclesfield itself comprises half of the new constituency. The former silk mill town has expanded greatly since the war, with the growth of new private estates pleasantly set on the edge of the Cheshire Plain just beneath the Peak District foothills. There are still terraced working-class houses in central and south Macclesfield, and council estates in Weston in the west and Hurdsfield in the NE, but more typical are the thousands of new private houses in estates like Tytherington and Bollinbrook in the NW of the town. But Winterton's majority is piled up in the highly affluent Cheshire commuter belt for Manchester: in Disley, Alderley Edge and Prestbury, where Rolls-Royces abound and the detached homes with external gas lamps and trim lawns are reminiscent of a wealthy American neighbourhood. Poynton and Bollington are less exclusive, but still fashionably set in the green belt west of the Peak hills.

Congleton's departure has taken much of the Liberal strength with it, at least at local level, and Winterton's style should continue to suit the electorate in this outermost belt of Cheshire commuterland.

1981	% Own Occ	70.0	1979 core seat Macclesfield
1981	% Loc Auth	21.4	C 40,116 58.5
1981	% Black/Asian	1	Lab 16,779 24.5
1981	% Mid Cl	58.6	L 11,726 17.1
1981	% Prof Man	25.0	MPs since 1945
1982	electorate 74,349		1945-71 Sir Arthur Harvey C
1979	notional result		1971- Nicholas Winterton C
	C 20,900		
Alliance		L	

Tatton

The new Cheshire constituency of Tatton is to be made up of the eastern half of Vale Royal District together with that part of the Borough of Macclesfield outside Nicholas Winterton's constituency. Basically the former area used to be in Northwich, the latter in Knutsford; but the affluent commuter town of Wilmslow, where many ICI managerial workers live, has also come in from the Cheadle constituency.

The twin towns of Northwich and Witton, and indeed the whole of the section of Vale Royal in Tatton, tend to vote Labour. There is a massive ICI chemical works at Winnington, near Northwich, and the region is heavily industrial, bearing the marks of the salt mining and canal communications constructed in the nineteenth century. Northwich was a Brunner Mond company town nearly 100 years ago, and it remained 77% working class in 1971. The rest of Tatton, however, is very much a different matter. Knutsford was the centre of a safe Tory seat held by Mrs Thatcher's close confidant, Jock Bruce-Gardyne; and Wilmslow shared little of Cheadle's Liberal tradition of the 1960s.

Tatton is named after a large area of uninhabited land, Tatton Park, at the heart of the constituency. Whether it can be forged into a unit is doubtful, for the two halves of the seat really have little in common. Nevertheless, Wilmslow and Knutsford should outvote Northwich to make Tatton a safe Conservative seat.

1981	% Own Occ	64.0	1979 core seat Knutsford		
1981	% Loc Auth	26.7	C	26,795	59.6
1981	% Black/Asian	1	Lab	8,992	20.0
1981	% Mid Cl	57.3	L	8,499	18.9
1981	% Prof Man	26.2	Ind C	690	1.5
1982	electorate 69,947		MPs since 1945		
1979	notional result		1945-70 Sir Walter Bromley-		
	C 14,700			Davenport C	
Alliance		SDP	1970-79 John Davies C		
			1979- Jock Bruce-Gardyne C		

Warrington North

It was in Warrington in July 1981 that the Social Democratic Party launched its first parliamentary election campaign in Britain. Their standard-bearer in the Warrington byelection was Roy Jenkins, later to be chosen as the first Leader of the Party. Although Labour's Doug Hoyle held on to the seat by 1,759 votes, Jenkins came close enough to prove that the SDP would be a force to be reckoned with in the years to come. One feels that however long Doug Hoyle remains the member here, Warrington will always be associated with Roy Jenkins and the SDP.

The seat that Hoyle and Jenkins fought was a rather curious one: a tiny core of the town, which had spread far beyond its administrative boundaries long before it was named as a New Town in 1968. Not only were the spreading Development Corporation estates of NE Warrington previously in the Newton constituency; but so were Penketh and Great Sankey to the west. The middle-class suburbs of Stockton Heath and Grappenhall south of the Manchester Ship Canal were in the Runcorn division. Now the whole of Greater Warrington is in Cheshire, and it is divided in two for parliamentary purposes. Most of the New Town housing together with the old town north of the Mersey goes into Warrington North.

North will undoubtedly be the better of the two seats for Labour. The SDP challenge in Old Warrington will fade now that Roy Jenkins is many hundreds of miles away in Glasgow. The Conservatives enjoy strong wards in outlying villages like Croft and Culcheth beyond the M62 to the north. But with the continued expansion of the New Town out into the flat lands of Risley Moss, Doug Hoyle should discover that this seat will never again be as much at risk as it was in the SDP's inaugural byelection.

1981	% Own Occ	53.3	1979 core seat Warrington		
1981	% Loc Auth	39.8	Lab	19,036	61.7
1981	% Black/Asian	1	C	9,032	28.8
1981	% Mid Cl	43.0	L	2,833	9.0
1981	% Prof Man	12.8	Ind	144	0.5
1982	electorate 68,751		MPs since 1945		
1979	notional result		1945-50 E. Porter Lab		
	Lab 7,200		1950-55 H.B.W. Morgan Lab		
Alliance		SDP	1955-61 Edith Summerskill Lab		
			1961-81 Thomas Williams Lab		
			1981- Doug Hoyle Lab		

Warrington South

The majority of Warrington's middle-class population is situated south of the Manchester Ship Canal, in suburbs like Stockton Heath, Appleton, Grappenhall, Thelwall and the small town of Lymm. All this has always been in Cheshire, and formed a solidly Conservative phalanx at the eastern end of Mark Carlisle's Runcorn seat.

Now this bloc is to be included in the newly created Warrington South. Another growing, mainly private residential area is to be found west of Warrington in Penketh and Great Sankey. Like much of Warrington's New Town development, Penketh/Great Sankey were included in the vast Newton constituency which almost surrounded Warrington. Penketh and Great Sankey are more marginal than the ex-Cheshire wards, but still voted Conservative in the 1979 elections. The only Labour stronghold in the new Warrington South is the inter-war council estate of Westy, which is set on an island between the River Mersey and the Ship Canal. But overall the South division will probably be safely Conservative. The seat is really the successor to Runcorn, and indeed part of the Halton Borough is included – the wards of Daresbury and Norton, which actually takes in some of Runcorn's New Town sprawl.

Warrington North has much the best claim to be the site of the historic 1981 byelection, when Labour held off Roy Jenkins's SDP challenge and the Conservatives lost their deposit. But Warrington South is quite different; it should end up as a Tory victory, and the Liberals have the Alliance nomination here.

1981	% Own Occ	62.5	1979 core seat Runcorn			
1981	% Loc Auth	31.7	C	32,907	51.5	
1981	% Black/Asian	1	Lab	22,226	34.8	
1981	% Mid Cl	50.1	L	8,783	13.7	
1981	% Prof Man	17.9	MPs since 1950			
1982	electorate 73,149		1950-64 D.F. Vosper C			
1979	notional result		1964- Mark Carlisle C			
	C 7,300					
Alliance		L				

Hartlepool

Hartlepool was the only parliamentary constituency to record
no swing at all between Labour and Conservative in the 1979
General Election. Since this was of course a year of decisive
Conservative victory, the Hartlepool poll actually represents
one of Labour's best ten results in England. Four of those
ten were to be found in the far northern counties, and it is
true to say that the response to Mrs Thatcher became
progressively less warm the further north one travelled.

Hartlepool is a very good example of the long-term swing to
Labour in the north. Labour only won it by 275 votes in
1945, and it was actually held by the Conservatives between
1959 and 1964, when the present member Ted Leadbitter
regained it for Labour. It is an archetypal North Eastern
industrial town, a few miles north of Teesside. The British
Steel plant and the docks employ fewer people than they used
to. Indeed Hartlepool has one of the worst records for
joblessness in the country, with 20.0% out of work in 1981.
Labour picks up votes both in the terraces near the harbour
and in the centre of the town, and in the newer council
estates on the edge of the town, such as Owton, Rossmere
and Brus. The Conservative vote comes mainly from the old
west end of the town, and from Seaton Carew by the
southern sands of the North Sea.

The boundary changes are relatively minor. Some
Conservative villages like Elwick and Greatham come in from
rural County Durham. It is a mark of Labour's strength
nowadays in Hartlepool that the new additions can be accepted
without a qualm on their part - Hartlepool's marginal days
seem to be over.

1981	% Own Occ	50.6	1979 core seat Hartlepool		
1981	% Loc Auth	43.3	Lab	27,039	55.1
1981	% Black/Asian	0.5	C	18,877	38.4
1981	% Mid Cl	37.2	L	3,193	6.5
1981	% Prof Man	10.6	MPs since 1945		
1982	electorate 70,415		1945-59 D.T. Jones Lab		
1979	notional result		1959-64 J.S. Kerans C		
	Lab 8,900		1964- Ted Leadbitter Lab		
Alliance		SDP			

Langbaurgh

The Cleveland hills overlook industrial Teesside. They are in themselves largely rural still, and their villages usually return Conservative majorities. Yet it was the ironstone discovered here that led to the boom of Middlesbrough as a steel town in the nineteenth century. The large local authority which administers the Cleveland hills and coast is the Langbaurgh Council. There is no place called Langbaurgh, and the name is difficult to pronounce; basically the constituency is similar to the old Cleveland and Whitby division, but Whitby is still in North Yorkshire and therefore must be transferred to another seat. Perhaps 'Cleveland' would therefore be a better name than Langbaurgh. Another change is that Langbaurgh also includes seven wards from south Middlesbrough, which are a mixture of peripheral council estates and favoured residential areas.

Cleveland and Whitby was held by the rising Tory economic expert Leon Brittan, who won it by around 7,000 votes in 1979. Langbaurgh would have been even closer, and one can see why Brittan launched a spirited defence of his existing constituency at the boundary inquiry. Labour must have hopes of taking Langbaurgh. Despite the presence of seaside resorts like Saltburn and market towns like Guisborough in the hills, there are Labour voters in semi-industrial communities like Skinningrove, Loftus and Marske on the coast as well as in the south Middlesbrough council estates.

Indeed Langbaurgh is a mixture throughout of peaceful countryside and notable industry. Unless Leon Brittan chooses to migrate far from Cleveland in search of another seat, he may well be the Cabinet Minister most in danger of defeat at the next General Election.

1981	% Own Occ	62.5	1979 core seat	Cleveland/Whitby	
1981	% Loc Auth	32.2	C	26,735	51.0
1981	% Black/Asian	3	Lab	19,818	37.8
1981	% Mid Cl	47.8	L	5,870	11.2
1981	% Prof Man	15.4	MPs since 1945		
1982	electorate 77,682		1945-52 O.G. Willey Lab		
1979	notional result		1952-59 Arthur Palmer Lab		
	C 4,300		1959-64 Wilfred Proudfoot C		
Alliance		L	1964-74 James Tinn Lab		
			1974- Leon Brittan C		

Middlesbrough

As before, the seat named Middlesbrough does not in fact contain all of the steel city between the Cleveland Hills and the River Tees. The SW of the town is donated to Stockton South; the south end to Langbaurgh. There do remain some Conservative, middle-class wards, like Acklam, Kirby and Linthorpe. But the Labour strength of this safe seat comes from the poor terraces of the town centre and the council estates under the Clevelands in SE Middlesbrough. Veteran MP Arthur Bottomley is retiring, but has been replaced by another popular local Labour moderate, Stuart Bell.

1981	% Own Occ	49.0	1979 core seat Middlesbrough		
1981	% Loc Auth	42.8	Lab	24,872	56.2
1981	% Black/Asian	4	C	13,463	30.4
1981	% Mid Cl	36.2	L	4,023	9.1
1981	% Prof Man	8.4	WRP	1,018	2.3
1982	electorate 64,533		Ind Lab	861	1.9
1979	notional result		MPs since 1945		
	Lab 12,900		1945-50 A. Edwards Lab (C)		
Alliance		L	1950-62 H.A. Marquand Lab		
			1962- A. Bottomley Lab		

Redcar

Although Redcar itself is a holiday resort on the North Sea, the constituency of this name is dominated by the ICI chemical complex at Wilton and by British Steel's works by the Tees near South Bank and Grangetown. Unglamorous, functional communities like Eston and Dormanstown provide a solid Labour vote. This region is now included within the local government District of Langbaurgh, but Redcar constituency is left unaltered by the Boundary Commission. It is represented by James Tinn, a member of the Union of Blastfurnacemen.

1981	% Own Occ	53.2	1979 same seat Redcar		
1981	% Loc Auth	42.5	Lab	25,470	53.7
1981	% Black/Asian	0.9	C	17,417	36.7
1981	% Mid Cl	38.5	L	4,225	8.9
1981	% Prof Man	9.5	Ind	333	0.7
1982	electorate 63,838		MP since 1974		
Alliance		SDP	1974- James Tinn Lab		

Stockton North

William Rodgers is probably the least well-known of the 'Gang' of four original leaders of the SDP. But despite his decision not to contest the leadership of the party, and his failure to be elected President, he has put a formidable amount of work into the organisation of the party and the Alliance, and indeed into the thought which lies behind it. He is undoubtedly a very senior and influential SDP MP. But can he hold on to his seat in Parliament?

Like several other SDP ex-Labour defectors, William Rodgers sits for a North Eastern constituency – in his case, Teesside, Stockton. As a Labour candidate, he won a comfortable 11,000 majority in this large division in 1979. In the redistribution, the seat becomes Stockton North. 20,000 electors are lost to Stockton South (formerly Thornaby), the constituency of another SDP founder member, Ian Wrigglesworth. The territory lost is mainly the Conservative, middle-class west end of Stockton – Bishopgarth, Hartburn, Fairfield and Parkfield wards. A rural ward, Whitton, is added, but overall the changes probably do not help Rodgers. If Stockton North resolves itself into a battle between the SDP and Labour, he would have liked more basically Conservative wards which might prefer the more centrist candidate of the two contenders. But as it is Stockton North looks like a very Labour seat, physically as well as in political terms. At Billingham the massive ICI chemicals plant dominates an industrial skyline. The centre of Stockton and the council estates to the NW are traditionally Labour ground, overshadowed by steelworks and other industry. Only two or three Conservative private housing estates remain, such as in west Billingham.

There were no 1982 local elections in Stockton, so it is difficult to assess the general strength of the SDP in the area. But Rodgers still has a chance to win through his personal vote, which may be considerable. Ironically, his chances of retaining the seat he has held since 1962 have not been made any easier by the loss of Tory west Stockton.

1981	% Own Occ	49.3	1979 core seat Stockton
1981	% Loc Auth	45.4	Lab 34,917 53.1
1981	% Black/Asian	1	C 23,790 36.2
1981	% Mid Cl	40.0	L 6,074 9.2
1981	% Prof Man	11.3	NF 384 0.6
1982	electorate 70,805		Oths 586 0.9
1979	notional result		MPs since 1945
	Lab 11,900		1945-62 G.R. Chetwynd Lab
Alliance		SDP	1962- William Rodgers Lab
			(SDP)

Stockton South

Ian Wrigglesworth did well to secure one of the six pro-Labour swings at the 1979 General Election in Thornaby upon Tees. But he did not have much time to enjoy his enlarged Labour majority, for in 1981 he was one of the first 13 to defect to the Social Democrats. Thornaby is the basis of the new Stockton South seat, which means that both Stockton divisions are to be defended by prominent SDP members. Unlike William Rodgers's Stockton North, Wrigglesworth's seat has always been a socially and politically mixed marginal. Thornaby was itself the direct successor to Middlesbrough West, always a tight contest between Labour and Conservative.

Even now, Stockton South contains a sizeable chunk of the town of Middlesbrough. Mostly this is not a district typical of that working-class steel town, but some high-status residential areas of SW Middlesbrough are included, along with the more unpretentious Ayresome further in towards the centre. All the boundary changes which converted Thornaby into Stockton South would have helped the Conservatives in the old days. Middle-class west Stockton is annexed. A number of Tory villages are taken in from Richmond - Yarm, Eaglescliffe, Preston and others. Even the parts of Middlesbrough included are more Conservative.

Ironically, all this means that the Labour Ian Wrigglesworth of 1979 vintage would almost certainly have failed to win the seat, had it existed then. Yet as a Social Democrat, he may benefit from the rise in the Conservative vote. Tories might vote for him tactically to keep Labour out. Stockton South looks like a genuine three-way marginal. Who would ever have thought in 1979 that William Rodgers would suffer and Ian Wrigglesworth gain through Stockton becoming more Labour and Thornaby more Conservative?

1981	% Own Occ	70.8		1979 core seat Thornaby		
1981	% Loc Auth	24.1		Lab	23,597	51.1
1981	% Black/Asian	2		C	18,073	39.1
1981	% Mid Cl	51.8		L	4,255	9.2
1981	% Prof Man	16.4		NF	251	0.5
1982	electorate 74,111			MPs since 1945		
1979	notional result			1945-51 G. Cooper Lab		
	C 900			1951-62 J.E.S. Simon C		
Alliance		SDP		1962-70 Jeremy Bray Lab		
				1970-74 John Sutcliffe C		
				1974- Ian Wrigglesworth Lab		
				(SDP)		

Falmouth and Camborne

Falmouth and Camborne was once known as the single predominantly Labour seat in Cornwall. Labour held it from its creation in 1950 to 1970, when Conservative David Mudd won it by 1,523 votes. But no constituency in Britain swung more to the Tories in the 1970s. By the 1979 Election, Mudd had amassed a majority of 16,600, or 30.8% of the vote – a swing of 19% to the right since 1966. What has accounted for this most dramatic of political transformations?

Labour used to be able to rely on substantial support at both ends of this seat, which extends from the Atlantic to the Channel coast of Cornwall. The ports of Falmouth and Penryn in the south elected a Labour MP in 1945; and the historian A.L. Rowse (then a left-winger) finished a strong second for Labour in 1935. The industrial belt around Camborne-Redruth to the north was once the centre of the Cornish tin mining industry. But now the mines are almost all closed. Falmouth's economy relies more on its role as a holiday resort than as a working port. Other factors work against Labour too. Nigh on 70% of the housing in the division is now owner occupied, for council dwellings have never been built extensively in Cornwall. Finally the MP David Mudd is a powerful and articulate figure. A former TV presenter, outspoken and independent, he stands on the populist right of the Conservative Party. Like several Cornish MPs, Mudd has been able to build up a formidable personal vote.

Labour still wins the odd council ward in Illogan, Camborne, Redruth and Falmouth. It will be interesting to see how the SDP do in their first contest in Falmouth and Camborne, where the Liberals have never made an impact. In the boundary changes, 8,000 voters are lost to the St Ives seat.

1981	% Own Occ	69.4	1979 core seat Falmouth/		
1981	% Loc Auth	18.4	Camborne		
1981	% Black/Asian	1	C	30,523	56.7
1981	% Mid Cl	45.9	Lab	13,923	25.9
1981	% Prof Man	16.1	L	7,489	13.9
1982	electorate 65,570		Meb Ker	1,637	3.0
1979	notional result		NF	280	0.5
	C 15,900		MPs since 1950		
Alliance		SDP	1950-66 F.H. Hayman Lab		
			1966-70 John Dunwoody Lab		
			1970- David Mudd C		

North Cornwall

If Falmouth and Camborne is a constituency which has lost its Labour tradition, North Cornwall is very much the place which never had one. Labour only ever saved its deposit in 1950-51 in North Cornwall. In 1979 the Labour candidate polled 1,514 votes, or 3.2% – their worst performance in Britain. But this does not mean that N Cornwall is a safe Tory seat. Far from it – there has been a long-standing Liberal strength which most recently has been personified by John Pardoe, who was MP from 1966 to 1979. Pardoe stood for the leadership of the party against David Steel, and undoubtedly ranked as the Liberal No.2 in Parliament, before his defeat by Tory solicitior Gerry Neale, who mobilised the holiday-home vote against Pardoe.

The Liberals had also won North Cornwall in every Election from 1929 to 1950. They tapped a strong Nonconformist and rural radical vote, and a distrust of 'English' Toryism down here in the far western peninsula. N Cornwall has been a Liberal-Tory marginal, traditionally displaying a very high level of turnout, for most of this century. Until the present redistribution, North Cornwall included Bude and Stratton, Launceston and the large holiday resort of Newquay (which was the Conservatives' best area). Now the town of Bodmin is added. Bodmin, standing on its bleak moor, has received London overspill population in the years since World War Two. It used to form the basis of its own constituency which also had a strong Liberal element, although former MP Paul Tyler lost by 10,000 in 1979.

John Pardoe has abandoned his career in the lower house, and it will be up to a new Liberal candidate to challenge Neale's 4,000 majority in North Cornwall. Such is this area's history of Liberals, that it must continue to rank as one of the party's brightest hopes at the next Election even without the bulky and powerful figure of Pardoe as candidate.

1981	% Own Occ	62	1979 core seat North Cornwall		
1981	% Loc Auth	20	C	24,489	51.7
1981	% Black/Asian	0.7	L	20,742	43.7
1981	% Mid Cl	43	Lab	1,514	3.2
1981	% Prof Man	19	E	442	0.9
1982	electorate 66,539		NF	224	0.5
1979	notional result		MPs since 1945		
	C 5,300		1945-50 T.L. Horabin L		
Alliance		L	1950-59 Sir H. Roper C		
			1959-66 Jim Scott-Hopkins C		
			1966-79 John Pardoe L		
			1979- Gerry Neale C		

St Ives

The constituency of St Ives covers the very south-western tip of the mainland of Britain, plus the Scilly Isles. Land's End and Lizard Point, and the towns of Penzance, St Ives, Helston and St Just are all in the seat, along with the Goonhilly Downs with their satellite communications aerial dishes. Most of this terrain is included in the Penwith and Kerrier Districts. St Ives is at present the seat of Falklands campaign Foreign Secretary John Nott, but Nott surprised many by his decision to retire from politics while very well known and scarcely past the age of 50.

The Liberals have never done as well here as elsewhere in rural Cornwall, so it is logical that the SDP will have the chance to try to mobilise support for the Alliance more effectively. The former Labour Prime Minister Harold Wilson was fond of taking his holidays in the Scilly Isles, but neither the Isles nor the rest of the St Ives constituency offers much hope for Labour, who scraped into a poor second place in 1979. In 1966 Labour achieved their best ever result here, just 3,000 votes behind Nott, who was contesting the seat for the first time. But the agriculture workers of Cornwall are no more inclined to militant trade unionism or socialism than other rural employees in Britain. The county's economy is heavily dependent on tourism and the summer season, never a good sign for Labour. There are few council house tenants, and of course scarcely any non-white residents, to bolster the left-wing support.

St Ives looks like remaining a safe Tory seat, providing a long-term seat in remotest Cornwall for John Nott's successor, David Harris, the present Euro-MP for Cornwall.

1981	% Own Occ	63.7	1979 core seat St Ives		
1981	% Loc Auth	19.1	C	22,352	54.0
1981	% Black/Asian	0.7	Lab	8,636	20.9
1981	% Mid Cl	42.5	L	8,299	20.1
1981	% Prof Man	18.0	Meb Ker	1,662	4.0
1982	electorate 64,118		E	427	1.0
1979	notional result		MPs since 1945		
	C 15,100		1945-50 N.A. Beechman C		
Alliance		SDP	1950-66 G.R. Howard C		
			1966- John Nott C		

South-East Cornwall

The Cornish constituency nearest to the Devon border used to be called Bodmin; but now Bodmin itself has been moved to N Cornwall, and replaced by Fowey from the Truro division. The redrawn seat is to be named SE Cornwall. The main towns now, besides Fowey, are Saltash and Torpoint over the Tamar from Plymouth; the twin seaside resort-ports of East and West Looe; and the inland towns of Liskeard and Lostwithiel near Restormel Castle. The bijou fishing village of Polperro, now heavily commercialised, is also in the division.

Bodmin was one of the several Liberal-Tory marginals in the county. Peter Bessell held it for the Liberals from 1964 to 1970, always narrowly. But it was never more marginal than when the Liberal Paul Tyler defeated Robert Hicks by nine votes in February 1974. Hicks won the seat back in October of the same year, and increased his majority over Tyler to 10,000 in 1979.

Robert Hicks was one of the moderate Conservatives thought most likely to defect to the SDP. But he has refrained from joining Christopher Brocklebank-Fowler of NW Norfolk, and remained within the Tory fold. He should be rewarded by a clear margin in SE Cornwall next time.

1981	% Own Occ	68	1979 core seat Bodmin		
1981	% Loc Auth	19	C	27,922	54.9
1981	% Black/Asian	0.7	L	17,893	35.2
1981	% Mid Cl	45	Lab	3,508	6.9
1981	% Prof Man	18	Meb Ker	865	1.7
1982	electorate 64,609		E	465	0.9
1979	notional result		NF	235	0.5
	C 7,600		MPs since 1945		
Alliance		L	1945-64 D. Marshall C		
			1964-70 Peter Bessell L		
			1970-74 Robert Hicks C		
			1974 Paul Tyler L		
			1974- Robert Hicks C		

Truro

In 1979 the Liberals lost their deputy leader, John Pardoe, defeated in North Cornwall. But some compensation was offered by the result in a neighbouring constituency. The Liberal position was strengthened substantially in the mid-Cornwall division of Truro, where David Penhaligon increased his majority from 464 to 8,708. Penhaligon is an abrasive and independent Cornishman, who seems now to have a safe seat and a very influential future in the Liberal Party. He defeated a rather inactive Conservative MP in October 1974, and has rapidly consolidated his position in Truro. He is a very suitable representative in a county which has the reputation for distrusting the English and the English parties.

Historically, Truro was not one of the Liberals' stronger seats in Cornwall. Indeed, the Labour Party were only 1,608 votes short of victory in 1966. But now Penhaligon has squeezed the Labour support so successfully that their percentage of the vote has been reduced from 37% (1966) to 7% (1979) - they are now 29,000 votes away from victory! The old Labour support came mainly from one of Cornwall's few industrial areas - the china clay mining belt around St Austell, Cornwall's largest town. St Austell is now the Liberal stronghold in the division, while the Tories still do well in the cathedral city of Truro itself.

Truro was formerly the largest seat in Cornwall by some way. The county's boundary changes are relatively minor, but over 10,000 voters are lost in the vicinity of Fowey to SE Cornwall. This should have little impact on Penhaligon's position, which is as strong as that of any Liberal MP.

1981	% Own Occ	67	1979 core seat Truro			
1981	% Loc Auth	19	L	33,571	52.8	
1981	% Black/Asian	0.7	C	24,863	39.1	
1981	% Mid Cl	46	Lab	4,689	7.4	
1981	% Prof Man	18	Meb Ker	227	0.4	
1982	electorate 68,376		NF	182	0.3	
1979	notional result		MPs since 1950			
	L 7,500		1950-70 H.G.B. Wilson C			
Alliance		L	1970-74 Piers Dixon C			
			1974-	David Penhaligon L		

Barrow and Furness

Tucked away beyond the Lake District in west Cumbria lies one of Britain's most depressed industrial districts. The largest of the towns here is Barrow, a port and shipbuilding centre strongly associated with the name of Vickers. Britain's nuclear submarines are constructed in the harbour here, but the economy has suffered all the threats and alarms to which single-industry towns are subject. Barrow's political response in 1979 was an iconoclastic swing in favour of the Labour Party, and the sitting MP, Cabinet Minister Albert Booth.

Barrow has actually been held by Labour since 1945, but often narrowly - yet their majority in 1979 was a healthy 8,000. The Labour vote is heavy in the low-cost private housing around the docks, and on Barrow Island and Walney Island. There are relatively few council estates in Barrow, where owner occupation surpasses 70%; local authority building is often restricted in what were once very much company towns. There are good Tory wards too, such as Hawcoat, in west and north Barrow.

Prior to the redistribution, the constituency included just the communities of Barrow and Dalton-in-Furness, which comprise the Borough of Barrow. Now 12,000 extra voters come in from the Furness peninsula, principally from the rather Conservative market and brewing town of Ulverston (formerly in Morecambe and Lonsdale). But the tide seems to be flowing Labour's way in this industrial backwater, and Albert Booth should be able to absorb the impact of Ulverston quite comfortably. The seat has been allocated to the SDP, but this is one of the weakest areas for the Alliance in the whole of England. Rather confusingly, the constituency name has been changed from Barrow in Furness to Barrow and Furness.

1981	% Own Occ	71.1	1979 core seat Barrow in	
1981	% Loc Auth	20.3	Furness	
1981	% Black/Asian	0.5	Lab 22,687	53.2
1981	% Mid Cl	39.8	C 14,946	35.1
1981	% Prof Man	10.8	L 4,983	11.7
1982	electorate 68,222		MPs since 1945	
1979	notional result		1945-66 W. Monslow Lab	
	Lab 5,400		1966- Albert Booth Lab	
Alliance		SDP		

Carlisle

Rather like Barrow, Carlisle is a working-class and industrial town tucked away in rural Cumbria. Its boundaries are unchanged by the Boundary Commission, which is a little odd, to say the least, for Carlisle's electorate in 1979 was only 53,000. Cumbria has been granted an extra seat because of the wildness and unmanageability of its Lake District terrain, yet the compact Carlisle remains the smallest in numbers as well as acreage! It does not expand to take in any of the villages which are now included in Carlisle City Council, a decision for which Labour must be thankful; they held Carlisle by only 4,566 votes in 1979, and an infusion of Tory rural hinterland would have threatened to unhinge their grip on the seat.

Carlisle is in many ways a city of suprises. For a long time it was the only part of England which boasted nationalised state pubs, but its MP Ron Lewis is a strict Methodist lay preacher teetotal Sabbatarian. It is a Labour seat entirely surrounded by William Whitelaw's massively Tory Penrith-Border seat. Lewis won Carlisle from the Conservatives in 1964, at a time when the local Tory Association was split, but he has held on fairly easily ever since. Unlike Barrow, Carlisle has a very high proportion of council housing estates, which ring this isolated city in Scottish border country. There is a variety of industry, but the largest single employer is Courtaulds textiles.

Ron Lewis is well into his 70s, but he has been readopted as Labour's candidate - and no-one can say that he isn't likely to continue to represent this provincial city in the far north-west of England for some time to come.

1981	% Own Occ	49.1	1979 same seat Carlisle	
1981	% Loc Auth	43.5	Lab 21,343	49.7
1981	% Black/Asian	0.6	C 16,777	39.1
1981	% Mid Cl	42	L 4,829	11.2
1981	% Prof Man	12	MPs since 1945	
1982	electorate 55,021		1945-50 E. Grierson Lab	
Alliance		SDP	1950-55 A. Hargreaves Lab	
			1955-64 D.M. Johnson C	
			1964- Ron Lewis Lab	

Copeland

The redistribution of the Cumbria seats posed a series of headaches for the Boundary Commissioners. Because of its geographical remoteness and ruggedness, the county was granted an extra seat to which it was not strictly entitled by population. Originally the Copeland seat was to contain the District of that name, plus some 14,000 electors from South Lakeland. After a bitter inquiry, however, it was decided to reduce the proposed seat simply to the Copeland District, which has only 52,000 electors.

Copeland is now exactly the same as the former Whitehaven seat. It still includes some of the most spectacular Lake District scenery, the quieter western lakes like Wastwater and Ennerdale Water. But the majority of the population is concentrated on the coast, which accounts for the fact that this division has been Labour since 1935. Whitehaven is a planned port of the eighteenth century, when it was created by the Lowther family. Haig Colliery, which overlooks Whitehaven harbour, is the only working pit left in Cumbria. There are also former coal mining towns like Cleator Morr and Egremont, and the remote Millom, which once possessed steelworks, at the south end of the constituency beyond the Black Combe mountain. Like most of the towns of west Cumbria, these communities seem old-fashioned and unchanging. Often unemployment is high and the memory of the 1930s is easily recalled. One stark exception to this is the nuclear power station at Windscale, the first in the world, sitting on the coastal plain in the centre of the constituency.

Swings between parties were often low in Whitehaven, and the renamed seat should remain reliable for Labour, barring a byelection such as the one which rocked them at the neighbouring seat of Workington in 1976.

1981	% Own Occ	45.0	1979 same seat Whitehaven		
1981	% Loc Auth	44.9	Lab	22,626	52.4
1981	% Black/Asian	0.3	C	17,171	39.8
1981	% Mid Cl	36.0	L	2,559	5.9
1981	% Prof Man	12.8	Ind	790	1.8
1982	electorate 55,019		MPs since 1945		
Alliance		SDP	1945-49 F. Anderson Lab		
			1959-70 J.B. Symonds Lab		
			1970- John Cunningham Lab		

Penrith and the Border

When Mrs Thatcher became Leader of the Conservative Party in 1975, she defeated William Whitelaw, for long a loyal lieutenant of former leader Edward Heath. But Whitelaw was again taken into the higher ranks of the party; he became Deputy Leader, and Home Secretary on the formation of a Tory government in 1979. Whitelaw's constituency of Penrith and the Border is little changed by the Boundary Commission's deliberations.

The seat contains nothing but villages apart from the small towns of Penrith and Wigton. It has remained loyal to Whitelaw since 1955. Indeed, in the Conservatives' defeat of February 1974 it gave him an emphatic personal vote of confidence by returning him with a greatly increased majority. The Liberals held this seat from 1945 to 1950, but they trailed a distant third behind Labour here in 1979.

It does not seem that the Alliance can threaten the Conservative grip on this border country any more than Labour can, even if Whitelaw should retire soon, as has been suggested in some quarters. This man of kindly and avuncular appearance has been subject to periodic attacks by the 'law-and-order' right wing of his own party, and it has on occasion been mooted that he might be unsuitable for a tough Thatcherite governmental strategy; but he has survived so far, and many think he plays an important role as the human face of Conservatism.

1981	% Own Occ	57	1979 core seat Penrith and the
1981	% Loc Auth	17	Border
1981	% Black/Asian	0.5	C 26,940 61.2
1971	% Mid Cl	37	Lab 9,844 22.4
1971	% Prof Man	16.5	L 7,257 16.5
1982	electorate 68,346		MPs since 1945
1979	notional result		1945-50 Wilfred Roberts L
	C 19,800		1950-55 R.D. Scott C
Alliance		L	1955- William Whitelaw C

Westmorland and Lonsdale

The former County of Westmorland used to form one complete constituency of its own. But in 1974 it was incorporated in the new County of Cumbria, and now it loses its independence in parliamentary terms as well.

It picks up the rural part of Lancashire, Lonsdale, which lies across the muddy expanse of Morecambe Bay from the body of that county. Lonsdale used to be associated with Morecambe in a Lancashire county division for electoral purposes. Another addition to Cumbria, and to Westmorland consitituency, is Kirkby Lonsdale (formerly in Skipton, Yorkshire). With 15% of the insured male population employed in agriculture, and a strong tourist industry centred on the southern Lake District, this will remain a solid Tory seat. Windermere is here, England's largest lake, and Ambleside, and Coniston Water; and Grasmere with its Wordsworthian associations. Indeed the attractions of Westmorland have attracted many poets and artists, and offer strong reasons for deep conservatism among the inhabitants.

The Liberals have turned in some useful performances in second place in the Westmorland seat. But that seems to be the position they are destined to keep. There is scarcely a Labour presence, even among the 20,000 residents of Kendal, Westmorland's largest town, despite its light industrial estates. The likely winner next time is the Conservative, Government Chief Whip Michael Jopling.

1981	% Own Occ	62.2	1979 core seat Westmorland		
1981	% Loc Auth	20.0	C	25,274	56.6
1981	% Black/Asian	0.5	L	12,867	28.8
1981	% Mid Cl	46.4	Lab	6,497	14.6
1981	% Prof Man	20.4	MPs since 1945		
1982	electorate 67,370		1945-64 W.M.F. Vane C		
1979	notional result		1964- Michael Jopling C		
	C 15,000				
Alliance		L			

Workington

One of the few completely unaltered constituencies in provincial England, Workington is the apparently safe Labour seat (which had even survived the disaster of 1931) which caused a shock by electing a Conservative in the 1976 byelection, which was caused by the elevation of the former Agriculture Minister Fred Peart to the House of Lords. It returned to the Labour fold in 1979, when Dale Campbell-Savours reversed his defeat at the hands of Richard Page three years before. But the legacy of doubt created by the byelection remains.

Indeed, at first sight Workington seems an odd division to be a Labour seat. Much of the acreage lies in the Lake District National Park, from Cockermouth to the busy tourist resort of Keswick by Derwent Water. Other renowned lakes such as Buttermere and Crummock Water are also included. In fact, though, this rural part of the seat is usually comnfortably outvoted by the coastal belt of West Cumbrian industry – Workington with its council estates and grimy steelworks, Maryport with its defunct docks, and the other small depressed communities of this declining and remote part of north-west England.

Workington had the highest unemployment rate of any Cumbrian constituency at the time of the 1981 Census – over 11%. Since that time the situation has certainly deteriorated. In such circumstances Labour seems unlikely to be upset again in Workington.

1981	% Own Occ	53.6	1979 same seat	Workington	
1981	% Loc Auth	35.3	Lab	24,523	53.2
1981	% Black/Asian	0.3	C	18,767	40.7
1981	% Mid Cl	36.9	L	2,819	6.1
1981	% Prof Man	13.2	MPs since 1945		
1982	electorate 56,680		1945-76 Fred Peart Lab		
Alliance		L	1976-79 Richard Page C		
			1979- Dale Campbell-Savours		
			Lab		

Amber Valley

This new constituency is based on the Amber Valley District, an industrial area in mid-Derbyshire formerly associated with the Ilkeston parliamentary division. The town of Ilkeston itself is now transferred to Erewash District and constituency. Amber Valley comprises three towns of 20,000 souls, Alfreton, Heanor and Ripley, together with surrounding villages like Ambergate, where the Amber flows into the Derwent, Derbyshire's main river.

This was once a coal-mining area, but it declined rapidly after the First World War, and although the Labour preferences remain, the last pits closed in the late 1960s. Now light industrial estates form the economic base. There is much hope advanced for the Amber Valley district. It is well connected by spur roads to the nearby M1, and the terraces of Victorian houses are now being brightened up with colourful touches of individuality.

The Ilkeston constituency had been steadily swinging away from Labour in recent elections. But Amber Valley remains a good prospect for the Labour candidate, David Bookbinder. Bookbinder is the Labour leader of Derbyshire County Council, and he was selected to replace sitting MP Ray Fletcher, who had admittedly been ailing for some years. Technically this counts as 'de-selection', but Fletcher took his removal in good part and there is no question of a split in the Labour vote as a result.

1981	% Own Occ	67.8	1979 core seat Ilkeston		
1981	% Loc Auth	25.0	Lab	29,760	50.6
1981	% Black/Asian	0.3	C	21,160	36.0
1981	% Mid Cl	36.9	L	7,879	13.4
1981	% Prof Man	13.2	MPs since 1945		
1982	electorate 67,407		1945-64 G.H. Oliver Lab		
1979	notional result		1964- Ray Fletcher Lab		
	Lab 6,200				
Alliance		L			

Bolsover

One of the most well-known parliamentary constituency names is Bolsover, a Derbyshire mining division. This is not because it enjoys marginal status or notably close contests but because of the fame of its aggressive Labour MP, Dennis Skinner, who is sometimes known as 'The Beast of Bolsover'.

But Skinner's controversial reputation in the House as a scourge of the Conservatives does not affect his massive majority in this constituency, which is dominated by large mining villages like Shirebrook and Temple Normanton. The town of Bolsover, perched on its crag, overlooks the industrial valley which houses the National Coal Board's North Derbyshire headquarters. This is the last true mining seat in Derbyshire, and it still ranks first among the list of seats employing men in mining throughout Britain.

Bolsover has taken in 10,000 electors from NE Derbyshire in the boundary revision, but the names of Dennis Skinner and Bolsover will remain closely coupled in the redrawn House of Commons.

1981	% Own Occ	49.6
1981	% Loc Auth	39.2
1981	% Black/Asian	0.3
1981	% Mid Cl	30.2
1981	% Prof Man	9.6
1982	electorate 65,287	
1979	notional result	
	Lab 18,500	

Alliance   SDP

1979 core seat Bolsover

Lab	27,495	66.6
C	10,116	24.5
L	3,688	8.9

MPs since 1945
1945-70 Harold Neal Lab
1970-   Dennis Skinner Lab

Chesterfield

Derbyshire's second-largest town is a bustling centre of industry. Although coal-mining has declined in North Derbyshire, Chesterfield's proximity to Sheffield is borne out by its many steelworking concerns, and the massive steel/chemical complex at Staveley lies within the constituency.

In the boundary changes, Chesterfield loses 10,000 electors from peripheral wards to North East Derbyshire, but it will remain a sound base for Labour's former Industry Secretary Eric Varley. Varley took on the task of Shadow Employment spokesman against Mrs Thatcher's administration, but remains a figure who attracts relatively little publicity for a leading politician. The only Conservative support of any significance in Chesterfield constituency is to be found in the Chesterfield West ward, an attractive residential area on the very fringe of the Peak District, but many of the town's professional and managerial workers commute from the town of Dronfield and from Peak villages outside the boundaries of the division.

Chesterfield will remain a typical northern industrial constituency, entirely safe for Labour and for Eric Varley. As a steelworking town it has every reason to fear the implications of the Conservative government's economic policies, and it is hard to predict a swing towards Thatcherism here.

1981	% Own Occ	49.6	1979 core seat	Chesterfield	
1981	% Loc Auth	41.6	Lab	31,048	57.4
1981	% Black/Asian	1	C	17,445	32.2
1981	% Mid Cl	41.3	L	5,617	10.4
1981	% Prof Man	12.3	MPs since 1945		
1982	electorate 68,628		1945-64 G. Benson Lab		
1979	notional result		1964- Eric Varley Lab		
	Lab 12,000				
Alliance		L			

Derby North

In 1979 Derby North was one of the most marginally held Labour seats in the country. Prominent moderate Phillip Whitehead beat off a powerful Conservative challenge by only 214 votes, which is the nearest Labour has come to losing a Derby seat since before World War Two. Whitehead did well to retain the seat at all, confining the swing to the Tories to just 3%.

Most of the more favoured residential areas in Derby are to be found in this division. Allestree and Darley, off the A6 towards Belper, are safe Conservative wards. However, Mickleover, a third Tory area, is one of the three western wards moved from city seats into South Derbyshire. Derby North continues to include Spondon and Chaddesden, two eastern wards towards Nottingham of mixed political characteristics. Most of the Labour strength is concentrated in the northern inner city and in the council estates at Mackworth and Breadsall.

Derby North is the more middle-class half of the city, but it also has more of Derby's council housing. It has the making of a classic marginal seat, but it has never been won by the Conservatives. The Liberals have never done well in Derby, but the impact of the SDP has probably been blunted by Whitehead's personal vote and his policies, which are likely to remain acceptable to the Derby N electorate. The SDP are not to oppose him at the next Election, but will leave the contest to their Alliance partners. With the removal of Mickleover, Labour need have fewer fears about this seat than before.

1981	% Own Occ	55.7	1979 core seat Derby North
1981	% Loc Auth	37.3	Lab 28,797 44.9
1981	% Black/Asian	2	C 28,583 44.5
1981	% Mid Cl	44.1	L 6,093 9.5
1981	% Prof Man	12.7	NF 592 0.9
1982	electorate 71,559		Eng Nat 122 0.2
1979	notional result		MPs since 1945
	Lab 1,500		1945-62 C.A.B. Wilcock Lab
Alliance		L	1962-70 Niall MacDermot Lab
			1970- Phillip Whitehead Lab

Derby South

Since the redistribution of the early 1970s, Derby South has
been by far the safer of the two Derby Labour seats. For
many years it was held by veteran peace campaigner Philip
Noel-Baker, and since 1970 by Walter Johnson, who was noted
for criticising Michael Foot's dress at the Cenotaph on
Armistice Day 1981.

It is in Derby South that the city's famous railway works are
to be found, and the Rolls-Royce aero factory, and Derby
County Football Club's 'Baseball Ground', surrounded by
dingy near-slum terraces. Here too live most of the city's
coloured population, mainly of Asian origin. There are council
estates, in the Peartree area for example, but more typical
are the Victorian terraces nearer the centre in Litchurch, the
ward represented by Derbyshire's Labour County Council
leader, David Bookbinder. The best ward for the
Conservatives is Littleover, mainly newish private housing on
the western edge of the city. Two wards, Chellaston and
Boulton, have been removed to the new South Derbyshire
seat, without altering the political balance; and some central
Derby territory has been gained from Derby N.

Walter Johnson's successor as Labour candidate is the former
Lincoln MP Margaret (Jackson) Beckett. She should be able to
rely on Derby South's continued loyalty, even though the
active Derby SDP is to contest this seat.

1981	% Own Occ	57.9	1979 core seat Derby South			
1981	% Loc Auth	30.7	Lab	26,945	50.0	
1981	% Black/Asian	15	C	20,853	38.7	
1981	% Mid Cl	40.6	L	5,196	9.6	
1981	% Prof Man	12.0	NF	587	1.1	
1982	electorate 69,924		Oth	268	0.5	
1979	notional result		MPs since 1945			
	Lab 3,900		1945-70 Philip Noel-Baker Lab			
Alliance		SDP	1970- Walter Johnson Lab			

Erewash

The new constituency of Erewash, based on the District of the same name, is an interesting amalgamation of the existing Conservative seat of SE Derbyshire with Ilkeston town. SE Derbyshire usually returned a Labour member between 1950 and 1970, when it was seized by Tory Peter Rost, but it has swung sharply to the right in the last decade. Ilkeston town was never the most Labour-inclined part of its constituency, and it too moved dramatically towards the Tories in 1979.

One of the reasons for the Conservative advance in Erewash has been the development of new owner-occupied estates in the last twenty years - now two-thirds of the housing is privately owned. This was particularly notable in the lace town of Long Eaton, the chief community in SE Derbyshire, which has risen from 50% to 70% owner occupied in two decades. Ilkeston too has increased from 40% to 60% private housing in the same time. Erewash is sandwiched between Derby and Nottingham, and many residents of Conservative communities like Sandiacre and West Hallam commute to one or the other city.

Erewash should be a marginal and volatile seat. There are chances for the Alliance too, here, with a long-standing Liberal strength in Kirk Hallam and an Independent Labour County Councillor in Sawley. The SDP have won the Alliance nomination for Erewash, and in a good year for the political centre, this rather large, skilled working-class, owner-occupier, commuter, expanding constituency could become a three-way marginal.

1981	% Own Occ	64.6
1981	% Loc Auth	24.7
1981	% Black/Asian	1
1981	% Mid Cl	39.8
1981	% Prof Man	12.6
1982	electorate 73,937	
1979	notional result	
	C 2,600	
Alliance		SDP

1979 core seat Derbyshire South-East

C	24,004	51.5
Lab	16,617	35.6
L	5,518	11.8
NF	498	1.1

MPs since 1945
1945-59 A.J. Champion Lab
1959-64 F.L.J. Jackson C
1964-70 Trevor Park Lab
1970-   Peter Rost C

High Peak

Although the Peak District was designated in 1946 as Britain's first National Park, and although the part of NW Derbyshire therein includes some of its finest scenery, the High Peak constituency has long been considered a marginal Conservative seat. Indeed, between 1966 and 1970 High Peak was held for Labour by Peter Jackson, a left-winger whose record showed the greatest number of rebellions against the Wilson government. Since 1970 the MP has been Tory Spencer le Marchant, an Etonian stockbroker who has served as Comptroller of Her Majesty's Household; but his majority has never exceeded 5,000. High Peak is now to gain some rural areas from Tory West Derbyshire, including Hathersage, fashionably set at the Sheffield end of the Hope Valley and popular with wealthy commuters to the steel city below the moors.

The reason why High Peak is not safely Tory is that over 80% of its population live in five small towns. The mill towns of Glossop and New Mills look as if they belong in Lancashire or Yorkshire, and share the owner-occupier marginality of the more northern Pennines, as does Chapel-en-le-Frith, which is dominated by Ferodo Brake Linings, and Whaley Bridge, increasingly popular with Manchester commuters. The spa town of Buxton is starkly divided. In the western half of the town are to be found the sleepy mansions where Victorians retired to take the waters. But the centre of Britain's limestone quarrying industry lies in the white-scarred landscape around Buxton, and Buxton's east end, Fairfield, harbours a heavy and reliable Labour vote. The other Labour stronghold in the High Peak is at Gamesley, a windy Manchester overspill estate on a hill outside Glossop.

Spencer le Marchant stands to benefit from the Boundary Commission's work. But Labour won every seat in the constituency in the 1981 County Council elections, except for the villages and West Buxton. Furthermore there may be a Social Democratic possibility, for David Marquand, close friend of Roy Jenkins in Brussels and now a Professor at Salford University, lives in the constituency, and may do well if he stands at the General Election.

1981	% Own Occ	64.3	1979 core seat High Peak		
1981	% Loc Auth	23.0	C	22,532	46.4
1981	% Black/Asian	0.1	Lab	17,777	36.6
1981	% Mid Cl	45.2	L	8,200	16.9
1981	% Prof Man	18.5	MPs since 1945		
1982	electorate 67,856		1945-61 Arthur Molson C		
1979	notional result		1961-66 David Walder C		
	C 6,400		1966-70 Peter Jackson Lab		
Alliance		SDP	1970-	Spencer le Marchant C	

North-East Derbyshire

NE Derbyshire, for many years a safe Labour seat due to its economic reliance on coal-mining and the heavy industry of the Chesterfield-Sheffield area, swung sharply to the Tories in the 1970s. This was partly due to boundary changes which came into effect in February 1974, and partly due to demographic and social changes.

There are still solidly Labour areas of NE Derbyshire: the mining towns of Killamarsh and Eckington are situated only a few miles from Sheffield and look over the county border to the socially similar Labour stronghold of Rother Valley. Clay Cross is south of Chesterfield, but is of course famous for its Labour councillors who rebelled against the policies of the 1970-74 Conservative government. But this kidney-shaped constituency, which curls around Chesterfield, also contains some substantial pockets of Conservative middle-class commuters. The Dronfield area has seen massive new private housing development schemes, most notably at Gosforth Valley, where modern semis and 'dets' have spread up the Peak District foothills in the 1970s. Dronfield residents mainly work in Sheffield. Meanwhile, Holymoorside, Wingerworth and Brampton are stone Peak District villages which have expanded to cater for affluent incomers, as they have become the most fashionable commuting bases for the Chesterfield bourgeoisie.

NE Derbyshire is a divided and mixed constituency, and as the mining industry continues to move into affluence, as the new private developments spread across the landscape, it may spring one of the major surprises of the 1980s, even though it is little altered in the boundary changes.

1981	% Own Occ	56.5	1979 core seat North-East
1981	% Loc Auth	35.2	Derbyshire
1981	% Black/Asian	0.4	Lab 27,218 48.1
1981	% Mid Cl	47.8	C 21,889 38.7
1981	% Prof Man	17.6	L 7,436 13.2
1982	electorate 68,854		MPs since 1945
1979	notional result		1945-59 H. White Lab
	Lab 5,700		1959-79 Tom Swain Lab
Alliance		SDP	1979- Ray Ellis Lab

South Derbyshire

The former constituency of Belper went through many ups and downs. For 25 years from 1945 it offered a seat to the controversial and colourful Labour right-winger George Brown, who unsuccessfully contested his party's leadership in 1963. But as the suburbs of Derby gradually encroached, it swung steadily to the Tories, and Brown was defeated in 1970, proclaiming that this was not the Belper he had once known. Nor was it. But in the redistribution which came into force between 1970 and 1974, the Derby sprawl was removed, and once more a Labour member held the seat from 1974-79. Then the present incumbent, Conservative dentist Mrs Sheila Faith, was elected by just 882 votes.

Now Belper town has been moved into the rural West Derbyshire. What remains is basically the District of South Derbyshire, together with three Derby wards, Boulton, Chellaston and Mickleover. South Derbyshire District is centred on Swadlincote, always the Labour citadel in Belper constituency. Swadlincote was once described by one famous son, the travel writer Rene Cutforth, as a 'hole in the ground', although he was referring to his childhood in the inter-war years. But S Derbyshire District also includes rural areas and small towns such as Melbourne and Repton, where there is a leading Midlands boys' public school. Furthermore, two of the three Derby wards added to the seat, Chellaston and Mickleover, are decidedly Conservative; Boulton is a Labour ward.

All in all it looks as if Belper's successor seat will produce close and exciting contests too. It would have been an extremely tight battle in 1979, and the seat should go to whichever party wins the General Election.

1981	% Own Occ	67.0	1979 core seat Belper		
1981	% Loc Auth	24.2	C	27,193	44.4
1981	% Black/Asian	1	Lab	26,311	42.9
1981	% Mid Cl	44.6	L	7,331	12.0
1981	% Prof Man	15.2	NF	460	0.8
1982	electorate 75,268		MPs since 1945		
1979	notional result		1945-70 George Brown Lab		
	Lab 900		1970-74 Geoffrey Stewart-Smith		
Alliance		SDP	C		
			1974-79 Roderick Macfarquhar		
			Lab		
			1979- Sheila Faith C		

West Derbyshire

West Derbyshire has for many years been the one truly rural seat in the county, and the one Conservative stronghold. Before the Second World War, the constituency was often the possession of the Marquess of Hartington, the son and heir of the chief local aristocrat, the Duke of Devonshire. It did rebel once or twice, to elect the populist Charlie White as a Common Wealther in 1944 and as a Labour candidate in 1945. But it has remained loyal to the Tories since 1950, usually with thumping majorities.

The old West Derbyshire seat contained the spa town of Matlock, Derbyshire's administrative capital, which with Darley Dale has a population of 20,000. Here too were three small towns of 5,000 people: Bakewell, Ashbourne and Wirksworth. Wirksworth is a quarrying town, covered in white lime dust, and boasting some Labour votes. But all the other communities in the division, including the hundreds of villages which make up the majority of the electorate, voted Conservative first, Liberal a long way second, and Labour nowhere. Bakewell, for example, has long been the seat of Derbyshire County Council Conservative group leader, Squadron Leader Norman Wilson. Surrounded by soft White Peak scenery, and the landed estates of Chatsworth and Haddon Hall, it typified the Conservatism of West Derbyshire.

In the redistribution, however, the town of Belper has been added to West Derbyshire. Belper is of course famous as the seat for 25 years of Labour Deputy Leader George Brown, and its inclusion somewhat alters the character of West Derbyshire. However, Belper town was never much more than marginally inclined to Labour, despite its Industrial Revolution textile mills, and the grip of the young Tory MP Matthew Parris, once Mrs Thatcher's private secretary, should not be shaken by Labour. The Liberals have turned in some respectable performances in second place here, and could conceivably provide an upset if there were to be an Alliance revival.

1981	% Own Occ	65.7	1979 core seat West Derbyshire
1981	% Loc Auth	18.6	C 21,478 52.5
1981	% Black/Asian	0.5	L 11,261 27.6
1981	% Mid Cl	46.3	Lab 8,134 19.9
1981	% Prof Man	19.7	MPs since 1945
1982	electorate 69,369		1945-50 C.F. White Lab
1979	notional result		1950-62 E.B. Wakefield C
	C 15,700		1962-67 Aidan Crawley C
Alliance		L	1967-79 Jim Scott-Hopkins C
			1979- Matthew Parris C

Exeter

Exeter is Devon's oldest city as well as its county town. Although much of the centre had to be rebuilt after the air raids of 1942, Exeter is still steeped in history. Geographically it is well sited at the heart of the large county of Devon; its strategic situation has also meant that it has become over-familiar to thousands of motorists who have been trapped over the years in its notorious traffic bottleneck. Exeter is an affluent market and commercial centre - 43% of its employed population work in non-manual occupations. This is usually a reliable indicator of Conservatism.

The City of Exeter is of almost exactly the right size to form a parliamentary seat on its own, and it is the only unaltered seat in Devon. Labour won the seat for the first time in 1966, when Mrs Gwyneth Dunwoody gained it from the Tories. But the present MP John Hannam regained Exeter in 1970 - Mrs Dunwoody's husband John lost another Labour West Country seat, Falmouth and Camborne, at the same time. The minor boundary changes were favourable to the Tories in 1974, and Hannam's majority is now 8,000 - Labour doesn't hold a single parliamentary seat south-west of Bristol any more, and it is unlikely that they can win Exeter again. They do have local strength in certain wards: Wonsford, Whipton and Stoke Hill. But Labour did not poll the most votes in Exeter even in the 1981 county council elections, one of their best years in recent times.

The SDP will contest Exeter on behalf of the Alliance. One might think that the Social Democrats may have an appeal in this cultured city, which possesses an attractive modern University. But there were no local elections in Exeter in 1982, so it is impossible to base any predictions of SDP performance on firm evidence. John Hannam seems the strong favourite to hold his seat at the next election.

1981	% Own Occ	59.9	1979 same seat Exeter		
1981	% Loc Auth	28.0	C	27,173	48.4
1981	% Black/Asian	1.3	Lab	19,146	34.1
1981	% Mid Cl	53.6	L	8,756	15.6
1981	% Prof Man	15.6	E	1,053	1.9
1982	electorate 71,656		MPs since 1945		
Alliance		SDP	1945-51 J.C. Maude C		
			1951-66 R.D. Williams C		
			1966-70 G. Dunwoody Lab		
			1970- John Hannam C		

Honiton

Devon is a large and diverse county. The different districts
have distinct individual characteristics. One can contrast the
brash and lively appeal of the 'Devon Riviera' of Torbay with
the undeveloped and unspoilt creek-indented coastline of the
South Hams. The 'Golden Coast' of North Devon around
Ilfracombe has a different nature again, and its towering dark
cliffs bear little resemblance to the gentler red cliffs of East
Devon. The Honiton constituency covers the bulk of the
District of East Devon.

Honiton is particularly associated with retirement houses –
over 30% of the population is of pensionable age, much the
highest figure in Devon. Resorts like Sidmouth, Seaton and
Budleigh Salterton are notably quiet, and tend not to cater
for the tastes of the younger generation. The largest town,
Exmouth, has some light industry, but this is very much a
residential and resort area. Inland there is some prosperous
farmland around Honiton itself, but in the boundary changes
the region around the country town of Ottery St Mary has
been transferred to Tiverton.

Honiton is one of the most Conservative constituencies in
Britain. Peter Emery retained the seat in a 1967 byelection
with a majority of 16,000, or 34.2% of the total vote. The lead
is now 25,231 (41.6%), one of the ten highest in the
country. The Liberals have finished second in Honiton on
most occasions since the war, but it is one of the few seats
in rural Devon where they have never had a chance of
victory, and they have donated the task of waging an uphill
battle to the SDP. It remains to be seen whether the elderly
electorate of Honiton will favour this youthful party. The
Conservatives still seem impregnable here in east Devon.

1981	% Own Occ	71.2	1979 core seat	Honiton	
1981	% Loc Auth	16.8	C	37,832	62.4
1981	% Black/Asian	1	L	12,601	20.8
1981	% Mid Cl	46.8	Lab	8,756	14.4
1981	% Prof Man	18.4	E	1,423	2.3
1982	electorate 71,836		MPs since 1945		
1979	notional result		1945-55 C. Drewe C		
	C 22,400		1955-67 R. Mathew C		
Alliance		SDP	1967- Peter Emery C		

North Devon

North Devon will always be associated with its MP of twenty years, the former leader of the Liberal Party Jeremy Thorpe. Thorpe won the seat from the Tories in 1959; previously it had been held by Richard Acland as a Liberal and later a Common Wealth MP from 1935 to 1945. Jeremy Thorpe became leader of his party in 1967, and presided over the Liberal revival of the early 1970s and their disappointments in the two 1974 Elections. But then scandal struck, as Norman Scott alleged that Thorpe had tried to have him killed after a homosexual affair between them. These charges were never substantiated in court, but some of the mud stuck. The North Devon electorate decisively rejected Jeremy Thorpe at the 1979 General Election, returning Conservative Tony Speller by an 8,000 majority.

Thorpe will not resume his political career in North Devon, and it remains to be seen whether the new Liberal candidate Roger Blackmore can recover the lost ground. He may be helped by the boundary changes, which remove the Bideford district, which was itself added in the last round of revisions in 1974. This is generally regarded as better Tory ground than most, especially the sea frontage around Westward Ho!. Thorpe managed to build up a powerful and broad coalition of support, not only in the largest town, Barnstaple (which has a substantial industrial element), but in the agricultural villages of the seat and even in holiday resorts like Ilfracombe. Perhaps the native Devonians were more inclined to Liberalism than people who came in from other parts of the country to retire, but in the years of triumph, Jeremy Thorpe's personal vote was strong throughout the seat.

Unless there is a national Liberal revival, it may well be that the 'Golden Coast' of N Devon will prove as Conservative as most tourist and agriculture areas are. But the experienced and active local Liberal organisation will be determined to prove that it can win the seat without Thorpe.

1981	% Own Occ	66	1979 core seat North Devon			
1981	% Loc Auth	17	C	31,811	50.1	
1981	% Black/Asian	0.8	L	23,338	36.7	
1981	% Mid Cl	44	Lab	7,108	11.2	
1981	% Prof Man	18	E	729	1.1	
1982	electorate 63,962		NF	237	0.4	
1979	notional result		Oth	281	0.5	
	C 6,900		MPs since 1945			
Alliance		L	1945-55	C.H.M. Peto C		
			1955-59	J.L. Lindsay C		
			1959-79	Jeremy Thorpe L		
			1979-	Tony Speller C		

Plymouth Devonport

Plymouth Devonport is one of the most famous constituency names. But its boundaries have changed radically many times. In the present review, the alterations were such that originally the new seat was to be named Plymouth North, and the name of Devonport was only revived after an inquiry by popular request. Indeed much of Devonport itself is no longer in the constituency, but has been transferred to the neighbouring Drake (or Central). The new 'Devonport' consists largely of the council estates which spread across the hills of north Plymouth, many of which were formerly in Drake. It would be a safer seat than before for Labour – except for the fact that the Devonport MP David Owen is now the No.2 man in the Social Democratic Party.

It is hard to say how well Owen will do in Devonport next time. There have been no local elections in Plymouth since the formation of the SDP and the Alliance, so no evidence is forthcoming from that source. Owen has done very well to hold a Plymouth seat as a Labour candidate since 1966. Originally he was elected at Sutton, then in 1974 after boundary changes he moved to Devonport to defeat the sitting member of 20 years, Dame Joan Vickers. (She had herself beaten Michael Foot at Devonport in 1955.) In 1979 Owen held on by 1,001 votes, against the national tide.

The question is – can the smooth, hard, still youthful SDP magnate David Owen mobilise the council estates of Budshead and Southway, and the Tamar frontage wards of St Budeaux and Keyham? Plymouth is a city of close-knit communities, and Owen has demonstrated that he has a personal vote here. There is a large Conservative minority who might be persuaded to vote for Owen now he is an SDP MP. He may well have almost the best chance of any SDP defector of being returned to Parliament next time.

1981	% Own Occ	40.6	1979 core seat Plymouth		
1981	% Loc Auth	48.3	Devonport		
1981	% Black/Asian	1	Lab	16,545	47.4
1981	% Mid Cl	34.4	C	15,544	44.5
1981	% Prof Man	7.8	L	2,360	6.8
1982	electorate 61,406		NF	243	0.7
1979	notional result		Ind	203	0.6
	Lab 2,800		MP since 1974		
Alliance		SDP	1974- David Owen Lab (SDP)		

Plymouth Drake

When Plymouth gained a third seat in the boundary changes
of the early 1970s, the additional constituency was named
Drake, after the hero of Plymouth Hoe; there is also an
island named after Drake in the Sound opposite the city
centre. Indeed Drake is the Plymouth Central seat, and would
have been renamed as such in the Boundary Commission's
original plan. That would have been an appropriate step, for
the seat actually contains major parts of those districts of
Plymouth commonly known as Devonport and Sutton.

Drake's first contest, in February 1974, saw a 2,000 vote
victory by the Conservative candidate, Miss Janet Fookes.
But in October of the same year, her majority was reduced to
just 34. Drake seemed a super-marginal seat. It contained the
highest proportion of Plymouth's council estates, concentrated
in the north of the city. But now Miss Fookes seems safe. In
1979 she increased her lead to over 4,000 votes, and in the
boundary changes most of the council estates were
transferred to the seat called Devonport (although part of
that port itself comes into Drake). Middle-class wards like
Compton and Stoke will now easily tip the balance. The
redefined Drake is clearly Conservative.

Plymouth City Centre was heavily bombed in the war, and
the reconstruction is clean, modern and elegant in style.
Plymouth is also of course one of the greatest of Royal Navy
ports, and Plymouth constituencies have a very high
proportion of service voters. As in Portsmouth this tends to
make them more Conservative than their class makeup
suggests. Drake is unlikely to be affected by the presence of
a leading Alliance MP next door - the nomination is still in
the hands of the Liberals, who lost their deposit last time.

1981	% Own Occ	52.9	1979 core seat Plymouth Drake		
1981	% Loc Auth	21.8	C	21,759	50.6
1981	% Black/Asian	2	Lab	17,515	40.7
1981	% Mid Cl	45.9	L	3,452	8.0
1981	% Prof Man	14.0	NF	279	0.6
1982	electorate 52,513		MP since 1974		
1979	notional result		1974-	Janet Fookes C	
	C 6,700				
Alliance		L			

Plymouth Sutton

The easternmost of the three Plymouth seats is by far the
most owner occupied, the most middle class, and the most
Conservative. Although it is still to be called Sutton, it is in
fact based on the communities of Plymstock and Plympton to
the east of the River Plym. Sutton ward itself is now in
Drake: an example of the anomalies created in the attempt to
save the existing constituency names in Plymouth.

Plymstock and Plympton are solidly Tory residential areas –
they were not included in a Plymouth seat until 1974, up to
then being part of the Tavistock county constituency. There
are three wards from west of the Plym which have always
been within the city – Mount Gould, Eggbuckland and the
only Labour ward, Efford. Sutton loses about 12,000 voters in
the redistribution, at Crownhill as well as at Sutton itself,
and the seat will now be even safer for the Conservatives.

The Tory MP here is Alan Clark. He is the son of Lord
(Kenneth) Clark, who became nationally known for his BBC
TV series 'Civilisation'. But Alan Clark is a military historian,
and a staunch right-winger, pro-hanging and anti-immigrant.
His trenchant views on defence go down well here in one of
the chief home bases of the Royal Navy. First elected after
boundary changes made Sutton a Conservative seat in
February 1974, he should continue to be a vocal and active
representative of the wealthiest and most respectable end of
Plymouth for many years to come.

1981	% Own Occ	67.3	1979 core seat Plymouth Sutton		
1981	% Loc Auth	19.1	C	28,892	54.8
1981	% Black/Asian	1	Lab	17,605	33.4
1971	% Mid Cl	50.7	L	6,226	11.8
1971	% Prof Man	13.6	MP since 1974		
1976	electorate 59,768		1974–	Alan Clark C	
1979	notional result				
	C 10,700				
Alliance		SDP			

South Hams

South Hams enjoys some of the most attractive scenery in England, but it is scarcely developed for tourism and is in no way ruined by commercial exploitation. Sea creeks penetrate deep inland along the wooded valleys of the Dart, the Avon and the Erme. But there are also grand cliffs and headlands, with names familiar to anyone used to sailing up the English Channel: Bolt Tail, Bolt Head, Prawle Point, Start Point. The towns are among the most elegant and stylish in Britain - the sophisticated yachting centres of Salcombe and the medieval town of Totnes further up the Dart.

In general, one finds that the more pleasant parts of the British coast and countryside vote Conservative, and understandably so; their residents have much to conserve. But the South Hams is likely to prove politically marginal. South Hams is a new seat, but it is quite similar to the old Totnes. However it does lose the district around Newton Abbot, and Ashburton-Buckfastleigh on the southern edge of Dartmoor, which pass into the Teignbridge division. In Totnes the Liberal candidate Anthony Rogers increased his vote and his share of the vote between October 1974 and 1979. Although the Totnes Conservative MP, former trade unionist Ray Mawby, held on by 10,000 votes last time, the Liberals must have good chances in both South Hams and Teignbridge next time. In 1979 the Labour vote in Totnes was reduced to a deposit-losing level, and with the departure of Newton Abbot their last reservoir of support disappears.

The centre of gravity of Liberalism in Devon may well be shifting southwards. The Thorpe era in North Devon is over, but Teignbridge and South Hams have charismatic and dynamic Liberal candidates. The South Hams may be less well known to tourists than the north coast, however unjustly; but it must appear on the political map as one of the ten best Liberal prospects next time.

1981	% Own Occ	67.3	1979 core seat Totnes		
1981	% Loc Auth	19.1	C	35,010	52.2
1981	% Black/Asian	1	L	24,445	36.4
1981	% Mid Cl	49.4	Lab	7,668	11.4
1981	% Prof Man	20.7	MPs since 1945		
1982	electorate 74,159		1945-55 R.H. Rayner C		
1979	notional result		1955- Ray Mawby C		
	C 13,700				
Alliance		L			

Teignbridge

When John Alderson was still Chief Constable of Devon and Cornwall, he had already become a nationally-known public figure for his advocacy of 'community policing' at a time when other leading policemen were calling for a tougher line in the face of mounting urban violence. Alderson retired from the force in 1981, and announced that he would be willing to embark on a political career. In October 1982 he was selected as the Liberal candidate for Teignbridge, Devon - which is generally thought to be one of the best Liberal prospects in the country. With his flair for attracting publicity, and a favourable seat, Alderson may well find that his path into a parliamentary career is easier than most find it.

Devon lost a seat in the last redistribution a decade ago. Now it is restored to a complement of 11 MPs. Teignbridge is the extra division, carved out of the northern half of the former Totnes and the southern end of Tiverton. It covers the coast between the Rivers Dart and Exe (between Torbay and Exeter), and its hinterland. It is centred on the River Teign, which enters the English Channel at the resort of Teignbridge. A little further up the river is the division's largest town, Newton Abbot. Other towns are Dawlish (on the sea) and Buckfastleigh and Ashburton (inland). Teignbridge also contains some of the prettiest scenery in Britain, near the eastern scarp of Dartmoor, around Moretonhampstead and Bovey Tracey.

John Alderson may well be thought the popular favourite to win Teignbridge at the next Election. But it should be remembered that the Conservatives held both Totnes and Tiverton fairly easily last time, and that in General Elections at least, 'personalities' and 'big names' do not always receive any extra boost. Indeed many have been cut down to size in the past. The Liberals still have work to do to win the new seat of Teignbridge.

1981	% Own Occ	67.4	New seat
1981	% Loc Auth	18.0	
1981	% Black/Asian	1	
1981	% Mid Cl	49.7	
1981	% Prof Man	18.6	
1982	electorate 67,751		
1979	notional result		
	C 9,800		
Alliance		L	

Tiverton

Tiverton is now the only constituency in Devon without a sea coast. Previously it did extend to the shore south of Exeter, but Dawlish and Teignmouth are now included in the new Teignbridge. Tiverton is based on the Mid-Devon District, with urban centres at Tiverton and Crediton and a large chunk of the rolling farmland at the centre of this largest of southern counties. The Liberals have finished second in Tiverton in the last three Elections, and when Robin Maxwell-Hyslop was first elected in 1960, they pressed him to a 3,000 vote margin. But Tiverton is not one of the Liberals' better hopes, and Maxwell-Hyslop can expect to be returned easily.

1981	% Own Occ	59.2	1979 core seat Tiverton
1981	% Loc Auth	23.9	C	33,444	56.7
1981	% Black/Asian	1	L	17,215	29.2
1981	% Mid Cl	48.4	Lab	8,281	14.0
1981	% Prof Man	19.0	MPs since 1945
1982	electorate 64,151		1945-60 D. Heathcoat-Amory C
1979	notional result		1960- R. Maxwell-Hyslop C
	C 14,400		
Alliance		L	

Torbay

The bustling seaside resorts of Torbay are perhaps too plebeian to justify the title of the Devon Riviera. But there can be no doubt that together Torquay, Brixham and Paignton form one of the most popular and famous of goals for holidaymakers in Britain. Torbay constituency loses 20,000 electors from three western wards to the new South Hams constituency. But Torbay, represented since 1955 by Sir Frederic Bennett, will remain an immensely safe Conservative seat, the epitome of England's Deep South.

1981	% Own Occ	71.7	1979 core seat Torbay
1981	% Loc Auth	12.2	C	36,099	54.6
1981	% Black/Asian	1	L	15,231	23.1
1981	% Mid Cl	50.5	Lab	12,919	19.6
1981	% Prof Man	18.5	E	1,161	1.8
1982	electorate 67,279		NF	647	1.0
1979	notional result		MPs since 1945
	C 16,000		1945-55 C. Williams C
Alliance		L	1955- Sir Frederic Bennett C

Torridge and West Devon

In 1974 the Devon constituencies of Torrington and Tavistock were abolished, and a single new seat of West Devon created. Tavistock was safely Tory; its destruction sent rapidly rising MP Michael Heseltine on a search for another seat - in the end he moved to Henley in Oxfordshire. But Torrington had briefly been won by the Liberal Mark Bonham-Carter in a 1958 byelection. He only held Torrington for a year before the Conservatives recaptured it. But his success was an augury of Jeremy Thorpe's victory in neighbouring North Devon in 1959.

In 1974 the Bideford area was not included in West Devon. But now the Torridge and West Devon constituency brings together Bideford, Torrington and Tavistock. It stretches from the old shipbuilding port of Appledore and the holiday resort of Westward Ho! far to the south, to include the bulk of Dartmoor. It takes in the bleak Princetown and its prison, and the small towns like Okehampton on the edge of the moor.

Despite Bonham-Carter's success in Torrington in 1958, West Devon has seen the Liberals under-perform. It is not too socially and economically dissimilar to North Devon, or to the Liberals' hopeful seats in South Devon. But at the last Election the Liberals could only garner 25% of the poll, 17,000 votes behind Conservative MP Peter Mills. It would therefore seem logical that the SDP might be given the Alliance nomination, to see if they could mobilise sections of support which the Liberals did not reach. But in fact the Liberals have retained the candidature themselves - they are fighting five of the six mainly rural seats in Devon. One feels it unlikely that they can challenge Peter Mills in Torridge and West Devon. Labour will be unlikely to save its deposit in the new seat.

1981	% Own Occ	67.3	1979 core seat West Devon	
1981	% Loc Auth	16.2	C 29,428	61.0
1981	% Black/Asian	0.8	L 12,256	25.4
1981	% Mid Cl	41.9	Lab 6,174	12.8
1981	% Prof Man	18.1	NF 393	0.8
1982	electorate 70,771		MPs since 1950	
1979	notional result		1950-58 G. Lambert C	
	C 15,400		1958-59 Mark Bonham-Carter L	
Alliance		L	1959-64 P.B. Browne C	
			1964- Peter Mills C	

Bournemouth East

The balmy south coast resort of Bournemouth is a monument to the Victorian love affair with the seaside. Attracted by the pine-clad slopes of the Bourne Valley, people came here to retire, or just to visit; they still do. It is even yet a highly successful and rather genteel retreat. The East division, which has now expanded to take in the centre of the town, has one of the smallest percentages of council housing in the country. This was the constituency of Churchill's friend, Brendan Bracken, and Suez rebel Nigel Nicolson, and also of John Cordle, whose political career was ended in 1977 by the Poulson fraud scandals. But his successor David Atkinson has one of the safest Tory seats in Britain.

1981	% Own Occ	65.6	1979 core seat Bournemouth E		
1981	% Loc Auth	8.9	C	25,808	62.6
1981	% Black/Asian	1	Lab	7,553	18.3
1981	% Mid Cl	52.4	L	6,738	16.4
1981	% Prof Man	16.9	Oths	1,104	2.7
1982	electorate 70,582		MPs since 1950		
1979	notional result		1950-52 Brendan Bracken C		
	C 21,500		1952-59 Nigel Nicolson C		
Alliance		L	1959-77 John Cordle C		
			1977- David Atkinson C		

Bournemouth West

Bournemouth West contains the town's only large council estates, and the only Labour ward of any importance, at Kinson. But it also boasts the most elegant hotels and villas of the resort, along the West Cliff towards Poole. Bournemouth was a little too small to justify two seats, so three wards are taken from NE Poole to make up the numbers. The MP, Sir John Eden, is vacating his safe seat; this will be inherited by John Butterfill, who was unfortunate enough to be defeated by the Liberal Bill Pitt in the 1981 Croydon NW byelection.

1981	% Own Occ	66.3	1979 core seat Bournemouth W		
1981	% Loc Auth	18.2	C	25,873	59.8
1981	% Black/Asian	1	Lab	9,247	21.4
1981	% Mid Cl	52.9	L	7,677	17.8
1981	% Prof Man	18.0	NF	438	1.0
1982	electorate 72,774		MPs since 1950		
1979	notional result		1950-54 Viscount Cranborne C		
	C 18,900		1954- Sir John Eden C		
Alliance		L			

Christchurch

The old Christchurch and Lymington seat had to be split up, for Lymington is still in Hampshire, whereas Christchurch was transferred to Dorset in the local government boundary changes of 1974, along with its larger neighbour Bournemouth. Lymington is now placed in the Hampshire county seat of New Forest. Christchurch, one of the smallest local authorities in the country - it is a full Borough although its population is only 38,000 - is now the core of a seat of its own.

Christchurch town is brought together with the suburban part of the Wimborne District north of Bournemouth - Ferndown, West Moors, St Leonards and St Ives, West Parley. Some of this strongly Tory territory was formerly in Hampshire in the New Forest seat, some in the North Dorset constituency.

Christchurch is one of only two seats in Dorset to be fought by the SDP, but there should be no problems for vocal right-winger Robert Adley, an active MP whose Christchurch/Lymington division was the third safest Conservative constituency in Britain at the 1979 General Election.

1981	% Own Occ	76
1981	% Loc Auth	11
1981	% Black/Asian	1
1981	% Mid Cl	58
1981	% Prof Man	24
1982	electorate 64,276	
1979	notional result	
	C 19,800	

Alliance   SDP

1979 core seat Christchurch/Lymington

C	29,817	66.0
L	7,654	16.9
Lab	6,722	14.9
E	965	2.2

MP since 1974
1974-   Robert Adley C

North Dorset

Dorset evokes the image of wild heaths and cliffs, especially to those who have read the novels of Thomas Hardy (and more recently John Fowles). But in fact five of Dorset's seven seats are more or less suburban, and another one, North Dorset, only becomes truly rural in the present boundary changes.

The commuter suburbs north of Bournemouth, part of the Wimborne District, are removed to Christchurch, leaving North Dorset as typified by small independent old market towns like Shaftesbury, Wimborne Minster and Blandford Forum. There is also the spectacular scenery of Cranborne Chase, the Blackmore Vale and the chalk downs. It joins Dorset West as a spacious and agricultural constituency of low population density.

North Dorset will surely remain safe for the sitting Conservative MP Nicholas Baker, an urbane lawyer. The Liberals could strengthen their second position; between 1945 and 1950 North Dorset was held by Frank (now Lord) Byers - but they were 23,000 votes adrift in 1979. Labour lost their deposit last time, and will struggle to save it in future too.

1981	% Own Occ	62		1979 core seat North Dorset		
1981	% Loc Auth	20		C	40,046	62.2
1981	% Black/Asian	1		L	16,750	26.0
1981	% Mid Cl	50		Lab	7,543	11.7
1981	% Prof Man	20		MPs since 1945		
1983	electorate 67,459			1945-50 Frank Byers L		
1979	notional result			1950-57 R.F. Crouch C		
	C 18,800			1957-70 Sir R.H. Glyn C		
Alliance		L		1970-79 David James C		
				1979- Nicholas Baker C		

Poole

Of all Dorset's seven safe Tory constituencies, Poole returned
the largest majority in 1979, giving new MP John Ward a
majority over Labour of 23,557. Poole is a successful,
expanding town, declared a growth area in the Strategic Plan
for the South East, which has attracted a variety of new
modern industry and new population. It had reached 119,000
inhabitants by 1981, and an electorate of 87,000. This means
that it can no longer stand as a single complete unit for
parliamentary purposes, and three of the town's 12 wards
have to be transferred to Bournemouth West.

Poole has often been regarded as a suburb of Bournemouth,
and indeed there are several attractive residential areas which
are suitable for use as commuting bases. But Poole is also
very much an independent town, and it has fewer economic
and social problems than almost any other in Britain - it
enjoys relatively low unemployment.

It is scarcely surprising that Poole will remain one of the
nation's safest Conservative seats.

1981	% Own Occ	67.6	1979 core seat Poole		
1981	% Loc Auth	21.6	C	38,848	57.0
1981	% Black/Asian	1	Lab	15,291	22.4
1981	% Mid Cl	47.8	L	14,001	20.5
1981	% Prof Man	15.2	MPs since 1950		
1982	electorate 70,436		1950-51 M.J. Wheatley C		
1979	notional result		1951-64 R.A. Pilkington C		
	C 18,000		1964-79 Oscar Murton C		
Alliance		L	1979- John Ward C		

South Dorset

The son and heir of the Marquess of Salisbury has the courtesy title of Viscount Cranborne, but he can sit in the House of Commons. Both names have been familiar in Tory politics since long before this century, and previous Marquesses of Salisbury have been influential within the party at all levels from Leader and Prime Minister down to highly esteemed pressure groups, usually on the right of the Conservative spectrum.

The present Viscount Cranborne, elected in 1979, is not the first of his line to represent South Dorset, which includes the seaside resort of Weymouth, the Portland naval base and the Isle of Purbeck, famed for its marble quarries. Indeed this must be one of the seats which has most frequently been represented by aristocrats, for Viscount Hinchingbrooke also held it until 1962.

There are pockets of Labour support in Weymouth and Portland, and Labour briefly held South Dorset after they had taken advantage of a split between pro- and anti-Common Market Conservatives in the 1962 byelection. But it returned to its traditional allegiance in the 1964 General Election, and the Viscount should have little trouble defending a 15,000 majority in a little altered county seat.

1981	% Own Occ	61.4	1979 core seat South Dorset	
1981	% Loc Auth	21.1	C	32,372	55.7
1981	% Black/Asian	1	Lab	17,133	29.5
1981	% Mid Cl	46.6	L	8,649	14.9
1981	% Prof Man	15.9	MPs since 1945	
1982	electorate 68,862		1945-62 Viscount Hinchingbrooke
1979	notional result		C
	C 13,600		1962-64 Guy Barnett Lab
Alliance		SDP	1964-79 Evelyn King C
			1979- Viscount Cranborne C

West Dorset

The most rural of the Dorset seats, West Dorset includes
Tolpuddle, whose early trade union martyrs have entered the
annals of Labour hagiography. But it is as far as can be from
a Labour stronghold. Rather, entrenched Toryism is the
order of the day among these small towns in Hardy country –
Dorchester and Sherborne, Beaminster and Bridport, Lyme
Regis on the coast. The Liberals finished second, and once
entertained hopes of victory here, but this almost unchanged
constitutency looks very safe for sitting Conservative Jim
Spicer.

1981	% Own Occ	57.1	1979 core seat West Dorset		
1981	% Loc Auth	24.5	C	26,281	58.7
1981	% Black/Asian	1	L	9,776	21.8
1981	% Mid Cl	48.4	Lab	7,999	17.9
1981	% Prof Man	18.9	NF	514	1.1
1982	electorate 61,129		Oth	192	0.4
1979	notional C 17,200		MPs since 1945		
Alliance		L	1945-74 K.S.D.W. Digby C		
			1974- Jim Spicer C		

Bishop Auckland

Durham is usually regarded as a citadel of heavy industry
and Labour strength. But in fact west Durham is mainly
rural, with farmland in the valleys among the high moors.
Bishop Auckland, the SW County Durham seat, includes
Teesdale, with Barnard Castle and Startforth, and the Wear
Valley with Bishop Auckland. All this is fairly Conservative;
the Bishop of Durham still has a palace at Bishop Auckland.
But the seat has been Labour continuously since 1935, when
it was won by Etonian economics expert Hugh Dalton. Mining
has declined in west Durham, but the New Town of Newton
Aycliffe offers renewed Labour support. Labour must continue
to hope that the urban east end of the seat outvotes the
rural wild west.

1981	% Own Occ	47	1979 core seat Bishop Auckland		
1981	% Loc Auth	41	Lab	27,200	48.7
1981	% Black/Asian	0.4	C	21,160	37.9
1981	% Mid Cl	39	L	7,439	13.3
1981	% Prof Man	14	MPs since 1945		
1982	electorate 71,831		1945-59 Hugh Dalton Lab		
1979	notional Lab 5,300		1959-79 James Boyden Lab		
Alliance		L	1979- Derek Foster Lab		

City of Durham

Rather like the City of Chester, the City of Durham is somewhat curiously named. Not only does it contain much else besides Durham itself, which only had a population of 26,000 in 1981, but it is designated as a <u>county</u> constituency. But there are reasons for its title. The constituency is now to be exactly the same as the 'City of Durham' local government unit; and it is well to distinguish this seat from the others in Durham county. Despite its modest size, Durham really is one of England's most historic and distinguished cities. It is noted for its fine cathedral, set on a crag in a bend of the Wear – and the bishopric of Durham has long been one of the most senior in the country. Durham University was the first to be founded in England outside Oxbridge, and still operates on a collegiate system. The city houses the administrative HQ for the county which bears its name, and many public servants as a result.

With its Establishment presence, it might be thought that Durham would be Conservative. But the seat has been safely Labour since 1935, and its character has been determined not so much by Church or University as by the fact that Durham is also at the geographical centre of the county's coalfield. Every year it is the site of a massive traditional miners' gala. Nonconformity has always been strong in this seat of Anglicanism. Besides the city itself, the seat contains the mining and ex-mining areas of Brandon-Byshottles, Coxhoe, Sherburn and the Deerness Valley to the west. Also Labour are the outlying Gilesgate and Framwellgate suburbs of Durham, and the Conservative vote is concentrated in the centre of the city and at Neville's Cross to the west. The SDP are locally believed to have a good chance of second place here.

Durham does lose some peripheral ex-mining areas to the new Sedgefield division, but it will almost certainly remain safe for Dr Mark Hughes. It seems fitting in the light of Durham's combination of distinguished privilege and left-wing politics that it should be represented by a Labour MP who is also a Balliol man.

1981	% Own Occ	47.3	1979 core seat Durham		
1981	% Loc Auth	44.9	Lab	30,903	52.3
1981	% Black/Asian	0.5	C	19,666	33.3
1981	% Mid Cl	51.3	L	8,572	14.5
1981	% Prof Man	16.1	MPs since 1945		
1982	electorate 67,079		1945-70 Charles Grey Lab		
1979	notional result		1970- Mark Hughes Lab		
	Lab 8,400				
Alliance		SDP			

283

Darlington

For most of the twentieth century, County Durham has been the very strongest Labour fortress in England. Its economy has been based on heavy industries, and in the main declining industries too - coal mining, steel, shipbuilding, heavy engineering. In local politics, many decades of unchallenged Labour control has not always been for the best, for the Labour Party or for the electorate, as office became a monopoly and corruption was not unknown. In parliamentary terms, Durham has returned an all-Labour delegation to the Commons since 1964. In that year, Labour's Ted Fletcher defeated the Conservative MP for Darlington; since then Darlington has remained the only marginal seat in Durham.

In many ways it is an anomaly. Unlike most Durham districts Darlington is not a mining town, and it is not on the coast. Rather it was created by the railway revolution of the nineteenth century. In 1825 it formed the central station on the world's first passenger line, from Shildon to Stockton. Its railway works are now closed, but Darlington has developed a series of light industries and in the North East it seems a relatively prosperous town still. It has a large Conservative middle-class vote in the west and south-west of the town. Only a quarter of the population live in council estates, although there are still decaying Victorian terraces around the centre. As in the whole of Durham, there is only a very small number of non-white immigrants. Darlington is actually the shopping centre for a large part of rural North Yorkshire, as well as for the more rough-hewn communities of County Durham. Nearly 40% of its population work in non-manual jobs.

Bearing in mind all this, it is quite possible to see why the Conservatives have won Darlington within living memory. But the fact remains that it has still stayed loyal to Durham's Labour traditions for nearly 20 years. It is unaltered in the boundary changes, although Ted Fletcher is now retiring in favour of a younger Labour candidate of similar political stance, Ossie O'Brien.

1981	% Own Occ	64.9
1981	% Loc Auth	26.0
1981	% Black/Asian	1.5
1971	% Mid Cl	47.1
1971	% Prof Man	13.5
1976	electorate 65,562	
Alliance		SDP

1979 same seat Darlington

Lab	22,565	45.5
C	21,513	43.4
L	5,054	10.2
NF	444	0.9

MPs since 1945
1945-51 D.R. Hardman Lab
1951-59 Sir F.F. Graham C
1959-64 Anthony Bourne-Arton
                    C
1964-   Ted Fletcher Lab

284

Easington

Easington is still associated by many with Manny Shinwell, the indestructible Labour politician who first entered Parliament in 1922 and represented an east Durham constituency from 1935 to 1970, when he was well over 80 years of age. In that year of 1935, Shinwell defeated the ex-Labour leader Ramsay Macdonald at Seaham. Shinwell switched to Easington when that seat was created in 1950, and for the last twenty years of his life in the Commons he remained an active and prominent member.

Now Seaham has again been reunited with Easington, effectively recreating the scene of Macdonald's triumphs in 1929 and 1931 and his humiliation in 1935. The Easington MP nowadays is Labour whip John Dormand, and he has enjoyed the same massive majorities that Shinwell did. The New Town of Peterlee is lost to the revived Sedgefield seat, but Seaham's Labour traditions are longer and even stronger than Peterlee's. Now the Easington seat is even more than ever dominated by the big colliery communities near the east coast of Durham - Horden, Murton and Easington itself. The mines are more modern and productive here, a far cry from the declining and defunct seams of west Durham. Some mines even extend beneath the North Sea bed. Easington will have the highest proportion of miners of any north-eastern seat. The local economy remains more buoyant than that in most parts of industrial Durham and Northumberland.

The Conservatives leave many seats unfought in local council elections here, and the Liberals form the main municipal opposition to Labour. But the Liberal activity cannot be turned into votes when it comes to electing a government, and Easington should continue to be a name identified with Labour landslides, as their rich seams of support continue to show no signs of exhaustion.

1981	% Own Occ	30.2	1979 core seat Easington		
1981	% Loc Auth	57.9	Lab	29,537	60.9
1981	% Black/Asian	0.2	C	11,981	24.7
1981	% Mid Cl	30.8	L	6,979	14.4
1981	% Prof Man	8.0	MPs since 1950		
1982	electorate 66,123		1950-70 Manny Shinwell Lab		
1979	notional result		1970- John Dormand Lab		
	Lab 21,500				
Alliance		L			

North Durham

North Durham is an amalgamation of parts of two old constituencies. The town of Chester-le-Street and its surrounding communities can no longer form the basis for a division of its own, now that the rapidly growing Washington New Town has been transferred into the Sunderland Borough in Tyne and Wear county. Now Chester-le-Street is joined by the working-class villages which made up the old Stanley Urban District, to create the North Durham seat. Stanley used to be in the Consett constituency, and it is still associated with Consett in the Derwentside District Council.

Labour had held Chester-le-Street since 1906, obtaining an 8,000 majority even in 1931, and successfully withstanding a Liberal byelection challenge in their boom year of 1973. Actually Chester-le-Street itself is quite a prosperous old town on the original route from Newcastle to London, and there is something of a Conservative vote in the east of the town towards the stately grounds of Lambton Park. But Chester-le-Street is surrounded by mining villages, and Stanley is more working class still. The North Durham seat should remain of firm Labour persuasion.

The present MP for Chester-le-Street is not a miner, as were some of his distinguished predecessors such as Jack Lawson (MP 1919-50). Giles Radice is something of a centre-right intellectual, educated at Winchester and Magdalen College, Oxford, and heavily involved in the Fabian Society and the Manifesto Group. But he has proved popular with his constituency party as well as with his constituents. Probably he will stand for the new North Durham seat, rather than following Washington into a Tyne and Wear seat.

1981	% Own Occ	50.3	1979 core seat Chester-le-Street
1981	% Loc Auth	44.0	Lab	38,672	60.4
1981	% Black/Asian	0.3	C	16,112	25.2
1981	% Mid Cl	47.1	L	9,247	14.4
1981	% Prof Man	13.1	MPs since 1945
1982	electorate 71,677		1945-50 Jack Lawson Lab
1979	notional result		1950-56 P. Bartley Lab
	Lab 23,400		1956-73 Norman Pentland Lab
Alliance		L	1973- Giles Radice Lab

North-West Durham

The new NW Durham constituency contains some industrial
scenery of an almost brutal nature. The old seat of this name
always included several lonely little mining towns among the
hills and moors around the Wear Valley - Tow Law, Crook and
Willington, Esh Winning. These isolated communities long ago
bred a tight-knit community spirit, of a determinedly
working-class nature which ensured often unopposed local
Labour politics. Mining has declined as the seams have been
exhausted in the high country of west Durham, but many of
the traditions have survived.
Now Brandon and Byshottles urban district is lost to the City
of Durham, and Spennymoor to Sedgefield. But the town
which replaces these is Consett, a town which suffered
economic and social disaster in the early 1980s when its steel
works were closed. Consett was very much a one-industry
town, and most of the male workers depended on the steel
industry directly or indirectly. Consett is on Derwentside
rather than in the Wear Valley, but it is nevertheless remote
and isolated. It is the highest town in County Durham, and
the ruined site of the steelworks stands on the top of the
hill, eerily dominating the red-stone town like a kind of
ghost.
Consett is a Labour stronghold, and NW Durham will remain
that rarity: a largely rural Labour constituency with a low
density of population. It is unclear as yet whether Consett's
David Watkins or Ernest Armstrong of NW Durham will win the
Labour nomination for this safe seat.

1981	% Own Occ	50	1979 core seat North-West	
1981	% Loc Auth	40	Durham	
1981	% Black/Asian	0.3	Lab 29,525	61.3
1981	% Mid Cl	44	C 14,245	29.6
1981	% Prof Man	12	L 4,394	9.1
1982	electorate 61,036		MPs since 1950	
1979	notional result		1950-55 J.D. Murray Lab	
	Lab 12,200		1955-64 J.W. Ainslie Lab	
Alliance		L	1964- Ernest Armstrong Lab	

Sedgefield

Although the total number of parliamentary constituencies tends to increase at each redistribution of boundaries, there are always a few casualties - constituencies that disappear, and MPs who lose their seats. Some find new pastures elsewhere, but one who never did was Labour member David Reed, whose Sedgefield seat was abolished in the last revision in 1974. This seems ironic now, for Sedgefield has been recreated by the Commission as the extra seat in County Durham this time.

Sedgefield is SE County Durham. It almost completely surrounds the town of Darlington, taking in all the rural wards of Darlington Borough. It takes the old mining district around Spennymoor from NW Durham, and Peterlee from Easington. The former Sedgefield Rural District is transferred from Durham. This is typified less by the old town of Sedgefield itself (pop. 4,000) with its racecourse and Shrove Tuesday football match, and more by the big colliery villages of Chilton, Ferryhill and Trimdon. All the pits which gave rise to these communities are now closed, and attempts have been made to establish new light industries in Peterlee and elsewhere. Peterlee was one of the three New Towns established in County Durham in the post-war years - the others were Newton Aycliffe and Washington (now in Tyne and Wear). It was named after Peter Lee, the Durham-born international miners' leader. Peterlee is a symbol of the new tasks and challenges set by the decline of Durham's coal industry through the twentieth century.

Sedgefield will be a safely Labour seat - David Reed will have cause to regret that it ever disappeared in the first place. The rural parts of Darlington Borough, and Sedgefield itself, are among the few Tory places in County Durham. But they will be swamped by the ex-mining villages, Spennymoor and Peterlee, which are all Labour strongholds.

1981	% Own Occ	37	New seat
1981	% Loc Auth	56	
1981	% Black/Asian	0.4	
1981	% Mid Cl	36	
1981	% Prof Man	10	
1982	electorate 61,954		
1979	notional result		
	Lab 13,100		
Alliance		SDP	

Basildon

Basildon is the largest of the British New Towns which were planned by the Reith Committee immediately after the Second World War. The designated area of the New Town has now reached a population of 90,000, and it has finally achieved a constituency of its own. Until now, it has always exercised a double influence on the seat in which it was included: providing a considerable, if volatile, Labour vote; and swelling the seat to among the largest in the country. Until 1974 Basildon New Town was incorporated in the vast Billericay division (123,000 electors in 1970), then in a seat named Basildon but including Billericay and Wickham from outside the New Town (103,500 electors in 1979).

Now after all this under-representation, Basildon has become a compact unit at last, about 65,000 electors strong in 1982. It should also finally lose its marginal status. The New Town itself voted Labour by 8,000 votes even in the 1979 local elections, when the inflated Basildon constituency went to extreme Conservative Harvey Proctor by over 5,000. Billericay and Wickham are really part of the Essex 'stockbroker belt', highly affluent Tory strongholds at all times. The old Basildon seat was one of the most divided, as well as one of the most marginal, in Britain. The New Town neighbourhoods of Fryerns, Lee Chapel, Pitsea and Vange have always returned a Labour majority, although they are inclined to high swings at election time. Langdon Hills and Nethermayne have a larger middle class presence.

But this should be a secure Labour constituency at last. The Alliance actually pushed their way into second place here in the 1982 local elections after a poor Conservative performance, and the Liberals won the Langdon Hills ward, but they only polled 27% to Labour's 48%, even in a bad Labour year. The percentage of council housing is declining, as New Town houses are sold off and private development undertaken. But this has not yet affected the political characteristics of Basildon New Town itself.

1981	% Own Occ	35.2	1979 core seat Basildon		
1981	% Loc Auth	63.3	C	37,919	46.9
1981	% Black/Asian	1	Lab	32,739	40.5
1981	% Mid Cl	43.6	L	9,280	11.5
1981	% Prof Man	12.4	NF	880	1.1
1982	electorate 65,515		MPs since 1974		
1979	notional result		1974-79 Eric Moonman Lab		
	Lab 8,200		1979- Harvey Proctor C		
Alliance		SDP			

Billericay

The Boundary Commissioners had one of their most protracted and difficult tasks in redrawing the old Basildon constituency. They succesively put forward three different proposals, and after two inquiries it was decided to separate the Basildon New Town from the more owner-occupied, middle-class communities of Billericay and Wickford. This has resulted in the re-creation of a Billericay seat. Billericay is a famous name in the legend of elections. In the 1960s it was consistently the first seat to announce its result on General Election night, despite the fact that at the time it was the largest seat in England. In those days Brentwood was included, as well as Basildon New Town.

The new Billericay creeps round to the south of Basildon to take in the Corringham-Fobbing, Orsett, Stanford le Hope and Homesteads wards of Thurrock. Billericay constituency is therefore almost cut into two quite separate parts, but this is not as illogical as it seems. The Thurrock wards are among the more middle class and Conservative in the Borough, especially Orsett, and a socially and politically homogeneous seat has been created.

Billericay will be a safe Conservative seat. The Conservative half of the old Basildon seat has become the base of the new Billericay, while the Labour half now forms a seat of its own. This adds up to two safe seats instead of one large marginal. If the young right-wing Conservative MP for Basildon, Harvey Proctor, can secure the nomination for Billericay, his political career will seem much more sure than appeared likely before the redistribution.

1981	% Own Occ	75.6	New seat
1981	% Loc Auth	19.8	
1981	% Black/Asian	1	
1981	% Mid Cl	57.7	
1981	% Prof Man	19.4	
1982	electorate 74,751		
1979	notional result		
	C 14,200		
Alliance		L	

Braintree

When the constituency of Braintree was carved out of Maldon in 1974, it was thought to be marginal. Indeed its first two contests were very close Tory victories, but with a 9% swing in 1979 the Conservative majority jumped to 12,500. The urban elements of the seat are close even in a bad Labour year - Bocking, the rapidly growing town of Witham, and the Braintree Central ward. But the villages around - Terling and Coggeshall, Black Notley and Hatfield Peverel and many more - are staunchly Conservative, and firmly tip the balance of the seat. A few thousand rural electors are lost in minor boundary changes, but it remains a seat Labour could only win in a landslide year.

1981	% Own Occ	55.3	1979 core seat Braintree		
1981	% Loc Auth	35.5	C	31,593	52.0
1981	% Black/Asian	2	Lab	19,075	31.4
1981	% Mid Cl	52.5	L	10,115	16.6
1981	% Prof Man	19.6	MP since 1974		
1982	electorate 73,823		1974- Anthony Newton C		
1979	notional C 11,500				
Alliance		SDP			

Brentwood and Ongar

Robert McCrindle, decided to stay with Brentwood when it was separated from his marginal Billericay seat in 1974. This was a good idea, for Brentwood and Ongar will remain a rock-solid Tory seat. It is not significantly altered in the boundary changes. Brentwood is situated just beyond the NE fringe of Greater London, on the road to Chelmsford. It is a modern town of mainly middle-class owner occupiers - Labour has chances only in the Brentwood South and Pilgrims Hatch wards. Brentwood and its large satellite, Hutton, are coupled with some much older villages and the town of Ongar in the Epping Forest district - all as Tory as it is.

1981	% Own Occ	67.9	1979 core seat Brentwood and		
1981	% Loc Auth	22.2	Ongar		
1981	% Black/Asian	1.5	C	29,113	60.4
1981	% Mid Cl	63.5	Lab	12,182	25.3
1981	% Prof Man	25.7	L	6,882	14.3
1982	electorate 66,703		MP since 1974		
1979	notional C 19,300		1974- Robert McCrindle C		
Alliance		L			

Castle Point

The Castle Point District, which is exactly the same as the new Castle Point constituency, has the highest proportion of owner occupiers in the United Kingdom - 84.3%. It consists of the towns of Benfleet and Canvey Island. The rapidly growing former seat of South East Essex also included Rayleigh, now transferred to Rochford. SE Essex also held the record for the highest proportion of owner-occupied housing in the old Parliament.

Castle Point will not be an overwhelmingly middle-class seat - certainly not the flat Canvey Island itself, dominated by its oil refinery, which was 72% working class in 1971. But the conservatism of owner occupiers should not be underestimated, and the concept of 'housing class' is gaining currency among academics. Castle Point is also remarkably homogeneous. The Conservatives won every seat in the 1979 local elections, and the Liberals did not contest a single one.

The Conservative majority at the last General Election in SE Essex was 24,500, after an 11.6% swing from Labour. Their lead in the Castle Point district was about 14,000. This new division is likely to be subject to very large swings, but it should remain a safe Conservative seat. The Alliance has no tradition on which to build, and seems unlikely to make a serious challenge in this Utopia of the property-owning democracy.

1981	% Own Occ	84.3	1979 core seat Essex South East		
1981	% Loc Auth	10.9	C	40,497	64.0
1981	% Black/Asian	1.2	Lab	15,965	25.2
1981	% Mid Cl	54.1	L	6,858	10.8
1981	% Prof Man	18.6	MP since 1955		
1982	electorate 64,532		1955-	Bernard Braine C	
1979	notional result				
	C 16,900				
Alliance		SDP			

Chelmsford

The county town of Essex is undeniably affluent and middle
class. Set in the heart of prosperous rolling farmland,
Chelmsford itself is popular with commuters as well as
enjoying its own life as an economic centre: the unemployment
rate of 4.3% in the constituency in 1981 was one of the lowest
in the country. Yet the Conservative hold on Chelmsford is
shaky in the extreme. The MP here is a nationally-known
figure, Norman St John-Stevas, the suave and civilised
aesthete who was sacked from Mrs Thatcher's Cabinet two
years into the government's life. But Liberal Stuart Mole
gathered over 28,000 votes against him in 1979 and
Chelmsford will mark one of the Liberals' strongest challenges
anywhere in Britain next time.

The boundary changes help the Liberals too. They have
always done best in Chelmsford itself, winning most of its
wards on the District Council in 1979 and all the Chelmsford
wards in the Essex County Council elections of 1981. The
Conservatives have fought back in the rural wards, in the
villages surrounding Chelmsford. But now 14,000 electors
from the rural part of the seat are removed to reduce its
size. The Chelmsford constituency does not now include the
northernmost and southernmost parts of the District - the
north end is in Braintree, the south end in Rochford.

The Liberals must have high hopes in Chelmsford, and it
would surely be one of the first half-dozen seats to fall in a
good Alliance year. But Norman St John-Stevas is a man of
considerable charm, and substance too, and with the full
weight of the powerful and resilient Conservative machine
working behind him he will prove hard to dislodge. The
Labour vote has already been squeezed down to a minimal
level.

1981	% Own Occ	65.3	1979 core seat Chelmsford		
1981	% Loc Auth	26.8	C	33,808	49.6
1981	% Black/Asian	2	L	28,377	41.6
1981	% Mid Cl	62.7	Lab	6,041	8.9
1981	% Prof Man	22.4	MPs since 1945		
1982	electorate 79,172		1945-50 E.R. Millington CW		
1979	notional result			(Lab)	
	C 3,500		1950-64 H. Ashton C		
Alliance		L	1964- N. St John-Stevas C		

Epping Forest

Epping Forest, just north-east of London, contains some of the best residential districts in Essex. The old Chigwell Urban District included Loughton and Buckhurst Hill as well as the affluent little town of Chigwell, which gave its name to the seat which preceded this one from 1955 to 1974. Epping and Theydon Bois are other attractive middle-class communities. Labour's only significant vote in a solidly Tory seat comes from the wards of Broadway, Paternoster and Dibden Green, and the town of Waltham Abbey. It should continue to be ultra-safe for a senior right-wing Conservative backbencher, Sir John Biggs-Davison.

1981	% Own Occ	63.1	1979 core seat Epping Forest		
1981	% Loc Auth	28.6	C	29,447	57.6
1981	% Black/Asian	1.5	Lab	13,994	27.4
1981	% Mid Cl	60.5	L	6,528	12.8
1981	% Prof Man	22.7	NF	1,110	2.2
1982	electorate 68,240		MP since 1955		
1979	notional C 15,400		1955-	Sir John Biggs-Davison	
Alliance		SDP			

Harlow

The post-war Harlow New Town lies tucked in a once rural corner of NW Essex. It is somewhat smaller than Basildon, and need the addition of about 10,000 electors from Epping Forest District, around North Weald, to make up a constituency. Harlow itself voted Labour by about 4,000 even after a 13% swing to the Tories at the 1979 General Election, but the inclusion of the Epping Forest villages brought Stan Newens's majority down to a shaky 1,392. There were Conservative wards in Harlow itself, at Old Harlow and in the south-western neighbourhoods of Great Parndon and Kingsmoor. But it would be surprising if Harlow were not to swing back to Labour next time, and the Alliance has shown some potential for forming the main opposition.

1981	% Own Occ	31.1	1979 core seat Harlow		
1981	% Loc Auth	66.2	Lab	22,698	42.7
1981	% Black/Asian	3	C	21,306	40.1
1981	% Mid Cl	49.8	L	8,289	15.6
1981	% Prof Man	15.1	NF	840	1.6
1982	electorate 70,641		MP since 1974		
1979	notional Lab 1,400		1974-	Stan Newens Lab	
Alliance		L			

Harwich

The Harwich constituency used to include the whole of NE Essex's Tendring District, but it was greatly oversized, with over 90,000 electors in 1979. Now it loses the western half of Tendring (places such as Brightlingsea), and the Essex University town of Wivenhoe. All are moved into North Colchester. That which remains should still be safely Conservative - the seaside resorts of Clacton and less brash Frinton and Walton; the east coast ferry port of Harwich; and some inland territory. Julian Ridsdale won a majority of over 20,000 in 1979, and despite a Liberal and Labour presence in parts of the seat, the reduction in size will reduce only the numerical majority, not the percentage.

1981	% Own Occ	78.3	1979 core seat Harwich		
1981	% Loc Auth	12.2	C	37,685	54.3
1981	% Black/Asian	1	Lab	16,998	24.5
1981	% Mid Cl	50.7	L	14,094	20.3
1981	% Prof Man	18.8	NF	597	0.9
1982	electorate 72,021		MPs since 1945		
1979	notional result		1945-54 Sir J.S. Holmes C		
	C 15,600		1954- Julian Ridsdale C		
Alliance		L			

North Colchester

Labour had hopes of seizing the Colchester seat for the first time since 1945 when the Boundary Commission originally proposed that the over-large division should be pared down to the town of Colchester itself. But after an inquiry, their hopes were shipwrecked. Colchester is now split down the middle along the line of the River Colne. Each half is diluted by a substantial rural area, and this ensures two safe Tory seats. In North Colchester the Labour wards of St Andrew's and Castle are overwhelmed by the western half of Tendring District and several rural wards of Colchester Borough.

1981	% Own Occ	70.4	1979 core seat Colchester		
1981	% Loc Auth	19.8	C	36,740	52.9
1981	% Black/Asian	2	Lab	22,877	33.0
1981	% Mid Cl	54.1	L	9,794	14.1
1981	% Prof Man	20.2	MPs since 1)45		
1982	electorate 77,251		1945-50 C.G.P. Smith Lab		
1979	notional result		1950-61 C.J.M. Alport C		
	C 15,300		1961- Antony Buck C		
Alliance		L			

Rochford

Essex has gained two extra seats as a result of redistribution. One of them is Rochford, in SE Essex. Rochford was created when the Commission put together Rayleigh from Bernard Braine's Essex SE, Rochford Rural District from Maldon, and some Chelmsford wards around Woodham Ferrers. Each of these is strongly Conservative and heavily owner-occupied. It is a region of residential growth and low unemployment - the expanding, prosperous face of Britain. Its creation forms a typical example of the way the Conservatives will benefit from the boundary changes.

1981	% Own Occ	82.1	New seat
1981	% Loc Auth	10.6	
1981	% Black/Asian	1	
1981	% Mid Cl	60.6	
1981	% Prof Man	20.7	
1982	electorate 68,563		
1979	notional C 20,200		
Alliance		L	

Saffron Walden

Saffron Walden is the most rural seat in Essex, and the only one to reach the nation's 100 most agricultural seats. Situated in the NW of the county, its only towns are Saffron Walden (population 10,000) and Halstead (9,000). This is a peaceful and pleasant corner of bustling Essex. Much of the county's countryside is now buried beneath sprawling housing estates and industry, but Saffron Walden is a welcome exception. It also has a long-term record of electing liberal Conservatives in a county noted for its adherence to the right. This was R.A. Butler's seat, and Sir Peter Kirk's. The present MP, Alan Haselhurst, lies in the same moderate tradition. Saffron Walden is scarcely disturbed by boundary changes.

1981	% Own Occ	62.3	1979 core seat Saffron Walden		
1981	% Loc Auth	23.5	C	28,563	53.8
1981	% Black/Asian	1	L	13,200	24.9
1981	% Mid Cl	53.6	Lab	10,547	19.9
1981	% Prof Man	24.0	Ind	425	0.8
1982	electorate 69,542		NF	342	0.6
1979	notional C 15,400		MPs since 1945		
Alliance		SDP	1945-65 R.A. Butler C		
			1965-77 Sir Peter Kirk C		
			1977- Alan Haselhurst C		

South Colchester and Maldon

Labour cried foul when the Boundary Commission reversed its
original plan to create a seat consisting entirely of the town
of Colchester. They would have had a fighting chance if they
could have contested a Colchester shorn of rural
appendages. But this possibility was washed away by the
revised recommendations presented by the Assistant
Commissioner, barrister C.W.F. Newman, after an inquiry
held at Chelmsford in March 1979. Now two Tory seats have
been drawn, each with half of Colchester and many external
wards.

Colchester south of the River Colne has now been placed
together with rural wards of Colchester Borough like West
Mersea and Tiptree, and the complete District of Maldon.
Within Colchester itself, Labour usually wins the wards of
Berechurch, Shrub End and New Town; but these are to be
swamped by Tory votes from outside. Maldon used to be the
base of a seat of its own, but half its electorate has been lost
to the new Rochford division.

The juxtaposition of Maldon and South Colchester is a happy
one for the Conservative Party. John Wakeham's majority in
Maldon was nearly 17,000 in 1979 in a seat of no more than
average size. Despite the presence of the better half of
Colchester for Labour, this new seat should be an excellent
bet for the Tories.

1981	% Own Occ	67.7	1979 core seat Maldon
1981	% Loc Auth	20.8	C 29,585 57.8
1981	% Black/Asian	1.5	Lab 12,848 25.1
1981	% Mid Cl	50.8	L 8,730 17.1
1981	% Prof Man	19.2	MPs since 1945
1982	electorate 79,134		1945-55 Tom Driberg Lab
1979	notional result		1955-74 Brian Harrison C
	C 13,000		1974- John Wakeham C
Alliance		SDP	

Southend East

Southend East appeared briefly in the national eye in 1980,
when Teddy Taylor, the former Conservative Secretary of
State for Scotland, was elected in a byelection. Taylor had
lost his seat at Glasgow Cathcart in the 1979 General Election,
and after accusations of carpetbagging in search of a safe
seat he won the Southend E byelection by only 430 votes.
This was a rare excellent Labour performance in a byelection,
and does not mean that this should be regarded as a marginal
seat. The Southend seats are unaltered, and although
Southend East is the more working-class end of the town,
having most of the small council tenant and non-white
population, Teddy Taylor's wanderings should end
satisfactorily here.

1981	% Own Occ	63	1979 same seat Southend East
1981	% Loc Auth	17	C 22,413 56.1
1981	% Black/Asian	4	Lab 11,639 29.1
1981	% Mid Cl	48	L 5,244 13.1
1981	% Prof Man	16	NF 676 1.7
1982	electorate 58,212		MPs since 1950
Alliance		SDP	1950-80 Sir Stephen McAdden C
			1980- Teddy Taylor C

Southend West

Southend West is a Liberal target seat, and the scene of
Liberal victories in local election wards like Leigh on Sea,
Prittlewell and Westborough. But it is also the more middle
class of the two Southend seats, and Paul Channon's lead at
the last Election was nearly 17,000. The Liberals have a long
way to go before they can capture this more elegant end of
one of London's favourite seaside resorts. Paul Channon's
father 'Chips' held this seat before him, and it has now been
safely in the family for nearly 50 years.

1981	% Own Occ	79	1979 same seat Southend West
1981	% Loc Auth	10	C 29,449 57.7
1981	% Black/Asian	2	L 12,585 24.6
1981	% Mid Cl	60	Lab 8,341 16.3
1981	% Prof Man	20	NF 680 1.3
1982	electorate 67,771		MPs since 1950
Alliance		L	1950-59 H.P.G. Channon C
			1959- Paul Channon C

Thurrock

The Borough of Thurrock stretches along the north bank of the Thames east of London from Purfleet through the dockland of Grays and Tilbury nearly to Canvey Island. The constituency used to be identical to the local authority district, but it was oversized at 91,000 electors in 1979, and the easternmost 25,000 have been lost to the new Billericay seat - Corringham, Orsett and Stanford le Hope.

Thurrock is a predominantly working class division, with a greater than average share of council housing. Here are to be found London's outermost docks, for Tilbury is the main container port for the capital. But Thurrock's wards do vary in social and political character. Labour's best areas are Tilbury, the Chadwell St Mary council estate, West Thurrock-Purfleet, Aveley and South Ockendon-Belhus. The Conservatives can fight back in Little Thurrock and much of Grays, especially the Grays North ward. There used to be a 20,000 Labour majority in Thurrock, but there was a massive swing of 11% to the Conservatives at the 1979 General Election. This reduced Labour MP Oonagh McDonald's margin to 6,419.

The electors removed in the redrawing are more Conservative than most in Thurrock, and Labour should have a slightly safer seat here. The wedge of England north and east of London showed the greatest swing to the right in 1979, and a further swing seems unlikely. The Alliance seems to have little appeal in Thurrock, polling under 15% in the 1982 local elections.

1981	% Own Occ	42.8	1979 core seat Thurrock			
1981	% Loc Auth	51.2	Lab	33,449	48.6	
1981	% Black/Asian	2	C	27,030	39.2	
1981	% Mid Cl	43.5	L	6,445	9.4	
1981	% Prof Man	11.1	NF	1,358	2.0	
1982	electorate 67,293		Oth	607	0.9	
1979	notional result		MPs since 1945			
	Lab 7,300		1945-50 L.J. Solley Lab			
Alliance		SDP	1950-76 Hugh Delargy Lab			
			1976-	Oonagh McDonald Lab		

Cheltenham

Cheltenham has long been perhaps the largest and most fashionable inland spa town in the country. Set in a bowl of hills in the Cotswolds, it is an artistic, cultural and educational centre - the site of such well-known establishments as Cheltenham College, Cheltenham Ladies' College, Cheltenham Grammar School and Dean Close School. It also has a booming industrial economy. It is increasingly favoured as a headquarters for firms moving out of London. It is conveniently sited on the A40 and near the M5 motorway. Another major employer in the town is the government communications centre, GCHQ. With this capacity for adapting to modern technology, and the streets of large elegant houses dating from previous centuries, one would think that Cheltenham would be a Tory stronghold.

Yet Labour nearly won Cheltenham in 1966, and although their challenge has now faded, the Liberals count it as one of their best hopes for a gain in the next General Election. Labour's strength lay in the council estates of Hester's Way, in the west of the town, and round Whaddon in the NE. The Liberals have achieved great municipal successes, particularly in central wards, and are now attracting Labour voters, who might prefer them to the Tories.

But the Conservatives can still count on several powerful weapons. Cheltenham has always been a centre of great affluence, such as in the suburb of Charlton Kings, one of the most middle-class places in Britain. Now Cheltenham is one of the few parts of the country where new wealth is clearly being created. The Conservative villages of Leckhampton and Prestbury are added in the boundary changes. Finally the Tories have a popular and worthy local MP in Charles Irving, a liberal bachelor who has twice been Mayor of Cheltenham. Cheltenham is usually one of the first seats to declare its results on election night. Charles Irving is likely therefore to be one of the first members elected to the new Parliament.

1981	% Own Occ	62	1979 core seat Cheltenham	
1981	% Loc Auth	22	C	25,618	51.0
1981	% Black/Asian	2	L	15,080	30.0
1981	% Mid Cl	55	Lab	9,185	18.3
1981	% Prof Man	16	NF	342	0.7
1982	electorate 76,600		MPs since 1945	
1979	notional result		1945-50 D.L. Lipson Ind	
	C 12,900		1950-64 W.W. Hicks Beach C	
Alliance		L	1964-74 Douglas Dodds-Parker C	
			1974- Charles Irving C	

Cirencester and Tewkesbury

If there is any single constituency which could be described as the heart of the Cotswolds, it is the east Gloucestershire seat of Cirencester and Tewkesbury. It includes many of the names most associated with those gentle hills: Bourton on the Water, Chipping Campden, Stow on the Wold, Fairford, Lechlade and Northleach, in addition to the two largest towns of the constituency title. As in many of the most attractive parts of Britain, there is a double reason for Conservatism: simply that the residents have much that is pleasant to conserve, and also that tourism tends to be a commercial pursuit carried on by private enterprise. This is a rural seat too, with sheep farming in the more rugged uplands and dairy farms elsewhere.

All in all, it is not hard to see why the Thatcherite junior Foreign Office Minister Nicholas Ridley was elected with a 19,000 majority over the Liberals in 1979. Labour can hardly win a single seat in the wards of the Cotswold and Tewkesbury Districts within this constituency, not even in Cirencester where there are sizeable council estates and pockets of industry. The Liberals do a little better, picking up a fair minority of votes right across the seat. But they have few councillors, and less of a local base than in Cheltenham, which lies as an enclave entirely surrounded by Cirencester and Tewkesbury.

Cirencester and Tewkesbury reached an electorate of 85,000 in 1979, and several thousand voters have been transferred to Cheltenham, whose suburbs have spread beyond its boundaries. Now Prestbury and Leckhampton are to be included in Cheltenham, although the spreading estates of Bishops Cleeve-Woodmancote remain in Cirencester and Tewkesbury. Nicholas Ridley should have no trouble winning re-election next time.

1981	% Own Occ	59	1979 core seat Cirencester/		
1981	% Loc Auth	22	Tewkesbury		
1981	% Black/Asian	1	C	37,651	56.0
1981	% Mid Cl	48	L	18,057	26.8
1981	% Prof Man	19	Lab	11,575	17.2
1982	electorate 79,929		MPs since 1945		
1979	notional result		1945-59 W.S. Morrison C		
	C 17,300		1959- Nicholas Ridley C		
Alliance		L			

Gloucester

Like Cheltenham, Gloucester expands to take in a couple of peripheral villages in the boundary changes. Like West Gloucestershire, Gloucester was once a fairly safe Labour seat which has moved towards the Conservatives on a long-term basis. In this case the Conservative victory came a little longer ago, not in 1979 but in 1970, when Sally Oppenheim defeated Labour's Jack Diamond. Mrs Oppenheim, who rose rapidly to become Consumer Affairs Minister under Mrs Thatcher, consolidated her hold on Gloucester through the 1970s, aided by the 1974 boundary changes, and Labour now look unlikely to regain the seat.

Gloucester has always been a functional, commercial town, less glamorous than its newer neighbour Cheltenham a few miles away. It was the lowest crossing point of the Severn before the opening of the bridge - this accounts for its prominence in Roman and medieval times, as one of the great towns of the West. It has always enjoyed a diversity of industry; once it was the home of Gloster Aircraft, now it houses one of the biggest ice cream factories in the world.

There is still enough of an industrial working-class population for Labour to do well in peripheral council estates like Matson, and further in towards the centre of the city; Gloucester possesses by far the greatest proportion of non-white immigrants in the county. But overall the percentage of council housing is low, and the Conservatives have several safe private housing wards on the edge of the city, like Kingsholm and Longlevens, Hucclecote and Tuffley. According to the 1982 local elections, though, Gloucester must rank as one of the best SDP chances in the country, for the Alliance polled 33% to the Conservatives' 40% in a good year. But all the ward victories were achieved by Liberals, and it is not clear to what extent Liberal voters will be prepared to support the SDP parliamentary candidate. But the Alliance is probably a greater threat to Mrs Oppenheim than Labour, who may well sink into third place in Gloucester.

1981	% Own Occ	68	1979 core seat Gloucester		
1981	% Loc Auth	22	C	25,163	48.7
1981	% Black/Asian	5	Lab	18,747	36.3
1981	% Mid Cl	48	L	7,213	14.0
1981	% Prof Man	13	NF	527	1.0
1982	electorate 74,673		MPs since 1945		
1979	notional result		1945-57 M. Turner-Samuels Lab		
	C 7,000		1957-70 Jack Diamond Lab		
Alliance		SDP	1970- Sally Oppenheim C		

Stroud

The District and constituency of Stroud is situated south of Gloucester. Much of it is still part of the Cotswold range of hills, although the countryside slopes down to the vale of the Severn around Berkeley. But compared with a neighbouring seat like Cirencester and Tewkesbury, there is more industry here, and fewer beauty spots. One or two dramatic industrial valleys prove striking sights: Chalford and the Golden Valley, and the Dursley-Cam district where Labour can win in a good year like 1981.

Stroud is safely Tory, like all the other Cotswold seats, but here Labour finish second and the Liberals third. Anthony Kershaw has held the constituency since 1955, but his majority over Labour was cut to 1,500 in 1966. It is ten times that now, but Labour did still poll some 17,000 votes in 1979, and may well achieve second place again next time – which might be a rare achievement in a predominantly rural seat in the south or south-west of England.

Stroud loses the villages of Quedgley and Hardwick, and Upton St Leonards, to Gloucester in the boundary changes, which are minor throughout Gloucestershire. It still includes a small section of the Cotswold local government District, around Tetbury (this is Labour's weakest area in the Stroud division). But fundamentally it is an almost unchanged constituency whose boundaries are almost coterminous with those of the Stroud District.

1981	% Own Occ	66	1979 core seat Stroud		
1981	% Loc Auth	23	C	32,534	52.6
1981	% Black/Asian	1	Lab	17,037	27.5
1981	% Mid Cl	47	L	12,314	19.9
1981	% Prof Man	17	MPs since 1945		
1982	electorate 78,021		1945-50 B.T. Parkin Lab		
1979	notional result		1950-55 W.R.D. Perkins C		
	C 15,500		1955- Anthony Kershaw C		
Alliance		L			

West Gloucestershire

West Gloucestershire is one of the small number of completely unchanged constituencies in the present redistribution. In fact it is very similar to the former Forest of Dean seat which existed before 1950. In 1931, when Labour was reduced to but fifty seats in the whole of Britain, they lost the Forest of Dean by only 1,500 votes, to a National Labour candidate. In fact, but for the interruption of 1931-5, Labour held the Forest of Dean seat from 1918 to 1979. But gradually what had once been one of the safest Labour seats swung to the Conservatives, and its fall at the 1979 Election was widely expected. What might account for such a transformation?

Once the Forest of Dean was an active coalfield, typified by little communities of miners around the tiny pits in the woods. But the coal seams are now worked out, and the last colliery closed in 1965, although some opencast mining continued. Stark towns like Coleford and Cinderford still stand as gaunt reminders of the Forest's industrial past, but more and more they have been outweighted by the advance of commuter suburbs around Gloucester; and the working-class traditions of West Gloucestershire, like the coal seams, have been exhausted, or at least eroded.

The history of West Gloucestershire is proof that political change does not have to be a result of boundary revision. Few parts of Britain so clearly show the connection between social and economic change and long-term party political swings. The phenomenon may still be operating in West Gloucestershire in which case it would be hard to see Paul Marland being defeated as the seat completes its cycle to become a safe Conservative division.

1981	% Own Occ	65.9	1979 same seat West		
1981	% Loc Auth	23.3	Gloucestershire		
1981	% Black/Asian	0.7	C	28,183	47.9
1981	% Mid Cl	45	Lab	24,009	40.8
1981	% Prof Man	16	L	6,370	10.8
1982	electorate 74,367		NF	270	0.5
Alliance		SDP	MPs since 1945		

MPs since 1945
1945-59 M.P. Price Lab
1959-74 Charles Loughlin Lab
1974-79 John Watkinson Lab
1979-   Paul Marland C

Aldershot

There are only a few constituencies in the country which are heavily influenced by the military vote, and most of them seem to be in Hampshire. It is known that Portsmouth and Gosport are more Conservative than their class makeup would suggest because of the presence of the Royal Navy and associated industries. Since the establishment of the Army camp in 1854, the name of Aldershot has been associated with the idea of square-bashing and basic training by many generations of soldiers, and others besides. The constituency also includes Farnborough, which claims to be the birthplace of aeronautical research and development, and brings thousands of visitors to its air show.

This district, the Borough of Rushmoor, is densely populated and rapidly expanding, and contains many thousands of non-service voters; but the flavour is pervasive. Like the naval ports on the Hampshire coast, Aldershot's politics are skewed to the right by the military interest. At the last Election Conservative MP Julian Critchley had a majority of 23,576 over the Liberals. Aldershot was far too large, with its 86,500 electorate, but now the expanding and ultra-middle-class town of Fleet is removed to the new East Hampshire division. Fleet is in Hart District, but some residential areas from Hart remain in Aldershot - Yateley, Hartney Wintney, Frogmore and Eversley.

There are Liberal pockets in the seat, and a working-class majority - but it will still be an unprecedented earthquake if the Tories should lose Aldershot. Perhaps surprisingly for this seat, Julian Critchley is one of the most prominent and outspoken 'wet' critics of the Thatcher government, but his own constituency party, like his constituency, still seems happy with him.

1981	% Own Occ	61.8	1979 core seat Aldershot
1981	% Loc Auth	22.0	C 38,014 57.5
1981	% Black/Asian	3	L 14,438 21.8
1981	% Mid Cl	50.2	Lab 13,698 20.7
1981	% Prof Man	18.7	MPs since 1945
1982	electorate 77,416		1945-54 O. Lyttleton C
1979	notional result		1954-70 Sir Eric Errington C
	C 19,400		1970- Julian Critchley C
Alliance		L	

Basingstoke

Basingstoke has been one of the most rapidly expanding towns in Britain for thirty years. In 1951 it was a Hampshire country town of 16,000 souls. By 1961 it had reached 26,000 and then the population doubled in ten years. It has now passed the 60,000 mark, as the massive private and council housing developments burgeon on the north and west sides of the town. Its political character has changed too. Safely Conservative even in 1945, the London overspill scheme voters have created a potential for Labour here, especially now that the constituency has been reduced to the new town core or 'doughnut' by the Commission. The electorate was over 99,000 in 1979, and still growing. Now a compact new seat has been formed around Basingstoke itself, which must offer the possibility of marginality.

Basingstoke swung heavily to the Conservatives at the last Election, and David Mitchell increased his majority to nearly 22,000. Clearly there weren't enough votes to sustain a Labour seat then, even if the Commission had already removed Conservative small towns and villages like Whitchurch, Kingsclere and Tadley, which are to go into the new NW Hampshire. But Labour might just have a chance in the new Basingstoke. In the 1981 County Council elections - admittedly one of Labour's best ever years - they probably won a majority in the new seat, as North and West Basingstoke outvoted the Conservative old town and the remaining villages.

It would probably take a swing to Labour of about 10% from the 1979 General Election to win Basingstoke. Even with continued demographic change, and the continued growth of the new Basingstoke, this seems unlikely. But this constituency does show that the boundary changes can sometimes help Labour, especially in expanding towns where Tory rural areas are chipped away from an over-large seat to leave a more working-class new town core. This has happened at The Wrekin (Telford), Stevenage, Basildon, Hemel Hempstead and now here at Basingstoke. It provides an interesting counterbalancing trend to the main current of the present boundary review.

1981	% Own Occ	53.2	1979 core seat Basingstoke		
1981	% Loc Auth	38.9	C	42,625	54.1
1981	% Black/Asian	2.5	Lab	20,879	26.5
1981	% Mid Cl	52.4	L	14,605	18.5
1981	% Prof Man	16.8	NF	677	0.9
1982	electorate 71,473		MPs since 1945		
1979	notional result		1945-55 P.W. Donner C		
	C 10,400		1955-64 D.K. Freeth C		
Alliance		SDP	1964- David Mitchell C		

306

East Hampshire

A long strip of the eastern border country of Hampshire has been designated as the new East Hants constituency. It is not entirely a new seat, for the old Petersfield division was very similar to the East Hampshire District, which provides the kernel of this seat of the same name. Most of the District is included - Petersfield, Liss, Liphook, Horndean and Whitehill for example - but Alton is transferred to Winchester. At the northern end of East Hampshire, the area around Fleet is annexed from the Aldershot constituency and the Hart District.

This is one of the most Conservative parts of Britain; it is very similar socially and politically to the Sussex and Surrey territory just across the county border - the constituencies of Chichester and Farnham (SW Surrey). Labour came extremely close to losing their deposit in Petersfield in 1979, scraping together only 12.6% of the vote, and they win no local wards. The Tory MP, former Army officer Michael Mates, beat the Liberal by 22,375 votes at the last General Election. The new addition, Fleet, is one of the most middle-class towns in Britain, with over 62% non-manual workers in 1971. Alton, which has departed, was one of the Liberals' better areas, along with Petersfield town itself.

Therefore it seems that the new East Hampshire may be even safer than the old Petersfield, although it will be about 10,000 votes smaller. This will scarcely make a dent in Mates's huge majority, or disturb the peace of this quiet corner of Tory southern England.

1981	% Own Occ	67.4	1979 core seat Petersfield		
1981	% Loc Auth	16.8	C	39,200	61.1
1981	% Black/Asian	2	L	16,825	26.2
1981	% Mid Cl	55.4	Lab	8,082	12.6
1981	% Prof Man	24.2	MPs since 1945		
1982	electorate 78,654		1945-51 Sir G.D. Jeffreys C		
1979	notional result		1951-60 Hon. P.R. Legh C		
	C 19,300		1960-74 Joan Quennell C		
Alliance		L	1974- Michael Mates C		

Eastleigh

Eastleigh Borough takes in much of the suburban belt just north and east of Southampton - Eastleigh itself, Chandlers Ford, Hiltingbury, Hedge End, West End, Botley, Bursledon and Hound. Now the parliamentary constituency of Eastleigh has invaded the city itself, to take the Woolston ward from the Southampton Itchen division. It has lost over 20,000 voters from the environs of Romsey to the new ·Romsey/ Waterside seat, so Eastleigh becomes even more of a compact, semi-urban borough seat than before. What will the effect of all this be in electoral terms?

The Conservative majority in the Eastleigh division in 1979 was 20,294. But this was after a large swing of 8.2% in a large seat; there was a time when it seemed it could be marginal. David Price held a slightly different Eastleigh by only 701 votes in 1966 - that didn't include Romsey, which makes it rather similar to the latest version. Eastleigh itself is a railway town, which gave Labour a majority even in 1979. But most of the rest of Eastleigh Borough consists of modern private housing developments. Labour gets hardly any votes, under 10% in fact, in Chandlers Ford and Hiltingbury, and doesn't do well in the post-war sprawl around Hedge End. This does tip the borough as a whole to the Conservatives. The Liberals are locally active in Chandlers Ford, but their support is thin and inconsistent. Woolston is by tradition a Labour ward in Southampton Itchen, and its transfer might in other circumstances have been of greater significance for marginal Itchen than for Eastleigh. But Itchen's MP Bob Mitchell has defected to the SDP, obscuring the situation. His survival as a Social Democrat probably does not depend as much on Woolston as it would if he were still the Labour candidate.

Eastleigh itself probably returns to the situation that it enjoyed between 1955 and 1970 - a Conservative seat which Labour can threaten in a landslide year. But Labour has so many centres of great weakness here, like the Chandlers Ford area, that a win for the left seems very unlikely.

1981	% Own Occ	70.3	1979 core seat Eastleigh		
1981	% Loc Auth	22.6	C	38,516	55.9
1981	% Black/Asian	1.5	Lab	18,222	26.5
1981	% Mid Cl	54.0	L	12,143	17.6
1981	% Prof Man	17.3	MP since 1955		
1982	electorate 82,197		1955-	David Price C	
1979	notional result				
	C 12,600				
Alliance		L			

Fareham

The Fareham constituency, which was created when Gosport and Fareham was divided in 1974, used to consist quite simply of the Fareham Borough, itself the same as the old Fareham Urban District. Now the situation is less clear. Two Fareham wards on the Solent have been shifted to Gosport, and re-placed by a considerable area of inland Hampshire countryside around Droxford and the Meon Valley. This will make Fareham much less of a compact urban seat than before, but no less safe an owner-occupied middle-class Conservative seat.

1981	% Own Occ	75.0	1979 core seat Fareham		
1981	% Loc Auth	15.3	C	28,730	59.0
1981	% Black/Asian	1.7	L	11,685	24.0
1981	% Mid Cl	54.4	Lab	8,041	16.5
1981	% Prof Man	18.6	NF	252	0.5
1982	electorate 71,677		MPs since 1974		
1979	notional result		1974-79 Reginald Bennett C		
	C 19,900		1979- Peter Lloyd C		
Alliance		L			

Gosport

In 1979 Gosport had the lowest percentage of professional and managerial workers of any Conservative constituency - only 7.3%. The professional/managerial figure is a good indicator of how working class a seat is, and usually of its political preferences. Yet this is no marginal, but one of the 50 safest Conservative seats. This extraordinary contradiction is to be explained by Gosport's high military vote, for the town is but a mile across the water from Portsmouth, and Royal Navy bases abound. Now the constituency expands to include two Fareham wards, Hill Head and Stubbington, just beyond Gosport's own Lee-on-Solent. But Gosport should remain one of the most working-class of Tory seats - and one of the most secure.

1981	% Own Occ	63.0	1979 core seat Gosport		
1981	% Loc Auth	22.9	C	24,553	61.8
1981	% Black/Asian	1.5	Lab	10,460	26.3
1981	% Mid Cl	40.1	L	4,741	11.9
1981	% Prof Man	11.0	MP since 1974		
1982	electorate 64,619		1974- Peter Viggers C		
1979	notional result				
	C 17,300				
Alliance		L			

Havant

The population of the Borough of Havant increased from 35,000 in 1951 to 109,000 in 1971. Until 1974 it was part of a Portsmouth seat, Langstone, which was of course greatly inflated by Havant's growth. It then earned a seat of its own, and in the redistribution it even loses two wards, Purbrook and Stakes, to Portsmouth N. These are two of the heavily Tory wards, and Havant does possess a Labour vote in modern council estates like Bondfields, Battins, Warren Park and Barncroft. But the Conservatives do very well elsewhere, in the holiday resort of Hayling Island, Emsworth, Cowplain and Havant-Waterloo itself. They should continue to have no trouble in winning by five-figure majorities in this seat.

1981	% Own Occ	57.1	1979 core seat Havant and	
1981	% Loc Auth	36.9	Waterloo	
1981	% Black/Asian	2	C	35,580	57.3
1981	% Mid Cl	50.5	Lab	15,240	24.5
1981	% Prof Man	17.4	L	11,274	18.2
1982	electorate 73,564		MP since 1974	
1979	notional C 16,100		1974- Ian Lloyd C	
Alliance		SDP		

New Forest

In 1979 New Forest MP Patrick McNair-Wilson won one of the ten largest Conservative majorities in Britain - 25,450. There have been extensive boundary changes. The port of Lymington has been taken in from Christchurch-Lymington, an enforced divorce because Christchurch is now in Dorset. The 'Waterside' parishes on the west side of Southampton Water have been taken away to be placed with Romsey in an extra Hampshire seat - these are Totton, Hythe, Dibden Purlieu and Fawley, famous for its oil refinery. The heart of the constituency remains the New Forest itself, with its affluent tourist towns of Lyndhurst, Brockenhurst and Ringwood. It will remain an epitome of Tory England.

1981	% Own Occ	71.6	1979 core seat New Forest	
1981	% Loc Auth	14.6	C	39,124	59.5
1981	% Black/Asian	1	L	13,674	20.8
1981	% Mid Cl	54.9	Lab	12,950	19.7
1981	% Prof Man	23.1	MPs since 1945	
1982	electorate 69,548		1945-68 Sir Oliver Crosthwaite-	
1979	notional C 20,900		Eyre C	
Alliance		L	1968- Patrick McNair-Wilson C	

North-West Hampshire

Hampshire has two extra seats as a result of the deliberations of the Boundary Commissioners. Because of the extensive and complex nature of the redrawing of parliamentary constituencies, it is not always clear which seats have the best claim to be the entirely new ones. But NW Hampshire must be reckoned as an extra seat. It contains some rural parts of western Basingstoke and Deane Borough, such as those around Whitchurch, Tadley, Overton and Kingsclere. These used to be in the Basingstoke seat. The other half of NW Hampshire is made up of the northern part of Test Valley Borough, centred on Andover, which was formerly associated with Winchester.

Andover was one of the towns chosen to expand to take in London overspill in the post-war period. In two decades after 1961 the population of this once sleepy country town doubled to 32,000. The number of council houses trebled in the 1960s alone. Clearly there is a large Labour vote in the northern half of Andover, but it didn't prevent the Conservatives winning Winchester constituency by 23,000 votes in 1979. Basingstoke also had a Tory majority of over 20,000, and the more Conservative parts join NW Hampshire. This new seat can therefore be nothing other than a Tory banker.

Some of the most attractive and comfortable villages in Hampshire are to be found in the north-west corner, places like Hurstbourne Tarrant and Kings Somborne. These small conservative communities are more typical of NW Hants than the overspill of Andover. The Liberals do have local election bases in Andover and in the ex-Basingstoke territory, and the Alliance may well push its way into second place in NW Hampshire. It looks like a typical phenomenon of this boundary review: yet another extra Tory vote in the Commons from the expanding southern shires.

1981	% Own Occ	51.5	New seat
1981	% Loc Auth	28.9	
1981	% Black/Asian	1.5	
1981	% Mid Cl	47.3	
1981	% Prof Man	19.4	
1982	electorate 65,549		
1979	notional result		
	C 15,800		
Alliance		L	

Portsmouth North

From 1966 to 1979, locally popular Labour moderate Frank Judd held on to Portsmouth West, and its successor Portsmouth North, by hair-raisingly narrow margins. He finally lost at the last General Election to Peter Griffiths, a Conservative who achieved notoriety in 1964, when he ousted Patrick Gordon Walker at Smethwick after an allegedly racist campaign. Portsmouth North is now one of the most working-class Conservative seats in the country, and its tendency to the right is usually explained by the Royal Navy connection.

At the last Election, Peter Griffiths has a better chance of holding North, the more marginal of the two Portsmouth seats. Two extremely Conservative wards come in from Havant, Purbrook and Stakes. Meanwhile the strongly Labour Charles Dickens ward, which includes HMS Victory in the naval dockyard, and much of the city centre, is transferred to Portsmouth S. These two changes might have increased the Conservative majority here from 2,000 to about 7,000. There are still Labour wards in western Portsea Island (Nelson Ward) and at the Paulsgrove council estate in the far NW. But the Conservatives win Drayton and Farlington, NE towards Havant, and Hilsea; Cosham and Copnor tend to swing with the tide.

Britain's premier naval port was never likely to be good ground for Labour, despite its working-class character and poor quality housing crowded on to Portsea Island or climbing the downs to the north. Portsmouth North will still be just the more marginal of the two 'Pompey' seats, but it won't be as good for Labour as before. Peter Griffiths may well build up a personal vote, such as that which kept Frank Judd in the Commons for many years, and he must be the favourite to hold the redrawn seat next time.

1981	% Own Occ	58	1979 core seat Portsmouth North		
1981	% Loc Auth	30	C	26,356	48.6
1981	% Black/Asian	2	Lab	24,045	44.4
1981	% Mid Cl	45	L	3,354	6.2
1981	% Prof Man	13	NF	298	0.6
1982	electorate 78,513		WRP	122	0.2
1979	notional result		MPs since 1974		
	C 6,900		1974-79 Frank Judd Lab		
Alliance		SDP	1979- Peter Griffiths C		

Portsmouth South

Southsea is the part of Portsmouth which plays the role of a seaside resort. Its hotels, piers and esplanade are situated along the southern coast of Portsea Island, not the western shore where the ferry port and naval bases open on to Portsmouth Harbour. Southsea is thoroughly Conservative, but the inland part of Portsmouth South, in the centre of the city, has Labour wards – Fratton, Milton and Charles Dickens, now gained from Portsmouth N. Labour has never won Portsmouth S, and the Liberals have no tradition here. As in other seats in the region, the Tories have consistently polled well here, and this Southsea seat will remain the safer of the two Portsmouth divisions.

1981	% Own Occ	62	1979 core seat Portsmouth South		
1981	% Loc Auth	12	C	26,835	54.7
1981	% Black/Asian	3	Lab	15,306	31.2
1981	% Mid Cl	43	L	6,487	13.2
1981	% Prof Man	11	NF	457	0.9
1982	electorate 74,563		MPs since 1945		
1979	notional C 11,200		1945-66 Sir J.M. Lucas C		
Alliance		SDP	1966- R. Bonner Pink C		

Romsey and Waterside

Hampshire's second extra constituency is a long north-south strip of terrain west of Southampton. It stretches from the old town of Romsey, at the bottom end of the Test Valley Borough, down through the Waterside parishes on Southampton Water's west bank. These latter communities are dominated day and night by the towers and flares of the Fawley oil refinery, where many of the inhabitants work. Totton and Hythe have grown enormously since the last war, mainly through private housing developments. Romsey was in Eastleigh constituency, the Waterside parishes in New Forest. The whole of this new seat is Conservatively inclined, and the Liberals may well take a clear second place.

1981	% Own Occ	70.1	New seat
1981	% Loc Auth	18.7	
1981	% Black/Asian	1	
1981	% Mid Cl	53.2	
1981	% Prof Man	18.8	
1982	electorate 70,714		
1979	notional C 20,800		
Alliance		SDP	

Southampton Itchen

The Southampton constituencies are named after the two rivers which flow into Southampton Water. Itchen is really the eastern half of the city, containing the mainly twentieth century part of Southampton beyond the River Itchen, but also some territory on the western bank. Both the constituencies are marginal, so even the slightest of boundary changes are significant. Itchen loses one ward, Woolston, from the south-eastern edge of the city to Eastleigh. Woolston was traditionally a Labour strongpoint, consisting of the Weston council estate and the old working-class community of Woolston itself. Itchen also takes in the whole of the city centre wards of Bargate and St Luke's now, west of the river; but no part of Portswood or Bassett.

These modifications would have eaten into Labour's tenuous 1,600 majority at the 1979 election. But fine calculations are less crucial now, for Labour MP Richard (Bob) Mitchell defected to the Social Democrats after the 1981 Labour Party Conference. Mitchell is popular locally, and he may well have one of the best chances of survival of all the SDP MPs. Itchen is the more working class of the two Southampton seats, but there is relatively little poverty and unemployment. There isn't too glaring a gap between council estates like Thornhill in Bitterne ward and the private housing of Bitterne Park and Harefield. All the wards are homogeneous and most are marginal, except perhaps for Bargate, where the small Asian population is concentrated. Here too, around Derby Road, is Southampton's famous red-light area.

In the 1982 local elections, the SDP only gathered 26% of the vote in Itchen to the Conservatives' 39% and Labour's 35½%. But if Labour recovers from the level of support in those days of the Falklands campaign, and if Mitchell's personal vote comes into operation, the seat could well become a battle between the SDP and Labour. In that case some Conservatives could vote for Mitchell on tactical grounds. It should be one of the most fascinating of contests next time.

1981	% Own Occ	55.7	1979 core seat Southampton
1981	% Loc Auth	30.2	Itchen
1981	% Black/Asian	6	Lab 28,036 46.3
1981	% Mid Cl	46.1	C 26,434 43.6
1981	% Prof Man	12.2	L 6,132 10.1
1982	electorate 73,580		MPs since 1950
1979	notional result		1950-55 R. Morley Lab
	Lab 800		1955-71 Horace King Lab
Alliance		SDP	(Speaker)
			1971- Richard Mitchell Lab
			(SDP)

Southampton Test

Southampton Test is one of the classic British marginal seats, changing hands in 1955, 1966, 1970, 1974 and 1979. It is also very similar in social and economic makeup to the national average. It is not surprising that the level of political contest and consciousness is keen, or that party membership is among the highest in the country.

Southampton is a great seaport, but more of a Merchant Navy and ferry base than a military zone, and it has none of the Royal Navy Conservatism of Portsmouth and Gosport. Test is west, as far as Southampton is concerned. The wards are actually not so homogeneous or marginal as in Itchen. Here we have the safest Conservative wards, at Bassett in the leafy north of the city, and at Shirley and Freemantle in the extensive middle-class residential area west of the Common. Here too is the safest Labour ward, Redbridge, a large council estate in the far west towards Totton; in that region Coxford and Millbrook are also usually won by Labour.

Unlike Itchen, Test does not have a sitting Social Democratic MP. But the Alliance polled 29% here in their first full-scale trial in the 1982 local elections, only 1% behind Labour with the Tories well ahead. The sitting Tory MP James Hill should therefore be the favourite to win Test next time, but his 1979 majority was only 2,000, and Test can never look like a safe seat for anyone. In the boundary changes Test loses the whole of the city centre, but picks up a small council estate in Bassett ward, and now includes the whole of Portswood. This will have little effect on the outcome. Any of the three groupings could win Test in a very good year; as before, it should go to the party which wins the General Election.

1981	% Own Occ	53.2
1981	% Loc Auth	33.8
1981	% Black/Asian	2.5
1981	% Mid Cl	47.7
1981	% Prof Man	13.8
1982	electorate 76,070	
1979	notional result	
	C 2,600	
Alliance		SDP

1979 core seat Southampton Test

C	27,198	46.4
Lab	25,075	42.7
L	6,393	10.9

MPs since 1950

1950-55 Horace King Lab
1955-64 J.M. Howard C
1964-66 Sir J. Fletcher-Cooke C
1966-70 Richard Mitchell Lab
1970-74 James Hill C
1974-79 Bryan Gould Lab
1979- James Hill C

Winchester

The revised Winchester seat consists of the Alton area of East Hampshire (formerly in Petersfield) together with the bulk of the old Winchester consituency. Winchester has lost Andover and its western end to the all-new North-West Hampshire division, and its southern end to Fareham.

Winchester is a city associated with the Establishment, with comfort and privilege. It has a renowned cathedral, and it is the centre of one of the main Church of England dioceses; in the Middle Ages there were suggestions that Winchester should be the seat of England's third archbishop. Winchester College is a public school with a social status second only to Eton, and an academic reputation second to none. But there is actually quite a strong Labour presence in the City of Winchester, which has a surprisingly high proportion of council housing. But the Alliance should now advance into second place in the constituency, for Labour's other source of support, the overspill town of Andover, has been removed.

The Alliance, SDP-led now, can challenge the Tories in Alton, Bishops Waltham, the Itchen Valley and some other rural areas. But the Conservatives poll strongly throughout the division, gaining a 23,000 majority in 1979, and must win the new, more compact Winchester in all normal circumstances.

1981	% Own Occ	58.3	1979 core seat Winchester
1981	% Loc Auth	25.6	C 38,198 55.9
1981	% Black/Asian	1.5	Lab 15,378 22.5
1981	% Mid Cl	55.5	L 14,228 20.9
1981	% Prof Man	21.9	Ind 395 0.6
1982	electorate 72,962		MPs since 1945
1979	notional result		1945-50 George Jeger Lab
	C 20,200		1950-64 P.H.B.O. Smithers C
Alliance		SDP	1964-79 Morgan Morgan-Giles C
			1979- John Browne C

Bromsgrove

Bromsgrove and Redditch was the largest seat in England at the 1979 General Election, with 104,375 voters. Since then it has continued to grow, and not only because of the expansion of Redditch New Town, but because this inner district of Hereford and Worcestershire is favoured by commuters to the West Midlands conurbation moving in to new private housing estates. Not surprisingly, Bromsgrove and Redditch has now been split in two by the Boundary Commission. Redditch is the major and most influential element in the new Mid Worcestershire seat, while Bromsgrove and the rest of the constituency are left as a new division with a 1976 electorate of 57,440.

Bromsgrove town is mixed and marginal. There are strong Labour wards at Sidemore in the north-west and Charford in the south-west, and there are many BL workers residing in the town. But automobile employees have developed a reputation for political volatility in recent Elections, and in 1979 Hilary (Hal) Miller could increase the Tory majority to nearly 16,000 in the Bromsgrove/Redditch seat. The east end of Bromsgrove is solidly Conservative - a former MP Sir John Higgs is still the County Councillor for Bromsgrove East ward.

But it is the expanded commuter villages of considerable affluence which really pile up the Conservative votes: Alvechurch, Wythall, Cofton Hackett and others. The loss of Redditch New Town should leave this as a safe Tory seat. Terry Davis won Bromsgrove for Labour in a byelection in 1971. This was to prove to be Labour's last byelection gain for over ten years. But Bromsgrove is now surely beyond their grasp. The poet A.E. Housman hailed from Fockbury near Bromsgrove; as he might put it, Bromsgrove is Labour's 'land of lost content', the happy highways where once they went, and cannot come again.

1981	% Own Occ	66.0	1979 core seat Bromsgrove/	
1981	% Loc Auth	25.8	Redditch	
1981	% Black/Asian	1.3	C 44,621	54.3
1981	% Mid Cl	54.4	Lab 28,736	35.0
1981	% Prof Man	21.6	L 8,066	9.8
1982	electorate 57,440		NF 752	0.9
1979	notional result		MPs since 1950	
	C 12,100		1950-55 John Higgs C	
Alliance		SDP	1955-71 James Dance C	
			1971-74 Terry Davis Lab	
			1974- Hal Miller C	

Hereford

Little altered in the boundary changes, Hereford will remain one of the Liberals' best hopes in the next Election. Hereford city itself has light industry and a surprisingly high proportion of council estates. This means that there is a substantial basic Labour vote for the Liberals to squeeze – Labour themselves were only 2,750 votes away from victory in the constituency in 1966. The Liberals have achieved some of their greatest municipal successes on the City of Hereford Council, approaching overall control on more than one occasion in the last few years.

The rural areas of southern Herefordshire are harder territory for the Liberals. Here are Ross and the Wye Valley, Abbey Dore and the Golden Valley, the Welsh border and the Black Mountains. This is an excellent stock raising area, and important for cereals, sugar beet and fruit. It is unsurprising that the Hereford seat has been Conservative since 1931, when the last Liberal member was defeated. But Colin Shepherd's Conservative majority was only 1,112 in October 1974, and still under 5,000 in their victorious year of 1979. With 7,000 Labour votes to bid for, the Liberals must still place Hereford at the top of their 'shopping list' of winnable seats next time.

There it will join several other Welsh Marcher seats: Leominster, Shrewsbury and Montgomery. Far removed from the Tory heartland of the Home Counties, this border country may emulate the Scottish Borders in Liberal preferences, should the Alliance make any breakthrough at all.

1981	% Own Occ	57.0	
1981	% Loc Auth	29.1	
1981	% Black/Asian	0.5	
1981	% Mid Cl	44.2	
1981	% Prof Man	16.2	
1982	electorate 64,145		
1979	notional result		
	C 5,000		
Alliance		L	

1979 core seat Hereford

C	23,012	47.7
L	18,042	37.4
Lab	7,150	14.8

MPs since 1945
1945-56 J.P.L. Thomas C
1956-74 David Gibson-Watt C
1974-   Colin Shepherd C

Leominster

Herefordshire and Worcestershire were merged in 1974, and the first parliamentary constituency to include territory from both former counties is the redrawn Leominster. Leominster used simply to be the northern half of Herefordshire, a remote but soft countryside of small towns and villages – Leominster itself, Kington, Bromyard, half-timbered Weobley. Now it stretches into the old Worcestershire to take in several western wards from the Malvern Hills District, such as Ledbury, and also the tiny spa of Tenbury Wells, formerly in Kidderminster constituency.

Leominster has one or two remarkable political features. Firstly, the Conservatives have beaten the Liberals by less than 3,000 votes on no fewer than seven occasions in General Elections since 1918. Secondly, Labour polled 2,099 votes or 5.3% in Leominster, their third lowest percentage anywhere in Britain. Finally, Leominster is the third most agricultural seat in England, with 24% employed on the land. One of the reasons why the Liberals have never quite taken the seat is that the Labour vote is too low to squeeze effectively. Tactical voting here would rely on the assumption that large numbers of Labour supporters would switch their support to the Liberals to remove the main Conservative enemy; but there simply aren't large numbers of Labour supporters in Leominster.

In October 1974, Liberal Roger Pincham lost to the Tory Peter Temple-Morris by only 579 votes. But Temple-Morris increased his majority to nearly 5,000 in 1979, and secured a overall majority of votes cast. In fact Leominster will remain a harder nut to crack than the majority suggests, and the boundary changes must have helped the Conservatives.

1981	% Own Occ	62.6	1979 core seat Leominster
1981	% Loc Auth	18.6	C 21,126 53.5
1981	% Black/Asian	0.5	L 16,261 41.2
1981	% Mid Cl	45.9	Lab 2,099 5.3
1981	% Prof Man	21.4	MPs since 1945
1982	electorate 66,144		1945-59 A.E. Baldwin C
1979	notional result		1959-74 Sir Clive Bossom C
	C 9,200		1974- Peter Temple-Morris C
Alliance		L	

Mid-Worcestershire

The Boundary Commission originally proposed that this seat should be called Redditch and Droitwich, and these two towns do form the main population centres, although there are also a number of villages from the old Droitwich Rural District north of Worcester. Redditch formed half of the huge Bromsgrove/Redditch division, which had swollen to 104,000 electors in 1979, 112,000 by 1981. Clearly this seat had to be split. Meanwhile, Droitwich and the villages used to be associated with Worcester, Peter Walker's constituency. Mid-Worcestershire forms the extra seat to which the County is entitled in the next Parliament.

Redditch was always the more Labour and working-class part of Bromsgrove and Redditch. It was designated a New Town in 1964, and its population rose by overspill from 34,000 in 1961 to 67,000 by 1981. In the 1979 General Election, Redditch probably accounted for only about 2,000 of Hal Miller's 16,000 majority, although it made up nearly half of the electorate of the constituency. At one time Bromsgrove-Redditch was regarded as a marginal, for it provided the only Labour gain in a byelection in the 1970s. Terry Davis won it in 1971, but lost it narrowly in February 1974.

The new seat of Mid-Worcestershire must therefore be regarded as an outside Labour chance. They polled more votes here than the Tories in the 1981 County Council elections, in an excellent Labour year. But Droitwich and the villages make it difficult for them. Droitwich is an old salt-mining and spa town, with a Labour majority at its northern end. But the villages among the orchards and rich farming country of mid-Worcestershire provided Peter Walker's best Conservative areas in Worcester, and will play the same role in this new constituency. As Redditch grows, it will dominate the seat even more, even though its name is not to be found in the title. Its continued expansion forms Labour's best chance of victory.

1981	% Own Occ	51.7	New seat
1981	% Loc Auth	42.3	
1981	% Black/Asian	3	
1981	% Mid Cl	48.0	
1981	% Prof Man	17.6	
1982	electorate 73,447		
1979	notional result		
	C 7,000		
Alliance		SDP	

South Worcestershire

South Worcestershire is the safest Conservative seat in Hereford and Worcester. Not only is the rolling farmland and fruit-growing country poor ground for the Labour Party, but there is no effective Liberal challenge here as in the Welsh Marches in Hereford and Leominster. This is the seat most associated with the late eccentric right-wing Conservative MP, Sir Gerald Nabarro, although Michael Spicer has held it since February 1974.

All the parts of South Worcestershire are strongly Tory. The Vale of Evesham contains some of the most extensive and prosperous orchards in England, and the small towns of Evesham and Pershore seem far removed from unemployment and other aspects of economic blight. The constituency stretches far and wide. In the centre are the fertile valleys of the Severn and the Avon, but to the east South Worcestershire reaches the corner of the Cotswolds at Broadway, that most twee and self-conscious of tourist trap villages. In the west the Malvern Hills emerge from the plain - the spa and inland tourist resort of Great Malvern is the largest town in the constituency. The home of Elgar (whose music captures so much of the spirit of 'Englishness' that he is sadly underrated abroad), Malvern seems the essence of comfortable Tory England like the South Worcestershire constituency as a whole.

Michael Spicer's Conservative majority at the last General Election was 20,654. Boundary changes remove some 12,000 voters to Worcester constituency, but this will have little impact on this identikit stronghold of Toryism and social harmony.

1981	% Own Occ	60.1	1979 core seat South		
1981	% Loc Auth	26.8	Worcestershire		
1981	% Black/Asian	0.5	C	34,926	57.1
1981	% Mid Cl	50.6	L	14,272	23.3
1981	% Prof Man	20.4	Lab	10,206	16.7
1982	electorate 73,547		E	1,722	2.8
1979	notional result		MPs since 1950		
	C 18,300		1950-55 R. de la Bere C		
Alliance		L	1955-66 Sir P.G. Agnew C		
			1966-74 Sir Gerald Nabarro C		
			1974- Michael Spicer C		

Worcester

Peter Walker has been for many years one of the leading
moderates in the upper echelons of the Conservative Party.
But his career has not yet reached the heights to which it
once seemed destined, when he entered Edward Heath's
Cabinet while he was still in his 30s. The temper of the
Conservative Party is no longer so suitable for Walker, and
he spent the first years of his time in Mrs Thatcher's Cabinet
in the relatively remote backwater of Agriculture and
Fisheries. Some think that the active leadership of the 'wet'
Conservatives has passed elsewhere, to James Prior perhaps.
But Peter Walker is still barely into his 50s, and the time for
his brand of politics may come again.

Since 1961, Peter Walker's constituency has been Worcester. It
is almost certainly true that he has done better in the city
than Conservative candidates for local office, for Worcester
City Council has often been controlled by the Labour Party.
There are excellent Labour wards in the council housing
estates in the east of the town, behind Shrub Hill station;
the Conservatives do best in Claines in the north, St Peter's
in the south and Bedwardine and St Clement's over the river
to the west. The terraces of the central Worcester wards are
marginal. Labour is very competitive in Worcester as a whole,
in local elections at least.

But Worcester has never quite been large enough to form a
seat of its own. Previously its numbers were made up by
Droitwich town and rural district to the north. Now the
constituency is to take in six rural wards to the east, places
with rolling Worcestershire names like Drakes Broughton,
Inkberrow and Upton Snodsbury. There will be 15,000 fewer
voters outside Worcester City than before, which must
improve Labour's chances. But it is hard to see this
unseating Peter Walker. Labour has never won Worcester,
failing in 1945 by just four votes. Their successes should
continue to be confined to municipal level.

1981	% Own Occ	64.0	1979 core seat Worcester		
1981	% Loc Auth	26.7	C	30,194	51.3
1981	% Black/Asian	1.5	Lab	18,605	31.6
1981	% Mid Cl	49.9	L	8,886	15.1
1981	% Prof Man	16.2	E	707	1.2
1982	electorate 66,891		NF	450	0.8
1979	notional result		MPs since 1945		
	C 11,100		1945-61 G.R. Ward C		
Alliance		SDP	1961- Peter Walker C		

Wyre Forest

It must first of all be pointed out that Wyre Forest has no connection at all with another new constituency, Wyre in Lancashire's North Fylde region. Wyre Forest is very much the successor to the old Kidderminster seat, and the Boundary Commission must have been tempted to retain that name. But the seat is identical to the local government District of Wyre Forest, which probably decided their choice.

The old Kidderminster division was very much more rural, including the Tenbury and Martley Rural Districts which have now been transferred to the ex-Herefordshire seat of Leominster. Wyre Forest has under half the acreage that Kidderminster did, but loses only 15,000 electors. Besides the carpet and staple manufacturing town of Kidderminster itself, it includes the canal town of Stourport on Severn, and Bewdley. Bewdley will forever be associated in politics with Stanley Baldwin, who represented it throughout his several periods as Prime Minister.

Wyre Forest will probably remain true to its tradition, a Conservative seat. But Labour does have a solid vote too, in parts of Kidderminster and in Stourport; and the Liberals are so active in local politics that Wyre Forest is one of their best chances for control among all District Councils. As yet this Liberal support has not been translated to General Elections – they only polled 16% in 1979. Wyre Forest is a nearly all-white constituency on the edge of the West Midlands metropolis, and like other such seats it showed itself very favourable to Thatcherite Conservatism in 1979. It should stay loyal to MP Esmond Bulmer, a member of the cider manufacturing family. Cider and Bulmer may indeed become almost as much a part of the Worcestershire scene as apples and Baldwin used to be.

1981	% Own Occ	67.2	1979 core seat Kidderminster

1981   % Own Occ   67.2   1979 core seat Kidderminster
1981   % Loc Auth   25.4   C   33,523   53.7
1981   % Black/Asian 1.1   Lab 17,871   28.6
1981   % Mid Cl   49.1   L   9,939   15.9
1981   % Prof Man   18.5   NF   1,052   1.7
1982   electorate 68,407   MPs since 1945
1979   notional result   1945-50 L. Tolley Lab
       C 12,700   1950-64 Gerald Nabarro C
Alliance   L   1964-74 Sir Tatton Brinton C
                              1974-   Esmond Bulmer C

Broxbourne

The East Hertfordshire seat was an oversized seat in 1979, with 96,000 electors. It had to be split up, and the Commission has been logical in basing a new seat on the Borough of Broxbourne, which clings to the western side of the River Lee in SE Hertfordshire on the Essex border. This incorporates a chain of communities bypassed by the A10 - from south to north, Waltham Cross, Cheshunt, Turnford, Wormley, Broxbourne itself, and Hoddesdon. All the wards are strongly Conservative except for one at each end of the seat (Waltham Cross on the Enfield border, and Rye Park, Hoddesdon) and one in the middle (Bury Green). The Northaw-Cuffley ward is included from Welwyn-Hatfield, which should boost the Tory majority by another 2,500 to about 15,000.

1981	% Own Occ	68.8	1979 core seat East
1981	% Loc Auth	24.6	Hertfordshire
1981	% Black/Asian	2	C	41,599	55.5
1981	% Mid Cl	55.5	Lab	20,139	26.9
1981	% Prof Man	19.6	L	11,393	15.2
1982	electorate 67,777		NF	1,819	2.4
1979	notional C 15,600		MP since 1955
Alliance		L	1955- Sir D. Walker-Smith C

Hertford and Stortford

The rump of the East Hertfordshire seat after the removal of Broxbourne is less urban, consisting of the villages and towns in NE Hertfordshire - the largest being Bishop's Stortford and Sawbridgeworth. These have now been amalgamated with Hertford and Ware, the more Conservative parts of the Hertford-Stevenage division. Indeed they were largely responsible for the defeat of Shirley Williams in 1979, producing a Tory majority of four thousand in a seat which she lost by only 1,296. There are no Labour wards at all in the former East Herts sections of Hertford and Stortford, which will be a very safe Tory seat.

1981	% Own Occ	61	New seat
1981	% Loc Auth	26	
1981	% Black/Asian	1	
1981	% Mid Cl	61.0	
1981	% Prof Man	26.5	
1982	electorate 67,473		
1979	notional C 12,100		
Alliance		SDP	

Hertsmere

The Borough of Hertsmere contains the communities of Potters Bar, Borehamwood-Elstree, Bushey and Radlett. All but Bushey were previously in the South Hertfordshire division, held with reasonable ease by the fast-rising Chairman of the Conservative Party, Cecil Parkinson. Now Bushey moves from SW Herts to join the rest of Hertsmere, and one ward from St Albans, London Colney, completes the constituency.

The old South Hertfordshire was decided by a political battle between Conservative Potters Bar, in folklore the last outpost of North London before the barbarian wastes of the north; and in the red corner Borehamwood, the 20,000 strong GLC out-estate, which provides a solid Labour bloc. Radlett is an affluent commuter town straddling the A5, the old Watling Street. Like the old Elstree village, it is solidly Conservative but smaller than Borehamwood and Potters Bar.

Only in the best of years could Labour mount a serious challenge in the old South Herts. Now, the importation of Bushey should tip this seat even more firmly towards the Conservatives, and leave Borehamwood looking even more like an isolated working-class outpost in comfortable Hertfordshire. Cecil Parkinson's remaining fears about the safety of his home base should be assuaged, and leave him free to rise, perhaps, to still higher things in his future career.

1981	% Own Occ	59.7	1979 core seat South
1981	% Loc Auth	32.2	Hertfordshire
1981	% Black/Asian	2.5	C 27,857 54.1
1981	% Mid Cl	62.5	Lab 16,059 31.2
1981	% Prof Man	23.8	L 7,001 13.6
1982	electorate 73,461		MP since 1974
1979	notional result		1974- Cecil Parkinson C
	C 12,600		
Alliance		L	

North Hertfordshire

The new North Hertfordshire is very much the same as the Hitchin seat which has existed since 1974. This is not the old Hitchin that Shirley Williams held from 1964 to 1974, which was a vast seat including Stevenage New Town. North Herts District consists of the towns of Hitchin, Letchworth, Baldock and Royston, together with the villages of the old Hitchin Rural District; of these, Codicote and Knebworth are not to be placed in the North Herts seat, but in the new Stevenage division.

In a good year for Labour they could think about winning Hitchin, but in 1979 Ian Stewart increased his Conservative majority from 3,000 to 13,000. North Hertfordshire may not be quite so safe, but the Conservatives can count on huge majorities in the villages, and in Royston in the northern tip of the county. South Hitchin and SW Letchworth are theirs too. Labour's strength lies mainly in Letchworth, which was the first Garden City to be founded by Ebenezer Howard in 1903. Howard believed that the garden city would be as great and significant an invention as the aeroplane, which first flew in the same year; both were 'harbingers of a new age'. He was wrong, and only one other garden city was built in England, also in Hertfordshire, at Welwyn. But the legacy survives in Letchworth's council housing majority. Baldock, next door, is another working-class town with many council estates; and Labour wins Oughton ward, NW Hitchin.

There is a relatively high non-white population in the constituency, and it is more working-class than, say, Welwyn-Hatfield which is a marginal. But North Hertfordshire will remain a hard nut for Labour to crack, and it won't crumble unless there is a left-wing landslide in Britain.

1981	% Own Occ	51.9	1979 core seat Hitchin		
1981	% Loc Auth	38.3	C	33,169	52.5
1981	% Black/Asian	5	Lab	19,940	31.6
1981	% Mid Cl	55.7	L	8,224	13.0
1981	% Prof Man	22.3	E	911	1.4
1982	electorate 75,635		NF	881	1.4
1979	notional result		MP since 1974		
	C 11,600		1974–	Ian Stewart C	
Alliance		L			

St Albans

St Albans is probably the oldest town in the modern county of Hertfordshire. But its political character is heavily influenced - and at the next Election, maybe crucially shaped - by a much younger town, Harpenden. Harpenden, which lies a few miles to the north, towards Luton, is the second most middle-class town in England, and it has grown rapidly in the post-war years. It is extremely Conservative, and in the West Common area of SW Harpenden it possesses one of the most affluent residential neighbourhoods in the country.

St Albans itself has traditionally been a Conservative town as well, but in the 1982 local elections the Alliance won nearly every ward. Only Harpenden prevented the new grouping from grasping the lead in the constituency as a whole, although they still polled 39% throughout the seat. In St Albans itself the only wards to escape the Alliance were the most Labour, Sopwell, south of the centre, and Marshalswick South, the most favoured residential area (NW St Albans). Other council estates (Batchwood) and private residential areas, old and new (St Peters and Verulam), went much the same way in 1982.

St Albans is little altered in the boundary changes. The Liberals were a poor second here in 1979, but long-time MP Victor Goodhew is retiring, and if the next General Election comes at a good time for the Alliance, it must be one of the seats to watch. The outlying wards, in Harpenden and Redbourn and Colney Heath, have resisted the appeal of the Alliance as yet, and may still save the Conservative Party here.

1981	% Own Occ	68.6	1979 core seat St Albans		
1981	% Loc Auth	21.0	C	31,301	53.1
1981	% Black/Asian	3.5	L	14,057	23.8
1981	% Mid Cl	68.2	Lab	13,638	23.1
1981	% Prof Man	29.3	MPs since 1945		
1982	electorate 73,096		1945-50 C.W. Dumpleton Lab		
1979	notional result		1950-59 J. Grimston C		
	C 15,800		1959- Victor Goodhew C		
Alliance		L			

South-West Hertfordshire

One of the safest of the nine Conservative constituencies in Hertfordshire at the 1979 Election was Herts SW, which is composed chiefly of the Three Rivers District. The first byelection of the new Parliament, caused by the retirement of Geoffrey Dodsworth, did not alter this picture. Three Rivers includes the affluent ultra-middle class communities of Rickmansworth and Chorleywood, together with satellites like Croxley Green and the private estate of Moor Park. Indeed Chorleywood is the most middle-class town in the whole of England, with 78% non-manual workers in 1971.

Now Bushey has been moved from SW Hertfordshire into S Herts, and replaced by the slightly smaller but equally Tory Berkhamsted (formerly in Hemel Hempstead). There are Labour voters in SW Herts too, though. They come largely from the large GLC overspill estate at South Oxhey, which fits in ill with its surroundings. In 1979 for example, Labour obtained only about 8% of the vote in Chorleywood ward, and 10% in Rickmansworth, but over 60% in South Oxhey. The Liberals have a local vote in Croxley Green, but have never challenged seriously in SW Hertfordshire as a whole.

Some of the best residential areas in the Home Counties are to be found in South-West Hertfordshire, in Chorleywood, Rickmansworth and Moor Park - the last, typically, is the home of a well-known public school (Merchant Taylors) and a famed golf course set around a country house clubhouse. South Oxhey is a quite anomalous intrusion, rather like its fellow former LCC estate of Borehamwood in Hertsmere. It is not large enough to disturb the Tory tenure of SW Hertfordshire.

1981	% Own Occ	63.6	1979 core seat Hertfordshire
1981	% Loc Auth	27.6	South-West
1981	% Black/Asian	2.5	C 33,112 54.7
1981	% Mid Cl	61.8	Lab 16,784 27.7
1981	% Prof Man	26.5	L 9,808 16.2
1982	electorate 74,802		NF 839 1.4
1979	notional result		MPs since 1950
	C 17,500		1950-74 Gilbert Longden C
Alliance		L	1974-79 Geoffrey Dodsworth C
			1979- Richard Page C

Stevenage

There are a few new constituencies where it is almost impossible to guess who would have been the victor had the 1979 General Election been fought on new boundaries. The Americans would say that they are 'too close to call'. One of these is Stevenage. In the local elections which took place on the same day, Labour were 3½ thousand votes ahead in Stevenage Borough wards. The new Stevenage seat also includes two rural wards from N Herts, and five from E Herts, some of which were uncontested Tory victories. Estimating General Election votes for such wards is very hazardous, but it would seem that Labour may have been about 500 votes ahead in the new Stevenage seat, but this is certainly well within the margin of error. It is best simply to consider the seat as super-marginal.

Stevenage New Town was of course part of the Hertford and Stevenage seat which dismissed Shirley Williams in 1979. But all its wards elected Labour councillors at the same time except for Old Stevenage. It was the other parts of her constituency which were responsible for the Tory majority which unseated Mrs Williams. Similarly it is the villages – Datchworth and Knebworth, Walkern and Watton-at-Stone, Cottered and Codicote – that provide the Tory vote now. But the non-New Town electorate is much reduced, from over 30,000 to under 10,000. Even without the effect of Shirley Williams's personal vote, the Tories will find it harder to win Stevenage next time.

But Labour will not have an easy victory. In 1982 the Alliance took seven seats on Stevenage Borough Council, and polled 36.3% – 310 votes less than Labour did. The 1982 local elections were not a great success for the Alliance in general, and Stevenage was one of their best results in Britain. They may even have been ahead in the constituency as a whole, for Labour has no strength outside the New Town. It should be one of the most interesting contests of the next Election.

1981	% Own Occ	39.0	1979 core seat Hertford/
1981	% Loc Auth	57.3	Stevenage
1981	% Black/Asian	3	C 31,729 45.1
1981	% Mid Cl	55.2	Lab 30,443 43.2
1981	% Prof Man	19.0	L 7,660 10.9
1982	electorate 68,046		NF 581 0.8
1979	notional result		MPs since 1974
	Lab 1,000		1974-79 Shirley Williams Lab
Alliance		SDP	1979- Petrie Bowen Wells C

Watford

Watford is the best example in Hertfordshire of a predominantly nineteenth century industrial town. For a long time too after the last war it was the safest, and on occasion the only, Labour seat in the county. Yet as the New Towns have grown, Watford is no longer the largest town in Herts, or its Labour citadel. Indeed, in the present redistribution it has been deemed to be too small to sustain a seat of its own, and it has had to take in communities from outside – Abbot Langley and Leavesden, Bricket Wood and Chiswell Green. These should add at least 2,500 votes to the 3,290 by which moderate Conservative Tristan Garel-Jones seized Watford in 1979. Watford will be even less of a Labour seat than before, and West Herts, Stevenage and Welwyn-Hatfield, all New Town seats, will all be better bets for Labour.

Watford town itself is still politically close. Labour can win most of the wards in an even year, without enjoying any massive strongholds. The Conservative votes are more concentrated, in the excellent residential area around Cassiobury Park and along the A411 in the NW of the town – Park and Nascot wards. The other safe Tory ward is Oxhey, south of the town centre. There aren't many council estates in Watford – Labour does well in the Callowland-Leggatts area of North Watford, and Holywell, west Watford. But there are Victorian industrial workers' terraces around the centre of the town (highly untypical of Hertfordshire), and here can be found much of Watford's 7% non-white population.

There was an 8% swing to the Tories in 1979, and the recapture of Watford was one of their best results in the General Election. The swing back will not be easy, for even without the boundary changes, the Conservatives were still ahead in Watford in the 1982 local elections. The Alliance polled only 23% in Watford then, and do not seem to pose the threat they do in Hertfordshire's other 'Old Town', St Albans.

1981	% Own Occ	64.0	1979 core seat Watford		
1981	% Loc Auth	25.2	C	21,320	47.6
1981	% Black/Asian	6	Lab	18,030	40.3
1981	% Mid Cl	56.7	L	5,019	11.2
1981	% Prof Man	19.1	NF	388	0.9
1982	electorate 72,603		MPs since 1945		
1979	notional result		1945-55 J. Freeman Lab		
	C 6,800		1955-64 F.W. Farey-Jones C		
Alliance		SDP	1964-79 Raphael Tuck Lab		
			1979- Tristan Garel-Jones C		

Welwyn-Hatfield

Hertfordshire is in many ways the most modern of English counties. Its population has shown the highest percentage increase over the last fifty years. Alone of the counties, it has two Garden Cities and four New Towns, all examples of the twentieth century's ideas of planned urban units. In a sense, Welwyn-Hatfield has two New Towns and one Garden City itself, for Hatfield is a Reith Committee New Town, and Welwyn Garden City also became a government-sponsored New Town after the war, although it began life as Ebenezer Howard's second privately financed garden city, following Letchworth, in 1920.

How do these test-tube communities vote? Like many New Towns, Welwyn and Hatfield are both marginal and volatile. In 1979 Labour held a slight lead in Hatfield, and a larger lead in the New Town estates of eastern Welwyn Garden City. But west of the railway tracks, in Welwyn's leafy inter-war garden city itself, the Conservatives lead in Handside and Sherrards wards. It is a divided town, west versus east on classic lines. The smaller communities which make up the District are all very Tory - old Welwyn, Brookman's Park and Northaw. But Northaw has now been moved out of the seat, and replaced by the smaller and less solidly Conservative Wheathampstead, from St Albans. A minor change, but it might have halved Christopher Murphy's 3,500 majority in 1979 - important in so close a seat.

Welwyn-Hatfield is one of the few predominantly middle-class seats that Labour might hope to win. The reason for this is clear: it is also predominantly local authority housing, although this percentage is dropping. The Alliance obtained only 23% of the vote here in 1982, lower than the national average, and Welwyn-Hatfield seems destined to remain an excellent reflector of the political tastes of modern southern England.

1981	% Own Occ	40.1	1979 core seat Welwyn and
1981	% Loc Auth	54.1	Hatfield
1981	% Black/Asian	2.3	C 28,892 48.6
1981	% Mid Cl	58.1	Lab 25,418 42.8
1981	% Prof Man	21.7	L 4,688 7.9
1982	electorate 73,445		NF 459 0.8
1979	notional result		MPs since 1974
	C 2,300		Feb-Oct 1974 Lord Balniel C
Alliance		SDP	1974-79 Helene Hayman Lab
			1979- Christopher Murphy C

West Hertfordshire

The Boundary Commission have indulged in some confusing name changes. Originally they were proposing to call this constituency Dacorum, after the local government District on which it is based, but after an inquiry the name was altered to West Herts, although the boundaries remained the same. It might be thought that both changes were unnecessary, because the seat will be dominated by the town of Hemel Hempstead. It is the direct successor to the marginal Hemel Hempstead constituency which changed hands in 1974 and 1979 (though not to the seat of this name which existed up to 1970, for that included ultra-Tory Harpenden). Indeed, Hemel Hempstead plays even more of a role here now, for Berkhamsted has been lost to SW Herts, leaving Tring as the only other town in the constituency.

This change will have a considerable impact on so marginal a contest. Berkhamsted is very Conservative, and its disappearance could effectively remove Hemel MP Nicholas Lyell's 5,000 majority. Lyell has taken such fright that he has migrated to stand at the safe Mid Beds seat. Since the former Labour MP. Robin Corbett, has not been reselected as candidate, West Hertfordshire could prove a rather unlikely site for Britain's first black MP for over 50 years: Paul Boateng, left-wing Chairman of the GLC's Police Committee, has been chosen to carry Labour's banner.

This may prove controversial, but otherwise Labour would have a good chance of winning West Herts. Hemel Hempstead itself is a New Town which has grown to become Hertfordshire's biggest town. Most of the neighbourhoods vote Labour, but Boxmoor, Central and Leverstock Green retain Tory votes from the old Hemel which existed before the New Town designation. The rest of West Herts is ultra-Conservative - Tring, and the villages - but there is less of this kind of country now. The destiny of this seat should depend on the West Hertfordshire electors' view of Paul Boateng.

1981	% Own Occ	48.0	1979 core seat	Hemel Hempstead	
1981	% Loc Auth	47.0	C	37,953	48.7
1981	% Black/Asian	2.5	Lab	32,964	42.3
1981	% Mid Cl	55.5	L	6,314	8.1
1981	% Prof Man	20.2	NF	649	0.8
1982	electorate 77,422		MPs since 1945		
1979	notional result		1945-59	Viscountess Davidson C	
	Lab 700		1959-74	James Allason C	
Alliance		SDP	1974-79	Robin Corbett Lab	
			1979-	Nicholas Lyell C	

Beverley

A town of 300,000 souls like Hull normally possesses enough of a middle-class professional or commercial element to produce sufficient Conservative votes to sustain at least one Tory parliamentary constituency. Where apparently there is no such Tory seat, as at Nottingham, Leicester and Hull, one may surmise that the city boundaries have been so drawn that the more desirable residential areas are to be found outside. In this eventuality, strongly Conservative dormitory constituencies exist, if one looks for them - Rushcliffe and Carlton near Nottingham, Blaby et al. for Leicester, and Haltemprice (now Beverley) for Hull.

Hull has three safe Labour divisions, but this is not to say that the big Humberside port has no wealthy and prosperous class of citizens. It is just that they tend to live in the suburbs of Cottingham and Haltemprice, Kirk Ella and Anlaby, and in the market town of Beverley. Beverley, noted for a superb cathedral-standard Minster, is to be the eponymous town of the constituency in future, but there are few changes from the old Haltemprice. Only a few wards - Cherry Holme, Skidby/Rowley, South Cave and Walkington - have been moved into the new Boothferry seat. This reduces the electorate by about 10,000.

But the minor changes of name and boundaries will not affect the position of the present MP, Major Patrick Wall (a right-wing Conservative, he is not to be confused with Bradford North's Militant Tendency Labour activist, Pat Wall). Major Wall secured a majority of nearly 20,000 over the Liberals in 1979. The Liberals have enjoyed some local success in Beverley itself, and Labour's best ward is Hessle, the northern terminus of the new Humber Bridge. But Haltemprice/Beverley will remain an excellent example of the way that solidly Tory suburban seats can be found even in the most remote corners of England.

1981	% Own Occ	72.3	1979 core seat Haltemprice
1981	% Loc Auth	18.3	C 34,525 55.8
1981	% Black/Asian	0.7	L 14,637 23.6
1981	% Mid Cl	60.8	Lab 12,743 20.6
1981	% Prof Man	22.2	MPs since 1950
1982	electorate 75,658		1950-54 R.K. Law C
1979	notional result		1954- Patrick Wall C
	C 17,400		
Alliance		L	

Boothferry

Boothferry will be one of the most heterogeneous and mixed constituencies in the country - mixed both geographically and politically. Its complexity is partly caused by the creation of the Humberside County in the early 1970s, which cut across the old boundaries of Lincolnshire, and East and West Yorkshire. The new Boothferry seat includes the port of Goole on the River Ouse (formerly in West Yorkshire); the flat plain of the Isle of Axholme west of Scunthorpe and the Trent (Lincolnshire); and a section of the hilly Wolds country around Market Weighton and Pocklington (East Riding of Yorkshire).

Its politics are as varied as the countryside. Goole is a Labour town, formerly the centre of a safe seat. It is an old company town, and the planned nineteenth-century streets still radiate geometrically from the town centre. Most of the mining area associated with Goole previously is now in South Yorkshire, in the Doncaster North seat. But the Isle of Axholme (formerly in Gainsborough) and the Wolds (ex-Howden) are farming districts of diverse character, and strongly Conservative. A region around South Cave on the north bank of the Humber is also brought in, from the Tory Haltemprice seat.

Boothferry is an artificial creation. Not only is it difficult to see a single member being able to represent such a range of different interests; but communications within the seat are seriously disrupted by the Rivers Ouse, Humber and Trent, and by the numerous canals of the low-lying part of the seat. It is the only Humberside constituency which combines districts from the former counties of Lincolnshire and Yorkshire. Like Humberside County itself, it will surely take time before Boothferry is accepted as a workable entity. It should be a safe Conservative seat, for the rural Wolds and the flat farmlands should outvote the industrial enclave around Goole.

1981	% Own Occ	64.8	1979 core seat Howden		
1981	% Loc Auth	22.6	C	26,550	56.0
1981	% Black/Asian	0.5	L	12,006	25.3
1981	% Mid Cl	44.5	Lab	8,827	18.6
1981	% Prof Man	17.8	MP since 1955		
1982	electorate 72,114		1955-	Sir Paul Bryan C	
1979	notional result				
	C 9,600				
Alliance		L			

Bridlington

The Bridlington constituency takes in the coast of what used to be the East Riding of Yorkshire from Spurn Head, a spit of land projecting into the North Sea which is a bird-watcher's paradise, up to the cliffs of Flamborough Head. Before the present redistribution the Bridlington seat used to extend further - through Filey almost to Scarborough. But this northernmost strip of the varied Yorkshire coast is now in the county of North Yorkshire, and must perforce be separated for electoral purposes from Bridlington.

To take the electorate up to 70,000 again, the seat is now to include more of the inland Wolds country, farming territory, such as that around the market town of Driffield, which used to be in the East Riding Howden seat.

After 30 years under the stewardship of the legless war veteran Richard Wood, a son of the Earl of Halifax, this safe Conservative seat was inherited by John Townend at the 1979 General Election. The SDP have the Alliance nomination, but they are unlikely to do better than the Liberals ever did in Bridlington, despite their hopes in the neighbouring Scarborough division.

1981	% Own Occ	68.4	1979 core seat Bridlington		
1981	% Loc Auth	18.6	C	27,988	54.8
1981	% Black/Asian	0.5	Lab	12,693	24.9
1981	% Mid Cl	47.6	L	10,390	20.3
1981	% Prof Man	18.9	MPs since 1950		
1982	electorate 76,662		1950-79 Richard Wood C		
1979	notional result		1979- John Townend C		
	C 16,900				
Alliance		SDP			

Brigg and Cleethorpes

The new Brigg and Cleethorpes constituency is produced by a reshuffle within the ex-Lincolnshire part of Humberside. The Borough of Cleethorpes formed the majority of the old seat named Louth, but Louth itself is still in Lincolnshire. Cleethorpes is brought together with the more rural part of the old outsized Brigg and Scunthorpe division, that around Brigg itself and Barton upon Humber.

Brigg and Scunthorpe was a very narrow Conservative gain in the 1979 General Election, but Brigg was always the more Conservative part of the division, and it should fit in well with the seaside resort of Cleethorpes. There is industry in the constituency - the oil refineries around the port of Immingham darken the South Humberside skyline. But there is no significant reservoir of Labour support in the new constituency. The Liberals did well in the old Louth seat, but not in the Brigg district.

In summary, then, Brigg and Cleethorpes takes the best Tory parts of two less than safe seats, to create an excellent prospect for the Conservative Party.

1981	% Own Occ	70.0	1979 core seat Louth		
1981	% Loc Auth	20.3	C	25,701	44.9
1981	% Black/Asian	0.5	L	19,026	33.2
1981	% Mid Cl	41.2	Lab	12,316	21.5
1981	% Prof Man	14.9	NF	261	0.5
1982	electorate 77,644		MPs since 1945		
1979	notional result		1945-70 Sir Cyril Osborne C		
	C 7,700		1970-74 Jeffrey Archer C		
Alliance		L	1974- Michael Brotherton C		

336

Glanford and Scunthorpe

Brigg and Scunthorpe was probably Labour's unluckiest loss at the 1979 General Election. The sitting MP John Ellis was beaten by only 486 votes, by a young right-wing Conservative, Michael Brown. But a Democratic Labour candidate took 2,000 votes, almost certainly splitting the Labour vote and causing Ellis's defeat.

This had been a Labour seat since 1935. Even though for much of that time the constituency had been named after the small market town of Brigg, the Labour strength had been determined for decades by the steel town of Scunthorpe, which had boomed in the nineteenth century. Now it seems likely that Scunthorpe will once again have a Labour MP, for nearly 30,000 mainly Tory electors around Brigg have been removed. The new Glanford/Scunthorpe seat will simply be composed of Scunthorpe itself and the communities near it on the west bank of the River Trent in Glanford Borough (there is no place called Glanford).

This is an industrial landscape. Scunthorpe, set on a bluff above the valley of the Trent, is dominated by the Frodingham steelworks. Down on the river-bank can be found power stations and chemical works like the one at Flixborough which exploded in the early 1970s. Half of Scunthorpe is comprised of council housing, and even in 1979 there was a Labour majority of over 4,000 in the town. The middle-class population is concentrated in a small enclave around Central Park in Kingsway ward, and beyond the town boundaries at Bottesford. The Social Democrats do have a tradition here, as in other parts of Lincolnshire, as the unofficial intervention in 1979 showed. The Alliance did well to poll 37% in Scunthorpe Borough in the 1982 local elections, but they will have to do even better to defeat Labour in a seat dominated by the threatened nationalised steel industry. Scunthorpe should return to Labour after a few anomalous Tory years.

1981	% Own Occ	58.9	1979 core seat Brigg/Scunthorpe		
1981	% Loc Auth	34.6	C	31,130	43.5
1981	% Black/Asian	2	Lab	30,644	42.8
1981	% Mid Cl	41.2	L	7,664	10.7
1981	% Prof Man	12.3	Dem Lab	2,042	2.9
1982	electorate 72,597		Ind	123	0.2
1979	notional result		MPs since 1945		
	C 800		1945-48 T. Williamson Lab		
Alliance		SDP	1948-74 E.L. Mallalieu Lab		
			1974-79 John Ellis Lab		
			1979- Michael Brown C		

Great Grimsby

Grimsby has been unusually loyal to the Labour Party. It was for 18 years the constituency of one of the most prominent theorists of the party, Anthony Crosland. In the April 1977 byelection caused by Crosland's sudden death, TV current affairs personality Austin Mitchell held the seat, on the same day as Labour were ousted by a 21% swing at Ashfield, Notts. In the 1979 General Election Mitchell increased his majority to over 6,000 - just about as large as Crosland enjoyed in 1974. The constituency is unchanged in the boundary revision, although its name is brought into line with the title of the local government Borough - Great Grimsby.

Grimsby is certainly a great fishing and container port. It has the largest accommodation capacity for frozen food in Europe. It has attempted to stave off depression by modernisation, and many Grimsby residents work in the petro-chemical complexes on the Humber Bank. Grimsby's Labour preferences can be guessed from the sight of the Victorian housing behind the docks, and peripheral council estates on the west and north sides of town. But there is a large Conservative middle-class residential area in the south-east, towards the seaside resort of Cleethorpes: the wards of Scartho, Wintringham, Wellow, Weelsby, Springfield, Clee. The political opinions of Grimsby wards seem very fixed, which accounts for the low swings that the seat has recorded.

The Alliance is unlikely to be able to break through Grimsby's set ways, and Austin Mitchell seems guaranteed a long career in Parliament; and should Labour ever return to government, once again Grimsby's representative may be one of the most articulate and intellectual of the holders of high office.

1981	% Own Occ	64.2	1979 same seat Grimsby		
1981	% Loc Auth	27.8	Lab	26,282	52.0
1981	% Black/Asian	0.8	C	20,041	39.7
1981	% Mid Cl	35.8	L	3,837	7.6
1981	% Prof Man	11.6	Mod Lab	214	0.4
1982	electorate 69,345		NF	137	0.3
Alliance		SDP	MPs since 1945		

MPs since 1945
1945-59 K.G. Younger Lab
1959-77 Anthony Crosland Lab
1977-   Austin Mitchell Lab

Kingston upon Hull East

The east end of Hull contains the Humber city's main
industrial area, several miles of commercial docks, and several
square miles of council estates. East is the safest of the three
Labour seats in Hull, returning the merchant seamen's
representative in Parliament, John Prescott, by 23,000 votes
in 1979. It seems, quite logically, to elect MPs of seafaring
interests - before Prescott the member for 25 years was
Commander Harry Pursey. A few thousand electors are transferred to North, but East will remain a Labour stronghold.

1981	% Own Occ	35	1979 core seat Hull East		
1981	% Loc Auth	60	Lab	39,411	62.5
1981	% Black/Asian	0.5	C	15,719	24.9
1981	% Mid Cl	36	L	7,543	12.0
1981	% Prof Man	7	NF	374	0.6
1982	electorate 70,827		MPs since 1945		
1979	notional result		1945-70 Harry Pursey Lab		
	Lab 19,300		1970- John Prescott Lab		
Alliance		L			

Kingston upon Hull North

The new North is very similar to the former Central seat held
by Kevin McNamara, although the commercial heart of the city
is transferred to West. Central used to be the least strongly
Labour of the three Hull seats, and its predecessor was won
by the Tories during the 1950s. It contained most of the
Conservative neighbourhoods within the city boundaries, like
Avenue and Newlands wards in NW Hull, not far from the
University. But the Stoneferry council estate is taken from
the oversized East, and North may well be safer for Labour
than the old Central ever was.

1981	% Own Occ	40	1979 core seat Hull Central		
1981	% Loc Auth	41	Lab	22,318	52.1
1981	% Black/Asian	1	C	14,725	34.4
1981	% Mid Cl	41	L	5,069	11.8
1981	% Prof Man	11	NF	422	1.0
1982	electorate 75,716		Oth	274	0.6
1979	notional result		MPs since 1945		
	Lab 10,500		1945-50 R.W.G. Mackay Lab		
Alliance		SDP	1950-59 W.R.A. Hudson C		
			1959-64 J.M. Coulson C		
			1964-66 H. Solomon Lab		
			1966- Kevin McNamara Lab		

Kingston upon Hull West

The third Labour working-class industrial seat in Hull is the West division. Here the fishing docks are situated, and now the city centre of Hull is gained from the old Central seat. The elctorate rises by about 15,000, and the seat will be even safer for Labour's new candidate Stuart Randall, who replaces the retiring veteran MP James Johnson

1981	% Own Occ	44	1979 core seat Hull West			
1981	% Loc Auth	36	Lab	19,750	55.8	
1981	% Black/Asian	1	C	11,592	32.7	
1981	% Mid Cl	36	L	3,656	10.3	
1981	% Prof Man	9	NF	411	1.2	
1982	electorate 59,407		MPs since 1955			
1979	notional result		1955-64 M. Hewitson Lab			
	Lab 9,700		1964-	James Johnson Lab		
Alliance		SDP				

Isle of Wight

Because it is a county of its own, the Isle of Wight must remain as a single constituency at the next Election, even though at 95,000 its electorate will be the largest of any in Britain; it does not quite attain the size needed to justify its division into two seats. In February 1974, the island was hit by a political tidal wave. Solidly Conservative for decades, the seat fell to Liberal Stephen Ross after the veteran Tory MP was involved in a financial scandal concerning Bembridge Harbour. Despite the circumstances of his election, Ross has held on by working hard and providing energetic constituency services, despite vigorous Tory challenges by able candidates like The Economist's Dudley Fishburn. The Labour vote, never strong in this seat where tourism and agriculture are the chief industries, has been squeezed throughout the island to a derisory minimum - the lowest percentage of any at the 1979 Election. This being so, Ross will have to pull out all the stops once more to secure another victory next time.

1981	% Own Occ	71.4	1979 same seat Isle of Wight		
1981	% Loc Auth	14.5	L	35,889	48.2
1981	% Black/Asian	0.2	C	35,537	47.7
1981	% Mid Cl	49.4	Lab	3,014	4.0
1981	% Prof Man	18.3	MPs since 1945		
1982	electorate 94,768		1945-59 Sir Peter Macdonald C		
Alliance		L	1959-74 Mark Woodnutt C		
			1974-	Stephen Ross L	

Ashford

This southern Kent seat is one of the few to escape the attentions of the Commission in unrevised form. It is also identical to the Ashford Borough, consisting of Ashford and Tenterden together with their associated rural districts. Tenterden is an affluent small town set in the wooded Weald of Kent, near the Sussex border, but Ashford is a larger centre which has taken in London overspill population in new council estates, particularly in the south of the town. This makes Ashford South a Labour ward, but does not threaten the comfortable lead of the former Navy Minister Keith Speed.

1981	% Own Occ	59.3	1979 same seat Ashford
1981	% Loc Auth	30.6	C 26,224 55.7
1981	% Black/Asian	1.7	Lab 12,586 26.7
1971	% Mid Cl	45.9	L 7,631 16.2
1971	% Prof Man	16.9	NF 678 1.4
1976	electorate 65,592		MPs since 1945
Alliance		SDP	1945-50 E.P. Smith C
			1950-74 William Deedes C
			1974- Keith Speed C

Canterbury

Conservative David Crouch won Canterbury by over 22,000 votes in 1979. It might be expected that the home of the chief see of the Church of England in the heart of prosperous Kent might be a Tory citadel, but actually Canterbury itself is the least strongly Conservative part of the seat, for there are Labour voters in the centre of the town. Over 20,000 voters have been lost as the seaside resort of Herne Bay is moved to North Thanet, which will reduce the Tory majority by four or five thousand: But the Conservatives can pile up their vote in the villages around Canterbury and in Whitstable (except in its western council estate of Seasalter). Canterbury will remain one of the safest Tory seats.

1981	% Own Occ	63.9	1979 core seat Canterbury
1981	% Loc Auth	22.5	C 38,805 58.3
1981	% Black/Asian	1.5	Lab 16,168 24.3
1981	% Mid Cl	54.5	L 10,665 16.0
1981	% Prof Man	20.0	NF 941 1.4
1982	electorate 73,690		MPs since 1945
1979	notional result		1945-53 J.B. White C
	C 18,500		1953-66 L.M. Thomas C
Alliance		L	1966- David Crouch C

Dartford

Dartford is the innermost constituency in Kent, nearest to East London, bordering Erith and Crayford in Bexley Borough. Since its post-war creation in 1955 it has always been regarded as a Labour seat, although it has twice been lost narrowly to the Conservatives, in 1970 and 1979. The present MP, Richard Dunn, won by only 1,392 last time, the smallest Conservative majority in Kent. But his chances of holding a difficult seat have been significantly improved by the addition of over 10,000 voters around Ash from the staunchly Tory Sevenoaks District.

It always was the rural part of this seat which gave the Conservatives a look-in. Dartford itself, and its smaller satellite town of Swanscombe, always turns in a Labour majority. The northern wards of Dartford, towards the tunnel, make up Labour's council estate stronghold, together with Swanscombe/Stone on the river between Dartford and Gravesend. The best residential zone in Dartford itself is in the west of the town, but the Conservatives do better the further away from the Thames one goes, towards the North Downs or into the Darent Valley. This is why the arrival of the ex-Sevenoaks villages might well tip the balance in this highly marginal seat.

It should remain true that Dartford is one of Labour's best bets in Kent. Since the war, Labour have held Gravesend, Rochester/Chatham, Faversham and Dover in good years; but only Dartford has ever seemed like a safe seat. However, Kent, like most of southern England, has slipped away from Labour in the last decade, and they could only draw level with the Conservatives in the new Dartford seat in the 1981 County Council elections, an oustanding year for them in general. Richard Dunn must therefore be the favourite to win Dartford at the next Election.

1981	% Own Occ	64.1	1979 core seat Dartford		
1981	% Loc Auth	27.7	C	21,195	45.9
1981	% Black/Asian	3.5	Lab	19,803	42.9
1981	% Mid Cl	55.4	L	4,407	9.5
1981	% Prof Man	17.9	NF	476	1.0
1982	electorate 72,275		Oth	328	0.7
1979	notional result		MPs since 1955		
	C 4,700		1955-70 Sydney Irving Lab		
Alliance		L	1970-74 Peter Trew C		
			1974-79 Sydney Irving Lab		
			1979- Richard Dunn C		

Dover

For many, Dover affords a first sight of England. It is one of only two English towns which the French dignify with their own version of its name, Douvres; the other is London. In the Second World War the famed cliffs of this major continental port became a symbol of bulldog patriotism and resistance, as well as sentiment. Yet its political preferences are not those of a stronghold of English nationalistic Toryism. Labour's David Ennals proved that Labour could win Dover by holding the seat from 1964 to 1970; but another frontbencher, Conservative Peter Rees, has won Dover comfortably since then. Now it is reduced to marginal status again by the removal of the Conservatives' best town, Sandwich, which joins South Thanet.

Besides the working-class population of Dover itself, this constituency contains the remnants of the Kent coalfield. Opened up in the inter-war years, the Kent field never reached true prosperity. Due to economic difficulties and its isolation from other mining areas, there was a shortage of labour and poor industrial relations which bred union militancy. There was an 'unpatriotic' strike in World War Two, only a few miles away from those white cliffs. Pit villages like Aylesham and the miners' Mill Hill district of Deal still maintain a strong Labour allegiance. But this mixed constituency also includes true blue seaside spots like Walmer (the other face of Deal from Mill Hill), St Margaret's-at-Cliffe and Capel-le-Ferne.

Dover is a truly heterogeneous marginal seat: which other division could include coal mining, seaside resorts, comfortable South of England villages and a major ferry port? It is certainly an unusual seat in any terms, and a surprising anomaly in Kent, that most south-eastern of counties in every sense.

1981	% Own Occ	59.8	1979 core seat Dover and Deal		
1981	% Loc Auth	26.4	C	30,606	50.0
1981	% Black/Asian	1	Lab	22,664	37.0
1981	% Mid Cl	41.4	L	6,906	11.3
1981	% Prof Man	12.9	Silly	642	1.0
1982	electorate 68,549		NF	378	0.6
1979	notional result		MPs since 1945		
	C 5,200		1945-50 J.R. Thomas Lab		
Alliance		SDP	1950-64 J.S.W. Arbuthnot C		
			1964-70 David Ennals Lab		
			1970- Peter Rees C		

Faversham

The Swale is the channel which divides the flat Isle of Sheppey from the mainland, and the Borough of Swale is the basis for the Faversham constituency. There are three major population centres: Sittingbourne, Faversham itself and Sheppey, together with some villages in the orchard-strewn countryside between. Sittingbourne has a population of nearly 40,000, and is the largest of the elements in the constituency, but the traditional name of Faversham has been retained. It was once a marginal - Labour held it very narrowly from 1945 right through till 1970. But Roger Moate won it then for the Conservatives, and by 1979 it had built up his majority to 12,000.

In the boundary changes some of the villages are lost - Hartlip and Upchurch to Gillingham, and Boughton and Courtenay to Canterbury. But this should reduce Moate's majority by only 1,500 or so. The Swale district is mixed in character. The Isle of Sheppey is no holiday paradise, but an industrial and working-class area which usually gives Labour a majority, especially in Sheerness. Sittingbourne is marginal, but has Labour wards, such as Milton Regis. Faversham and the villages are safely Tory. All the areas have seen a growth of owner-occupied housing in the last two decades, and together with the general trend to the Conservatives in the SE of England this has caused a long-term swing away from Labour in this constituency.

Faversham seems to be lost to Labour for good. In the 1982 local elections they were reduced to third place, as the Alliance forced its way into second with 30% of the vote, still over 10% behind the Tories. What is more, some of the Conservatives' best rural wards were not contested in 1982, so it seems that Moate should be returned without serious opposition again next time.

1981	% Own Occ	64.8	1979 core seat Faversham		
1981	% Loc Auth	25.2	C	33,513	54.4
1981	% Black/Asian	1	Lab	21,351	34.6
1981	% Mid Cl	45.5	L	6,349	10.3
1981	% Prof Man	16.2	NF	439	0.7
1982	electorate 76,942		MPs since 1945		
1979	notional result		1945-64 P.L. Wells Lab		
	C 10,400		1964-70 Terence Boston Lab		
Alliance		SDP	1970- Roger Moate C		

Folkestone and Hythe

The southernmost stretch of the Kent coast is probably its most attractive. This constituency includes two of the medieval Cinque Ports, Hythe and Romney, as well as the Romney Marsh country and Lydd, and the Elham Valley inland. Folkestone, second only to Dover as a continental ferry port, has more charm as a resort than its functional rival 7 miles north. Folkestone and Hythe remains identical to Shepway District. It is a very safe Conservative seat, and the Liberals are the main challengers, at their strongest in Folkestone North and Romney Marsh; the Tories do best in Hythe and the inland villages. The present MP, Albert Costain, is in his 70s and may well retire at the next Election.

1981	% Own Occ	65.3	1979 same seat F'stone & Hythe		
1981	% Loc Auth	17.1	C	26,837	55.7
1981	% Black/Asian	1.4	L	10,817	22.5
1981	% Mid Cl	49.4	Lab	10,015	20.8
1981	% Prof Man	17.9	NF	478	1.0
1982	electorate 67,808		MPs since 1950		
Alliance		L	1950-59 H.R. Mackeson C		
			1959- Albert Costain C		

Gillingham

Gillingham is the largest of the 'Medway towns', and the least industrial. It is almost entirely a residential area, with three-quarters of the housing owner occupied. This implies a safe Conservative seat, even though Gillingham is not particularly high in status. It has scarcely a higher proportion of professional and managerial workers than Gravesend or Dartford, and a much lower percentage than Canterbury or Maidstone. There was a Liberal challenge here in the early 1970s, and one feels that the Alliance always proves a greater potential threat than Labour: they did well to jump to 34% of the vote here in 1982. The present MP is Sir Freddie Burden, the oldest member of the House, born in the year 1905.

1981	% Own Occ	75	1979 core seat Gillingham		
1981	% Loc Auth	14.5	C	26,791	53.1
1981	% Black/Asian	4	Lab	16,292	32.3
1981	% Mid Cl	52.4	L	6,219	12.3
1981	% Prof Man	14.4	NF	528	1.0
1982	electorate 69,636		Oths	593	1.2
1979	notional C 11,200		MP since 1950		
Alliance		L	1950- Sir Frederick Burden C		

Gravesham

Rather like Dartford, Gravesend constituency used to see a
battle between the Labour voters in the towns on the River
Thames and the Tories of the rural hinterland, which ran
south to the North Downs escarpment and east across the
marshes to the Isle of Grain and the River Medway. In 1979
there was no doubt which side came out on top, for after an
8% swing the Conservative Tim Brinton gained Gravesend with
a majority of 9,346. But whereas the undersized Dartford
gains extra villages in the redistribution, Gravesend loses
20,000 voters as it is reduced to the same dimensions as
Gravesham Borough, from which it takes its new name. The
territory which is lost is the Conservative rural and suburban
district near Strood on the west bank of the Medway, now in
the Rochester upon Medway Borough and the Medway
constituency.

Gravesend North and Northfleet, on the bank of the Thames,
are Labour's strongholds in Gravesham; but Gravesend is a
working-class town, and Labour can also count on the
support of the council estate of Singlewell on its southern
edge. Gravesham has the highest percentage of non-white
voters of any constituency in Kent too, concentrated in
central Gravesend. The Conservative strength will lie in the
villages, like Meopham, Higham and Shorne, and a minority
vote in Gravesend; but losing the Strood hinterland will be a
blow to Tim Brinton.

Labour probably need a swing of only about 4% to take
Gravesham next time. If they win the General Election, it
should fall. With the non-white population increasing – the
percentage has doubled in the last ten years – Gravesham
should prove one of the brighter hopes for Labour in their
gloomy southern region.

1981	% Own Occ	62.7	1979 core seat Gravesend
1981	% Loc Auth	28.5	C 37,592 52.0
1981	% Black/Asian	6.8	Lab 28,246 39.0
1981	% Mid Cl	51.3	L 5,917 8.2
1981	% Prof Man	17.1	NF 603 0.8
1982	electorate 71,922		MPs since 1945
1979	notional result		1945-47 G. Allighan Lab
	C 6,600		1947-55 Sir Richard Acland Lab
Alliance		SDP	1955-64 Peter Kirk C

Maidstone

The constituency based on Kent's county town was seriously oversized in 1979, with 93,000 electors. Now the north-eastern sector of the Borough is removed, together with two wards from Maidstone itself, to the new Mid Kent division. This would have reduced the Tory majority last time from 21,000 to about 15,000 – still safe, it would seem. But in the early 1980s Maidstone saw a Liberal surge which makes this seat one of the best chances for an Alliance surprise in the country.

In the 1982 local elections the Alliance polled the highest number of votes in the wards within the new, smaller, Maidstone seat. But only 12 of the 20 wards were actually up for election that year, so it is hard to say that this would imply a Liberal gain in a parliamentary election. It should be remembered too that all over the country the Liberals have done better locally than in national elections. But they are undeniably strong in the town of Maidstone itself, and in 1982 the SDP showed an ability to do well in Labour's only area of strength, SE Maidstone (Shepway and Park Wood). The villages in this constituency are traditionally excellent Tory ground. This is hop-growing country, and the Conservatives seem to do as well at this initial stage of the brewing industry as they do everywhere else associated with the drink trade.

Labour obtain derisory votes in the rural part of central Kent, and the Liberals find it harder ground too. But now that the constituency is reduced to more of a Maidstone core, their chances have been done no harm. Few Conservative MPs can be so worried about a 21,000 majority as Maidstone's John Wells.

1981	% Own Occ	63.0	1979 core seat Maidstone		
1981	% Loc Auth	26.1	C	37,727	52.6
1981	% Black/Asian	2	L	16,676	23.2
1981	% Mid Cl	56.0	Lab	16,632	23.2
1981	% Prof Man	19.5	NF	703	1.0
1982	electorate 71,081		MPs since 1945		
1979	notional result		1945-59 Sir A.C. Bossom C		
	C 14,000		1959- John Wells C		
Alliance		L			

Medway

Rochester and Chatham used to be one of those rare seats in Kent that Labour might hope to win in a good year. But the boundary changes have worked against them here. Rochester and Chatham have been split, and each half lumped in with some Conservative rural terrain.

The Medway seat consists of Rochester and Strood, together with 20,000 new voters from the west side of the River Medway, formerly in Gravesend. Although it attracts some tourism because of its early cathedral in the old town in the loop of the Medway, and because of its association with Dickens, Rochester is every bit as prone to vote Labour as its less glamorous twin town of Chatham, which is now submerged in Mid Kent. But this marginal Rochester should in future be swamped by the Conservative villages and suburbs in the flat lands across the Medway. This includes that caravan site of a seaside resort, Allhallows-on-Sea, the Isle of Grain with its dominating oil refinery, and the marshes also known for Dickensian connections.

Rochester and Chatham was a natural and long-respected unit. But with 80,000 electors it was rather too large to survive in its old form. In some cases when faced with this type of problem the Boundary Commission maintained the essentials of a seat by chipping some wards off the edge, as at Cambridge and Ipswich. This may well help Labour by pruning the seat down to an urban core. But where the Commission split the town and add rural wards to each half, it almost always hurt Labour by diluting their urban vote. Not surprisingly the party fought very hard indeed against the proposals in the Medway area, and a second inquiry was held. But it looks as if Labour's expectations in both Medway and Mid-Kent are significantly worse than they ever were in Rochester and Chatham. They must be reduced to a Micawberish hope that something will turn up out of the blue.

1981	% Own Occ	62.0	1979 core seat Rochester/
1981	% Loc Auth	25.9	Chatham
1981	% Black/Asian	5	C 27,574 47.5
1981	% Mid Cl	44.7	Lab 24,886 42.8
1981	% Prof Man	13.9	L 5,219 9.0
1982	electorate 63,148		NF 417 0.7
1979	notional result		MPs since 1950
	C 3,700		1950-59 Arthur Bottomley Lab
Alliance		SDP	1959-64 Julian Critchley C
			1964-70 Anne Kerr Lab
			1970-74 Peggy Fenner C
			1974-79 Robert Bean Lab
			1979- Peggy Fenner C

348

Mid Kent

This new constituency is rather a curious mixture. On the
one hand is the working-class, military and rather tough town
of Chatham (40,000 electors); on the other it includes
extremely Conservative North Downs villages and stretches
right into Maidstone itself (25,000). Chatham was part of the
highly marginal Rochester/Chatham seat, but the further
south one travels away from the Medway the worse the
territory becomes for Labour. The industrial scene shades
into the Garden of England, with its hop fields and orchards,
and finally bites into the middle-class neighbourhoods of NE
Maidstone. Labour objected strenuously to the creation of this
rather illogically drawn seat; but after two inquiries, its
boundaries stand. It should be an extra Conservative seat in
Kent, whose allocation rises from 15 seats to 16.

1981	% Own Occ	68.4	New seat
1981	% Loc Auth	22.2	
1981	% Black/Asian	3	
1981	% Mid Cl	54.2	
1981	% Prof Man	18.9	
1982	electorate 66,255		
1979	notional C 8,800		
Alliance	L		

North Thanet

The Isle of Thanet was split into two seats in the early
1970s, each on the small side. They were still both under
50,000 electors in 1979, and ripe for redistribution. Now
Thanet West gains 20,000 from Canterbury in the highly Tory
shape of Herne Bay, and becomes North Thanet - a built-up
strip of resorts along the north coast of Kent: Herne Bay,
Birchington, Westgate, Margate and Cliftonville. Labour gets
close only in central Margate. It should remain very safe for
Tory William Rees-Davies, a Thanet MP since 1953.

1981	% Own Occ	69.6	1979 core seat Thanet West		
1981	% Loc Auth	15.4	C	18,122	55.4
1981	% Black/Asian	1.5	Lab	8,576	26.2
1981	% Mid Cl	51.5	L	6,017	18.4
1981	% Prof Man	18.5	MP since 1974		
1982	electorate 66,431		1974-	William Rees-Davies C	
1979	notional C 14,100				
Alliance		SDP			

349

Sevenoaks

West Kent is socially and politically very similar to Surrey just over the county boundary. Sevenoaks is close enough to London to fall within the middle-class commuting zone, and the affluent villages around Westerham and Edenbridge are rarely dependent on agriculture. The only Labour vote is in Swanley, which is rather close to Dartford. It is of course a very safe Conservative seat. The loss of the northern end around the Darent Valley to Dartford will make scarcely a dent in the 22,000 majority of Conservative MP Mark Wolfson. It will remain the most upper-class seat in Kent.

1981	% Own Occ	62.4	1979 core seat Sevenoaks		
1981	% Loc Auth	23.9	C	36.697	57.4
1981	% Black/Asian	1.5	Lab	14,583	22.8
1981	% Mid Cl	59.5	L	11,839	18.5
1981	% Prof Man	24.4	NF	821	1.3
1982	electorate 72,017		MPs since 1945		
1979	notional result		1945-50 C.E. Ponsonby C		
	C 18,700		1950-79 Sir John Rodgers C		
Alliance		L	1979- Mark Wolfson C		

South Thanet

South Thanet is the old Thanet East - Ramsgate and Broadstairs - plus Sandwich from Dover. It is slightly less completely devoted to tourism than North Thanet. Broadstairs is a thoroughly respectable resort and the home town of Edward Heath, but Ramsgate is a working hovercraft and ferry port, and there are Labour council estate wards inland at Newington and Northwood. But Sandwich is a new addition very much to the taste of the Conservative Party, and there should be no problems for the multi-talented Tory whizz-kid MP Jonathan Aitken

1981	% Own Occ	68.5	1979 core seat Thanet East		
1981	% Loc Auth	18.8	C	20,367	57.2
1981	% Black/Asian	1	Lab	10,128	28.4
1981	% Mid Cl	57.2	L	4,755	13.3
1981	% Prof Man	21.6	NF	376	1.1
1982	electorate 62,298		MP since 1974		
1979	notional result		1974- Jonathan Aitken C		
	C 13,600				
Alliance		L			

350

Tonbridge and Malling

In the last redistribution in the early 1970s, the old Tonbridge seat was split in two as Tunbridge Wells was hived off into a constituency of its own. It seems as if the Boundary Commission managed to get its Tonbridges and Tunbridges sorted out, for neither Tonbridge/Malling nor Tunbridge Wells are in any way altered this time. Tonbridge and Malling is a rock-solid Tory seat set amongst the orchards of central Kent. There is some local Liberal success around the Mallings themselves, but no problems on the horizon for Housing Minister John Stanley.

1981	% Own Occ	64.9	1979 same seat Tonbridge and		
1981	% Loc Auth	24.2	Malling		
1981	% Black/Asian	1.3	C	29,534	54.5
1981	% Mid Cl	57.2	Lab	13,282	24.5
1981	% Prof Man	21.6	L	10,904	20.1
1982	electorate 72,718		NF	429	0.8
Alliance		SDP	MP since 1974		
			1974-	John Stanley C	

Tunbridge Wells

Spa towns have always tended to the Conservatives, and Kent's example, Royal Tunbridge Wells, is no exception. Every ward in the division is ordinarily Conservative in preference, in the elegant inland resort itself and right down the Sussex border through Southborough to comfortable Hawkhurst and Cranbrook. Tunbridge Wells was the safest of all the fifteen Conservative seats in Kent at the last Election, and it may well turn in the largest numerical majority too next time. Its boundaries are unaltered, and like Tonbridge and Malling it remains coterminous with local government Districts of the same name.

1981	% Own Occ	57.1	1979 same seat Tunbridge Wells		
1981	% Loc Auth	21.7	C	31,928	59.5
1981	% Black/Asian	1.7	Lab	11,392	21.2
1981	% Mid Cl	57.1	L	9,797	18.3
1981	% Prof Man	21.7	NF	509	0.9
1982	electorate 74,213		MP since 1974		
Alliance		L	1974-	Patrick Mayhew C	

Blackburn

The Lancashire textile town of Blackburn is still popularly associated with the redoubtable Labour politician Barbara Castle, who represented the town from 1945 to 1979. But Mrs Castle has now retired from Westminster (although she is still the leader of Labour's group of Euro-MPs), and the Blackburn MP is Jack Straw, a former President of the National Union of Students and already a Labour front-bench economics spokesman. Jack Straw clearly has a bright future within the party.

He must of course look after his constituency. Blackburn has been expanded by some 20,000 voters in the boundary changes, mainly in the SW of the town, and the seat is now the largest in Lancashire. The county has a curious disparity of 24,000 between the electorates of the largest seat (Blackburn, 76,000) and the smallest (Morecambe and Lunesdale, 52,000). But Labour should still be able to regard Blackburn as a good bet – 20% of the population is non-white, mainly Asians who have settled in terraced rows such as those at Whalley Range. There are also council estates like those on the edge of the town at Shadworth and Whitebirk. The Conservatives fight back in affluent residential areas such as those around Corporation Park and in Billinge and Revidge wards in NW Blackburn – but many members of the town's middle classes live out in Ribble Valley villages like Wilpshire.

Blackburn is not a town without problems. There is a large and growing non-white minority, and the far-right National Party led by John Kingsley Read actually won a couple of seats here on the town council in the early 1970s. Now united as a single community, this gritty and self-contained northern town will still provide interesting contests. Jack Straw, like Barbara Castle, will need to exercise all his skills and ability to retain his position as the town's MP.

1981	% Loc Auth	61.2	1979 core seat Blackburn		
1981	% Loc Auth	33.7	Lab	19,683	50.7
1981	% Black/Asian	20	C	14,193	36.6
1981	% Mid Cl	38.8	L	4,371	11.3
1981	% Prof Man	11.5	NF	565	1.5
1982	electorate 76,863		MPs since 1955		
1979	notional result		1955-79 Barbara Castle Lab		
	Lab 2,400		1979- Jack Straw Lab		
Alliance		SDP			

Blackpool North

It might be thought that Blackpool, traditionally the Mecca of the northern working classes, would be one of the safest Conservative towns in the country. Its economy dependent on tourism, scarcely more than 10% of its housing council owned: together with the image of the Blackpool seaside landlady, this scarcely seems promising for the left. Yet in fact there are hardly any overwhelming Tory wards, and Labour achieves a solid minority in most wards. In the North division they usually lead in Claremont ward, just beyond the North Pier, and in the inland ward of Park. In Labour's high-water mark year of 1981, they returned most of the Blackpool county councillors. Blackpool is a commercial centre, but it is not 'posh'. Labour should continue to achieve a good second place here.

1981	% Own Occ	71	1979 same seat Blackpool North		
1981	% Loc Auth	15	C	23,209	53.7
1981	% Black/Asian	0.5	Lab	12,980	30.0
1981	% Mid Cl	46	L	6,127	14.2
1981	% Prof Man	13	NF	943	2.2
1982	electorate 59,065		MPs since 1945		
Alliance		L	1945-62 T.A.R.W. Low C		
			1962- Norman Miscampbell C		

Blackpool South

Both the Blackpool constituencies survive the redistribution unscathed. The dividing line between the N and S seats lies, logically, at the level of the central of Blackpool's three piers. This leaves the town centre and the Tower in North, but South has the amusement park and its share of the Golden Mile. Its political characteristics are very similar to North's - Labour wards at Hawes Side, Clifton and Victoria inland, small Tory leads elsewhere. It should continue to provide a moderate majority for Foreign Office Minister Peter Blaker.

1981	% Own Occ	75	1979 same seat Blackpool South		
1981	% Loc Auth	10	C	21,762	51.5
1981	% Black/Asian	0.5	Lab	12,914	30.6
1981	% Mid Cl	42	L	7,057	16.7
1981	% Prof Man	13	NF	524	1.2
1982	electorate 57,884		MPs since 1945		
Alliance		SDP	1945-64 J.R. Robinson C		
			1964- Peter Blaker C		

Burnley

The new constituency is now identical to Burnley Borough, which includes areas surrounding the town itself. This raises the electorate from an undersized 51,000 to 68,000, and probably halves the 1979 Labour majority of 6,000. The additions, the town of Padiham and the former Burnley Rural District, have come from the safely Tory Clitheroe constituency.

Burnley itself is not without its middle-class residential districts, north-east towards Nelson and up Rose Hill south towards Rawtenstall. But despite the fact that Burnley is a town largely of owner occupiers, like many in Lancashire, Labour have held it since 1935 without serious trouble. Many of the little terraced cottages survive from Burnley's cotton-weaving period, not necessarily gentrified. It is a local tradition that newly marrieds buy their own inexpensive houses, and it doesn't imply affluence. There is an Asian population of about 3,000, although this is much fewer than in the neighbouring town of Blackburn. Padiham was the best Labour area in Clitheroe, so it shouldn't create too much of an inroad into the Labour margin in Burnley. But the old Burnley Rural District was composed of solidly middle-class villages like Worsthorne, a couple of miles out to the east beyond Turf Moor football ground.

MP Dan Jones is retiring, like many members over 70 years of age. His Labour successor Peter Pitt will have a larger, and less safe constituency. But unless there is a further swing against Labour, beyond the low point of 1979, he should still take over without too many alarums.

1981	% Own Occ	69.6	1979 core seat Burnley		
1981	% Loc Auth	24.0	Lab	20,172	50.8
1981	% Black/Asian	3.6	C	14,062	35.4
1981	% Mid Cl	38.8	L	5,091	12.8
1981	% Prof Man	12.6	Oth	352	0.9
1982	electorate 68,301		MPs since 1945		
1979	notional result		1945-59 W.A. Burke Lab		
	Lab 5,100		1959- Dan Jones Lab		
Alliance		L			

Chorley

Chorley has for some years been one of the Lancashire marginals which swung with the tide at General Elections. It was won by the Conservatives in 1970 and 1979, by Labour in 1974. With 81,000 electors, it was oversized, and Leyland has now been transferred into the new South Ribble division. Chorley Borough and Chorley constituency are now almost identical; two wards are added from West Lancashire District to bring the electorate to 66,000, almost exactly the average in England.

These changes should slightly benefit the Tories, without putting Chorley finally out of Labour's reach. Leyland will be the best Labour area in South Ribble. Parbold and Wrightington, the two West Lancashire wards in the new Chorley, are both extremely Conservative. Chorley town itself, however, is solidly Labour, most of all in the East and SW wards. The best residential area in Chorley is the NW ward. Outside Chorley itself, Coppull is Labour; Euxton, Clayton-le-Woods and Whittle-le-Woods Conservative. The Alliance achieved under 20% in the 1982 borough elections here and seems not to pose a threat to the constituency's two-party marginal status.

The Tories may well have had a lead of three or four thousand votes here in 1979 – some wards were not fully contested, which makes the calculation of a notional result more inaccurate. But Labour did very well in the 1981 and 1982 local elections, and proved that they can approach striking distance of victory in Chorley.

1981	% Own Occ	75.9	1979 core seat	Chorley		
1981	% Loc Auth	17.6	C	31,125	46.8	
1981	% Black/Asian	1	Lab	28,456	43.0	
1981	% Mid Cl	49.3	L	6,388	9.6	
1981	% Prof Man	18.6	NF	376	0.6	
1982	electorate 72,930		MPs since 1945			
1979	notional result		1945-70	Clifford Kenyon	Lab	
	C 3,300		1970-74	Constance Monks	C	
Alliance		SDP	1974-79	George Rodgers	Lab	
			1979-	Den Dover	C	

Fylde

The Fylde is the peninsula jutting into the Irish Sea about half-way up the coast of Lancashire. Its most well known town is Blackpool. But South Fylde achieved political fame as a constituency too. In 1979 it returned the largest Conservative majority, 32,247. This was also the largest majority on the mainland of Great Britain, exceeded only in Northern Ireland's huge seats. Nor was this an isolated achievement. South Fylde has consistently been noted for producing the biggest Tory margin.

However, one of the reasons for this was that South Fylde's electorate was well above the quota - 93,000 in 1979. Now about 40,000 electors from the Preston suburbs around Penwortham have been moved into the new South Ribble division. This leaves the core of the new constituency as the local government Borough of Fylde, basically Lytham St Anne's and Kirkham. One rural ward from Preston completes the picture. Lytham St Anne's is a rather genteel seaside resort and residential area. It is south of bustling, plebeian Blackpool, and bears a calmer flavour. It has the kind of overwhelming Conservatism that Blackpool itself lacks. It is solidly owner occupied, and much new private housing development has taken place, inland in St Anne's especially.

The numerical majorities gained in the new Fylde seat will probably drop out of the record range to around 20,000. But it will be just as safe for the Tories as before. The present MP is lawyer Edward Gardner, who found a safe haven at South Fylde in 1970 after previously undergoing a more risky existence as the member for one of England's most marginal seats, Billericay. Gardner is in his seventies now, but still very active, and he has not announced his retirement.

1981	% Own Occ	72.0
1981	% Loc Auth	13.2
1981	% Black/Asian	0.7
1981	% Mid Cl	60.3
1981	% Prof Man	23.1
1982	electorate 62,506	
1979	notional result	
	C 22,200	
Alliance		L

1979 core seat South Fylde

C	45,883	63.4
Lab	13,636	18.8
L	11,938	16.5
NF	941	1.3

MPs since 1945
1945-70 Claude Lancaster C
1970-   Edward Gardner C

Hyndburn

The Hyndburn constituency is the same as the Hyndburn Borough, and very similar to the old Accrington division. This east Lancashire seat is made up of a number of small ex-textile towns between Blackburn and Burnley. The political contest here is keen. Although Labour haven't lost Accrington since the war, the majority has always been narrow. Hyndburn should be even closer.

All the wards of the former seat were marginal. Accrington and Church tended to Labour, Clayton le Moors, Rishton and Oswaldtwistle to the Tories. Now arrive Great Harwood, from the Conservative county seat of Clitheroe, and the rural ward of Altham. Few constituencies will have a higher proportion of owner occupiers than Hyndburn. It is predominantly a working-class seat, but the tight-knit little terraced communities seem just as designed for political marginality as the Pennine towns further east.

The Conservatives achieved a clear majority in the 1979 local elections in Hyndburn, yet Arthur Davidson held Accrington by 3,000 votes. Part of the discrepancy is due to the new additions, Great Harwood and Altham. But it does also seem clear that Davidson did better than his Labour local election running-mates: a rare example of a discernible gap between local and national voting patterns. Davidson may well have a personal vote, which could prove a vital factor in the close-run contests that Hyndburn will certainly undergo. The Alliance only achieved 24% of the vote here in 1982, and will probably be squeezed into third place.

1981	% Own Occ	77.8	1979 core seat Accrington		
1981	% Loc Auth	16.0	Lab	19,576	48.9
1981	% Black/Asian	4	C	16,282	40.7
1981	% Mid Cl	40.1	L	3,646	9.1
1981	% Prof Man	12.8	NF	508	1.3
1982	electorate 59,940		MPs since 1945		
1979	notional result		1945-66 H. Hynd Lab		
	Lab 2,900		1966- Arthur Davidson Lab		
Alliance		SDP			

Lancaster

The centre of gravity of the Lancaster seat has been shifted southwards in the redistribution. It is still dominated by Lancaster itself, of course. But whereas before the seat moved north to take in Carnforth and the Lunesdale area, now it moves south to take in the fertile farmland around Garstang, Great Eccleston and Pilling from the Wyre Borough. Wyre is virtually the old ultra-Tory North Fylde seat, and inclusion of part of it should decide the destiny of this seat. Lancaster itself is marginal, containing mixed areas like Scotforth and Skerton and Labour wards like Bulk. It is the rural hinterland that should continue to keep this seat Tory.

1981	% Own Occ	67.7	1979 core seat Lancaster
1981	% Loc Auth	21.1	C 19,400 47.6
1981	% Black/Asian	1	Lab 15,174 37.3
1981	% Mid Cl	44.9	L 5,949 14.6
1981	% Prof Man	15.6	NF 196 0.5
1982	electorate 56,547		MPs since 1945
1979	notional result		1945-55 F.H.R. Maclean C
	C 7,900		1955-66 Humphrey Berkeley C
Alliance		L	1966-70 Stanley Henig Lab
			1970- Elaine Kellett-Bowman C

Morecambe and Lunesdale

This seat is the northern half of the District of Lancaster. Morecambe and Heysham were previously associated with Lonsdale, formerly a detached part of Lancashire across Morecambe Bay, now in Cumbria. This is replaced by Lunesdale, confusingly, a similar name, but previously included in the Lancaster seat. The alterations should have no political effect in a very safe Tory seat. The only Labour ward is the railway town of Carnforth, just off the M6, and the Alliance has no strong tradition here.

1981	% Own Occ	76.3	1979 core seat Morecambe and
1981	% Loc Auth	8.3	Lonsdale
1981	% Black/Asian	0.5	C 29,068 55.4
1981	% Mid Cl	50.4	Lab 13,253 25.3
1981	% Prof Man	19.7	L 10,150 19.3
1982	electorate 53,117		MPs since 1945
1979	notional result		1945-58 Sir W.J.I. Fraser C
	C 12,200		1958-64 B.R.V.Z. de Ferranti C
Alliance		SDP	1964-79 Alfred Hall-Davis C
			1979- Mark Lennox-Boyd C

Pendle

The Borough of Pendle takes its name from the distinctive mountain whose mass overshadows the small towns of NE Lancashire. This new constituency, which is coterminous with Pendle Borough, incorporates the whole of the Nelson and Colne seat, together with Barnoldswick and Earby from the Yorkshire division of Skipton and a few villages from Clitheroe.

Nelson and Colne was one of the great marginal Lancashire seats. It was held narrowly for many years by Sydney Silverman, renowned for his part in the abolition of capital punishment. After his death in 1968 it alternated between Labour and Tory. It was composed of a group of small ex-textile towns. 'Red' Nelson has long been known for its Labour preferences, while Colne is good ground for the Liberals at municipal level, and Reedley-Brierfield and Barrowford are Conservative. Of the additions, Barnoldswick and Earby are pretty close between the major parties, while the rural wards tip the balance of this seat to the advantage of the Conservatives. There is a large Asian presence, particularly in Nelson.

The contest in Pendle will be very tight. The Conservatives would have pulled ahead in the 1979 General Election, but Labour can easily carry the seat, while the Liberals make it a three-way marginal in local elections. The Liberal Party has never managed to reproduce this form in national polls, though, and it remains to be seen whether the Alliance can build on local successes at the next General Election.

1981	% Own Occ	75.5	1979 core seat Nelson and Colne
1981	% Loc Auth	17.8	C 17,522 45.0
1981	% Black/Asian	6.9	Lab 17,086 43.9
1981	% Mid Cl	36.6	L 4,322 11.1
1981	% Prof Man	12.7	MPs since 1945
1982	electorate 65,552		1945-68 Sydney Silverman Lab
1979	notional result		1968-74 David Waddington C
	C 2,000 (RW)		1974-79 Doug Hoyle Lab
Alliance		L	1979- John Lee C

Preston

The former seats of Preston North and Preston South were among the most marginal in the country. The smallest majority at the 1979 Election was gained by Conservative Robert Atkins at Preston North - just 29 votes. Labour's Stan Thorne won Preston South, traditionally rather better for his party, by 621 votes. Yet the new constituency of Preston should be a safe seat for Labour at all times, and would probably have given them a majority of over 6,000 votes even in 1979.

What accounts for this suprising phenomenon? The answer is that both the Preston seats previously crossed the boundaries of Preston itself to take in other towns. South included Walton-le-Dale, now in South Ribble District and constituency. North included Fulwood, a strongly Conservative dormitory town which certainly ensured Robert Atkins's victory in 1979. Fulwood and some rural areas are incorporated in Preston Borough, but they are transferred in parliamentary elections to Ribble Valley, a Tory constituency where their political impact will be absorbed. Preston itself is an old cotton town, the home of Richard Arkwright of spinning jenny fame. It has a large Asian community, terraced working-class streets, council estates like the Labour fortress of Ribbleton, and only two regularly Conservative wards, Ashton and Tulketh.

The Alliance have made little impact here, as yet, and Preston's history of producing close battles should now come to an end. It is not clear whether left-winger Stan Thorne will inherit the new safe seat, as it is equally composed of wards from the old North and South seats. Whoever the Labour candidate is, he or she can breathe more easily than anyone who has contested in Preston for fifty years.

1981	% Own Occ	74.6	New seat
1981	% Loc Auth	18.9	
1981	% Black/Asian	11	
1981	% Mid Cl	35.3	
1981	% Prof Man	11.8	
1982	electorate 65,859		
1979	notional result		
	Lab 8,500		
Alliance		SDP	

Ribble Valley

This will be one of the most uniformly solid Conservative constituencies in the new Parliament. The Borough of Ribble Valley is made up of small towns and rural areas which were formerly in the safe Tory Clitheroe seat. Clitheroe itself is the largest town in the Borough, with 13,000 people. Other communities are Longridge and Whalley, but there is much douce countryside here. This is the Lancashire equivalent of the Yorkshire Dales, including much of the Forest of Bowland.

There are no good Labour wards in Ribble Valley. Besides the rural areas and small towns, the Borough incorporates some affluent suburbanised villages around Blackburn, which were formerly in the Darwen division. Wilpshire and Mellor are the largest of these. They are often conceded uncontested to the Conservatives in local elections. Finally, the Ribble Valley constituency picks up one town from outside the Ribble Valley Borough – Fulwood, the strongly Conservative dormitory town from Preston North, 87% owner occupied and 3% local authority housing.

In previous Parliaments, the 'left-over' parts of Central Lancashire outside the major towns were gathered together in two Conservative seats, Darwen and Clitheroe. The former has been broken up by the creation of the Rossendale/Darwen seat. The latter has also lost population – Padiham to Burnley, Great Harwood to Hyndburn. Ribble Valley picks up the remnants of Clitheroe and Darwen, together with Fulwood from a Preston seat. It is a constituency which must effectively be conceded to the Tories, a concentration of their suburban and rural strength. They may even regret having so much of their support confined here, rather than spread about to influence more constituencies.

1981	% Own Occ	79.7
1981	% Loc Auth	10.2
1981	% Black/Asian	1
1981	% Mid Cl	57.7
1981	% Prof Man	21.1
1982	electorate 60,117	
1979	notional result	
	C 14,100	
Alliance		SDP

1979 core seat Clitheroe

C	25,081	57.1
Lab	13,502	30.7
L	5,362	12.2

MPs since 1945
1945-50 H.E. Randall Lab
1950-59 R. Fort C
1959-70 Frank Pearson C
1970-79 David Walder C
1979-   David Waddington C

Rossendale and Darwen

Geographically, this is a rather illogically drawn new constituency. The former Rossendale seat was a compact unit, with good internal lines of communication along a group of east Lancashire Pennine valleys - from Rawtenstall west to Haslingden, east to Bacup, south to Ramsbottom. Now, the boundaries climb across a range of hills to Darwen, in Blackburn Borough several miles to the west. Ramsbottom is lost, as it is now part of Bury Metropolitan Borough, but Whitworth is gained from Heywood and Royton.

Rossendale was a classic marginal seat, given to modest swings but yet usually electing a member of whichever party won the General Election. Rawtenstall, Bacup and Haslingden are full of even wards, homogeneous in nature and politically 50-50. Ramsbottom, however, was much gentrified and the most Conservative part of the old seat. With its forcible departure across the county boundary into Greater Manchester, Rossendale had to look further afield for extra electors; it had been a small seat for some time. Darwen was the main town in the strongly Conservative seat of that name. Although Darwen itself is actually a three-way marginal, with a strong Liberal presence, some of its Tory environs have come with it, notably part of ultra-middle-class Turton. These parts of Blackburn Borough will tip the balance of the Rossendale and Darwen seat to the Conservatives.

As the M66 has brought the Rossendale Valley within reach, its solid terraces of private houses have become more desirable as commuting bases for Greater Manchester. Similarly, Darwen is losing its character as a mill town, although the dramatic mill chimneys and steep terraces still remain. This seat could still be won by Labour in a very good year, but the boundary changes are probably exacerbating a general slide away from Labour in Anthony Greenwood's old territory.

1981	% Own Occ	68.8	
1981	% Loc Auth	25.4	
1981	% Black/Asian	2	
1981	% Mid Cl	40.9	
1981	% Prof Man	14.5	
1982	electorate 75,079		
1979	notional result		
	C 5,700		
Alliance		L	

1979 core seat Rossendale

C	20,370	48.0
Lab	18,497	43.6
L	3,543	8.3

MPs since 1945
1945-70 Anthony Greenwood Lab
1970-74 Ronald Bray C
1974-79 Michael Noble Lab
1979-   David Trippler C

South Ribble

Fortunately for the Boundary Commissioners, the 1976 electorate of the Borough of South Ribble was of almost exactly the right size for a parliamentary constituency - 65,000 electors. It is not very near Ribble Valley, a more rural area further inland. South Ribble is situated just south of Preston. It includes the towns of Leyland (formerly in Chorley) and Walton-le-Dale (Preston South), together with Penwortham, Longton and other suburban parishes from the old Preston Rural District. These last were all in the massively Tory South Fylde seat.

Leyland and Walton-le-Dale are politically closely contested, as their origin in marginal seats might suggest. But (again as expected) the ex-South Fylde contingent tips South Ribble decisively into the Tory column. This will be a mixed and interesting seat. Leyland is the home of BL's truck division, the largest commercial vehicle factory in Britain. New industries are being attracted too, for the bulk of the Central Lancashire New Town developments lie in South Ribble - three new housing developments and two industrial estates, at Walton Summit and Moss Side, Leyland. The total population of the Borough is expected to rise from 90,000 to 120,000 by the end of the century.

What effect the New Town element will have on the politics of South Ribble is unclear. Labour obtained a 300 vote margin here in 1981 during their best ever performance in Lancashire county council elections. But in all normal years it should be a Conservative seat. It is an entirely new division, and it is unclear whether any sitting MP will risk a contest here.

1981	% Own Occ	76.7	New seat
1981	% Loc Auth	18.6	
1981	% Black/Asian	0.9	
1981	% Mid Cl	52.1	
1981	% Prof Man	15.6	
1982	electorate 73,247		
1979	notional result		
	C 8,900		
Alliance		L	

West Lancashire

West Lancashire will be a starkly divided constituency. On the one hand, it includes the fertile and prosperous west Lancashire plain, with the town of Ormskirk. This is all excellent territory for the Conservative Party, with many overwhelmingly strong wards. On the other hand, though, West Lancashire incorporates the New Town of Skelmersdale, which has one of the highest rates of unemployment in England. Skelmersdale is as Labour as the rest of west Lancashire is Tory. Formerly it was part of the safely Labour Ince constituency. Which face of West Lancashire will dominate?

The constituency is more or less the same as the District of West Lancashire, although two wards of the latter are transferred to Chorley. Previously Ormskirk, Aughton, Burscough and the other villages on the plain formed a Conservative minority in an inaptly named Ormskirk constituency which was in fact awarded to Labour by the inclusion of the vast Liverpool overspill estate of Kirkby. Skelmersdale very much takes Kirkby's place as the Labour counterbalance, but it is only about half as large as Kirkby. This means that in most years West Lancashire should be a Conservative seat.

It is rather odd that Skelmersdale might have a Tory MP. This windy hill town has never been one of the more successful New Towns. Besides the notorious unemployment, it has had difficulty attracting and keeping population, and a large number of houses remain empty. The attempt to sell them at knock-down prices - under £3,000 in some cases - has not worked well. The contrast with the comfortable Ormskirk district is dramatic. Ormskirk should outvote Skelmersdale normally, but in 1981 (an excellent year for Labour) the total number of votes polled in West Lancashire in the county council elections for Labour and Conservative was almost equal. The Tories romped ahead in 1982, though, and the Alliance only achieved 22% of the vote.

1981	% Own Occ	57.8	1979 core seat Ormskirk		
1981	% Loc Auth	35.1	Lab	37,222	50.0
1981	% Black/Asian	0.7	C	36,364	48.9
1981	% Mid Cl	50.5	WRP	820	1.1
1981	% Prof Man	19.0	MP since 1974		
1982	electorate 74,098		1974– Robert Kilroy-Silk Lab		
1979	notional result				
	C 5,000 (RW)				
Alliance		SDP			

Wyre

The Borough of Wyre is named after the River Wyre which cuts off the northern end of the Fylde peninsula from the Lancaster/Morecambe region. It has no connection with Wyre Forest, which is in Worcestershire. The whole of the new Wyre constituency was formerly in North Fylde, which had a Conservative majority of 22,000 in 1979. It is a fairly compact unit north of Blackpool, including the fishing port of Fleetwood, residential Thornton Cleveleys and Poulton-le-Fylde, and Preesall. Garstang Rural District has been transferred to the Lancaster seat, but this will remain a Tory constituency of great loyalty and permanence.

1981	% Own Occ	80.6	1979 core seat North Fylde		
1981	% Loc Auth	12.1	C	36,366	60.8
1981	% Black/Asian	0.5	Lab	14,376	24.0
1981	% Mid Cl	51.1	L	8,630	14.4
1981	% Prof Man	16.8	NF	481	0.8
1982	electorate 66,522		MPs since 1950		
1979	notional result		1950-66 R.O. Stanley C		
	C 15,300		1966- Walter Clegg C		
Alliance					

Blaby

All three seats in Leicester were won by Labour in 1979. Rather like its fellow East Midlands city, Nottingham, this is due to the fact that a large proportion of the middle class suburbs lie outside the boundaries. The safe Conservative constituency of Blaby wraps itself around the south and west of Leicester in a kidney-shape, and extends south through open countryside to Lutterworth. The seat is unchanged by the Boundary Commission, and will remain a seat almost purpose-built for Conservatism - in this case personified by confident Cabinet Minister Nigel Lawson.

1981	% Own Occ	78	1979 same seat Blaby		
1981	% Loc Auth	14	C	33,221	58.1
1981	% Black/Asian	2	Lab	12,581	22.0
1981	% Mid Cl	54	L	9,277	16.2
1981	% Prof Man	19	NF	2,056	3.6
1982	electorate 72,017		MP since 1974		
Alliance		L	1974- Nigel Lawson C		

Bosworth

Bosworth is one of the constituencies which has shown a long-term swing to the Conservatives in the last thiry years, regardless of the movement of national preferences. Labour held the seat right through the years of the Tory governments of 1951 and 1964, but lost it in 1970 to Adam Butler (son of Rab), and have never recaptured it. For much of this time the Labour MP was the well-known right-wing warrior Woodrow Wyatt. But in 1979 it was Adam Butler who enjoyed a healthy majority of 8,435. Much of the decline of the Labour vote can probably be attributed to the reduction of the influence of the old Leicestershire coalfield, and the growth of new private housing around Hinckley.

Now the boundary changes should finally put Bosworth beyond Labour's reach. The best area for Labour was always Coalville, which was the mining centre its name implied. But Coalville is now transferred to the new NW Leicestershire seat, and Bosworth is reduced to just about the same boundaries as the local authority of Hinckley-Bosworth. The only rural ward which votes Labour is the mining village of Bagworth; and Hinckley itself is a growing Conservative town of 55,000 people.

Coalville's removal reduces Bosworth's inflated electorate of 90,000 by nearly 25,000. It also removes nearly every ward which voted Labour in 1979, and this should increase Adam Butler's majority by a good 5,000. It seems very likely that the onward march of history in this west Leicestershire seat means that there will be no more close battles in Bosworth.

1981	% Own Occ	74.2	1979 core seat Bosworth		
1981	% Loc Auth	18.8	C	37,030	48.5
1981	% Black/Asian	0.7	Lab	28,595	37.5
1981	% Mid Cl	42.3	L	10,032	13.1
1981	% Prof Man	15.5	NF	682	0.9
1982	electorate 72,627		MPs since 1945		
1979	notional result		1945-59 A.C. Allen Lab		
	C 14,800		1959-70 Woodrow Wyatt Lab		
Alliance		SDP	1970- Adam Butler C		

Harborough

In the last parliamentary redistribution in the early 1970s it was found necessary to create an extra seat in south Leicestershire as Harborough's electorate had reached 103,000 at the 1979 Election. The new seat of Blaby was carved out of the western half of Harborough, leaving Harborough as the SE Leicestershire county division. But the boundaries at this end of the county seem to have been sorted out satisfactorily, for neither Blaby nor Harborough are altered at all in the most recent redistribution. The Commissioners have switched their attention to the northern end of the county, where an extra seat is awarded.

Harborough is a safe Conservative seat. It includes some urban areas - the middle-class owner-occupier Oadby, and the more mixed Wigston - and much rolling Leicestershire countryside around Market Harborough. John Farr has been MP for over 20 years and enjoyed a majority of nearly 22,000 in 1979. This formula - a mixture of affluent Leicester suburbs and rural areas - seems likely to create at least three ultra-safe Conservative seats (Blaby, Harborough and Rutland-Melton), an interesting counterbalance to the three Labour inclined seats in Leicester itself. There is also a contrast between the nearly all-white suburbs and the city, which is over 20% non-white (mainly Asian) - which strengthens the Conservatism of such areas as Oadby, just beyond the Leicester city boundaries.

Labour can only compete in the central area of Wigston, and the Liberals finished in third place in Harborough last time. There is no evidence that the SDP will have any appeal here, so it seems a foregone conclusion that John Farr will be elected for the eighth successive time.

1981	% Own Occ	78	1979 same seat Harborough		
1981	% Loc Auth	14	C	33,328	60.4
1981	% Black/Asian	3	Lab	11,350	20.6
1981	% Mid Cl	52	L	9,529	17.3
1981	% Prof Man	19	NF	1,002	1.8
1982	electorate 72,352		MPs since 1945		
Alliance		L	1945-50 H.C. Attewell Lab		
			1950-59 J.M. Baldock C		
			1959- John Farr C		

Leicester East

Tom Bradley was first elected as Labour MP for Leicester NE in a byelection in 1962. When Leicester was reduced from four to three seats in 1974, he was returned for Leicester East. In 1979 he suffered from a swing of only 1.3% to the Conservatives, and held on when other Labour seats of similar marginality were falling elsewhere in the Midlands. Bradley had served the Labour Party well; he was a member of their NEC and had been Chairman of the Party in 1975-6. But in 1981 he defected to the Social Democrats on their foundation, and he intends to contest Leicester East as an Alliance candidate at the next Election. This may well turn the constituency into a three-way marginal.

The old textile town of Leicester has become known since the Second World War as one of the centres of Asian immigration to Britain. After the first wave from the Asian sub-continent in the 1950s and 1960s, there was a particular boost after General Amin expelled the Ugandan Asians in 1972. Many found their way from East Africa to Leicester, and settled in the privately-rented and owner-occupied terraces of the centre of the town. Both Leicester South and East divisions were around 26% non-white at the time of the 1981 Census. This certainly helps to account for Leicester's unusual warmth towards the Labour Party in the 1979 Election.

Leicester East undergoes only minor boundary changes. There is as yet no clue about Bradley's chances of holding the seat for the SDP, for there have been no local elections in Leicester since the Alliance's formation in 1981. The Labour candidate is Patricia Hewitt, of the National Council for Civil Liberties. Traditionally Labour have done best in the inner-city wards like Charnwood and Latimer, while the Conservatives have fought back in outer residential suburbs like Evington. The Tories might be strong enough even to win if the Asian vote and the anti-government vote is split between Labour and the SDP.

1981	% Own Occ	53	1979 core seat Leicester East
1981	% Loc Auth	35	Lab 23,844 46.9
1981	% Black/Asian	26	C 20,988 41.3
1981	% Mid Cl	38	L 4,623 9.1
1981	% Prof Man	12	NF 1,385 2.7
1982	electorate 68,036		MP since 1974
1979	notional result		1974- Tom Bradley Lab (SDP)
	Lab 2,700		
Alliance		SDP	

Leicester South

Leicester South was one of the half-dozen constituencies which swung to Labour at the last election, giving a much needened boost to Jim Marshall's fragile majority - 1,133 in October 1974. Marshall had gained South from the Tories in that election, and in many ways it is surprising that Labour have been able to win the seat at all. Here are the best residential areas within Leicester itself, especially in Knighton ward. Mansions line the A6 as it leaves Leicester on its way south-east towards Market Harborough. The former Leicester SE, which was abolished in 1974, was safely Conservative.

Yet there is another face to Leicester South. It contains the city centre, and a sizeable proportion of Leicester's Asian community - over a quarter of the constituency's population in 1981, a figure which had substantially increased in the 1970s. The innermost wards, such as Wycliffe, are sufficient to counteract the vote of Knighton and the other leafy suburbs. There are council estates in Aylestone, in the SW of the division. Leicester South is the most middle-class and the most heavily owner-occupied of the three seats within the city - but all three look like rejecting the Conservative Party once again next time. One of the Tories' problems is that most of the affluent suburbs are outside the city boundaries, in Leicestershire County constituencies.

Leicester has real racial tensions. But so far at least the solidity and discipline of the Asian vote has benefited Labour - the turnout is quite high and very reliable. There has not been much sign of a white reaction in electoral terms at least, although the National Front did well in Leicester local elections in the early 1970s. Leicester was certainly one of Britain's urban pressure-cookers, and serious trouble may come unless an improvement is made in racial integration and relations. Its political preferences will continue to be closely scrutinised, and it will remain one of the hardest districts to predict, electorally, as we pass into the 1980s.

1981	% Own Occ	54	1979 core seat Leicester South		
1981	% Loc Auth	27	Lab	24,548	46.4
1981	% Black/Asian	26	C	22,550	42.6
1981	% Mid Cl	42	L	4,856	9.2
1981	% Prof Man	14	NF	940	1.8
1982	electorate 74,879		MPs since 1974		
1979	notional result		1974	Tom Boardman C	
	Lab 3,600		1974-	James Marshall Lab	
Alliance		L			

Leicester West

Leicester West is the 'council-estate' seat in the East Midlands city. It also has the fewest non-white residents by far; this is not entirely unconnected, for Asians prefer to live together in owner-occupied or privately rented houses rather than dispersed among council estates, and in any case they rarely collect enough housing points to qualify for local authority accommodation. Leicester West is also the safest Labour seat of the three in the city, although it did demonstrate a slightly larger swing to the right in 1979.

The MP is a senior Labour backbencher, the Jewish barrister Greville Janner. The seat has been in the family for a long time – its predecessor Leicester NW had been held by Greville's father Barnett Janner since 1945. When Greville was adopted on his father's retirement in 1970, some thought that pressure may have been applied to secure the hereditary succession. But there is no doubt that Greville Janner has been a lively, active, competent and popular member for Leicester West.

Like the other Leicester seats, West is little altered by the Boundary Commission. It is a mixture of peripheral private estates and local authority developments, the latter predominating. Janner should be safe in West, which is Leicester's only safe seat; the SDP have the Alliance nomination, but they will probably concentrate their efforts in the city on preserving Tom Bradley's position in the East division.

1981	% Own Occ	42	1979 core seat Leicester West		
1981	% Loc Auth	45	Lab	26,032	53.6
1981	% Black/Asian	12	C	17,194	35.4
1981	% Mid Cl	36	L	4,032	8.3
1981	% Prof Man	10	NF	1,308	2.7
1982	electorate 68,615		MP since 1974		
1979	notional result		1974–	Greville Janner Lab	
	Lab 7,400				
Alliance		SDP			

Loughborough

Despite the continuation of the name, the newly drawn Loughborough seat is very different from the old. Almost the only part in common is the town of Loughborough itself. The constituency used to be completed by the bulk of the Leicestershire coalfield which is now in the brand-new NW Leics division. This was the keystone of Labour's victories in Loughborough from 1945 to 1974. But the territory which replaces the coalfield presents very different characteristics.

The valley of the River Soar, north of Leicester, contains many large suburban villages which stretch to the boundary of the city itself. All are solidly Conservative - Barrow upon Soar, Quorndon, Mountsorrell, Anstey, Sileby and the largest of all, Birstall. This Soar Valley district was previously in the Melton seat, which had a Conservative majority of over 24,000. Loughborough itself, also in Charnwood Borough, is still good ground for Labour. There is one middle-class Conservative residential ward, Burleigh, but much of this industrial engineering town consists of old terraces and large council estates. There is also a noticeable non-white presence. But Loughborough cannot outweigh the suburban and rural elements of the seat, and the Conservatives would probably have won the seat by well over 10,000 in 1979.

The Conservative victor in 1979 was Stephen Dorrell, the youngest MP in the new House, and one who quickly gained a reputation as one of the most moderate Conservatives. He defeated John Cronin, the representative of 25 years' standing. As in the case of Bosworth, it now seems that Labour can no longer hope to win Loughborough back, although they have the consolation of knowing that the discarded parts of the two seats have been brought together to create a new Labour constituency, NW Leicestershire.

1981	% Own Occ	71	1979 core seat Loughborough			
1981	% Loc Auth	19	C	29,788	48.0	
1981	% Black/Asian	4	Lab	24,589	39.6	
1981	% Mid Cl	50	L	6,650	10.7	
1981	% Prof Man	20	E	595	1.0	
1982	electorate 70,771		NF	484	0.8	
1979	notional result		MPs since 1945			
	C 10,100		1945-55 M. Follick Lab			
Alliance		SDP	1955-79 John Cronin Lab			
			1979-	Stephen Dorrell C		

North-West Leicestershire

NW Leicestershire seems at first sight to be an attempt to create a Labour seat in rural Leicestershire, despite the fact that their support in the area has been declining in recent years. From their point of view, the better parts of Bosworth and Loughborough - both Conservative gains in the 1970s - have been gathered together in a new constituency based on the declining Leicestershire coalfield. In fact the Boundary Commission has not acted in a politically partisan manner, of course. They have simply based this extra Leicestershire seat on the local government district of NW Leics, which forms the whole of the seat with the addition of the small town of Shepshed in Charnwood Borough.

Coalville will be the largest town in the new constituency. As in other coalfields, mining communities in Leicestershire are generally small, and the old Coalville Urban District included the villages of Whitwick, Ellistown and Thringstone. Again as in other coalfields, it should not be assumed that villages are necessarily Conservative. There is a tradition of industrial villages along the Leicestershire/Warwickshire border, and NW Leics is very similar in many ways to another new seat, not far away, North Warwickshire. The Conservative parts of the NW Leics seat include a historic small town, Ashby de la Zouch, and the area around Castle Donington, the site of the East Midlands airport. Shepshed is marginal.

Labour would definitely have won NW Leics in 1979, even though it was a very bad year for the party. But the number employed by the coalfield is gradually being reduced, and the long-term swing to the Tories in this district may eventually be resumed.

1981	% Own Occ	66.2	New seat
1981	% Loc Auth	25.2	
1981	% Black/Asian	0.5	
1981	% Mid Cl	40.1	
1981	% Prof Man	15.4	
1982	electorate 68,791		
1979	notional result		
	Lab 800		
Alliance		L	

Rutland and Melton

The smallest county in England, Rutland, lost its administrative independence when it was absorbed into Leicestershire in 1974. But it had already been associated with another county for parliamentary purposes, in the shape of the constituency of Rutland and Stamford (Lincolnshire). Now this arrangement has had to be revised, and Rutland (still a local government District) is now tied to Melton Mowbray.

Melton already had an electorate of 87,000 in 1979, when Tory Michael Latham won a 24,000 majority. But it makes room for Rutland by losing most of the suburban Soar Valley to Loughborough, although it retains the big villages of Thurmaston, Syston, East Gosford and Queniborough. So this NE Leicestershire seat contains varied countryside stretching from the very edge of the city of Leicester past the industrial and market town of Melton Mowbray to the pleasant rolling countryside of the Leicestershire Wolds and the Vale of Belvoir.

There has been much controversy over the plan to open up a new coalfield in the northernmost tip of rural Leicestershire near the Duke of Rutland's seat of Belvoir and not far from Mrs Thatcher's home town of Grantham, Lincolnshire. Even if mining - and miners - do come to disturb the fox-hunting and quiet of the Vale, the political impact on Rutland and Melton would be negligible. The constituency is still monolithically Tory. The Leicester suburbs are as Conservative in this constituency as in other points of the compass. Rutland and rural Leicestershire are prosperous farming areas, and feudal elements survive. The small towns of Melton Mowbray, Oakham and Uppingham were all Conservative even in the 1981 County Council elections when Labour enjoyed their best year in recent times.

1981	% Own Occ	65.1	1979 core seat Melton		
1981	% Loc Auth	19.4	C	40,242	58.6
1981	% Black/Asian	1	Lab	15,882	23.1
1981	% Mid Cl	44.3	L	12,596	18.3
1981	% Prof Man	17.8	MPs since 1945		
1982	electorate 75,478		1945-56 H.A. Nutting C		
1979	notional result		1956-74 Miss Mervyn Pike C		
	C 19,700		1974- Michael Latham C		
Alliance		L			

East Lindsey

East Lindsey spills down from the prosperous hills of the Lincolnshire Wolds to the seaside resorts of the east coast. It is based on the constituency of Horncastle, but the eponymous town has been transferred along with Wragby and Woodhall Spa to join Gaisnborough. The numbers are made up by the inclusion of Louth, which has lost most of its own old constituency to Humberside county. East Lindsey is essentially NE Lincolnshire, and it contains a fair selection of the variety of types of terrain to be found within this big county.

The popular impression of Lincolnshire is that it is composed entirely of flat fields growing vegetables and flowers under a huge sky. But this is belied by the Wolds, a green hilly landscape of mixed and wealthy farming. The windswept and rather untidy towns of East Anglia are far away in spirit and in appearance from the affluent and elegant Louth, with its towering church spire. (In the nineteenth century Louth was known as the 'nest of rooks' because it was full of black-coated clergymen hiding from their rural parishes.) Meanwhile the resort towns of Skegness, Mablethorpe and Sutton-on-Sea form a mecca for Midlanders travelling east to the North Sea. They compensate for their flatness by making a virtue out of the 'bracing' winds off the sea.

Horncastle and Louth were both Conservative seats with a strong Liberal presence. The MPs have contrasting styles. Horncastle's Peter Tapsell is a highly intelligent, sophisticated and independent member who has never been a Minister. Louth's Michael Brotherton is a vocal right-winger, frequently figuring in the press with a quote and a reaction. Whichever Conservative contests East Lindsey next time should hold a lead over the Liberals, except in a disastrous year for the Government.

1981	% Own Occ	64	1979 core seat Horncastle		
1981	% Loc Auth	17	C	21,362	55.1
1981	% Black/Asian	0.5	L	10,833	28.0
1981	% Mid Cl	40	Lab	6,240	16.1
1981	% Prof Man	17	NF	319	0.8
1982	electorate 69,100		MPs since 1945		
1979	notional result		1945-66 Sir J.F.W. Maitland C		
	C 11,400		1966- Peter Tapsell C		
Alliance		L			

Gainsborough and Horncastle

In the north-western corner of Lincolnshire are to be found the District of West Lindsey and the parliamentary constituency of Gaisnborough. This, like much of Lincolnshire, seems rather a corner of England, off the beaten track and 'a long way round whichever way you go'. The Gainsborough seat hugs the eastern bank of the River Trent. The Trent is broad up here near its junction with the Humber, and with road bridges only every 10 or 15 miles the West Lindsey area is decidedly cut off.

Now in the boundary changes the low-lying Isle of Axholme at the north end of the constituency on the other (west) bank of the Trent is lost, for it is now in the county of Humberside. To make up the numbers, Gainsborough encroaches eastwards further into the hilly Lincolnshire Wolds to take a few thousand voters from East Lindsey District. These include the small towns of Wragby, Woodhall Spa and Horncastle. Horncastle is pretty much the centre of the Wolds, and it did give its name to a previous Lincolnshire constituency. Justly that name survives, coupled with Gainsborough in the title of this new seat.

Remote it may be, but the politics of Gainsborough were always interesting. Here the Liberals mounted a challenge to the right-wing Tory MP, fox-hunting Marcus Kimball. Labour did well in the south part of Gainsborough itself, an industrial town on the Trent, but the Liberals kept up a more sustained performance both in the flatlands of the Trent Valley and up on the Wolds. The new additions are not so good for the Liberals, particularly the little inland resort of Woodhall Spa, but then neither was the Isle of Axholme. In a breakthrough year for the Alliance, Gainsborough and Horncastle could provide one of the shock results of the Election, and in political terms at least this part of Lincolnshire will no longer be a forgotten land.

1981	% Own Occ	62	1979 core seat Gainsborough		
1981	% Loc Auth	20	C	24,040	46.4
1981	% Black/Asian	0.5	L	16,885	32.6
1981	% Mid Cl	40	Lab	10,335	19.9
1981	% Prof Man	16	Ind C	570	1.1
1982	electorate 67,088		MPs since 1945		
1979	notional result		1945-56 H.F.C Crookshank C		
	C 7,400		1956- Marcus Kimball C		
Alliance		L			

Grantham

Grantham made little impact on the national political scene
until it achieved a kind of fame as Margaret Thatcher's home
town. In a radio poll in the early 1980s it was voted (almost
certainly unfairly) Britain's most boring town. In the 1979
General Election, the Grantham constituency provided an
18,000 Conservative majority for Douglas Hogg, the son of
Quintin, Lord Hailsham. This seems only proper.

In fact the semi-industrial town of Grantham makes up under
a third of the electorate of this constituency, which covers
most of west central Lincolnshire. It used to stretch all the
way to the suburbs of Lincoln and curl around the county
town, but now North Hykeham, Bracebridge Heath,
Skellingthorpe and the other overgrown villages are more
logically included with Lincoln itself. This reduced the
Grantham electorate by 15,000, and leaves Grantham and
Sleaford as the main population centres, surrounded by
scores of villages in the mainly flat and fertile countryside of
agricultural Lincolnshire. There are Labour voters in the
Earlesfield and Harrowby wards of Grantham, and the little
town of Metheringham saw one of the isolated independent
social democratic successes in 1981, before the party had
officially been established.

But it is hard to see Grantham falling, unless Mrs Thatcher
herself should fall in a very big way indeed. Douglas Hogg
seems set for a political career as lengthy as his father's. His
predecessor was Joseph Godber, for some considerable time
the Minister of Agriculture - a very suitable post.
Lincolnshire has more seats in the list of the 50 with the most
employed in agriculture in England than any other county.
There are six, and Grantham is one of them.

1981	% Own Occ	57.7	1979 core seat Grantham
1981	% Loc Auth	26.2	C 36,697 55.5
1981	% Black/Asian	1	Lab 18,547 28.1
1981	% Mid Cl	40.0	L 10,852 16.4
1981	% Prof Man	14.5	MPs since 1945
1982	electorate 75,062		1945-50 W.D. Kendall Ind
1979	notional result		1950-51 E.M. Smith C
	C 15,200		1951-79 Joseph Godber C
Alliance		L	1979- Douglas Hogg C

Holland with Boston

In 1966 Labour were only 316 votes away from victory in the south-east Lincolnshire seat of Holland with Boston. But the Conservative MP Richard Body benefited from an enormous 8% swing in 1970, and another favourable swing in February 1974 even though Labour won the General Election. By 1979 Body's majority had increased to 17,500. There are fewer better examples of the collapse of Labour's vote in rural areas, although a similar long-term swing can be seen in Norfolk and in the Cornwall seat of Falmouth and Camborne.

Holland used to be the southernmost of Lincolnshire's three administrative parts - the others were Lindsey and Kesteven. It was named Holland because of its similarity to the flat monotony of the farming nation across the North Sea, and a large number of Dutch familes have done well here - Van de Bergh and Geest are two well-known names. Agriculture and related industries certainly do predominate, particularly vegetable production. There is no constituency in England with a greater proportion of workers employed on the land than Holland with Boston.

In the boundary changes the district around the flower-growing town of Spalding is removed, and the Holland/Boston electorate reduced by over 25,000. Labour is quite competitive in Boston Borough, but the Conservatives do very well in South Holland, both in the villages among the Fens and in small towns near the Wash like Holbeach and Long Sutton. In appearance this countryside is very un-English. Few of its inhabitants are wealthy. But the political party which proves most to its taste is English enough - the Conservative Party, which has increasingly found the agricultural regions fertile ground in recent years.

1981	% Own Occ	58.8
1981	% Loc Auth	30.2
1981	% Black/Asian	0.5
1981	% Mid Cl	39.6
1981	% Prof Man	15.1
1982	electorate 63,749	
1979	notional result	
	C 10,200	
Alliance	L	

1979 core seat Holland with Boston

C	35,440	55.5
Lab	17,908	28.1
L	10,480	16.4

MPs since 1945
1945-66 Sir H.W. Butcher C
1966- Richard Body C

Lincoln

Lincoln achieved a place in social democratic history in 1973, when its MP Dick Taverne resigned from the Labour Party and fought a triumphant byelection as an independent Democratic Labour candidate opposed to Labour's leftward drift. Taverne held his seat in the first General Election of 1974, and throughout the decade the Democratic Labour group was active in local Lincoln politics. Even in 1979 it may be surmised that the votes cast for a Dem Lab candidate let in the Conservative for the first Tory victory in the Lincoln constituency since 1935.

Indeed Lincoln's appearance is still reminiscent of a Labour seat. Thousands of tourists visit Lincoln's magnificent cathedral and castle set on a limestone ridge above the River Witham and the quaint streets of the old town below. But the view from the top of the ridge is of heavy engineering industry and terraced housing below to the south, and there are sprawling council estates behind the cathedral to the north. Lincoln has returned to its Labour allegiance in local elections in the early 1980s, and if the seat were to be fought on unchanged boundaries next time the tenure of first-term Conservative MP Kenneth Carlisle would look shaky indeed.

But help has arrived in the form of the middle-class suburbs beyond Lincoln's boundaries, in Grantham constituency and North Kesteven District. These are now added to the city they serve, which might add around 3,000 to Kenneth Carlisle's majority of just 602. It might be thought that a threat might also come from the SDP. After all, Lincoln saw almost the beginning of the Long March of social democracy. But in fact that storm seems to have blown out, for in the 1982 local elections the Alliance was third in Lincoln with 24.5% of the vote, and didn't win a single ward. The new Lincoln should be a tight Lab-Con marginal, with the SDP nowhere in sight.

1981	% Own Occ	57.2	
1981	% Loc Auth	33.1	
1981	% Black/Asian	1	
1981	% Mid Cl	43.7	
1981	% Prof Man	12.4	
1982	electorate 73,391		
1979	notional result		
	C 3,800		
Alliance		SDP	

1979 core seat Lincoln

C	17,777	41.8
Lab	17,175	40.4
L	5,638	13.3
Dem Lab	1,743	4.1
Oths	184	0.5

MPs since 1945
1945-50 George Deer Lab
1950-62 Geoffrey de Freitas Lab
1962-74 Dick Taverne Lab (Dem Lab)
1974-79 Margaret Jackson Lab
1979- Kenneth Carlisle C

Stamford and Spalding

The new SW Lincolnshire seat has had to be cobbled together. The soft rolling countryside around the prosperous and multi-spired town of Stamford had previously been associated with Rutland, but the smallest county has passed into Leicestershire for the purposes of administration and of parliamentary representation. It has been replaced by Spalding, famed for its flower festival, from the flat lands further to the east towards the Fens and the Wash, in the old Lincolnshire parts of Holland.

Lincolnshire is noted for its early, albeit inconsistent, tendency to favour the Social Democratic ideal. Dick Taverne was elected in the historic 1973 byelection at Lincoln, and Democratic Labour candidates were active in Lincoln city politics for many years subsequently. A crucial intervention was made at Brigg and Scunthorpe in the north of the county (now Humberside) by an independent Social Democrat in the 1979 General Election. In the 1981 Lincolnshire County Council elections independent Social Democrats won two wards even before the launch of the Social Democrats as an official campaigning party. These two victories came not in Lincoln or Scunthorpe, but in other parts of the county - at Metheringham in the Fens and in Spalding NW.

The Social Democrats are still very active in Spalding, and do indeed have the nomination for Stamford and Spalding for the Alliance. But nevertheless the new seat should remain safe for Kenneth Lewis, Tory MP for Rutland and Stamford since 1959.

1981	% Own Occ	60.8	1979 core seat Rutland and
1981	% Loc Auth	27.5	Stamford
1981	% Black/Asian	0.5	C 26,198 56.5
1981	% Mid Cl	44.5	Lab 11,383 24.5
1981	% Prof Man	17.5	L 8,801 19.0
1982	electorate 65,890		MPs since 1945
1979	notional result		1945-50 Lord Willoughby de
	C 16,100		Eresby C
Alliance		SDP	1950-59 Sir R.E.J. Conant C
			1959- Kenneth Lewis C

Great Yarmouth

Great Yarmouth is the largest holiday resort and the largest
working port in Norfolk. It is a ferry centre for travel to
Northern Europe and a base for North Sea oil and gas
exploitation. Yarmouth itself is also known for a solid Labour
vote. In 1981 Labour won six of the seven county council
wards in the town. Even in 1979, when Labour lost the
General Election, they held their own in Yarmouth, winning
the Lichfield/Cobholm, Magdalen, Nelson, Shrublands and
South wards comfortably. Labour held the Yarmouth seat in
Parliament from 1945 to 1951, and 1966 to 1970.

It is not the town of Yarmouth itself which has kept
Conservative Anthony Fell as MP here for most of the last
thirty plus years, but the villages of the coast and the rural
hinterland. Now the boundary changes are to reduce their
influence. A few villages which were previously in Suffolk are
brought in - Bradwell, Hopton and Burgh Castle, for
example. But a considerable portion of the old Blofield and
Flegg Rural District is lost to the Broadland local government
District, and the Mid Norfolk constituency. Now the Great
Yarmouth seat is to be identical to the Borough of the same
name, which means that its electorate is about 13,000 smaller
than previously.

Anthony Fell, the New Zealand born member for Yarmouth, is
retiring at the next Election. In a good year, Labour must
have a better chance than before of taking Great Yarmouth,
now that the town itself plays a greater role in the seat
named after it. The Liberals have had some local success, but
lost their deposit at the last General Election, and seem likely
to be squeezed into third place again next time.

1981	% Own Occ	61.6	1979 core seat Yarmouth		
1981	% Loc Auth	28.5	C	28,066	50.4
1981	% Black/Asian	1.0	Lab	20,838	37.4
1981	% Mid Cl	44.0	L	6,112	11.0
1981	% Prof Man	16.4	NF	640	1.2
1982	electorate 63,076		MPs since 1945		
1979	notional result		1945-51 E. Kinghorn Lab		
	C 1,700		1951-66 Anthony Fell C		
Alliance		L	1966-70 Hugh Gray Lab		
			1970- Anthony Fell C		

Mid Norfolk

In 1974 Norfolk lost a parliamentary seat when Central Norfolk was abolished, sending Ian Gilmour off in search of a new constituency. Now Norfolk regains its 8-strong delegation, and again there is to be a seat which almost surrounds Norwich, and touches neither the sea nor Norfolk's boundary with any other county. Mid Norfolk is its name, and it takes rural inland territory from Yarmouth, North and SW Norfolk. It includes part of the Broads, and one or two small towns from East Dereham across the interior of the big county to Acle. Like the old Central Norfolk, it will be safely Conservative, even though now no affluent Norwich suburbs are included.

1981	% Own Occ	68.6	New seat
1981	% Loc Auth	18.1	
1981	% Black/Asian	1	
1981	% Mid Cl	48.4	
1981	% Prof Man	18.5	
1982	electorate 68,581		
1979	notional result		
	C 14,800		
Alliance		SDP	

North Norfolk

Norfolk had the rare distinction of being an agricultural seat electing a Labour MP from 1945 to 1970. But then farm-workers' union official Bert Hazell was beaten, and in 1974 a number of Tory middle-class Norwich suburbs were added from the old Central Norfolk. Now the suburbs are removed again, but no-one would suggest that the new North Norfolk will be vulnerable to Labour, whose East Anglian rural vote has collapsed very rapidly. This seat also includes a stretch of the holiday coast around Cromer and Sheringham, and part of the Norfolk Broads. Ralph Howell should hold it easily.

1981	% Own Occ	59.3	1979 core seat North Norfolk		
1981	% Loc Auth	22.3	C	43,952	56.9
1981	% Black/Asian	0.7	Lab	22,126	28.6
1981	% Mid Cl	40.8	L	10,643	13.8
1981	% Prof Man	17.5	NF	548	0.7
1982	electorate 65,125		MPs since 1945		
1979	notional result		1945-64 E.G. Gooch Lab		
	C 12,000		1964-70 Bert Hazell Lab		
Alliance		SDP	1970- Ralph Howell C		

North-West Norfolk

The only Conservative MP who defected to the Social Democrats was Christopher Brocklebank-Fowler of North West Norfolk. His chances of political survival seem slender. NW Norfolk was based on the former King's Lynn seat, which Labour won in good years like 1945 and 1950, and 1964 and 1966. But the Conservatives have done increasingly well in rural Norfolk. When Brocklebank-Fowler first won the seat for the Tories in 1970, his majority was just 33. By 1979 the lead had increased to 8,000, and not just because of boundary changes.

In the present redistribution, NW Norfolk loses about 20,000 electors in all, mainly around Walsingham and Wells-next-the-Sea, which are transferred to North Norfolk. This will improve Labour's chances, for their strength is concentrated in King's Lynn. Lynn is an industrial town, as well as a port which was once the third most important in the nation. The prosperous town houses in the centre of Lynn still give evidence of its affluent past, but now it has taken in much overspill population from London. Like other East Anglian ports (Lowestoft and Great Yarmouth), King's Lynn usually gives a majority of its votes to Labour. In 1981 Labour took all four county council seats. The Conservatives do well in the holiday resort of Hunstanton, in the orbit of royal influence around Sandringham, and in the wind-blown agricultural villages of west Norfolk, where cereals and sugar beet form the base of the economy.

Brocklebank-Fowler seems to be in great danger of being squeezed out in this Conservative-Labour marginal. It is unclear if he will split the Tory vote – he is after all a unique case. One imagines that the Conservative support will hold together well, which should make the Government favourites to win NW Norfolk next time.

1981	% Own Occ	59
1981	% Loc Auth	25
1981	% Black/Asian	0.7
1981	% Mid Cl	40
1981	% Prof Man	17
1982	electorate 69,038	
1979	notional result	
	C 6,100	

Alliance   SDP

1979 core seat North-West Norfolk

C	33,796	51.0
Lab	25,868	39.0
L	6,588	9.9

MPs since 1945
1945-51 F.J. Wise Lab
1951-59 R. Scott-Miller C
1959-64 D.G. Bullard C
1964-70 Derek Page Lab
1970- Christopher
        Brocklebank-Fowler C (SDP)

Norwich North

The City of Norwich has remained remarkably loyal to the Labour Party. In 1979, when the Conservatives won the General Election easily, Labour retained both Norwich parliamentary seats and won 39 of the 48 seats on the city council. There are two reasons for this unusually strong showing. One is that Norwich has a very high proportion of council housing: over 50% within the city council area in 1981. The other is that a considerable part of the owner-occupied middle-class Tory-voting districts of Norwich actually lie outside the city boundaries in Broadland District. These suburbs are at present in the North Norfolk seat, which reached an electorate of over 98,000 in 1979. The two Norwich seats, on the other hand, were distinctly under-sized.

Now, however, Sprowston, Thorpe St Andrew and Hellesdon are to be incorporated in a compact Norwich North constituency, together with five Labour-voting wards from the present North seat. This will prove a close and fascinating contest. About 30,000 electors, or half of the new seat, live in the working-class northern fringes of the city. One can see the serried rows of council houses from Mousehold Heath, once the scene of Robert Ket's famous rebellion in 1549. This is the core of David Ennals's current Norwich N constituency, the safest Labour seat in East Anglia. But the suburbs are also 30,000 strong, and previously contributed to Ralph Howell's 22,000 Tory majority in N Norfolk. However, not all of Sprowston, Thorpe St Andrew and Hellesdon is affluent, even if it is mainly composed of private housing, and in an even year Labour would probably be competitive.

The inclusion of the Broadland wards in a Norwich city seat is logical – they are in its social and economic gravitational field. But nevertheless it has the effect of making the new North more marginal even than the Norwich S seat. The two disparate halves of the constituency will battle it out for political victory around Mousehold Heath.

1981	% Own Occ	58.4	1979 core seat Norwich North		
1981	% Loc Auth	33.8	Lab	17,927	50.8
1981	% Black/Asian	1	C	12,336	34.9
1981	% Mid Cl	46.5	L	4,253	12.0
1981	% Prof Man	13.0	E	334	0.9
1982	electorate 63,264		NF	250	0.7
1979	notional result		Oth	198	0.6
	C 3,500		MPs since 1950		
Alliance		L	1950-64 J. Paton Lab		
			1964-74 G. Wallace Lab		
			1974- David Ennals Lab		

Norwich South

Through much of the medieval period, Norwich was the second city of England. Since that time it has been overtaken by many others in population, but it remains an important provincial centre. The fine cathedral and town houses of the historic centre bear witness to its time as a wool trading town and rich commercial metropolis. Norwich South contains the city centre, the cathedral close, and also the University of East Anglia on the SW edge of Norwich. It also includes the one strongly Tory ward in the city, the top residential area of Eaton by the River Yare.

In the redistribution, this marginal seat moved further into the territory of the former safe Labour Norwich North: Bowthorpe, Heigham and Thorpe Hamlet are transferred between the two Norwich seats. South now incorporates over two-thirds of the City of Norwich, 11 of its 16 wards. In the past it has tended to swing with the national tide - it was Conservative between 1950-64 and 1970-74. But Labour MP John Garrett did well to hold on by 1,000 votes in 1979, and his position will be further strengthened by the boundary changes.

Municipally, Norwich is a strongly pro-Labour city, apparently proud of its local authority's activity, with its extensive council estates and cheap public transport. The odds must be that it will again return two Labour MPs next time. The SDP have the Alliance nomination for the South seat (the Liberals take the North). But the SDP only polled 26% in the 1982 local elections in Norwich South, and the Alliance failed to win a single ward in the city - the pattern of 13 Labour wards and three Conservative remained unshaken.

1981	% Own Occ	37.2	1979 core seat Norwich South
1981	% Loc Auth	51.2	Lab 16,282 44.9
1981	% Black/Asian	1	C 15,042 41.6
1981	% Mid Cl	48.5	L 4,618 12.8
1981	% Prof Man	14.8	NF 264 0.7
1982	electorate 64,987		MPs since 1950
1979	notional result		1950-55 H.G. Strauss C
	Lab 2,800		1955-64 Geoffrey Rippon C
Alliance		SDP	1964-70 C. Norwood Lab
			1970-74 Tom Stuttaford C
			1974- John Garrett Lab

South Norfolk

South Norfolk is a constituency which had undergone a transformation since the last war. As in many other rural Norfolk seats, Labour had a strong presence here through the 1950s and 1960s. Christopher Mayhew (in the 1970s a Liberal) had represented South Norfolk for Labour from 1945 to 1950, then the Conservatives won it six consecutive times with a majority of less than 3,500. There was a change of Conservative MP: in 1955 the courtly, charming John Hill replaced P.A.D. Baker, who was expelled from the House and sentenced to seven years' imprisonment for uttering forged documents. But Hill himself won paper-thin majorities for year after year in an agricultural seat of little over 40,000 electors.

But in the 1970s the situation changed dramatically. The seat was enlarged in the 1974 boundary changes. Thetford was designated an industrial boom town and overspill area for London. By 1979 the electorate was over 100,000; and the present Tory MP John MacGregor enjoyed a 19,000 majority. Clearly the strength of the Labour Party, based on the agricultural workers' union, had collapsed.

Equally clearly the seat had to be reduced in size, and in the new revision of boundaries Thetford and the Wayland Rural District departed into Breckland District and the SW Norfolk constituency. The seat is left as identical to the South Norfolk District, based on the small towns of Diss and Wymondham and the rural districts of Depwade, Forehoe/Henstead and Loddon near the Suffolk border. S Norfolk should remain safely Conservative, for Labour's appeal in rural East Anglia has in all probability gone for ever.

1981	% Own Occ	67.9
1981	% Loc Auth	20.0
1981	% Black/Asian	0.7
1981	% Mid Cl	50.9
1981	% Prof Man	19.5
1982	electorate 73,377	
1979	notional result	
	C 14,500	
Alliance		L

1979 core seat South Norfolk

C	42,792	54.5
Lab	23,755	30.2
L	11,990	15.3

MPs since 1945
1945-50 C. Mayhew Lab
1950-54 P.A.D. Baker C
1954-74 John Hill C
1974- John MacGregor C

South-West Norfolk

SW Norfolk has one of the most extraordinary and interesting post-war electoral histories in the country. Indeed the political writer R.W. Johnson found it possible to write an article about this one seat in the journal Parliamentary Affairs in 1972. The facts are remarkable. Seven times between 1945 and 1966 the majority of the winning candidate in SW Norfolk was less than 1,000. Four times the seat swung against the national trend. There is a saying - 'Norfolk do different'. In politics, at least, SW Norfolk certainly did.

Sidney Dye won the seat by 53 votes in 1945, held it by 260 in 1950, but lost it to Tory D.G. Bullard by 442 the next year. Dye regained it - by 193 - in 1955, but on his death in 1959 the new Labour candidate A.V. Hilton increased the majority to a princely 1,354. In the General Election of the same year, though, Hilton's lead was reduced to 78, and in 1964 Paul Hawkins gained the seat for the Tories (against the tide) by 123. Hawkins has held it ever since - by 775 in 1966, and steadily increasing his majority to its present level of nearly 11,000. SW Norfolk is a clearer example than any other of the fading of rural radicalism in Norfolk, for its boundaries have not altered since 1950.

Now, however, Thetford and a large part of the lonely heath of Breckland is to come in from South Norfolk. Much of East Anglia resembles an armed camp, and this district is no exception. There is a large forbidden battle area north of Thetford, and big airfields adorn the flat countryside. The little towns of Swaffham, Downham Market and Watton vote Conservative nowadays, and the Thetford overspill estates will offer the only solid Labour support here now. Norfolk no longer 'do different' - politically it behaves much as any other part of rural England does.

1981	% Own Occ	60	1979 core seat South-West		
1981	% Loc Auth	26	Norfolk		
1981	% Black/Asian	1	C	14,767	54.8
1981	% Mid Cl	40	Lab	14,063	31.1
1981	% Prof Man	17	L	6,363	14.1
1982	electorate 70,945		MPs since 1945		
1979	notional result		1945-51 S. Dye Lab		
	C 10,600		1951-55 D.G. Bullard C		
Alliance		L	1955-59 S. Dye Lab		
			1959-64 A.V. Hilton Lab		
			1964- Paul Hawkins C		

Corby

For many years Corby has seemed like a striking anomaly in the East Midlands county of Northamptonshire. In the inter-war years the town boomed almost from nothing as steelworks were constructed to exploit the local resources of iron ore. Many workers came down from industrial Scotland, migrating from the grime of Clydeside to rural Northants. Then in 1950 Corby was designated as a government-sponsored New Town, and its population further expanded to its present level of over 50,000. Recently however Corby has been submerged under the pall of a deep depression as the steelworks suffered decline and closure, and unemployment was running at 27% in 1981. It has been said that Corby is in danger of becoming a ghost town.

As a steelworking district and a New Town, it is scarcely surprising that Corby is the Labour stronghold in Northants. Since the war it has kept the Kettering seat Labour, although by only 1,478 votes in 1979. Now it has a constituency of its own – or not quite, for the new Corby has over 23,000 electors from East Northants District as well as the 37,000 of Corby itself. Corby is as Labour as ever, but East Northants includes much of the rural north of the county, such as the countryside around the prosperous town of Oundle, which is the site of a well-known public school and the heart of hunting territory. The only Labour district in the East Northants section is the small town of Irthlingborough.

Overall it can be calculated that Corby itself would have produced a Labour majority of about 5,000 in 1979, but that the East Northants wards voted Conservative by between 4,000 and 5,000. As before, Corby is nearly swamped by Tory terrain, but just manages to tip the balance for Labour as it did in Kettering. In the prevailing climate of high unemployment and economic difficulties, it is hard to see Corby doing anything other than swinging to Labour next time.

1981	% Own Occ	41.4	New seat
1981	% Loc Auth	52.8	
1981	% Black/Asian	1	
1981	% Mid Cl	37.6	
1981	% Prof Man	13.0	
1982	electorate 63,461		
1979	notional result		
	Lab 400		
Alliance		L	

Daventry

When Reg Prentice left the Labour Party during the 1974-79 Parliament he did not trifle with Liberals, social democrats or centrist notions of any kind - he crossed the floor to become a Conservative MP. Not surprisingly he did not stand as a Tory in his Newham NE seat in the 1979 General Election, but managed to find a rock-solid Conservative constituency distant from East London in every way: Daventry, south Northants. He was duly elected with a majority of over 21,000, and joined Mrs Thatcher's front bench team. But his Tory ministerial career did not last long, and he returned to the back benches, retaining his ironclad Conservative seat in hunting country in the shires.

His majority should be reduced next time, if only because the seat loses a third of its 90,000 electorate in the boundary changes. The old Daventry included a good half of the acreage of Northants, curling almost completely around Northampton itself, in addition to incorporating the southern half of the county. Now the northernmost part, around Brixworth, goes to Kettering, and the suburban belt near Northampton around Roade and Blisworth goes to Northampton South. What is left is a mixture of South Northants and Daventry Districts. Daventry is an expanding overspill town, with sprawling new housing estates and a confusing major road structure. Nowhere else is any real Labour strength to be found, not in the villages nor in the small towns like Brackley and Towcester.

It is unclear what the future shape of Reg Prentice's career might be, whether he will return to the public eye or remain becalmed in a backwater of politics. But at least he need have little fear of the Labour Party any more, for they continue to pose no threat in Daventry.

1981	% Own Occ	60.4	1979 core seat Daventry		
1981	% Loc Auth	28.5	C	41,422	56.6
1981	% Black/Asian	1	Lab	19,939	27.3
1981	% Mid Cl	48.8	L	11,286	15.4
1981	% Prof Man	20.0	NF	522	0.7
1982	electorate 63,730		MPs since 1945		
1979	notional result		1945-62 Sir R.E. Manningham-		
	C 13,100			Buller C	
Alliance		SDP	1962-79 Arthur Jones C		
			1979- Reg Prentice C		

Kettering

The constituency named Kettering has been Labour since 1945, and usually considered safe; but this will no longer be the case as Labour's mainstay of Corby has been removed and put into a separate seat. The Borough of Kettering remains, with an electorate of 50,000 - it would undoubtedly have given the Tories a majority in 1979 - and it is joined by ten thousand electors from the Daventry District and constituency, which is solidly Conservative.

Kettering itself has never been a Labour town. Unlike Corby, whose economy was perilously (and eventually disastrously) based on a single industry, Kettering has a variety of light industries. It is a prosperous commercial centre with a substantial middle class. Associated with it are a number of the small semi-industrial towns that are so common in central Northants - Burton Latimer, Desborough and Rothwell - and 23 villages near the Welland Valley. The main industries are engineering, clothing, footwear and ironstone quarrying, but there are agricultural districts too, and commuters, particularly in the Brixworth area taken from Daventry, which is handy for travel to Northampton.

The new Kettering seat would have voted Conservative even in Labour's best year in recent times, 1981. It should be ranked as a safe Tory seat. Without Corby, the whole character of the Kettering seat changes, socially, economically and politically. Sitting Labour MP Bill Homewood would be well advised to seek nomination for the Corby constituency. Although it might appear at first sight that the Labour Corby is the extra seat in Northants created by the redistribution, in fact the Conservatives should come out one seat to the good - for the way that Kettering changes hands outweighs the creation of Corby.

1981	% Own Occ	68.2	1979 core seat Kettering		
1981	% Loc Auth	23.7	Lab	31,579	45.0
1981	% Black/Asian	2	C	30,101	42.9
1981	% Mid Cl	46.9	L	8,424	12.0
1981	% Prof Man	12.9	MPs since 1945		
1982	electorate 62,733		1945-64 G.R. Mitchison Lab		
1979	notional result		1964-79 Sir Geoffrey de Freitas		
	C 8,800			Lab	
Alliance		SDP	1979- Bill Homewood Lab		

Northampton North

Northampton was one of the last places to be designated as a New Town, in 1968; yet unlike most New Towns, the subsequent arrival of overspill population and of swathes of modern local authority housing does not seem to have pushed the politics of Northampton towards Labour. Of course, Northampton was already a major county town of over 100,000 people, and not a green field site awaiting an entirely new community. But it was also held by Reginald Paget for Labour from 1945 to 1974. How did Northampton come to have two Conservative MPs in 1979?

Paget was something of an eccentric, a fox-hunting pro-hanging Labour MP on the far right of his own party. Northampton seems to go in for controversial MPs, for the Labour member for the North division after 1974's split was Maureen Colquhoun. She got into hot water with her local party and achieved notoriety for her professed lesbianism. There is evidence that the 8% swing which defeated her in North was partly due to personal unpopularity. Northampton gained a second seat in the early 1970s because of New Town growth, and North is the seat which contains most of it as it sprawls NE towards Wellingborough, north of the River Nene. Here we have hypermodern neighbourhoods like Lumbertubs and Thorplands, Ecton and Lings, swallowing up old villages and farmland. These nests of oddly shaped little boxes do tend to give Labour a slender majority; but North also includes some of the better residential areas of Northampton, in Abington and Park wards, and out in Welford. Only the older council estate of Dallington-Kings Heath, in the NW, really counts as a Labour stronghold.

Northampton never completed its planned growth, and its population now only justifies 1½ seats, so North is somewhat expanded, although it is the seat which remains entirely within the Borough. It would undoubtedly have voted last time for the present MP, Tony Marlow, one of the most vitriolic and vociferous right-wing Tories in the House. But with the removal of the Colquhoun factor, and the continued New Town growth, it must be very marginal.

1981	% Own Occ	60.0	1979 core seat Northampton		
1981	% Loc Auth	35.4	North		
1981	% Black/Asian	4	C	18,597	48.2
1981	% Mid Cl	47.2	Lab	13,934	36.1
1981	% Prof Man	12.9	L	5,659	14.7
1982	electorate 67,248		NF	373	1.0
1979	notional result		MPs since 1974		
	C 5,100		1974-79 Maureen Colquhoun Lab		
Alliance		L	1979- Tony Marlow C		

Northampton South

Labour never quite managed to win Northampton South after its creation in 1974, when Northampton was divided into two seats. They lost to Conservative Michael Morris by 179 votes in February 1974 and by 141 votes in October. On both occasions the Labour candidate was the unfortunate John Dilks, who had also lost to Dick Taverne in the 1973 Lincoln byelection, and who has never even yet entered Parliament.

Now it looks as if Labour never will take Northampton South, for this undersized constituency is to take in thirteen villages from the rural South Northants District, despite a rearguard action by the Labour Party at the boundary inquiry. The villages, like Roade and Kislingbury, are safely Conservative, and some of them house affluent commuters to the Northamptonshire county town. The urban part of the new Northampton South division does contain Labour wards like Castle in the town centre and the old council estates of Delapre, but also good residential areas like Weston Favell.

If Labour couldn't win the seat without the villages, it is hard to see them triumphing after their inclusion.

1981	% Own Occ	62.9	1979 core seat Northampton		
1981	% Loc Auth	28.5	South		
1981	% Black/Asian	5	C	19,125	49.7
1981	% Mid Cl	50.0	Lab	15,491	40.2
1981	% Prof Man	16.8	L	3,478	9.0
1982	electorate 67,324		NF	407	1.1
1979	notional result		MP since 1974		
	C 9,700		1974–	Michael Morris C	
Alliance		SDP			

Wellingborough

Wellingborough was held by Labour for all but five years between 1945 and 1969, throughout the Tory fifties, in fact. But Peter Fry then gained it at a byelection, and Labour has never won it back.

Now the seat loses 25,000 mainly rural, mainly Tory voters from the north of the county to the new Corby division, but even this is unlikely to make Wellingborough marginal again, never mind a Labour seat. Fry won by over 12,000 last time. Clearly the small towns of the division, Wellingborough, Rushden and Higham Ferrers are swinging towards the Tories on a long-term basis.

This development has occurred despite the fact that there is council as well as new private housing construction in the district, and a substantial non-white presence. Rushden and Wellingborough used to be primarily shoemaking and textile towns, but have now diversified into a variety of light industries. Wellingborough in particular is expanding, like its large neighbour Northampton, and new population and prosperity are being brought to an old industrial area. Peter Fry seems likely to continue to represent the smaller Wellingborough seat.

1981	% Own Occ	62.7	1979	core seat	Wellingborough	
1981	% Loc Auth	31.1	C	37,812	52.3	
1981	% Black/Asian	6	Lab	25,278	34.9	
1981	% Mid Cl	43.0	L	8,506	11.8	
1981	% Prof Man	14.6	NF	529	0.7	
1982	electorate 67,944		Ind	209	0.3	
1979	notional result		MPs since 1945			
	C 7,600		1945-59	G.S. Lindgren	Lab	
Alliance		L	1959-64	Michael Hamilton	C	
			1964-69	Harry Howarth	Lab	
			1969-	Peter Fry	C	

Berwick upon Tweed

For many years, the Liberal Chief Whip Alan Beith performed a skilful balancing act in Berwick upon Tweed. When he won the seat from the Tories in a byelection in November 1973, the Liberal revival of the early 1970s was already petering out into disappointment, and Beith only crept home by 57 votes. In the General Election of February 1974 his majority rose to a princely 443, but in October of that year it was reduced again, to 73 votes this time. After all this brinkmanship it was a genuine surprise when he romped home by over 5,000 in 1979, when the Tories won the General Election!

Given Beith's relative landslide at the last Election, he shouldn't be worried too much about gaining nearly 10,000 voters from Morpeth constituency in the boundary changes. Some of the villages transferred, like Chevington and Ellington, house enough miners to provide solid Labour support. Beith has already managed to squeeze the Labour vote in the small towns of this seat - Berwick, Alnwick and Amble - so he should welcome the arrival of electors from a Labour seat who might prefer him to the Tory candidate. Beith's position is now strong throughout Berwick constituency, despite the Tory influence of the Percy family of Alnwick Castle, and despite the tourist industry attracted by the dramatic coastline.

Berwick did have something of a Liberal tradition - Sir Edward Grey was the member from 1885 to 1916, and Sir William Beveridge was briefly MP here at the end of the war. But modern Liberalism in Berwick owes much to Alan Beith. Like so many Liberal MPs, it seems that once he had managed to enter Parliament at a byelection, he has been able to capitalise on his personal vote and to provide exceptional constituency services. He has already shown himself to be one of the great political survivors, and it would now be a major shock if he were actually to lose England's northernmost constituency.

1981	% Own Occ	37.3	1979 core seat Berwick	
1981	% Loc Auth	37.4	L 19,351	54.3
1981	% Black/Asian	0.3	C 13,663	38.4
1981	% Mid Cl	39.2	Lab 2,602	7.3
1981	% Prof Man	15.9	MPs since 1945	
1982	electorate 53,647		1945-51 R.A.F. Thorp C	
1979	notional result		1951-73 Lord Lambton C	
	L 5,300		1973- Alan Beith L	
Alliance		L		

Blyth Valley

Blyth is one of those constituencies which has become well known because of a close fight by an MP at odds with his party to keep his seat. Often when a Labour member is involved, the cause for the battle was ideological, as in the case of forerunners of the SDP like Dick Taverne of Lincoln. But at Blyth the independently-minded Eddie Milne was dropped by the local party before the February 1974 election in favour of a right-winger, Ivor Richard. Milne beat Richard as an Independent Labour candidate in February, but lost to another Labour QC, John Ryman, in October. Milne's vote did not fade rapidly, as has happened to some MPs who have persisted in seeking election. In 1979 he still polled 18,000 votes to take second place, and there is still a functioning Independent Labour Party in Blyth Valley District.

Blyth is one of those gritty northern towns of resolute and remorseless industrial aspect. The skyline is overshadowed by the power station, and by the coal mine and the dockyards. Bare council estates ring the town, which has very few middle-class roads. The constituency, tucked into the SE corner of Northumberland, also includes ex-mining villages like Seghill and Seaton Delaval. The most rapidly growing area is the private housing 'New Town' of Cramlington. Opinions about Cramlington are mixed, and despite the fact that the number of owner-occupied houses in Blyth Valley District doubled in the 1970s, little trace can be found of a movement to the Conservatives here. In the boundary changes, the working-class town of Bedlington is removed to Wansbeck constituency.

It is unclear whether the Independent Labour Party will again contest Blyth at the next General Election. Their appeal does seem to be fading, so Ryman should face fewer problems at their hands. Cramlington will play a more important role as it grows in a more compact seat. It may show the volatility associated with private housing estates and New Towns, and the Conservatives may well move into second place in Blyth Valley. But it is hard to see them ever approaching Labour in what is traditionally one of their strongest areas.

1981	% Own Occ	49.3	1979 core seat Blyth		
1981	% Loc Auth	43.6	Lab	25,047	40.1
1981	% Black/Asian	0.4	Ind Lab	17,987	28.8
1981	% Mid Cl	45.4	C	14,194	22.7
1981	% Prof Man	12.9	L	5,176	8.3
1982	electorate 58,030		MPs since 1950		
1979	notional result		1950-60 Alf Robens Lab		
	Lab 5,000 (RW)		1960-74 E. Milne Lab (Ind Lab)		
Alliance		SDP	1974- John Ryman Lab		

Hexham

Hexham is the single surviving Conservative constituency in Northumberland. The other rural seat, Berwick, fell to the Liberals in 1973, and south-east Northumberland is a heavily populated, industrial Labour stronghold typified by coal-mining and shipbuilding. But Hexham seems almost to be designed to gather together Tory voters.

The Upper Tyne Valley is predominantly argicultural, with market centres at the prosperous small towns of Hexham and Corbridge. The most complete section of the remains of Hadrian's Wall form a focus for tourism, together with the associated Roman forts. The only Labour support is to be found at the industrial enclave of Prudhoe. But Conservative votes pile up at the affluent residential Newcastle commuter base of Ponteland-Darras Hall, where nearly all of the houses are detached and owner occupied.

Hexham loses 15,000 mainly Labour voters around Wideopen and Newcastle Airport to Tyne and Wear county and Newcastle city seats. It will therefore be even safer in future for the sitting MP, former Minister Geoffrey Rippon.

1981	% Own Occ	56.5	1979 core seat Hexham			
1981	% Loc Auth	24.5	C	25,483	48.0	
1981	% Black/Asian	0.5	Lab	16,935	31.9	
1981	% Mid Cl	53.8	L	10,697	20.1	
1981	% Prof Man	23.8	MPs since 1945			
1982	electorate 54,474		1945-51 D. Clifton Brown C			
1979	notional result			(Speaker)		
	C 7,200		1951-66 R.M. Speir C			
Alliance		L	1966-	Geoffrey Rippon C		

Wansbeck

The new Wansbeck constituency is based on the old Morpeth,
but it is probably more appropriately named now. Morpeth is
an old market town on the A1 Great North Road, and it now
houses many affluent commuters to Newcastle. As such it is
marginal politically, and socially unlike the tough working-
class communities of the Northumberland coalfield nearby. The
seat is now to take its title from the River Wansbeck, and
from the local authority District of the same name.

Labour won Morpeth in every General Election after the
Second World War with great comfort. The Labour preferences
were determined by the presence of the large mining town of
Ashington, home of the footballing Charlton brothers, and
industrial Newbiggin by the coast, where retired pit ponies
graze by the sea. In the boundary changes, another rough-
hewn mining community, Bedlington, comes in from Blyth to
replace some villages lost to Berwick.

Wansbeck will be an even safer seat for Labour than Morpeth
was. In the late 1960s the career of Morpeth MP Will Owen
was clouded by (unproven) allegations that he had passed
information to the Soviet Union. But his successor George
Grant has sat quietly in the Commons since 1970, and seems
likely to continue to take his place among the battery of
Labour MPs from north-eastern mining seats.

1981	% Own Occ	42.1
1981	% Loc Auth	42.2
1981	% Black/Asian	0.4
1981	% Mid Cl	38.6
1981	% Prof Man	10.9
1982	electorate 63,987	
1979	notional result	
	Lab 18,400	
Alliance		L

1979 core seat Morpeth
Lab	21,744	56.3
C	9,913	25.7
L	6,972	18.0

MPs since 1950
1950-54 R.J. Taylor Lab
1954-70 Will Owen Lab
1970-   George Grant Lab

Ashfield

In 1977 the Nottinghamshire mining constituency of Ashfield sprung one of the greatest surprises in the history of British byelections. On the same day as Labour held a much more marginal seat at Grimsby, they lost a 23,000 majority to Conservative Tim Smith. The seat was regained for Labour by Frank Haynes in 1979, but an explanation for the byelection reverse is still sought. Was it a specific response to the departure of David Marquand to join Roy Jenkins at the EEC, and his replacement with another non-miner candidate? Or was it a result of some dramatic change in the political nature and anatomy of Ashfield?

At that time, Ashfield consisted of a slice of the older part of the Notts coalfield, set back to back with the Derbyshire border, over which lies Dennis Skinner's Bolsover fiefdom. Its three main towns were Sutton in Ashfield, Kirkby in Ashfield and Hucknall. Now Hucknall has been moved into the new seat of Sherwood. But it has been replaced by Eastwood, smaller than Hucknall but at least as inclined to vote Labour. All in all, the constituency has lost 12,000 voters. The greatest Tory strength is situated in the new private estate of Ravenshead, south of Mansfield. But Ashfield is changing - the percentage of owner occupiers in Ashfield District rose from 50% in 1971 to 58% in 1981.

Ashfield should remain a sound seat for Labour and for ex-Bevin Boy Frank Haynes. But west Notts is an area where coal mining is declining, pits threatened with closure. This area was opened up in the nineteenth century, and lacks the certainty of the massive 1920s pits further east. A mixture of other industries already employs more; this region has long been known for hosiery and other textiles, with a predominantly female work-force. Ashfield will probably not return a Labour majority of 20,000 again, and with its political temper remaining volatile, Labour should never take Ashfield for granted again.

1981	% Own Occ	58.4	1979 core seat Ashfield		
1981	% Loc Auth	33.8	Lab	33,116	52.8
1981	% Black/Asian	0.5	C	25,319	40.4
1981	% Mid Cl	31.3	L	3,914	6.2
1981	% Prof Man	10.3	NF	397	0.6
1982	electorate 70,277		MPs since 1945		
1979	notional result		1945-53 Seymour Cocks Lab		
	Lab 5,800		1953-66 W.N. Warbey Lab		
Alliance		L	1966-77 David Marquand Lab		
			1977-79 Tim Smith C		
			1979- Frank Haynes Lab		

Bassetlaw

Before the redistribution, all Nottinghamshire parliamentary constituencies neatly matched the local government District boundaries. With the creation of an eleventh seat in the county, Sherwood, this arrangement has been disturbed. In the far north of the county, for example, Bassetlaw has lost some Conservative rural areas and the marginal market town of East Retford, and gained the mining town of Warsop. All in all, like several Notts seats, it ends up with about 12,000 fewer voters.

There is no place called Bassetlaw. The seat is named after a medieval 'hundred', or group of parishes. The chief town, however, is undoubtedly Worksop. Worksop is still an active mining centre, boasting three working pits - Manton, Steetley and Shireoaks. But it is also a prospering residential community, with burgeoning new estates in the north-east providing Conservative votes to add to those in Worksop's hilly south ward. There remains a Labour majority in Worksop's council estates and internal pit villages, like Manton and Rhodesia. But the heaviest Labour vote in the constituency will come from Harworth and Warsop, both of which are dominated by massive twentieth century pits.

Bassetlaw will remain a predominantly mining seat, and it will be even more of a stronghold for its well-known MP, Joe Ashton, an articulate representative of the centre of his party. Ashton is from Sheffield, which is the nearest metropolis to Bassetlaw, an area which regards itself as intransigently northern, unlike much of Nottinghamshire. It is not a depressed or endangered area. But its confidence in the future, and the miners' new-found affluence, should not unseat Ashton under any foreseeable circumstances.

1981	% Own Occ	49.4	1979 core seat Bassetlaw		
1981	% Loc Auth	34.5	Lab	29,426	50.2
1981	% Black/Asian	0.5	C	22,247	38.0
1981	% Mid Cl	37.0	L	6,913	11.8
1981	% Prof Man	13.5	MPs since 1945		
1982	electorate 65,938		1945-68 Fred Bellenger Lab		
1979	notional result		1968- Joe Ashton Lab		
	Lab 9,300				
Alliance		SDP			

Broxtowe

Nottingham City elected three Labour MPs in 1979. The
monopoly of Labour representation is largely because
Nottingham's three main middle class residential areas lie
outside the city boundaries: West Bridgford in Rushcliffe,
Carlton and Arnold in Gedling, and Beeston in Broxtowe.
Broxtowe is very similar to the Beeston seat which was first
fought in 1974, but it has lost 12,000 electors to Ashfield.
Otherwise it is composed of the whole of the Broxtowe
District, which lies to the west of Nottingham.

The old Beeston was originally thought to be a marginal seat,
and produced two close Elections in 1974. However, there was
an 8% swing to the sitting MP Jim Lester in 1979, which
produced a 10,000 majority. This may have been partly due to
an 8% rise in the level of owner occupation in the 1970s. Now,
the boundary changes will have a marked effect on the
politics of the district. The voters to be lost are mainly from
the town of Eastwood. Eastwood was the Labour stronghold in
the old Beeston, and although all its pits are now closed, it
will forever be associated with D.H. Lawrence's early years.

In the new division of Broxtowe, politics vary from marginal
Labour support in Central Beeston and Stapleford to strongly
Conservative in Bramcote, Toton and Chilwell. But the
constituency is now comprised almost entirely of twentieth-
century owner-occupied dwellings, largely occupied by white
commuters, and it should be regarded as a safe Tory seat.

1981	% Own Occ	69.8	1979 core seat Beeston		
1981	% Loc Auth	19.6	C	33,273	52.6
1981	% Black/Asian	1	Lab	23,077	36.5
1981	% Mid Cl	51.3	L	6,935	11.0
1981	% Prof Man	18.0	MP since 1974		
1982	electorate 69,838		1974-	Jim Lester C	
1979	notional result				
	C 10,900				
Alliance		L			

Gedling

The new constituency of Gedling, compactly sited on the north-eastern fringe of Nottingham, is very similar to the old Carlton division. There is a small town called Gedling, but the seat's name was chosen because of the existence of a local government Borough of Gedling, which shares the same boundaries as the present Carlton constituency. Gedling itself is an old mining district, which still possesses a large colliery, but the political cast of the seat is more shaped by the middle-class towns of Carlton and Arnold.

In fact Gedling will be a suburban middle-class commuting base for Nottingham, rather like Rushcliffe south of the River Trent. At the inner edge of the seat, wards like Mapperley Plains touch the city boundaries and are socially and politically indistinguishable from the desirable residential parts of the city itself. Further out, overgrown villages like Burton Joyce will simply add to the renamed seat's likely Conservative majority.

Gedling has lost some 12,000 electors compared with its predecessor, Carlton. The mining village of Calverton, for example, has been transferred to Nottinghamshire's new and eleventh constituency, Sherwood. There Calverton will join other mining communities, and its departure leaves Gedling a more homogeneous suburban owner-occupied Tory seat.

1981	% Own Occ	72.4	1979 core seat Carlton		
1981	% Loc Auth	19.3	C	31,762	52.6
1981	% Black/Asian	2.5	Lab	18,989	31.4
1981	% Mid Cl	51.6	L	9,077	15.0
1981	% Prof Man	15.9	NF	606	1.0
1982	electorate 66,917		MPs since 1945		
1979	notional result		1945-66 Sir Kenneth Pickthorn		
	C 11,800			C	
Alliance		SDP	1966-	Philip Holland C	

Mansfield

Mansfield now has a strong claim to be regarded as one of the two or three most important mining centres in the country. It is a large enough town to enjoy other industries – traditionally hosiery and more recently such as Metal Box – and an attractive middle-class residential area in the south of the town, around Berry Hill. But with the rise of the modern Nottinghamshire coalfield as one of the mainstays of the twentieth-century coal industry, Mansfield has become the metropolis for the miners of a dozen pits within ten miles of the town centre.

As older fields like those of South Wales, Durham and Lancashire have declined in the last fifty years, Nottinghamshire has become the leading producer and employer, along with South Yorkshire. Certainly it is the most profitable district under the National Coal Board, and its affluence blends with a moderate tradition to produce a well-known lack of militancy among the Notts miners in industrial relations. Nevertheless Nottinghamshire mining constituencies have retained a loyalty to the Labour Party, and Mansfield is no exception.

The new seat differs little from the old. It still contains the towns of Mansfield and Mansfield Woodhouse, but Warsop is lost to the Bassetlaw constituency. Mansfield will remain a safe bet for Labour's Don Concannon, at present the Shadow Spokesman on N Ireland, and a contender for Cabinet office in a prospective Labour government.

1981	% Own Occ	57.0	1979 core seat Mansfield		
1981	% Loc Auth	34.8	Lab	29,051	52.3
1981	% Black/Asian	0.5	C	17,720	31.9
1981	% Mid Cl	36.1	L	8,536	15.4
1981	% Prof Man	11.1	NF	259	0.4
1982	electorate 65,912		MPs since 1945		
1979	notional result		1945-66 Bernard Taylor Lab		
	Lab 8,300		1966- Don Concannon Lab		
Alliance		SDP			

Newark

Labour held the east Nottinghamshire constituency of Newark from 1950 to 1979. By most standards it could be ranked as a safe Labour seat. In 1979 Conservative Richard Alexander defeated the former Agriculture Minister Ted Bishop to break the pattern. Now, the siphoning off of Labour's colliery village strongholds in the west of the constituency to the new Sherwood division should leave Alexander with a secure seat. Labour always relied on mining votes for victory - from Ollerton, Blidworth, Clipstone, Edwinstowe, and Bilsthorpe. All now disappear from Newark constituency.

The town of Newark on Trent itself, once known as the Key to the North, earned a reputation for cropping up in English history, most notably as a Royalist base in the Civil War. But despite its castle, old market square, town houses and streets named 'gates' as in York, Newark's residential areas are more typified by large council estates at the north and south ends of the town. Its private housing is not outstanding either, yet Newark gave the Conservatives a majority in 1979. More Conservative still are the cathedral town of Southwell and commuter villages like Collingham and Winthorpe. Now, rather similar parts of Bassetlaw District and constituency further down the Trent have been added: the market town of East Retford, marginal in politics, and large villages like Tuxford. All adds up to a homogeneous seat: two market towns each of 20,000 souls and their surrounding rural communities.

Newark's new guise is in many ways more logical than the highly differentiated constituency that gave Labour a majority for thirty years. There was never much contact or sympathy between Newark, Southwell and the coalfield. Newark's industries are brewing and engineering, less committed to Labour than mining. From fifteenth position in the list of mining seats in the 1970s, Newark's mining population will drop almost to zero. Its political character must be transformed as a result.

1981	% Own Occ	57.9	1979 core seat Newark	
1981	% Loc Auth	30.6	C	27,711	45.8
1981	% Black/Asian	0.5	Lab	25,960	42.9
1981	% Mid Cl	43.9	L	6,773	11.2
1981	% Prof Man	16.8	MPs since 1945	
1982	electorate 64,046		1945-50 S. Shephard C	
1979	notional result		1950-64 George Deer Lab	
	C 5,100		1964-79 Ted Bishop Lab	
Alliance		SDP	1979- Richard Alexander C	

Nottingham East

In 1979 Labour only polled a majority of about 8,000 in Nottingham. But they were fortunate in the way that the city's three seats were drawn, for they managed to win each of them with a majority of between 2,500 and 3,500 - a very efficient use of resources. But after the Boundary Commission's redistribution they are not nearly so lucky. In 1979 almost the whole of their city-wide majority would have been packed into the new North division, leaving East and South among the most marginal country. Indeed, if one uses the standard methods of calculating the notional result in 1979 in East, Labour's majority comes out around 400 votes! Since this is no more than an estimate, it really would have been 'too close to call', as the Americans say.

East was the safest of the three Nottingham Labour seats in 1979. So what has happened in the redrawing? East used to be the inner-city seat, taking in the commercial heart of Nottingham, the industrial 'Meadows' between the city centre and the Trent, and the West Indian St Ann's district east of the centre. Now much of the central area and the Meadows are lost, while East becomes a long strip on the edge of Nottingham, stretching up to annex the strongly Conservative Mapperley region from the North. East is now a classically divided marginal. In its southern half are to be found inner council estates, and a proportion of Nottingham's considerable non-white population. In the north the streets become hilly and tree-lined, near the border with the middle-class Tory suburb of Carlton.

East's MP, Jack Dunnett, is now a leading national soccer official, Chairman of the Football League, and long ago announced that he is retiring at the end of the present Parliament. His successor Martyn Sloman will have a much more marginal seat to fight - possibly the one which would have produced the closest result in the country in 1979.

1981	% Own Occ	41.7	1979 core seat Nottingham East		
1981	% Loc Auth	41.8	Lab	15,433	50.5
1981	% Black/Asian	12	C	12,199	39.9
1981	% Mid Cl	37.9	L	2,270	7.4
1981	% Prof Man	10.5	NF	426	1.4
1982	electorate 67,993		Oth	252	0.8
1979	notional result		MPs since 1950		
	Lab 400		1950-55 I. Winterbottom Lab		
Alliance		SDP	1955-64 J.K. Cordeaux C		
			1964- Jack Dunnett Lab		

Nottingham North

Nottingham is an industrial East Midlands city of 300,000 people, whose economy is more than usually dominated by three major employers – Raleigh Cycles, Players Cigarettes and Boots chemists. It is also the home of excellent breweries, and in general it is characterised by good value and a relatively low cost of living. It has a high non-white population, and around 50% of the housing in the city is council-owned – a recipe for good Labour ground.

NW Nottingham is undoubtedly the most working-class and strongly Labour part of the city. Here are to be found the large peripheral council estates, in Strelley, Aspley and Bilborough wards and also the old working-class community of Bulwell, where perennial Communist candidate John Peck was nearly elected to the council in 1979 (Peck has stood as a CP candidate for North in the last eight General Elections). This is the edge of mining country, and North will be the only truly safe Labour seat in Nottingham after the boundary changes. The Commissioners' revisions here are considerable. Most of the council estates were previously in the 65% local authority West constituency, held by Michael English. Bulwell was in North, represented since 1959 by William Whitlock, who achieved momentary attention as the junior FO minister involved in the Anguilla dispute in the West Indies in 1969. The old North has donated its more Conservative elements around Mapperley to the undersized East.

Every ward in the new North would have been won by Labour even in 1979, with the single exception of Beechdale. It is not really in Labour's interests to concentrate all their best wards into one constituency like this. Indeed in the USA, where partisan redistricting exists, it is a known brand of gerrymandering to pack as many opposition supporters into one seat as possible. Nobody would accuse the British Boundary Commission of such practices, and indeed Labour was fortunate to spread their vote so effectively in previous years.

1981	% Own Occ	29.1	1979 core seat Nottingham North		
1981	% Loc Auth	67.1	Lab	25,028	46.9
1981	% Black/Asian	6	C	21,956	41.1
1981	% Mid Cl	30.4	L	4,900	9.2
1981	% Prof Man	7.4	CP	1,071	2.0
1982	electorate 73,196		NF	454	0.9
1979	notional result		MPs since 1955		
	Lab 8,900		1955-59 J. Harrison Lab		
Alliance		SDP	1959- William Whitlock Lab		

Nottingham South

A second ultra-marginal seat in Nottingham in 1979, besides East, would have been Nottingham South. The city is completely redrawn, and South consists of at least three very different neighbourhoods. The city centre and the industrial and working-class territory between the centre and Trent Bridge come from East. South is not the same seat as the old marginal division of that name which existed before 1974, which included the heavily Tory suburb of West Bridgford. Rather the bulk of the new South originates in the abolished Nottingham West, itself a very mixed division.

The mansions of Wollaton, near the rolling green campus of the University of Nottingham, offer a heavy Conservative vote. Nearer the centre is the old west end of the city, the Park estate, which is spaciously laid out in crescents and 'circuses' - and still all-white, even though West Indians and Asians dominate the terraces on the other side of the Derby Road. But south of the River Trent, rather remote from the rest of Nottingham, is the enormous post-war Clifton council estate, now the strongest Labour area in the constituency.

The present member for Nottingham West is Michael English, one of the constitutional experts of the House of Commons. English is a valued and respected member, one of the most active and hard-working in the House. But there can be no doubt that the Conservatives would have taken South, albeit by only a few hundred votes, in 1979. Wollaton and Park would have outvoted Clifton and the city centre Meadows area. If Michael English is going to stand for the new South division, he must hope for a positive swing to Labour at the next Election.

			1979 core seat Nottingham West		
1981	% Own Occ	42.3			
1981	% Loc Auth	48.0	Lab	26,301	46.5
1981	% Black/Asian	3	C	23,801	42.1
1981	% Mid Cl	43.9	L	5,497	9.7
1981	% Prof Man	13.1	NF	718	1.3
1982	electorate 69,143		WRP	192	0.3
1979	notional result		MPs since 1955		
	C 600		1955-59 T. O'Brien Lab		
Alliance		L	1959-64 Peter Tapsell C		
			1964- Michael English Lab		

Rushcliffe

Rushcliffe, the southernmost constituency in Notts, is one of the seats unchanged in the present distribution. It is also identical to the local government District of Rushcliffe. This makes it very easy to calculate its 'vital statistics' - and the figures tell the political story too. Rushcliffe's housing is 71% owner occupied, only 15.5% council; in 1971 50% of the economically active and retired population was employed in non-manual jobs. Less than 2% of the population live in households with a non-white head. The Conservative majority in 1979 was 22,484.

There is no town called Rushcliffe. The largest community in the District is West Bridgford, the 60% middle-class commuter suburb which lies across Trent Bridge from the centre of Nottingham. The Nottingham Forest football ground, the Test cricket ground, and the Notts County Council HQ all lie technically in West Bridgford, which indicates that it can really be counted as an integral part of Nottingham. The rest of Rushcliffe is more rural, but it includes prosperous small towns like Ruddington and Bingham. The only Labour ward is Cotgrave, where the first coal mine south of the Trent was sunk in the early 1960s. Cotgrave is seen as distinctly unusual within Rushcliffe, and has suffered some social difficulties and deprivations in its time.

This seat should continue to provide a safe haven for rising young Conservative front-bencher Kenneth Clarke. Liberal success has been thin in Nottinghamshire for many years.

1981	% Own Occ	70.8	1979 same seat Rushcliffe			
1981	% Loc Auth	15.9	C	34,196	62.2	
1981	% Black/Asian	1.7	Lab	11,712	21.3	
1981	% Mid Cl	60.3	L	9,060	16.5	
1981	% Prof Man	24.0	MP since 1974			
1982	electorate 70,863		1974-	Kenneth Clarke C		
Alliance		L				

Sherwood

Sherwood is an entirely new, extra, eleventh constituency in Nottinghamshire. Unlike the present ten, it is not based on a local authority District, but it includes elements of Ashfield, Gedling and Newark - formerly Ashfield, Carlton and Newark constituencies. But it does have a common economic base to tie it together. Coal is King here, and the new seat should rise straight into the top five in the national list of divisions dominated by employment in mining. As such, it is a logical creation, and should hold together better than some of its predecessors.

For example, the area taken from Newark constituency is effectively the new Dukeries coalfield which was opened up in the 1920s, transforming a district previously known for its large aristocratic estates in the remnants of Sherwood Forest. The coal mining communities created to cater for the new pits still vote Labour, despite the fact that this is one of the most prosperous coalfields in the nation - no one is proposing any pit closures in east Nottinghamshire. Ollerton, Bilsthorpe, Edwinstowe, Blidworth and Clipstone always formed the Labour strength in Newark, and did not blend easily with the rural part of the seat and with the Conservative market town of Newark-on-Trent itself. Similarly, Calverton, a modern mining village, is now removed from Gedling (Carlton), and Hucknall (Ashfield) is an old-established mining town in the Leen Valley, which was opened up in the nineteenth century.

The removal of the coalfield from Newark should push that seat permanently on to the Conservative side. But Labour's compensation in Nottinghamshire is that the new Sherwood division should vote as solidly for their party as any in the county.

1981	% Own Occ	59.0	New seat
1981	% Loc Auth	24.1	
1981	% Black/Asian	0.5	
1981	% Mid Cl	40.2	
1981	% Prof Man	14.3	
1982	electorate 69,589		
1979	notional result		
	Lab 6,300		
Alliance		SDP	

Banbury

The new Banbury seat will contain all of the Cherwell District except for Kidlington; it will also include two or three villages from West Oxfordshire District, principally the Bartons. This means that its electorate will be drawn mainly from the expanding towns of Banbury and Bicester, the remainder being made up of the villages of NE Oxon. It might be thought that this is an identikit Tory seat in the comfortable South Midlands, but both Banbury and Bicester now have large council estates and new industrial developments. Banbury especially is a Labour voting town in an even year, as wards like Neithrop, Ruscote and the new Hardwick estate turn out heavily for them.

In the redistribution, Banbury constituency has lost NW Oxfordshire to the new Witney seat, this including Chipping Norton and Woodstock. It is also losing its long-established and widely respected MP, Neil Marten, who is retiring. All in all, the Tory majority should be reduced, perhaps to about half its present level of 14,000. However, it is hard to see Labour taking the seat, even in a very good year, and much of the new housing in Banbury and Bicester is privately owned. The proportion owner occupied in Cherwell rose from 48% to 58% between 1971 and 1981.

The constituency remains somewhat misnamed. Banbury itself may continue to vote Labour; and probably it will continue to be outvoted by Bicester and the villages. The new Conservative candidate, Tony Baldry, should succeed Neil Marten, effectively as the representative for Cherwell District.

1981	% Own Occ	54.6	1979 core seat Banbury		
1981	% Loc Auth	29.6	C	31,137	54.7
1981	% Black/Asian	2	Lab	16,623	29.2
1981	% Mid Cl	44.8	L	8,658	15.2
1981	% Prof Man	16.3	NF	504	0.9
1982	electorate 64,753		MPs since 1945		
1979	notional result		1945-59 A.D. Dodds-Parker C		
	C 13,000		1959- Neil Marten C		
Alliance		SDP			

Henley

As well as Sir Ian Gilmour, another well-known Conservative who was displaced by the last Boundary Commission in the early 1970s was Michael Heseltine. His Devon seat of Tavistock was abolished, and he had to go 'on the road' in search of safe pastures. Also like Gilmour, he found a super-safe seat - in his case, Henley, in Oxfordshire. Heseltine can have no complaints about the present review, for it leaves him with an even more overwhelmingly safe seat.

The only substantial base of Labour support in the old Henley was in Oxford's eastern fringe, where the city's sprawl spilt beyond its administrative and parliamentary boundaries. Now Littlemore, and parts of Oxford's Rose Hill and Wood Farm council estates, have rightly been shifted into the new Oxford East constituency. This leaves only one Labour ward in Henley, the highly untypical and raw little overspill estate of Berinsfield, outside Dorchester on Thames. More redolent of the constituency's political flavour are the ever-fashionable towns of Henley on Thames, at the southern end of the seat, and Thame at the north end. Here too are Goring, beside the river; Wheatley, just off the A40; and Rotherfield Peppard and Sonning Common, which are favoured by Reading's well-off commuters.

Labour will be almost completely eliminated now, and the pockets of Liberal strength in South Oxfordshire should ensure a second place for the Alliance. But Michael Heseltine's political career cannot be threatened from this source. He should not have constituency trouble again, and few contenders for future high office could have a more secure or attractive base than Henley.

1981	% Own Occ	70	1979 core seat Henley
1981	% Loc Auth	14	C 29,982 58.7
1981	% Black/Asian	1.5	L 11,693 22.9
1981	% Mid Cl	55	Lab 9,435 18.5
1981	% Prof Man	23	MPs since 1945
1982	electorate 62,134		1945-50 Sir G.W.G. Fox C
1979	notional result		1950-74 John Hay C
	C 17,900		1974- Michael Heseltine C
Alliance		L	

Oxford East

This is not the Oxford of dreaming spires, tourism and privileged ease, but the nine wards of the city east of the Rivers Cherwell and Thames, together with the built-up areas of Littlemore, Marston and Risinghurst, which are outside the city boundaries in South Oxfordshire District, but physically part of Greater Oxford.

Traditionally East Oxford has been the better half of the city for the Labour Party since the arrival of the motor industry in the inter-war years. Here BL's Cowley complex - Pressed Steel and Morris Motors - straddles the eastern bypass, literally miles from the University dominated centre of the city. Here too are peripheral council estates: post-war prefabricated Barton; Wood Farm; Rose Hill; Northway; and Blackbird Leys, the sprawling 1960s development where most of Oxford's small West Indian population is to be found. Further in, just across Magdalen Bridge from the city centre, lies St Clements, which is Oxford's nearest thing to an inner city area. There is terraced housing off the Cowley Road, and a concentration of Asians in East and St Clements wards, which have swung to the left since the days when they were the homes of deferentially Conservative or Liberal college servants.

But although the new East Oxford will be better for Labour than the city as a whole, and the addition of Littlemore is certainly a major aid, the seat will remain marginal in a good Tory year. Some of the best residential areas in Oxford are to be found in Old Headington, along the road to London and especially in the private roads of Headington Hill, near the headquarters of Robert Maxwell's Pergamon Press. Oxford is still basically an affluent city, although perceived threats to Cowley may well lead to a larger anti-Government swing than elsewhere at the next Election.

1981	% Own Occ	50
1981	% Loc Auth	31
1981	% Black/Asian	7
1981	% Mid Cl	44
1981	% Prof Man	14
1982	electorate 64,245	
1979	notional result	
	Lab 200	
Alliance		L

1979 core seat Oxford

C	27,459	45.3
Lab	25,962	42.8
L	6,234	10.3
E	887	1.5
Ind	72	0.1

MPs since 1945
1945-50 Quintin Hogg C
1950-59 H. Turner C
1959-66 Monty Woodhouse C
1966-70 Evan Luard Lab
1970-74 Monty Woodhouse C
1974-79 Evan Luard Lab
1979- John Patten C

Oxford West and Abingdon

When the City of Oxford was broken up in the Boundary Commission's present review, six of the fifteen wards will join parts of the Abingdon constituency, until 1974 part of Berkshire. These six wards, west of the Rivers Cherwell and Thames, contain the whole of the historic walled city of Oxford, the bulk of the University, the main shopping centre and the town and county halls. It also includes the well-known intellectual and professional residential areas of North Oxford.

West Oxford is the more Conservative, less industrial half of the city – Cherwell and Wolvercote wards, in the far north, are the strongest Tory bastions. It does however also include the working-class enclaves of Jericho and Osney, and the highly volatile student vote of the University-dominated Central ward, which has elected Conservative, Labour and Alliance councillors in its brief existence since 1979. But both Abingdon itself and most particularly the owner-occupied sprawl between the two towns – Radley and Kennington – are Conservative too. In 1979 the Conservatives would probably have won this seat by about 8,500 votes, if it had been contested.

There was one of the most prolonged quarrels between the Liberal Party and the SDP concerning the candidature for this seat. The Liberals have a strong tradition in Abingdon and the villages; the SDP feel that the academic centre of Oxford must be highly fertile ground for cultivation. Certainly Labour can have few hopes in this seat, so perhaps their vote can be squeezed enough to make Oxford West and Abingdon into a Conservative-Alliance marginal. The SDP won the battle in the carve-up, and selected Evan Luard, twice elected as Labour MP for Oxford. In a new seat old loyalties may have been weakened, but the Conservatives must start strong favourites.

1981	% Own Occ	58.5	New seat
1981	% Loc Auth	19.6	
1981	% Black/Asian	2	
1981	% Mid Cl	59.4	
1981	% Prof Man	22.6	
1982	electorate 67,712		
1979	notional result		
	C 10,500		

Alliance   SDP

Wantage

The majority of the electorate of the old oversized Abingdon constituency has been designated as joining the new Wantage division. All of it was in Berkshire before the county boundary changes of the early 1970s. The main towns are Wallingford and Didcot from South Oxfordshire District, and Faringdon and Wantage from the Vale of White Horse.

Didcot, which has a famous place as a junction in railway mythology, and a massive power station, is a Labour town. Wallingford is Liberal, at least at local level. Wantage has an early SDP recruit, Alec Spurway, as its County Councillor, elected back in May 1981. But in spite of these deviations, the new seat will be generally Conservative, for the Tories command huge majorities in the large villages that make up the balance of this seat - Marcham and Drayton, Shrivenham, Harwell (near the Atomic Energy Research Establishment), and many more.

It is likely that the Conservative MP for Abingdon, Tom Benyon, will move to Wantage to allow Oxford's John Patten to contest the Oxford West and Abingdon division. Benyon is the brother of the Tory MP for Buckingham. He should have little trouble in Wantage. The Alliance challenge is a long shot to be watched on Election night, but it must remain an outside bet.

1981	% Own Occ	56	1979 core seat Abingdon	
1981	% Loc Auth	24	C 41,211	53.7
1981	% Black/Asian	1.5	Lab 18,920	24.7
1981	% Mid Cl	54	L 16,164	21.1
1981	% Prof Man	20	Ind 381	0.5
1982	electorate 64,050		MPs since 1945	
1979	notional result		1945-53 Sir R.G.C. Glyn C	
	C 13,600		1953-79 Airey Neave C	
Alliance		SDP	1979- Tom Benyon C	

Witney

The new Witney seat is based on the West Oxfordshire local
government District, and contains most of the old Mid Oxon
constituency. Mid Oxon has had only a brief decade of life
since its first contest in 1974. Its speedy replacement is an
indication of the rapid growth of population in Oxfordshire,
which obtained an extra seat in the boundary redistributions
of both the 1970s and the 1980s.

Witney itself is a growing industrial and residential town, 20
miles west of Oxford; the renowned blanket works has been
joined by new factories on industrial estates. Other urban
centres include Chipping Norton, Carterton, Eynsham,
Charlbury, Woodstock and Kidlington, all growing dormitories
for Oxford. Taking into account the smaller villages that make
up the electorate, every part of the constituency is inclined
to the Conservatives.

Witney should provide a safe bastion for Foreign Office
Minister Douglas Hurd, who has been on the fringe of Cabinet
office for many years. Hurd has been MP for Mid Oxon
throughout its life as a constituency, but should have no
difficulty due to the boundary changes.

1981	% Own Occ	60.6	1979 core seat	Mid Oxon	
1981	% Loc Auth	22.4	C	28,465	56.9
1981	% Black/Asian	1	Lab	13,004	26.0
1981	% Mid Cl	47.4	L	8,367	16.7
1981	% Prof Man	17.1	Ind	174	0.3
1982	electorate 69,016		MP since 1974		
1979	notional result		1974-	Douglas Hurd C	
	C 14,000				
Alliance		L			

Ludlow

The Liberals have not given up many of their most hopeful constituencies to their SDP partners in the Alliance. But one example where they have given way is that of Ludlow in South Shropshire, one of a chain of Tory seats in the Welsh Marches where the Liberals have been active in recent years.

Ancient small towns like Church Stretton, Bishop's Castle and Ludlow itself seem deep in the countryside. These were already parliamentary borough constituencies when their eighteenth-century politics were studied and anatomised by the historian Lewis Namier. But the Bridgnorth district is much more in the orbit of the West Midlands conurbation. This part of the Ludlow constituency is much strengthened by the boundary changes, for some 9,000 voters near Bridgnorth are gained from The Wrekin.

These changes will benefit the Conservatives, and it is hard to see the SDP causing Eric Cockeram MP as much trouble as the Liberals would have done.

1981	% Own Occ	58.0	1979 core seat Ludlow			
1981	% Loc Auth	21.8	C	20,906	52.8	
1981	% Black/Asian	0.6	L	12,524	31.6	
1981	% Mid Cl	44.0	Lab	5,717	14.4	
1981	% Prof Man	19.9	NF	354	0.9	
1982	electorate 61,525		Ind	106	0.3	
1979	notional result		MPs since 1945			
	C 12,500		1945-51 U. Corbett C			
Alliance		SDP	1951-60 C.J. Holland-Martin C			
			1960-79 Jasper More C			
			1979- Eric Cockeram C			

North Shropshire

The Leader of the House of Commons, John Biffen, is commonly regarded as one of the brightest and most original of Mrs Thatcher's Cabinet Ministers, principled, hard-working and respected even by his political opponents - he is a hard-line monetarist and an anti-marketeer. Biffen has never had serious trouble in his Oswestry constituency since his initial election in a 1961 byelection.

Now Oswestry gains over 10,000 of The Wrekin's more Conservative electors, around the little market town of Newport, which should only increase Biffen's majority. The Liberals have not pressed as hard for victory here as in other divisions on the Welsh border, and could in fact do no better than third in the 1979 General Election. The seat is renamed North Shropshire.

It remains a collection of small towns and rural terrain on the very fringes of Wales, where remnants of Wat's Dyke and Offa's Dyke offer reminders of the time when this was Mercia's - and England's - front line against Celtic raids.

1981	% Own Occ	58.0	1979 core seat Oswestry
1981	% Loc Auth	26.0	C 23,551 54.6
1981	% Black/Asian	0.5	Lab 10,150 23.5
1981	% Mid Cl	43.7	L 9,405 21.8
1981	% Prof Man	17.5	MPs since 1945
1982	electorate 73,424		1945-50 O.B.S. Poole C
1979	notional result		1950-61 W.D. Ormsby-Gore C
	C 14,000		1961- John Biffen C
Alliance		L	

Shrewsbury and Atcham

Shropshire politics remained dominated by the landed and wealthy long after the introduction of universal enfranchisement. The Earl of Plymouth and Viscount Bridgeman both represented county constituencies in their commoner days. Shrewsbury was represented by the present Earl of Harrowby, and when he (once) lost the seat it was to a Liberal multi-millionaire. The sitting Conservative MP Sir John Langford-Holt has held the seat since 1945 and is now retiring. Local Conservatives rejected the overtures of Warren Hawksley who wanted to migrate from the neighbouring, marginal Wrekin division and have instead brought in Derek Conway from Newcastle-upon-Tyne.

The constituency is dominated by the county town and the Boundary Commissioners have changed only the name to give recognition to the local government Borough of Shrewsbury and Atcham. South of Shrewsbury, in Meole Brace and Bayston Hill, the Liberals are strong. But the constituency runs west to the Welsh border and it is in the rural areas as well as in the wealthier wards of Shrewsbury, like Kingsland, that Conservative support is strongest.

The Liberals moved into second place in February 1974 and have remained there since. The Liberals benfited from one of the first Social Democrat organisations established in the country (before the official SDP was founded) but it would be surprising if they overcame the 10,500 majority which Langford-Holt bequeaths. The railway workers (diminished in numbers) no longer give unstinting support to Labour, nor do agricultural workers. Perhaps the order of the parties in Shrewsbury will remain the same as before. Mr Conway is 29, the same age as Langford-Holt when he inherited the seat, and he must hope for as long a leasehold on the property.

1981	% Own Occ	62.5	1979 same seat Shrewsbury
1981	% Loc Auth	24.7	C	23,548	48.6
1981	% Black/Asian	0.8	L	13,364	27.6
1981	% Mid Cl	52.9	Lab	11,558	23.8
1981	% Prof Man	17.7	MP since 1945
1982	electorate 66,478		1945-	Sir John Langford-Holt
Alliance		L		C

The Wrekin

The great cone-shaped peak of the Wrekin dominates the mid-Shropshire countryside. But the landscape which can be viewed from the top of the hill is not merely the soft scenery of agriculture. For nearby is one of the birthplaces of the world's first industrial revolution: the forge of Abraham Darby's works at Coalbrookdale, where iron was smelted with coke in the first decade after 1700. A mile away is another famous eighteenth century achievement, the iron bridge of 1779 over the gorge of the Severn, which forms the heart of Britain's most extensive industrial museum. As time passed other industrial towns joined Coalbrookdale, Ironbridge and Coalport: Dawley, Wellington, and the coal-mining community of Oakengates. This produced a substantial built-up area, scarred by productive industry, which has now been unified by the establishment of the Telford New Town in the 1960s.

Of course, Telford is an isolated Labour outpost in Shropshire. The Wrekin has been won by Labour eight times in General Elections since 1923. But it was never as safe as it might be, because electors from rural Shropshire were always included as well as the industrial communities; by 1979 the electorate was over 92,000. Conservative Warren Hawksley edged out the Labour MP Gerald Fowler in that year's Election, the fifth time Wrekin has changed hands since the 1945 Election.

Now Conservative districts around Newport and around Shifnal are removed by the Boundary Commissioners, and The Wrekin is reduced to a compact core around Telford New Town. It should be safely Labour. As in the case of other expanding overspill towns, Labour has benefited from the removal of extraneous rural regions.

1981	% Own Occ	41.5	1979 core seat The Wrekin	
1981	% Loc Auth	53.6	C 32,672	45.6
1981	% Black/Asian	3	Lab 31,707	44.2
1981	% Mid Cl	39.4	L 7,331	10.2
1981	% Prof Man	12.6	MPs since 1945	
1982	electorate 76,569		1945-55 I.O. Thomas Lab	
1979	notional result		1955-66 W. Yates C	
	Lab 1,400		1966-70 Gerald Fowler Lab	
Alliance		SDP	1970-74 Anthony Trafford C	
			1974-79 Gerald Fowler Lab	
			1979- Warren Hawksley C	

Bridgwater

Bridgwater Borough Council was well known in the late 1960s as one of the few local authorities which remained loyal to Labour in the darkest days of Harold Wilson's government. The town of Bridgwater, with its decaying docks now stranded inland, still votes for the Labour Party at local level. But it is now part of the new Sedgemoor District, and as before, untypical of Bridgwater constituency, which has been Conservative since 1950. The seat stretches NW from Bridgwater through the Quantock Hills to the Somerset coastline at Minehead and Watchet. The seaside resort of Burnham-on-Sea has been moved into Wells, and Bridgwater has lost just over 10,000 voters; but it should remain safe for Tory Environment Secretary Tom King.

1981	% Own Occ	59.9	1979 core seat Bridgwater		
1981	% Loc Auth	27.8	C	31,259	54.1
1981	% Black/Asian	0.7	Lab	16,809	29.1
1981	% Mid Cl	41.1	L	9,693	16.8
1981	% Prof Man	15.7	MPs since 1945		
1982	electorate 64,236		1945-50 Vernon Bartlett Ind		
1979	notional C 10,900		1950-70 Sir George Wills C		
Alliance		SDP	1970-	Tom King C	

Somerton and Frome

The new east Somerset seat of Somerton and Frome contains elements from the old divisions of Wells and Yeovil. It is essentially the fifth and extra seat that Somerset's population growth justifies. Frome is a semi-industrial town not far from the depressed former Somerset coalfield around Norton-Radstock. But mostly Somerton and Frome is a rural constituency. Somerton itself has a population of only 2,000 - much the same size as Wincanton, Bruton, Castle Cary and Langport. Like most of the extra seats in England created by the present Boundary Commission, Somerton and Frome will elect a Conservative MP to Westminster.

1981	% Own Occ	62.5	New seat
1981	% Loc Auth	23.2	
1981	% Black/Asian	1	
1981	% Mid Cl	42.5	
1981	% Prof Man	18.1	
1982	electorate 64,474		
1979	notional C 10,700		
Alliance		SDP	

Taunton

Since 1956 the west Somerset division of Taunton has been represented by Edward du Cann, now one of the most respected and influential of Conservative backbenchers, Chairman of the 1922 Committee, and mentioned often as a possible Speaker or an alternative candidate for high office.

The Taunton constituency, little altered in the boundary changes, consists of the Borough of Taunton Deane together with some wards of the District of West Somerset, which stretches through the little town of Dulverton across Exmoor to the Devon border. Taunton Deane includes Wellington as well as the county town itself, which has its share of light industry, council estates and Labour voters, particularly in east Taunton.

Labour managed to cut the Conservative majority to 3,000 in their great year of 1966. But it remains hard to see du Cann losing his seat under any normal circumstances. This is not one of the Liberals' West Country strongholds, and the SDP have been granted the Alliance nomination.

1981	% Own Occ	58.7	1979 core seat Taunton			
1981	% Loc Auth	28.8	C	28,483	53.2	
1981	% Black/Asian	1	Lab	15,759	29.4	
1981	% Mid Cl	50.6	L	7,928	14.8	
1981	% Prof Man	16.1	E	1,403	2.6	
1982	electorate 70,300		MPs since 1945			
1979	notional result		1945-50 V.J. Collins Lab			
	C 12,800		1950-56 H.L. Hopkinson C			
Alliance		SDP	1956- Edward du Cann C			

Wells

The Liberal candidate Alan Butt Philip has achieved a strong second place in the last three General Elections in the Mendips in the Wells constituency. The core of the seat lies in the historic communities of Wells and Glastonbury - Wells with its famous cathedral, Glastonbury with its abbey and its Tor, a mound with mystical prehistoric associations. This is the countryside of Camelot, with its mythical Arthurian connotations: the Mendip hills look over the flat plain of the Somerset Levels.

There is also industry here: Street is an old shoe-making town, and Frome used to be in the seat, although it is now transferred to Somerton and Frome in the boundary changes. With 10,000 Labour votes to squeeze, the Liberals can still entertain reasonable hopes of a gain in Wells in a good year.

The addition of Cheddar and the seaside resort of Burnham-on-Sea will not make Butt Philip's task easier. Nevertheless, the right-wing Tory MP, war veteran Robert Boscawen, can expect a further stiff challenge at the next General Election.

1981	% Own Occ	66.5	1979 core seat Wells			
1981	% Loc Auth	21.4	C	30,400	51.3	
1981	% Black/Asian	1	L	18,204	30.7	
1981	% Mid Cl	46.5	Lab	10,024	16.9	
1981	% Prof Man	20.1	Oth	576	1.0	
1982	electorate 62,116		MPs since 1945			
1979	notional result		1945-51 D.C. Boles C			
	C 11,900		1951-70 S.L.C. Maydon C			
Alliance		L	1970-	Robert Boscawen C		

Yeovil

The Conservatives have held the south Somerset seat of Yeovil since its creation in 1918, without a break. For over 30 years the MP has been John Peyton, who was Transport Minister in Mr Heath's government. But Yeovil is also one of the few places where the Liberals did better in 1979 than in 1974. The dynamic candidate Paddy Ashdown pushed them up into a clear second place last time, with over 30% of the vote for the first time since the war. John Peyton is retiring at the next Election. In the 1981 county council elections, the Liberals won every seat in Yeovil town. Yeovil really must be one of the Alliance's brightest prospects.

In the boundary changes, 20,000 voters are lost as the northern half of the division is transferred to Somerton/Frome. This should help the Liberals, for their support is concentrated in the semi-industrial eponymous town of the constituency. The largest employer in Yeovil is Westland Helicopters, who have a number of plants in and around the town. Other major centres of population are Chard, Crewkerne and Ilminster, all within striking distance of the Dorset border.

Labour used to do quite well in Yeovil. In 1966 Peyton's majority was cut to its smallest ever figure, 2,080 - and it was Labour who finished in second place. But Labour are now consigned firmly to the 'bronze medal position', and if Paddy Ashdown can persuade their remaining supporters (14,000 in 1979) to vote Liberal to keep the Tories out, Yeovil must seem one of the government's most vulnerable seats.

1981	% Own Occ	60.3	1979 core seat Yeovil		
1981	% Loc Auth	29.2	C	31,321	47.9
1981	% Black/Asian	1	L	19,939	30.5
1981	% Mid Cl	44.4	Lab	14,098	21.6
1981	% Prof Man	15.7	MPs since 1945		
1982	electorate 66,074		1945-51 W.H. Kingsmill C		
1979	notional result		1951- John Peyton C		
	C 8,900				
Alliance		L			

Burton

There have been times when Burton upon Trent has seemed a marginal constituency. The Conservatives only held it by 277 votes in 1966, for example. Yet Labour hasn't won the seat, except in their annus mirabilis of 1945, despite the fact that it is more working class in composition than, say, Newcastle under Lyme or the old Lichfield and Tamworth. The centre of Burton, with its terraces of small nineteenth-century houses, looks like Labour territory. There is an Asian population in the town. Why, then, has it always returned Conservatives since 1950?

Burton is one of Britain's great brewing towns, and the traditional connection between the Tory Party and the brewing trade may affect the constituency's politics. But Burton itself did vote Labour, albeit narrowly, even in 1979. More crucial, perhaps, than the brewing link is the fact that the seat contains the whole of the East Staffordshire District, which stretches north through rural areas past Uttoxeter. Stapenhill, on the hill across the Trent from Burton, is a Tory ward. So are Tutbury, Rolleston and the rural Needwood Forest and Yoxall, and the small market town of Uttoxeter, the second largest unit in the seat. Rural and agricultural areas always prove themselves more willing to vote Conservative than urban districts of the same class makeup.

The percentage of owner occupiers in East Staffordshire rose by over 10% in the 1970s. The constituency of Burton, not altered in the boundary revision, seems to be becoming safer for its right-wing Conservative MP, Ivan Lawrence.

1981	% Own Occ	65.5
1981	% Loc Auth	23.6
1981	% Black/Asian	3.4
1981	% Mid Cl	42.2
1981	% Prof Man	14.8
1982	electorate 72,672	
Alliance		L

1979 same seat Burton

C	29,821	54.0
Lab	20,020	36.3
L	5,383	9.7
NF	414	0.6

MPs since 1945
1945-50 A.W. Lyne Lab
1950-55 W.A. Colegate C
1955-74 J.G. Jennings C
1974- Ivan Lawrence C

Cannock and Burntwood

From 1945 to 1970 Cannock was the constituency of Jennie Lee, while she was Aneurin Bevan's wife and widow. When she was defeated by Conservative Patrick Cormack, she said that this was not the same Cannock that it once had been. She was right, for the growth of many large commuter villages for the West Midlands conurbation had changed the political characteristics of the seat. But by 1974 this Conservative territory had been removed to form the core of the new seat of SW Staffordshire, and Cannock was left as a safe Labour seat once more. It has been held by Gwilym Roberts without difficulty ever since. Patrick Cormack sensibly followed the bulk of his supporters into SW Staffs.

In the present boundary changes, Cannock loses the growing town of Rugeley across Cannock Chase, and gains Burntwood from Lichfield and Tamworth. This will if anything strengthen Labour's position further, for Rugeley included many burgeoning private housing estates, while Burntwood is very much part of the south Staffordshire mining tradition which includes Brownhills and Cannock itself. Cannock Chase is heathland of sandy and wild ruggedness, but it looks down on the sprawl of a semi-urban landscape created by coal mining. Most of the pits have now closed, but Cannock's Labour preferences live on.

The Liberals never made any impact in Cannock, and the SDP have won the Alliance nomination for the new Cannock-Burntwood seat. It is unclear what chances they have of victory, and it is unlikely that another Labour MP will have cause to be disappointed with the Cannock constituency in the near future.

1981	% Own Occ	60.7	1979 core seat Cannock		
1981	% Loc Auth	32.7	Lab	25,050	52.8
1981	% Black/Asian	1	C	17,704	37.3
1981	% Mid Cl	43.9	L	4,729	10.0
1981	% Prof Man	14.6	MPs since 1945		
1982	electorate 66,075		1945-70 Jennie Lee Lab		
1979	notional result		1970-74 Patrick Cormack C		
	Lab 5,500		1974- Gwilym Roberts Lab		
Alliance		SDP			

Mid Staffordshire

Like many shire counties in England, Staffordshire's population growth entitles it to an extra seat in the new Parliament. It is fair to say that the additional division is Mid Staffordshire, a curiously drawn long thin constituency which seems designed to take in bits overflowing from other seats. Lichfield comes in from the huge Lichfield/Tamworth seat. Rugeley is annexed from Cannock. The Mid Staffs constituency then skirts Stafford to take Stone and its surrounding villages from Hugh Fraser's Stafford/Stone seat.

Also like most extra seats in England, Mid Staffs will prove a boon for the Conservative Party. Lichfield is a rapidly expanding residential area. This cathedral town was always the most Conservative element in the key marginal Lichfield and Tamworth, and at the last Election it swung heavily to help to elect Tory MP John Heddle. Rugeley has a modern coal mine (Lea Hall) and associated massive power stations. But it also has rapidly growing private housing estates, and has doubled in size in the last twenty years; Rugeley marginally voted Conservative in the 1979 General Election. Stone, and especially the villages of central Staffordshire, are pushed to the right by their agricultural characteristics.

With its high proportion of low-cost private housing and skilled workers, Mid Staffordshire could well prove a volatile constituency, subject to large swings between all parties. But whoever wins the Conservative nomination will surely be the strong favourite to win the seat.

1981	% Own Occ	63.7	New seat
1981	% Loc Auth	27.4	
1981	% Black/Asian	1	
1981	% Mid Cl	48.7	
1981	% Prof Man	17.4	
1982	electorate 67,632		
1979	notional result		
	C 8,000		

Alliance   L

Newcastle under Lyme

The Borough of Newcastle under Lyme, to the west of Stoke on Trent and commonly considered to be part of the Potteries, is a region of great variety. There are mining communities at Silverdale, Chesterton and Knutton; good residential areas in parts of Wolstanton, Porthill, Thistleberry and Westlands; spice is added by Keele University and its population; and the mixture is completed by rural elements out to the west, although Madeley has been removed to Stafford. Small wonder that Frank Bealey, Jean Blondel and W.P. McCann decided to analyse Newcastle under Lyme at book length in 1965 in Constituency Politics.

Yet despite these diverse characteristics, Newcastle under Lyme has remained loyal to Labour since the war. At the last election, John Golding, a well-known right-wing Labour and Co-Operative activist on the NEC, held a majority of over 4,000. This is slightly surprising, for Newcastle's middle-class and professional/managerial percentages are only fractionally below average. The latter especially is usually an excellent indicator of party preference. There are more council tenants than average, and more miners, although this is not a 'mining seat' by any means. Perhaps the answer is partly regional, for the Potteries have remained marvellous ground for Labour. At the 1979 Election, Newcastle, like Stoke, swung only 3% to the Tories compared with 5% nationally.

The Potteries are not a fashionable part of England, nor an affluent or expanding one. Although Newcastle under Lyme escapes much of the grime and substandard housing that still besets parts of Stoke, it may well continue to be a better bet for Labour, and Golding, than other seats of its social class makeup.

1981	% Own Occ	58.3	1979 core seat Newcastle under		
1981	% Loc Auth	34.6	Lyme		
1981	% Black/Asian	1	Lab	28,649	48.5
1981	% Mid Cl	41.8	C	24,421	41.3
1981	% Prof Man	14.3	L	5,878	9.9
1982	electorate 66,123		Ind	156	0.3
1979	notional result		MPs since 1945		
	Lab 5,600		1945-51 J.D. Mack Lab		
Alliance		L	1951-69 Stephen Swingler Lab		
			1969- John Golding Lab		

South Staffordshire

This is in fact the old SW Staffordshire, represented since its creation in 1974 by Conservative Patrick Cormack, and now renamed in line with the local authority District with which it is coterminous. Before 1974, this growing area formed part of the Cannock constituency, and it was largely responsible for the defeat of Labour's Jennie Lee there in 1970.

On its creation, SW Staffs was one of the few seats in the country to be composed entirely of Rural District Councils. Yet although there are no large towns, its voters come almost entirely from the newish suburban communities fringing the western edge of the West Midlands conurbation - Wombourne, Codsall, Brewood, Great Wyrley. 22% of the housing is local authority owned, but 67½% is owner occupied - almost all built since the war. It is this element, and the new West Midlands middle class spawned by the affluence of the 1950s and 1960s, that gives this constituency its powerful Conservatism. Less than 1% of the population is of West Indian or Asian origin, yet the politics of South Staffordshire are effectively influenced by the racial mix of the inner conurbation. This is one of the 'snow-white' areas which moved to the right in response to immigration.

Patrick Cormack, undoubtedly a lively and active MP, achieved a 17,000 majority in 1979, and it is hard to see him having any more trouble next time. The seat is still growing, and presents the new face of the West Midlands young middle class - only 9% of the voters are over 65. Its modern housing typifies a thoroughly modern milieu.

1981	% Own Occ	67.5	1979 same seat South-West		
1981	% Loc Auth	23.4	Staffordshire		
1981	% Black/Asian	0.7	C	32,153	60.4
1981	% Mid Cl	54.7	Lab	14,720	27.6
1981	% Prof Man	21.9	L	5,460	10.3
1982	electorate 72,687		NF	912	1.7
Alliance		L	MP since 1974		
			1974-	Patrick Cormack C	

South-East Staffordshire

The new constituency of SE Staffordshire is based on the Borough of Tamworth. Tamworth is one of the fastest growing towns in England, although it is not a designated New Town. It has risen from a population of 23,000 in 1951 to 64,000 in 1981. The development has been both of council housing and, slightly outstripping that, private estates. Most of the new residents have come from the West Midlands conurbation, as the local accent testifies. Tamworth looks very different now from its former self, with tower blocks rising immediately above the historic town centre, and burgeoning housing sprawl in most directions.

Tamworth was previously part of the large and marginal Lichfield and Tamworth division. Both halves have grown enormously, but Lichfield was generally regarded as the more Conservative. Most of the wards in Tamworth are rather evenly balanced politically, but in May 1979 Labour polled 500 more votes than the Tories in the borough elections. This indicates that Labour might have a good chance in SE Staffordshire. But Tamworth is likely to be outvoted by the Lichfield District wards that are also included in SE Staffs – small towns and villages like Alrewas, Shenstone and Fazeley. In addition, Labour's chances in SE Staffordshire are weakened by the fact that the politics of expanding towns like Tamworth are always unpredictable. Frequently their inhabitants seem to cast aside the traditions of their upbringing to adopt new politics in their new surroundings – especially if now they own their own houses. There is no substantial black and Asian population in Tamworth despite its proximity to Birmingham.

SE Staffs is an extra seat, created by the population growth in the southern half of the county. South Staffordshire has for some years been more volatile and rapidly changing, demographically and politically, than the Potteries further north. It is doubtful if any sitting MP will risk a contest here. In 1979, the Conservatives would have won the seat, if narrowly. But the SE Staffordshire of 1979 is already gone, as expansion continues apace. It may well be that this will make the Tory Party the beneficiary of a long-term swing.

1981	% Own Occ	58.1	New seat
1981	% Loc Auth	35.9	
1981	% Black/Asian	1	
1981	% Mid Cl	46.3	
1981	% Prof Man	17.7	
1982	electorate	63,660	
1979	notional C	4,900	
Alliance			

Stafford

One of the most long-serving MPs is Hugh Fraser, the member for Stafford and Stone since 1945. If he does not retire at the next Election, but rather contests the new Stafford seat, he will be the sole Conservative survivor of the 1945 intake, the earliest still to be represented in the House. Fraser is a senior backbencher, once married to the writer Lady Antonia; and he would continue to be elected without difficulty in the redrawn Stafford, even though his majority would be reduced by the transfer of over 20,000 electors around Stone to the extra Mid Staffs seat. Loggerheads, Madeley and Whitmore wards are taken from Newcastle under Lyme Borough.

Stafford is itself a marginal town, with a variety of industry and a historic centre ringed by hideous major road development. There are strongly Labour wards in the council estates by the railway tracks to the south of Stafford, and in Coton in the NE of the town. But the Conservatives fight back in the private estates of Holmcroft and Highfields, Weeping Cross and Wildwood.

But Stafford's population of 55,000 is not enough to sustain a seat on its own, and the balance is firmly tipped by the fact that a considerable agricultural hinterland is still appended. This lies mainly to the west of Stafford, around little towns like Gnosall and Eccleshall. It is firmly Conservative territory, and Hugh Fraser can rely on the villages and county estates of this most softly rural of all parts of Staffordshire. One thing will change – for the first time he will have an opponent from the Social Democratic Party. But he can confidently expect Stafford to return him to Parliament for a twelfth term, should he wish it.

1981	% Own Occ	65.1	1979 core seat Stafford/Stone
1981	% Loc Auth	23.4	C 34,387 52.4
1981	% Black/Asian	2	Lab 21,210 32.3
1981	% Mid Cl	54.0	L 10,049 15.3
1981	% Prof Man	18.6	MP since 1945
1982	electorate 71,246		1945– Hugh Fraser C
1979	notional result		
	C 8,400		

Alliance   SDP

Staffordshire Moorlands

The new consituency of Staffordshire Moorlands is to be coterminous with the District of the same name, which is situated at the north end of the county bordering Cheshire and Derbyshire's Peak District. It was all previously part of the Leek constituency, but Leek has now lost Kidsgrove to Stoke on Trent North.

Some of the finest countryside in the Midlands is situated in Staffordshire – much of Dovedale and many other Peak District dales, the Manifold Valley and the Churnet Valley around Alton Towers and its pleasure gardens. The rugged hill farmers of the high moors and the dairy farms of the gentler slopes produce a solid Conservative vote. But for many years the old Leek seat seemed safe for Labour. This was mainly due to the coal-mining and heavy industry of towns like Kidsgrove and Biddulph, which are physically part of the Pitteries, which has been as strong a Labour region as any in England. Leek itself, with its textile industry, remained marginal. But the seat slipped away from Labour in the 1970s. There was a rapid rise of owner-occupation throughout the division as new private estates were built. Many commuters for Stoke or Crewe found the area a source of relatively cheap housing. By 1981, 77.5% of housing in the constituency was owner occupied, 10% more than in 1971 and among the highest figures in Britain.

David Knox had already established himself as an invulnerable MP for Leek by the end of the 1970s, and with the loss of Kidsgrove, the new constituency should be safely Conservative. There has been no strong tradition of Liberal activity, and the Social Democrats seem unlilely to make any impact.

1981	% Own Occ	77.5	1979 core seat Leek		
1981	% Loc Auth	14.0	C	36,508	51.9
1981	% Black/Asian	0.1	Lab	25,937	36.9
1981	% Mid Cl	44.3	L	6,474	9.2
1981	% Prof Man	16.8	R	1,451	2.1
1982	electorate 72,808		MPs since 1945		
1979	notional result		1945-70 Harold Davies Lab		
	C 13,000		1970- David Knox C		
Alliance		SDP			

Stoke on Trent Central

Stoke on Trent is almost certainly the most favourable city in England for the Labour Party. In municipal elections, it was one of the few local authorities in the country which never passed out of Labour control in the dark days of the late 1960s. In the 1979 local elections, only one of Stoke's twenty wards returned Conservative victors (Trentham Park). This indicates that there is no substantial middle-class residential area within the city, nothing to provide the basis for a solid Tory vote.

Why is this? Partly it is a function of the fact that the City of Stoke on Trent is made up of many small semi-independent communities, more even than the 'Five Towns' of Arnold Bennett. As in the Black Country, each town in the Potteries is a working-class and industrial unit. The industries of the district are in general long-established: all stages of pottery production, of course, and an old coalfield. Stoke on Trent still bears its industrial scars more clearly than most British cities. There are relatively few tower blocks, more Victorian houses blackened by the once ferocious grime. It vies with Sheffield for the title of the most resolutely working-class city in England, but unlike Sheffield it has no leafy Tory constituency within its boundaries. Indeed there have been, and will still be, three safe Labour seats in Stoke.

Central is made up of the administrative headquarters of Stoke itself, the shopping centre of Hanley, and a number of other wards like Hartshill and Berryhill. It is expanded, but not significantly altered in the redistribution, and although Labour MP Robert Cant is retiring, his successor Mark Fisher should encounter no trouble in holding on to the seat.

1981	% Own Occ	52.9	1979 core seat Stoke on Trent Central
1981	% Loc Auth	37.1	
1981	% Black/Asian	3	Lab 24,707 60.2
1981	% Mid Cl	31.3	C 12,104 29.5
1981	% Prof Man	8.1	L 4,260 10.4
1982	electorate 67,704		MPs since 1945
1979	notional result		1945-66 B. Stross Lab
	Lab 14,500		1966- Robert Cant Lab
Alliance		SDP	

Stoke on Trent North

The northern part of Stoke on Trent is made up in the main of two of Bennett's Five Towns, Burslem and Tunstall – solidly working-class Labour territory, and not given to high swings. To this core is added Kidsgrove, and a few other wards of Newcastle Borough. These were previously in Leek constituency, but are not included in the new Staffordshire Moorlands seat. They were very much the Labour part of Leek, and their inclusion, and 17,000 more voters, will not weaken Labour's 12,000 majority. Quite the reverse, in fact: 3,000 votes might be added. The northern Potteries are not good ground for Conservatives or Alliance, and there is a complete slate of wholly-Labour wards within this seat.

1981	% Own Occ	60.2	1979 core seat Stoke on Trent
1981	% Loc Auth	33.8	North
1981	% Black/Asian	1	Lab 25,652 59.4
1981	% Mid Cl	31.5	C 13,228 30.6
1981	% Prof Man	8.7	L 3,984 9.2
1982	electorate 76,201		NF 341 0.8
1979	notional Lab 13,400		MPs since 1945
Alliance		SDP	1945-53 A.E. Davies Lab
			1953-66 Harriet Slater Lab
			1966- John Forrester Lab

Stoke on Trent South

The third safe Labour constituency in Stoke on Trent has been associated since 1966 with the deaf MP Jack Ashley, a much admired fighter for the cause of the disabled. Fenton, Longton and Meir are typically solid Potteries Labour wards, but the one Conservative ward in the whole of Stoke on Trent is here too, at Trentham Park. But the three Stoke constituencies are, overall, very similar. The small middle-class population is so widely dispersed and evenly spread as to be ineffective, politically, and Labour can count on a full slate of MPs in the city in the new Parliament.

1981	% Own Occ	58.1	1979 core seat Stoke on Trent
1981	% Loc Auth	34.6	South
1981	% Black/Asian	1	Lab 31,610 58.8
1981	% Mid Cl	32.7	C 17,364 32.3
1981	% Prof Man	10.0	L 4,829 9.0
1982	electorate 70,927		MPs since 1945
1979	notional Lab 12,500		1945-66 E. Smith Lab
Alliance		L	1966- Jack Ashley Lab

Bury St Edmunds

At the last General Election, the Conservative Eldon Griffiths won the NW Suffolk seat of Bury St Edmunds by over 20,000 votes. The historic and affluent town of Bury St Edmunds lies at the centre of prosperous rolling countryside. But this is by no means an identikit rural Tory constituency. In 1971, only 43% of the housing was owner-occupied. This was because of two factors - a large council overspill development at Haverhill; and a high proportion of armed service voters in camps such as the Air Force base at Mildenhall. It was also a very large seat, of over 95,000 voters. The southern end around Haverhill has now been transferred to South Suffolk, which should reinforce Eldon Griffiths's position in the much smaller Bury St Edmunds seat.

1981	% Own Occ	51.3	1979 core seat Bury St Edmunds		
1981	% Loc Auth	29.0	C	41,426	56.8
1981	% Black/Asian	1	Lab	21,167	29.0
1981	% Mid Cl	40.9	L	10,386	14.2
1981	% Prof Man	14.4	MPs since 1950		
1982	electorate 72,698		1950-64 W.T. Aitken C		
1979	notional result		1964- Eldon Griffiths C		
	C 15,400				
Alliance		SDP			

Central Suffolk

Eye used to be the smallest town after which a constituency was named - it had a population of only 1,500 in 1981. The new Central Suffolk seat is based on parts of the rural Eye constituency, but it also includes four wards from the northern edge of Ipswich. Two of these are Conservative - Broom Hill and Castle Hill - and two Labour, Whitton and Whitehouse. These cancel each other out. There was a Liberal MP for Eye as recently as 1951, but Central Suffolk should be safe for the moderate Eye Tory, John Selwyn Gummer.

1981	% Own Occ	63.2	1979 core seat Eye		
1981	% Loc Auth	24.0	C	28,707	52.0
1981	% Black/Asian	1	Lab	13,686	24.8
1981	% Mid Cl	43.9	L	12,259	22.2
1981	% Prof Man	16.1	Oths	592	1.1
1982	electorate 75,560		MPs since 1945		
1979	notional result		1945-51 E.L. Granville L		
	C 9,900		1951-79 Sir Harwood Harrison C		
Alliance		L	1979- John Selwyn Gummer C		

Ipswich

The largest town in Suffolk has had one of the most curious electoral histories in recent years. Labour held Ipswich continuously from 1938 to 1970 - latterly the MP being Sir Dingle Foot. It was then won for the Conservatives by just 13 votes by Ernle Money. Money retained the seat against the national swing in February 1974, when Labour was returned to power. His majority increased to 259. But a popular local moderate Labour candidate, Ken Weetch, triumphed in October 1974 by a princely 1,733 margin. In 1979, when Mrs Thatcher won the Election, Labour obtained their second best result anywhere in the country in Ipswich - a positive swing of 1.4% and a majority of nearly 4,000.

East Anglia has had a tradition of 'doing different' and like Norwich, Ipswich has been one of Labour's happiest towns in recent years. Weetch is undoubtedly well thought of in Ipswich. But it is difficult to explain the pro-Labour swing in 1979 in terms of social, racial or economic developments, as is possible in the heavily Asian Bradford West, the one seat which swung more to Labour.

In the boundary changes, Ipswich loses four wards from its northern edge - over 20,000 voters in all. Two of the wards are strongly Tory, two strongly Labour. They are all transferred into the new, additional Central Suffolk division. This should not worry Ken Weetch too much - and neither should the Alliance, which obtained little more than 20% in the 1982 local elections in Ipswich. The nomination is to be taken by the Liberals, who have always counted Suffolk as one of their very weakest areas. Ipswich is an industrial town and an active port. It is also independently-minded - but Ken Weetch seems likely to continue to benefit from Ipswich's favours.

1981	% Own Occ	56.3	1979 core seat Ipswich		
1981	% Loc Auth	33.3	Lab	34,444	48.2
1981	% Black/Asian	3	C	30,703	43.0
1981	% Mid Cl	44.1	L	5,772	8.1
1981	% Prof Man	12.0	NF	449	0.6
1982	electorate 67,882		WRP	115	0.2
1979	notional result		MPs since 1945		
	Lab 3,400		1945-57 R.R. Stokes Lab		
Alliance		L	1957-70 Sir Dingle Foot Lab		
			1970-74 Ernle Money C		
			1974- Ken Weetch Lab		

South Suffolk

The southern strip of Suffolk along the Essex border is mainly archetypal Tory rural England; the Constable country along the Stour, the 'film-set' former wool towns of Lavenham and Long Melford. There are London overspill estates at Haverhill and Sudbury - which used to form the basis of its own constituency. But South Suffolk, most of which is composed of the Babergh District, must be a safe bet for the Tory candidate, probably Sudbury MP Keith Stainton.

1981	% Own Occ	58.4	1979 core seat Sudbury/
1981	% Loc Auth	29.7	Woodbridge
1981	% Black/Asian	1	C 39,544 55.0
1981	% Mid Cl	45.3	Lab 18,972 26.4
1981	% Prof Man	18.6	L 13,435 18.7
1982	electorate 76,120		MPs since 1950
1979	notional result		1950-63 J.H. Hare C
	C 13,500		1963- Keith Stainton C
Alliance		L	

Suffolk Coastal

Suffolk is entitled to an extra seat in the present redistribution of parliamentary boundaries. The Suffolk Coastal division, which is exactly coterminous with the local authority district of the same name, is made up almost equally of voters from the former Eye and Sudbury/Woodbridge divisions. The whole of the North Sea coast is included, except for that around Lowestoft in the Waveney division. Felixstowe is a bustling port and active seaside resort. Aldeburgh is smaller, an elegant mecca for music lovers - the Snape Maltings lie just inland. Woodbridge is a lively town a few miles up the River Deben. Both Eye and Sudbury/Woodbridge were safely Conservative, so it is not surprising that Suffolk Coastal will provide a safe haven for an additional Tory member of the House.

1981	% Own Occ	60.9	New seat
1981	% Loc Auth	19.9	
1981	% Black/Asian	0.9	
1981	% Mid Cl	48.0	
1981	% Prof Man	19.1	
1982	electorate 71,196		
1979	notional result		
	C 16,800		
Alliance		SDP	

Waveney

James Prior has taken the brunt of the role of the unofficial leader of the 'wet' left-wing Tories who worry about the effects of the government's harsh economic policies. Their adherence to the 'one-nation' tradition of Disraeli has not endeared the 'wets' to the predominant grouping within the Conservative Party, which now seems to owe more to nineteenth-century Gladstonian laissez-faire liberalism. Consigned to a difficult role as Northern Ireland Secretary, Prior has still managed to cut an effective and dignified figure in the Cabinet.

But besides being in an embattled minority within his own party, Prior does not enjoy the benefit of a safe seat. He won the Suffolk constituency of Lowestoft from Labour in 1959, but his majority has never been vast. It was cut to 358 in 1966, and 2,000 as recently as October 1974. Lowestoft is the fourth largest fishing port in Britain, and entertains a shipbuilding industry and a large Birds Eye frozen food plant as well. Like other east coast ports, such as King's Lynn and Yarmouth, Lowestoft has a strong Labour presence. Labour won all seven county council wards here in the 1981 elections. Even in 1979, Prior needed to rely on the smaller towns of the division - Beccles, Bungay, Halesworth and the elegant little seaside resort of Southwold.

The seat is now identical to the local government District of Waveney. This accounts for the change of name from Lowestoft, but it must be doubted how many Britons can identify the location of Waveney. In the boundary changes, 10,000 mainly Tory voters are transferred over the Norfolk border into Great Yarmouth. Prior must look to ensure his seat in the Commons if he is to continue his political career - even if he avoids internecine strife within his own party.

1981	% Own Occ	67.6	1979 core seat Lowestoft		
1981	% Loc Auth	20.8	C	33,376	50.5
1981	% Black/Asian	0.5	Lab	25,555	38.6
1981	% Mid Cl	39.7	L	6,783	10.3
1981	% Prof Man	14.1	E	435	0.7
1982	electorate 77,773		MPs since 1945		
1979	notional result		1945-59 E. Evans Lab		
	C 7,100		1959- James Prior C		
Alliance		SDP			

Chertsey and Walton

Surrey's eleven seats, all little altered in the boundary review, all rank as safely Conservative. Surrey has an image as the essence of the London commuter belt for the middle classes and the wealthy, especially now that the inner part of the old county of Surrey has been incorporated in Greater London. Given this, one might think that the parliamentary constituencies of Surrey are not sufficiently heterogeneous in character to warrant a detailed description of their political anatomy. Yet in the case of Chertsey and Walton there are indeed internal variations worthy of note, even if these are not enough to make the seat marginal.

The old Urban District of Walton included Weybridge and Hersham. St George's Hill, Weybridge, belies its past as a haunt of the primitive communist Diggers in the 1640s to rank as the best known of the private estates of the super-rich, with its multi-million pound valued houses widely spaced and jealously guarded. Burwood Park ranks only a little way further down the scale of affluence. But there are council estates in Hersham, and Walton on Thames itself is on favourable occasions a Labour seat on Surrey County Council. Similarly, Chertsey town is mixed politically and socially. The old Chertsey Urban District also includes Conservative Addlestone and New Haw.

Minister for the RAF Geoffrey Pattie was elected in 1979 on a minority vote, although with the opposition equally divided between Liberal and Labour, he obtained a healthy 12,000 majority. It is unlikely that the solid Tory vote here can be cracked, but the substantial numbers of opposition voters should remind us that even Surrey is not a kingdom of identikit equals.

1981	% Own Occ	65.7	1979 core seat Chertsey and Walton
1981	% Loc Auth	20.4	

1981	% Black/Asian	2.5	C	25,810	49.0
1981	% Mid Cl	62.1	L	13,786	26.2
1981	% Prof Man	25.8	Lab	12,211	23.2
1982	electorate 70,938		NF	819	1.6

1979   notional result
       C 12,000

Alliance   SDP

MPs since 1945
1945-50 A. Marsden C
1950-70 Sir Lionel Heald C
1970-74 Michael Grylls C
1974-   Geoffrey Pattie C

East Surrey

The Conservative Chancellor of the Exchequer, Sir Geoffrey Howe, represents the comfortable semi-rural constituency of East Surrey, which stretches to the Kent border in Winston Churchill country, near Chartwell. East Surrey is one of the few unchanged seats, and a proposal to rename it Tandridge, after the local authority, was reversed after an inquiry. Sir Geoffrey has never had much to fear from the little towns of Oxted and Lingfield, Caterham and Warlingham, or from the affluent villages of his seat, which has always been more worried by fears of inflation rather than unemployment.

1981	% Own Occ	69.2	1979 same seat East Surrey
1981	% Loc Auth	19.4	C 28,266 62.8
1981	% Black/Asian	1.8	L 8,866 19.7
1981	% Mid Cl	64.1	Lab 7,398 16.4
1981	% Prof Man	29.4	NF 452 1.0
1982	electorate 58,874		MPs since 1945
Alliance		L	1945-51 M.L. Astor C
			1951-70 C. Doughty C
			1970-74 Sir W. Clark C
			1974- Sir Geoffrey Howe C

Epsom and Ewell

Epsom and Ewell will be a smaller seat at the next Election, for Leatherhead has been moved into Mole Valley, while parts of Banstead have been added. The basis of the seat remains, however, and since it gave Tory Archie Hamilton a 26,000 majority in 1969 there can be no prediction of any political change. This is horse racing country, as well as the home of the mid-Surrey commuter - Tattenhams is one of the Banstead wards joining Epsom and Ewell. The Alliance can hope for little more than a clear second place here, and Epsom should remain Tory by the equivalent of a good twenty lengths.

1981	% Own Occ	75.2	1979 core seat Epsom/Ewell
1981	% Loc Auth	16.7	C 39,104 61.9
1981	% Black/Asian	3	L 12,746 20.2
1981	% Mid Cl	70.8	Lab 11,315 17.9
1981	% Prof Man	26.8	MPs since 1945
1982	electorate 70,842		1945-47 Sir A.R.S. Southby C
1979	notional result		1947-55 M.S. McCorquodale C
	C 23,000		1955-78 Sir Peter Rawlinson C
Alliance		L	1978- Archie Hamilton C

Esher

In the 1979 Election, Esher could boast the safest of all the Tory majorities in Surrey, and one of the half- dozen safest in Britain. It was a small seat of 47,000 electors. Now it is increased to 62,000 by the addition of some Guildford wards such as Clandon and Horsley, Effingham and Send. Esher Urban District consisted of Esher itself, Cobham, the Dittons, the Moleseys, Oxshott and Hinchley Wood: solidly affluent owner-occupier territory, conveniently and expensively situated just outside the Greater London boundary across the river from Hampton Court. It will remain an overwhelming stronghold for its right-wing Tory MP, ex-colonel Carol Mather.

1981	% Own Occ	74.0	1979 core seat Esher
1981	% Loc Auth	15.0	C 24,152 65.1
1981	% Black/Asian	2	L 7,311 19.7
1981	% Mid Cl	71.5	Lab 5,634 15.2
1981	% Prof Man	34.9	MPs since 1950
1982	electorate 62,448		1950-70 Sir W. Robson Brown C
1979	notional C 22,400		1970- Carol Mather C
Alliance		L	

Guildford

Guildford is not merely a commuting town for London. Like Reigate and Woking, it is big enough to act as a commercial and employing centre of its own; and like them, it has extensive council estates, here in the west and north of the town. Guildford itself, then, is not universally Tory, but the seat also includes more affluent villages like Worplesdon, and now Cranleigh, Ewhurst and Bramley from Waverley District, SW Surrey. Cabinet Minister David Howell gained a 20,000 majority in 1979 - it was one of the earliest, and most predictable, results to be declared. Labour, and the Alliance, should receive a respectable five-figure vote at Guildford; but there can be few worries for Howell at the next Election.

1981	% Own Occ	66	1979 core seat Guildford
1981	% Loc Auth	22	C 31,595 57.2
1981	% Black/Asian	2	Lab 11,689 21.2
1981	% Mid Cl	60	L 11,673 21.2
1981	% Prof Man	25	Ind 232 0.4
1982	electorate 75,659		MPs since 1945
1979	notional C 19,400		1945-50 Sir J.J. Jarvis C
Alliance		SDP	1950-66 G.R.H. Nugent C
			1966- David Howell C

Mole Valley

In the present redistribution, a considerable exercise in the renaming of constituencies has taken place. Often the title of the local government District has been used, as here in the case of Mole Valley, which is based on the former seat of Dorking. The town of Dorking itself, which has a population of 20,000, is set in the midst of the highest hills in Surrey. It is still partly country town, and partly suburbanised. Now it is to be joined by Leatherhead, which includes Ashtead, Bookham and Fetcham, and which was previously in Epsom and Ewell. Mole Valley will be one of the safest Tory seats, while the Alliance is a good bet for retaining second place.

1981	% Own Occ	65.4	1979 core seat Dorking
1981	% Loc Auth	20.2	C	29,003	61.4
1981	% Black/Asian	1.5	L	9,240	19.6
1981	% Mid Cl	66.1	Lab	8,970	19.0
1981	% Prof Man	29.4	MPs since 1950
1982	electorate 65,508		1950-64 Sir G.C. Touche C
1979	notional C 19,600		1964-79 Sir George Sinclair C
Alliance		L	1979- Keith Wickenden C

North-West Surrey

Surrey Heath District, on which the constituency of NW Surrey is based, was the only one in the country to have a 100% Conservative representation amongst its councillors in 1979 - 36 councillors, 36 Tories. The absence of independents indicates that this is a thoroughly suburban seat. It includes the growing private residential towns of Camberley and Frimley, with their strong military presence - Sandhurst, Bagshot, Bisley and other well-known Army haunts fringe the constituency. The other part of the seat is even more high-status: Egham, which includes Virginia Water, with its Wentworth estate which rivals St George's Hill for the title of most exclusive in Britain. The Tory majority here at the last Election was over 25,000, and its boundaries are unchanged.

1981	% Own Occ	68.6	1979 same seat North-West
1981	% Loc Auth	18.6	Surrey
1981	% Black/Asian	3	C	36,219	63.7
1981	% Mid Cl	61.4	Lab	10,763	18.9
1981	% Prof Man	26.5	L	9,037	15.9
1982	electorate 78,680		NF	796	1.4
Alliance		L	MP since 1974
			1974- Michael Grylls C

Reigate

Some of the rare Labour-supporting local authority and county council wards in Surrey are to be found in Reigate, in the council estates east and south of the town, and in Redhill, its less favoured neighbour. Down towards Horley the propinquity of Gatwick Airport becomes very noticeable, both due to the congestion of traffic on the ground and because of the aircraft noise. All this is somewhat less desirable than much of the rest of the favoured commuting county.

But the Reigate seat also includes excellent residential areas such as NW Reigate up against the shoulder of the North Downs, and places like Tadworth where the village atmosphere is not quite extinguished. However, some of the most attractive wards, in Banstead, have been moved into Epsom and Ewell.

Although the MP, lively and combative Thatcherite George Gardiner, should continue to benefit from the remorseless Conservatism of this owner-occupied division, it is less clearly dominated by the 'gin-and-Jag' set than many seats, and both Labour and the Alliance are capable of achieving a five-figure vote.

1981	% Own Occ	66.3	1979 core seat Reigate and		
1981	% Loc Auth	21.6	Banstead		
1981	% Black/Asian	2.5	C	33,767	59.8
1981	% Mid Cl	63.6	Lab	12,454	22.1
1981	% Prof Man	25.0	L	10,257	18.2
1982	electorate 71,025		MPs since 1945		
1979	notional result		1945-50 G.S. Touche C		
	C 18,800		1950-70 Sir J. Vaughan-Morgan		
Alliance		SDP	C		
			1970-74 Sir Geoffrey Howe C		
			1974- George Gardiner C		

Spelthorne

Spelthorne is that part of Surrey north of the Thames. It used to be in Middlesex, but the residents preferred not to be included in Greater London; the county of Surrey seems better to suit their tastes and self-image. The main communities are Staines, Sunbury on Thames, Ashford and Shepperton.

Jammed between London's great western reservoirs and Heathrow Airport, it might not seem to be a very attractive residential area. Indeed, there are few of the large detached houses, private roads and leafy suburbs associated with Surrey. Yet in 1979 Humphrey Atkins won a Tory majority of over 16,000. There is a large Labour minority, which is most notable in the Stanwell council estate, and the proportion of professional and managerial workers is clearly the lowest in the county. Humphrey Atkins has lost his position in Mrs Thatcher's Cabinet, another casualty of the Falklands dispute.

But despite these factors, Spelthorne should retain its preference for right-wing politics, and it is difficult to see the Alliance's soft centre having much appeal here. The seat is unaltered in the boundary review.

1981	% Own Occ	69.4	1979 same seat Spelthorne		
1981	% Loc Auth	20.0	C	31,290	57.4
1981	% Black/Asian	2.8	Lab	15,137	27.8
1981	% Mid Cl	61.7	L	7,565	13.9
1981	% Prof Man	21.5	NF	518	1.0
1982	electorate 72,807		MPs since 1945		
Alliance		SDP	1945-50 G. Pargiter Lab		
			1950-70 Sir G. Craddock C		
			1970- Humphrey Atkins C		

South-West Surrey

Outer Surrey, towards the Sussex and Hampshire borders, contains some of the most pleasant countryside and residential areas in England. The three main towns are Godalming, Haslemere and Farnham, which gives its name to the current seat on which the new division of SW Surrey is based. Farnham, which is very similar to the Waverley District, has provided a sound political base for a former Prime Minister's son, Maurice Macmillan, since 1966. The Liberals did challenge strongly in 1974, and still command a clear second place. But who can be surprised that this highly comfortable and attractive corner of England should continue to endow the Conservative Party with its chief favours?

1981	% Own Occ	66	1979 core seat Farnham		
1981	% Loc Auth	20	C	30,127	58.3
1981	% Black/Asian	2	L	13,658	26.4
1981	% Mid Cl	58	Lab	7,497	14.5
1981	% Prof Man	23	Oth	374	0.7
1982	electorate 69,967		MPs since 1945		
1979	notional result		1945-66 Sir G. Nicholson C		
	C 17,000		1966- Maurice Macmillan C		
Alliance		L			

Woking

Woking is the largest town in Surrey. The new Woking Borough, like the former Woking Urban District, includes surrounding communities like Byfleet and Horsell; it makes up the bulk of the seat, the remainder being Ash and Pirbright from Guildford Borough. Woking is large enough to have its council estates, and terraced central streets. Labour forced its way into second place in 1979. But this was 18,000 votes behind Thatcherite Minister Cranley Onslow, who need have nothing to fear, barring an unlikely political earthquake in Woking.

1981	% Own Occ	68.7	1979 core seat Woking		
1981	% Loc Auth	20.3	C	31,719	57.0
1981	% Black/Asian	4	Lab	13,327	24.0
1981	% Mid Cl	62.3	L	9,991	18.0
1981	% Prof Man	25.2	NF	564	1.0
1982	electorate 77,938		MPs since 1950		
1979	notional result		1950-64 H.A. Watkinson C		
	C 18,400		1964- Cranley Onslow C		
Alliance		L			

Bexhill and Battle

This Sussex constituency is based on the former seat of Rye, but the easternmost stretch of the county's coastline around Rye and Winchelsea is now drawn together with Hastings. What remains in Bexhill and Battle is the coastal strip between Hastings and Eastbourne, and the fertile and wooded countryside behind. This is the area most associated with the Norman Conquest of England, for William I landed at Pevensey and defeated the army of the Anglo-Saxon regime at Battle, the heart of the inland part of this new seat. But there is little chance that there will be much significant political warfare here, for this will be one of the safest Conservative seats in England.

The Liberals came second in the Rye constituency in the last Election, and have some local strength in Battle and the villages. Labour suffered one of their 21 lost deposits in the 1979 Election in Rye, but do have one county council ward in Bexhill North. But Bexhill as a whole is very Conservative, and over half of its permanent population is made up of retired people. Tory MP Bryant Goodman Irvine is retiring at the next Election, but he won a majority of over 23,000 last time. He will bequeath to his lucky successor Charles Wardle a seat every bit as safe as Rye.

The constituency is based largely on the District of Rother. This River Rother flows into the Channel at Rye, and forms the Kent-East Sussex border for part of its length. The environment it waters couldn't be more different from that other constituency of Rother Valley and the town of Rotherham. If that is the Socialist Republic of South Yorkshire, Bexhill and Battle is in the Tory citadel of southern England.

1981	% Own Occ	72	1979 core seat Rye		
1981	% Loc Auth	14	C	35,516	62.7
1981	% Black/Asian	1	L	12,438	22.0
1981	% Mid Cl	54	Lab	6,852	12.1
1981	% Prof Man	23	E	1,267	2.2
1982	electorate 61,816		NF	552	1.0
1979	notional result		MP since 1955		
	C 18,400		1955-	Bryant Godman Irvine C	
Alliance		L			

Brighton Kemptown

Labour has only ever won one seat in Sussex, and that seat is Brighton Kemptown. It was something of a shock when Dennis Hobden seized Kemptown in 1964 - and he swept in by the margin of fully seven votes. Hobden had the temerity to win again in 1966, but in 1970 the seat reverted to the Conservative fold, where it has remained since, in the hands of Andrew Bowden. In 1979 Bowden's majority was a healthy 8,000, and with the creation of the new Crawley seat Kemptown will no longer be the brightest Labour hope in Sussex.

Kemptown is the east end of Brighton, not only geographically, but sociologically too. Here we have the more plebeian, less fashionable side of the south's most famous seaside resort, around and beyond the East (Palace) Pier. Well behind the front, council estates climb up into the South Downs. Labour can normally count on success in wards like Moulsecoomb, Woodingdean and Hanover, and there is a left-wing Sussex University presence up near Falmer. As might be expected, the Tories do better on the sea-front, especially at Rottingdean, which produced nearly half of Bowden's majority on its own in 1979. The Social Democrat Tom Forester has had much success in Hanover ward in local elections; it remains to be seen whether the Alliance can make any impact in Kemptown as a whole.

Like most popular and successful holiday resorts, Brighton has a seamy and inelegant side. But with an economy so dependent upon tourism, the service industries and commerce, this is rarely translated into support for the Labour Party. Despite Kemptown's working-class characteristics, Dennis Hobden's renowned success looks like a singular product of the high-water mark of Labour's fortunes in the late 1960s. There are only minor adjustments in the boundaries of the Brighton seats.

1981	% Own Occ	52
1981	% Loc Auth	30
1981	% Black/Asian	2
1981	% Mid Cl	46
1981	% Prof Man	13
1982	electorate 61,959	
1979	notional result	
	C 7,800	

Alliance   SDP

1979 core seat Brighton Kemptown

C	25,512	53.6
Lab	17,504	36.8
L	4,179	8.8
NF	404	0.8

MPs since 1950
1950-59 H.S. Johnson C
1959-64 David James C
1964-70 Dennis Hobden Lab
1970-   Andrew Bowden C

Brighton Pavilion

The safe Tory seat in Brighton is the west or Pavilion division. This is the most elegant end of the seafront, towards genteel Hove: in few other towns could there be a ward named Regency. Inland there are the comfortable suburbs with a high proportion of London commuters, Preston and Patcham. Labour can fight back only at Stanmer, near the radical plate-glass of Sussex University. Pavilion is held by a prominent back-bench right-winger from a famous Conservative family, Julian Amery.

1981	% Own Occ	60	1979 core seat	Brighton Pavilion	
1981	% Loc Auth	10	C	22,218	53.7
1981	% Black/Asian	3	Lab	12,099	29.3
1981	% Mid Cl	55	L	5,965	14.4
1981	% Prof Man	18	E	469	1.3
1982	electorate 60,399		NF	320	0.9
1979	notional C 10,400		MPs since 1950		
Alliance		SDP	1950-69 Sir L.W.B. Teeling C		
			1969- Julian Amery C		

Eastbourne

There are only two constituencies in Great Britain where over 30% of the population is aged over 65. Both are in Sussex. One is Worthing in W Sussex, and the other is Eastbourne. This resort beneath the towering cliffs of Beachy Head was founded in the 18th century like Brighton, but it is decidedly quieter and more staid. The Liberals do well in local elections in wards like Downside and Langney, and they approached within 7,500 votes of victory in Eastbourne in the February 1974 Election. But their vote collapsed in subsequent General Elections, and the Tory majority in 1979 was 26,084. Labour wins just one council estate ward, Hampden Park. Eastbourne loses a few thousand voters to Bexhill/Battle, but it should remain safe for Ian Gow, Mrs Thatcher's Parliamentary Private Secretary.

1981	% Own Occ	72	1979 core seat	Eastbourne	
1981	% Loc Auth	14	C	37,168	63.0
1981	% Black/Asian	1.5	L	11,084	18.8
1981	% Mid Cl	57	Lab	10,166	17.2
1981	% Prof Man	19	NF	533	0.9
1982	electorate 72,767		MPs since 1945		
1979	notional C 24,100		1945-74 Sir Charles Taylor C		
Alliance		L	1974- Ian Gow C		

Hastings and Rye

The easternmost constituency in East Sussex, Hastings and Rye, is a combination of the old slightly undersized Hastings seat and 10,000 voters from Rye – taking in the old Cinque Ports of Rye and Winchelsea and the modern beach resort of Camber Sands. Hastings is by no means a Tory stronghold. Labour cut the majority to only 2,000 in 1966, and enjoys safe wards in Hollington, Ore and Mount Pleasant. But the addition of Rye would have boosted Kenneth Warren's Hastings majority to a comfortable 12,000 in 1979.

1981	% Own Occ	60	1979 core seat Hastings		
1981	% Loc Auth	17	C	21,311	51.5
1981	% Black/Asian	1.5	L	6,474	15.7
1981	% Mid Cl	51	Ind	839	2.0
1981	% Prof Man	16	NF	344	0.8
1982	electorate 70,025		MPs since 1945		
1979	notional result		1945-70 Sir E.M. Cooper-Key C		
	C 12,500		1970– Kenneth Warren C		
Alliance		L			

Hove

The only unaltered constituency in East Sussex comprises Brighton's twin town of Hove, the westernmost part of East Sussex. This is an almost entirely residential area stretching back from the Regency squares and crescents on the seafront to sheltered hollows in the South Downs. The only hint of industry is found at Portslade, near the eastern arm of Shoreham harbour – Labour's only ward is Portslade North. Hove is a massively certain seat for Tim Sainsbury, a member of the grocery chain family, who successfully resisted the Liberal revival of the time when first elected in the 1973 byelection. If the Liberals couldn't win Hove in that year (when they took Ripon, the Isle of Ely and Berwick upon Tweed), they never will.

1981	% Own Occ	57.8	1979 same seat Hove		
1981	% Loc Auth	14.8	C	30,256	60.1
1981	% Black/Asian	2.3	Lab	10,807	21.5
1981	% Mid Cl	59.0	L	8,771	17.4
1981	% Prof Man	20.6	NF	508	1.0
1982	electorate 71,841		MPs since 1950		
Alliance		L	1950-65 A.A.H. Marlowe C		
			1965-73 Martin Maddan C		
			1973– Timothy Sainsbury C		

Lewes

The county town of East Sussex is the centre of another of
the Tory bastions in the county. In the boundary changes it
loses part of the old Hailsham Rural District, now in Wealden,
and with it some 14,000 electors. Besides Lewes itself, the
constituency includes the seaside resort of Seaford, and the
rather depressed ferry port of Newhaven, Peacehaven and the
inland country behind the Brighton-Eastbourne coast. Labour
has some votes in Newhaven and Lewes, but could do no
better than third in 1979 - and the Liberals were over 21,000
votes behind the Tory MP, Tim Rathbone.

1981	% Own Occ	70	1979 core seat Lewes		
1981	% Loc Auth	16	C	33,992	58.4
1981	% Black/Asian	1	L	12,279	21.1
1981	% Mid Cl	57	Lab	11,152	19.2
1981	% Prof Man	22	NF	764	1.3
1982	electorate 67,470		MPs since 1945		
1979	notional result		1945-74 Sir Tufton Beamish C		
	C 18,200		1974- Tim Rathbone C		
Alliance		L			

Wealden

The Sussex Weald is a largely agricultural and heavily wooded
district of soft southern English scenery. The new Wealden
constituency is similar to the former East Grinstead division,
but East Grinstead itself is now in West Sussex, and must be
replaced by part of Hailsham Rural District. There are no
large towns in Wealden, but the largest are Crowborough,
Hailsham, Uckfield and Forest Row. Wealden is the only one
of the eight East Sussex seats without a sea frontage, and it
stretches into the far north of the county almost to
Tunbridge Wells. It will be an overwhelmingly Conservative
seat.

1981	% Own Occ	75	1979 core seat East Grinstead		
1981	% Loc Auth	11	C	28,279	62.0
1981	% Black/Asian	1.5	L	11,102	24.4
1981	% Mid Cl	57	Lab	6,196	13.6
1981	% Prof Man	23	MPs since 1945		
1982	electorate 69,011		1945-55 R.S. Clarke C		
1979	notional result		1955-65 Hon. Mrs E.V.E. Emmet		
	C 19,000			C	
Alliance		SDP	1965- Geoffrey Johnson-Smith		
				C	

Arundel

There were only three Conservative majorities of over 30,000
at the 1979 General Election, and one of these was achieved
by Michael Marshall at Arundel. The little town of Arundel
itself accounted for only just over 2% of the large electorate
of 91,000, most of the population being concentrated on the
coastal strip from Bognor Regis to Worthing.

This constituency used to be identical to the local government
District of Arun. Now 25,000 electors at the eastern end of
the strip, around Rustington, East Preston and Angmering,
have been moved into Shoreham. This shouldn't affect the
safeness of the seat, although the numerical majority will of
course be reduced. Bognor Regis, Arundel and the villages
are strongly Conservative, with the Liberals taking second
place. The Liberals have done very well in local elections
next door in Adur, the District on which Shoreham is based,
but they have made little impact in Arun District or Arundel
constituency. Labour can win the industrial section of the
ancient port of Littlehampton.

But the constituency is an epitome of Tory Sussex. The River
Arun flows down through the lush scenery of the South
Downs through the gap at Arundel to the westernmost coast
in Sussex, passing through the Duke of Norfolk's sphere of
influence. It is a representative seat for West Sussex, a
comfortable and affluent corner of England, apparently with
every reason to pursue a policy which is conservative in
every sense.

1981	% Own Occ	73	1979 core seat Arundel		
1981	% Loc Auth	14	C	43,968	65.0
1981	% Black/Asian	1	L	13,208	19.5
1981	% Mid Cl	56	Lab	10,509	15.5
1981	% Prof Man	23	MP since 1974		
1982	electorate 74,324		1974-	Michael Marshall C	
1979	notional result				
	C 23,600				
Alliance		L			

Chichester

The south and south-east of England has increasingly become a kind of desert for the Labour Party. They did not win any of the 11 seats in Surrey, or the 15 seats in Kent, or the 14 seats in Sussex at the 1979 General Election. There is a case to be made for saying that Sussex is the most Conservative of all counties. In the first election for the European Parliament in 1979, there were only two British constituencies with a Tory majority of over 100,000. They were the two Sussex seats. A typical example of the secureness of Conservative parliamentary seats in Sussex is Chichester. Anthony Nelson won it with a majority of 23,776 last time. It would take a swing of 22%, to the Liberals, to dislodge him.

Chichester's boundaries are not altered in the present revision. The constituency is the western part of West Sussex. It runs along the Hampshire border from the Channel coast at Selsey Bill and the creek territory of the Witterings and Bosham through Chichester itself and the South Downs to the douce little towns of Midhurst and Petworth. Chichester town has its share of council estates, but Labour can rarely win a single local authority ward, and finishes a poor third in the seat as a whole. The aristocratic influence is strong in this attractive neck of the woods – the stately homes include Cowdray Park at Midhurst, Petworth House and the Goodwood House of the Dukes of Richmond and Gordon.

It might be said in jest that Chichester will be in the hands of the Conservative Party until the Revolution. But it seems quite probable that even after the Revolution the Workers' Soviet for Chichester would be Tory.

1981	% Own Occ	59.7	1979 same seat Chichester		
1981	% Loc Auth	23.5	C	34,696	62.3
1981	% Black/Asian	1.4	L	10,920	19.6
1981	% Mid Cl	53.1	Lab	8,569	15.4
1981	% Prof Man	21.5	Ind	863	1.5
1982	electorate 77,434		E	656	1.2
Alliance		SDP	MPs since 1945		

1945-58 Hon. L.W. Joynson-Hicks C
1958-69 W.H. Loveys C
1969-74 Christopher Chataway C
1974- Anthony Nelson C

449

Crawley

The New Town of Crawley, designated in 1946, formed a red blot on the county's landscape to many Sussex residents' minds. With its large London overspill population and predominance of local authority housing, it contrasts sharply with the affluent middle-class norm of Sussex. Its political impact, however, was always limited by its inclusion within the Horsham seat, which had grown to an electorate of 100,000 by 1979. Now Crawley acquires a seat of its own - but ironically enough, the Conservatives would have won it in 1979.

Crawley itself probably gave Labour a majority in the last General Election - it certainly cast 600 more votes to Labour than the Conservatives in the local elections which took place in the New Town on the same day. But although Crawley has finally shaken off the influence of Horsham, it is still not large enough to stand quite alone. It gains 5,000 or so voters from some very Tory villages from Mid Sussex - Copthorne, Worth and Balcome, which would just have tipped the balance in 1979. Crawley itself has Tory wards too, mainly in the south and east of the town - Furnace Green, Pound Hill, Three Bridges. Labour does best in Langley Green, Ifield, West Green, Tilgate and Broadfield. Each neighbourhood is planned as a self-contained unit, and they have varied statuses and characteristics - there are 'good' and 'bad' sides of town even in a post-war planned community like Crawley.

The proportion of council housing in Crawley Borough has declined from 66% in 1971 to 54% in 1981 as local authority housing has been sold and new private estates developed. Despite its reputation, Crawley itself is near enough politically marginal. But the new constituency must still be Labour's best bet in Sussex. Labour did well to come out top of the poll even in the 1982 local elections. The Alliance obtained only 24% of the vote, and seems to pose no threat to the two older parties in Crawley.

1981	% Own Occ	41	New seat
1981	% Loc Auth	53	
1981	% Black/Asian	5	
1981	% Mid Cl	53	
1981	% Prof Man	15	
1982	electorate 70,856		
1979	notional result		
	C 1,500 (RW)		
Alliance		SDP	

Horsham

In October 1974 Peter Hordern's Conservative majority in Horsham and Crawley was reduced to 3,699. But now he will be able to rely on one of the safest seats in Britain, for the threat posed by Crawley's Labour tendencies has been removed. His seat will now simply be Horsham District – the old Horsham Urban and Rural Districts and the former Chanctonbury RD to the south, which is picked up from Shoreham. Horsham, a market town and commuting base for London, is the only large unit. The rest of this prosperous seat in central Sussex is composed of the small towns of Pulborough, Billingshurst and Steyning and many affluent villages.

1981	% Own Occ	65.5	1979 core seat Horsham and		
1981	% Loc Auth	23.2	Crawley		
1981	% Black/Asian	1.7	C	42,529	52.2
1981	% Mid Cl	57.7	Lab	27,508	33.8
1981	% Prof Man	23.9	L	10,920	13.4
1982	electorate 79,791		NF	493	0.6
1979	notional result		MPs since 1945		
	C 15,500		1945-51 Earl Winterton C		
Alliance		SDP	1951-64 C.F.H. Gough C		
			1964- Peter Hordern C		

Mid Sussex

Three quarters of the electorate of Mid Sussex is contained within four towns – the old towns of East Grinstead and Cuckfield, and the modern commuting bases of Haywards Heath and Burgess Hill. East Grinstead is a solidly Conservative acquisition from the county of East Sussex, but Mid Sussex was already one of the 25 safest Tory seats in Britain. The only relief from a full slate of Conservative/Independents on the Mid Sussex District Council is provided by two Liberals from Burgess Hill. But the Alliance can hope for no better a placing than second in Mid Sussex.

1981	% Own Occ	73	1979 core seat Mid Sussex		
1981	% Loc Auth	14	C	32,548	61.2
1981	% Black/Asian	2	L	11,705	22.0
1981	% Mid Cl	63	Lab	8,260	15.5
1981	% Prof Man	26	Ind C	697	1.3
1982	electorate 76,860		MP since 1974		
1979	notional result		1974- Timothy Renton C		
	C 22,600				
Alliance		L			

Shoreham

Shoreham is the parliamentary seat based on the Adur District Council. Adur is one of the few authorities where the Liberals can seriously mount a challenge for control. But they trailed 21,500 votes behind Tory Richard Luce at the last General Election, so it seems clear that they cannot translate their support into national elections. In the boundary changes, Shoreham has lost some inland territory, but now includes coastal communities on both sides of Worthing, taking those to the west from Arundel. There is some industry in the ports of Shoreham and Southwick, but Labour can get nowhere in this seat.

1981	% Own Occ	73	1979 core seat Shoreham		
1981	% Loc Auth	19	C	34,339	60.9
1981	% Black/Asian	1	L	12,754	22.6
1981	% Mid Cl	52	Lab	8,867	15.7
1981	% Prof Man	20	NF	406	0.7
1982	electorate 70,400		MP since 1974		
1979	notional result		1974-	Richard Luce C	
	C 21,500				
Alliance		L			

Worthing

Over a third of the population of the seaside town of Worthing is over 65 years of age – the highest proportion of any parliamentary constituency in Britain. Worthing will be one of the few seats undisturbed by the Boundary Commission's work. The town is renowned for its mild climate; but the only threat to the tenure of Tory MP Terence Higgins has come not from Liberals or Labour, who have never made any impact here, but from those within his own party who have thought him too moderate. Having survived a serious attempt to oust him in 1970, though, Higgins seems set for a long continuation of his career in the House.

1981	% Own Occ	76.3	1979 same seat Worthing		
1981	% Loc Auth	11.6	C	33,624	61.2
1981	% Black/Asian	1	L	13,244	24.1
1981	% Mid Cl	60.0	Lab	7,163	13.0
1981	% Prof Man	20.7	NF	893	1.6
1982	electorate 76,371		MPs since 1945		
Alliance		L	1945-64 Sir Otho Prior-Palmer C		
			1964-	Terence Higgins C	

North Warwickshire

Warwickshire was once one of the most populous counties in England. But with the removal of the city of Coventry and the great West Midlands conurbation, Warwickshire is left as a highly truncated rump which only possesses five parliamentary constituencies. One of the seats which was split in two by the creation of the West Midlands Metropolitan County was Meriden, a highly marginal and over-large division. The part of Meriden which remains in Warwickshire makes up the North Warwicks Borough. The new constituency of the same name also includes most of the town of Bedworth, formerly in Nuneaton.

North Warwickshire will be better for Labour than the old Meriden was. The ex-Meriden electorate is spread across small towns and villages of varying types. Some of them are Conservative commuter bases, like Coleshill and Water Orton. But there are also Labour-supporting industrial communities around the old Warwickshire coalfield - places like Arley, Baddesley Ensor and Atherstone. All in all, North Warwickshire Borough might have given the Conservatives a narrow majority of a thousand or so in 1979. But Bedworth is very much a working-class suburb of Nuneaton, and its inclusion tips the new N Warwicks seat towards Labour in an even year.

Indeed Bedworth is so strong for Labour that the Nuneaton MP Leslie Huckfield feels its departure will seriously weaken his own chances. But Huckfield's loss is North Warwickshire's gain, and the new seat seems set to join the small band of semi-rural Labour constituencies.

1981	% Own Occ	62.0	New seat
1981	% Loc Auth	28.1	
1981	% Black/Asian	0.5	
1981	% Mid Cl	41.2	
1981	% Prof Man	14.5	
1982	electorate 69,339		
1979	notional result		
	Lab 3,100		
Alliance		SDP	

Nuneaton

Nuneaton is, by tradition, a Labour stronghold. The Conservatives haven't won it since 1931 (and then only by 2,000 votes). When Harold Wilson decided to appoint the transport union leader Frank Cousins to the government in 1965, he found a safe seat at Nuneaton. The experiment of bringing in new blood at top level from outside Parliament has never really proved a success in peacetime, and Cousins resigned to create another byelection just two years later. (The ex-CBI chief John Davies also met problems when imported as Conservative MP for Knutsford in the 1970s.)

But Leslie Huckfield, youngest MP when elected in the 1967 byelection, had no trouble at Nuneaton for a dozen years. In 1979, though, a 9.3% swing to the Conservatives cut his majority from 17,000 to 7,000; and when the Boundary Commission announced plans to remove the town of Bedworth and replace it with three rural wards, Huckfield decided to accept nomination for a safe seat at Wigan. Some feel that it is bad for a captain to abandon a sinking ship in this manner.

But is Nuneaton sinking beneath the deep-blue Tory waves? Surely a 50-year tradition of Labour representation cannot be so fragile that it is vulnerable to fairly minor boundary changes. Nuneaton itself is still a predominantly Labour town. There are middle-class residential areas at Whitestone and in NE Nuneaton, but Labour piles up the votes at Camp Hill and Attleborough, Stockingford and Chilvers Coton. The added outlying wards - Wolvey, Fosse and Earl Craven in Rugby Borough - are Conservative, but they only account for about 8,000 of the electorate of 63,000. Huckfield's move should prove to have been unnecessary, at least unless there is a further swing against Labour next time.

1981	% Own Occ	65.8	1979 core seat Nuneaton		
1981	% Loc Auth	27.0	Lab	31,403	49.9
1981	% Black/Asian	3	C	23,715	37.7
1981	% Mid Cl	42.8	L	6,184	9.8
1981	% Prof Man	15.0	NF	718	1.3
1982	electorate 66,674		Ind Lab 629		1.0
1979	notional result		MPs since 1945		
	Lab 1,400		1945-65 F.G. Bowles Lab		
Alliance		SDP	1965-67 Frank Cousins Lab		
			1967- Les Huckfield Lab		

Rugby and Kenilworth

Rugby was a constituency with one of the most peculiar electoral histories in the country. First of all, it elected W.J. Brown as an Independent during the war, in 1942, and then again in 1945 against official Labour and Conservative opposition. It then developed as a marginal with the habit of swinging against the national tide - towards the Conservatives in 1964, towards Labour in 1970, and towards the Conservatives again in October 1974. Finally in 1979 it came resoundingly into line, and the Labour MP William Price was beaten by an 8% pro-Tory swing.

Now the situation has changed significantly, for in comes the Coventry commuter town of Kenilworth from Warwick Borough. Kenilworth's sophisticated electorate has on occasion elected local Liberal councillors, but it is one of the most affluent and middle-class towns in Britain, and it is hard to see the new Rugby/Kenilworth division as anything other than safe Conservative. Kenilworth was always the most Conservative part of Warwick and Leamington constituency, and its removal will of course tip that seat in the opposite direction.

Despite its encapsulation of the spirit of the nineteenth century public school (William Webb Ellis, Thomas Arnold, Tom Brown), Rugby itself is a heavy engineering centre and a Labour town. Wards like Hillmorton, Newbold and Benn produced large Labour majorities even in 1979. But Rugby will now be swamped by the affluent villages nearby, and by Kenilworth, which is growing all the time. First term Tory MP James Pawsey can hope for a consolidated majority next time.

1981	% Own Occ	72	1979 core seat Rugby
1981	% Loc Auth	18	C 24,417 47.3
1981	% Black/Asian	4	Lab 21,688 42.0
1981	% Mid Cl	56	L 4,945 9.6
1981	% Prof Man	20	NF 551 1.1
1982	electorate 75,094		MPs since 1945
1979	notional result		1945-50 W.J. Brown Ind
	C 4,300		1950-59 J. Johnson Lab
Alliance		L	1959-66 A.E. Wise C
			1966-79 William Price Lab
			1979- James Pawsey C

Stratford on Avon

It might be thought that Stratford on Avon would prove one of the most civilised of English constituencies. Famed throughout the world as the home of the most favoured of all playwrights, Stratford welcomes all kinds of sophisticates as well as the more humble types of tourist. At the last General Election Stratford gave the intelligent, logical Angus Maude a 22,000 majority. Yet in some ways south Warwickshire is deep and mysterious countryside, where dark rumours abound. It is said that the last witch-lynching in Britain took place here, as late as the 1940s. There were surprising newspaper reports a few years ago that the little town of Southam was the British headquarters of the Ku Klux Klan.

This is the only truly rural constituency in Warwickshire, extending from the plain of the Avon around Stratford up the scarp of Edgehill into the Cotswold hills. Not far from Stratford can be found remote villages and strong rural working-class accents – the mythical 'Ambridge' of the radio soap opera 'The Archers' would probably be in south Warwickshire. Primitive or sophisticated, town or country, this constituency is strongly Conservative. Apart from Stratford itself, the towns are too small to be independent of their agricultural hinterland. Southam, Kineton and Alcester are all only of around 5,000 population. In the north, around Wooton Wawen and Henley in Arden can be found the comfortable homes of long-distance commuters to Birmingham. The Liberals can pull into second place, but they have few locally active centres of strength.

The constituency is identical to the Stratford on Avon District. It is little altered, losing a few thousand suburban voters around Hockley Heath to Solihull Borough. Angus Maude, who has held Stratford since the 1963 byelection caused by the resignation of the disgraced John Profumo, is retiring. The first candidate selected as his successor was Robin Hodgson, formerly member for Walsall N (1976-79). But Hodgson gave up the nomination on personal grounds. He was almost certainly turning down the opportunity of a life tenure of one of England's safest Tory seats.

1981	% Own Occ	59.4	1979 core seat Stratford on Avon		
1981	% Loc Auth	24.8			
1981	% Black/Asian	0.7	C	35,470	60.4
1981	% Mid Cl	50.5	L	12,916	22.0
1981	% Prof Man	22.8	Lab	10,334	17.6
1982	electorate 76,619		MPs since 1950		
1979	notional result		1950-63 John Profumo C		
	C 21,200		1963- Sir Angus Maude C		
Alliance		L			

Warwick and Leamington

Warwick and Leamington might be thought an archetypal safe Tory seat. This was Sir Anthony Eden's constituency; Royal Leamington Spa is the most well-known of the Midlands inland watering-holes; and at the last Election Dudley Smith won a Conservative majority of 16,500. But in fact it could now almost become a marginal in a good Labour year. The reason for this is that 20,000 electors have been lost as Kenilworth, the most Conservative part of the seat, leaves to join Rugby. This may well reduce the Conservative majority by as much as 6,000 - and in 1966 the Tory majority was only 8,500.

In fact, both Warwick and Leamington have substantial blocs of Labour support. Warwick has a large council estate in the west of the town, while South Leamington harbours one of the largest Asian communities in any small town in Britain. Labour took about 42% of the vote in the Leamington Spa local elections in 1979, even in a bad year for them (it was the same day as the General Election). Leamington is also an industrial town - Automotive Products are the best known of the employers. Its spa and tourist functions are fairly much dormant, and its politics seem likely to continue to belie the elegant impression given by the fine streets of the centre and north of the town.

Warwick and Leamington will be a much closer contest than before, but it would still be a surprise if Labour won. Besides the two major towns of the constituency, there are a number of villages such as Whitnash, Radford Semele and Cublington, where the Tories do have a massive lead - even in Barford, where a pub is named after a local man, Joseph Arch, the founder of agricultural trade unionism.

1981	% Own Occ	62	
1981	% Loc Auth	23	
1981	% Black/Asian	7	
1981	% Mid Cl	50	
1981	% Prof Man	18	
1982	electorate 71,357		
1979	notional result		
	C 13,200		
Alliance		SDP	

1979 core seat Warwick/
Leamington

C	35,925	54.3
Lab	19,367	29.3
L	9,905	15.0
E	905	1.4

MPs since 1945

1945-57 Sir Anthony Eden C
1957-68 Sir John Hobson C
1968-   Dudley Smith C

Devizes

Of all the English counties, Wiltshire is probably the least
altered in the boundary changes - its five seats were already
of an acceptable size, and conformed closely to the local
government boundaries. Devizes was before, and is now, a
mixture of the Kennet District of NE Wiltshire and part of
Thamesdown - it almost completely surrounds Swindon. The
seat sweeps down from Highworth in the NE corner of the
county across the Marlborough Downs into the Vale of
Pewsey. Labour have support in the edge of Swindon and in
Devizes itself; they were 2,500 votes short of victory in 1966.
But a senior moderate Conservative backbencher, Charles
Morrison, had built up his majority to 16,000 plus by 1979.

1981	% Own Occ	57.3	1979 core seat Devizes		
1981	% Loc Auth	25.5	C	32,439	50.9
1981	% Black/Asian	1.5	Lab	16,351	25.7
1981	% Mid Cl	46.0	L	14,059	22.1
1981	% Prof Man	16.8	Oths	855	1.3
1982	electorate 82,835		MPs since 1945		
1979	notional result		1945-55 M.C. Hollis C		
	C 16,200		1955-64 H.P. Pott C		
Alliance		SDP	1964- Charles Morrison C		

North Wiltshire

There is no significant difference between the new North
Wiltshire seat and the old Chippenham, which was one of the
Liberals' best hopes for many years - they were within about
3,000 votes of the Tories in 1966 and in both 1974 Elections.
Labour is squeezed down to a deposit-losing level. The
Liberals do best in the small towns, Calne, Cricklade and
Chippenham itself, while the Conservatives pull ahead in the
rolling countryside of NW Wiltshire. The very moderate
Conservative MP, Richard Needham, is likely to have another
close fight on his hands next time.

1981	% Own Occ	59.5	1979 core seat Chippenham		
1981	% Loc Auth	25.5	C	29,308	49.2
1981	% Black/Asian	1.4	L	24,611	41.3
1981	% Mid Cl	45.6	Lab	5,146	8.6
1981	% Prof Man	16.8	E	521	0.9
1982	electorate 76,179		MPs since 1945		
1979	notional result		1945-62 Sir D.M. Eccles C		
	C 4,700		1962-79 Daniel Awdry C		
Alliance		L	1979- Richard Needham C		

Salisbury

The Liberals have two target seats in Wiltshire. One is North Wiltshire (Chippenham); the other is right at the other end of the county, Salisbury. The City of Salisbury itself is far too small to merit a compact urban seat of its own, and the Salisbury division effectively spreads over much of south Wiltshire – it includes Amesbury, Stonehenge and much of the Salisbury Plain. A far cry from the days before 1832 when the deserted Old Sarum returned two MPs! In the minor boundary changes which will come into effect at the next Election, it gains the district around Tisbury in the very SW corner of the county from Westbury.

Why do the Liberals do well in parts of Wiltshire? Part of Wessex, Wiltshire is scarcely a peripheral county of the Celtic fringe, where the Liberal Party's strength has survived longer than elsewhere. Liberalism in Salisbury is of more recent date. As in Chippenham, the Liberals have been able to rely on an active local organisation which has sometimes contrasted with that of the Conservatives. They have also been able to tap a large working-class vote, both in Salisbury itself and in the army camps on Salisbury Plain – this seat has one of the highest proportions of servicemen in the country. Labour obtained 45% of the vote in Salisbury in 1966, but only 12.6% in 1979.

There is to be an infusion of new blood in the Salisbury Conservative Party at the next Election – Michael Hamilton is to retire in favour of Robert Key. Key will have to work hard to resist the Liberal advance in Salisbury, which must be one of the seats most vulnerable to an Alliance breakthrough.

1981	% Own Occ	51.3	1979 core seat Salisbury		
1981	% Loc Auth	26.0	C	24,962	49.9
1981	% Black/Asian	1.5	L	18,718	37.4
1981	% Mid Cl	46.2	Lab	6,321	12.6
1981	% Prof Man	15.6	MPs since 1945		
1982	electorate 72,640		1945-65 J.G. Morrison C		
1979	notional result		1965- Michael Hamilton C		
	C 7,100				
Alliance		L			

Swindon

Swindon is an isolated red spot on the political map of southern England. With the defection of MPs to the Social Democrats, Labour now have no representatives on the south coast, and nothing in the south-west or Wessex except for three seats in Bristol - and Swindon. What accounts for this Wiltshire outpost in so much hostile territory? The answer takes us back to the arrival of the Great Western Railway in 1835, followed shortly by one of the largest locomotive works in the world. Swindon had become an industrial town.

Swindon has always since remained one of Britain's great railway junctions. But its industrial character has been reinforced by modern developments following the 1952 Town Development Act, which has brought Plesseys, Burmah Oil and countless other employers. Swindon is well situated for a boom town, just off the M4 within easy reach of London. Along with industrial estates have come housing estates, which has meant that Swindon has expanded outwards in every direction. To the west there is Toothill, to the north Moredon and Whitworth, and to the SE Dorcan, Park and Eldene. Some of this is low-cost private housing, not council, but all of it helps Labour; there are Conservative wards only in the old middle-class residential areas in the south of the town, most notably in the Lawns ward.

The Conservatives did hold Swindon for a few months after a byelection in Labour's dark year of 1969. But apart from that, it has been safely Labour since 1945. Despite its continued growth, Swindon is little altered in the redistribution. David Stoddart lost his first contest here in 1969, but he has won four times since, and should continue to do so in the foreseeable future.

1981	% Own Occ	58.1	1979 core seat Swindon
1981	% Loc Auth	37.1	Lab	25,218	50.2
1981	% Black/Asian	3	C	19,319	38.4
1981	% Mid Cl	44.7	L	5,709	11.4
1981	% Prof Man	12.3	MPs since 1945
1982	electorate 76,727		1945-55 T. Reid Lab
1979	notional result		1955-69 F.E. Noel-Baker Lab
	Lab 5,900		1969-70 C.J.F. Ward C
Alliance		SDP	1970- David Stoddart Lab

Westbury

The small towns of West Wiltshire contain a surprising degree of industry, and most of them are far from picturesque. Westbury is actually the smallest of the five towns in the constituency which bears its name. The others are Melksham and Bradford-on-Avon, which both have Avon Rubber Company factories; the military centre of Warminster, which is also the UFO sighting capital of the United Kingdom; and the largest of all, the county town of Trowbridge, which started as a weaving centre but has diversified into foodstuffs and brewing.

Bradford-on-Avon's physical attractions mean that it is much more Conservative than the other towns. It is set amid a ring of hills, near the beautiful Limpley Stoke valley, and is suitable for commuters to Bath and Bristol. Warminster, in the Upper Wylye Valley, is in that part of Wiltshire which resembles a large armed encampment; it too tends to the right. Trowbridge is marginal, Westbury and (especially) Melksham decidedly Labour. Yet Labour, which came within 3,000 votes of victory here in 1966, finished third in Westbury in 1979. As elsewhere in Wiltshire, the Liberals actually did better in the General Election than they do in local elections, a rare state of affairs for a small party. The Conservatives can rely on the rural parts of the seat, from Holt in the north to Mere in the south, and seem as safe as in the Westbury constituency as in any in Wiltshire.

Westbury loses a few thousand voters around Tisbury to Salisbury in the boundary changes. Rather curiously, two independent candidates, one a 'Wessex Regionalist', polled almost 4,500 votes here in 1979. But no matter who stands against him, the sitting Tory member, company director Dennis Walters, should have no trouble retaining the seat next time.

1981	% Own Occ	65.4	1979 core seat Westbury		
1981	% Loc Auth	23.6	C	29,929	47.2
1981	% Black/Asian	1.7	L	15,950	25.2
1981	% Mid Cl	46.1	Lab	12,532	19.8
1981	% Prof Man	17.2	Ind	2,547	4.0
1982	electorate 80,126		Wessex R	1,905	3.0
1979	notional result		E	554	0.9
	C 13,100		MPs since 1945		
Alliance		L	1945-64 R.V. Grimston C		
			1964-	Dennis Walters C	

Harrogate

Harrogate is the largest spa town in the North of England, an elegant inland holiday resort 15 miles north of Leeds beyond Harewood House. Harrogate is larger than Leamington Spa or Tunbridge Wells, and almost rivals Bath in the grandeur of its architecture and facilities. Like many spa towns, Harrogate has always been strongly Conservative, and although it is no longer fashionable to take the waters, it has developed into a major conference centre. It is also a very popular growing residential site - new private houses spring up to join the Victorian mansions set around Harrogate's many green parks.

The constituency, little altered in the redistribution, also includes the prosperous town of Knaresborough set in a bend of the River Nidd, and a series of villages stretching across Marston Moor to the gates of York. The Liberals are competitive in local elections in Harrogate itself, but this never pushed them into better than a poor second place in General Elections. Next time the SDP will see if they can enjoy better luck. Labour only just saved its deposit last time, and can only win one ward, Harrogate Bilton, even in a good year.

Harrogate is also the only place in the country to have a Whig county councillor - Cecil Margolis of Harlow ward, who beat off Liberal, Labour and Conservative opposition in the 1981 elections. Mr Margolis stood for the Harrogate constituency in the October 1974 General Election, and polled 719 votes. But it shouldn't be thought that Harrogate's politics are typified by eccentricity. The Conservative Robert Banks secured an 18,000 majority in 1979, and seems set for a long career in politics, regardless of whether he is opposed by Labour, Liberal, SDP or Whig.

1981	% Own Occ	71	1979 core seat Harrogate		
1981	% Loc Auth	11	C	30,551	59.5
1981	% Black/Asian	1	L	12,021	23.4
1981	% Mid Cl	62	Lab	8,221	16.0
1981	% Prof Man	23	NF	585	1.1
1982	electorate 73,273		MPs since 1950		
1979	notional result		1950-54 C. York C		
	C 19,300		1954-74 James Ramsden C		
Alliance		SDP	1974- Robert Banks C		

Richmond (Yorks)

Yorkshire is vast, and diverse. Even the County of North Yorkshire alone contains three of the largest-area parliamentary constituencies in England (Richmond, Ryedale, Skipton and Ripon). Here in Richmond is to be found some of the finest unspoilt scenery in the country, the remoter northern half of the Yorkshire Dales National Park, around the beautiful valleys of Swaledale and Wensleydale. This deeply Conservative farming country is so far removed from the industry of the cities of South and West Yorkshire that one can see why some Yorkshiremen think that their homeland could be a state in itself.

The politics is as varied as the scenery, and as the economy. The huge seat of Richmond, in the far NW of the county, contains no large towns. Yet its electorate is larger than average, and still greater after the boundary changes, for now Thirsk is to be included. Northallerton is the county town of North Yorkshire, and Richmond an ancient stronghold at the foot of Swaledale. Thirsk is a market town known for its horse-racing. Another centre of population is provided by the army camp at Catterick. But there are hundreds of villages, often little more than hamlets, among the hilly sheep and dairy farms made famous by James Herriot's Yorkshire vet novels.

The municipal politics of the Richmondshire and Hambleton districts show a sturdy independence. But this is in fact one of the safest Conservative seats in the country, offering Edward Heath's friend and ally Sir Timothy Kitson a 19,000 majority over the Liberals in 1979. This is one of the few rural seats in the country with more than 20% privately rented housing. It is also one of the most agriculturally-based of all seats. Richmond is not really an affluent constituency – but socialism and state control seem far removed from the yeoman philosophy of the Dales.

1981	% Own Occ	56.9	1979 core seat Richmond
1981	% Loc Auth	21.6	(Yorks)
1981	% Black/Asian	1	C 28,958 61.5
1981	% Mid Cl	43.9	L 9,964 21.2
1981	% Prof Man	19.5	Lab 8,173 17.4
1982	electorate 74,870		MPs since 1945
1979	notional result		1945-59 Sir T.L. Dugdale C
	C 21,000		1959- Sir Timothy Kitson C
Alliance		L	

Ryedale

The local government District of Ryedale is the largest in acreage in England. The new constituency of this name includes almost the whole of that District, but also extends to Easingwold in the Vale of York and Filey on the coast near Scarborough - two towns nearly 50 miles apart. Ryedale is based on the old Thirsk and Malton seat in NE Yorkshire, a vast rural tract from the edge of York through flatlands, then hills to the North York Moors. This is solidly Conservative country, for a long time held by one family, the Turtons. The Liberals' few local successes are not translated into General Election votes. Labour cannot win a single ward.

1981	% Own Occ	67.3	1979 core seat Thirsk and
1981	% Loc Auth	17.1	Malton
1981	% Black/Asian	0.7	C 32,520 59.2
1981	% Mid Cl	46.5	Lab 11,924 21.7
1981	% Prof Man	17.7	L 10,533 19.2
1982	electorate 78,399		MPs since 1945
1979	notional result		1945-74 Sir Robin Turton C
	C 20,300		1974- John Spence C
Alliance		L	

Scarborough

The dramatic coast from Scarborough to Whitby, and the North Yorkshire Moors behind it, might seem to be natural Conservative territory. Scarborough is the major Yorkshire seaside resort, and along with tourism agriculture forms the main basis of the economy here. It is indeed a safe Conservative seat, yet there is actually a considerable Labour vote in local elections in Scarborough and Whitby, an odd reversal of roles, for it is the Liberals who usually do better in local elections than General Elections. In the boundary changes Whitby and the Moors come in from Cleveland, and some inland country around Pickering is lost to Ryedale.

1981	% Own Occ	65	1979 core seat Scarborough
1981	% Loc Auth	21	C 23,669 53.2
1981	% Black/Asian	0.5	Lab 11,344 25.5
1981	% Mid Cl	45.0	L 9,025 20.3
1981	% Prof Man	16.4	Ind 487 1.1
1982	electorate 73,177		MPs since 1945
1979	notional result		1945-66 Sir A.C.M. Spearman C
	C 12,800		1966- Michael Shaw C
Alliance		SDP	

Selby

The countryside south of York around Selby is so flat that it is more prone to major flooding than anywhere else in Britain. Selby itself was an inland port on the Ouse, and the big rivers of the plain are now tapped by massive power stations like those at Drax near the A1(M) trunk road. But now a new industry is growing on, or rather under, the Selby flatlands - the most modern coalfield in the country, where high technology is used to exploit deep and concealed seams. Unlike the Vale of Belvoir development, the Selby coalfield does not threaten a beautiful district - the scenery here is monotonous at best. But will it cause a political upheaval?

There is no doubt that this new constituency would have been Conservative in 1979. Most of it was in the now divided Barkston Ash seat, which gave Tory MP Michael Alison an 18,000 majority. There is already a Labour presence in the marginal small towns of Selby itself, Tadcaster and Sherburn in Elmet. The University of York is situated in the constituency at Heslington. But this is still primarily rural Britain, not traditional Labour country. Even when the coalfield is fully productive, some of the miners might commute into the area from their present homes further west; others will be absorbed into existing communities, for new colliery villages are not planned.

The population of the Selby seat is already increasing. But it may turn out to be a wise guess which contends that the impact of mining will not prevent the Conservatives from being able to regard Selby as a safe seat.

1981	% Own Occ	66.0	1979 core seat Barkston Ash		
1981	% Loc Auth	22.1	C	40,381	56.2
1981	% Black/Asian	0.5	Lab	21,670	30.2
1981	% Mid Cl	47.7	L	7,909	11.0
1981	% Prof Man	21.3	E	1,829	2.5
1982	electorate 65,102		MPs since 1945		
1979	notional result		1945-64 Sir L. Ropner C		
	C 10,000		1964- Michael Alison C		
Alliance		L			

Skipton and Ripon

The new Skipton and Ripon seat consists of the countryside which most people would consider to be the heart of the Dales - Settle, Skipton, Ripon and Wharfedale. These southern dales are more accessible to the great population centres of industrial Lancashire and West Yorkshire, and as a result villages like Grassington and Burnsall have a softer, more commercial air than the more rugged communities further north. Here are tourist targets like Bolton Priory, Fountains Abbey and Malham Tarn. There are some old textile mills in Skipton, but the constituency's economy is heavily dependent upon tourism and farming.

Skipton and Ripon brings together two old seats, both formerly in the West Riding. Skipton has lost the small mill towns of Barnoldswick and Earby, which are now in Lancashire, and Sedbergh and Dentdale, which are now in Cumbria. Barnoldswick and Earby were Labour's only source of any strength at all in the Skipton seat, which was very much a Liberal-Conservative marginal. Ripon has lost the Conservative towns of Ilkley and Otley in Lower Wharfedale, for they are now in the Metropolitan County of West Yorkshire. Ripon too was a constituency with a Liberal tradition in recent years, for the bookseller David Austick won it in their boom year of 1973 at the same time as Clement Freud won the Isle of Ely. But Austick could hold Ripon for less than a year, and by 1979 Conservative academic Keith Hampson had increased his majority to 16,000 there.

Do the Liberals have a good chance in this huge rural seat in the SW of North Yorkshire? It is after all a combination of two seats which offered them some of their brightest hopes in the 1970s. In October 1974 the dynamic Liberal candidate Claire Brooks lost at Skipton by only 590 votes. But the Liberal challenge seemed to be declining rapidly in the late 1970s, and it may well be that their time of opportunity here in the southern Dales has passed by.

1981	% Own Occ	70	1979 core seat Skipton		
1981	% Loc Auth	14	C	23,177	51.2
1981	% Black/Asian	0.7	L	17,484	38.6
1981	% Mid Cl	47	Lab	4,632	10.2
1981	% Prof Man	18	MPs since 1945		
1982	electorate 69,597		1945-79 Burnaby Drayson C		
1979	notional result		1979- John Watson C		
	C 13,600				
Alliance		L			

York

After an inquiry, the Commission decided to maintain the City of York as a single unit for parliamentary purposes, even though its electorate is well over the average at 77,000. This means that the seat is unchanged, and next time another fascinating three-way struggle may be expected in this marginal seat. In 1979 the sitting Labour MP Alex Lyon was fortunate enough to restrict the pro-Tory swing to 2% and to hold on by 1,250 votes - an average swing would have defeated him. The Tories have a considerable reserve of strength in York, which they held from 1950 to 1966. To complete the picture, the Liberals have had great local election success in three wards in west York - Backfield, Westfield and Foxwood.
York is a city of great interest and diversity. It is of course famed for its cathedral and its medieval walls, which attract a vast throng of visitors. The central ward, Guildhall, is Conservative, full of elegant town houses and twee shops. But York is also a notable railway centre, and a manufacturing metropolis for chocolate, cocoa and confectionery, and egineering, leather and chemicals. The Rowntree Quaker tradition may have something to do with the Liberal vote, but for a long time Liberalism was dormant in York, so it may be a phenomenon of much more recent origin. In any case the Liberals were very unsuccessful in General Elections - they lost their deposit in 1979, while polling about 20% in the local elections in the same wards on the same day. This may be one reason why the SDP has gained the Alliance nomination for the next Election. The Alliance's strong showing in 1982 may not represent a promising chance of victory in a contest for national honours.
Alex Lyon is an independently minded and active MP. He is a libertarian who is very concerned with matters such as race relations and social issues. He was dismissed from James Callaghan's government because of disagreements over its immigration policy in 1976. Lyon seems very popular in York, and must be favourite to retain the seat at the next Election.

1981	% Own Occ	58.3	1979 same seat York		
1981	% Loc Auth	31.3	Lab	26,703	44.7
1981	% Black/Asian	1.0	C	25,453	42.6
1981	% Mid Cl	44.4	L	6,752	11.3
1981	% Prof Man	12.4	Ind	569	1.0
1982	electorate 79,008		NF	221	0.4
Alliance		SDP	MPs since 1945		

MPs since 1945
1945-50 J. Corlett Lab
1950-59 H. Hylton-Foster C
1959-66 C.B. Longbottom C
1966-   Alex Lyon Lab

Roxburgh and Berwickshire

The Liberal leader David Steel finds that his Roxburgh, Selkirk and Peebles constituency is divided in the boundary changes. Roxburgh is united with Berwickshire in a seat which was originally named East Borders. It is felt that Steel will choose to stand for the West Borders (Tweeddale, Ettrick and Lauderdale). This means that Roxburgh and Berwickshire may well prove to be a Conservative seat, even though neither half has a Tory MP at present.

Roxburgh includes the largest town in the Borders, Hawick, and the smaller Kelso and Jedburgh. This is good farming country, and it includes many tourist attractions such as the border abbeys at Jedburgh, Kelso and Dryburgh. The towns have traditionally been the centre of the tweed and knitwear industry. Local elections are not normally fought on party lines, and it is difficult to test the theory that the Liberalism of Roxburgh is closely tied to David Steel personally, and will not be transferred to another Liberal candidate. Berwickshire is the most Conservative part of the present Berwick and East Lothian seat, which is a marginal Labour seat. Berwickshire was a very small county, and actually only has a population of 18,000. Nevertheless, there is no Liberal tradition there, and the Conservatives will probably start favourites in the all-new Roxburgh/Berwickshire seat.

The Borders are somewhat fortunate to be allocated two seats by the Boundary Commission. There are only 78,000 electors in the whole Region, and both the proposed divisions are very small. Scotland is over-represented by comparison with England. Its seats average 53,000 electors, compared with 65,000 south of the border. Yet this has not prevented the Commission from awarding Scotland an extra and 72nd seat in the present review, the first time this century that Scotland has departed from its legal minimum of 71 seats.

1981	% Own Occ	32.7	New seat
1981	% Loc Auth	48.8	
1981	% Mid Cl	37.7	
1981	% Prof Man	15.5	
1978	electorate 41,766		
1979	notional result		
	L 300		
Alliance		L	

Tweeddale, Ettrick and Lauderdale

David Steel was the youngest MP when he gained Roxburgh, Selkirk and Peebles for the Liberals as he turned 27 in March 1965. On occasions it has seemed that his hold on his seat was tenuous, especially after his sponsorship of legislation to make abortion more easily available in the late 1960s – not an entirely popular position in this respectable Borders country. He also opposed the South African rugby tour in 1969. But Steel survived by 550 votes in 1970, and his position strengthened dramatically through the next decade. In 1976 he was elected Party Leader by a ballot of the entire membership, and in 1979 he won Roxburgh, Selkirk and Peebles by over 10,000 votes – a landslide compared with most Liberal MPs.

Steel is now joint leader of the Liberal-SDP Alliance, which entertains ambitions of doing well enough to form a government, or at least hold the balance of power after the next Election. Although still only in his early 40s, Steel is recognised to be one of the most formidable politicians in Britain, a tough and even ruthless campaigner. His leadership of the Liberals is unquestioned, and some feel that he would be the ideal man to be an Alliance Prime Minister.

Nor need he have any fears about his local base nowadays. The Borders will now enjoy two compact seats, and Steel will almost certainly choose the western Tweeddale, Ettrick and Lauderdale seat – effectively the old Selkirk and Peebles. Steel lives in his constituency, at Ettrick Bridge, a pillar of the church and a family man. He now does well among the farmers of the seat, as well as in the textile towns such as Galashiels and Selkirk and Peebles. The SNP and Labour lost their deposits last time, and the Conservatives' hopes of dislodging Steel are fading away. Steel's seat is more compact than before, even if its new name is just as long!

1981	% Own Occ	40.6	1979 core seat Roxburgh,
1981	% Loc Auth	43.9	Selkirk and Peebles
1981	% Mid Cl	45.7	L 25,993 53.1
1981	% Prof Man	17.4	C 15,303 31.3
1978	electorate 36,299		Lab 4,150 8.5
1979	notional result		SNP 3,502 7.2
	L 4,500		MPs since 1955
Alliance		L	1955-65 C.E.M. Donaldson C
			1965- David Steel L

Clackmannan

The former constituency of Clackmannan and East
Stirlingshire was the site of one of the strongest Scottish
Nationalist performances of their 1970s revival. It was one of
the seven seats they won in February 1974, as broadcaster
and journalist George Reid defeated the sitting Labour MP,
Dick Douglas. Reid increased his majority to 7,000 in October
1974, and he only just lost the Clackmannan/E Stirlings seat
in much bleaker circumstances for the SNP in 1979. Martin
O'Neil regained the seat for Labour by just 984 votes.

Reid was always ranked as a gradualist as far as
independence for Scotland was concerned, and as a left-
winger in other political matters. There is good reason for
such policies, in this seat, for it is a working-class
stronghold. The Conservatives have never made a significant
impact, and neither have the Liberals - the SDP have the
nomination for the Alliance, but cherish little hope of
success. It seems that again Clackmannan will be effectively a
straight fight between Labour and the SNP.

In the boundary changes the East Stirlingshire section of the
seat has been shared between the two new Falkirk divisions,
leaving the old County of Clackmannan (still surviving as a
District) as the core of its own seat. Even small Scottish
towns tend to have a majority of council housing, and those
in Clackmannan are no exception - Alva, Tillicoultry, Alloa
and Dollar. There is no mining left in Clackmannan now, but
it remains an industrial and working-class part of Central
Scotland.

1981	% Own Occ	29	
1981	% Loc Auth	65	
1981	% Mid Cl	38	
1981	% Prof Man	12	
1978	electorate 47,000		
1979	notional result		
	Lab 3,300		
Alliance			SDP

1979 core seat Clackmannan/East
Stirlingshire

Lab	22,780	41.9
SNP	21,796	40.1
C	9,778	18.0

MPs since 1945
1945-70 Arthur Woodburn Lab
1970-74 Dick Douglas Lab
1974-79 George Reid SNP
1979- Martin O'Neil Lab

Falkirk East

Until the present redistribution, there were still some Scottish
constituencies which consisted of collections of towns or
burghs, which did not form a contiguous constituency but
were associated even though separated by several miles of
countryside incorporated in other seats. One such division
was Stirling, Falkirk and Grangemouth. Now however, the
eastern part of the town of Falkirk is placed together with
the oil refining community of Grangemouth and Bo'ness
(formerly in West Lothian). This compact seat at the inner
end of the Firth of Forth should remain safely Labour.

1981	% Own Occ	25	1979 core seat Stirling, Falkirk	
1981	% Loc Auth	71	and Grangemouth	
1981	% Mid Cl	37	Lab 29,499	56.5
1981	% Prof Man	12	C 13,881	26.6
1978	electorate 52,200		SNP 8,856	17.0
1979	notional result		MPs since 1945	
	Lab 11,700		1945-48 J.C. Westwood Lab	
Alliance		SDP	1948-71 Malcolm Macpherson Lab	
			1971- Harry Ewing Lab	

Falkirk West

The western half of the Falkirk District consists of part of
the town of Falkirk, and also the small burghs of Denny and
Dunipace from the old Stirlingshire East and Clackmannan. All
are traditionally Labour, working-class communities, and
despite the SNP challenge of the 1970s Labour should have
few problems in Falkirk West.

1981	% Own Occ	24	New seat
1981	% Loc Auth	72	
1981	% Mid Cl	38	
1981	% Prof Man	12	
1978	electorate 53,200		
1979	notional result		
	Lab 8,400		
Alliance		L	

Stirling

The majority of the acreage of the Central Region of Scotland is situated in the new Stirling constituency, which closely follows the lines of the Stirling District. It is a mixture of terrain drawn from a number of former seats. The historic City of Stirling itself comes from the Stirling, Falkirk and Grangemouth burghs seat. Much of the southern half of the seat was formerly in West Stirlingshire. The northern part, which includes Dunblane, Callander and the Trossachs, was in Kinross and W Perthshire.

Not only is Stirling a mixed seat of varied origins, but it is likely also to be very marginal. Stirling itself is as inclined to the Labour Party as are most Scottish towns. West Stirlingshire was held by Labour's energetic left-winger Dennis Canavan, but most of his support was concentrated in small towns like Kilsyth, Denny and Dunipace which have been removed to seats other than Stirling. Kinross and West Perthshire is hopeless for Labour, and traditionally Tory - it was for many years Alec Douglas-Home's seat. The SNP have recently been strong in both West Stirlingshire and West Perthshire.

It is very hard to calculate a notional result for the Stirling seat using local election figures, for there are many uncontested elections in this scattered and heterogeneous District. This much is clear: Stirling will be a Labour-Conservative marginal, with an outside chance of an SNP impact. The Alliance, Liberal-led here, may well finish fourth in Stirling. It will be a seat well worth watching, especially if the fiery Canavan takes the Labour nomination.

1981	% Own Occ	39	New seat
1981	% Loc Auth	49	
1981	% Mid Cl	46	
1981	% Prof Man	16	
1978	electorate 47,000		
1979	notional result		
	C 700		
Alliance		L	

Dumfries

Dumfriesshire has been one of the two or three safest Conservative seats in Scotland since the war. It never succumbed to the Nationalist challenge of 1974, and Hector Monro had a comfortable 9,000 majority over Labour in 1979. There is a Labour presence among the many council estates of Dumfries, but their other source of support has been removed: Dumfries loses 10,000 voters in Upper Nithsdale to Galloway, in order to equalise the electorate of the two Dumfries/Galloway seats. Upper Nithsdale includes some mining districts at Kirkconnel and Sanquhar near the Ayrshire border. Monro will win Dumfries again easily.

1981	% Own Occ	39	1979 core seat Dumfries		
1981	% Loc Auth	45	C	22,704	45.2
1981	% Mid Cl	38	Lab	13,700	27.3
1981	% Prof Man	13	L	7,159	14.3
1978	electorate 54,800		SNP	6,647	13.2
1979	notional result		MPs since 1945		
	C 7,700		1945-63 N.M.S. Macpherson C		
Alliance		SDP	1963-64 D.C. Anderson C		
			1964- Hector Monro C		

Galloway and Upper Nithsdale

Galloway is the far south-west of Scotland, the old Counties of Kirkcudbright and Wigtown. Although in the Lowlands, Galloway has its mountains and lochs, glens and forests, and remains a quiet and accessible miniature version of the Highlands themselves. Its politics resemble much of rural Scotland much further north - safely Conservative for many years until 1974, then falling to the SNP. Galloway fell in the second (October) SNP revolution of that year, and was one of the seats which was expected to return to the Tory fold in 1979. It duly did, and may be safe for new MP Ian Lang.

1981	% Own Occ	41	1979 core seat Galloway		
1981	% Loc Auth	39	C	15,306	45.8
1981	% Mid Cl	38	SNP	12,384	37.1
1981	% Prof Man	17	L	2,852	8.5
1978	electorate 50,600		Lab	2,841	8.5
1979	notional result		MPs since 1945		
	C 5,200		1945-59 J.H. Mackie Ind C (C)		
Alliance		L	1959-74 John Brewis C		
			1974-79 George Thompson SNP		
			1979- Ian Lang C		

Central Fife

One of the best known, and perhaps one of the most misunderstood, Members of Parliament is Willie Hamilton, the present Labour MP for Fife Central. Hamilton is known by most people simply as the arch-caviller at royal privilege, as a man with none of the traditional British respect for the institutional and personal majesty of monarchy. As such he is seen as a wild man, an unpopular and isolated minority figure, and even as a dangerous left-winger. The last criticism is inaccurate and unfair. Willie Hamilton stands on the right of the Labour Party. He is in favour of the EEC. He has even recently had to survive a very serious left-wing attempt to unseat him, which involved a tied vote in his reselection conference resulting in a second ballot – in which he was narrowly successful. Hamilton is actually one of that threatened species which the press usually rushes to support: the 'moderate' Labour MP.

More trouble may be caused for Willie Hamilton by the sweeping boundary changes in Fife. The new Central Fife is very different from the current seat, and even more from the West Fife constituency which Hamilton held from 1950 to 1974. Central Fife is now centred not on the Fife coalfield but on the New Town of Glenrothes. It extends to the coast to take in the industrial ports of Buckhaven and Methil from Kirkcaldy and Leven from East Fife. It should still be a safe Labour seat, even though Glenrothes has the mixed and volatile politics common to New Towns everywhere. But Hamilton may have to stave off another selection challenge in the revised seat. His left-wing opponent last time was Henry McLeish, a leading Regional councillor, who represents Kennoway and Windygates ward, which is in the new constituency.

Willie Hamilton has had a long and active career in the Commons. It is unlikely that the voters will end it, despite the publicity given to his republicanism. Ironically, it is the growing revolutionary feeling in the Labour Party which threatens Hamilton's own position.

1981	% Own Occ	20	1979 core seat Fife Central		
1981	% Loc Auth	75	Lab	27,916	58.0
1981	% Mid Cl	35	C	9,597	20.2
1981	% Prof Man	9	SNP	9,208	19.3
1978	electorate 51,100		Comm 1,172		2.5
1976	notional result		MP since 1974		
	Lab 12,300		1974– Willie Hamilton Lab		
Alliance		L			

Dunfermline East

Fife receives an extra seat in the boundary changes. As is often the case, it is difficult to say which the new constituency is, for several of the Fife divisions are radically altered. But Dunfermline East has as good a claim as any, for Dunfermline previously enjoyed only one seat, most of which is in the Dunfermline West division. The town of Dunfermline itself is entirely within the West seat. East includes Inverkeithing and Rosyth from the old Dunfermline, but it is centred on Cowdenbeath and Lochgelly from Willie Hamilton's Fife Central.

Cowdenbeath and Lochgelly lie at the heart of the Fife coalfield, which has had a long left-wing, even Communist tradition. Willie Gallacher was MP for West Fife from 1935 to 1950, at a time when there were only at most two Communist members in the country (Phil Piratin represented Mile End, Stepney, from 1945 to 1950). Even yet, there are Communist local councillors: in the 1982 Regional elections W. Clarke won Ballingry for the Communists with 73.4% of the poll, defeating a Labour candidate. The little mining communities here were once known as 'Little Moscows': Lumphinnans, Kelty, Kinglassie and others; the attachment to Communism is still greater than anywhere else in Britain except possibly the Rhondda Valley in South Wales.

Dunfermline East will be an extra safe Labour seat in Fife. Despite the local Communist support, there is no realistic chance of the Party candidate even saving his or her deposit; but Dunfermline East will still be one of the most radical constituencies in the nation.

1981	% Own Occ	25	New seat
1981	% Loc Auth	65	
1981	% Mid Cl	33	
1981	% Prof Man	8	
1978	electorate 48,000		
1979	notional result		
	Lab 14,800		
Alliance		L	

Dunfermline West

Dunfermline was for six centuries Scotland's capital, and seven kings of Scotland are buried there. As befits such an ancient and distinguished town, Dunfermline's politics are very mixed – four different parties won wards in Dunfermline itself in the 1982 Regional elections (Labour, Conservative, Liberal and SDP). Dunfermline constituency has lost the industrial districts east of the town itself, but still extends west up the Forth to Culross and Kincardine. Dunfermline West should be a slightly less safe Labour seat than the old Dunfermline was.

1981	% Own Occ	40	
1981	% Loc Auth	50	
1981	% Mid Cl	42	
1981	% Prof Man	13	
1978	electorate 47,200		
1979	notional result		
	Lab 6,100		
Alliance		SDP	

1979 core seat Dunfermline

Lab	22,803	44.3
C	15,490	30.1
SNP	7,351	14.3
L	5,803	11.3

MPs since 1945
1945-50 W.M. Watson Lab
1950-59 J. Clarke Lab
1959-64 A.E. Thompson Lab
1964-79 Adam Hunter Lab
1979-   Dick Douglas Lab

Kirkcaldy

The 'Lang Toun' of Kirkcaldy has a mile-long esplanade, but the birthplace of Adam Smith and Robert Adam is not really a seaside resort: it is an industrial, working-class town of solid Labour support. The constituency is pared down by 10,000 voters as the ports of Buckhaven and Methil are transferred to Central Fife. Burntisland and Kinghorn are tourist attractions on the Forth. Even they still vote Labour in an even year, and the shrunken Kirkcaldy will remain safe for Labour.

1981	% Own Occ	28	
1981	% Loc Auth	65	
1981	% Mid Cl	37	
1981	% Prof Man	10	
1978	electorate 52,200		
1979	notional result		
	Lab 8,700		
Alliance		SDP	

1979 core seat Kirkcaldy

Lab	25,449	53.9
C	12,386	26.2
SNP	9,416	19.9

MPs since 1945
1945-59 T.F. Hubbard Lab
1959-   Harry Gourlay Lab

North-East Fife

Half of the acreage of Fife is contained within the NE Fife seat, which is of an entirely different character from the rest of the ancient kingdom which is now a Region. Here are elegant tourist resorts and fishing villages, and prosperous farming country between the Tay and the Forth, and the ancient University town of St Andrews. There are a large number of small, respectable burghs – there were 14 towns with burgh status in the former East Fife constituency, and only one, Leven, is lost as the boundaries are reduced to fit exactly those of the NE Fife District.

The politics of NE Fife couldn't be more different from the rest of the Region either. It has been solidly Conservative (or National Liberal) for many decades. Its views are, perhaps, eloquently represented by one of Auchtermuchty's most famous sons, the eccentric and vituperative right-wing Sunday Express columnist, John Junor. Auchtermuchty is but one of the old, stable, middle-class communities of NE Fife – others include Cupar, Newport, Kilrenny and the Anstruthers, Crail, Elie/Earlsferry, Tayport and of course St Andrews, a city of time-honoured Conservatism. If any single constituency can bear that honour, this is the true home of the game of golf.

However, a strong challenge can be expected from one quarter: the Liberal Party has been active in local elections, and pushed their way forward into second place at the 1979 General Election (although still nearly 10,000 votes behind Tory MP Barry Henderson). The Liberals do regard NE Fife as one of their outside chances – but the Conservatives have a great weight of tradition and history on their side here in the rural part of the kingdom and Region of Fife.

1981	% Own Occ	48.7	1979 core seat Fife East			
1981	% Loc Auth	34.3	C	20,117	43.0	
1981	% Mid Cl	47.7	L	10,762	23.0	
1981	% Prof Man	18.8	Lab	9,339	19.9	
1978	electorate 47,800		SNP	6,612	14.1	
1979	notional result		MPs since 1945			
	C 8,600		1945-61 Sir J. Henderson-			
Alliance		L			Stewart C	
			1961-79 Sir John Gilmour C			
			1979-	Barry Henderson C		

Aberdeen North

Aberdeen is Scotland's third largest city. It also ranks as Britain's only boom town, due to its status as the chief onshore port for the exploitation of the North Sea oil field. New houses are being built. Property values are rising. The city centre is buzzing with multinational financial activity. But Aberdeen still has its vast swathes of working-class council estates, and relatively impoverished citizens. These are concentrated in the northern half of the city and the Aberdeen North parliamentary constituency.

It is interesting that neither of the Aberdeen seats came near to being won by the Nationalists in 1974, in spite of the salience of the oil issue. The Conservatives held South against a strong Labour challenge, while Labour's grip on North was hardly weakened. There are only minor boundary changes in Aberdeen, and it seems likely that the major parties will continue to dominate the political representation.

Robert Hughes should hold Aberdeen North easily. Three-quarters of the housing is council owned. Like Glasgow, Edinburgh and Dundee, most of the council estates are concentrated on the edge of the city: in Aberdeen, far away from the North Sea and its wealth can be found Northfield, Mastrick and other local authority developments in the NW of the city. North also includes quaint Old Aberdeen, around St Machar's Cathedral and King's College. The SDP have the nominations for both the Aberdeen seats, but it is unlikely that they will make any more impact than the Liberals or the Nationalists have in either seat in the city.

1981	% Own Occ	17	1979 core seat Aberdeen North		
1981	% Loc Auth	74	Lab	26,771	59.3
1981	% Mid Cl	36	C	7,657	17.0
1981	% Prof Man	8	SNP	5,796	12.8
1978	electorate 62,900		L	4,887	10.8
1979	notional result		MPs since 1945		
	Lab 17,500		1945-70 Hector Hughes Lab		
Alliance		SDP	1970- Robert Hughes Lab		

Aberdeen South

Despite a considerable amount of pressure, Labour has only ever won Aberdeen South once, in 1966. Then Donald Dewar defeated the long-serving Conservative MP, Lady Tweedsmuir, but in 1970 Iain Sproat regained the seat. Dewar later found a safe haven at Glasgow Garscadden (1978). Sproat meanwhile has hung on to Aberdeen South four times despite the fact that on three occasions his majority has been less than 1,100. Sproat is one of the best known and most vocal members of the Commons: a right-wing polemicist who is one of his own best publicists. Aberdeen South is perenially at the top of Labour's list of target seats in Scotland, both because of the thinness of the majority and because they would dearly love to oust Sproat personally.

South is traditionally the respectable middle-class end of the granite city. There are still solid Tory wards - the mansions of Rubislaw, the owner occupiers of Hazlehead, Rosemount and Holburn. But it is also a deeply divided seat, with some strongly Labour wards. These are to be found in the centre of the city (St Nicholas and St Clements wards) and in the peripheral council estates constructed relatively recently, such as Torry south of the River Dee. Also beyond the Dee, the Nigg ward is included, but Kincorth is not - both are dominated by council housing and are heavily Labour.

Labour and Conservative voters in Aberdeen South are very committed, very solid. There is little opportunity for the Alliance and the Nationalists in so tight a contest. The Conservatives retained a narrow majority in the wards which make up the constituency in the 1982 Regional elections. Sproat seems a great survivor, and considering the oil boom too, he has a fighting chance of continuing to make his abrasive presence felt in future Parliaments.

1981	% Own Occ	49	1979 core seat Aberdeen South
1981	% Loc Auth	37	C 20,820 40.7
1981	% Mid Cl	51	Lab 20,048 39.2
1981	% Prof Man	18	L 5,901 11.5
1978	electorate 55,900		SNP 4,361 8.5
1979	notional result		MPs since 1945
	C 500		1945-46 Sir J.D.W. Thomson C
Alliance		SDP	1946-66 Lady Tweedsmuir C
			1966-70 Donald Dewar Lab
			1970- Iain Sproat C

Banff and Buchan

The bulk of East Aberdeenshire is brought together with the coastal part of Banff in the new Banff and Buchan seat - its boundaries are coterminous with the Grampian District of the same name. Both Banff and East Aberdeenshire were held by the Scottish Nationalists from 1974 to 1979. Indeed this NE corner of Scotland beyond Aberdeen was the true heartland of SNP success, for Winnie Ewing won Moray and Nairn too. Previously all three seats had been safely Tory; indeed from 1924 to 1958 E Aberdeenshire had been held by the colourful and independent Tory battler Robert Boothby. But by now all three have returned to the Tory fold, none by a majority of more than 2,000.

Banff and Buchan is traditionally fishing and farming country, now affected by the discovery of North Sea oil. The main towns in the old E Aberdeens were Fraserburgh and Peterhead. Peterhead, rapidly expanding through oil, is better for the SNP than Fraserburgh. There are several other small burghs, of determined independence - Banff, Macduff, Portsoy, Turriff, Rosehearty, Aberchirder and others. These are canny communities, always willing to shift their political loyalty according to their perception of their interest.

There is little real ideological difference between the Tories and their local Nationalists - both Douglas Henderson of East Aberdeenshire and Hamish Watt of Banff were clearly on the right wing of their party, and were accused by some of being 'tartan Tories'. Should there be a Nationalist revival, Banff and Buchan would still be one of the first Tory seats to fall.

1981	% Own Occ	41.1	1979 core seat Aberdeenshire	
1981	% Loc Auth	47.2	East	
1981	% Mid Cl	36.6	C	16,827	42.8
1981	% Prof Man	12.6	SNP	16,269	41.4
1978	electorate 56,800		Lab	6,201	15.8
1979	notional result		MPs since 1945	
	C 1,300		1945-58 Robert Boothby C	
Alliance		SDP	1958-74 Patrick Wolrige-Gordon C	
			1974-79 Douglas Henderson SNP	
			1979- Albert McQuarrie C	

Gordon

Aberdeenshire West has been for some time the best Liberal
hope of a gain in rural Scotland. It was won in 1966 by
Liberal James Davidson, but he decided not to defend the
seat in 1970. His replacement as a Liberal candidate was
Laura Grimond, wife of the former Party Leader Jo Grimond
of Orkney and Shetland. But Mrs Grimond was defeated easily
by Lieutenant-Colonel Colin Mitchell, 'Mad Mitch' of Aden.
Mitchell's campaign was dominated by a single issue, the
preservation of the Argyll and Sutherland Highlanders. He
too became a single term MP by choice like Davidson, and left
Parliament voluntarily in February 1974. His successor Russell
Fairgrieve is a very substantial figure, once Chairman of the
Scottish Tories and now a junior Scottish Minister in Mrs
Thatcher's government.
Fairgrieve still has a tough Liberal challenge on his hands.
His majority over the Liberals has varied between 1,640 and
2,766. In the boundary changes Aberdeenshire West loses
Royal Deeside to Kincardine/Deeside, and gains part of E
Aberdeenshire on the coast around Ellon. It is renamed
Gordon but remains recognisably the same seat. It contains
much soft farming country, but the scenery becomes more
rugged as it climbs away from the coastal belt up towards the
Grampians. It also includes some of the expanding and
prosperous suburbs of Aberdeen, around the Don.
Labour and the SNP have never made an impact here, and
Gordon remains the only realistic chance of a Liberal gain
from the Tories in Scotland. Fairgrieve's hold is still tenuous,
but he is a much respected and responsible figure, and he
may well gradually consolidate his position in Gordon.

1981	% Own Occ	53	1979 core seat West
1981	% Loc Auth	28	Aberdeenshire
1981	% Mid Cl	40	C	21,086	40.9
1981	% Prof Man	16	L	18,320	35.5
1978	electorate 54,500		Lab	7,907	15.3
1979	notional result		SNP	4,260	8.3
	C 5,200		MPs since 1950
Alliance		L	1950-59 H.R. Spence C
			1959-66 A.F. Hendry C
			1966-70 James Davidson L
			1970-74 Colin Mitchell C
			1974- Russell Fairgrieve C

Kincardine and Deeside

The southernmost constituency in the Grampian Region is Kincardine and Deeside. There are three distinct elements in the new seat. Kincardineshire was formerly part of the constituency of Angus North and Mearns - a district of fishing ports and farming which provided the setting for Lewis Grassic Gibbon's novels, such as 'Cloud Howe'. Stonehaven is the biggest town. Deeside, or more strictly the south bank of the Dee, was in West Aberdeenshire. It has, of course, strong royal connections centred on Balmoral Castle, and extends to the edge of the Grampians at Braemar. Finally, part of the suburban overspill for Aberdeen is included - council estates like Kincorth and owner-occupied residential areas.

As might be expected, this means that there is mixed political support in Kincardine and Deeside. Deeside has Liberal tendencies. But Angus North and Mearns has been Conservative since its creation in 1950, very safely on all occasions except during the height of the SNP thrust of 1974. The Liberals did not even contest the seat in 1979. Alick Buchanan-Smith has been MP since 1964, and remains popular locally and nationally despite his resignation as Shadow Secretary of State for Scotland in December 1976 over Tory failure to support devolution. Buchanan-Smith is now an Agriculture Minister and as a farmer himself seems well placed to represent this Kincardine and Deeside seat. The south Aberdeen suburbs are varied in character and cancel each other out politically.

Alick Buchanan-Smith is generally regarded as one of the brightest and most thoughtful and urbane of Scottish Tories. He must be the strong favourite to win Kincardine and Deeside, especially with the opposition so equally divided.

1981	% Own Occ	49
1981	% Loc Auth	29
1981	% Mid Cl	39
1981	% Prof Man	16
1978	electorate 55,800	
1979	notional result	
	C 9,700	
Alliance		L

1979 core seat Angus North and Mearns

C	18,302	57.5
SNP	7,387	23.2
Lab	6,132	19.3

MPs since 1950
1950-64 C.N. Thornton-Kemsley
              C
1964-   Alick Buchanan-Smith C

Moray

It is sometimes said that the Scottish National Party presents whichever political face is most attractive to the voters of a neighbourhood: left-wing in industrial Strathclyde, right-wing in the rural east and north. Winnie Ewing offers living proof that this slur is not entirely justified, for she has been elected for both industrial and rural seats. She won the historic 1967 Hamilton byelection, and held the seat until 1970. Then she produced an equally dramatic upset - the defeat of Scottish Secretary Gordon Campbell at Moray and Nairn in February 1974. She was ousted by Alex Pollock in 1979, but only by 422 votes. Winnie Ewing is still successful and active in politics in North Eastern Scotland, for she was elected Euro MP for the Highlands in a tight multi-sided contest in June 1979.

In the boundary changes, Nairn is transferred to Inverness, for that little county has been placed in the Highland Region. The old county of Moray remains the centre of the constituency, and it is now matched with the inland part of Banffshire. Since Banff was also a Nationalist seat between 1974 and 1979, the new Moray remains a good SNP prospect. The largest community is the cathedral town of Elgin, but there are many other small burghs - Buckie, Keith, Forres, Dufftown, Cullen and Lossiemouth, where Ramsay Macdonald was born. The rolling farmland of Speyside cuts through the heart of the seat.

Moray is now identical to the District of the same name. The Labour and Liberal Parties have great difficulty saving their deposits here, and it will remain a straight fight between the Tories and the SNP.

1981	% Own Occ	41.2	1979 core seat Moray/Nairn		
1981	% Loc Auth	40.2	C	14,222	40.1
1981	% Mid Cl	36.6	SNP	13,800	38.9
1981	% Prof Man	13.4	L	4,361	12.3
1978	electorate 56,500		Lab	3,104	8.7
1979	notional result		MPs since 1945		
	SNP 70		1945-59 J. Stuart C		
Alliance		L	1959-74 Gordon Campbell C		
			1974-79 Winnie Ewing SNP		
			1979- Alex Pollock C		

Caithness and Sutherland

By 1979 the northernmost constituency on the mainland of Great Britain, Caithness and Sutherland, already had the unique distinction of having been represented by MPs of four different affiliations since the war. Then Robert Maclennan, the Labour MP, made it _five_ different parties by deserting to the SDP in 1981! The first shock that Caithness and Sutherland has provided came in 1945, when E.L. Gandar-Dower was elected as a Conservative by six votes over Labour, with the Leader of the Liberal Party, Sir Archibald Sinclair, losing his seat in third place, another 55 votes behind. Gandar-Dower later became an Independent, and so did Sir David Robertson who succeeded him in 1950. In 1964 Caithness and Sutherland was won by a Liberal, and in 1966 Maclennan took over, with a majority of 64.

This is a vast seat, of varying landscape - Caithness is flat and prosperous farmland, in the far NE corner of Scotland, stretching to John o'Groats. It is smaller than Sutherland but has the bulk of the population of the seat. Sutherland is a wild and untamed world, with a population of 11,000 spread amongst over a million acres of inaccessible moorland and weirdly shaped mountains like Suilven.

It only has 30,000 electors, but it clearly has one of the most complex political anatomies of any seat. It was felt that the growth of Thurso associated with the nuclear reactor at Dounreay helped Maclennan to hold the division as a Labour candidate from 1966, adding to their traditional crofter support. Wick is usually regarded as the most Liberal part of the seat. The Tories are more than just the lairds' party. Finally, the SNP has done well in Caithness and Sutherland of recent years, and it is not beyond the bounds of possibility that they might become the sixth party to represent the seat since the war! However, Maclennan must have a better chance than most SDP defectors of holding his seat, in this far northern land of personal votes and individualistic politics.

1981	% Own Occ	37.5	1979 core seat C'ness & S'land		
1981	% Loc Auth	42.8	Lab	9,613	41.5
1981	% Mid Cl	41.2	C	7,074	30.5
1981	% Prof Man	16.7	SNP	6,487	28.0
1979	electorate 29,564		MPs since 1945		
1979	notional result		1945-50 E.L. Gandar-Dower C		
	Lab 2,500		(Ind C)		
Alliance		SDP	1950-64 Sir D. Robertson C		
			(Ind C)		
			1964-66 George Mackie L		
			1966- R. Maclennan Lab		
			(SDP)		

Inverness, Nairn and Lochaber

Until the boundary changes, Inverness was the largest constituency in area in Britain. Now it loses the isle of Skye and the Aird district of Invernessshire to Ross and Cromarty, which takes over its mantle as the giant of all divisions. But Inverness does expand to take Nairn and Grantown on Spey from Banff and Moray and Nairn, and Kinlochleven and Ardnamurchan from Argyll. It is still a vast seat.

Its politics are also individual to the point of uniqueness. Inverness has been held for the Liberals by Russell Johnstone since 1964, often narrowly. Yet this still represents only 33% of the vote, and the opposition was almost evenly divided between the three other parties, all of whom can count on substantial blocs of support. This is the heart of the hunting, shooting and fishing Highlands, packed with Conservative patriarchs and their estates. The Nationalists are aided by the Gaelic culture of the west coast and can count on some working-class support. Labour's candidate Brian Wilson started the well-known local radical paper, the West Highland Free Press, based in Skye; there are also large council estates in the city of Inverness, besides the small estates which are found in villages throughout Scotland. Kinlochleven is a depressed aluminium company town in the heart of some of the most beautiful scenery in Scotland.

Russell Johnstone obviously has a personal following throughout his constituency. But the boundary changes will not help him, for there is no Liberal tradition in the Nairn or Argyll sections of the new seat. The loss of Skye will hurt the SNP and Labour. It seems as if the Tories are the main beneficiaries of the revision, and will challenge strongly in Inverness, Nairn and Lochaber.

1981	% Own Occ	40	1979 core seat Inverness		
1981	% Loc Auth	45	L	15,716	33.7
1981	% Mid Cl	41	C	11,559	24.8
1981	% Prof Man	13	SNP	9,603	20.6
1978	electorate 61,900		Lab	9,586	20.6
1979	notional result		Oth	112	0.2
	L 900		MPs since 1945		
Alliance		L	1945-50 Sir M. Macdonald Ind L		
			1950-54 Lord M. Douglas-Hamilton C		
			1954-64 N.L.D. McLean C		
			1964- Russell Johnstone L		

Orkney and Shetland

The Highlands and Islands of Northern Scotland demonstrate some of the most unusual and independent political preferences in the UK. This takes a multiplicity of forms. The four northernmost constituencies in Britain have MPs of four different parties. The Orkney and Shetland seat is very much one of a kind. Its independence from Scotland is shown by the derisory 4% vote gained by the SNP candidate in the 1979 General Election, and by its vote against a Scottish assembly. Orkney and Shetland might even secede itself from an independent Scotland!

For over 30 years Orkney and Shetland has elected Jo Grimond, who was Leader of the Liberal Party from 1956 to 1967. The elegant and sophisticated Grimond was much responsible for modernising the image of the Liberals and revivifying the party after their dark period after World War Two. No other party has been able to approach Grimond's vote recently, but now he has announced his retirement. It remains to be seen whether his vote can be transferred to another Liberal, or whether it was largely personal.

The Orkney and Shetland contest will be one of the most open in Britain. The Conservatives finished second in 1979, but still polled only 21%. Labour finds it difficult to mobilise the crofting vote in this most heavily agricultural of Scottish seats, and there are fewer council houses here than in most Scottish divisions. In fact, the greatest challenge to the Liberals might even come from an independent islander candidate. In the local elections in Shetland, the unofficial Shetland Movement did very well; but there are of course also sharp differences between Orkney and Shetland. If the Liberals can find a candidate of personal weight and standing matching or even approaching Jo Grimond's, they should hold on. Otherwise, it's anyone's game.

1981	% Own Occ	50.2	1979 same seat Orkney and		
1981	% Loc Auth	29.6	Shetland		
1981	% Mid Cl	37.3	L	10,950	56.4
1981	% Prof Man	14.3	C	4,140	21.3
1979	electorate 28,884		Lab	3,385	17.4
Alliance		L	SNP	935	4.8

MPs since 1945
1945-50 B.H.H. Neven-Spence C
1950-   Jo Grimond L

Ross, Cromarty and Skye

Another of the massive Scottish Highlands seats, Ross and Cromarty expands still further to take in the island of Skye, Lochalsh and part of NW Invernessshire. It now has the largest area of any constituency. It stretches right across Scotland from the lowland east coast at Cromarty and the fertile Black Isle, through rolling Easter Ross to the stark grandeur of the Wester Ross wilderness and the west coast. Skye boasts the most dramatic scenery of any Scottish island, with its rounded Red Cuillin mountains and razor-backed Black Cuillins.

Yet in all its two million acres, the seat houses only 44,500 voters, which makes canvassing and campaigning a personal business. Ross and Cromarty never paid very much attention to national political trends. As recently as 1970 there was a Liberal MP here, Alasdair Mackenzie, but his vote proved to be a product of loyalty to the man, not the party. The Liberal vote collapsed in the 1970s, and the SDP have been granted the Alliance nomination now. Despite the panorama of mountains, lochs and glens and moors on the west coast, most of the population is centred in Easter Ross. Here can be seen a twin picture of boom and decay: oil refineries and rigs are planned, while the Invergordon aluminium smelter is condemned.

Since 1970 the Conservative Hamish Gray has consolidated his position, and now seems to have a safe seat (despite the folk-memory of the nineteenth-century Highland clearances). The accession of Skye will help Labour and the SNP, but they still seem destined to be battling it out for second place behind Gray.

1981	% Own Occ	44	1979 core seat Ross/Cromarty
1981	% Loc Auth	38	C 10,650 42.4
1981	% Mid Cl	42	SNP 5,915 23.6
1981	% Prof Man	17	Lab 5,055 20.1
1978	electorate 44,500		L 3,496 13.9
1979	notional result		MPs since 1945
	C 5,600		1945-64 J. MacLeod C
Alliance		SDP	1964-70 Alasdair Mackenzie L
			1970- Hamish Gray C

Western Isles

The Outer Hebrides are the only part of Scotland with a majority of Gaelic speakers - 79% in 1981. As in Wales, the higher the proportion of those who can speak the Celtic language, the stronger the Nationalism of the constituency. The leader of the SNP, Donald Stewart, was first elected in 1970 - the party's only success in that General Election. The number of SNP MPs has since risen and fallen, but it seems likely that if the party should ever be reduced to one member, then it will again be Donald Stewart acting as the voice of Scotland, and of the Western Isles.

The Western Isles seat is unchanged by the Boundary Commission (although there was at one stage a suggestion that Skye might be added): it consists of Lewis, Harris, Benbecula, the Uists and the smaller islands of the Hebridean chain. These bare treeless islands rely on fishing and farming. There are only a dozen Scottish seats with a majority of owner-occupied houses, but Western Isles is one of them. Yet these are not wealthy residents: the proportion of non-manual workers is one of the lowest in Scotland. There are still a large number of crofters, small producers who have traditionally voted Labour. Malcolm Macmillan held Western Isles for Labour continuously from 1935 (when he was 22 years old) to 1970, and Labour remains second in the seat. The Tories have lost their deposit in the last three Elections; indeed Donald Stewart himself represents the values of social conservatism with great determination.

Donald Stewart may well hold Western Isles with a personal vote for many years, just as Malcolm Macmillan did. Here in these windblown outposts of Scotland, politics is an intense, local, inward-looking business, little related to national development - even the national currents of Scotland, never mind Westminster, 600 miles and a sea crossing away.

1981	% Own Occ	64.3	1979 same seat Western Isles		
1981	% Loc Auth	24.1	SNP	7,941	52.5
1981	% Mid Cl	32.8	Lab	4,878	32.3
1981	% Prof Man	11.3	C	1,600	10.6
1979	electorate 22,393		L	700	4.6
Alliance		L	MPs since 1945		

1945-70 Malcolm Macmillan Lab
1970-   Donald Stewart SNP

East Lothian

Berwick and East Lothian used to be one of the most tightly contested and quirky constituencies in Britain. Labour's John Mackintosh lost it in February 1974 despite the national anti-Tory swing; he regained it in October of the same year, and on his death in 1978 another Labour moderate, John Home Robertson, retained the seat in Labour's best byelection result of the 1974-9 Parliament. Now the seat loses the former County of Berwickshire, now in the Borders Region. Always the minor partner in Berwick and E Lothian, Berwickshire contained neither Berwick itself, which is in England, nor North Berwick, which is in East Lothian.

Berwickshire was also the most Conservative part of the seat. East Lothian becomes less and less Labour the further one moves away from Edinburgh. The Labour strength in the old coalfield around Tranent, Ormiston, Preston and Prestonpans is now joined by Musselburgh, formerly in Edinburgh East. These should outweigh the Tory farming, market and seaside towns further out - Cockenzie, Haddington, East Linton, Dirleton, North Berwick and Dunbar.

The swapping of Musselburgh for Berwickshire should convert an ultra-marginal seat into one safe for Labour - although of course the loss of Musselburgh will make Gavin Strang's task of holding Edinburgh East for Labour much harder. The constituency is now identical to the East Lothian District.

1981	% Own Occ	30.4	1979 core seat Berwick and East
1981	% Loc Auth	60.1	Lothian
1981	% Mid Cl	47.7	Lab 21,977 43.5
1981	% Prof Man	15.2	C 20,304 40.2
1978	electorate 60,203		L 4,948 10.0
1979	notional result		SNP 3,300 6.5
	Lab 9,600		MPS since 1945
Alliance		L	1945-51 J.J. Robertson Lab

1951-66 Sir W. Anstruther-Gray
             C
1966-74 John Mackintosh Lab
1974   Michael Ancram C
1974-78 John Mackintosh Lab
1978-   John Home Robertson
             Lab

Edinburgh Central

Edinburgh loses one of its seven seats in the boundary changes. With its puny electorate of 37,700, Edinburgh Central looked like a candidate for abolition, but in fact it has survived, and North is the seat to disappear, split four ways. The former Central was based on Edinburgh's Old Town, containing Arthur's Seat, the Castle and the Royal Mile, and the brooding tenements of the ancient walled city. Its northern boundary was Princes Street, but now it extends beyond into the eighteenth-century terraces of the New Town. Thus is united both types of the superb architecture of the heart of Edinburgh. The Central constituency must be one of the most culturally and historically blessed of any in Britain.

There was always a political divide, as well as architectural and physical ones, between the Old Town and the New Town. Tribunite Robin Cook held Central for Labour, gathering votes from the high-density tenements of the Old Town ridge, which extends west to Gorgie and Daltry. The New Town was the centre of sophisticated but solidly Tory Edinburgh North, the seat of junior minister Alex Fletcher. Cook will have great difficulty holding the new Central, for another addition is the solidly middle-class Murrayfield ward, the home of Scottish Rugby Union. Central will now be a Conservative seat in an even year.

Almost untouched by war bombing, the centre of Edinburgh is a fascinating and colourful district, steeped in history and character. Now that the New Town is included in the seat, it is fully sized, and still contains relatively less constructed in the last century than any other seat in Britain. It is a worthy seat of, and for, Scotland's capital.

1981	% Own Occ	60	1979 core seat Edinburgh		
1981	% Loc Auth	11	Central		
1981	% Mid Cl	55	Lab	12,191	47.8
1981	% Prof Man	15	C	7,530	29.6
1978	electorate 57,400		L	3,096	12.2
1979	notional result		SNP	2,486	9.8
	C 2,000		Ind	176	0.7
Alliance		SDP	MPs since 1945		

1945-51 A. Gilzean Lab
1951-74 Thomas Oswald Lab
1974-   Robin Cook Lab

Edinburgh East

East returned the largest Labour majority in Edinburgh at the
1979 General Election, in fact the largest majority any party
won in the city. But this is highly unlikely to be the case
next time. The old East stretched beyond the city boundary
to take in the East Lothian town of Musselburgh, which is a
Labour stronghold. Now Musselburgh is removed, and in the
1982 Regional elections the Tories polled the most votes in the
new East, admittedly in an excellent year for them. They may
have done particularly well in Lothian because of the well-
publicised battle between the former Labour authority and the
Westminster government over public spending cuts.

This is basically that part of Edinburgh east and south-east
of Arthur's Seat. It is a very mixed constituency, socially
and politically. Craigmillar and Bingham are amongst the most
impoverished council estates in Edinburgh. On the other
hand, there are good residential areas on the coast around
Portobello, which is a Tory ward, and inland at Craigentinny
and Jock's Lodge. At the north end of the seat, at Lochend,
it fringes into Leith, another Labour constituency, and it also
now takes a small chunk of the abolished North division.

Gavin Strang should be able to hold East for Labour in all
but a disastrous year. The Alliance did less well here than in
several of the Edinburgh seats in its first trial in 1982,
polling only 19%, and the Nationalists are weak throughout the
Scottish capital. But Strang's 1979 majority of 8,000 plus
should be halved by the disappearance of Musselburgh, and
East will no longer have a council housing majority.

1981	% Own Occ	48	1979 core seat Edinburgh East
1981	% Loc Auth	44	Lab 23,477 53.7
1981	% Mid Cl	51	C 14,660 33.5
1981	% Prof Man	14	SNP 5,296 12.1
1978	electorate 52,000		Comm 173 0.4
1979	notional result		WRP 124 0.3
	Lab 6,800		MPs since 1945
Alliance		L	1945-47 G.R. Thomson Lab
			1947-54 J.T. Wheatley Lab
			1954-70 E.G. Willis Lab
			1970- Gavin Strang Lab

Edinburgh Leith

Undoubtedly the most controversial of the Edinburgh MPs is Ron Brown, the Labour MP for Leith. He is not to be confused with the other Ron Brown, SDP member for Hackney South and Shoreditch, for the Leith MP is a left-winger who reached the national eye after his endorsement of Russian policy after a visit to Afghanistan. Ron Brown is one of the most active of the 1979 intake to Parliament.

His chances of remaining in the Commons have certainly been enhanced by the boundary changes. Leith was the smallest seat in Edinburgh in 1979, with only 37,204 electors. Now it has expanded south, to take in the Inverleith and Warriston sections of the abolished North constituency; these are Conservative. But more relevantly, Leith has also moved west to take in the West Pilton/Muirhouse council estate. This is a highly depressed area, with many abandoned houses and flats. Not surprisingly, the Conservatives polled but 3% in Pilton in the 1980 city council elections. All these changes would have boosted Brown's majority in 1979 from 4,000 to over 7,000. Leith itself is of course the port for Edinburgh, an old-fashioned industrial area of glowering dark stone tenements, warehouses and cobbled streets. The old seat also included the Tory wards of Trinity and Newhaven though, to set against Leith itself and the half of the Granton-Pilton-Muirhouse council estate which was already in the seat.

Despite Ron Brown's reputation as an extremist, the Alliance may pose little threat in Leith. In 1982 they only polled 22.5% in the new constituency - nowhere near their strength in the Tory constituencies of Pentlands, West and South. Brown should survive to play a similar role in the new Parliament.

1981	% Own Occ	55	1979 core seat Edinburgh Leith		
1981	% Loc Auth	25	Lab	12,961	46.3
1981	% Mid Cl	50	C	8,944	32.0
1981	% Prof Man	11	L	3,382	12.1
1978	electorate 62,900		SNP	2,701	9.7
1979	notional result		MPs since 1945		
	Lab 8,100		1945-70 J.H. Hoy Lab		
Alliance		SDP	1970-79 Ronald King Murray Lab		
			1979- Ron Brown Lab		

Edinburgh Pentlands

When one is confronted by the massive tower block of the
1970s council development at Wester Hailes, it is almost
impossible to believe that one is in a Conservative
constituency. This peripheral estate is a concrete city in its
own right, far removed in all senses from the elegance of
central Edinburgh. Add the information that at the last
Election Edinburgh Pentlands also included large council
estates of an earlier vintage at Sighthill and Stenhouse, and
it becomes a deeper mystery why Malcolm Rifkind won the
seat for the Tories. Yet the fact is that this constituency in
SW Edinburgh, named after the Pentland Hills which
overshadow it, is one of the most deeply divided socially in
the whole of Britain.

Rifkind actually owed his victory to the excellent residential
areas of owner-occupied housing which are to be found on the
south-western edge of the city - the mansions of Colinton,
the bungalows of Fairmilehead - and the suave terraces of the
inner south side at Merchiston. The last named is lost in the
redistribution to South, but Rifkind should have a safer
constituency, for the Stenhouse council estate passes into
West, and Pentlands reaches out beyond the old city
boundary to take in the Tory residential area of Currie-
Balerno, formerly in Midlothian. Labour slipped to third place
in the new Pentlands in 1982, well behind the Alliance, as
their support was confined to the Wester Hailes/Sighthill
corner of the constituency.

Rifkind is a successful and rising young politician, first
elected as MP at 27 years of age and now a junior Scottish
Minister. In some quarters he is tipped as a future Secretary
of State. He has done well to hold the mixed Pentlands seat -
it had more council housing than any other Tory seat in
Scotland in 1979 - and his frail majority should be boosted by
the boundary changes.

1981	% Own Occ	49	1979 core seat Edinburgh		
1981	% Loc Auth	45	Pentlands		
1981	% Mid Cl	58	C	17,684	39.3
1981	% Prof Man	17	Lab	16,486	36.6
1978	electorate 57,800		L	5,919	13.1
1979	notional result		SNP	4,934	11.0
	C 6,400		MPs since 1950		
Alliance		SDP	1950-64 Lord John Hope C		
			1964-74 Norman Wylie C		
			1974- Malcolm Rifkind C		

Edinburgh South

South is the least altered of all the constituencies in Edinburgh, making only minor swaps with next door Pentlands, gaining Merchiston and losing part of Morningside. Nowadays South is a marginal seat, although Labour has never won it; in the 1950s and 1960s Labour support grew in several Edinburgh seats as peripheral council estates were constructed. Here, Liberton and Gilmerton are part of a series of developments which fringe the southern edge of the city. In political terms Liberton and Gilmerton battle against the inner south side: Newington, Morningside, Merchiston - wards which epitomise the elegance and grace of bourgeois Edinburgh districts.

Edinburgh is a relatively middle-class city. In 1979 South was one of the four seats in the city with over 50% non-manual workers. As in London and Cardiff, professional jobs are thick on the ground in this capital city, even if Scotland has not attained home rule or its own Assembly. In Edinburgh South, the presence both of large blocs of middle-class housing and a higher than average percentage of council tenants gave both Conservatives and Labour a heavy vote - the Tories' Michael Ancram coming out 2,460 votes ahead in 1979.

But another factor should be added to this complex mixture. In 1982 the Alliance did very well in all the wards of the South constituency, achieving 31% which would have been good enough to win second place if there had been a seat-wide contest. This was only 7% behind the Conservatives, and the Alliance may have their best chance in Edinburgh here. The SDP have gained the Alliance nomination. Edinburgh South is certainly the nearest seat in the city to a three-way marginal.

1981	% Own Occ	55	1979 core seat Edinburgh South
1981	% Loc Auth	36	C 17,986 39.7
1981	% Mid Cl	59	Lab 15,526 34.3
1981	% Prof Man	20	L 7,400 16.3
1978	electorate 60,800		SNP 3,800 8.4
1979	notional result		E 552 1.2
	C 3,600		MPs since 1945
Alliance		SDP	1945-57 Sir W.Y. Darling C
			1957-79 M.C. Hutchison C
			1979- Michael Ancram C

Edinburgh West

In 1979 Edinburgh West produced the largest numerical and percentage majority of the four Tory seats in the Scottish capital. After the redistribution there will be even less doubt about West's status as the most middle-class division and as the safest Conservative stronghold. Previously this north-western segment of the city included West Pilton, probably the most decrepit council estate in Edinburgh and certainly one of the most decayed districts in Britain. Now West Pilton/Muirhouse, the only Labour ward in Edinburgh West, is transferred to Leith, there to join the rest of the Pilton-Granton estate.

West is left as a solid bastion of the Edinburgh upper orders. Taking in part of Edinburgh North, it now contains the sought-after residential areas of Cramond, Barnton, Corstorphine, Blackhall and Ravelston. It is not surprising that the top boys' public schools are to be found here, Fettes College and Stewart Melville's, their pinnacled towers proudly facing each other. Here is the girls school, Mary Erskine College, in the heart of Jean Brodie-land, and so too is Edinburgh High School, widely regarded as the best state school in the city. Its reputation is such that it has become very desirable to live in its catchment area – which makes the council estate of Clermiston one of the most up-market in Edinburgh. The Stenhouse council estate is taken from the Pentlands seat.

West is now thoroughly middle class. The anomalous near-slum has vanished, and is replaced by some of the best residential parts of the former Conservative Edinburgh North. The MP here is Lord James Douglas-Hamilton. He had a 7,000 majority over Labour in 1979, but Labour sank to 18.2% of the vote here in 1982. The Alliance offered a far greater threat, polling 37% to the Tories' 40%, and seizing the Corstorphine wards. Clearly they have much to offer the tastes of one of the most sophisticated electorates in Britain.

1981	% Own Occ	65	1979 core seat Edinburgh West
1981	% Loc Auth	25	C 19,360 45.4
1981	% Mid Cl	68	Lab 12,009 28.2
1981	% Prof Man	22	L 7,330 17.2
1978	electorate 57,700		SNP 3,904 9.2
1979	notional result		MPs since 1945
	C 6,400		1945-59 Sir G.I.C. Hutchison C
Alliance		L	1959-74 J.A. Stodart C
			1974- Lord James Douglas-Hamilton C

Linlithgow

Tam Dalyell of West Lothian is one of the most independent and active MPs in the House of Commons. He is the only Etonian Labour MP. He is known for his sharp objections to devolution proposals and to demands for Scottish independence. But he has clearly been shown to be a man of great popularity among the Scots. In his West Lothian constituency he has fended off the challenge of former Chairman of the SNP William Wolfe seven times, starting with his victory in a byelection in 1962. In 1979 he extended his majority to over 20,000. Now boundary changes are to reduce the swollen electorate of West Lothian considerably, as the New Town of Livingston is removed completely. The old name for the County of West Lothian was Linlithgowshire, and now once again a seat is to be based on Linlithgow, the ancient burgh near the Forth.

The local election results of 1982 suggest that there may be tight contests in Linlithgow as there were in West Lothian. Labour polled 38% overall, the SNP 36%. What is more, it was the Social Democrats who won the Linlithgow ward itself, ahead of the SNP and the Tories, with Labour fourth. The SNP also do well in the old shale mining area around Whitburn, Bathgate and Armadale. The mining has been replaced by new industries such as the BL car works at Bathgate, but its legacy remains in the ugly and massive slag heaps which dominate the otherwise flat countryside, giving it a unique aspect. The strongly Labour Bo'ness is transferred to Central Region, and Queensferry and Kirkliston are included even though they are now part of Edinburgh city.

If Dalyell decides to stand in Linlithgow, he should be able to tap a richly deserved personal vote built up over 20 years. But if he decides to seek election elsewhere, Linlithgow could well provide a shock result, as it remains an outside chance for the SNP and even for the SDP-Alliance.

1981	% Own Occ	26	1979 core seat West Lothian	
1981	% Loc Auth	69	Lab	36,713	54.9
1981	% Mid Cl	37	SNP	16,613	24.9
1981	% Prof Man	10	C	13,162	19.7
1978	electorate 54,500		Comm	404	0.6
1979	notional result		MPs since 1945	
	Lab 12,100		1945-51 G. Mathers Lab	
Alliance		SDP	1951-62 J. Taylor Lab	
			1962- Tam Dalyell Lab	

Livingston

The New Town of Livingston lies half-way between Edinburgh and Glasgow, and has drawn its population from the overspill of both major Scottish cities. It is the only New Town in the Lothian Region; East Kilbride and Cumbernauld and Irvine are all in Strathclyde, Glenrothes in Fife. Like many of the government-designated New Towns in both England and Scotland, it has a high level of social dislocation - uneployment, welfare cases, mental illness. Despite the variety of architecture, the housing appears low-cost and poor. Despite the variety of 'neighbourhoods', Livingston seems a soulless and depressing place.

Yet also like other New Towns, it demonstrates far greater political volatility than the working-class districts from which many of the residents of Livingston originally came. The SNP polled a quarter of the votes in both Livingston wards in the 1982 Regional elections. Also the SDP won the Livingston S ward from Labour, and the Liberals were second in Livingston North. Labour has a slightly more comfortable lead in the other parts of the seat, the ex-mining district around Broxburn and the Calders. But this untried constituency will be well worth close scrutiny. The Liberals have the Alliance nomination, and will be hoping to translate their local votes into parliamentary terms. The SNP has done well many times in the former West Lothian seat, from which part of the new Livingston is drawn.

The two large divisions of West Lothian and Midlothian may well have been divided into three Labour seats by the Boundary Commission. But neither Linlithgow nor Livingston ssem rock-safe, and the Nationalists and the Alliance will cherish hopes of success - particularly in whichever seat in which they will not have to face Tam Dalyell as Labour candidate.

1981	% Own Occ	22	New seat
1981	% Loc Auth	73	
1981	% Mid Cl	39	
1981	% Prof Man	11	
1978	electorate 46,200		
1979	notional result		
	Lab 10,600		
Alliance		L	

Midlothian

The Scottish parliamentary constituencies are on average smaller than those in England, Wales and Northern Ireland. But Midlothian and West Lothian are the two largest seats in Scotland, and in 1979 Midlothian had reached an electorate of over 101,000, the fifth largest on the mainland, and nearly twice the Scottish quota. This situation, caused largely by the growth of Livingston New Town, obviously had to be remedied. Basically what has happened now is that Midlothian and West Lothian have been split into three new seats, Linlithgow, Livingston and Midlothian.

The new Midlothian seat is identical to Midlothian District, which means that the constituency loses its western end around the Calders and the New Town. Its heart is the largely defunct Midlothian coalfield, with its little communities of unrelieved working-class character which almost entirely consist of council housing - Loanhead, Bonnyrigg/Lasswade, Dalkeith, Easthouses, Gorebridge, Newtongrange and others. There are a few private residential areas, such as at Penicuik beneath the Pentland Hills, which offer some Tory votes. But one of the favourite districts for middle-class Edinburgh commuters, Currie and Balerno, has been transferred into the city itself and the Pentlands constituency. Midlothian as a whole had a total of 60.9% council housing at the 1981 census.

Though more compact than before, the new Midlothian seat should be just as safe for Labour now that the Nationalist surge of the mid-1970s is over. Alex Eadie's majority was cut to 4,000, or 6%, in October 1974, but the SNP collapsed into third place in 1979 and Eadie beat the Tory by 17,000 votes. Barring an SNP revival, Labour should gain a clear extra seat from the population growth of the outer Lothian area.

1981	% Own Occ	27.5	1979 core seat Midlothian			
1981	% Loc Auth	62.0	Lab	37,733	47.8	
1981	% Mid Cl	46.5	C	20,797	26.4	
1981	% Prof Man	13.1	SNP	13,260	16.8	
1978	electorate 59,288		L	7,129	9.0	
1979	notional result		MPs since 1955			
	Lab 12,500		1955-59 D.J. Pryde Lab			
Alliance		SDP	1959-66 J.M. Hill Lab			
			1966- Alexander Eadie Lab			

Argyll and Bute

The vast constituency of Argyll was usually the last in
Britain to declare its result, as votes were brought by boat
from Mull, Jura and Islay, as well as even smaller islands like
Coll, Tiree and Colonsay. Argyll also included vast tracts of
moorland on the mainland, divided by deep sea-lochs which
make communications within the seat very difficult. In the
boundary changes, another island is added: Bute, which was
previously a county of its own, associated with North
Ayrshire for electoral purposes. But the electorate actually
declines, for Bute only has a population of 14,000, while
Argyll has lost its northern end beyond Oban and Mull to the
Highland Region – remote Ardnamurchan disappears, and
Ballachulish, and the depressed aluminium smelting town of
Kinlochleven. But Argyll and Bute will remain one of the
largest and most difficult seats geographically – nearly 2
million acres of rough terrain. It may also well remain
difficult to predict politically.
Argyll is the heart of laird paternalism, and it was safely
Tory until February 1974 when, after the retirement of
Conservative frontbencher Michael Noble, it was gained by
Scottish Nationalist Iain MacCormick in a surprise late result.
MacCormick held on until 1979, when Argyll was recovered for
the Tories by John Mackay. MacCormick is now a Social
Democrat, but Argyll and Bute must remain a good Nationalist
prospect. 10% of the population speak Gaelic, and the isles of
the western coast (even here in the south) are sturdily
independent in politics, culture and religion.
Strathclyde is generally thought of as a heavily urban,
industrial Region. But this seat, which takes up half its
acreage, gives the lie to that. All the parties will have to
canvass vigorously, by boat and on foot as well as by road,
if they are to hope to win this Highland seat in Strathclyde.

1981	% Own Occ	40.9	1979 core seat Argyll
1981	% Loc Auth	37.9	C 12,191 36.8
1981	% Mid Cl	42.8	SNP 10,545 31.8
1981	% Prof Man	18.0	Lab 5,283 15.9
1978	electorate 47,100		L 5,113 15.4
1979	notional result		MPs since 1945
	C 4,100		1945-58 D. McCallum C
Alliance		L	1958-74 Michael Noble C
			1974-79 Iain MacCormick SNP
			1979- John Mackay C

Ayr

The Secretary of State for Scotland in Mrs Thatcher's government is George Younger, a scion of the brewing family. Younger sits for the Ayr constituency, which he has held since 1964. Yet despite his high office, and his long period of tenure, Younger can never have regarded Ayr as a safe seat. His majority was reduced to 484 in 1966, and it was still under 3,000 in 1979.

Ayr is a divided town, socially and politically. The northern half contains most of the council estates, and the commercial harbour. It is strong Labour territory. Southern Ayr is a fashionable residential area and seaside resort. The constituency also includes Prestwick, and now, for the first time, the golfers' paradise of Troon. The Ayrshire seaside resorts are all Conservative in disposition, and Troon's inclusion will undoubtedly strengthen George Younger's grip on Ayr. Ayr is a seat of peculiarly Scottish characteristics. Over 40% middle class even back in 1971, it ranks as one of the more high-status seats in Britain. But not far off half of the population live in council houses, a much more common form of tenure north of the border than in England or Wales.

The odds are now that George Younger will cling on to Ayr at the next Election for the seventh successive time. In one way at least he deserves his good fortune. He was the Tory candidate who stood down at the last minute to allow Alec Douglas-Home to enter the Commons as member for Kinross and West Perthshire in 1963. If he had not given way to his new leader, he would still be representing that very safe seat. Ayr was never so attractive a prospect, and six close contests have reminded Younger of his self(?)-sacrifice. Now the accession of Troon will ease Younger's position as the most vulnerable Cabinet Minister.

1981	% Own Occ	46	1979 core seat Ayr		
1981	% Loc Auth	47	C	18,907	43.3
1981	% Mid Cl	48	Lab	16,139	36.9
1981	% Prof Man	17	L	4,656	10.7
1978	electorate 62,700		SNP	3,998	9.1
1979	notional result		MPs since 1950		
	C 4,300		1950-64 Sir T.C.R. Moore C		
Alliance		L	1964- George Younger C		

Carrick, Cumnock and Doon Valley

Carrick, Cumnock and Doon Valley is essentially the old South Ayrshire constituency. It has to be renamed because Ayrshire no longer exists, but is absorbed into the vast Strathclyde Region. The new lengthy name does however do justice to the disparate nature of the seat. Carrick is soft coastal country, with the seaside resort of Girvan and farmland around the town of Maybole just inland. Cumnock and Doon Valley are the heart of the South Ayrshire coalfield, where stark communities like Dalmellington and New Cumnock lie isolated amongst the rugged moors, offering as bleak an industrial scene as any in Britain.

The political divisions of the constituency follow the lines which might be predicted. Carrick is Conservative, Doon Valley and Cumnock normally very heavily Labour. In October 1974 the largest numerical majority in Scotland was obtained by South Ayrshire's Labour MP, Jim Sillars. Sillars was regarded as a bright young prospect in the party, with a liveliness and intellectual acumen not always associated with Labour MPs for Scottish seats. But he became disaffected with the Labour Party, particularly over lack of progress towards devolution, and resigned the whip in 1976 to become one of the two 'Scottish Labour Party' MPs. In the 1979 election he was narrowly defeated by the official Labour candidate, George Foulkes, and now Sillars has joined the SNP. It is not clear whether he will fight his old seat on behalf of the Nationalists, who lost their deposit in S Ayrshire last time.

In the boundary changes, 6,000 voters are gained from the Conservative Ayr constituency. But barring another split Labour vote, it is impossible to imagine the Tories winning here, among the remote mining communities of the Mauchline basin, the Doon Valley, and Cumnock.

1981	% Own Occ	23	1979 core seat South Ayrshire		
1981	% Loc Auth	68	Lab	14,271	35.2
1971	% Mid Cl	35	SLP	12,750	31.4
1971	% Prof Man	12	C	10,287	25.4
1978	electorate 56,300		SNP	3,233	8.0
1979	notional result		MPs since 1945		
	Lab 3,300		1945-46 A. Sloan Lab		
Alliance		SDP	1946-70 Emrys Hughes Lab		
			1970-79 Jim Sillars Lab (SLP)		
			1979- George Foulkes Lab		

Clydebank and Milngavie

Scotland seems to harbour more bizarrely drawn seats than the rest of the United Kingdom put together. In particular, it specialises in combining very Conservative towns and very Labour towns in the same constituency. All three of the former Dunbartonshire seats were of this nature. West Dunbartonshire included the former Communist stronghold of Vale of Leven and the Tory seaside town of Helensburgh. East Dunbartonshire brought together the Cumbernauld New Town and Bearsden, the most middle-class town in Britain. Central Dunbartonshire combined Clydebank and Milngavie, an association continued in this new seat.

Clydebank is the epitome of a working-class shipbuilding town, 22% middle class and possessing 78% council housing. Milngavie, like its neighbour Bearsden, is one of the most desirable residential areas for Glasgow commuters, 61% middle class and 55% owner occupied. Clydebank normally votes about six times as heavily for Labour as for the Conservatives. In Milngavie the proportions are nearly reversed. Clydebank is much larger than Milngavie (although in the redistribution Milngavie is reinforced with a few thousand voters from Bearsden), and Central Dunbartonshire was a safe Labour seat. Clydebank and Milngavie will be too.

The Conservatives can never do well enough to worry Labour in this deeply divided seat. In 1974, however, there was a threat from quite a different direction. Jimmy Reid stood as a Communist candidate. Reid was the charismatic spokesman for the men who tried to 'work-in' to prevent the closure of the Upper Clyde shipyards. For a while it was felt that Reid's personal popularity, allied to the effect of the economic blizzard which had hit Clydebank, would make him a serious contender. He did indeed poll 5,928 votes in February 1974, which made him the first Communist to save his deposit for many years. But it proved a flash in the pan, and the Communist poll of 177 votes (0.3%) in 1979 shows that it was mainly due to Reid's personal talents than any deep or lasting streak of revolutionary feeling here on Clydeside.

1981	% Own Occ	26	1979 core seat Dunbartonshire Central			
1981	% Loc Auth	70				
1981	% Mid Cl	48	Lab	20,515	53.1	
1981	% Prof Man	12	C	8,512	22.0	
1978	electorate 51,700		SNP	6,055	15.7	
1979	notional result		L	3,099	8.0	
	Lab 11,500		Oth	312	0.8	
Alliance		SDP	Comm	117	0.3	

MP since 1974

1974- Hugh McCartney Lab

Clydesdale

When the New Town of East Kilbride was taken out of the Lanark seat in 1974, 'The Scotsman' predicted that the rump of Lanark would be Tory. Indeed Judith Hart survived only narrowly in both 1974 Elections, first against a Tory challenge and then beating the SNP by 698 votes. But in 1979 she pulled clear of both rivals. Now, after relatively minor changes, which include a change of name to Clydesdale, the seat should be easier still for Dame Judith, a recent Chairman of the Labour Party. The seat contains large areas of sparsely populated moorland, and at one time elected Alec Douglas-Home (Lord Dunglass), but it is really part of the Strathclyde industrial belt.

1981	% Own Occ	36	1979 core seat Lanark
1981	% Loc Auth	55	Lab 18,118 43.2
1981	% Mid Cl	41	C 12,979 30.9
1981	% Prof Man	12	SNP 7,902 18.8
1978	electorate 58,400		L 2,967 7.1
1979	notional result		MPs since 1945
	Lab 9,900		1945-50 T. Steele Lab
Alliance		SDP	1950-51 Lord Dunglass C
			1951-59 P.F. Maitland C
			1959- Judith Hart Lab

Cumbernauld and Kilsyth

The New Town of Cumbernauld, set on a windy hill 15 miles NE of Glasgow, is now brought together with Kirkintilloch and Bearsden in the E Dunbartonshire seat. This is highly illogical, for Cumbernauld houses mainly Glasgow overspill, while Bearsden is an ultra-Tory middle-class suburb NW of Glasgow. Not surprisingly, E Dunbartons was very marginal. Now Cumbernauld is joined with Kilsyth, formerly in W Stirlings, to form a seat of its own - small now, but growing. The SNP offers the only real opposition to Labour, who will probably choose the present E Dunbartons MP Norman Hogg.

1981	% Own Occ	27.8	New seat
1981	% Loc Auth	71.0	
1981	% Mid Cl	50.7	
1981	% Prof Man	11.4	
1978	electorate 39,000		
1979	notional result		
	Lab 7,200		
Alliance		SDP	

Cunninghame North

Cunninghame North would have produced one of the closest results in Scotland had it existed in 1979, and it will form one of the relatively few marginal seats north of the border. Indeed, it is very hard to be certain about which party would have won it. Using the standard method of calculating notional results adopted by the BBC and ITN, it would have gone to Labour by a few hundred votes. This is within the margin of error and doubt.

Cunninghame North is based on the old North Ayrshire and Bute seat, held by 4,000 in 1979 by Conservative John Corrie. This was a safe Tory constituency, formerly occupied by writer, adventurer and explorer Fitzroy Maclean. But in the boundary changes Bute is transferred to join Argyll. There are still islands in Cunninghame N - the large Arran, and the small Cumbraes in the Firth of Clyde. These, together with the seaside resort of Largs, form the Conservative strongholds in the division. But Labour could always rely on the working-class coastal towns of Ardrossan and Saltcoats. Although their neighbour Stevenston is lost to Cunninghame South (the former Central Ayrshire), the old inland mining district of the Garnock Valley is gained in return.

In the 1982 Regional elections, Strathclyde electoral district 91 (Garnock Valley) and 92 (Ardrossan/Saltcoats) voted Labour by over two to one. ED 93 (Arran/Largs) voted Conservative by five to one, but this was not quite sufficient to prevent Labour gaining a majority of votes (of about 500) in the territory due to make up Cunninghame North. Unless John Corrie can find a safer seat, he has great cause for worry here in what used to be North Ayrshire.

1981	% Own Occ	42	1979 core seat North Ayrshire	
1981	% Loc Auth	49	and Bute	
1981	% Mid Cl	40	C 17,317	45.7
1981	% Prof Man	15	Lab 13,004	34.3
1978	electorate 52,400		SNP 5,272	13.9
1979	notional result		L 2,280	6.0
	Lab 300		MPs since 1945	
Alliance		SDP	1945-59 Sir C.G. MacAndrew C	
			1959-74 Sir Fitzroy Maclean C	
			1974- John Corrie C	

Cunninghame South

Irvine is the only one of Scotland's five New Towns to be sited on the coast; and indeed the only New Town in Britain next to the sea. It is scheduled to have an ultimate population of over 100,000, and its growth has already persuaded the Boundary Commission to cut down the Central Ayrshire division, of which it was a part, to a more compact core around Irvine. The new seat is to be named Cunninghame South.

The working-class port of Stevenston is added from North Ayrshire, but the Labour Garnock Valley is moved in the opposite direction, and the Tory seaside resort of Troon is transferred to Ayr. Nevertheless Cunninghame South is clearly based on the old Ayrshire Central, which has been securely Labour since 1959, and represented by David Lambie since 1970.

Irvine has taken much overspill from Glasgow, and Cunninghame South will be an even safer Labour seat than Ayrshire Central was. Both the Nationalists and the Liberals lost their deposit last time.

1981	% Own Occ	23	1979 core seat Ayrshire Central
1981	% Loc Auth	73	Lab 27,438 51.1
1981	% Mid Cl	39	C 15,734 29.3
1981	% Prof Man	13	SNP 5,596 10.4
1978	electorate 46,000		L 4,896 9.1
1979	notional result		MPs since 1950
	Lab 10,000		1950-55 A.C. Manuel Lab
Alliance		L	1955-59 D.L.S. Nairn C
			1959-70 A.C. Manuel Lab
			1970- David Lambie Lab

Dumbarton

This new seat, which is identical to the Scottish District of Dumbarton, is very similar to the old Dunbartonshire West.

The constituency is by no means socially homogeneous. It is generally accepted that Labour must concede the seaside town of Helensburgh to the Tories, especially since it has become popular with commuters to Glasgow. The Tories concede the Vale of Leven, an old textile-working valley which was once known as one of Britain's 'Little Moscows', rare citadels of Communism and militant working-class consciousness. This being so, the contest is usually decided in the town of Dumbarton itself, whose 25,000 inhabitants make up the third significant centre of population in the division. Dumbarton is a working-class town, and three-quarters of the housing is owner occupied. It is Dumbarton's continued allegiance which has ensured that Labour have never lost West Dunbartonshire since the Second World War.

The present sitting member is a moderate, Ian Campbell. Now that he has fought off a reselection challenge from the left in his own party, he should be safe in the renamed seat at the next Election.

1981	% Own Occ	35.0	1979 core seat Dunbartonshire
1981	% Loc Auth	55.1	West
1981	% Mid Cl	45.3	Lab 21,166 48.4
1981	% Prof Man	13.2	C 14,709 33.7
1978	electorate 55,900		SNP 7,835 17.9
1979	notional result		MPs since 1945
	Lab 6,400		1945-50 A. McKinlay Lab
Alliance		SDP	1950-70 Tom Steele Lab
			1970- Ian Campbell Lab

East Kilbride

The creation in 1974 of the New Town seat of East Kilbride south of Glasgow offered a haven to Dr Maurice Miller, the Labour MP for Kelvingrove, who was not selected for one of the new seats in the city after the boundary changes. Miller has clung on to East Kilbride since then, although he had to overcome strong challenges by the SNP, which polls well in several of the Scottish New Towns. The Nationalist appeal has faded, and Miller should have no trouble in a slightly more compact East Kilbride seat after the redistribution.

1981	% Own Occ	30.2	1979 core seat East Kilbride	
1981	% Loc Auth	68.0	Lab	31,401	53.9
1981	% Mid Cl	52.8	C	17,128	29.4
1981	% Prof Man	15.7	SNP	9,090	15.6
1978	electorate 60,100		Comm	658	1.1
1979	notional result		MP since 1974	
	Lab 8,900		1974- Maurice Miller Lab	
Alliance		SDP		

Eastwood

A large proportion of such middle class as there is in Glasgow lives in dormitory suburbs just outside the city boundaries - Bearsden in the north, and Eastwood District to the SW. There are no Tory seats in the City of Glasgow any more, but the old E Renfrewshire division was really a suburban division. Clarkston, Newton Mearns and Giffnock are physically part of the conurbation. It was probably the most Conservative and the most middle-class constituency in Scotland. The one Labour outpost, the industrial town of Barrhead, remains in the little altered but renamed Eastwood seat.

1981	% Own Occ	71	1979 core seat East	
1981	% Loc Auth	26	Renfrewshire	
1981	% Mid Cl	68	C	25,910	49.9
1981	% Prof Man	30	Lab	12,672	24.4
1978	electorate 56,600		L	9,366	18.0
1979	notional result		SNP	3,989	7.7
	C 11,500		MPs since 1945	
Alliance		SDP	1945-59 E.G.R. Lloyd C	
			1959-79 Betty Harvie Anderson C	
			1979- Allan Stewart C	

Glasgow Cathcart

Labour gained only one seat from the Conservatives anywhere in Britain at the 1979 General Election. But the Tory MP who lost his seat was Teddy Taylor, who would probably have been Secretary of State for Scotland in Mrs Thatcher's new government. The seat concerned was Glasgow Cathcart. Why did it fall to Labour? The answer is twofold. The Conservatives did not do nearly so well in the rest of Britain, and there were many examples of pro-Labour swings north of the border. But also Cathcart had been moving towards Labour for many years, due to the continued growth of the massive Castlemilk council estate in the southern half of the constituency.

Before Castlemilk began to spread up the slopes of the bowl of hills around Glasgow, Cathcart was a very safe Tory seat. In 1955, for example, they won it with a majority of 15,751, or 45.2% of the total vote. Here are to be found the most respectable, owner-occupied residential districts within the city south of the Clyde - King's Park, Mount Florida, Cathcart, Newlands. The sturdy bungalows and semis always turn in a reliable Conservative vote. But gradually they were outnumbered as the 1950s and 1960s passed by the massive peripheral development of Castlemilk, which so transformed the politics of the Catchart seat that it was said that Teddy Taylor held on only through his personal independent appeal. In 1979 he finally lost, to John Maxton - a nephew of Jimmy Maxton, the Clydeside ILPer of the 1930s.

Ironically the boundary changes help the Conservatives in Cathcart. Part of Castlemilk is lost to Rutherglan, and owner-occupied Pollokshaws comes in from Pollok. The Tory middle-class half of the seat down the slopes to the north is strengthened. Taylor would probably not have lost this new Cathcart had it existed in 1979. But with his departure to the very different climes of Southend East, it is unlikely that the Tories can find a candidate strong enough to regain Cathcart.

1981	% Own Occ	49
1981	% Loc Auth	41
1981	% Mid Cl	57
1981	% Prof Man	15
1978	electorate 52,600	
1979	notional result	
	C 1,700	
Alliance		SDP

1979 core seat Glasgow Cathcart

Lab	17,550	45.9
C	15,950	41.8
SNP	2,653	6.9
L	2,042	5.3

MPs since 1945
1945-46 F. Beattie C
1946-64 J. Henderson C
1964-79 Teddy Taylor C
1979-   John Maxton Lab

Glasgow Central

Glasgow has an active and grand centre fitting for Scotland's largest city and the heart of Strathclyde's industrial belt. But the housing around the city centre has long been known as some of the poorest in Britain. The Victorians built dark tenements, such as those in the once notorious and fearsome Gorbals, which have now been almost entirely cleared. This has meant an enormous loss of population in the central seats of Glasgow. By 1982 the number on the register in the old Central had fallen to 17,000, the fewest of any constituency. Govan had 24,000 electors; Queen's Park, Kelvingrove and Shettleston little over 30,000 each.

The new Central seat crosses the Clyde for the first time. It now comprises most of the old Central seat, north of the river. To the south there is the eastern end of the old Govan, and most of Queen's Park, which forms the single largest element in the redrawn constituency. There have been three byelections in Glasgow seats since 1979. Besides Roy Jenkins's Hillhead triumph, Labour have held both Central (in 1980) and Queen's Park (1982) easily, following the deaths of the sitting MPs. In Queen's Park Mrs Helen McElhone replaced her husband Frank, who collapsed and died after a march in support of the health workers.

The SNP moved into second place in both the byelections within the new Central seat, but in each case Labour maintained a very substantial lead. The Conservatives and the Liberals lost their deposits in the byelection. The main contest will probably be for the Labour nomination in this super-safe seat in the heart of Glasgow's grime.

1981	% Own Occ	12	1979 core seat Glasgow Queen's Park
1981	% Loc Auth	70	
1981	% Mid Cl	32	Lab 15,120 64.4
1981	% Prof Man	6	C 5,642 24.0
1978	electorate 55,700		SNP 2,276 9.7
1979	notional result		Oths 454 1.9
	Lab 12,900		MPs since 1974
Alliance		L	1974-82 Frank McElhone Lab
			1982- Helen McElhone Lab

Glasgow Garscadden

Glasgow has long had a tradition as one of the roughest, toughest and poorest cities in Europe. This working-class, industrial community on the Clyde was once known for its ferocious nineteenth-century tenement slums in the centre of the city. Now much of that inner city is cleared. The Gorbals have almost vanished. Govan has been depopulated. But districts of an unrelievedly impoverished and working-class nature are still to be found. Many people have been moved out from the centre to vast inter-war and post-war council estates on the edge of Glasgow. These are areas of multiple social and economic devastation, with inadequate social facilities and remote from the activity and life of the heart of the city to boot.

Such a place is Garscadden. This NW Glasgow seat contains the inter-war council estates of Yoker and Knightswood, and the stark post-war development of Drumchapel under the Kilpatrick Hills, six miles from the city centre. Drumchapel borders middle-class Bearsden, but they are miles apart socially. There are no owner occupiers. A third of the population is unemployed. In the constituency as a whole 73% of the residents do not have a car, and 89% are council tenants. Rather like other peripheral estates, like Easterhouse in the NE and Castlemilk in the south, Drumchapel has become a byword for crime and vandalism, degradation and social dislocation. Knightswood is more respectable, a more settled community – but the politics of Garscadden are homogeneous: all wards vote Labour.

Donald Dewar retained this safe seat for Labour in a 1978 byelection, and there seems no serious challenge to his continued tenure on the horizon. It is hard to see why Garscadden should have any love for the Conservative Party, and Nationalism has never made a breakthrough here. It is scarcely altered in the boundary changes.

			1979 core seat Glasgow		
1981	% Own Occ	7	Garscadden		
1981	% Loc Auth	89	Lab	23,591	61.5
1981	% Mid Cl	40	C	8,393	21.9
1981	% Prof Man	7	SNP	6,012	15.7
1978	electorate 52,700		Comm	374	1.0
1979	notional result		MPs since 1974		
	Lab 15,000		1974-78 William Small Lab		
Alliance		SDP	1978- Donald Dewar Lab		

Glasgow Govan

Govan is the Glasgow constituency most associated with shipbuilding, but many of the yards here on the south bank of the Clyde have closed, although derricks still point skywards as mute reminders of Glasgow's great industrial past. Over a quarter of the old Govan's male population was unempoyed at the time of the 1981 census, and the total has grown since then. Govan is in SW Glasgow, marching along the south bank of the Clyde from opposite the city centre to the boundary with Renfrew. Here is Ibrox, and the home of the Protestant Rangers Football Club. But this district has been heavily depopulated, and the existing Govan seat had only 24,000 electors in 1979. Not surprisingly, it has been much enlarged in the boundary changes.

Most of the new Govan will in fact be drawn from the abolished Craigton division - Crookston and Hillington, Penilee and Cardonald, Mossparks and Bellahouston. Craigton was the seat of Labour's Scottish Secretary Bruce Millan, and it was itself heavily Labour and predominantly council owned. But it is further away from the river and from the city centre than the former Govan division, and now comes more into the category of peripheral constituencies than inner city seats. It was held by a Conservative before 1959, but has swung gradually to Labour ever since.

Govan was held briefly for the SNP by the charismatic Margo Macdonald between the November 1973 byelection and the February 1974 General Election. But she found the Labour vote rock-hard and resilient too, and held Govan for only four months. The Nationalists never made much headway in the ex-Craigton terrain which forms the bulk of the new Glasgow Govan. It should be a safe Labour seat.

1981	% Own Occ	25	1979 core seat Glasgow Craigton		
1981	% Loc Auth	65	Lab	19,952	59.9
1981	% Mid Cl	43	C	9,480	28.5
1981	% Prof Man	11	SNP	3,881	11.7
1978	electorate 55,800		MPs since 1955		
1979	notional result		1955-59 J.N. Browne C		
	Lab 13,200		1959- Bruce Millan Lab		
Alliance		L			

Glasgow Hillhead

Following his promising performance in the SDP's inaugural byelection at Warrington in July 1981, Roy Jenkins found a place in Parliament by winning Glasgow Hillhead from the Conservatives on 25 March 1982. Jenkins received 10,106 votes; the Tories polled 8,068; Labour 7,846. By the end of 1982 Roy Jenkins had become Leader of the Social Democratic Party and the Alliance's prospective candidate for Prime Minister.

At first sight the rugged City of Glasgow might seem a surprising haven for a very English Welshman of notably sophisticated and intellectual tastes. But Hillhead is a very special part of Glasgow - the only Conservative seat left in the city after the 1979 Election, Hillhead was one of the most middle-class seats in Britain. Its population had the highest educational achievement of any in Scotland. The mansions of Kelvindale and Anniesland, Jordanhill and Broomhill from the classic west end of Glasgow, traditionally Tory. Nearer the Clyde were poorer areas, more favourable to Labour: Scotstoun and Partick.

In the boundary changes, Hillhead is expanded to include the southern half of the abolished constituency of Kelvingrove, centred on Glasgow University. Kelvingrove has been a Labour seat for twenty years, and Labour may well pose as great a threat to Jenkins as the Conservatives in the new seat of Hillhead. It should be a genuine three-way marginal. In the 1982 Regional elections in the wards which make up the new seat, the three groupings were almost neck and neck. The Labour candidates received 7,627 votes, the Conservatives' 7,462 and the Alliance's 7,452. But Jenkins's personal vote as leader of the party must give him an excellent chance of retaining Hillhead, even against stout opposition from both the two older parties.

1981	% Own Occ	50	1979 core seat Glasgow Hillhead		
1981	% Loc Auth	23	C	12,368	41.0
1981	% Mid Cl	60	Lab	10,366	34.4
1981	% Prof Man	20	L	4,349	14.4
1978	electorate 56,100		SNP	3,050	10.1
1979	notional result		MPs since 1945		
	Lab 2,000		1945-48 J.S.C. Reid C		
Alliance		SDP	1948-82 Thomas Galbraith C		
			1982- Roy Jenkins SDP		

Glasgow Maryhill

The new Maryhill seat is a mixture of the old North Glasgow
division of the same name (a peripheral council estate
constituency of formidable Labour strength) and the northern
half of the abolished Kelvingrove. Kelvingrove was part of
the old west end of the city, with a low proportion of council
housing and a relatively high percentage of privately rented
houses and non-white residents for Glasgow. Despite its more
heterogeneous character, Maryhill will still be a very safe
Labour division.

1981	% Own Occ	15	1979 core seat	Glasgow	Maryhill	
1981	% Loc Auth	65	Lab	22,602	66.2	
1981	% Mid Cl	38	C	5,106	15.0	
1981	% Prof Man	9	SNP	3,812	11.2	
1978	electorate 56,700		L	2,332	6.8	
1979	notional result		Comm	287	0.8	
	Lab 13,300		MPs since 1945			
Alliance		L	1945-74 William Hannan Lab			
			1974- James Craigen Lab			

Glasgow Pollok

Pollok, SW Glasgow, was a Conservative seat until 1964, and
then again from the 1967 byelection to 1970. Since then the
Labour MP, Protestant anti-abortion campaigner James White,
has strengthened his hold. The boundary changes will further
help, adding the Labour Crookston/Cowglen ward in exchange
for the Tory Pollokshaws/Newlands. Pollok is now mainly a
peripheral council estate division centred on the stark
Priesthill and Nitshill developments - only Pollokshields/
Shawlands break the Labour pattern.

1981	% Own Occ	25	1979 core seat	Glasgow Pollok	
1981	% Loc Auth	62	Lab	21,420	49.2
1981	% Mid Cl	46	C	12,928	29.7
1981	% Prof Man	12	SNP	4,187	9.6
1978	electorate 53,500		L	3,946	9.1
1979	notional result		Oths	1,014	2.3
	Lab 13,400		MPs since 1945		
Alliance		SDP	1945-55 T.D. Galbraith C		
			1955-64 J.C. George C		
			1964-67 A. Garrow Lab		
			1967-70 Esmond Wright C		
			1970- James White Lab		

Glasgow Provan

Glasgow Provan is a distinguished seat in one way. It holds the record for the highest percentage of council-owned houses in a constituency in Britain. In 1971 that figure reached a remarkable 96.9%, with just 0.7% of the housing owner occupied. By 1981 the council housing percentage was still as high as 93.3%, and the owner occupiers had shot up to 2.6%. The boundary changes are only minimal, so Provan will retain its primary position among 'council estate constituencies'.

The development of overspill estates here on the edge of NE Glasgow has transformed the political character of the Provan seat since its creation in 1955. Then the Labour candidate defeated the Conservative by just 180 votes. The population of Provan ward increased from 24,000 in 1951 to 75,000 in 1961. After a series of massive swings, Provan is now Labour's seventh safest seat in Britain, boasting a majority of 18,844 or 54.4% of the vote. Much of this is due to the growth of Easterhouse, the vast and reputedly violent and gang-ridden estate on the very fringe of Glasgow. But all the neighbourhoods of the Provan seat are socially similar - dreary and often grim council estates on each side of the M8 as it enters the city. At the time of the 1981 census, 31.3% of the men in the constituency were out of work, the second highest figure in Scotland.

It is hard to see the SDP or the SNP making any impact on Hugh Brown's majority here. The proportion of council housing in Scotland is much higher than in England or Wales, but nowhere is it as dominant as in Glasgow Provan. Nor are these stable and happy communities. Despondency and desperation stalk the streets, and degradation seems only just around the corner.

1981	% Own Occ	2.5	1979 core seat Glasgow Provan		
1981	% Loc Auth	93	Lab	24,083	69.5
1981	% Mid Cl	35	C	5,239	15.1
1981	% Prof Man	5	SNP	4,767	13.8
1978	electorate 57,100		Oths	570	1.7
1979	notional result		MPs since 1955		
	Lab 18,800		1955-64 W. Reid Lab		
Alliance		SDP	1964- Hugh Brown Lab		

Glasgow Rutherglen

Rutherglen was until recently an ancient burgh, independent of Glasgow in administrative terms although almost swallowed up by it physically. Rutherglen's first charter was granted in 1126, but in the local government reorganisation of the early 1970s the burgh was finally incorporated into the City of Glasgow. Now its parliamentary constituency is perforce moved from the defunct Lanarkshire County to become a Glasgow city seat. The boundary changes are not very substantial: part of the Castlemilk council estate comes in from Glasgow Cathcart, and the district around Carmyle is lost to Shettleston.

The Labour MP Gregor Mackenzie won Rutherglen from the Tories in a byelection in May 1964, and he has held it six times since then. Now, however, the greatest challenge comes from a possibly unexpected source: the Liberal Party. The Liberals do badly in industrial Scotland, and they rarely challenged in Rutherglen before they suddenly doubled their vote in the 1979 General Election. In the 1982 local elections they moved into a clear second place in the aggregate vote of the three Regional wards which make up the new Glasgow Rutherglen – Toryglen/Rutherglen, Glenwood/Fernhill and Cambuslang/Halfway.

Gregor Mackenzie must remain the favourite in Rutherglen, but the Liberals have worked hard to build on local election success. Rutherglen will now be by far their best hope in Glasgow, and indeed one of their two or three best in the whole of industrial Scotland.

1981	% Own Occ	35	1979 core seat Rutherglen
1981	% Loc Auth	60	Lab 18,546 46.7
1981	% Mid Cl	50	C 10,523 26.5
1981	% Prof Man	14	L 7,315 18.4
1978	electorate 57,400		SNP 3,325 8.4
1979	notional result		MPs since 1945
	Lab 12,800		1945-51 G. McAllister Lab
Alliance		L	1951-64 R.C. Brooman-White C
			1964- Gregor Mackenzie Lab

Glasgow Shettleston

Shettleston is the old east end of Glasgow, a district of working-class tenements and radical politics, associated between the wars with the 'red Clydesiders' and ILPers - Wheatley and McGovern. The present Shettleston is now too small to survive as a seat. It is extended towards the centre of the city to take in Parkhead, home of the Catholic Celtic FC; and away from the city to Mount Vernon, Carmyle and Garrowhill, now in Bothwell and Rutherglen. It will remain an iron-clad Labour seat.

1981	% Own Occ	17	1979 core seat Glasgow		
1981	% Loc Auth	71	Shettleston		
1981	% Mid Cl	36	Lab	13,955	64.1
1981	% Prof Man	7	C	4,794	22.0
1978	electorate 52,900		SNP	3,022	13.9
1979	notional result		MPs since 1945		
	Lab 13,500		1945-59 J. McGovern ILP (Lab)		
Alliance		L	1959-79 Sir Myer Galpern Lab		
			1979- David Marshall Lab		

Glasgow Springburn

The new Springburn will be the largest of Glasgow's 11 seats, with an electorate of 60,000. To the old Springburn seat in North Glasgow is added 20,000 electors, mainly from Maryhill. Springburn will remain very working class, very strongly Labour. Here the tower blocks of Barmulloch and Balornock hang over the city centre, here are the remains of the Cowlairs rail yard, and of the inner-city district of Dennistoun. Springburn's stark aspect typifies Glasgow's harsh urban problems.

1981	% Own Occ	16	1979 core seat Glasgow		
1981	% Loc Auth	75	Springburn		
1981	% Mid Cl	35	Lab	18,871	66.1
1981	% Prof Man	6	C	6,100	21.4
1978	electorate 60,000		SNP	3,587	12.6
1979	notional result		MPs since 1945		
	Lab 18,300		1945-64 J.C. Forman Lab		
Alliance		L	1964-79 Richard Buchanan Lab		
			1979- Michael Martin Lab		

Greenock and Port Glasgow

There have been very few Labour-Liberal marginal constituencies in Britain in recent years. Most good Liberal prospects have been Conservative seats, most Liberal parliamentary gains at the Tory expense. But one exception to this pattern is to be found in Strathclyde, at Greenock. Here on the industrial lower reaches of the Clyde the Conservatives are so weak that they did not even put up a candidate in 1970 - the only place where this has happened in Britain for many years. In 1970 Labour beat the Liberals in more or less a straight fight by 3,000 votes. Both in municipal and parliamentary politics the Liberals offer the strongest opposition to Labour in the Greenock/Inverclyde district.

Now however the situation has become very much more complex, for Dickson Mabon (Labour MP for Greenock since 1955) has defected to the SDP. After many years of opposing Mabon, the local Liberals quite understandably were reluctant to concede the nomination for a little-changed Greenock/Port Glasgow seat to the SDP. After a protracted wrangle, the Liberals have secured the nomination here, leaving Mabon to fight the neighbouring Renfrew West/Inverclyde division.

Ironically the 1982 Strathclyde Regional elections suggest that the Renfrew West seat may even be the better bet for the Alliance. The Labour vote in the tough, working-class Clydeside shipbuilding towns of Greenock and Port Glasgow is holding up firmly, and the Liberal challenge may once again falter at the last gasp.

1981	% Own Occ	19	1979 core seat Greenock/Port		
1981	% Loc Auth	74	Glasgow		
1981	% Mid Cl	35	Lab	24,071	53.0
1981	% Prof Man	8	L	12,789	28.2
1978	electorate	60,200	C	4,926	10.9
1979	notional result		SNP	3,435	7.6
	Lab 12,000		WRP	176	0.4
Alliance		L	MPs since 1945		

MPs since 1945
1945-55 H. McNeil Lab
1955-   Dickson Mabon Lab
                    (SDP)

Hamilton

Winnie Ewing became the first SNP MP for over 20 years when she seized the Lanarkshire county town of Hamilton in a 1967 byelection. Labour regained the seat in 1970, and prominent moderate George Robertson fought off home-town girl Margo Macdonald's challenge in another byelection in 1978. This failure to repeat their success of a decade before augured ill for the SNP, and their vote collapsed completely in 1979. Robertson now seems very safe in a slightly enlarged but still predominantly working-class constituency.

1981	% Own Occ	29	1979 core seat Hamilton
1981	% Loc Auth	67	Lab 24,593 59.6
1981	% Mid Cl	40	C 9,794 23.8
1981	% Prof Man	12	SNP 6,842 16.6
1978	electorate 59,800		MPs since 1945
1979	notional result		1945-67 Tom Fraser Lab
	Lab 16,200		1967-70 Winnie Ewing SNP
Alliance		L	1970-78 Alex Wilson Lab
			1978- George Robertson Lab

Kilmarnock and Loudoun

This is an unchanged constituency, identical to the old Kilmarnock, but its name is brought into line with that of the local government District. The seat was held for 33 years by a Labour Scottish Secretary, the centrist Willie Ross, but it is now represented by a left-winger, Willie McKelvey. The town of Kilmarnock is best known for Johnnie Walker whisky, but this Ayrshire seat also includes Stewarton and the small ex-mining towns of the Irvine Valley.

1981	% Own Occ	29.9	1979 same seat Kilmarnock
1981	% Loc Auth	66.3	Lab 25,718 52.6
1981	% Mid Cl	41.6	C 14,251 29.1
1981	% Prof Man	12.1	SNP 8,963 18.3
1979	electorate 60,351		MPs since 1945
Alliance		SDP	1945-46 Mrs C.M. Shaw Lab
			1946-69 Willie Ross Lab
			1969- Willie McKelvey Lab

Monklands East

The eastern half of Monklands District consists of the town of
Airdrie and some territory from the old North Lanarkshire
division around Chapelhall and Salsburgh. Although this
latter appears rural, it does include some of the industrial
plain between Glasgow and Edinburgh near the M8. It has
sometimes been said that the engineering town of Airdrie has
Protestant and Conservative traditions, whereas Coatbridge
was Catholic and Labour. But there is no evidence for this
theory in election results. Both Monklands seats will be
Labour strongholds.

1981	% Own Occ	20	1979 core seat Coatbridge/
1981	% Loc Auth	77	Airdrie
1981	% Mid Cl	39	Lab 27,598 60.9
1981	% Prof Man	10	C 12,442 27.5
1978	electorate 47,600		SNP 5,260 11.6
1979	notional result		MPs since 1945
	Lab 12,700		1945-59 Mrs J. Mann Lab
Alliance		L	1959-82 James Dempsey Lab
			1982- Tom Clarke Lab

Monklands West

The Monklands District is similar to the former Coatbridge
and Airdrie constituency, which was safely Labour - Tom
Clarke held it easily in a byelection even in Labour's poor
year of 1982, during the period of Falkands fever. Monklands
West is centred on the rugged heavy industrial town of
Coatbridge, together with parts of North Lanarkshire and
East Dunbartons - Chryston and the Kelvin Valley in
Strathkelvin District. It will be yet another safe Labour seat
on Strathclyde.

1981	% Own Occ	22	New seat
1981	% Loc Auth	73	
1981	% Mid Cl	40	
1981	% Prof Man	11	
1978	electorate 49,300		
1979	notional result		
	Lab 12,300		
Alliance		SDP	

Motherwell North

About half of the old constituency of Bothwell is incorporated in the new Motherwell North: that part east of the M74 motorway - Bellshill, Tannochside, Mossend, Birkenshaw and other strongly working-class and council-owned districts. But substantial parts of Lanarkshire North around Shotts are also included. It is an ex-mining area, and as in so many Scottish industrial seats, the Labour Party still seems almost immune from challenge.

1981	% Own Occ	20	1979 core seat Bothwell	
1981	% Loc Auth	75	Lab	26,492	55.0
1981	% Mid Cl	42	C	11,275	23.4
1981	% Prof Man	10	L	5,225	10.8
1978	electorate 55,500		SNP	5,202	10.8
1979	notional result		MPs since 1945	
	Lab 16,000		1945-64 J. Timmons Lab	
Alliance		L	1964- James Hamilton Lab	

Motherwell South

Motherwell South is very similar to the former Motherwell and Wishaw constituency. It is overshadowed by the vast and threatened Ravenscraig steelworks, and its hopes of prosperity rise and fall with those of the Scottish steel industry. The MP is an Englishman, Dr Jeremy Bray, who formerly represented another steel area, Middlesbrough West (1962-70). The SNP did not do well in Motherwell in 1979, even though they held it briefly in 1945. 80% of the housing is council owned, and it should remain a rock-solid Labour seat, especially in difficult times for its main industry.

1981	% Own Occ	17	1979 core seat Motherwell/	
1981	% Loc Auth	81	Wishaw	
1981	% Mid Cl	44	Lab	22,263	56.9
1981	% Prof Man	11	C	11,326	28.9
1978	electorate 52,500		SNP	4,817	12.3
1979	notional result		Comm	740	1.9
	Lab 11,400		MPs since 1945	
Alliance		SDP	1945-54 A. Anderson Lab	
			1954-74 George Lawson Lab	
			1974- Jeremy Bray Lab	

Paisley North

Paisley is Scotland's fifth largest town, and previously formed a single seat on its own. Now it is divided down the middle, and each half is joined by urban parts of the West Renfrewshire seat. In the case of Paisley North, it is Renfrew itself which is added. The town of Renfrew is strongly Labour, and although the middle-class Abercorn ward of Paisley is in the seat, Paisley North will be safe for the Labour Party. The previous Paisley member, John Robertson, defected to the short-lived Scottish Labour Party, but he did not contest the seat in 1979 and the SLP collapsed.

1981	% Own Occ	26
1981	% Loc Auth	66
1981	% Mid Cl	41
1981	% Prof Man	11
1978	electorate 48,800	
1979	notional result	
	Lab 10,600	
Alliance		SDP

1979 core seat Paisley

Lab	25,894	55.8
C	12,139	26.2
SNP	7,305	15.7
Oths	1,078	2.3

MPs since 1945
1945-48 Viscount Coverdale Lab
1948-61 D.W. Johnstone Lab
1961-79 John Robertson Lab
                   (SLP)
1979-   Allen Adams Lab

Paisley South

The southern half of Paisley is paired with the town of Johnstone and the troubled Linwood car plant. Paisley's main industries have been thread mills, cars and engineering, but all have suffered economic insecurity. Paisley South will be even more solidly Labour than Paisley North. This was once H.H. Asquith's seat, and the Liberals nearly won Paisley in the 1961 byelection and in 1964 - but their vote has almost entirely disappeared of recent years.

1981	% Own Occ	15
1981	% Loc Auth	76
1981	% Mid Cl	36
1981	% Prof Man	9
1978	electorate 52,200	
1979	notional result	
	Lab 8,000	
Alliance		L

New seat

Renfrew West and Inverclyde

The old Renfrewshire West seat was one of the largest in Scotland, with over 78,000 electors in 1979. In the boundary changes, two very strong Labour areas, Johnstone-Linwood and Renfrew, have been incorporated in the two new Paisley divisions. The rump which is left is much more mixed, with a number of middle-class privately-owned residential districts. The senior and much respected Tribunite MP for Renfrewshire West, Norman Buchan, must feel his majority to be vulnerable to the Tories after the boundary changes. What is more, another formidable contender has come forward: Dickson Mabon, the Labour MP for Greenock for over 25 years, who is to try his luck in Renfrew West and Inverclyde as an SDP candidate.

It could be a genuine three-way marginal. In the 1982 Regional elections, Labour polled 35% in the wards of the new seat, the Alliance 34%. The Liberal candidate won the Inverclyde West ward by a landslide, demonstrating an ability to take middle-class votes in a part of Scotland where the Conservatives have rarely been able to mobilise their potential vote. The Labour vote, though now reduced, may prove hard to crack. Buchan is a great survivor and may have something in the way of personal support.

As well as the industrial towns of Greenock and Port Glasgow, Inverclyde includes some desirable residential areas: Gourock, Wemyss Bay and Kilmalcolm. West Renfrew, on the other hand, still has some Labour wards in Strathgryffe and at the expanding town of Erskine. But the Renfrew West/ Inverclyde seat will offer a fascinating contest, and one whose outcome is as hard to predict as any in Britain.

1981	% Own Occ	50	1979 core seat Renfrewshire
1981	% Loc Auth	43	West
1981	% Mid Cl	55	Lab 28,236 44.5
1981	% Prof Man	18	C 19,664 31.0
1978	electorate 48,400		SNP 8,333 13.1
1979	notional result		L 7,256 11.4
	Lab 1,800		MPs since 1945
Alliance		SDP	1945-50 T. Scollan Lab
			1950-64 J.S. Maclay C
			1964- Norman Buchan Lab

Strathkelvin and Bearsden

The former seat of East Dunbartonshire had a strong claim to be the most bizarrely drawn in Britain, combining as it did the New Town of Cumbernauld with Bearsden, the most middle-class town in the United Kingdom. The politics of the seat reflected this lack of homogeneity. When first contested in February 1974, East Dunbartonshire elected a Conservative, Barry Henderson. In October of that year, though, there was almost a three-way dead heat: the Conservatives, Labour and the winning SNP candidate Margaret Bain all polled just over 15,000 votes. Mrs Bain's majority was 22. Then in 1979, East Dunbartonshire's third election produced a third different winning party: Labour moved up from third place to first, as the SNP vote collapsed.

In the boundary changes, the worst casualties are removed as Cumbernauld is granted a seat of its own. The new Strathkelvin and Bearsden consists of three towns within commuting distance of Glasgow - Kirkintilloch, Bishopbriggs and Bearsden. Bearsden is still a middle-class stronghold, with 82% non-manual workers and 90% owner occupiers, but Kirkintilloch and the north Glasgow suburb of Bishopbriggs are both mixed in tenure and marginal politically. The Conservatives would evidently have been ahead in this seat if it had been fought in 1979, but their hold is weakened by Liberal success in local elections in Bearsden, once the dour and respectable epitome of Scottish Toryism.

It is extraordinary that a place like Bearsden, which is far more middle-class in census terms than even deepest Surrey or Sussex, should have a Labour MP. Yet it has not been part of a seat represented by a Conservative since the war, except for a few months between the 1974 Elections. Now it should finally form the core of a Conservative constituency, as long as too many of its citizens do not indulge their local election taste for Liberalism, and thus let Labour in yet again.

1981	% Own Occ	60	1979 core seat East
1981	% Loc Auth	30	Dunbartonshire
1981	% Mid Cl	67	Lab 23,268 37.9
1981	% Prof Man	25	C 20,944 34.1
1978	electorate 54,100		SNP 12,654 20.6
1979	notional result		L 4,600 7.5
	C 7,700		MPs since 1974
Alliance		L	1974 Barry Henderson C
			1974-79 Margaret Bain SNP
			1979- Norman Hogg Lab

Angus East

For many years, until a shock in 1974, the County of Angus formed some of the Conservatives' best territory in Scotland. Angus stretches from the edge of the Highlands and the fringes of the Grampians to the outskirts of Dundee. The mainstay of the economy is agriculture, with some textile industry. There are also some small coastal tourist resorts, all of which are included in the new Angus seat. The small communities of the constituency are still bleak ground for Labour. Montrose, Brechin and Arbroath are ancient and highly respectable burghs. The golfing town of Carnoustie and Monifieth near Dundee are fashionable resorts and residential areas.

Most of Angus East was formerly in South Angus, which was held by Mrs Thatcher's friend and confidant Jock Bruce-Gardyne with massive majorities until 1974, when the Tory lead was first cut back and then overcome by the SNP. Peter Fraser recovered South Angus for the Tories in 1979, but only by a 1,000 vote majority over the Scottish Nationalist MP Andrew Welsh. The minor part of Angus East (including Brechin and Montrose) was formerly in North Angus and Mearns, which never fell to the SNP, and is now a much safer Conservative seat than Angus South.

Should there be an SNP revival in rural Scotland, Angus East will be one of the most vulnerable Tory seats. The east coast was particularly aware of the discovery of 'Scottish' oil in the North Sea, and the Nationalists may add to their positive vote by acting as the recipients of any protest votes against Mrs Thatcher's government, for they are clearly in second place here. Labour lost their deposit in Angus South last time. The SDP have the Alliance nomination, but their Liberal partners have been very weak in Angus recently.

1981	% Own Occ	41	1979 core seat South Angus
1981	% Loc Auth	44	C 20,029 43.6
1981	% Mid Cl	43	SNP 19,066 41.5
1981	% Prof Man	16	Lab 4,623 10.1
1978	electorate 57,100		L 2,218 4.8
1979	notional result		MPs since 1950
	C 6,500		1950-64 J.A.L. Duncan C
Alliance		SDP	1964-74 Jock Bruce-Gardyne C
			1974-79 Andrew Welsh SNP
			1979- Peter Fraser C

Dundee East

The Scottish National Party achieved very little in electoral terms before the early 1970s. Dr Robert McIntyre held Motherwell for a few months after winning a wartime byelection in 1945. Winnie Ewing held Hamilton for three years after another byelection success in 1967. Donald Stewart has won the highly independent and individualistic Gaelic speaking Western Isles since the 1970 General Election. But it was the discovery of oil in the North Sea which fuelled the great post-war Nationalist resurgence. Many Scots decided that the proceeds of the North Sea finds should pass into their pockets. The SNP won seven seats in February 1974, 11 in October of the same year.

But the phenomenon proved transient, lacking the consistency of the more linguistically and culturally based Welsh Nationalism. In 1979 only two SNP seats survived - but one of them was Dundee East, now the only Nationalist constituency in industrial Scotland. Its singular loyalty to the SNP is probably due to two features, one positive, one negative: the good service provided as MP by SNP Deputy Leader Gordon Wilson; and the fact that the Labour candidate was the ex-Communist trade unionist Jimmy Reid. Many traditional Labour voters must have been alarmed by the policies and reputation of the Upper Clyde Shipbuilders' work-in leader.

Dundee East is slightly more middle class than its western neighbour, possessing a large Tory residential area among the private housing of Broughty Ferry and Balgillo. But it has its fair share of Dundee's inner-city desolation, and of its massive inland peripheral council estates. Gordon Wilson will always have to fight hard to resist a Labour challenge in Dundee East, and against any other candidate than a newly-converted Jimmy Reid, he might have grave difficulty.

1981	% Own Occ	25	
1981	% Loc Auth	63	
1981	% Mid Cl	42	
1981	% Prof Man	11	
1978	electorate 63,500		
1979	notional result		
	SNP 2,200		
Alliance		L	

1979 core seat Dundee East

SNP	20,497	41.0
Lab	17,978	36.0
C	9,072	18.2
L	2,317	4.6
WRP	95	0.2

MPs since 1950
1950-52 T.F. Cook Lab
1952-73 George Thomson Lab
1973-74 George Machin Lab
1974-   Gordon Wilson SNP

Dundee West

Unlike Dundee East, West has avoided the temptation to elect a Nationalist MP, remaining loyal to Labour since its creation in 1950. Scotland's fourth city does have middle-class and traditionally Tory residential districts, in both west and east. Winston Churchill was a Coalition Liberal MP for Dundee from 1918 to 1922; he was then beaten by Labour's E.D. Morel and the 'Labour Prohibitionist' Edwin Scrymgeour.

Dundee West does have Tory wards still, but the Conservative vote has crumbled of late and in 1979 they finished third in both seats. More typical of Dundee West are the post-war council estates which climb the hills behind the city, away from the Tay beyond the Dundee Law (Dundee's central hill, its own version of Edinburgh's Arthur's Seat). Two-thirds of the housing in Dundee West is council owned, and the tower block developments reinforce the impression of a working-class industrial city.

Dundee was once 'Juteopolis', the centre of the world's jute mill industry. The mills were particularly concentrated in the working-class district of Lochee, West Dundee. But the jute industry was moved out to the Indian sub-continent in the early twentieth century, and Dundee has had to look for ways of diversifying its economy. Tribunite Ernie Ross seems safe in Dundee West, although the Nationalists cut the Labour majority to under 3,000 in October 1974. Neither of the Dundee seats is significantly altered in the boundary changes.

1981	% Own Occ	22.5	1979 core seat Dundee West	
1981	% Loc Auth	66	Lab	23,654	47.3
1981	% Mid Cl	43	SNP	13,197	26.4
1981	% Prof Man	11	C	12,892	25.8
1978	electorate 64,500		Comm	316	0.6
1979	notional result		MPs since 1950	
	Lab 10,500		1950-63 John Strachey Lab	
Alliance		SDP	1963-79 Peter Doig Lab	
			1979- Ernest Ross Lab	

North Tayside

The now-abolished County of Perthshire used to be divided
into western and eastern sections for parliamentary
purposes. West Perthshire was placed together with the tiny
county of Kinross; East Perthshire was less extensive in
acreage because it included the City of Perth. Now the
Boundary Commission have shifted the dividing line, so that
there are southern and northern constituencies. Perth is now
partnered by Kinross in the south, and a vast division on the
edge of the Highlands is created - North Tayside. This takes
in the northernmost sections of three former seats in Tayside:
Kinross/West Perths, Perth/East Perths, and South Angus.

The only town of any size, Forfar, comes from the latter
seat, but most of the acreage comes from Kinross and West
Perthshire, a constituency which is usually associated with
Sir Alec Douglas-Home. When the Conservative chieftains
decided to pick Home as the successor to Harold Macmillan as
party leader and Prime Minister, he was sitting in the
Lords. He had to disclaim his earldom and find a seat in the
Commons in rapid time. George Younger (later Scottish
Secretary) was persuaded to give way at Kinross-W Perths.,
and Home was elected with ease in November 1963.

Home held the seat until 1974, when he returned to the Lords
(this time as a life peer) and was replaced by the colourful
Nicholas Fairbairn as Conservative MP. Fairbairn held the
seat against a strong Nationalist challenge by only 53 votes,
but he has probably strengthened his position since despite
his resignation from the post of Solicitor General for Scotland
in 1982.

1981	% Own Occ	48	1979 core seat Kinross/West		
1981	% Loc Auth	30	Perthshire		
1981	% Mid Cl	48	C	15,523	50.5
1981	% Prof Man	21	SNP	9,045	29.4
1978	electorate 50,300		L	3,572	11.6
1979	notional result		Lab	2,593	8.4
	C 2,000		MPs since 1945		
Alliance		L	1945-55 W.M. Snedden C		
			1955-63 W.G. Leburn C		
			1963-74 Alec Douglas-Home C		
			1974- Nicholas Fairbairn C		

Perth and Kinross

Like many Scottish seats, Perth and East Perthshire was safely Conservative until 1974, when it was won by the Scottish National Party. Perth fell in the October Election, when five-term MP Ian Macarthur was defeated by Douglas Crawford. Again following the Scottish pattern, the Tories regained the seat in 1979, even though their candidate William Walker was temporarily confined to a wheelchair following a gliding accident. In the boundary changes the southern half of the constituency around Perth itself is placed together with the old County of Kinross.

This is a prosperous part of Lowland Scotland. Livestock and fruit growing are the main agricultural bases, and the town of Perth itself is still expanding and suffers from relatively low unemployment. Like most Scottish towns, Perth does have a substantial Labour vote, particularly in the west Perth Letham/Tulloch district. But overall Labour will be lucky to retain their deposit in Perth and Kinross.

The Nationalists will still pose the main challenge to the Tories, and their chances of victory are bound to depend more on their national standing than on local issues. In May 1982 they only won one of the nine Tayside Regional electoral districts in the new seat, and the SNP are not as strong in Kinross as in the old Perth/E Perths seat. The Conservative William Walker is therefore the favourite to win Perth and Kinross at the next Election.

1981	% Own Occ	40
1981	% Loc Auth	43
1981	% Mid Cl	50
1981	% Prof Man	17
1978	electorate 60,000	
1979	notional result	
	C 5,200	
Alliance		L

1979 core seat Perth/East Perthshire

C	20,153	41.9
SNP	17,050	35.5
Lab	6,432	13.4
L	4,410	9.2

MPs since 1945
1945-59 A. Gomme-Duncan C
1959-74 Ian Macarthur C
1974-79 Douglas Crawford SNP
1979-   William Walker C

528

Alyn and Deeside

Clwyd is the NE corner of Wales, incorporating the old counties of Flintshire and Denbighshire. Socially and economically it is a mixed district, ranging from the Welsh-speaking hill farms of the Denbigh moors to the seaside resorts of the north coast and the heavy coal and steel industries of Wrexham and Deeside. Clwyd's existing seats are larger than the Welsh average, and it gains a fifth constituency in the boundary revision.

Alyn and Deeside is one of the more industrial seats. It is based on the old East Flintshire, but loses Flint and Holywell to Delyn. It is now a compact division set at the head of the Dee estuary, on the very border with Cheshire and England. The main towns are Connah's Quay, Buckley, Hawarden and Shotton. Despite the historical connection between Hawarden and Liberalism (this was the site of Gladstone's country house), East Flintshire was a safe Labour constituency. Since its creation, when Flintshire was divided in 1950, it was held successively by Mrs Eirene White and Barry Jones, a leading moderate in the party. The stark remains of the steelworks at Shotton give a clue to the reason for Labour's strength on Deeside; this is a solidly working-class district, now afflicted with a near 20% unemployment rate, and suffering from decline and depression.

Although Flint and Holywell were Labour towns, Barry Jones must start the favourite in Alyn and Deeside. This is an English-speaking constituency – indeed, it extends as far as the suburbs of Chester – so the Welsh Nationalists have no strength. The SDP will fight Alyn/Deeside for the Alliance, but Barry Jones hardly seems the type of MP most vulnerable to their appeal. He can expect to be returned to be an influential member of his party in the new Parliament.

1981	% Own Occ	66.9	1979 core seat East Flintshire		
1981	% Loc Auth	26.2	Lab	29,339	48.3
1981	% Welsh Sp	7	C	23,116	38.1
1981	% Mid Cl	44.7	L	6,736	11.1
1981	% Prof Man	12.9	PC	1,198	2.0
1981	electorate 56,443		Comm	307	0.5
1979	notional result		MPs since 1950		
	Lab 5,000		1950-70 Eirene White Lab		
Alliance		SDP	1970- Barry Jones Lab		

Clwyd North-West

The North Wales holiday coast is one of the most Conservative parts of the principality. It varies in character, from the open flat sands and amusement arcades of Rhyl through Abergele to the elegant sweep of wooded Colwyn Bay. But it is all solidly Tory, as is the hinterland, which includes the tiny cathedral city of St Asaph and Rhuddlan, with its Norman castle. Clwyd NW takes in coastal parts of both Denbigh and West Flintshire – it has the best claim to be the extra seat which Clwyd gains in the boundary changes. It would be logical for either sitting Tory MP – Geraint Morgan or Anthony Meyer – to move in to such a safe seat.

1981	% Own Occ	68.5	New seat
1981	% Loc Auth	17.6	
1981	% Welsh Sp	20	
1981	% Mid Cl	49.6	
1981	% Prof Man	18.0	
1981	electorate 61,618		
1979	notional C 11,700		
Alliance		L	

Clwyd South-West

Clwyd SW will be the most heavily Welsh-speaking of the five Clwyd seats. It is centred on the District of Glyndwr, around Denbigh and Llangollen of Eisteddfod fame. But it also includes the rural southern part of Colwyn Borough and a section of Wrexham Maelor around Ruabon. It is said that the SDP member for Wrexham, Tom Ellis, will choose to fight Clwyd SW. Certainly the Liberals have taken the nomination for Wrexham itself, so Ellis must move. But Clwyd SW is similar to the old Denbigh seat, safely Conservative since the war, and one of the only three Tory seats in Wales in 1966. One must have grave doubts about Ellis's chances against sitting Conservative Geraint Morgan.

1981	% Own Occ	52.8	1979 core seat Denbigh		
1981	% Loc Auth	35.2	C	23,683	44.9
1981	% Welsh Sp	40	L	14,833	28.1
1981	% Mid Cl	43.7	Lab	9,276	17.6
1981	% Prof Man	15.7	PC	4,915	9.3
1981	electorate 55,703		MPs since 1945		
1979	notional C 3,200		1945-50 Sir J.H. Morris-Jones C		
Alliance		SDP	1950-59 E.H.G. Evans C		
			1959- Geraint Morgan C		

530

Delyn

Delyn will be the most marginal seat in Clwyd. It draws its electorate almost evenly from East Flint (which was always Labour) and West Flint (always Conservative, even in 1966). The towns in Delyn also fit this divided pattern. Flint is an industrial centre, even boasting a number of tower blocks. Holywell too is a strong working-class, Labour town. But Mold is the administrative and cultural headquarters of Clwyd, as it was of the old Flintshire. Prestatyn is one of the flat holiday resorts of the north coast, familiar to many through its Butlin's holiday camp. Which half will shape the political destination of the new seat? The ex-W Flint section is slightly larger, and in the Tory year of 1979 would probably have swung Delyn to the right. But it could prove a classical marginal, swinging with national opinion.

1981	% Own Occ	71.1	1979 core seat West Flint		
1981	% Loc Auth	22.3	C	26,364	49.0
1981	% Welsh Sp	18	Lab	16,678	31.0
1981	% Mid Cl	46.5	L	9,009	16.8
1981	% Prof Man	15.6	PC	1,720	3.2
1981	electorate 61,992		MPs since 1950		
1979	notional C 5,600		1950-70 Sir Nigel Birch C		
Alliance		L	1970-	Sir Anthony Meyer C	

Wrexham

Wrexham was once the mining capital of N Wales, surrounded by a coalfield which reached public notice after the Gresford colliery disaster of 1934. Gresford has closed now, as have all the pits except one. But Wrexham remains a great industrial centre and Labour stronghold. The present MP Tom Ellis has defected to the SDP, but he will not contest Wrexham again, leaving the uphill struggle to the Liberals. 20,000 electors are lost, mainly to Clwyd SW, but Wrexham should be safe for the new Labour candidate John Marek.

1981	% Own Occ	50.4	1979 core seat Wrexham		
1981	% Loc Auth	41.8	Lab	30,405	49.2
1981	% Welsh Sp	14	C	18,256	29.5
1981	% Mid Cl	45.6	L	11,389	18.4
1981	% Prof Man	14.6	PC	1,740	2.8
1981	electorate 60,200		MPs since 1945		
1979	notional result		1945-55 R. Richards Lab		
	Lab 9,600		1955-70 J.I. Jones Lab		
Alliance		L	1970-	Tom Ellis Lab (SDP)	

Carmarthen

In recent years, Carmarthen has been noted for its tight contests between Labour and Plaid Cymru, the Welsh National party. Most spectacularly, Labour candidate Gwynoro Jones held off the challenge of long-standing PC president Gwynfor Evans by only three votes in February 1974. But Evans has been successful in Carmarthenshire. He upset Labour in a byelection in July 1966 caused by the death of Lady Megan Lloyd George (herself once a Liberal MP). Gwynoro Jones (who is now a Social Democrat, and was the SDP candidate for Gower in the 1982 byelection) did hold Carmarthen from 1970 to October 1974, but Gwynfor Evans returned triumphantly in that autumn Election. In 1979 Evans was beaten by a new Labour candidate, Dr Roger Thomas – one of three Thomases standing in the contest!

Why is Carmarthen typified by the Labour-Plaid Cymru marginality? It is generally regarded as one of the three most 'Welsh' seats in Wales – two-thirds of the population can speak Welsh, which is the first language in many parts of the constituency. Like all Welsh-speaking areas, it is not good ground for Tories. The Tory candidate polled a wretched 5.7% in October 1974, although there was a recovery in 1979. This is Labour's last remaining seat in rural Wales, and it is easily the most agricultural seat they hold in Britain. Indeed, there are only three seats anywhere which contain more workers employed in agriculture. The Liberals held Carmarthen until 1957, but they did not do well in 1979, even though their candidate was the well-known rugby coach, Clem Thomas. The SDP are to see if they can do better next time.

Even though he is now in his 70s, the great warrior Gwynfor Evans is due to stand again at Carmarthen next time. And in such a fascinatingly close seat, who is to say that the Nationalists might not once again pull off a victory?

1981	% Own Occ	64.8	1979 core seat Carmarthen		
1981	% Loc Auth	22.7	Lab	18,667	35.8
1981	% Welsh Sp	63	PC	16,689	32.0
1981	% Mid Cl	41.4	C	12,272	23.6
1981	% Prof Man	15.1	L	4,186	8.0
1981	electorate 63,613		NF	149	0.3
1979	notional result		Oth	126	0.2
	Lab 1,200		MPs since 1945		
Alliance		SDP	1945-57 R.H. Morris L		
			1957-66 Megan Lloyd George Lab		
			1966-70 Gwynfor Evans PC		
			1970-74 Gwynoro Jones Lab		
			1974-79 Gwynfor Evans PC		
			1979- Roger Thomas Lab		

Ceredigion and Pembroke North

Cardiganshire was traditionally one of the strongest Welsh-speaking parts of Celtic rural west Wales. The new seat of Ceredigion and Pembroke N still has the fourth highest proportion of Welsh speakers of all division, a clear majority of the population. But here the political defence of Welsh culture has not fallen to Plaid Cymru, who finished bottom here last time. Rather, Cardiganshire has probably the longest tradition of Liberalism of any British constituency. Apart from a Labour interlude between 1966 and 1974, it has been solidly Liberal for over a century.

The Liberal MP for Cardigan since 1974 has been Geraint Howells, reputedly a fine orator in his first language. Although the seat is extended to include about 15,000 voters from Pembrokeshire, this is Welsh-speaking North Pembs, around Fishguard north of Preseli Mountains, not the Tory 'Little England beyond Wales' of Tenby and Haverfordwest. Howells should be able to absorb this influence, for he has built up a considerable local reputation. The Conservatives did well throughout rural Wales in 1979, and leapt up from 9% in Cardigan in October 1974 to 30% last time – their largest increase in Britain. Labour have thus been displaced from second position, and a revival seems unlikely.

Ceredigion is a district of hill farms, and little Welsh-speaking towns like Tregaron and Newcastle Emlyn. It boasts wild moors and one of the largest bogs in Britain. The 'English' parties' support is concentrated on the superb holiday coast of Cardigan Bay, and in the University town of Aberystwyth. As long as Geraint Howells continues to gather the Welsh-speaking and anti-government vote, he should hold on in the personal politics of the tight-knit communities of Ceredigion.

1981	% Own Occ	64.5	1979 core seat Cardigan			
1981	% Loc Auth	18.7	L	13,227	35.6	
1981	% Welsh Sp	60	C	11,033	29.7	
1981	% Mid Cl	46.9	Lab	7,488	20.2	
1981	% Prof Man	20.5	PC	5,382	14.5	
1981	electorate 59,662		MPs since 1945			
1979	notional result		1945-66 Roderic Bowen L			
	L 1,000 (RW)		1966-74 Elystan Morgan Lab			
Alliance		L	1974- Geraint Howells L			

Llanelli

Llanelli is the only Labour stronghold in Dyfed. This is not unconnected with the fact that it is not so much a rural West Wales seat as an outpost of the South Wales valley constituencies. It is most famous for digging coal, anthracite. But there is also a great tinplate works, and many other industries. Here too can be found many of the cultural characteristics of the South Wales valleys – a famous rugby team, singing, Nonconformist chapels. But it is also a Welsh-speaking district, where over half the population is still bilingual. In that sense at least it does belong with Dyfed, and the west, rather than with the English-influenced Glamorgan counties.

All this makes life for the Conservatives here miserable. At the last Election it returned one of the 15 largest Labour numerical majorities in Britain. Indeed the Liberals finished second in the October 1974 election, and the Tories were relegated to fourth behind Plaid Cymru. In an almost unchanged constituency, nobody seems able to beat the Labour MP, barrister Denzil Davies. Davies is already a front bench spokesman, and would be considered for Cabinet rank in a Labour government. He stands on the moderate wing of his party, but had no trouble being reselected as candidate for Llanelli.

The westernmost of the great folded valleys of South Wales is as loyal to Labour as any other. From Llanelli up to Ammanford and Glanaman under the Black Mountains, the communities find Labour voting as much a part of their tradition as any other. The strength of socialism, like the sound of singing, reverberates round the valleys.

1981	% Own Occ	60.6	1979 core seat Llanelli		
1981	% Loc Auth	33.6	Lab	30,416	59.5
1981	% Welsh Sp	55	C	10,471	20.5
1981	% Mid Cl	39.2	L	5,856	11.4
1981	% Prof Man	11.8	PC	3,793	7.4
1981	electorate 64,776		Comm	617	1.2
1979	notional result		MPs since 1945		
	Lab 20,600		1945-70 James Griffiths Lab		
Alliance		L	1970- Denzil Davies Lab		

Pembroke

Pembroke is another Dyfed constituency with a curious electoral history. In 1945 Major Gwilym Lloyd George, son of David, held the seat by 168 votes over Labour. Lloyd George was endorsed by both the Liberal and the Conservative parties. Then in 1950 Desmond Donnelly captured Pembroke for Labour, and he was re-elected six times with some ease, except in 1955 when once again a combined Liberal and Conservative candidature entered the lists. But after 1966 Donnelly's politics became increasingly eccentric. He first resigned the whip to sit as Independent Labour, then formed his own Democratic Party. In 1970 he secured over 12,000 votes, standing as a Democrat, and split the Labour support sufficiently to let the Tory Nicholas Edwards in.

Edwards is still there, and now he is Secretary of State for Wales. By 1979 Pembroke was looking like a safe Conservative seat, benefiting from the strong pro-Tory movement in rural Wales, even before the present redistribution removes the Conservatives' poorer areas, the Welsh-speaking North Pembs around Fishguard. Pembroke constituency is now even more clearly 'Little England beyond Wales'. English-speaking settlers fortified this district against the Welsh after the Norman Conquest, and even yet there is a strongly English spirit in towns like Tenby and Saundersfoot on the coast, and Haverfordwest. Pembroke is a port and county town, and Milford Haven a growing working-class oil refining port. There is also a fine wild coastline, dotted with offshore islands like Skomer and Skokholm, and the smallest cathedral city in Britain, St David's.

Nicholas Edwards must be one of Labour's main targets, certainly in Wales at least. But the boundary changes will make the task even more difficult for a new Labour candidate, Oxford law don Alan Griffiths.

1981	% Own Occ	55.7	1979	core seat Pembroke		
1981	% Loc Auth	31.2	C	30,483	49.2
1981	% Welsh Sp	12	Lab	23,015	37.1
1971	% Mid Cl	43.4	L	6,249	10.1
1971	% Prof Man	16.5	PC	1,573	2.5
1981	electorate 66,998		E	694	1.1
1979	notional result		MPs since 1945		
	C 6,300		1945-50	Gwilym Lloyd George
Alliance		SDP			L-C
			1950-70	Desmond Donnelly Lab
				(Ind Lab) (Dem)
			1970-	Nicholas Edwards C

Bridgend

The creation of a separate seat of Bridgend in Mid-Glamorgan gives the Tories hopes of one seat at least in this most forbidding of counties for them. They are competitive in the market and commercial centre of Bridgend itself, which is not a coal-mining town, but belongs to the more fertile Vale of Glamorgan. The Conservatives can expect a lead in votes cast on the coastline, in the small resorts of Porthcawl and Ogmore by Sea. They should do as well in the farmland here as in the neighbouring Vale of Glamorgan constituency around Cowbridge. Their only major difficulties in this southern half of the District of Ogwr come in the industrial communities around Bridgend - Pencoed, Bryncethin, Tondu and Aberkenfig; and in the Pyle/Cornelly/Kenfig district not far from the Margam and Port Talbot steelworks.

Bridgend looks very like a marginal seat. It is difficult to calculate a notional result for 1979 due to an irregular candidature pattern in the local elections which were fought on the same day. But there can be no better hope for the Tories in Mid-Glamorgan than Bridgend. This is not the coal-mining valley country of northern Ogwr - Ogmore Vale, Maesteg and Pontycymmer. The only three Conservative councillors in the county were elected here, in Bridgend, Porthcawl and in the Ogmore by Sea ward of the old Penybont Rural District.

Yet the fact remains that Labvour will start favourites in the new and untried Bridgend division - a testament to the depth of their strength, and of the Conservative weakness, in South Wales.

1981	% Own Occ	66.2	New seat
1981	% Loc Auth	26.7	
1981	% Welsh Sp	6	
1981	% Mid Cl	50.8	
1981	% Prof Man	17.3	
1976	electorate 53,154		
1979	notional result		
	Lab 1,000 (RW)		

Alliance   SDP

Caerphilly

Caerphilly's Labour MP Ednyfed Hudson Davies defected to
the SDP in 1982. But his assessment of his chances of holding
the seat is clear. In the Alliance carve-up, Caerphilly has
been allocated to the Liberals, even though they lost their
deposit last time. Davies is clearly seeking safer pastures
elsewhere. Caerphilly has not always been quite such a
certain Labour prospect, for in a byelection in July 1968 Plaid
Cymru came within 2,000 votes of a shock victory, even in an
English-speaking seat. But that was the height of the
unpopularity of Harold Wilson's government and this little
altered seat in the Lower Rhymney Valley should now justify
Davies's fears, and return to Labour at the next Election.

1981	% Own Occ	58.6	1979 core seat Caerphilly		
1981	% Loc Auth	33.8	Lab	27,280	58.8
1981	% Welsh Sp	6	C	8,783	18.9
1981	% Mid Cl	41.9	PC	6,931	14.9
1981	% Prof Man	12.1	L	3,430	7.4
1981	electorate 63,400		MPs since 1945		
1979	notional result		1945-68 Ness Edwards Lab		
	Lab 19,400		1968-79 Fred Evans Lab		
Alliance		L	1979- E.H. Davies Lab (SDP)		

Cynon Valley

This is one of the most famous of all the South Wales coal
mining valleys, set between Merthyr Tydfil and the Rhondda
at the heart of Mid Glamorgan. The seat used to be named
after the main community, Aberdare, but it is in fact little
altered in the boundary changes. It is now coterminous with
the Cynon Valley Borough. The communities along the 11 mile
valley from Abercynon through Mountain Ash to Hirwaun are
bedrock Labour territory. Apart from isolated Nationalist
successes, it has never seemed like springing any surprises.

1981	% Own Occ	65.7	1979 core seat Aberdare		
1981	% Loc Auth	26.6	Lab	26,716	71.5
1981	% Welsh Sp	11.1	C	6,453	17.3
1981	% Mid Cl	35.5	PC	3,652	9.8
1981	% Prof Man	10.6	Comm	518	1.4
1981	electorate 51,053		MPs since 1945		
1979	notional result		1945-46 G.H. Hall Lab		
	Lab 20,900		1946-54 D.E. Thomas Lab		
Alliance		SDP	1954-74 Arthur Probert Lab		
			1974- Ioan Evans Lab		

Merthyr Tydfil and Rhymney

Merthyr Tydfil was the first great boom town of the South
Wales Industrial Revolution. At the end of the eighteenth
century it became one of the leading iron and coal working
towns in the world. In 1801 it was the largest town in Wales,
a hurly-burly melting pot of recent immigrants, where
fortunes were to be made very rapidly. Through the
nineteenth century the names of Dowlais, Cyfarthfa and many
other works made Merthyr one of the most famous industrial
towns in Britain. But its growth stopped early, and it has
been losing population for a century.

Now Merthyr has an electorate of under 40,000, and must look
elsewhere to make up the numbers. It finds them in the
neighbouring Upper Rhymney Valley to the east, taking
voters from Michael Foot's Ebbw Vale and Neil Kinnock's
Bedwellty. This should boost the majority of Labour FO
spokesman Ted Rowlands to one of the highest in the country
- not far short of 30,000.

But Merthyr has given Labour some shocks in recent years.
In 1970 the octogenarian MP S.O. Davies was not reselected
by the party on grounds of age. He stood as an Independent
and won easily. On his death in 1972, the Welsh Nationalists
ran Rowlands very close in the byelection. They have never
won a South Welsh industrial seat, although they have
threatened on a number of occasions. Now however the new
Merthyr/Rhymney seat looks impregnable. The first Labour
parliamentary leader, James Keir Hardie, sat for Methyr
Tydfil between 1900 and his death in 1915. His tradition has
not been forgotten, here in the cradle of valley industrialism.

1981	% Own Occ	52.8	1979 core seat Merthyr Tydfil		
1981	% Loc Auth	41.3	Lab	22,386	71.3
1981	% Welsh Sp	8	C	4,426	14.1
1981	% Mid Cl	33.6	PC	2,926	9.4
1981	% Prof Man	9.6	L	1,275	4.1
1981	electorate 59,981		Oth	337	1.1
1979	notional result		MPs since 1945		
	Lab 26,300		1945-72 S.O. Davies Lab (Ind		
Alliance		L		Lab)	
			1972-	Ted Rowlands Lab	

Ogmore

Ogmore by Sea is a small resort on the soft Glamorgan coast near Porthcawl. But the Ogmore seat is in fact a mining valley constituency, named after Ogmore Vale between Maesteg and Pontypridd. In the boundary changes, it loses what mixed character it had. It no longer reaches the Bristol Channel, at Ogmore by Sea or anywhere else. It no longer includes the marginal town of Bridgend, now the centre of its own seat. Rather it becomes a resolutely industrial, much more safely Labour seat in the coal-rich hills, full of famous names like Maesteg and Pontycymmer in the Garw Valley, and Price Town. There should be no problems for first-term Labour MP Ray Powell.

1981	% Own Occ	60.3	1979 core seat Ogmore		
1981	% Loc Auth	33.5	Lab	29,867	53.4
1981	% Welsh Sp	8	C	13,780	24.6
1981	% Mid Cl	32.4	L	9,812	17.5
1981	% Prof Man	9.2	PC	2,450	4.4
1981	electorate 51,951		MPs since 1950		
1979	notional Lab 14,800		1950-79 Waltter Padley Lab		
Alliance		L	1979- Ray Powell Lab		

Pontypridd

In 1979 the Tories polled over 17,000 votes in Pontypridd - it was by no means the stereotype of a Welsh valley constituency. Indeed it passed south through the lush (and Conservative) Vale of Glamorgan around Cowbridge to the coast west of Barry. Now, however, much of this farming territory is in South Glamorgan, and Pontypridd is a more compact, safer Labour seat. Its electorate is reduced from 75,000, one of the largest in Wales, to 60,000. It is now composed mainly of the Taff and Ely Valleys, around Pontypridd and the Royal Mint town of Llantrisant. It will stay safe for a leading Labour moderate, Brynmor John MP.

1981	% Own Occ	64.9	1979 core seat Pontypridd		
1981	% Loc Auth	29.3	Lab	32,801	56.0
1981	% Welsh Sp	27	C	17,114	29.2
1981	% Mid Cl	46.8	L	6,228	10.6
1981	% Prof Man	15.0	PC	2,200	3.8
1981	electorate 60,671		NF	263	0.4
1979	notional result		MPs since 1945		
	Lab 15,000 (RW)		1945-70 A. Pearson Lab		
Alliance		SDP	1970- Brynmor John Lab		

Rhondda

There is no Labour majority in Britain larger than that in the Rhondda constituency - 31,481 in 1979. The two Rhonddas - Fach and Fawr - are the archetypes of the popular image of the South Wales mining valleys. The names of the communities strung like beads along the valley bottom, or clinging to the steep sides of the hills, are as famous as their chapels and male voice choirs: Treherbert, Treorchy, Tonypandy, Ton Pentre, Tylorstown, Ferndale and Mardy, which was a Communist citadel in the 1930s. The only Communist county councillor in England and Wales is to be found in the Rhondda - Annie Powell of Penygraig. The Communists came second in a General Election in a Rhondda seat as recently as 1966.

But it is for Labour voting that the Rhondda is most known. Before 1974 it enjoyed two seats, one in each valley. There is an unbroken tradition of Labour MPs here right back to the election of the Lib-Lab W. Abraham (Mabon) in 1885. Although mining has declined in the Rhondda valleys, the proud little owner-occupied communities of terraced houses retain much of their traditional proletarian spirit. There are scarcely any council houses in the Rhondda. One exception is the windy, bleak post-war estate of Penrhys, on the top of the hill between the two valleys; Penrhys has been notably less successful as a harmonious unit than the older settlements.

It is hard to see any challenge to Labour's hegemony here. The Communists polled 15,761 votes in Rhondda East in 1945, 972 fewer than Labour. Plaid Cymru came within 3,000 in Rhondda West in a 1967 byelection. The SDP will contest the seat for the first time at the next Election, but their task seems as hopeless as all the other parties. Unaffected by the work of the Boundary Commissioners, Rhondda may well provide once again Labour's largest majority, and safest seat.

1981	% Own Occ	76.1	1979 same seat Rhondda	
1981	% Loc Auth	17.7	Lab	38,007	75.1
1981	% Welsh Sp	9.5	C	6,526	12.9
1981	% Mid Cl	32.8	PC	4,226	8.4
1981	% Prof Man	9.4	Comm 1,819	3.6
1981	electorate 63,412		MP since 1974	
Alliance		SDP	1974- Alec Jones Lab	

Cardiff Central

Cardiff Central is in fact based on the former Cardiff N seat, which was safely Conservative. Not only does it include the fine city and civic centre of the capital, but also a large middle-class residential area around Penylan, Cyncoed and Pentwyn. There are in fact very few council tenants in the seat at all, although there is quite an amount of privately-rented terraced housing. The proportion of non-white residents is the highest in Wales, around 5%, but Conservative MP Ian Grist should have little trouble holding a 50% middle-class seat.

1981	% Own Occ	67	1979 core seat Cardiff North		
1981	% Loc Auth	12	C	17,181	47.3
1981	% Welsh Sp	6	Lab	13,133	36.2
1981	% Mid Cl	58	L	4,921	13.6
1981	% Prof Man	20	PC	1,081	3.0
1981	electorate 55,683		MP since 1974		
1979	notional result		1974-	Ian Grist C	
	C 5,000 (RW)				
Alliance		SDP			

Cardiff North

This is the successor to the old Cardiff NW, held by the late Conservative Michael Roberts, not to the former North seat. It consists of a swathe of middle-class commuter wards – Rhiwbina, Whitchurch, Llanishen - all safely Conservative. Capital cities always have a higher proportion of non-manual workers than elsewhere, due to the concentration of bureaucrats and service workers. Cardiff NW's figure of 57.6% in 1971 was exceeded only in 22 constituencies in Britain, and nowhere in Wales. Reinforced by one or two rural areas outside Cardiff, the new North seat will remain solidly Tory.

1981	% Own Occ	75	1979 core seat Cardiff North		
1981	% Loc Auth	19	West		
1981	% Welsh Sp	7	C	17,925	51.0
1981	% Mid Cl	66	Lab	11,663	33.2
1981	% Prof Man	22	L	4,832	13.7
1981	electorate 53,467		PC	743	2.1
1979	notional result		MP since 1974		
	C 6,700		1974-83 Michael Roberts C		
Alliance		L			

Cardiff South and Penarth

The most likely man to be the Father of the next House of Commons - that is, the longest-serving member - is James Callaghan, the former Labour leader and Prime Minister. He has represented a southern Cardiff seat since 1945, and is thought to have taken his oath of allegiance before any of the other survivors of the 1945 intake. Now, however, his faithful constituency has been much altered in name and character. The seaside town of Penarth, in the Vale of Glamorgan District and at present in the oversized Conservative division of Barry, has been added to South Cardiff to create a seat of rare social and economic variety.

The basis of James Callaghan's vote has always been situated in the docklands of the Welsh capital, in the Labour strongholds of Splott, Rumney and Bute Town, the slightly seedy, disreptuable 'Tiger Bay' of literature, the home area of singer Shirley Bassey. Cardiff has a working port as well as the manicured grounds and classic architecture of the fine Civic Centre, and South Cardiff is very different from the comfortable residential areas of the northern half of the city, where the bureaucrats and professional classes live. But Penarth is 50% middle-class, and has always contributed towards the Tory majority in Barry constituency.

Although in an even year a seaside town of 20,000 people should not be able to shake Jim Callaghan's grip, or to outvote his heartland in the Cardiff docks, his majority may well be reduced. There is no significant vote for the Alliance, or for Plaid Cymru in this English speaking seat.

1981	% Own Occ	55	1979 core seat Cardiff South		
1981	% Loc Auth	29	East		
1981	% Welsh Sp	4	Lab	23,871	59.3
1981	% Mid Cl	45	C	15,170	37.7
1981	% Prof Man	14	PC	628	1.6
1981	electorate 59,917		Oths	619	1.5
1979	notional result		MPs since 1945		
	Lab 4,900		1945-	James Callaghan Lab	
Alliance		L			

Cardiff West

Cardiff West is the constituency of the current Speaker of the House of Commons, George Thomas. It has on occasion been suggested that the Speaker should not represent a full-sized seat like other members, for it is difficult for him to offer certain constituency services or to ask questions in the House. He is also forbidden from campaigning at election time, even for himself, but the Conservatives and Liberals at least rarely oppose the Speaker, as a matter of principle. He was re-elected with a massive majority in 1979 against Plaid Cymru and National Front candidates, whose vote was inflated only slightly by the lack of competition.

George Thomas has already announced that he will not serve as Speaker in the next Parliament, so it is worthwhile assessing the political characteristics of the little changed Cardiff West seat. The Labour candidate David Seligman must be the favourite to win. George Thomas held Cardiff West for Labour for nearly 30 years before he was chosen as Speaker. Local election evidence suggests that Labour might have won Cardiff W by about 5,000 votes on 3 May 1979, had it been fought on party lines. There is a large council estate at Ely-Caerau on the SW edge of the city, and despite the presence of a Conservative ward at Llandaff (site of Cardiff's cathedral), this is a more working-class constituency than most in South Glamorgan.

George Thomas will be a loss to the House, and to Cardiff West as well, despite his limited role as MP in recent years. This courtly bachelor is a product of the South Welsh chapel, choral and Labour traditions, but he has been a widely respected and non-partisan steward of the best principles of the Commons.

1981	% Own Occ	50	1979 core seat Cardiff West
1981	% Loc Auth	35	Spkr 27,035	85.6
1981	% Welsh Sp	6	PC 3,272	10.4
1981	% Mid Cl	45	NF 1,287	4.1
1981	% Prof Man	13	MP since 1950
1981	electorate 58,857		1950- George Thomas Lab
1979	notional result		(Speaker)
	Speaker 25,000 (RW)		
	(Lab 5,200)		
Alliance		SDP	

Vale of Glamorgan

The Vale of Glamorgan is very different in its economic and political characteristics from most of South Wales. There are no coal miners here, and no strong history of Labour support. The previous parliamentary constituency, Barry, was one of the three in Wales which remained Conservative in 1966. Only 6% of the population can speak Welsh at all, and Nationalism has never been a force here.

There is industry in Barry itself, which boomed as a coal port after 1880 and still has working docks. Barry is politically marginal, with Tory votes in west Barry (Baruc ward) which has some appeal as a holiday resort, but Labour strength around Barry Dock. But Sir Raymond Gower has been enabled to hold on to the Barry constituency for over 30 years because of the Conservatism of the hinterland. In the boundary changes, the resort of Penart and Tory villages like Lisvane are transferred to Cardiff constituencies. Barry was one of the largest seats in Wales, with over 75,000 electors. It does however pick up equally Conservative rural and coastal terrain from Pontypridd - Llantwit Major and Rhoose, and the soft farming country around Cowbridge.

Labour cut Raymond Gower's majority to 1,394 in 1966. But it had recovered to 9,000 in 1979, and the Vale of Glamorgan seat will be at least as safe as Barry was. The SDP have the Alliance nomination, but they are untested here in South Glamorgan, which has had no local elections since their foundation. The Conservatives remain favourites to win in the Vale.

1981	% Own Occ	64	1979 core seat Barry		
1981	% Loc Auth	22	C	30,720	50.9
1981	% Welsh Sp	6	Lab	21,928	36.3
1981	% Mid Cl	55	L	6,105	10.1
1981	% Prof Man	20	PC	1,281	2.1
1981	electorate 61,813		NF	312	0.5
1979	notional result		MPs since 1950		
	C 7,000 (RW)		1950-51 Mrs D.M. Rees Lab		
Alliance		SDP	1951- Sir Raymond Gower C		

Aberavon

The mighty steelworks of Abbey and Margam, near Port Talbot, dominate the constituency of Aberavon, which lies behind the sand dunes between the Bristol Channel and the South Wales mountains. Port Talbot is situated at the mouth ('Aber') of the River Afan, which gives its name to the local government District here. But this is an English-speaking constituency, full of immigrants from further east, who came in to work at the industry of Port Talbot from the eighteenth century onwards. Naming it Aberavon rather than Port Talbot does at least make the seat the first in the national alphabetical list; that is its only electoral distinction, for it returns Labour's former Welsh Secretary John Morris by a massive margin.

It will be even safer than before, for the one Conservative element in the constituency, the seaside resort of Porthcawl, is now in the County of Mid Glamorgan and therefore transferred to the Bridgend seat. In the boundary changes Aberavon gains a few thousand voters across the River Neath towards Swansea, from places such as Skewen and Jersey Marine. These were previously in the Neath division. Aberavon also reaches up into the hills which form a backdrop to the steel plant on the flat plain, to take in the old mining town of Glyncorrwg at the top of its blind valley near Maesteg.

Aberavon was Ramsay Macdonald's seat during his period of office as the first ever Labour Prime Minister in 1924, although he migrated to Seaham in Durham for his second term from 1929. John Morris may not be quite so distinguished, but he would still have a good chance of again being a Labour government's Secretary of State for Wales, should they win an Election.

1981	% Own Occ	53.5	1979 core seat Aberavon		
1981	% Loc Auth	42.6	Lab	31,665	61.7
1981	% Welsh Sp	10	C	12,692	24.7
1981	% Mid Cl	33.3	L	4,624	9.0
1981	% Prof Man	7.6	PC	1,954	3.8
1981	electorate 54,129		Comm	406	0.8
1979	notional result		MPs since 1945		
	Lab 16,100		1945-50 W.G. Cove Lab		
Alliance		L	1959-	John Morris Lab	

Gower

Gower is a constituency of two very distinct and different parts. The Gower peninsula itself is well known for its holiday beaches, its chalets and bungalows, and its homes of wealthy commuters to nearby Swansea. But on the other side of Swansea are the Llwchwr and Swansea Valleys, with stark working-class industrial communities like Gorseinon, Pontardulais and Pontardawe. The Labour votes piled up in this Welsh-speaking and anthracite mining territory have in the past easily outweighed the Gower peninsula's contribution.

When the veteran Labour MP Ifor Davies died in 1982, Gareth Wardell held Gower very easily for Labour in the byelection, although the SDP's Gwynoro Jones did well to come second, polling 9,875 to Wardell's 17,095. But all is not completely rosy for Gareth Wardell. In the boundary changes, the influence of the Gower peninsula is to be increased, as the Mumbles ward is transferred from Swansea West. The Mumbles are great rocks jutting out into Swansea Bay, and around them has grown an affluent residential area and popular seaside resort. The inclusion of Mumbles should cut Labour's majority by about 3,000, and this effect should be doubled by the removal of the Upper Swansea Valley around Ystalyfera to Neath constituency.

Now the Conservatives can hope to regain second place in the General Election in Gower, and even to press Labour closely in a good year. The working-class towns north of Swansea should still determine the destination of this division's preferences, but the Tory Gower peninsula will have more of a say than ever before in the seat which bears its name.

1981	% Own Occ	63.1	1979 core seat Gower			
1981	% Loc Auth	31.3	Lab	24,963	53.2	
1981	% Welsh Sp	30	C	14,322	30.5	
1981	% Mid Cl	54.3	L	4,245	9.1	
1981	% Prof Man	19.4	PC	3,357	7.2	
1981	electorate 56,110		MPs since 1945			
1979	notional result		1945-59 David Grenfell Lab			
	Lab 6,200		1959-82 Ifor Davies Lab			
Alliance		SDP	1982- Gareth Wardell Lab			

Neath

Neath is one of those many industrial South Wales valley constituencies which run in N-S strips along the dips in the ridged and folded landscape. It includes most of the Neath and Dulais valleys, and now the Upper Swansea Valley too. At the southern end of the seat is the medium-sized town of Neath itself. The lower reaches of the valleys are almost entirely given over to industry - coal, aluminium and engineering; many of the hillsides have been afforested for timber. Neath has been safely Labour since 1922, and this state of affairs will not be altered by the minor boundary changes.

1981	% Own Occ	63.1	1979 core seat Neath	
1981	% Loc Auth	31.3	Lab 27,071	64.5
1981	% Welsh Sp	20	C 8,455	20.2
1981	% Mid Cl	39.6	PC 6,430	15.3
1981	% Prof Man	10.9	MPs since 1945	
1981	electorate 55,678		1945-64 D.J. Williams Lab	
1979	notional result		1964- Donald Coleman Lab	
	Lab 16,000			
Alliance		SDP		

Swansea East

The north and east sides of Swansea form that city's industrial heartland. Here are the docks, the steel, tinplate and copper works, and most of the council estates - concentrated in working-class wards like Morriston and Llansamlet and Penderry. In the minor boundary changes, East loses its share of the city centre. Swansea East is as much a Labour stronghold as any in Wales, and has been so for many years - it even survived Labour's disaster in 1931. It now returns Methodist lay preacher Donald Anderson, who was Labour MP for Monmouth 1966-70. Anderson will not find Swansea E so marginal and uncertain a prospect!

1981	% Own Occ	58.1	1979 core seat Swansea East	
1981	% Loc Auth	37.0	Lab 31,909	69.9
1981	% Welsh Sp	12	C 10,689	23.4
1981	% Mid Cl	37.4	PC 2,732	6.0
1981	% Prof Man	8.9	Comm 308	0.7
1981	electorate 57,807		MPs since 1945	
1979	notional result		1945-63 D.L. Mort Lab	
	Lab 19,900		1963-74 Neil McBride Lab	
Alliance		L	1974- Donald Anderson Lab	

Swansea West

Swansea is Wales's second city, and with the creation of West Glamorgan County it is confirmed as undoubtedly the metropolis of the western valleys. It has been known as a great industrial centre at the mouth of the River Tawe since the eighteenth century. But it also has its leafy suburbs, its University college, and a fine new city centre rebuilt after the bomb destruction of 1941. All these are in Swansea West, which is also the city's marginal seat - the only marginal in West Glamorgan.

Along with leafy suburbs goes Tory voting, even in a city with so gritty a reputation as Swansea. There are strongly Conservative wards like Sketty, Ffynone and St Helen's, west of the city centre on the gentle slopes above Swansea Bay. Labour fights back in the inner wards, and in the peripheral industrial ward of Fforestfach, but the Conservatives won Swansea West in 1959, and Alan Williams's Labour majority was reduced to 401 in 1979. But help is at hand for Labour. In the boundary changes, the outermost western Conservative ward of Mumbles is transferred to Gower, and the whole of the city centre is now in Swansea West. This should make it a safe seat for Labour under any normal circumstances.

Plaid Cymru have no strength in the English-speaking community of Swansea, and the Liberals lost their deposit too last time. The SDP will take the Alliance nomination, but Alan Williams is a Labour moderate, and indeed there were suggestions that he might be in trouble with left-wing elements within his own party. He has been reselected, and with the help of the boundary changes, he now seems in a much safer position to win Swansea West next time.

1981	% Own Occ	57.4	1979 core seat Swansea West
1981	% Loc Auth	29.8	Lab 24,175 46.1
1981	% Welsh S⸝	9	C 23,774 45.3
1981	% Mid Cl	52.8	L 3,484 6.6
1981	% Prof Man	15.9	PC 1,012 1.9
1981	electorate 58,700		MPs since 1945
1979	notional result		1945-59 P. Morris Lab
	Lab 3,200		1959-64 J.E.H. Rees C
Alliance		SDP	1964- Alan Williams Lab

Blaneau Gwent

Ebbw Vale is one of the most famous of all constituency names. From 1929 to 1960 Ebbw Vale was represented by Aneurin Bevan. Since then it has been held by Bevan's friend and biographer Michael Foot - the present Leader of the Labour Party. But the name of Ebbw Vale will not be found in the new Parliament. One of the three valley head towns of the old constituency, Rhymney, has been transferred to Merthyr Tydfil. The other towns, Tredegar and Ebbw Vale, are to be included in Blaenau Gwent ('Blaenau' means 'uplands' in Welsh). There they are joined by Brynmawr, from Brecon and Radnor, and the northern half of the Abertillery division.

Jeffrey Thomas, the MP for Abertillery, is now a Social Democrat, but Abertillery has on occasion been the safest seat in the whole of Britain. Thomas is not going to risk a contest against Michael Foot, and the Alliance nomination for Blaenau Gwent has been left to the Liberals. Foot need have no worries about his renamed constituency. Coal mining and steel production have declined in these eastern valleys, and a number of light industries have been attracted in recent decades. All the same, unemployment reached a severe level of 18% in 1981. But the essential characteristics of these working-class communities remain, and Foot should receive an extra boost now that he is leader of the party. Only 2% of the population speak Welsh at all, so Plaid Cymru has never posed a threat.

It is sad that the end is coming after 50 years in which the name of Ebbw Vale has been associated with the leaders of the Old Left, famed for oratory and a commitment to the history and traditions of parliamentary democracy. But Blaenau Gwent will certainly remain loyal to the beliefs of Michael Foot, rather than the new-fangled attractions of Thatcherism, the Alliance, or Nationalism.

1981	% Own Occ	55.5	1979 core seat Ebbw Vale		
1981	% Loc Auth	40.4	Lab	20,028	69.2
1981	% Welsh Sp	2	C	3,937	13.6
1981	% Mid Cl	31.6	L	3,082	10.7
1981	% Prof Man	8.0	PC	1,884	6.5
1981	electorate 56,952		MPs since 1945		
1979	notional result		1945-60 Aneurin Bevan Lab		
	Lab 23,300		1960- Michael Foot Lab		
Alliance		L			

Islwyn

One of the most rapidly rising Labour politicians of the last decade is Neil Kinnock. Still only just into his 40s, the smoothly articulate Kinnock is widely tipped as a future Labour Party leader, possibly even the next one. His seat is right next door to Michael Foot, whose politics are very much in the same tradition. Kinnock was first elected at Bedwellty in 1970, and has never had any trouble piling up massive majorities. The logical successor to the abolished Bedwellty is another constituency with a name which causes difficulties for the English tongue – Islwyn.

Islwyn contains most of the old Bedwellty seat – Mynyddislwyn and Risca – together with the western part of Abertillery (Abercarn). Basically the three small seats of Ebbw Vale, Abertillery and Bedwellty have been collapsed into two, but there are probably no problems of nomination, for the Labour MP for Abertillery, Jeffrey Thomas, has defected to the Social Democrats, and is unlikely to contest any of the seats in the eastern valleys. Islwyn will be identical to the strongly Labour local authority of the same name.

The South Wales coalfield has declined greatly. Only a tenth as much coal is produced now as at the end of the First World War, and under 40 pits survive in the whole of South Wales. It is no longer one of the nation's major coalfields, and many of the remaining mines are uneconomic and in danger of closure. Islwyn is one of the districts which has enlisted government support in attracting new light industry, and unemployment is not as severe as in many of the other valleys. Bedwellty was safely Labour from its creation in 1918 to its demise. Islwyn should provide as sound a platform, from which Neil Kinnock's ambition may vault.

1981	% Own Occ	52.3	1979 core seat Bedwellty		
1981	% Loc Auth	38.7	Lab	28,794	71.3
1981	% Welsh Sp	3.0	C	8,358	20.7
1981	% Mid Cl	35.3	PC	2,648	6.6
1981	% Prof Man	11.2	E	556	1.4
1981	electorate 50,372		MPs since 1945		
1979	notional result		1945-50 Sir C. Edwards Lab		
	Lab 21,200		1950-70 H. Finch Lab		
Alliance		SDP	1970- Neil Kinnock Lab		

Monmouth

There was for a long time a dispute about whether Monmouthshire was in Wales or England. The coal mining valleys of Ebbw Vale and Abertillery and Pontypool clearly do belong to the culture and tradition of South Wales. Monmouthshire is the basis of the new County of Gwent, which is indubitably in Wales. Bu the Monmouth constituency itself shows why there was ever cause for debate. Over 97% of the population speak English only. Plaid Cymru obtain derisory votes - 641, or 1%, at the last Election. The soft and fertile green farmland of the Usk and Wye valleys is of a type found only on the English borders. And finally Monmouth has shown a most un-Welsh devotion to the Conservative Party.

Only once, in 1966, has Monmouth been won by Labour - and that was at a time when the Tories were reduced to only three seats in the whole of Wales. The 1966 result saw the defeat of front-bencher Peter Thorneycroft, who had won Monmouth even in 1945; Thorneycroft later entered the Lords and became Chairman of the Conservative Party. But Monmouth is not really marginal. The affluent and comfortable small county towns of Monmouth, Abergavenny and Crickhowell near the Black Mountains seem more typical of English rural areas - certainly in their political preferences. The villages of the Wye and Usk valleys are steeped with Anglo-Saxon culture and history - Tintern Abbey, Raglan Castle. Labour's only strongpoint lies at the site of another mighty Norman castle, Chepstow; even Chepstow is situated on the Wye border with Gloucestershire and the Severn Road Bridge to Avon.

Before the boundary changes, Monmouth was the most populous seat in Wales, with over 80,000 electors. Now Caerleon and the coastal strip of Magor and St Mellons are lost, as Newport and Monmouth are rearranged as three new seats. But Monmouth will still be one of the five safest Tory seats in Wales, which is good news for Conservative Whip John Stradling Thomas.

1981	% Own Occ	61.4	1979 core seat Monmouth
1981	% Loc Auth	28.1	C 33,547 50.5
1981	% Welsh Sp	2	Lab 23,785 35.8
1981	% Mid Cl	51.9	L 8,494 12.8
1981	% Prof Man	20.2	PC 641 1.0
1981	electorate 55,943		MPs since 1945
1979	notional result		1945-66 Peter Thorneycroft C
	C 9,200		1966-70 Donald Anderson Lab
Alliance			1970- John Stradling Thomas
			C

Newport East

Newport is the third largest town in Wales, a port which has served the eastern valleys since industry came to South Wales. The previously unified Newport was safely Labour, but now it has been divided along the line of the River Usk, which flows through the centre of Newport, and each half has been diluted with Conservative rural territory from the Monmouth seat. Both Newport constituencies may now be vulnerable to the Tories in a bad year for Labour.

East is the better of the two divisions for the Labour Party. Here can be found the vast Llanwern steelworks, Newport's largest single employer. Labour can rely on the support of the threatened steelworkers and others living in the peripheral eastern council estates of Ringland, Lliswerry and Alway. The rest of Newport east of the Usk is more mixed, but wards like St Julian's and Victoria still tend to Labour. The M4 sweeps dramatically through the hills of this part of the seat, on its way to soaring across the Usk. The Conservative vote comes mainly from the outlying wards around Magor and Langstone, and along the coast into Monmouth Borough nearly as far as Chepstow.

It is difficult to imagine Newport East falling to the Tories. Llanwern has been considered for closure, like many steelworks. Dead or alive, Llanwern's stark grandeur will dominate the political scene as well as the skyline in east Newport. Sitting Labour MP Roy Hughes will probably stand for this, the more hopeful of the two Newport constituencies for his party.

1981	% Own Occ	62.9	1979 core seat Newport			
1981	% Loc Auth	30.4	Lab	30,919	51.7	
1981	% Welsh Sp	2	C	21,742	36.3	
1981	% Mid Cl	42.9	L	6,270	10.5	
1981	% Prof Man	13.4	PC	473	0.8	
1981	electorate 52,354		NF	454	0.8	
1979	notional result		MPs since 1945			
	Lab 5,600		1945	Ronald Bell C		
Alliance		SDP	1945-56 P. Freeman Lab			
			1956-66 Frank Soskice Lab			
			1966-	Roy Hughes Lab		

Newport West

Newport West will be a very marginal seat. If Labour had won it in 1979, it would have been close. This is all rather surprising, for Newport has been regarded as a safe Labour division since 1945. The problem for Labour is twofold. The more Conservative middle-class residential wards within Newport are mainly situated west of the river, most notably at Allt-yr-yn, although Malpas is also marginal. But as well as this, a number of rural and commuter communities previously in the oversized Monmouth seat are included in a Newport division for the first time. All are Conservative in an even year: Rogerstone, Bassaleg, Marshfield and the former Roman town of Caerleon set in its bend of the River Usk.

Labour fights back in the large peripheral council estates of Bettws and St Woolos, and the town centre is also west of the river. Here, and in the old dockland to the south, is to be found Newport's old terraced housing and its small non-white population. Very few West Indians or Asians have migrated to Wales, so it is not worth reporting the percentage of non-whites in every Welsh seat. Only in Cardiff and Newport does the average pass 1%. It is between 2% and 3% in Newport West. This is also very much English-speaking Wales - only 2% speak Welsh at all, and Plaid Cymru received only 473 votes, or 0.8% of the total in Newport in 1979.

The Liberals contest Newport West for the Alliance, while the SDP have the nomination for East. Neither has much expectation of success. Newport West will be a major-party battle, and one so uncertain that no sitting MP is likely to stand. Labour will nevertheless start as narrow favourites.

1981	% Own Occ	58.6	New seat
1981	% Loc Auth	34.2	
1981	% Welsh Sp	2	
1981	% Mid Cl	52.3	
1981	% Prof Man	16.7	
1981	electorate 53,640		
1979	notional result		
	Lab 3,100		
Alliance		L	

Torfaen

Torfaen is the furthest east of the series of great South Welsh industrial valleys. The base of its economy has changed more than most. Mining is no longer significant here, but light and varied industry has been attracted. Indeed the largest centre of population in the valley is now the post-war New Town of Cwmbran, which houses nearly 45,000 people. But the name with which this valley constituency has always been most associated is that of Pontypool. In fact, when the Boundary Commission originally suggested that the town of Pontypool itself should be detached to join parts of Islwyn, the neighbouring valley, the sitting Pontypool MP led a storm of protest. The Commission changed its mind, and the Torfaen valley has been saved as a parliamentary unit - it is little different from the old Pontypool seat.

As such, it will remain a Labour stronghold. To the east of Torfaen, the mining valleys give way to rural border country, which is heavily Conservative. But the growth of Cwmbran has raised the proportion of council houses in Torfaen to the highest in Wales; and the old Pontypool was one of those seats which remained loyal to Labour even in 1931. From 1935 to 1946 Roy Jenkins's father was Labour MP for Pontypool, and the future SDP leader went to school in the constituency at Abersychan Grammar School.

In 1958 the present MP was returned in a byelection. Leo Abse has long been known as an active and independent backbencher, particularly noted for his work in social reform - homosexual law and divorce reform, opposition to abortion. His political autobiography 'Private Member' shows an unusual interest in psychology, and its ambiguous title reflects the drift of Abse's contribution as a backbench MP specialising in the most personal of issues. Abse is one of the most colourful figures in the House, and since his constituency is now preserved he should be returned to continue his familiar role as the psychoanalyst of the next Parliament.

1981	% Own Occ	39.5	1979 core seat Pontypool		
1981	% Loc Auth	56.9	Lab	27,651	61.8
1981	% Welsh Sp	2.5	C	10,383	23.2
1981	% Mid Cl	39.6	L	5,508	12.3
1981	% Prof Man	10.2	PC	1,169	2.6
1981	electorate 58,630		MPs since 1945		
1979	notional result		1945-46 A. Jenkins Lab		
	Lab 17,400		1945-58 D.G. West Lab		
Alliance		SDP	1958- Leo Abse Lab		

Caernarfon

There is no more purely 'Welsh' constituency than Caernarfon.
Over 80% of the population speak Welsh, which is the first
language in many parts of the seat. The MP is the
parliamentary leader and President of Plaid Cymru, Dafydd
Wigley, who polled twice as many votes as anyone else in the
seat in 1979. One of the previous members was the great
Welsh wizard, David Lloyd George, who represented the
Caernarvon district of boroughs from 1890 to 1945 without a
break. But Caernarvon's Liberal tradition gave way to
Labour, in the person of Goronwy Roberts, who represented
Caernarvon from 1945 to February 1974. Then Roberts was
defeated by Wigley.
The Welsh Nationalism of Caernarfon is clearly more than a
flash in the pan. Wigley has increased his majority in each of
the three Elections in which he has been victorious.
Caernarfon is little altered in the boundary changes, although
the spelling of the name has been adjusted to the Welsh
version. It is made up of the District of Dwyfor, and the
southern half of the Borough of Arfon. It includes the Lleyn
peninsula, much of it wild and remote but incorporating a
district popular with holidaymakers around Portmadoc,
Criccieth and Pwllheli. The main town of Caernarfon is
predominantly Welsh-speaking as well, but rather
incongruously it boasts a great Norman castle and was the
site of the investiture of the (very English) Prince of Wales.
Dafydd Wigley seems to have an assured future in
Caernarfon. He has annexed most of the former Labour
support. The SDP are standing for the first time in
Caernarfon, but their prospects seem limited here in the
depths of Wales. The Conservatives are also too English a
party ever to have a chance in this land of Nonconformist
radicalism, the Welsh language and the memory of Lloyd
George. Wigley stands to inherit most of the political
traditions powerful in Caernarfon, and it will surely be the
last seat ever to abandon Plaid Cymru.

1981	% Own Occ	62.8	1979 core seat Caernarvon		
1981	% Loc Auth	23.8	PC	17,420	49.7
1981	% Welsh Sp	81	Lab	8,696	24.8
1981	% Mid Cl	45.8	C	6,968	19.9
1981	% Prof Man	17.7	L	1,999	5.7
1981	electorate 43,893		MPs since 1945		
1979	notional result		1945-74 Goronwy Roberts Lab		
	PC 8,700		1974- Dafydd Wigley PC		
Alliance		SDP			

Conwy

Gwynedd is often thought of as the most 'Welsh' of counties, and indeed it does include the only two current constituencies held by Plaid Cymru. But not all of West Wales is dominated by Celtic influence. In the south, in Dyfed, Pembroke behaves more like an English coastal constituency. The North Wales coast too is noted for its caravan parks and its dependence on tourism. Welsh speakers are in a minority in the existing seat of Conway, and the 'English' parties predominate. The Plaid Cymru candidate lost his deposit in 1979.

Conway is little altered in the boundary changes, but its name is to be spelt in the Welsh style. Like Conway, it consists of the northen half of the old Caernarvonshire: the University town of Bangor, the large holiday resort of Llandudno, the walled town of Conwy, the smaller seaside resorts of Penmaenmawr and Llanfairfechan, Bethesda on the way up towards Snowdon.

Like most seaside districts largely dependent on tourism, Conwy will be inclined to the Conservatives. Peter Thomas, later Secretary of State for Wales, held Conway for 15 years from 1951. Thomas was ousted by Ednyfed Hudson Davies, now SDP member for Caerphilly, in the Welsh Labour Party's annus mirabilis of 1966. But in 1970 Conway returned to its usual allegiance, electing Wyn Roberts – who still holds the seat with some comfort. Conwy will in fact be one of the safest Conservative seats in Wales, and Roberts has little to worry about concerning his 'renamed' seat.

1981	% Own Occ	60.4	1979 core seat Conway		
1981	% Loc Auth	26.4	C	18,142	44.7
1981	% Welsh Sp	40	Lab	12,069	29.7
1981	% Mid Cl	48.8	L	6,867	16.9
1981	% Prof Man	18.0	PC	3,497	8.6
1981	electorate 51,482		MPs since 1950		
1979	notional result		1950-51 W.E.E. Jones Lab		
	C 5,800		1951-66 Peter Thomas C		
Alliance		L	1966-70 E.H. Davies Lab		
			1970- Wyn Roberts C		

Meirionydd Nant Conwy

In the USA 'ethnic minority' districts are sometimes created to provide representation for blacks or Hispanics. The nearest thing to this in Britain is the Welsh-speaking seat of Meirionydd Nant Conwy. The Commission originally proposed uniting Merioneth with much of Tory English speaking Conway on the north coast. This caused a storm of protest, not least as it would have eliminated one of Plaid Cymru's two seats. After an inquiry, the Commission decided to expand Merioneth only slightly, taking just the sparsely populated mountainous southern part of Aberconwy District, to become the clumsily named Meirionydd Nant Conwy.

Both Plaid Cymru MPs sit for divisions in the NW corner of Wales, around the Snowdon mountain range. The party leader Dafydd Wigley represents Caernarvon, and at present his colleague and neighbour is Dafydd Elis Thomas, first elected like Wigley in February 1974. Also like Wigley, Thomas has consolidated his position ever since, and now stands very well in a small seat. But unlike Wigley, Thomas stands on the far left of the British parliamentary system - he is a professed socialist, and inclined to more drastic measures in pursuit of his nationalism than some of his colleagues. His defeat by Wigley in a leadership contest in the early 1980s suggests that he remains in a minority in his party.

Like Caernarvon, Merioneth passed through a pre-war Liberal stage and a post-war period of Labour support. This is not good ground for Tories. There are holiday resorts, like Harlech, with its medieval castle, and Barmouth. The Conservatives achieved second place last time. But the largest centre of population is the unique slate-mining town of Blaenau Ffestiniog, which has suffered from economic depression since many quarries closed. Slate tips hang over the town, which has the functional character of a single-industry community. Blaenau Ffestiniog was once solidly Labour, but Plaid Cymru are now very competitive here. Thomas has little to fear from a seat which still only contains 30,000 electors, and still forms a tight-knit Welsh-speaking community.

1981	% Own Occ	60.6	1979 core seat Merioneth		
1981	% Loc Auth	24.4	PC	9,275	40.8
1981	% Welsh Sp	68	C	5,365	23.6
1981	% Mid Cl	39.6	Lab	5,332	23.5
1981	% Prof Man	16.5	L	2,752	12.1
1981	electorate 30,443		MPs since 1945		
1979	notional result		1945-51 E.O. Roberts L		
	PC 1,400		1951-70 T.W. Jones Lab		
Alliance		L	1970-74 Will Edwards Lab		
			1974- Dafydd Elis Thomas PC		

Ynys Mon

The island of Anglesey remains a parliamentary constituency on its own, but moves from the beginning almost to the end of the alphabetical list of seats due to the Commission's decision to use its Welsh name, Ynys Mon.

This is fairly logical - 61% of the population do speak Welsh, many employing it as their first language. But this is not a seat noted for its strength of Welsh Nationalism, although it has been contested several times by the militant Welsh singer Dafydd Iwan, standing as the Plaid Cymru candidate. From 1929 to 1951 Anglesey was held by David Lloyd George's daughter Megan, at that time a Liberal (although later Labour MP for Carmarthen). From 1951 to 1979, a similar personal popularity was held by Cledwyn Hughes, Welsh Secretary under Harold Wilson and now the leading Labour politician in the House of Lords. But on Cledwyn Hughes's retirement in 1979, little-fancied Conservative Keith Best came as if from nowhere to seize the island, defeating the former Labour MP for Cardigan, Elystan Morgan. This should not have been so surprising. The Tories did well throughout rural Wales, and Anglesey is a generally affluent island with a strong tradition of tourism.

Ynys Mon-Anglesey is the most heavily Welsh-speaking seat that the Conservatives hold. This in itself must cast doubts on its safety. But Labour will need a 4% swing next time to recover the island, and it is difficult to foresee a Liberal revival or the first SDP or Plaid Cymru breakthrough. The percentage of owner occupiers increased by over 10 points in the 1970s. The unsung Keith Best now seems the favourite to hold Ynys Mon.

1981	% Own Occ	59.0	1979 same seat Anglesey
1981	% Loc Auth	28.0	C	15,100	39.0
1981	% Welsh Sp	61.0	Lab	12,283	31.7
1981	% Mid Cl	43.3	PC	7,863	20.3
1981	% Prof Man	16.4	L	3,500	9.0
1981	electorate 49,793		MPs since 1945
Alliance		SDP	1945-51 Megan Lloyd George L
			1951-79 Cledwyn Hughes Lab
			1979- Keith Best C

Brecon and Radnor

Powys is the smallest of the Welsh counties. With only 84,000 electors in all, this sparsely populated tract of Mid Wales is scarcely entitled to more than one seat in its own right. The Boundary Commission originally suggested that Powys should be united with Gwent, and that there should be an Abergavenny and Brecon seat which would cross the county boundary. But as in many other cases, the local inquiry reinforced the principle of 'minimum change'. Powys retains its two representatives in Parliament, and its constituencies of Brecon/Radnor and Montgomery. This is despite the fact that both divisions are much smaller than average in electorate, even for Wales. But the vast acreage of these mid-Wales border seats may offer an excuse and an explanation for this apparent over-representation.

Brecon and Radnor is not actually an unchanged seat. It loses part of the northern fringe of the mining valleys, around Brynmawr, to Blaenau Gwent. This is a significant change, for Brecon and Radnor is a marginal seat, won by the Tories in 1979 for the first time since 1931. There is still some Labour mining territory in the SW corner of Brecon district, at Ystradgynlais in the Upper Swansea Valley. But Brecon and Radnor is an enormous seat, encompassing the Brecon Beacon mountains. The economy is mainly dependent on agriculture. More typical than Ystradgynlais are the little spa towns of Builth Wells and Llanwrtyd Wells and Llandrindod Wells, and the market centres of Brecon and Hay on Wye. The former tiny County of Radnor is very English border terrain.

All in all, the capture of Brecon and Radnor was one of the best examples of the long-term swing to the Tories in rural Wales. The loss of Brynmawr may well mean that Labour cannot win it back. Ironically, the new Conservative MP for Brecon and Radnor is Tom Hooson, the cousin of Emlyn Hooson, the former Liberal MP for Montgomery - who was another prominent victim of that Tory surge in rural Wales.

1981	% Own Occ	57.7	1979 core seat Brecon/Radnor		
1981	% Loc Auth	25.3	C	22,660	47.2
1981	% Welsh Sp	17	Lab	19,633	40.9
1981	% Mid Cl	41.0	L	4,654	9.7
1981	% Prof Man	16.4	PC	1,031	2.1
1981	electorate 46,800		MPs since 1945		
1979	notional result		1945-70 Tudor Watkins Lab		
	C 2,600		1970-79 Caerwyn Roderick Lab		
Alliance			1979- Tom Hooson C		

Montgomery

When the Conservatives pulled off a surprise victory in Montgomery in 1979, they ended a century of Liberal dominance in the Mid Wales border county. Since 1962 the member had been Emlyn Hooson, QC. Before that Montgomery had been held by Clement Davies, the Leader of the Liberal Party from 1945 to 1956. The unbroken Liberal tradition extends well back into Victorian times.

Mongtomery has another claim to fame. In 1971, 30.3% of the employed population was engaged in agriculture - the highest proportion of any seat in Britain. Some of the farms rear sheep, up in the hills; but Montgomeryshire is not in general wild countryside, but fertile rolling land near the English boundary. The rural and agricultural nature of Montgomery was once even more distinct. For here is the smallest of the designated New Towns, the appropriately named Newtown (it has actually existed for centuries). Newtown has doubled in population since the war, but it is still only 9,000 altogether. This still makes an impact in a constituency of only 37,000 electors in total, and Newtown may well have moved to the Conservatives in 1979 as significantly as the English New Towns did.

Emlyn Hooson will not attempt to regain Montgomery. He has already taken a seat in the House of Lords. It may well be that the new member Delwyn Williams can consolidate his position in Montgomery, and that his stewardship will not be a brief aberration, but will mark the end of the Liberal reign in Montgomery.

1981	% Own Occ	52.1	1979 same seat Montgomery			
1981	% Loc Auth	30.1	C	11,751	40.3	
1981	% Welsh Sp	24.0	L	10,158	34.9	
1981	% Mid Cl	38.5	Lab	4,751	16.3	
1981	% Prof Man	15.9	PC	2,474	8.5	
1981	electorate 37,421		MPs since 1945			
Alliance		L	1945-62 Clement Davies L			
			1962-79 Emlyn Hooson L			
			1979- Delwyn Williams C			

Belfast East

If west Belfast is generally regarded as the centre of that troubled city's Catholic Republicanism, east Belfast has a strong claim to be a stronghold of Orange Protestant Loyalism. The residential areas stretch from inner city terraces out to attractive suburban residential areas in Knock and Belmont. There is a diversity of industry, such as the Harland and Wolff shipyard and the Short aircraft factory.

Belfast East was held from February 1974 to 1979 by William Craig, the Leader of the Vanguard Unionist party and a man one considered to be a dark force on the extreme wing of mainstream unionist politics. But in 1979 Craig, now an Official Unionist, was outflanked by an even more militant Protestant, 30 year old Peter Robinson of Ian Paisley's Democratic Unionist Party. Robinson only beat Craig by 64 votes, and overall Belfast East proved to be the closest contest of any in the UK, for Alliance Party Leader Oliver Napier finished within a thousand votes of victory in third place - Robinson, Craig and Napier all polled between 15,000 and 16,000 votes. The Catholic parties all declined to contest Belfast East.

In the boundary changes Belfast East loses several thousand voters to North Down and Strangford, but it still extends beyond the city boundaries to take in four wards from Castlereagh District. Robinson is strong in Castlereagh as well as within the city boundaries, and may well strengthen the DUP hold on East Belfast next time. It is ironic that this constituency, which includes Stormont Castle, may well continue to return one of the most virulent Protestant opponents of the British government's attempts at power-sharing between the Northern Irish communities.

1971	% RC	10	1979 core seat Belfast East		
1979	electorate 59,207		DUP	15,994	31.4
1979	notional result		OUP	15,930	31.2
	OUP 600		All	15,066	29.5
MPs since 1945			UPNI	2,017	4.0
1945-50 T.L. Cole UU			NI Lab 1,982		3.9

1950-59 A.J. McKibbin UU
1959-74 Stanley McMaster UU
1974-79 Wiliam Craig Vanguard
1979-   Peter Robinson DUP

Belfast North

Belfast North produced an extraordinary result at the 1979 General Election. There was a seven-way contest for the seat vacated by the retiring Official Unionist, John Carson. A remarkably even spread of votes produced a victory for the Paisleyite Democratic Unionist John McQuade, even though he polled only 27.6% - the lowest winning percentage in the UK, and indeed the lowest for many elections. McQuade may also be one of the oldest 'freshmen' MPs in recent times: his exact age is not published.

The wards which make up the Belfast North seat contain some grim reminders of the tragic and turbulent troubled recent history of the Northern Irish capital: Ardoyne and New Lodge, Crumlin, Shankill and Woodvale. There is a substantial Catholic minority in the constituency - Catholic parties polled 23% of the vote in 1979 - but the predominant tone is unionist. There are many Protestant working-class areas here, such as that around the Shankill Road, although there is also a pleasant residential area along the Antrim Road. As in Belfast East, the voters turned to a Paisleyite activist in 1979, narrowly ahead of an Official Unionist. The more moderate and non-sectarian parties such as the UPNI, the Alliance Party, and the NI Labour Party were squeezed out last time, and probably will be again.

Belfast North is relatively little altered in the boundary changes. It still extends from the edge of the city to the battered slums which form the cockpit of the UK's greatest urban and civil strife. Its future electoral development remains as unpredictable and fragmented in general prospect as the future development of Northern Ireland itself.

1971	% RC	30	1979 core seat Belfast North		
1979	electorate 65,723		DUP	11,690	27.6
1979	notional result		OUP	10,695	25.3
	OUP 2,500		SDLP	7,823	18.5
MPs since 1945			UPNI	4,220	10.0
1945-50 W.F. Neill UU			All	4,120	9.7
1950-59 H.M. Hyde UU			Rep C 1,907		4.5
1959-74 W.S. Mills UU			NI Lab 1,889		4.4
1974-79 John Carson UU					
1979- John McQuade DUP					

Belfast South

South Belfast is traditionally regarded as the most affluent and middle-class part of the city. Here is to be found the Queen's University campus, and many of the most select residential areas of the Northern Irish capital, such as the Malone Road. It was relatively isolated from the worst of the 'troubles', but that no part of Belfast is immune from violence was brutally shown in 1981 by the assassination of the Official Unionist MP, Robert Bradford, at one of his advice centres.

The subsequent byelection was won convincingly by the Grand Master of the Orange Order of Northern Ireland, Martin Smyth, who like Bradford is a minister of religion. Smyth stood in the OUP interest, and beat off challenges from the Alliance Party and the Paisleyite DUP, and seems now to have one of the safest seats in the turbulent Northern Ireland political scene. The main threat to his continued tenure is likely to come from the Alliance Party, which is not to be confused with the British Liberal-SDP alliance. The Alliance Party is a non-sectarian liberal centrist grouping of about a decade's existence, with prominent figures such as Oliver Napier (who is a Catholic) and the Belfast South candidate Basil Glass.

The Alliance receives a considerable degree of support from the middle-class professional, managerial and intellectual classes of southern Belfast. There is very little SDLP support here, and none of the militant nationalist parties have stood in a recent General Election. The boundaries are little altered in N Ireland's sweeping review.

1971	% RC	15	1979 core seat Belfast South		
1979	electorate 57,938		OUP	28,875	61.7
1979	notional result		All	11,745	25.1
	OUP 14,400		SDLP	3,694	7.9
MPs since 1945			UPNI	1,784	3.8
1945-52 C.H. Gage U			Oth	692	1.5
1952-63 Sir D.C. Campbell UU					
1963-74 R.J. Pounder UU					
1974-81 Robert Bradford OUP					
1981- Martin Smyth OUP					

Belfast West

West Belfast has long been the chief battleground of unionist-nationalist rivalry. It is an area with considerable unemployment and shocking social and housing problems in addition to the all-too-familiar violence associated with the names of parts of the seat such as the Falls Road, the Divis Flats and Andersonstown. No constituency in the United Kingdom looks so degraded, so war-torn.

Since 1945 the political competition for the representation of Belfast West has been largely between unionist and some brand of labour candidate such as Jack Beattie (Irish Labour Party) and more recently Gerry Fitt (Republican Labour). Fitt has held the seat since 1966 with great popularity and showing much bravery, despite the enmity of the Protestants and of more extreme nationalists. The constituency is becoming more strongly Catholic, but Fitt's survival now seems in doubt.

Fitt was a founder-member of the SDLP in 1970, but in 1979 he resigned and now sits as an independent socialist. In 1981 the District Council election still showed the SDLP ahead of other republican candidates. But inside a year Gerry Adams (Sinn Fein) had topped the poll in the Assembly elections (fought on the old boundaries), and his party had taken 30% of the vote compared with the SDLP's 20%. The Catholic vote seems certain to be split several ways, and any prediction of the General Election result in Belfast West would be treading on dangerous ground indeed.

1971	% RC	65	1979 core seat	Belfast West	
1979	electorate 61,179		SDLP	16,480	49.5
1979	notional result		OUP	8,245	24.8
	SDLP 12,500		DUP	3,716	11.1
MPs since 1950			Rep C	2,282	6.9
1950-51	T.L. Teevan UU		All	2,024	6.1
1951-55	J. Beattie Irish Lab		NI Lab	540	1.6
1955-64	Mrs F.P.A. McLaughlin				
	UU				
1964-66	J. Kilfedder UU				
1966-	Gerry Fitt Rep Lab				
	(SDLP) (Ind Soc)				

East Antrim

This new seat of East Antrim consists of two complete District Council areas, Larne and Carrickfergus, and nine wards from Newtownabbey, lying between the M2 motorway and Belfast Lough. Some 60% of the new seat, the Paisleyite strongholds of Larne and Carrickfergus, comes from North Antrim; the remainder, apart from a ward drawn from North Belfast, is removed from the former South Antrim division.

E Antrim is essentially a coastal constituency lying between the Antrim hills and the sea. The northern part of the seat consists of headlands and glens and picturesque villages. But the south, from Carrickfergus to Belfast, is almost continuously urban. The constituency is dominated by the latter section. Carrickfergus has suffered severely from the closure of ICI and Courtaulds, the makers of man-made fibres, and several related industries. Larne is a very busy sea ferry port with some heavy engineering industry and a power station. Although a protestant district, East Antrim has by no means escaped from the dire effects of the recession and the decimation of the artificial fibre industry in the province.

East Antrim will return a unionist Member of Parliament; but the question is - of what variety? Democratic Unionists polled better than Official Unionists in this area in the District Council elections of 1981. However the fortunes of the OUP revived somewhat in the Assembly elections of 1982. The DUP may still be ahead but the outcome could well depend on the personality of the candidate selected. The SDLP vote in the area is very small but the Alliance Party is fairly strong with around 20% of the vote.

1971	% RC	17	New seat
1979	electorate 58,985		
1979	notional result		
	DUP 5,900		

East Londonderry

This new constituency comprises two complete District Council areas, Limavady and Coleraine, and twelve of Magherafelt's fifteen wards. Approximately two-thirds of the seat is derived from the old division of Londonderry, with about a quarter from Mid Ulster and the remainder from North Antrim.

However, despite the name (which some feel is a concession to Protestant feeling), the constituency is predominantly rural and an important agricultural area. In the west the seat backs into the Sperrins but the northern coast, fringing Lough Foyle and the Atlantic, is much more fertile. The main urban centres are Coleraine, Magherafelt and Limavady, but there are numerous small market towns such as Kilrea, Maghera, Dungiven and Castledawson. Coleraine is the centre for the New University of Ulster. There is also a tourist industry based on the north coast and Portrush in particular.

East Londonderry is predominantly unionist but with pockets of intense republican feeling. This territory has traditionally been represented by an Official Unionist but there are signs of change. Democratic Unionists have improved their position in the 1981 District Council elections and in the 1982 Assembly elections. At the same time the SDLP have gained in the Limavady area but have had to concede ground to Sinn Fein in the traditional republican areas. Official Unionists are the largest party in the constituency - which will probably be contested by the current Londonderry MP William Ross - but the margin over the Democratic Unionists may be small.

1971	% RC	33	New seat
1979	electorate 63,486		
1979	notional result		
	OUP 17,500		

Fermanagh and South Tyrone

The consituency is one of the least changed in the Northern
Irish boundary revision. It comprises two complete District
Council areas, Fermanagh and Dungannon. It is a border seat
sharing a very long frontier with the Republic. It is rural
and agricultural with a significant tourist business based on
the Erne lakes. The main urban centres are Enniskillen and
Dungannon, at different ends of the seat.
   This is traditionally one of the cockpits of unionist-
nationalist rivalry. There is a small Catholic majority, but like
neighbouring Mid Ulster the elections have often been decided
by abstentionism and vote-splitting. The electoral history is
convoluted and bitter. In 1955 a convicted felon was elected
for Sinn Fein but disqualified, and the seat was represented
by a unionist until 1970. Frank McManus won the seat as a
Unity candidate in 1970 but lost it on a split vote to Unionist
Party Leader Harry West in February 1974. Frank Maguire
united the Catholic vote and held the seat from October 1974
until his death in 1980. But the byelection was won by
hunger striker Bobby Sands, who died in the H Block protest
the next month. New legislation on the disqualification of
candidates followed, but amid international attention and new
heights of feeling Sands's election agent Owen Carron held
the vote in the second byelection of 1981. He has not taken
his seat at Westminster either.
   Neither Sands nor Carron were opposed by the SDLP, but it
is likely that the nationalist vote will be split at the next
General Election. This could well let in the stronger of the
unionist parties, the OUP, which had around 43% of the vote
in the Assembly elections of 1982, compared with 28% for
Carron and 20% for the SDLP.

1971	% RC	55
1979	electorate 66,129	
1979	notional result	
	Ind Rep 5,000	

MPs since 1950
1950-55 C. Healy Nationalist
1955   P. Clarke Sinn Fein
1955-64 R.G. Grosvenor UU
1964-70 Marquess of Hamilton
                      UU
1970-74 F. McManus Unity
1974   Harry West UU
1974-80 Frank Maguire Ind Rep
1981   Bobby Sands Ind
1981-   Owen Carron Ind

1979 core seat Fermanagh/South
Tyrone

Ind Rep	22,398	36.0
OUP	17,411	28.0
SDLP	10,785	17.3
UUUP	10,607	17.0
All	1,070	1.7

Foyle

For many years the politics of the City of Londonderry demonstrated the most stark example of gerrymandering in the United Kingdom. The ward boundaries were so drawn that Derry's Roman Catholic majority was confined to one of the City Council's four divisions, thus maintaining permanent Protestant control. In parliamentary terms too, the Catholics of the Bogside and the other famous Derry ghettoes have been outvoted due to the inclusion of Protestant rural areas. Now however a Catholic seat is created, and it is interesting to note that it is named Foyle, after the river, rather than 'Londonderry' with its English connotations.

Foyle includes the whole of the City of Londonderry District and seven wards of Strabane, including the town itself, which was formerly in Mid Ulster. Foyle includes scenic areas bounded to the west by the River Foyle and Donegal beyond, to the north by Lough Foyle and to the east by the Sperrin mountains. But its politics will be dominated by the urban areas: the City of Derry and Strabane, the town with persistently the highest unemployment level in the UK.

The politics of the seat will be controlled by the City of Londonderry. In 1981 the SDLP gained an overall majority on the District Council with 41% of the vote. But in the Assembly elections of 1982, Martin McGuinness (Sinn Fein) polled 8,207 first preference votes, 13.5%. The SDLP candidates amassed 31.5%, and were thus clearly ahead of the more extreme Sinn Fein challenge. The unionist vote in the new seat is fairly evenly divided between the DUP and the OUP but they are competing for little more than a third of the electorate. With Sinn Fein committed to contest, and the SDLP committed to oppose them it promises to be an interesting contest. But Foyle probably has a clear SDLP majority and its opponents consider that it was drawn for SDLP Leader John Hume, who has not yet been a Westminster MP.

1971	% RC	60	1979 core seat Londonderry		
1979	electorate 63,486		OUP	31,592	49.6
1979	notional result		SDLP	19,185	30.2
	SDLP 2,000		All	5,830	9.2
MPs since 1945			IIP	5,489	8.6
1945-51 Sir R.D. Ross UU			Rep C	888	1.4
1951-55 W. Wellwood UU			Oth	639	1.0
1955-74 R. Chichester-Clark					
	UU				
1974- William Ross OUP					

Lagan Valley

This new constituency is centred on the Lisburn District
Council area, now the second most populous after Belfast,
and one ward, Carryduff, from Castlereagh. About two-thirds
of the electorate comes from the old South Antrim, a quarter
from North Down and the remainder from Belfast South and
South Down.

The area is fairly compact and densely populated, and takes
its name from the River Lagan. In addition to the substantial
urban population of Lisburn, there are a number of smaller
communities, such as Hillsborough, Moira and Glenavy. The
M1 motorway bisects the constituency.

The political complexion of this predominantly Protestant seat
is strongly unionist. The Democratic Unionist Party improved
its position in the local elections of 1981, and is now very
competitive in Lisburn. However, Official Unionists are
equally strong - so personality could be a factor in
determining the successful candidate. The rival Unionists will
fight it out for victory in Lagan Valley, for the SDLP and
Alliance are too weak to secure success or representation in
an election which is not decided on a system of proportional
representation such as pertains in Northern Irish local and
Assembly elections. Lagan Valley will return an extra
Protestant to Westminster.

1971	% RC	15	New seat
1979	electorate 57,906		
1979	notional result		
	OUP 22,700		

Mid Ulster

Mid Ulster is one of the two rural constituencies in the province which have Catholic and nationalist majorities, and the most turbulent electoral histories in the United Kingdom. Like Fermanagh and South Tyrone, its contests have been marked by abstentionism, disqualification, vote splits between rival factions and controversial byelections. Mid Ulster has had an anti-unionist majority of several thousand for many years, but after the disqualification of Sinn Feiner T.J. Mitchell as a convicted felon in 1955, the Catholic vote divided to let in the Unionist G. Forrest. On his death in 1969 the seat was won by the 21 year old Bernadette Devlin (later McAliskey) as a nationalist Unity candidate. But she lost it to the OUP's John Dunlop on another split vote in February 1974, and he has benefited from further Catholic schisms since.

The seat is little altered in the boundary changes. It includes two complete Districts, Omagh and Cookstown, and part of Strabane and Magherafelt Districts. It is rural and scenic and contains parts of the Sperrin mountains.

John Dunlop may not stand again, and the unionist standard could well pass to the DUP, who have recently increased their strength in the area. The split between more moderate and more extreme nationalism may well continue, with the vote split almost equally between the SDLP and Sinn Fein. The unionists seem better able to unite their support in Mid Ulster and are likely to continue to reap the electoral rewards.

1971	% RC	55	1979 core seat	Mid Ulster	
1979	electorate 62,628		UU	29,249	44.7
1979	notional result		SDLP	19,266	29.4
	OUP 8,800		IIP	12,055	18.4
MPs since 1950			All	3,481	5.3
1950-51 A. Mulvey Nat			Rep C	1,414	2.2
1951-55 M. O'Neill Nat					
1955-56 T.J. Mitchell Sinn Fein					
1956-69 G. Forrest UU					
1969-74 Bernadette Devlin Unity					
1974- John Dunlop UU					

Newry and Armagh

This new constituency includes all the wards of the Armagh District and seventeen wards from Newry and Mourne. It draws about 85% from the old Armagh and the remainder from South Down. Both these seats are currently represented by Official Unionists, but Newry and Armagh has been so drawn as to provide a Catholic and nationalist majority. This caused the DUP to launch a protest at the Northern Ireland Boundary Commission inquiry, but to no avail.

Newry-Armagh is predominantly rural and agricultural with a major apple growing industry. The largest centres are the City of Armagh, the ecclesiastical capital of Ireland, and Newry. Both have traditional industries but also considerable unemployment. The southern part of the seat, near the long border with the Republic, has seen some of the most violent incidents of the troubles.

The SDLP should in theory be favourites to exploit the anti-unionist majority in Newry and Armagh. But their vote may well be weakened by a Sinn Fein challenge, as it was in the 1982 Assembly elections. If there were a single unionist candidate, the seat might fall to the Protestants as a result of such a split. But if the SDLP can field such a strong candidate as Seamus Mallon they may squeak home.

1971	% RC	55	1979 core seat Armagh		
1979	electorate 61,463		OUP	31,668	48.6
1979	notional result		SDLP	23,545	36.1
	OUP 2,300		DUP	5,634	8.6
MPs since 1945			Rep C	2,310	3.5
1945-48 Sir W.J. Allen UU			All	2,074	3.2
1948-54 J.R.E. Harden UU					
1954-59 C.W. Armstrong UU					
1959-74 John Maginnis UU					
1974- Harold McCusker OUP					

North Antrim

The eminence grise of the Northern Irish political scene in the last decade has been the Reverend Ian Paisley, founder and Leader of the Democratic Unionist Party. This brooding giant has now forced his way into prime position among Ulster's Protestant politicians. He received a vote of great confidence when elected to the European Parliament in 1979, and since he ousted Official Unionist Henry Clark in 1970 he has been returned to Westminster with increasingly massive majorities from his home district of North Antrim.

The redrawn North Antrim seat comprises three complete District Council areas: Ballymena, Ballymoney and Moyle. It is drawn almost completely from the old seat of the same name, with the exception of about one per cent gained from South Antrim. It is largely rural and agricultural and very scenic. The north coast is bounded by the Atlantic and has beaches and the renowned Giants Causeway. The east coast has a narrow coastal road opening into the glens. The Antrim hills fall away towards the River Bann to the west. The main urban centres are Ballymena, Ballymoney and Ballycastle. There is some industry, both of an agriculturally based kind and of more modern types.

Although the new North Antrim has lost Larne and Carrickfergus, the recent elections in the area show that the DUP has lost none of its strength. The Official Unionists are the second largest party in the area. Support for the SDLP is scattered, but it is usually enough to save the deposit. However, the political outcome of the Election would appear to be the clearest in this constituency of any in the Six Counties: a large majority for the heavyweight sitting member, the inevitable return of Ian Paisley, the 'Big Fella' from Ballymena.

1971	% RC	20	1979 core seat North Antrim		
1979	electorate 62,505		DUP	33,941	51.7
1979	notional result		OUP	15,398	23.4
	DUP 14,100		All	7,797	11.9
MPs since 1945			SDLP	4,867	7.4
1945-52 Sir R.W.H. O'Neill UU			ILP	3,689	5.6
1952-59 P.R.H. O'Neill UU					
1959-70 Henry Clark UU					
1970- Ian Paisley DUP					

North Down

The new North Down constituency comprises the North Down District and six wards from Castlereagh District in the Belfast suburbs. Three-quarters of the revised seat is derived from the old oversized North Down, and the remainder comes from Belfast East, which previously extended far beyond the city boundary. Much of the constituency is urban, with Bangor, Holywood and Dundonald providing the bulk of the population. It is a popular dormitory area for Belfast. Each of the main centres does have local industry. The seat contains some large public authority housing areas, but also contains very select areas between Holywood and Bangor once favoured by the Northern Ireland Office for visiting civil servants.

The constituency of North Down has traditionally returned an Official Unionist with a very large majority. Indeed, the proportion of Roman Catholics is among the lowest of any Northern Irish division. The current member, James Kilfedder, gained just such a vast majority in 1970 – 41,433. But the constituency exemplifies the splits which have occurred in the unionist family of parties since then. Kilfedder was expelled from the United Ulster Unionist Coalition in October 1975 and was severely critical of other Unionist MPs at Westminster. Shortly before the General Election of May 1979 he resigned from the Official Unionist party but was reelected as an Independent Ulster Unionist against an OUP candidate. In January 1980 Kilfedder launched his own party, the Ulster Popular Unionists, and has contested elections since then under that label. He topped the poll in the old North Down area in the 1982 Assembly elections and was elected Speaker of the Assembly.

However, Democratic Unionists have also polled well since 1981 and the fortunes of the OUP have revived. In addition, the Alliance Party has very respectable support – in 1979 it pushed the OUP into third place. The outcome may well be determined by personality factors or by a decision of Kilfedder to stand in the new Strangford seat instead.

1971	% RC	10	1979 core seat North Down		
1979	electorate 59,563		Ind UU	36,989	59.6
1979	notional result		All	13,364	21.5
	Ind UU 10,500		OUP	11,728	18.9

MPs since 1945
1945-46 J. Little
1946-50 C.H. Mullen UU
1950-53 Sir W.D. Smailes UU
1953-55 Mrs P. Ford UU
1955-70 George Currie UU
1970-   James Kilfedder UU

South Antrim

The constituency of South Antrim has for many years held more than one electoral record. In the old House of Commons, it was the largest seat in population and electorate, with over 132,000 voters in 1982. Thus it offered the clearest justification for the award of five extra seats to Northern Ireland, to bring the total to 17. South Antrim also frequently produced the largest majority in the House: over 50,000 for Knox Cunningham in 1959, when he polled 95.1% of the vote as a Unionist candidate; and the highest majority in the 1979 General Election, 38,868 for Official Unionist Leader James Molyneaux.

The new South Antrim comprises only about 43% of the previous vastly oversized seat. It includes the Antrim District and twelve wards from Newtownabbey. It stretches from Lough Neagh and the River Bann in the west to the borders of Belfast and East Antrim in the east. South Antrim is mainly rural but with the M2 motorway running westwards it has excellent communications between the urban and industrial areas. These are Antrim, Randalstown and Ballyclare and Glengormley on the fringes of Belfast. The seat has been affected by the sharp decline in the man-made fibre industry in the last twenty years. It has a very important agricultural sector and a valuable eel fishing industry based at Toome. It also contains Aldergrove Airport and the service industries associated with it.

Although the seat is much reduced in size, James Molyneaux seems as safe as ever here. The DUP improved their position in the area in 1981 but the Official Unionists are clearly ahead. Support for the Alliance Party and the Catholic parties is relatively small.

1971	% RC	20
1979	electorate 58,743	
1979	notional result	
	OUP 18,500	

MPs since 1945
1945-50 S.G. Haughton UU
1950-55 D.L. Savory UU
1955-70 Knox Cunningham UU
1970-   James Molyneaux OUP

1979 core seat South Antrim		
OUP	50,782	68.9
All	11,914	16.2
SDLP	7,432	10.1
Ind Lab	1,895	2.6
Rep C	1,615	2.2

South Down

When the controversial figure of Enoch Powell returned to his spiritual home, Parliament, in October 1974, it was as Official Ulster Unionist MP for South Down. Powell had long been associated with the Unionist cause, but it still surprised many that he should so quickly enter the maelstrom of Northern Irish politics after leaving the Conservative Party.

If Powell decides to contest South Down again, he may well face severe problems, for it has been significantly altered in the boundary changes. It has lost some mainly Protestant territory in its northern half, and now consists of the whole of Down District (46% RC in 1971), eight wards from Banbridge (25% RC) and thirteen from Newry and Mourne (63% RC). The constituency is predominantly rural with a rolling countryside and a very important agricultural sector. It has a tourist industry based on the seaside town of Newcastle, the Mourne Mountains and forest parks. Fishing is centred on Kilkeel, Annalong and Ardglass. The most important urban unit is Downpatrick which is also an administrative centre for a number of government services. On Carlingford Lough the port of Warrenpoint serves as a roll-on roll-off freight facility to serve Newry and its hinterland.

Besides the new-found Catholic near-majority, Powell will face hearty opposition from the DUP, who have little sympathy for the brand of unionism represented by the sitting member. But it is likely that both republican and unionist sides will be split, for Sinn Fein may well attract some SDLP votes. The SDLP control the Newry and Mourne Council and are the largest party in Down, but the outcome should depend on whose vote is most internally split.

1971	% RC	50	1979 core seat South Down			
1979	electorate 58,743		OUP	32,254	50.0	
1979	notional result		SDLP	24,033	37.3	
	OUP 600		All	4,407	6.8	
MPs since 1950			IIP	1,853	2.9	
1950-74 L.P.S. Orr UU			Rep C	1,682	2.6	
1974-	Enoch Powell OUP		Oths	247	0.4	

Strangford

This all-new constituency is based on the Ards District Council area with the addition of eight wards from the neighbouring Castlereagh District. About seventy per cent of the new seat is derived from the former grossly oversized North Down; the remainder is from Belfast South and Belfast East. Strangford could justly be described as one of the five extra Northern Irish constituencies created in the present review.

The focus of the constituency is the Ards peninsula and Strangford Lough, notwithstanding the inclusion of parts of metropolitan Belfast. Despite the recent outflow of population from Belfast to Newtownards, Comber and Donaghee, the area is fairly thinly populated and rural. It has an intensive agricultural sector, a fishing industry, tourism and significant industries in Newtownards and Comber. However, much of the employment is provided by Belfast, the province's first city.

Politically the outcome of the election is dependent on whether the popular sitting member, Independent Unionist James Kilfedder, decides to stand for Strangford or North Down, both largely carved out of his present seat. The DUP were slightly ahead of the Official Unionists in the 1981 District Council elections, but Kilfedder could probably defeat either if he stood in Strangford. The seat also has a sizeable Alliance vote but one insufficient so far to shake the main unionist parties. There is no significant Roman Catholic population in Strangford.

1971	% RC	10	New seat
1979	electorate 61,903		
1979	notional result		
	Ind UU 7,900		

Upper Bann

This new constituency comprises the Craigavon District Council area and almost half of the Banbridgre District. It is named after the River Bann which flows into Lough Neagh. The seat is based on the northern part of the old Armagh constituency, which makes up some 70% of Upper Bann; it also draws about 28% from South Down and a small portion from South Antrim.

The constituency is mainly rural with a strong dependence upon agriculture but it also contains some sizeable towns. Lurgan and Portadown are the twin towns on which the new city of Craigavon was founded, but its centre just did not grow to meet expectations. Both towns have their own industries and have direct access to the M1 which runs through the centre of the constituency. Banbridge is an important market town on the dual carriageway and main route to the Border and Dublin. There is an important tourist attraction in the excellent coarse fishing in the River Bann.

Politically, Armagh has been associated with Official Unionism. The northern part of the old constituency was the unionist stronghold. The OUP is stronger than the DUP and in the Assembly elections returned three members to one Paisleyite. The new seat seems safe for the sitting member for Armagh, Harold McCusker.

1971	% RC	30	New seat
1979	electorate 59,613		
1979	notional result		
	OUP 10,500		

LIST OF MAPS

1 South West England

579

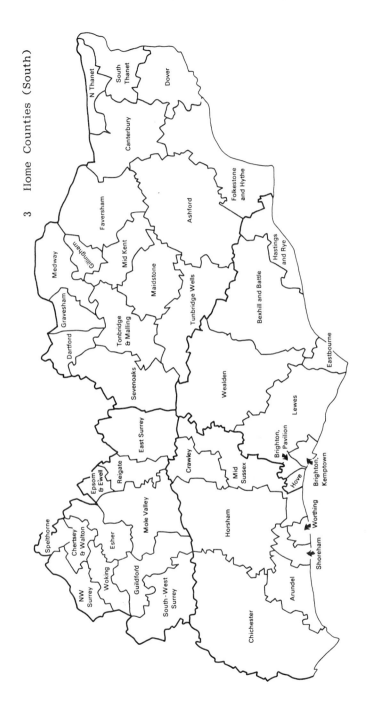

4 South London

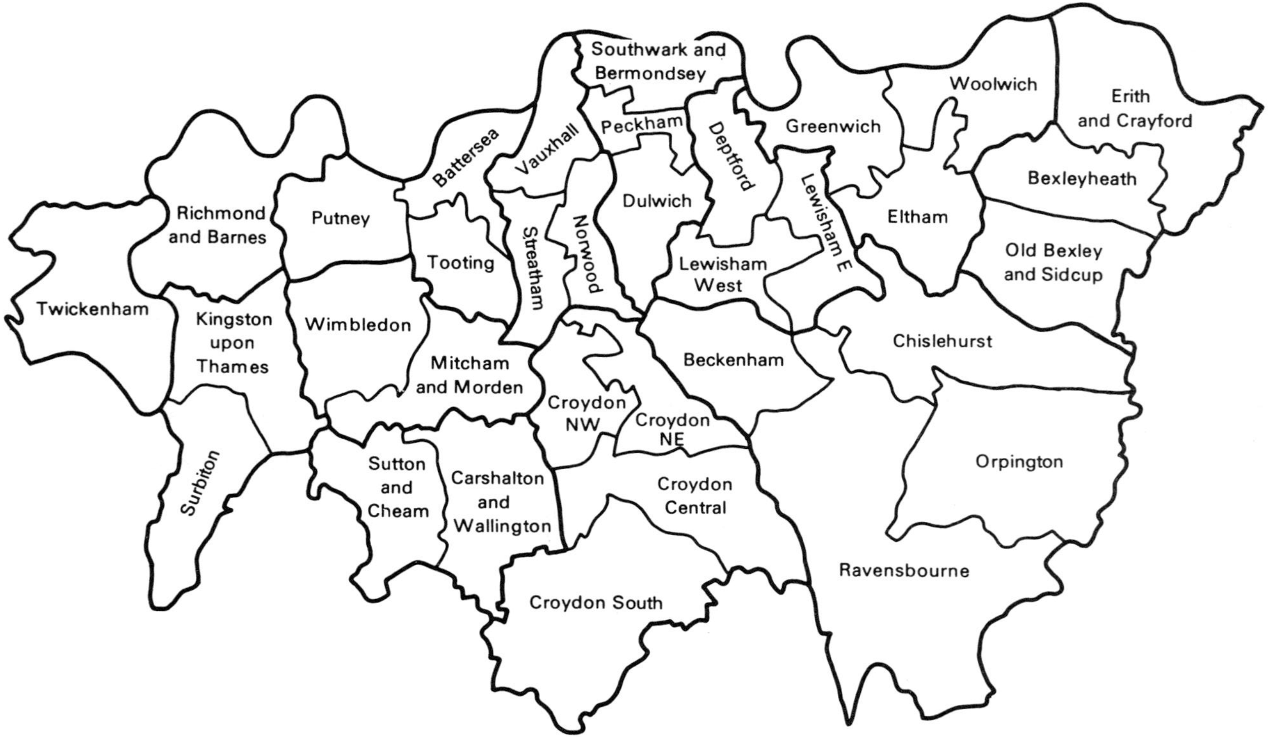

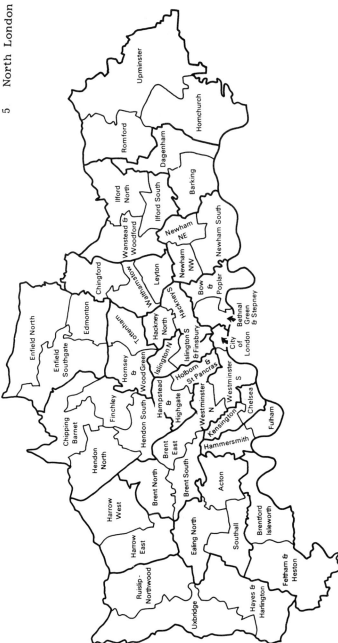

Upminster

Romford

Homchurch

Dagenham

Ilford
North

Ilford South

Barking

Wanstead &
Woodford

Newham
NE

Newham South

Newham
NW

Chingford

Leyton

Bow
&
Poplar

Walthamstow

Hackney
S

Bethnal
Green
& Stepney

Enfield North

Edmonton

Hackney
North

City
of
London

Enfield
Southgate

Tottenham

Wood Green

Islington N

Islington S
& Finsbury

Hornsey
&

Holborn
&
St Pancras

Westminster
S

Finchley

Hendon South

Hampstead
&
Highgate

N

Westminster

Kensington

Chelsea

Chipping
Barnet

Brent
East

Fulham

Hendon
North

Brent South

Hammersmith

Harrow
West

Brent North

Acton

Brentford
Isleworth

Harrow
East

Ealing North

Southall

Feltham &
Heston

Ruislip-
Northwood

Uxbridge

Hayes &
Harlington

Coventry North-East

Coventry South-East

Coventry North-West

Coventry South-West

Meriden

Sutton Coldfield

Birmingham, Erdington

Birmingham, Hodge Hill

Birmingham, Yardley

Birmingham, Sparkbrook

Solihull

Aldridge-Brownhills

Birmingham, Perry Barr

Birmingham, Small Heath

Birmingham, Hall Green

Walsall South

West Bromwich East

Birmingham, Ladywood

Birmingham, Edgbaston

Birmingham, Selly Oak

Walsall North

Warley East

Wolverhampton North-East

Wolverhampton South-East

West Bromwich West

Warley West

Birmingham, Northfield

Wolverhampton SW

Dudley East

Halesowen and Stourbridge

Dudley West

1   Liverpool, Walton
2   Liverpool, Riverside
3   Liverpool, Mossley Hill
4   Liverpool, Broadgreen
5   Liverpool, West Derby

15 North Yorkshire and Humberside

1　Tyne Bridge
2　Gateshead E

Berwick upon Tweed

Wansbeck

Blyth Valley

Wallsend

Newcastle
upon Tyne

Tynemouth

South Shields

Hexham

Jarrow

N
C E
1 2

Sunderland North

Sunderland South

Blaydon

Houghton & Washington

N Durham

Easington

Carlisle

City of
Durham

North West
Durham

Penrith and the Border

Sedgefield

Workington

Bishop Auckland

Darlington

Copeland

Westmorland and Lonsdale

Barrow and
Furness

Monmouth

Newport East

Torfaen

Newport West

Blaenau
Gwent

Islwyn

Cardiff S
& Penarth

Cardiff
C

Caerphilly

Cardiff
North

Cardiff W

Merthyr Tydfil
&
Rhymney

Pontypridd

Cynon Valley

Rhondda

Vale of Glamorgan

Ogmore

Neath

Aberavon

Bridgend

Swansea
E

Swansea
W

Gower

East Lothian

Leith
E
C
S
W
Edinburgh
Pentlands
Midlothian
Livingston
Linlithgow

Tweedale, Ettrick and
Lauderdale

Roxburgh
and Berwickshire

Dumfries

Galloway and Upper Nithsdale

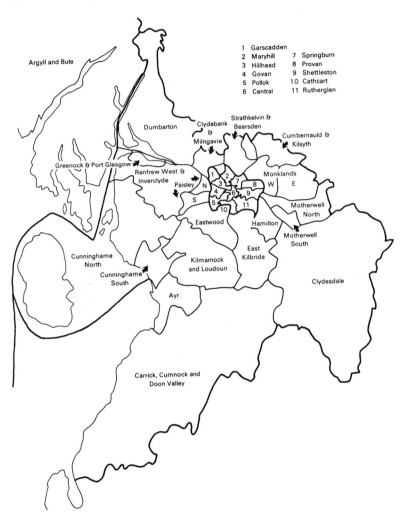

1 Garscadden
2 Maryhill
3 Hillhead
4 Govan
5 Pollok
6 Central
7 Springburn
8 Provan
9 Shettleston
10 Cathcart
11 Rutherglen

Argyll and Bute

Dumbarton

Clydebank & Milngavie

Strathkelvin & Bearsden

Cumbernauld & Kilsyth

Greenock & Port Glasgow

Renfrew West & Inverclyde

Paisley

N
S

Monklands

W   E

Motherwell North

Eastwood

Hamilton

Motherwell South

Cunninghame North

Cunninghame South

Ayr

Kilmarnock and Loudoun

East Kilbride

Clydesdale

Carrick, Cumnock and Doon Valley

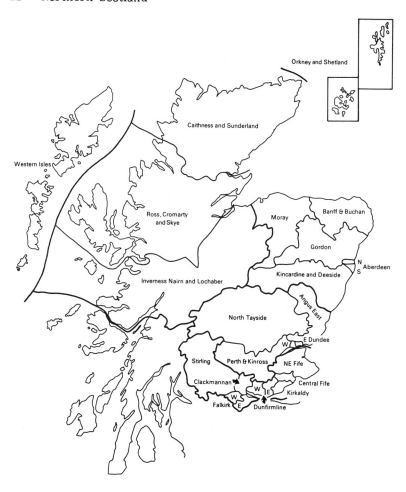

Orkney and Shetland

Caithness and Sunderland

Western Isles

Ross, Cromarty and Skye

Moray

Banff & Buchan

Gordon

Inverness Nairn and Lochaber

Kincardine and Deeside

N
Aberdeen
S

Angus East

North Tayside

E Dundee

W

Stirling

Perth & Kinross

NE Fife

Clackmannan

Central Fife

W E
Kirkaldy

Falkirk
W
E
Dunfirmline

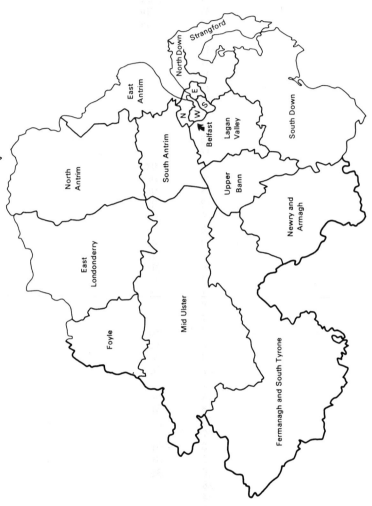

INDEX